ADVANCED

Human
and
Social
BIOLOGY

Glenn Toole
Vice Principal, Pendleton Sixth Form College, Salford

Susan Toole
**Head of Biology, The Hulme Grammar School for Girls, Oldham
and Former Team Leader and Examiner for A-level Biology**

Stanley Thornes (Publishers) Ltd

First published in 1997 by
Stanley Thornes (Publishers) Ltd
Ellenborough House
Wellington Street
CHELTENHAM GL50 1YW

A catalogue record of this book is available from the
BritishLibrary.

ISBN 0 7487 2790 9

Book plus Student's Art Notebook
ISBN 0 7487 2911 9

5-Pack Student's Art Notebook
ISBN 0 7487 2910 0

97 98 99 00 / 10 9 8 7 6 5 4 3 2 1

Artwork by Tech-Set Ltd, Geoff Jones, Annabel Milne,
Angela Lumley, Mark Dunn, Tim Smith, David Oliver, and
Peters and Zabransky (UK) Ltd
Typeset by Tech-Set Ltd, Gateshead, Tyne & Wear
Printed & bound in Slovenia
by Printing House DELO – Tiskarna
by arrangement with Korotan Ljubljana

Acknowledgements

To Annabel Milne for permission to reproduce artwork on
pp. 53, 57, 362, 415, 416, 441, 455.

To the following for permission to reproduce photographs:

Biological Sciences Review: p.448; Biophoto Associates:
pp.52, 54, 56, 57 (top, bottom), 60, 104, 111, 120, 156, 168, 245
(top left, bottom left), 317, 361 (bottom), 380, 434 (top and
bottom), 489 (bottom), 495, 512 (bottom); Bruce Coleman
Ltd: pp.172 (Jane Burton), 173 (top, bottom) (Kim Taylor),
275, 314 (bottom) (John Murray), 335 (Dr Norman Myers),
348 (bottom) (Adrian Davies); Ecoscene: pp.345 (Andrew
D.R. Brown), 348 (top) (Nick Hawkes); FLPA: p.316 (D.T.
Grewcock); Gene Cox: pp.206, 368; GSF Picture Library:
pp.248, 293 (bottom), 333 (D. Hoffman); Holt Studios
International: pp.115; 286, 525 (Inga Spence), 326, 332
(bottom) (Nigel Cattlin), 332 (top) (Richard Anthony); ICCE:
p.350 (top and bottom) (Jacolyn Wakeford); J & S
Professional Photography: p.525 (top) (Jim Lowe); Martyn
F. Chillmaid: p.297; Oxford Scientific Films: pp.174 (J.K.
Burras), 179 (Scott Camazine), 295 (K.G. Vock, Okapia), 298,
318, 347 (middle) (Kathie Atkinson), 323 (Colin Milkins),
346 (Ian West); Panos Pictures: pp.293 (Rob Cousins), 314
(top) (J. Hartley), 532 (Sean Sprague); Ralston Photography:
p.530; Science Photo Library: pp.474 (bottom), 21 (Richard
Kirby), 47 (David Scharf), 94 (Simon Fraser/RVI,
Newcastle-upon-Tyne), 96 (Phillippe Plailly/Eurelios), 98
(David Parker), 104, 400 (Biophoto Associates), 117
(Moredun Animal Health), 210 (bottom), 416, 558 (top,
bottom) (Prof. P. Motta, Dept. of Anatomy, University 'La
Sapienza', Rome), 249, 521 (James Holmes, Celltech Ltd),
267 (J.C. Revy), 337, 342, 462, 510 (CNRI), 361 (top), 385
(Martin Dohrn), 365 (top) (Astrid and Hanns-Frieder
Michler), 365 (bottom) (Manfred Kage), 376, 478 (top) (Bill
Longcore), 391 (Professors P.M. Motta and S. Correr), 396
(Eamonn McNulty), 455, 458 (Dr Don Fawcett), 470 (Dr
Colin Chumbley), 474 (top) (Tim Beddow), 474 (middle)
(Catherine Pouedras), 491 (bottom) (Secchi-Lecaque,
Roussel-UCLAF, CNRI), 546 (BSIP, VEM), 563 (Clinique
STE Catherine, CNRI); Science Pictures Ltd: pp. 154, 207,
210 (top), 218, 244, 245 (right), 256, 258, 375, 392, 440, 449,
457, 489 (top), 491 (top), 550; University of Oxford: p.67;
Wildlife Matters: p.340.

To the following examination boards for permission to
reproduce questions from examination papers:

Associated Examining Board (AEB)
Edexcel Foundation, London Examinations (ULEAC)
Northern Examinations and Assessment Board (NEAB)
University of Cambridge Local Examinations Syndicate
(UCLES), reproduced by permission of University of
Cambridge Local Examinations Syndicate

Contents

Preface ix

Part I

Levels of Organization

Part II — The Continuity of Life

Inheritance in context

Part IV — Transport and Exchange Mechanisms

Why humans need transport and exchange mechanisms

Part V — Coordination, Response and Control

Part VI — Microorganisms, biotechnology and disease

Chapter 22
Human heath and disease

Chapter 23
Food, diet and health

Preface

The popularity of Human and Social Biology has increased over recent years. As a result not only have more examination boards introduced syllabuses in these subjects at AS and A-Level, but there has also been expansion of the human and social aspects of Biology syllabuses. Modularization of many syllabuses has made it possible for examination boards to offer a wide range of modules which, in appropriate combinations, can lead to A-Levels and AS in either Biology or Human/Social Biology.

This book has been written to cover the core material from all the examination board syllabuses in Human/Social Biology and most of the optional material as well. The most popular options such as health and disease, microorganisms and biotechnology, and those concerned with food, human evolution, physiology, ecology, reproduction and genetics are all comprehensively covered as well as the social aspects of biology. Intended primarily for students taking AS and A-Level Human/Social Biology syllabuses, the text will also be valuable to students studying Scottish Higher Grade examinations, GNVQ Science (Advanced) or the International Baccalaureat.

Building upon the success of *Understanding Biology for Advanced Level* it has been decided to adopt a similar format and style. Where core material is the same the content has been amended to suit human biology syllabuses. In addition there are totally new sections on populations, human evolution, human health and disease and food, food production and health. The human and sociological aspects in all areas of the book have been expanded. Short, informative sections on selected topics have been highlighted under a new title – *Focus*. These are referred to in the text and allow in-depth consideration of selected items without disrupting the flow of the main theme being followed. Project suggestions have been chosen to cover human/social aspects of biology and are intended as ideas for enquiry and to stimulate innate curiosity. *Did you Know?* offers fascinating and often surprising facts about us and our world. While introducing a light-hearted note, they also provide worthwhile factual information about the topic being studied.

All nomenclature in this book is consistent with the recommendations made by the Institute of Biology and the Association for Science Education. Samples of recent questions of the Examining Boards have been included at the end of each chapter. Overall the book is intended to provide a clear, highly accessible text that is sufficiently detailed to satisfy the requirements of all major syllabuses but without unnecessary detail which can sometimes cloud the underlying issues. As human and social biology are about us, they are inherently of interest and we hope that this book will provide both information needed for examination success and the stimulus to investigate and enquire further.

Finally we should like to express our gratitude to all those at Stanley Thornes (Publishers) Ltd without whose encouragement, patience and hard work this book would never have been completed. To Margaret O'Gorman and John Hepburn we express our special thanks for their unstinting efforts in making it all possible.

Glenn and Susan Toole

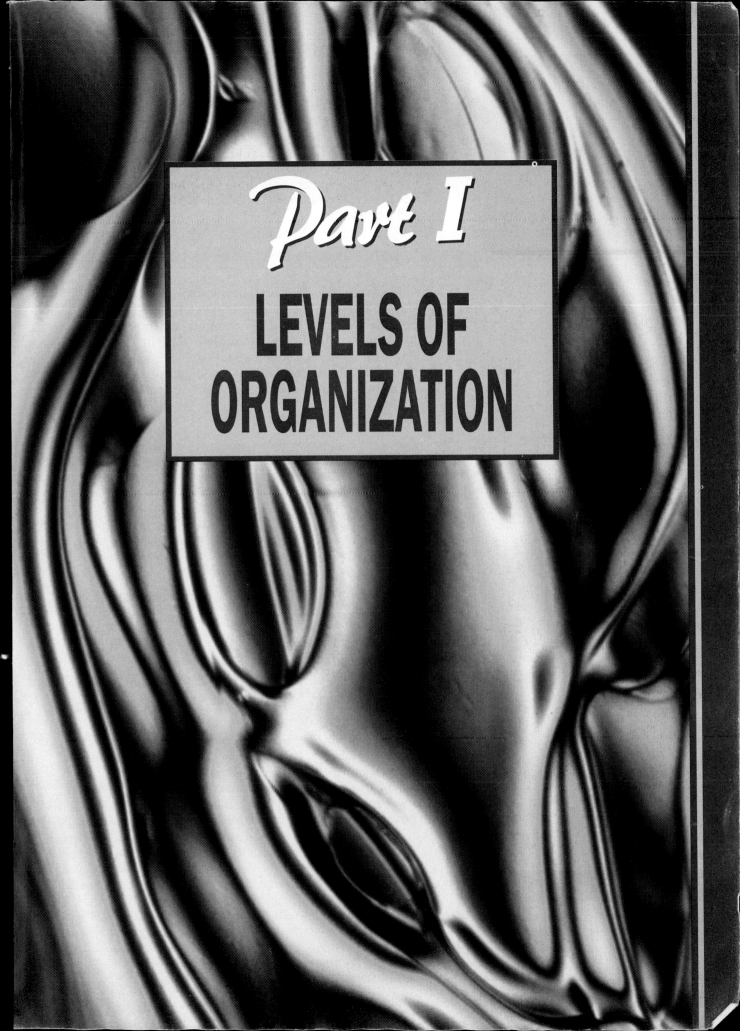

Part I

LEVELS OF ORGANIZATION

1 Size and complexity

Within the range of living organisms, including man, it is possible to recognize seven levels of organization, each of which forms the basis of the next. The most fundamental unit is the **atom**; atoms group to form **molecules**, which in turn, may be organized into **cells**. Cells are grouped into **tissues** which collectively form **organs**, which form **organisms**. A group of organisms of a single species may form a **population**.

TABLE 1.1 **Metric units**

Units of size			
1 kilometre	(km)	=	1000 (10^3) metres
1 metre	(m)		
1 centimetre	(cm)	=	1/100 (10^{-2}) metre
1 millimetre	(mm)	=	1/1000 (10^{-3}) metre
1 micrometre (micron)	(μm)	=	1/1 000 000 (10^{-6}) metre
1 nanometre	(nm)	=	1/1 000 000 000 (10^{-9}) metre
1 picometre	(pm)	=	1/1 000 000 000 000 (10^{-12}) metre

1.1 Atomic organization

Atoms are the smallest unit of a chemical element which can exist independently. They comprise a nucleus which contains positively charged particles called **protons**, the number of which is referred to as the **atomic number**. For each proton there is a particle of equal negative charge called an **electron**, so the atom has no overall charge. The electrons are not within the nucleus, but orbit in fixed quantum shells around it (see Fig. 1.1). There is a fixed limit to the number of electrons in any one shell. There may be up to seven such shells each with its own energy level; electrons in the shells nearest the nucleus have the least energy. The addition of energy, e.g. in the form of heat or light, may promote an electron to a higher energy level within a shell. Such an electron almost immediately returns to its original level, releasing its newly absorbed energy as it does so. This electron movement is important biologically in processes such as photosynthesis (Chapter 11).

Did you know?

The most common element by number of atoms in the human body is hydrogen, 63%, next is oxygen, 25.5%.

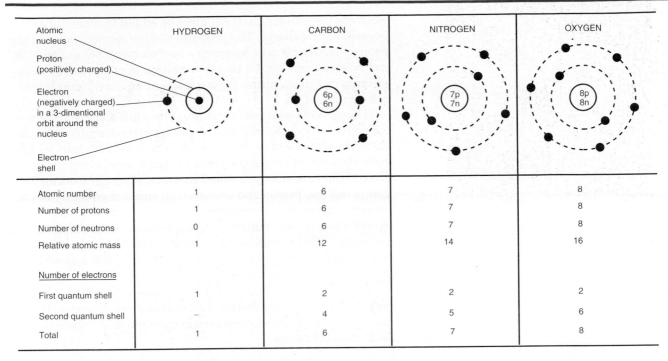

	HYDROGEN	CARBON	NITROGEN	OXYGEN
Atomic number	1	6	7	8
Number of protons	1	6	7	8
Number of neutrons	0	6	7	8
Relative atomic mass	1	12	14	16
Number of electrons				
First quantum shell	1	2	2	2
Second quantum shell	–	4	5	6
Total	1	6	7	8

Fig. 1.1 Atomic structure of four commonly occurring biological elements

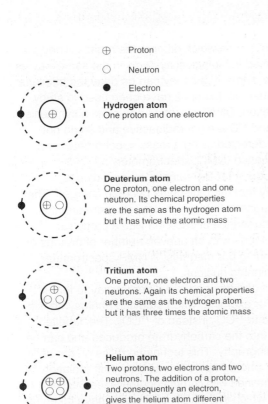

Fig. 1.2 Atomic structure of the atoms of hydrogen, deuterium, tritium and helium

The nucleus of the atom also contains particles called **neutrons** which have no charge. Protons and neutrons contribute to the mass of an atom, but electrons have such a comparatively small mass that their contribution is negligible. However, the number of electrons determines the chemical properties of an atom. (See Fig. 1.2.)

1.1.1 Ions

As we have seen, atoms do not have any overall charge because the number of protons is always the same as the number of electrons and both have equal, but opposite, charges. If an atom loses or gains electrons it becomes an **ion**. The addition of electrons produces a negative ion while the loss of electrons gives rise to a positive ion. The loss of an electron is called **oxidation**, while the gain of an electron is called **reduction**. The atom losing an electron is said to be oxidized, while that gaining an electron is said to be reduced. The loss of an electron from a hydrogen atom, for instance, would leave a hydrogen ion, comprising just a single proton. Having an overall positive charge it is written as H^+. Where an atom, e.g. calcium, loses two electrons its overall charge is more positive and it is written Ca^{2+}. The process is similar where atoms gain electrons, except that the overall charge is negative, e.g. Cl^-. Ions may comprise more than one type of atom, e.g. the sulphate ion is formed from one sulphur and four oxygen atoms, with the addition of two electrons, SO_4^{2-}.

1.1.2 Isotopes

The properties of an element are determined by the number of protons and hence electrons it possesses. If protons (positively charged) are added to an element, then an equivalent number of electrons (negatively charged) must be added to maintain an overall neutral charge. The properties of the element would then change – indeed it now becomes a new element. For example, it can be seen from Fig. 1.1 that the addition of one proton, one electron and one neutron to the carbon atom, transforms it into a nitrogen atom.

If however, a neutron (not charged) is added, there is no need for an additional electron and so its properties remain the same. As neutrons have mass, the element is heavier. Elements which have the same chemical properties as the normal element, but have a different mass, are called **isotopes**. Hydrogen normally comprises one proton and one electron and consequently has an atomic mass of one. The addition of a neutron doubles the atomic mass to two, without altering the element's chemical properties. This isotope is called **deuterium**. Similarly, the addition of a further neutron forms the isotope **tritium**, which has an atomic mass of three (Fig. 1.2).

Isotopes can be traced by various means, even when incorporated in living matter. This makes them exceedingly useful in tracing the route of certain elements in a variety of biological processes.

NOTEBOOK

Using isotopes as tracers

Isotopes are varieties of atoms which differ in their mass. They are usually taken up and used in biological systems in the same way as the 'normal' form of the element, but they can be detected because they have different properties. Isotopes have been used to study photosynthesis, respiration, DNA replication and protein synthesis. Isotopes such as ^{15}C and ^{13}C are not radioactive and so do not decay but they can be detected using a mass spectrometer or a nuclear magnetic resonance (NMR) spectrometer.

To use a mass spectrometer the sample to be studied is vaporized is such a way that the molecules become charged. They then pass through a magnetic field which deflects them and the machine records the abundance of each ion with a particular charge : mass ratio. Isotopes with an uneven number of protons or electrons spin, like spinning bar magnets. A NMR spectrometer detects each type of spinning nucleus.

Radioactive isotopes can be used in a different way to follow biological processes. For example, when studying photosynthesis leaves may be exposed to $^{14}CO_2$ instead of $^{12}CO_2$. The 'labelled' carbon is incorporated into the carbohydrate produced and can be detected using autoradiography. This technique relies on the ability of radioisotopes to 'fog' photographic film as they emit radiation. When the process is combined with chromatography (see Section 14.3) it is possible to identify which individual compounds have taken up the radioactive carbon. If an accurate measure of the radioactivity in a sample is required a scintillation counter can be used.

Radioisotopes in medicine

Radioisotopes can be used both for diagnosis and treatment of disease as well as for research into possible causes. A particularly important isomer used to study lung and heart complaints is ^{99m}technetium. It has a half life of only 6 hours and so decays very rapidly. It can be used as an aerosol, in very low concentrations, to show up available air spaces in patients' lungs. It may be used to label red blood cells so that the distribution of blood within the spaces of the heart or in deep veins can be shown. This is useful if there is a possibility of blood clots having formed.

The radiation emitted by a radioisotope can be used to destroy damaged tissue. For example ^{137}caesium is inserted in a sealed probe to destroy cancerous cells in the cervix. ^{131}Iodine is taken up selectively by the thyroid gland and can be used in carefully calculated doses to destroy a specific amount of that gland.

^{90}Yttrium in a silicate injection kills synovial tissues which are eroding the ends of the bones in sufferers of rheumatoid and osteo arthritis.

1.2   Molecular organization

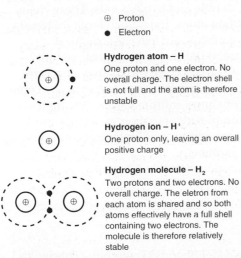

⊕ Proton
● Electron

Hydrogen atom – H
One proton and one electron. No overall charge. The electron shell is not full and the atom is therefore unstable

Hydrogen ion – H⁺
One proton only, leaving an overall positive charge

Hydrogen molecule – H₂
Two protons and two electrons. No overall charge. The eletron from each atom is shared and so both atoms effectively have a full shell containing two electrons. The molecule is therefore relatively stable

Fig. 1.3 Atomic structure of a hydrogen atom, a hydrogen ion and a hydrogen molecule

We have seen that the electron shells around an atom may each contain a maximum number of electrons. The shell nearest the nucleus may possess a maximum of two electrons and the next shell a maximum of eight. An atom is most stable, i.e. least reactive, when its outer electron shell contains the maximum possible number of electrons. For example, helium, with a full complement of two electrons in its outer shell, is inert. In a hydrogen atom, the electron shell has a single electron and so the atom is unstable. If two hydrogen atoms share their electrons they form a hydrogen **molecule**, which is more stable. The two atoms are effectively combined and the molecule is written as H_2. The sharing of electrons in order to produce stable molecules is called **covalent bonding**.

The oxygen atom contains eight protons and eight neutrons in the nucleus with eight orbiting electrons. The inner quantum shell contains its maximum of two electrons, leaving six electrons in the second shell (Fig. 1.1). As this second shell may contain up to eight electrons, it requires two electrons to complete the shell and become stable. It may therefore combine with two hydrogen atoms by sharing electrons to form a water molecule (Fig. 1.4). In this way the outer shells of the oxygen atom and both hydrogen atoms are completed and a relatively stable molecule is formed.

Carbon with its six electrons (Fig. 1.1) has an inner shell containing two, leaving four in the outer shell. It requires four

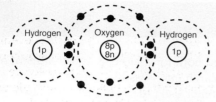

Water molecule (H₂O)
The oxygen atom shares 2 electrons with each hydrogen atom.
Both molecules thereby complete their outer shell - the
hydrogen atom with 2 electrons, the oxygen atom with 8

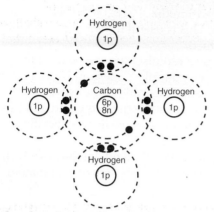

Methane molecule (CH₄)
The carbon atom shares 2 electrons with each hydrogen atom.
Each hydrogen atom thus completes its outer shell with 2
electrons, while the carbon atom completes its outer shell with 8

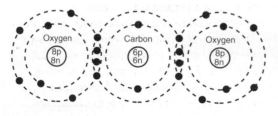

Carbon dioxide molecule (CO₂)
The carbon atom shares 4 electrons with each oxygen atom. All
three atoms thereby complete their outer shells with 8 electrons

*Fig. 1.4 Atomic models of the molecules of
water, methane and carbon dioxide*

TABLE 1.2   **Relative abundance by weight of
elements in humans compared to the earth's crust**

Element	Human	Earth's crust
Oxygen	63.0	46.5
Carbon	19.5	0.1
Hydrogen	9.5	0.2
Nitrogen	5.0	0.0001
Phosphorus	0.5	1.5

more electrons to fill this shell. It may therefore combine with four hydrogen atoms each of which shares its single electron. This molecule is called methane CH_4 (Fig. 1.4). It may also combine with two oxygen atoms, each of which shares two electrons. This molecule is carbon dioxide (Fig. 1.4).

When an atom, e.g. hydrogen, requires one electron to complete its outer shell it is said to have a **combining power (valency)** of one. Oxygen, which requires two electrons to complete its outer shell, has a combining power of two. Likewise nitrogen has a combining power of three and carbon of four.

When two atoms share a single electron, the bond is referred to as a **single bond** and is written with a single line, e.g. the hydrogen molecule is H—H and water may be represented as H—O—H. If two atoms share two electrons a **double bond** is formed. It is represented by a double line, e.g. carbon dioxide may be written as O=C=O. To form stable molecules, hydrogen must therefore have a single bond; oxygen two bonds (either two singles or one double); nitrogen must have three bonds (either three singles, or one single and one double); and carbon must have four bonds. It should now be apparent that these four atoms can combine in a number of different ways to form a variety of molecules. This partly explains the abundance of these elements in living organisms although some are relatively rare in the earth's crust (Table 1.2).

Carbon in particular can be seen to be almost 200 times more abundant in living organisms than in the earth's crust. Why should this be so? In the first place, carbon with its combining power of four can form molecules with a wide variety of other elements such as hydrogen, oxygen, nitrogen, sulphur, phosphorus and chlorine. This versatility allows great diversity in living organisms. More importantly, carbon can form long chains linked by single, double and triple bonds. These chains may be thousands of carbon atoms long. Such large molecules are essential to living organisms, not least as structural components. Furthermore, these chains have great stability – another essential feature. Carbon compounds may also form rings. These rings and chains may be combined with each other to give giant molecules of almost infinite variety. Examples of the size, diversity and complexity of carbon molecules can be found among the three major groups of biological compounds: carbohydrates, fats and proteins.

These are discussed in more detail in Chapter 2.

1.2.1 Ionic bonding

In addition to forming covalent bonds through the sharing of electrons, atoms may stabilize themselves by losing or gaining electrons to form ions. The loss of an electron (oxidation) leaves the atom positively charged (oxidized). The gain of an electron (reduction) leaves the atom negatively charged (reduced). Oppositely charged atoms attract one another forming **ionic bonds**. Sodium, for example, tends to lose an electron forming a Na^+ ion; chlorine tends to gain an electron forming a Cl^- ion. These two oppositely charged ions form ionic bonds and form sodium chloride (common salt).

1.2.2 Hydrogen bonds

The electrons in a molecule do not distribute themselves evenly but tend to group at one position. This region will consequently be more negative than the rest of the molecule. The molecule is said to be **polarized**. The negative region of such a molecule will be attracted to the positive region of a similarly polarized molecule. A weak electrostatic bond between the two is formed. In biological systems this type of bond is frequently a hydrogen bond. These bonds are weak individually, but collectively form important forces which alter the physical properties of molecules. Water forms hydrogen bonds which, as we shall see in Chapter 17, significantly affect its properties and hence its biological importance.

1.3 Cellular organization

In 1665, Robert Hooke, using a compound microscope, discovered that cork was composed of numerous small units. He called these units, **cells**. In the years which followed, Hooke and other researchers discovered that many other types of material were similarly composed of cells. By 1838, the amount of plant material shown to be composed of cells convinced Matthias Schleiden, a German botanist, that all plants were made up of cells. The following year, Theodor Schwann reached the same conclusion about the organization of animals. Their joint findings became known as the **cell theory**. It was of considerable biological significance as it suggested a common denominator for all living matter and so unified the nature of organisms. The theory makes the cell the fundamental unit of structure and function in living organisms. Hooke had originally thought the cell to be hollow, and that the wall represented the living portion. It soon became clear that cells were far from hollow. With the development of better light microscopes, first the nucleus and then organelles such as the chloroplasts became visible. One hundred years after Schleiden and Schwann put forward the cell theory, the development of the **electron microscope** revolutionized our understanding of cell structure. With its ability to magnify up to 500 times more than the light microscope, the electron microscope revealed the fine structure of cells including many new organelles. This detail is called the **ultrastructure** of the cell. The complexity of cellular structure so revealed led to the emergence of a new field of biology, **cytology** – the study of cell ultrastructure. This shows that while organisms are very diverse in their structures and cells vary considerably in size and shape, there is nevertheless a remarkable similarity in their basic structure and organization. This structure and organization is studied in Chapter 4.

1.4   Colonial organization

The first colonies may have arisen when individual unicells failed to separate after cell division. Within colonies each cell is capable of carrying out all the essential life processes. Indeed, if separated from the colony, any cell is capable of surviving independently. The only advantage of a colonial grouping is that the size of the unit probably deters some predators and thus increases the group's survival prospects.

If one cell in a colony should lose the ability to carry out a vital process, it could only survive by relying on other cells in the colony to perform the process on its behalf. The loss of one function, however, might permit the cell to perform one or other of its functions more efficiently, because the energy and resources required by the missing function could be directed towards the remaining ones. In this way, the individual cells within a colony could have become different from one another in both structure and function, a process known as **differentiation**. Further changes of this type would finally result in cells performing a single function. This is known as **specialization**. Clearly specialization must be organized in such a way that all essential functions are still performed by the colony as a whole. With increasing specialization, and the consequent loss of more and more functions, any cell becomes increasingly dependent on others in the colony for its survival. This **interdependence** of cells must be highly organized. Groups of cells must be coordinated so that the colony carries out its activities efficiently. Such coordination between the different cells is called **integration**. Once the cells become so dependent on each other that they are no longer capable of surviving independently, then the structure is no longer a colony but a **multicellular organism**.

1.5   Tissue organization

A tissue is a group of similar cells, along with any intercellular substance, which performs a particular function. Some cells, e.g. unicellular protozoans and algae, perform all functions which are essential to life. It is impossible for such cells to be efficient at all functions, because each function requires a different type of cellular organization. Whereas one function might require the cell to be long and thin, another might require it to be spherical. One function might require many mitochondria, another, very few. Acid conditions might suit one activity but not another. No one cell can possibly provide the optimum conditions for all activities. For this reason, cells are specialized to perform one, or at most a few, functions. To increase efficiency, cells performing the same functions are grouped together into a tissue. The study of tissues is called **histology**. Some organisms, e.g. cnidarians, are at the tissue level of organization. Their physiological activities are performed by tissues rather than organs.

1.6 Organ level of organization

An organ is a structural and functional unit of a plant or animal. It comprises a number of tissues which are coordinated to perform a variety of functions, although one major function often predominates. The majority of plants and animals are composed of organs. Most organs do not function independently but in groups called **organ systems**. A typical organ system is the digestive system which comprises organs such as the stomach, duodenum, ileum, liver and pancreas. Certain organs may belong to more than one system. The pancreas, for example, forms part of the **endocrine (hormone)** system as well as the digestive system, because it produces the hormones insulin and glucagon, as well as the digestive enzymes amylase and trypsinogen.

1.7 Social level of organization

A **population** is a number of individuals of the same species which occupy a particular area at the same time. In itself, a population is not a level of organization as no organization exists between the individual members. In some species, however, the individuals do exhibit some organization in which they cooperate for their mutual benefit. Such a population is more accurately termed a **society**. It differs from a colony (although the term is often used) in that the individuals are not physically connected to one another, but totally separate. As with a colony, the individuals can survive independently of others in the society, although usually somewhat less successfully. Unlike most colonies, there is considerable coordination between the society members and communication forms an integral part of their organization. Humans form the most advanced of all societies.

2 Molecular organization

2.1 Inorganic ions

Water is the most important inorganic molecule in biology and its chemical structure and properties are described in Chapter 17. Dissolved in the water within humans are a large number of inorganic ions. Typically they constitute about 1% by weight, but they are nonetheless essential. They are divided into two groups: the **macronutrients** or **major elements** which are needed in very small quantities, and the **micronutrients** or **trace elements** which are needed in minute amounts (a few parts per million).

TABLE 2.1   **Inorganic ions, their functions and sources in humanss**

Inorganic ions	Functions	Food source	Notes
Nitrate NO_3^- Ammonium NH_4^+	Nitrogen is a component of amino acids, proteins, vitamins, coenzymes and nucleotides. Some hormones contain nitrogen, e.g. insulin	Meat, milk, eggs and other protein foods	Deficiency of protein causes kwashiorkor
Phosphate PO_4^{3-} Orthophosphate $H_2PO_4^-$	A component of nucleotides, ATP and some proteins. Used in the phosphorylation of sugars in respiration. A major constituent of bone and teeth. A component of cell membranes in the form of phospholipids	Meat and dairy products	Deficiency can result in a form of bone malformation called rickets
Sulphate SO_4^{2-}	Sulphur is a component of some proteins and certain coenzymes, e.g. acetyl coenzyme A	Meat, milk, eggs and other protein foods	Sulphur forms important bridges between the polypeptide chains of some proteins, giving them their tertiary structure
Potassium K^+	Helps to maintain the electrical, osmotic and anion/cation balance across cell membranes. Assists active transport of certain materials across the cell membrane. Necessary for protein synthesis and is a co-factor in respiration.	Meat, fish and vegetables	Potassium plays an important role in the transmission of nerve impulses. Deficiency causes muscle weakness, heart and nerve problems
Calcium Ca^{2+}	The main constituent of bones and teeth. Needed for the clotting of blood and the contraction of muscle	Dairy products	Deficiency leads to rickets and delay in the clotting of blood
Sodium Na^+	Helps to maintain the electrical, osmotic and anion/cation balance across cell membranes. Assists active transport of certain materials across the cell membrane	Added to many prepared foods e.g. cheese and bacon	Necessary for the functioning of the kidney, nerves and muscles; deficiency may cause muscular cramps. Sodium ions have much the same function as potassium ions and may be exchanged for them

cont.

TABLE 2.1 *cont.*

Inorganic ions	Functions	Food source	Notes
Chlorine Cl^-	Helps to maintain the electrical, osmotic and anion/cation balance across cell membranes. Needed for the formation of hydrochloric acid in gastric juice. Assists in the transport of carbon dioxide by blood (chloride shift)	Added to many prepared foods e.g. cheese and bacon	Deficiency may cause muscular cramps
Magnesium Mg^{2+}	An activator for some enzymes, e.g. ATPase. A component of bone and teeth	Green vegetables	Deficiency causes dilation of blood vessels, irregular heart rhythm and nervous disorders
Iron Fe^{2+} or Fe^{3+}	A constituent of electron carriers, e.g. cytochromes, needed in respiration. A constituent of certain enzymes, e.g. dehydrogenases, decarboxylases, peroxidases and catalase. Forms part of the haem group in the respiratory pigments haemoglobin and myoglobin	Liver, kidneys, other meat and vegetables	Deficiency leads to anaemia
Manganese Mn^{2+}	An activator of certain enzymes e.g. phosphatases. A growth factor in bone development	Vegetables and cereal grains	Deficiency leads to muscle and nerve disorders and bone deformations
Copper Cu^{2+}	A constituent of some enzymes, e.g. cytochrome oxidase and tyrosinase. Needed for blood formation	Seafood and liver	Deficiency causes fatigue and anaemia
Iodine I^-	A constituent of the hormone thyroxine, which controls metabolism	Seafood and iodized salt	Deficiency causes cretinism in children and goitre in adults
Cobalt Co^{2+}	Constituent of vitamin B_{12}, which is important in the synthesis of RNA, nucleoprotein and red blood cells	Meat	Deficiency causes pernicious anaemia
Zinc Zn^{2+}	An activator of certain enzymes, e.g. carbonic anhydrase	Most foods but especially meat	Carbonic anhydrase is important in the transport of carbon dioxide in blood
Fluorine F^-	A component of teeth and bones	Drinking water	Associates with calcium to form calcium fluoride which strengthens teeth and helps prevent decay

2.2 Carbohydrates

Carbohydrates comprise a large group of organic compounds which contain carbon, hydrogen and oxygen and which are either aldehydes or ketones. The word carbohydrate suggests that these organic compounds are hydrates of carbon. Their general formula is $C_x(H_2O)_y$. The word carbohydrate is convenient rather than exact, because while most examples do conform to the formula, e.g. glucose —$C_6H_{12}O_6$, sucrose $C_{12}H_{22}O_{11}$, a few do not, e.g. deoxyribose —$C_5H_{10}O_4$. Carbohydrates are divided into three groups: the **monosaccharides** ('single-sugars'), the **disaccharides** ('double-sugars') and the **polysaccharides** ('many-sugars').

The functions of carbohydrates, although variable, are in the main concerned with storage and liberation of energy. A full list of individual carbohydrates and their functions is given in Table 2.2 on page 18.

2.3   Monosaccharides

Monosaccharides are a group of sweet, soluble crystalline molecules of relatively low molecular mass. They are named with the suffix -ose. Monosaccharides contain either an aldehyde group (—CHO), in which case they are called **aldoses** or **aldo-sugars**, or they contain a ketone group (C = O), in which case they are termed **ketoses** or **keto-sugars**. The general formula for a monosaccharide is $(CH_2O)_n$. Where n = 3, the sugar is called a **triose** sugar, n = 5, a **pentose** sugar, and n = 6, a **hexose** sugar.

NOTEBOOK

The mole

The mole is the scientific unit for the amount of a substance and is expressed as the symbol – **mol**. One mole of any substance contains the same number of particles (atoms, molecules or ions). This number is known as **Avogadro's constant** and is equal to 6.023×10^{23}. To give you some idea of the vast size of this number, it is equal to the total human population of one hundred million million worlds identical to ours!

Different atoms (and therefore molecules and ions) have different masses. Chemists use the atomic weight of carbon, set at 12, as a standard against which to compare the weight of other atoms. Thus hydrogen which has a mass one twelfth that of carbon is given the mass of 1. These are known as relative atomic masses. The relative atomic mass of an element in grams always contains a mole of its atoms (i.e. 6.023×10^{23} atoms). The same is true of the relative **molecular** mass of a molecule. Thus:

a mole of hydrogen atoms (H) has a mass of 1 g
a mole of hydrogen molecules (H_2) has a mass of 2 g
a mole of oxygen atoms (O) has a mass of 16 g
a mole of oxygen molecules (O_2) has a mass of 32 g
a mole of water molecules (H_2O) has a mass of 18 g.

To find out the number of moles in a given mass of a substance we simply divide the mass (in grams) by the mass of one mole,

e.g. in 90 g of water there are $\frac{90}{18}$ moles

$= 5$ moles (or $5 \times 6.023 \times 10^{23}$ molecules)

When dealing with gases, we use volume rather than weight to measure amounts. A mole of any gas at standard temperature and pressure (0 °C and 1 atmosphere) occupies $22.4 \, dm^3$ (litres). At room temperature (20 °C) this volume expands to $24 \, dm^3$. That all gases, regardless of the mass of the molecules they comprise, should occupy the same volume may seem surprising. In a gas however, the molecules are so far apart, that the size of the molecule itself is unimportant in terms of the volume occupied. Imagine several balls bouncing around inside a large hall – they could all be fitted in whether they were golf balls, tennis balls or footballs.

The concentration of a solution can be expressed in moles. A $1 \, mol \, dm^{-3}$ solution (1M solution) contains 1 mol in each dm^3 of the

2.3.1 Structure of monosaccharides

Probably the best known monosaccharide, glucose, has the formula $C_6H_{12}O_6$. All but one of the six carbon atoms possesses an hydroxyl group (—OH). The remaining carbon atom forms part of the aldehyde group. Glucose may be represented by a straight chain of six carbon atoms. These are numbered beginning at the carbon of the aldehyde group. Glucose in common with other hexoses and pentoses easily forms stable ring structures. At any one time most molecules exist as rings rather than a chain. In the case of glucose, carbon atom number 1 may combine with the oxygen atom on carbon 5. This forms a six-sided structure known as a **pyranose** ring. In the case of

solution. In other words to make up a 1 mol dm^{-3} (1 M) solution of a substance we add the relative molecular mass in grams of that substance to 1 dm^3 (litre) of water. In the case of sucrose ($C_{12}H_{22}O_{11}$) this is:

Molecule	Number in sucrose	Relative atomic mass (g)	Total mass (g)
CARBON	12	12	$12 \times 12 = 144$
HYDROGEN	22	1	$22 \times 1 = 22$
OXYGEN	11	16	$11 \times 16 = 176$
			Total 342 g

Hence we dissolve 342 g of sucrose in 1 dm^3 of water

To convert moles into number of molecules, mass or volume and vice versa simply follow the scheme below.

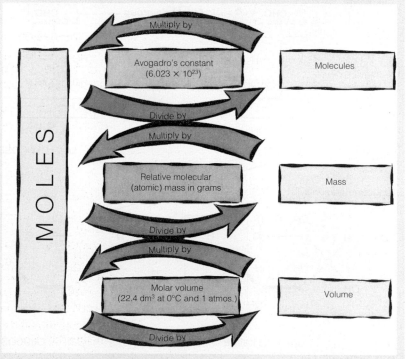

Conversion to and from moles

fructose, it is carbon atom number 2 which links with the oxygen on carbon atom 5. This forms a five-sided structure called a **furanose** ring (Fig. 2.1). Both glucose and fructose can exist in both pyranose and furanose forms.

Glucose, in common with most carbohydrates, can exist as a number of **isomers** (they possess the same molecular formula but differ in the arrangement of their atoms). One type of isomerism, called **sterioisomerism**, occurs when the same atoms, or groups, are joined together but differ in their arrangement in space. One form of sterioisomerism, called **optical isomerism**, results in isomers which can rotate the plane of polarized light (light which is vibrating in one plane only). The isomer which rotates the plane of polarized light to the right is called the **dextro(D or +) form**; the isomer rotating it to the left is called the **laevo(L or −) form**. (By present convention, however, the D and L forms are named by different criteria, regardless of the direction in which they rotate polarized light.) While the chemical and physical properties of the two forms are the same, many enzymes will only act on one type. There would seem to be no reason why one form should be preferred to another, and yet almost all naturally occurring carbohydrates are of the D(+) form. It must be assumed that at an early stage in evolution the D(+) form was selected by chance and the consequent development of enzymes specific to this type ensured that all subsequent development was based on this form. Both D(+) and L(−) forms of glucose are shown in Fig. 2.1. The D(+) and L(−) forms of glucose arise because the relevant carbon atom has four different groups attached to it. This is called an **asymmetric carbon atom.** Another asymmetric carbon atom arises when

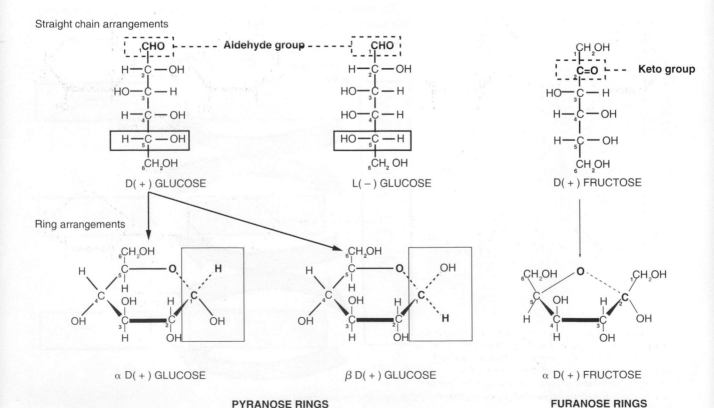

Fig. 2.1 *Structure of various isomers of glucose and fructose*

glucose forms a ring structure. This gives rise to two further isomers, the α-**form** and the β-**form**. Both types occur naturally and, as we shall see later, result in considerable biological differences when they form polymers. Fig. 2.1 again illustrates both types.

2.4   Disaccharides

Monosaccharides may combine together in pairs to give a **disaccharide** (double-sugar). The union involves the loss of a single water molecule and is therefore a **condensation reaction**. The addition of water, under suitable conditions, is necessary if the disaccharide is to be split into its constituent monosaccharides. This is called **hydrolysis** 'water-breakdown' or, more accurately, 'breakdown *by* water'. The bond which is formed is called a **glycosidic bond**. It is usually formed between carbon atom 1 of one monosaccharide and carbon atom 4 of the other, hence it is called a 1–4 glycosidic bond (see Fig. 2.2). Any two monosaccharides may be linked in this way to form a disaccharide of which maltose, sucrose and lactose are the most common.

   Disaccharides, like monosaccharides, are sweet, soluble and crystalline. Maltose and lactose are reducing sugars, whereas sucrose is a non-reducing sugar. The significance of this is considered in Section 2.5.4.

maltose (malt sugar) = glucose + glucose

sucrose (cane sugar) = glucose + fructose

lactose (milk sugar) = glucose + galactose

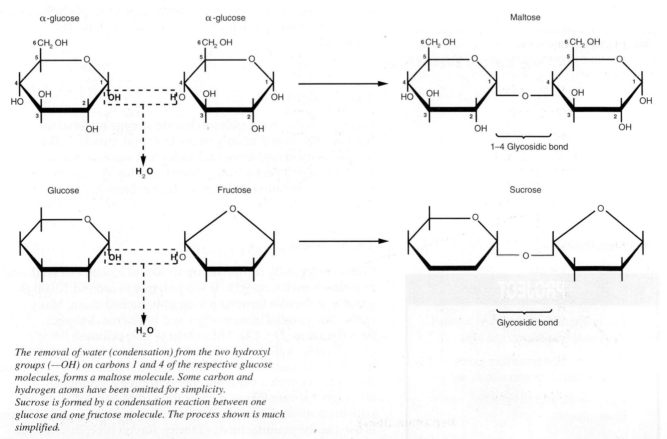

The removal of water (condensation) from the two hydroxyl groups (—OH) on carbons 1 and 4 of the respective glucose molecules, forms a maltose molecule. Some carbon and hydrogen atoms have been omitted for simplicity.
Sucrose is formed by a condensation reaction between one glucose and one fructose molecule. The process shown is much simplified.

Fig. 2.2 Formation of maltose and sucrose

2.5   Polysaccharides

In the same way that two monosaccharides may combine in pairs to give a disaccharide, many monosaccharides may combine by condensation reactions to give a **polysaccharide**. The number of monosaccharides which combine is variable and the chain produced can be branched or unbranched. The chains may be folded, thus making them compact and therefore ideal for storage. The size of the molecule makes them insoluble – another feature which suits them for storage as they exert no osmotic influence and do not easily diffuse out of the cell. Upon hydrolysis, polysaccharides can be converted to their constituent monosaccharides ready for use as respiratory substrates. Starch and glycogen are examples of storage polysaccharides.

Starch and glycogen are degraded in the digestive tract by α-amylase, β-amylase and amylo-α (1→6)-glucosidase.

α-amylase is an endoglucosidase which randomly hydrolyses α- (1→4) linkages of the side chains of glycogen and amylopectin. It can cleave either side of a branch point except in very highly branched regions.

β-amylase, an exoglycosidase, sequentially removes β-maltose from the ends of the outer branches but stops cleavage before any branch points are reached.

The structures remaining after hydrolysis by α- and β-amylase are called limit dextrins and comprise about three dozen glucose residues.

Amylo-α-(1→6)-glucosidase, the debranching enzyme, catalyses the hydrolysis of the α- (1→6) glycosidic bonds of the limit dextrins, thereby permitting further breakdown by α- and β-amylase.

2.5.1 Starch

Starch is a polysaccharide which is found in most parts of the plant in the form of small granules. It is a reserve food formed from any excess glucose produced during photosynthesis. It is common in the seeds of some plants, e.g. maize, where it forms the food supply for germination. Indirectly these starch stores form an important food supply for humans.

Starch is a mixture of two substances: amylose and amylopectin. Starches differ slightly from one plant species to the next, but on the whole they comprise 20% amylose, 79% amylopectin, and 1% of other substances such as phosphates and fatty acids. A comparison of amylose and amylopectin is given in Fig. 2.3.

2.5.2 Glycogen

Glycogen is the major polysaccharide storage material in humans. It is stored mainly in the liver and muscles. Like starch it is made up of α-glucose molecules and exists as granules. It is similar to amylopectin in structure but it has shorter chains (10–20 glucose units) and is more highly branched.

2.5.3 Cellulose

Cellulose typically comprises up to 50% of a plant cell wall, and in cotton it makes up 90%. It is a polymer of around 10 000 β-glucose molecules forming a long unbranched chain. Many chains run parallel to each other and have cross linkages between them (Fig. 2.4). These help to give cellulose its considerable stability which makes it a valuable structural material. The stability of cellulose makes it difficult to digest and therefore not such a valuable energy source for humans although it is valuable as dietary fibre (roughage). Cellulose's structural strength has long been recognized by humans. Cotton is used in the manufacture of fabrics. Rayon is produced from cellulose extracted from wood and its remarkable tensile

PROJECT

1. Put scrapings from round and wrinkled pea seeds on a microscope slide.

2. Stain with iodine/potassium iodide solution and cover with a cover slip.

3. Compare the starch grains from both types of seed.

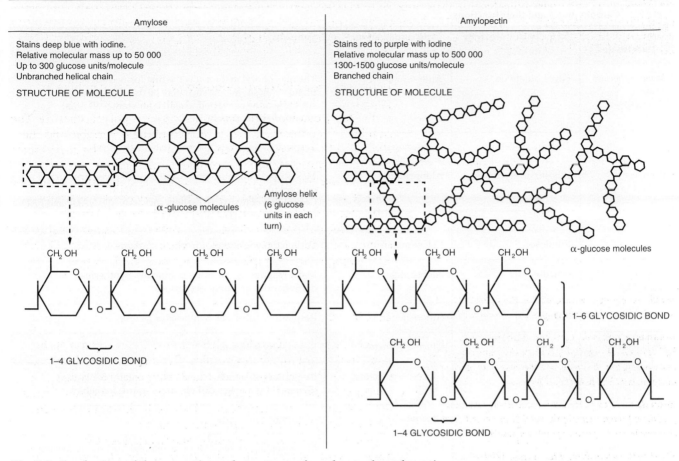

Amylose	Amylopectin
Stains deep blue with iodine. Relative molecular mass up to 50 000 Up to 300 glucose units/molecule Unbranched helical chain	Stains red to purple with iodine Relative molecular mass up to 500 000 1300-1500 glucose units/molecule Branched chain
STRUCTURE OF MOLECULE	STRUCTURE OF MOLECULE

Fig. 2.3. Comparison of the properties and structures of amylose and amylopectin

strength makes it especially useful in the manufacture of tyre cords. Cellophane, used in packaging, and celluloid, used in photographic film, are also cellulose derivatives. Paper is perhaps the best known cellulose product.

Being composed of β-glucose units, the chain, unlike that of starch, has adjacent glucose molecules rotated by 180°. This allows hydrogen bonds to be formed between the hydroxyl (—OH) groups on adjacent parallel chains which help to give cellulose its structural stability.

Simplified representation of the arrangement of glucose chains

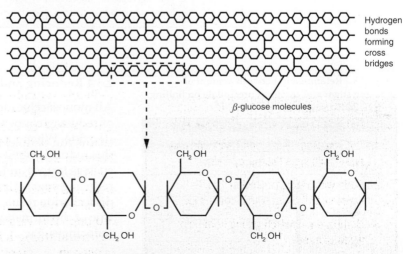

Fig. 2.4 Structure of the cellulose molecule

TABLE 2.2 **Carbohydrates and their functions**

Group of carbohydrates	Name of carbohydrate	Type/composition	Function
Monosaccharides Trioses $(C_3H_6O_3)$	Glyceraldehyde	Aldose sugar	The phosphorylated form is the first formed sugar in photosynthesis, and as such may be used as a respiratory substrate or be converted to starch for storage. It is an intermediate in glycolysis
	Dihydroxyacetone	Ketose sugar	Respiratory substrate. Intermediate in glycolysis
Pentoses $(C_5H_{10}O_5)$	Ribose/deoxyribose	Aldose sugars	Makes up part of nucleotides and as such gives structural support to the nucleic acids RNA and DNA. Constituent of hydrogen carriers such as NAD, NADP and FAD. Constituent of ATP
	Ribulose	Ketose sugar	Carbon dioxide acceptor in photosynthesis
Hexoses $(C_6H_{12}O_6)$	Glucose	Aldose sugar	Major respiratory substrate in humans. Synthesis of disaccharides and polysaccharides
	Galactose	Aldose sugar	Respiratory substrate. Synthesis of lactose
Disaccharides	Sucrose	Glucose + fructose	Respiratory substrate.
	Lactose	Glucose + galactose	Respiratory substrate. Human milk contains 5% lactose, therefore it is a major carbohydrate source for babies
	Maltose	Glucose + glucose	Respiratory substrate
Polysaccharides	Amylose Amylopectin } starch	Unbranched chain of α-glucose with 1–4 glycosidic links + branched chain of α-glucose units with 1–4 and 1–6 glycosidic links	Major storage carbohydrate in plants and food source for humans
	Glycogen	Highly branched short chains of α-glucose units with 1–4 glycosidic links	Major storage carbohydrate in humans
	Cellulose	Unbranched chain of β-glucose units with 1–4 glycosidic links + cross bridges	Gives structural support to cell walls

TABLE 2.3 **Relationship between amount of reducing sugar and colour of precipitate on boiling with Benedict's reagent**

Amount of reducing sugar	Colour of solution and precipitate
No reducing sugar	Blue
Increasing quantity of reducing sugar	Green
	Yellow
	Brown
	Red

2.5.4 Reducing and non-reducing sugars

All monosaccharides, whether aldo- or keto-sugars, are capable of reducing copper (II) sulphate in Benedict's reagent to copper (I) oxide. When monosaccharides combine to form disaccharides this reducing ability is often retained with the result that sugars such as lactose and maltose, although disaccharides, are still reducing sugars. In a few cases, however, the formation of a disaccharide results in the loss of this reducing ability. This is true of the formation of sucrose which is therefore a non-reducing sugar.

2.6   Lipids

Lipids are a large and varied group of organic compounds. Like carbohydrates, they contain carbon, hydrogen and oxygen, although the proportion of oxygen is much smaller in lipids. They are insoluble in water but dissolve readily in organic solvents such as acetone, alcohols and others. They are of two types: fats and oils. There is no basic difference between these two; fats are simply solid at room temperatures (10–20°C) whereas oils are liquid. The chemistry of lipids is very varied but they are all esters of **fatty acids** and an alcohol, of which **glycerol** is by far the most abundant. Glycerol has three hydroxyl (—OH) groups and each may combine with a separate fatty acid, forming a **triglyceride** (Fig. 2.5). It is a condensation reaction and thus hydrolysis of the triglyceride will again yield glycerol and three fatty acids.

The three triglycerides may all be the same, thereby forming a simple triglyceride, or they may be different in which case a mixed triglyceride is produced. In either case it is a condensation reaction.

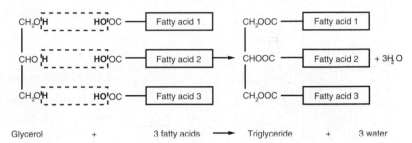

Fig. 2.5 Formation of a triglyceride

2.6.1 Fatty acids

As most naturally occurring lipids contain the same alcohol, namely glycerol, it is the nature of the fatty acids which determines the characteristics of any particular fat. All fatty acids contain a carboxyl group (—COOH). The remainder of the molecule is a hydrocarbon chain of varying length (examples are given in Table 2.4). This chain may possess one or more double bonds in which case it is said to be **unsaturated**. If, however, it possesses no double bonds it is said to be **saturated**.

It can be seen from Table 2.4 that the hydrocarbon chains may be very long. Within the fat they form long 'tails' which extend from the glycerol molecule. These 'tails' are **hydrophobic**, i.e. they repel water.

TABLE 2.4   **Nature and occurrence of some fatty acids**

Name of fatty acid	General formula	Saturated/ unsaturated	Occurrence
Butyric	C_3H_7COOH	Saturated	Butter fat
Linoleic	$C_{17}H_{31}COOH$	Unsaturated	Linseed oil
Oleic	$C_{17}H_{33}COOH$	Unsaturated	All fats
Palmitic	$C_{15}H_{31}COOH$	Saturated	Animal and vegetable fats
Stearic	$C_{17}H_{35}COOH$	Saturated	Animal and vegetable fats
Arachidic	$C_{19}H_{39}COOH$	Saturated	Peanut oil
Cerotic	$C_{25}H_{51}COOH$	Saturated	Wool oil

2.6.2 Phospholipids

Phospholipids are lipids in which one of the fatty acid groups is replaced by phosphoric acid (H_3PO_4) (Fig. 2.6). The phosphoric acid is **hydrophilic** (attracts water) in contrast to the remainder of the molecule which is **hydrophobic** (repels water). Having one end of the phospholipid attracting water while the other end repels it affects its role in the cell membrane.

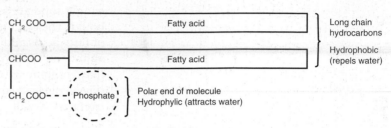

Fig. 2.6 Structure of a phospholipid

2.6.3 Functions of lipids

1. An energy source – Upon breakdown they yield $38\,kJ\,g^{-1}$ of energy. This compares favourably with carbohydrates which yield $17\,kJ\,g^{-1}$.

2. Storage – On account of their high energy yield upon breakdown, they make excellent energy stores. For the equivalent amount of energy stored they possess less than half the mass of carbohydrate. This makes them especially useful because locomotion requires mass to be kept to a minimum.

3. Insulation – Fats conduct heat only slowly and so are useful insulators. If fat is to be stored because of its concentrated energy supply, it may as well be put to a secondary use. It is stored beneath the skin (subcutaneous fat) where it helps to retain body heat.

4. Protection – Another secondary use to which stored fat is put is as a packing material around delicate organs. Fat surrounding the kidneys, for instance, helps to protect them from physical damage.

5. Waterproofing – Skin produces an oily secretion from its sebaceous glands, which waterproofs the body.

6. Cell membranes – Phospholipids are major components of the cell membrane and contribute to many of its properties (see Section 4.2.2).

2.6.4 Steroids

Steroids are related to lipids, and **cholesterol** is perhaps the best known. It is found in humans where it is important in the synthesis of steroid hormones, such as oestrogen and cortisone. Other important steroids include vitamin D and bile acids.

Cholesterol

Cholesterol

Cholesterol is a lipid containing four rings of carbon and hydrogen atoms with a branched side chain. A single hydroxyl group (OH^-) gives the molecule a small charge as the result of ionization. Cholesterol is very hydrophobic.

Most cholesterol in the body is found in the membranes of cells. The plasma membrane has the most, almost one cholesterol molecule for each phospholipid. In internal membranes the ratio is closer to $1:10$.

Cholesterol is essential for the functioning of plasma membranes where it plays two main roles. Firstly it limits the uncontrolled leakage of small molecules (water and ions) in and out of the plasma membrane. The cell can thus control the passage of solutes and ions using specialized membrane proteins and without wasting energy counteracts their leakage. Cholesterol is an important constituent of myelin and helps to prevent the outward flow of ions which would 'short circuit' the movement of nerve impulses along the axon. The second role of cholesterol in membranes is to pull together the fatty acid chains in phospholipids, restricting their movement, but not making them solid. Cholesterol is also used by the liver for making bile salts and, in small quantities, is used to make steroids in the ovaries, testes and adrenal glands.

In total the body contains a pool of about 120–150 g of cholesterol which is maintained by biosynthesis in the liver and intestine and by ingestion of meat, seafood, eggs and dairy produce. Vegans take in no cholesterol but most other diets result in an intake of approximately 0.5 g, the body making a further 0.5 g, per day. Cholesterol is lost from the body mainly as bile salts, but also as bile, in cells from the lining of the intestine and a tiny percentage as steroid hormones in the urine.

Cholesterol is insoluble in water but can be carried in the blood plasma in the form of lipoproteins. The balance of these lipoproteins is usually maintained by special receptors in the livers cells but saturated fats in the diet decrease their activity and hence lead to a rise in plasma cholesterol. Deposits of crystalline cholesterol and droplets of cholesterol esters can cause thickening of the artery walls (atherosclerosis). This can lead to heart attacks (from blocking of coronary arteries), strokes (brain arteries blocked) or blockages of arteries in the legs. **Atherosclerosis** may follow damage caused to the artery walls by high blood pressure and smoking. Smoking considerably decreases the concentration of the antioxidant vitamins E and C in the blood resulting in the oxidation of some lipoproteins.

The products of oxidation are often toxic to the cells of the artery and cause them to behave abnormally. The damaged cells release substances which cause the blood to clot and the artery to contract. Macrophages which degrade the oxidized lipoproteins are unable to deal with the cholesterol it carries. Eventually they fill with cholesterol and die, depositing the cholesterol back into the artery.

T.S. human aorta with a fatty atheroma partially obstructing the interior

2.7 Proteins

Proteins are organic compounds of large molecular mass (up to 40 000 000 for some viral proteins but more typically several thousand, e.g. haemoglobin = 64 500). They are not truly soluble in water, but form colloidal suspensions. In addition to carbon, hydrogen and oxygen, they always contain nitrogen, usually sulphur and sometimes phosphorus. Whereas there are relatively few carbohydrates and fats, the number of proteins is almost limitless. A simple bacterium such as *Escherichia coli* has around 800, and humans have over 10 000. They are specific to each species. Glucose is glucose in whatever organism it occurs, but proteins vary from one species to another. Indeed, it is the proteins rather than the fats or carbohydrates which determine the characteristics of a species. Proteins are rarely stored in organisms, except in eggs or seeds where they are used to form the new tissue. The word protein (from the Greek) means 'of first importance' and was coined by a Dutch chemist, Mulder, because he thought they played a fundamental rôle in cells. We now know that proteins form the structural basis of all living cells and that Mulder's judgement was sound.

PROJECT

Breakfast cereals have labels on the outside of the packet indicating the amounts of the various ingredients

Use your knowledge of the various food tests to find out if the claims on the labels are correct.

2.7.1 Amino acids

Amino acids are a group of over a hundred chemicals of which around twenty commonly occur in proteins. They always contain a basic group, the amino group (—NH_2) and an acid group, the carboxyl group (—COOH). (See Fig. 2.7.) Most amino acids have one of each group and are therefore neutral, but a few have more amino groups than carboxyl ones (basic amino acids) while others have more carboxyl than amino groups (acidic amino acids). With the exception of glycine, all amino acids have an asymmetric carbon atom and therefore exhibit optical isomerism, having both D(+) and L(−) forms. Whereas all naturally occurring carbohydrates are of the D(+) form, all naturally occurring amino acids are of the L(−) form. Amino acids are soluble in water where they form ions. These ions are formed by the loss of a hydrogen atom from the carboxyl group, making it negatively charged. This hydrogen atom associates with the amino group, making it positively charged. The ion is therefore **dipolar** – having a positive and a negative pole. Such ions are called **zwitterions** (see Fig. 2.8). Amino acids therefore have both acidic and basic properties, i.e. they are **amphoteric**. Being amphoteric means that amino acids act as **buffer solutions**. A buffer solution is one which resists the tendency to alter its pH even when small amounts of acid or alkali are added to it. Such a property is essential in biological systems where any sudden change in pH could adversely affect the performance of enzymes.

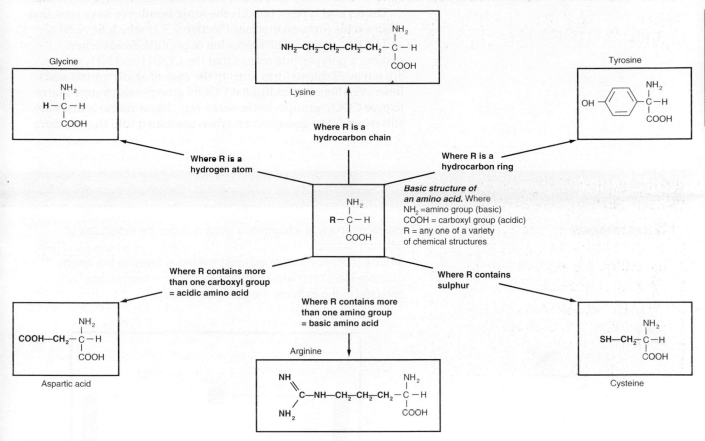

Fig. 2.7 *Structure of a range of amino acids*

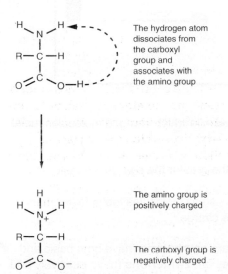

Fig. 2.8 *Zwitterion formation in amino acids*

2.7.2 Formation of polypeptides

We have seen that monosaccharides may be linked to form disaccharides and polysaccharides by the loss of water (condensation reaction). Similarly, fats are formed from condensation reactions between fatty acids and glycerol. The formation of polypeptides follows the same pattern. A condensation reaction occurs between the amino group of one amino acid and the carboxyl group of another, to form a **dipeptide** (see Fig. 2.9, on page 26). Further combinations of this type extend the length of the chain to form a **polypeptide** (see Figs. 2.10 and 2.11).

A polypeptide usually contains many hundreds of amino acids. Polypeptides may be linked by forces such as disulphide bridges to give proteins comprising thousands of amino acids.

2.7.3 Structure of polypeptides

The chains of amino acids which make up a polypeptide have a specific three-dimensional shape (see Fig. 2.12). This shape is important in the functioning of proteins, especially enzymes. The shape of a polypeptide molecule is due to four types of bonding which occur between various amino acids in the chain.

The first type of bond is called a **disulphide bond**. It arises between sulphur-containing groups on any two cysteine molecules. These bonds may arise between cysteine molecules in the same amino acid chain (intrachain) or between molecules in different chains (interchain).

The second type of bond is the **ionic bond**. We have seen that amino acids form zwitterions (Section 2.7.1) which have NH_3^+ and COO^- groups. The formation of peptide bonds when making a polypeptide means that the COOH and NH_2 groups are not available to form ions. In the case of acidic amino acids, however, there are additional COOH groups which may ionize to give COO^- groups. In the same way, basic amino acids may still retain NH_3^+ groups even when combined into the structure

NOTEBOOK

Electrophoresis

Electrophoresis is a technique used to separate molecules of different electrical charge. Under the influence of an electrical field, **anions** (negatively charged ions) will move towards the **anode** (positive electrode) while **cations** (positively charged ions) are attracted to the cathode (negative electrode).

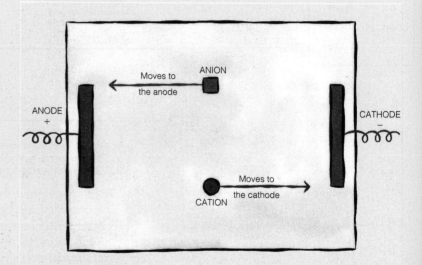

Two factors affect the speed with which charged molecules move towards an electrode:

1. The amount of charge – the greater the charge the faster the molecule moves.
2. The size of the molecule – small molecules move faster than larger ones with the same charge.

Amino acids and proteins are **amphoteric** (have both basic and acidic properties) because they are **zwitterions** (have positively and negatively charged groups).

The amount of positive or negative charge is affected by pH. Each molecule has a specific pH at which the total positive charge is exactly equal to the total negative charge, i.e. it is electrically neutral and has no tendency to move to either the anode or cathode of an electric field. This is known as the **isoelectric point**. At higher pH protein and amino acid molecules become more negatively charged while at lower pH they become more positively charged.

of a polypeptide. In addition NH_3^+ and COO^- can occur at the ends of a polypeptide chain. Any of these available NH_3^+ and COO^- groups may form ionic bonds which help to give a polypeptide molecule its particular shape. These ionic bonds are weak and may be broken by alterations in the pH of the medium around the polypeptide.

The third type of bond is the **hydrogen bond**. This occurs between certain hydrogen atoms and certain oxygen atoms

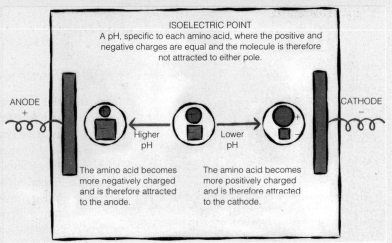

The molecules being separated have to be supported in an appropriate medium such as paper or a thin layer of gel.

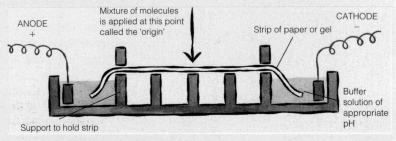

Typical apparatus for carrying out electrophoresis

Either end of a strip of the medium is dipped in a small reservoir of buffer solution of the appropriate pH. Each reservoir also contains an electrode.

The electrical field is applied for a specific period of time and then the position of the molecules is determined by adding a suitable stain to colour them. The molecules are separated according to their charges; the negatively charged ones moving to the anode with the most negatively charged ones moving furthest. The positively charged ones move to the cathode and again the more positive they are the closer they get to the cathode.

It is possible to treat the mixture being separated in such a way that all the molecules are equally negatively charged. These can then be loaded at the cathode end of the apparatus and will be attracted to the anode. The distance they travel in a given time will then depend not on their charge but their size, the smaller molecules moving further than the larger ones.

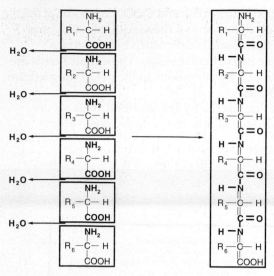

Amino acid molecules
(where R_1, R_2, R_3 etc. represent
any of the 20 or so groups
found in naturally-occurring amino
acids)

Polypeptide
(part of)

Fig. 2.10 Formation of a polypeptide

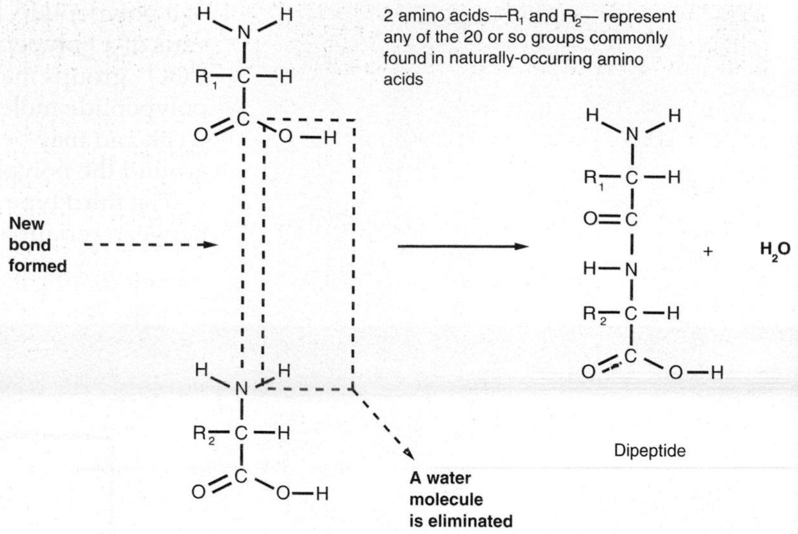

A simplified representation of a polypeptide chain to show three types of bonding responsible for shaping the chain. In practice the polypeptide chains are longer, contain more of these three types of bond and have a three dimensional shape.

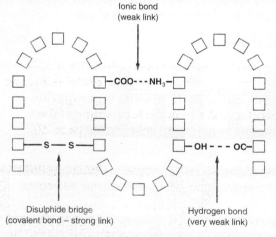

Ionic bond
(weak link)

—COO- - -NH₃—

Disulphide bridge
(covalent bond – strong link)

Hydrogen bond
(very weak link)

—OH - - - OC—

—S — S—

Fig. 2.11 Types of bond in a polypeptide chain

2 amino acids—R_1 and R_2— represent any of the 20 or so groups commonly found in naturally-occurring amino acids

New
bond
formed

A water
molecule
is eliminated

Dipeptide

+ H_2O

Fig. 2.9 Formation of a dipeptide

within the polypeptide chain. The hydrogen atoms have a small positive charge on them (electropositive) and the oxygen atoms a small negative charge (electronegative). The two charged atoms are attracted together and form a hydrogen bond. While each bond is very weak, the sheer number of bonds means that they play a considerable rôle in the shape and stability of a polypeptide molecule.

The fourth type is **hydrophobic interactions** which are interactions between non-polar R groups. These cause the protein to fold as hydrophobic side groups are shielded from water.

2.7.4 Fibrous proteins

The fibrous proteins have a primary structure of regular repetitive sequences. They form long chains which may run parallel to one another, being linked by cross bridges. They are very stable molecules and have structural rôles within organisms. Collagen is a good example. It is a common constituent of human connective tissue, especially in structures requiring physical strength, e.g. tendons. It has a primary structure which is largely a repeat of the tripeptide sequence, glycine – proline – alanine, and forms a long unbranched chain. Three such chains are wound into a triple helix, with cross bridges linking them to each other and providing additional structural support. (Compare the repeating glucose units, parallel chains and cross links of the structural carbohydrate cellulose.)

2.7.5 Globular proteins

In contrast to fibrous proteins, the globular proteins have highly irregular sequences of amino acids in their polypeptide chains. Their shape is also different, being compact globules. If a fibrous protein is likened to a series of strands of string twisted into a rope, then a globular protein can be thought of as the same string rolled into a ball. These molecules are far less stable and have metabolic rôles within organisms. All enzymes are globular proteins. Globular and fibrous proteins are compared in Table 2.5, on page 28.

FOCUS

Hair perming

The protein keratin, which makes up human hair, has a high percentage of the amino acid cysteine. The disulphide bridges formed between cysteine molecules are largely responsible for the shape of the hair. Hair is straight or curly because the keratin contains disulphide linkages that enable the molecules to hold their particular shapes. When hair is permed it is first treated with a reducing agent that breaks some of the —S—S— bonds.

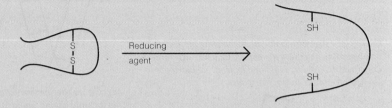

This allows the molecules to become more flexible and the hair is then set into the desired shape, using rollers or curlers. An oxidizing agent is then added which reverses the above reaction, forming new disulphide bonds, which now hold the molecules together in the desired positions. The straightening of curly hair is done in the same way. 'Perms' are not of course truly permanent. The hair keeps growing and the new hair has the same disulphide linkages as the original hair.

2.7.6 Conjugated proteins

Many proteins incorporate other chemicals within their structure. These proteins are called **conjugated proteins** and the non-protein part is referred to as the **prosthetic group**. The prosthetic group plays a vital rôle in the functioning of the protein. Some examples are given in Table 2.6 (see page 29).

Fig. 2.12 Fine structure of the fibrous protein collagen

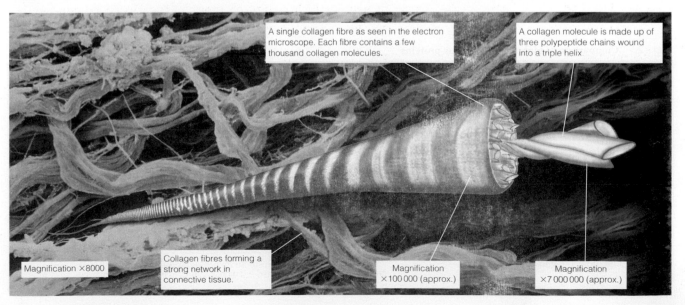

A single collagen fibre as seen in the electron microscope. Each fibre contains a few thousand collagen molecules.

A collagen molecule is made up of three polypeptide chains wound into a triple helix.

Magnification ×8000

Collagen fibres forming a strong network in connective tissue.

Magnification ×100 000 (approx.)

Magnification ×7 000 000 (approx.)

(a) *The primary structure of a protein is the sequence of amino acids found in its polypeptide chains. This sequence determines its properties and shape. Following the elucidation of the amino acid sequence of the hormone insulin, by Frederick Sanger in 1954, the primary structure of many other proteins is now known.*

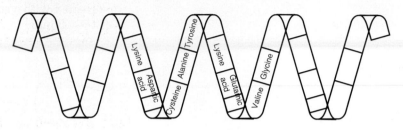

| | Lysine | Aspartic acid | Cysteine | Alanine | Tyrosine | Lysine | Glutamic acid | Valine | Glycine | |

(b) *The secondary structure is the shape which the polypeptide chain forms as a result of hydrogen bonding. This is most often a spiral known as the α-helix, although other configurations occur.*

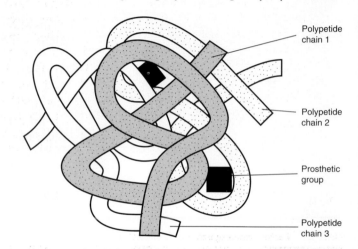

(c) *The tertiary structure is due to the bending and twisting of the polypeptide helix into a compact structure. All three types of bond, disulphide, ionic and hydrogen, contribute to the maintenance of the tertiary structure.*

(d) *The quarternary structure arises from the combination of a number of different polypeptide chains, and associated non-protein groups, into a large complex protein molecule.*

Polypetide chain 1

Polypetide chain 2

Prosthetic group

Polypetide chain 3

Fig. 2.13 Structure of proteins

TABLE 2.5 **Comparison of globular and fibrous proteins**

Fibrous proteins	Globular proteins
Repetitive regular sequences of amino acids	Irregular amino acid sequences
Actual sequences may vary slightly between two examples of the same protein	Sequence highly specific and never varies between two examples of the same protein
Polypeptide chains form long parallel strands	Polypeptide chains folded into a spherical shape
Length of chain may vary in two examples of the same protein	Length always identical in two examples of the same protein
Stable structure	Relatively unstable structure
Insoluble	Soluble – forms colloidal suspensions
Support and structural functions	Metabolic functions
Examples include collagen and keratin	Examples include all enzymes, some hormones (e.g. insulin) and haemoglobin

TABLE 2.6   Examples of conjugated proteins

Name of protein	Where found	Prosthetic group
Haemoglobin	Blood	Haem (contains iron)
Mucin	Saliva	Carbohydrate
Casein	Milk	Phosphoric acid
Cytochrome oxidase	Electron carrier pathway of cells	Copper
Nucleoprotein	Ribosomes	Nucleic acid

2.7.7 Denaturation of proteins

We have seen that the three-dimensional structure of a protein is, in part at least, due to fairly weak ionic and hydrogen bonds. Any agent which breaks these bonds will cause the three-dimensional shape to be changed. In many cases the globular proteins revert to a more fibrous form. This process is called **denaturation**. The actual sequence of amino acids is unaltered; only the overall shape of the molecule is changed. This is still sufficient to prevent the molecule from carrying out its usual functions within an organism.

Denaturation may be temporary or permanent and is due to a variety of factors as shown in Table 2.7.

TABLE 2.7   Factors causing protein denaturation

Factor	Explanation	Example
Heat	Causes the atoms of the protein to vibrate more (increased kinetic energy), thus breaking hydrogen and ionic bonds	Coagulation of albumen (boiling eggs makes the white more fibrous and less soluble)
Acids	Additional H^+ ions in acids combine with COO^- groups on amino acids and form $COOH$. Ionic bonds are hence broken	The souring of milk by acid (e.g. *Lactobacillus* bacterium produces lactic acid, lowering pH and causing it to denature the casein, making it insoluble and thus forming curds)
Alkalis	Reduced number of H^+ ions causes NH_3^+ groups to lose H^+ ions and form NH_2. Ionic bonds are hence broken	
Inorganic chemicals	The ions of heavy metals such as mercury and silver are highly electropositive. They combine with COO^- groups and disrupt ionic bonds. Similarly, highly electronegative ions, e.g. cyanide (CN^-), combine with NH_3^+ groups and disrupt ionic bonds	Many enzymes are inhibited by being denatured in the presence of certain ions, e.g. cytochrome oxidase (respiratory enzyme) is inhibited by cyanide
Organic chemicals	Organic solvents alter hydrogen bonding within a protein	Alcohol denatures certain bacterial proteins. This is what makes it useful for sterilization
Mechanical force	Physical movement may break hydrogen bonds	Stretching a hair breaks the hydrogen bonds in the keratin helix. The helix is extended and the hair stretches. If released, the hair returns to its normal length. If, however, it is wetted and then dried under tension, it keeps its new length – the basis of hair styling

TABLE 2.8   **Functions of proteins**

Vital activity	Protein example	Function
Nutrition	Digestive enzymes, e.g. trypsin amylase lipase	Catalyses the hydrolysis of proteins to polypeptides Catalyses the hydrolysis of starch to maltose Catalyses the hydrolysis of fats to fatty acids and glycerol
	Mucin	Prevents autolysis. Lubricates gut wall
	Casein	Storage protein in milk
Respiration and transport	Haemoglobin	Transport of oxygen
	Myoglobin	Stores oxygen in muscle
	Prothrombin/fibrinogen	Required for the clotting of blood
	Mucin	Keeps respiratory surface moist
	Antibodies	Essential to the defence of the body, e.g. against bacterial invasion
Growth	Hormones, e.g. thyroxine	Controls growth and metabolism
Excretion	Enzymes, e.g. urease; arginase	Catalyse reactions in ornithine cycle and therefore help in protein breakdown and urea formation
Support and movement	Actin/myosin	Needed for muscle contraction
	Ossein	Structural support in bone
	Collagen	Gives strength with flexibility in tendons and cartilage
	Elastin	Gives strength and elasticity to ligaments
	Keratin	Tough for protection, e.g. in nails and skin
	Lipoproteins	Structural components of all cell membranes
Sensitivity and coordination	Hormones, e.g. insulin/glucagon ACTH vasopressin	Control blood sugar level Controls the activity of the adrenal cortex Controls blood pressure
	Rhodopsin/opsin	Visual pigments in the retina, sensitive to light
Reproduction	Hormones, e.g. prolactin	Induces milk production
	Chromatin	Gives structural support to chromosomes

2.8   Nucleic acids

Like proteins, nucleic acids are informational macromolecules. They are made up of chains of individual units called **nucleotides**. The structure of nucleic acids and their constituent nucleotides are closely related to their functions in heredity and protein synthesis. For this reason the details of their structure will be left until the nature of the genetic code is discussed in Chapter 5.

2.9 Questions

1. In an investigation, a student tested a number of supermarket desserts.

(a) Complete the table, which shows the results of five tests on a 'Caramel Dessert'.

Test	Result of test	Conclusion
Iodine in potassium iodide solution added	Pale yellow colour	
Boiled with Benedict's or Fehling's solution	Blue colour	
Boiled with dilute acid then boiled with Benedict's or Fehling's solution	Brick-red colour	
Shaken with ethanol, ethanol decanted into water	White emulsion	
Biuret solution added	Lilac colour	

(5 marks)

(b) The drawing shows part of a cellulose molecule.

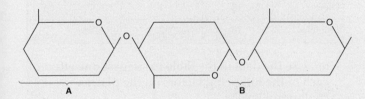

    A   B

(i) Name the monomer labelled **A** on the diagram. *(1 mark)*

(ii) Name the reaction which produced the bond labelled **B** on the diagram. *(1 mark)*

(iii) Explain how the structure of the cellulose molecule is related to its role as a component of plant cell walls. *(2 marks)*

(Total 9 marks)

NEAB February 1995, Paper BY1, No. 1

2. *(a)* Name a polymer that is formed from amino acids by condensation reactions. *(1 mark)*

(b) The diagram shows part of the structural formula of an amino acid.

(i) Complete the structural formula of the amino acid. *(1 mark)*

(ii) With reference to the diagram, explain what is meant by deamination. *(1 mark)*

(iii) Describe what happens, in the liver, to the products of the deamination process.

(3 marks)

(Total 6 marks)

NEAB February 1995, Paper BY3, No. 6

3. An experiment was carried out to separate three amino acids, X, Y and Z, dissolved together in a buffer solution at pH 7.6. A piece of filter paper was soaked in the buffer and supported to allow its ends to dip into separate troughs of the same buffer. A drop of the amino acid mixture was applied to the centre of the paper before an electric current was passed through it. The current was switched off and the paper was removed and dried before being dipped in ninhydrin solution. The diagram shows the final appearance of the paper.

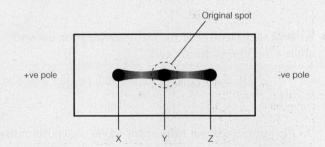

(a) What is this separation technique called?

(1 mark)

(b) Why was the paper dipped in ninhydrin solution? *(1 mark)*

(c) What conclusions can you draw from these results about the three amino acids, **X, Y** and **Z**? *(3 marks)*

(Total 5 marks)

AEB June 1993, Paper 1, No. 7

4. Give **one** precise function for each of the following:

(a) thrombin *(1 mark)*
(b) collagen *(1 mark)*
(c) trypsin *(1 mark)*
(d) albumin *(1 mark)*
(e) insulin *(1 mark)*

(Total 5 marks)

AEB June 1992, Paper 1, No. 12

5. Complete the table with a tick (✓) if the statement is true or a cross (×) if it is not true.

Statement	Biochemical substance				
	Starch	Protein	Triglyceride	DNA	RNA
Contains carbon, hydrogen and oxygen only					
Contains nitrogen					
Contains phosphate groups					
Gives a positive reaction when boiled with Benedict's reagent					
Is hydrolysed to smaller units during digestion					
Contains uracil					

(5 marks)

AEB June 1992, Paper 1, No. 2

6. Write an account of the structure of proteins and their functions in living cells.

ULEAC June 1995, Paper 1, No. 15(b)

7. Phospholipids are important molecules with many roles in the body.

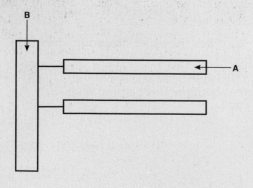

(a) (i) Complete a copy of the diagram to show the structure of a phospholipid by adding the missing component. *(2 marks)*
(ii) Name **A** and **B**. *(1 mark)*
(b) With reference to phospholipids explain the term *hydrophilic*. *(1 mark)*
(c) Many chemicals which are toxic to the human body, such as DDT, are very soluble in lipids. Suggest how a DDT molecule could:
(i) enter a cell; *(1 mark)*
(ii) accumulate in the body. *(1 mark)*
(Total 6 marks)

AEB June 1995, Paper 1, No. 5

8. The table shows the effect of fatty acids in the diet on plasma cholesterol levels in humans.

Fatty acid	Number of carbons in fatty acid	Number of double bonds	Effect on plasma cholesterol level
Caprylic	8	0	None
Lauric	12	0	Increases
Myristic	14	0	Increases greatly
Stearic	18	0	Increases
Oleic	18	1	None
Linoleic	18	2	Reduces

(a) Use the data in the table to suggest **one** effect of each of the following factors on the plasma cholesterol level:
(i) The number of double bonds in dietary fatty acids *(1 mark)*
(ii) The number of carbon atoms in dietary fatty acids *(1 mark)*
(b) (i) How are the carbon atoms arranged in a fatty acid? *(1 mark)*
(ii) What is meant by an *unsaturated* fatty acid? *(1 mark)*

(c) Describe **one** way in which the body uses plasma cholesterol and **one** way in which it may be harmed by plasma cholesterol.

(2 marks)
(Total 6 marks)

AEB June 1995, Paper 1, No. 1

3 Enzymes

Until recently it was thought that all biological catalysts were enzymes. We now know that other substances may carry out catalytic functions in living organisms. **Abzymes** are antibodies with catalytic properties and **ribozymes** are molecules of RNA which act catalytically on themselves. Most biological catalysts however are globular proteins known as enzymes. A catalyst is a substance which alters the rate of a chemical reaction without itself undergoing a permanent change. As they are not altered by the reactions they catalyze, enzymes can be used over and over again. They are therefore effective in very small amounts. Enzymes cannot cause reactions to occur, but only speed up ones which would otherwise take place extremely slowly. The word 'enzyme' means 'in yeast', and was used because they were first discovered by Eduard Buchner in an extract of yeast.

3.1 Enzyme structure and function

Enzymes are complex three-dimensional globular proteins, some of which have other associated molecules. While the enzyme molecule is normally larger than the substrate molecule it acts upon, only a small part of the enzyme molecule actually comes into contact with the substrate. This region is called the **active site**. Only a few of the amino acids of the enzyme molecule make up the active site. These so-called **catalytic amino acids** are often some distance apart in the protein chain but are brought into close proximity by the folding of that chain (see Fig. 3.1).

The catalytic amino acids A, B and C, although some distance apart in the chain, are close together when the protein is folded.

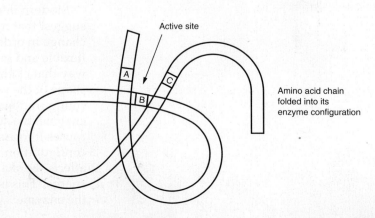

Fig. 3.1 Catalytic amino acids forming the active site

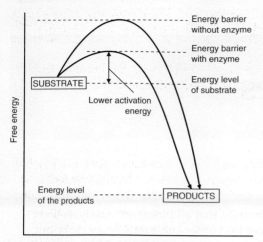

Fig. 3.2 How enzymes lower the activation energy

3.1.1 Enzymes and activation energy

Before a reaction can take place it must overcome an energy barrier by exceeding its activation energy. Enzymes operate by lowering this activation energy and thus permit the reaction to occur more readily (Fig. 3.2). As heat is often the source of activation energy, enzymes often dispense with the need for this heat and so allow reactions to take place at lower temperatures. Many reactions which would not ordinarily occur at the temperature of an organism do so readily in the presence of enzymes.

3.1.2 Mechanism of enzyme action

Enzymes are thought to operate on a **lock and key mechanism**. In the same way that a key fits a lock very precisely, so the substrate fits accurately into the active site of the enzyme molecule. The two molecules form a temporary structure called the **enzyme–substrate complex**. The products have a different shape from the substrate and so, once formed, they escape from the active site, leaving it free to become attached to another substrate molecule. The sequence is summarized in Fig. 3.3.

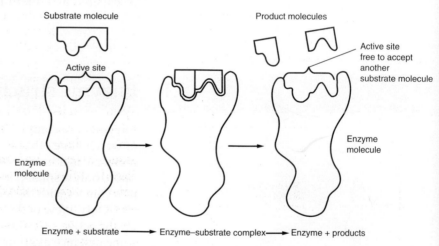

Fig. 3.3 Mechanism of enzyme action

Modern interpretations of the lock and key mechanism suggest that in the presence of the substrate the active site may change in order to suit the substrate's shape. The enzyme is flexible and moulds to fit the substrate molecule in the same way that clothing is flexible and can mould itself to fit the shape of the wearer. The enzyme initially has a binding configuration which attracts the substrate. On binding to the enzyme, the substrate disturbs the shape of the enzyme and causes it to assume a new configuration. It is this new configuration which is catalytically active and which in turn affects the shape of the substrate thus lowering its activation energy. This is referred to as an **induced fit** of the substrate to the enzyme.

3.2 Properties of enzymes

The properties of enzymes can be explained in relation to the lock and key mechanism of enzyme action, and the theory of induced fit.

3.2.1 Specificity

All enzymes operate only on specific substrates. Just as a key has a specific shape and therefore fits only complementary locks, so only substrates of a particular shape will fit the active site of an enzyme. Some locks are highly specific and can only be opened with a single key. Others are opened by a number of similar keys; yet others may be opened by many different keys. In the same way, some enzymes will act only on one particular isomer. Others act only on similar molecules; yet others will break a particular chemical linkage, wherever it occurs.

3.2.2 Reversibility

Chemical reactions are reversible, and equations are therefore often represented by two arrows to indicate this reversibility. (See opposite.)

At any one moment the reaction (shown left) may be proceeding predominantly in one direction. If, however, the conditions are changed, the direction may be reversed. It may be that the reaction proceeds from left to right in acid conditions, but in alkaline conditions it goes from right to left. In time, reactions reach a point where the reactants and the product are in **equilibrium** with one another. Enzymes catalyze the forward and reverse reactions equally. They do not therefore alter the equilibrium itself, only the speed at which it is reached. Carbonic anhydrase is an enzyme which catalyzes a reaction in either direction depending on the conditions at the time. In respiring tissues where there is much carbon dioxide it converts carbon dioxide and water into carbonic acid. In the lungs, however, the removal of carbon dioxide by diffusion means a low concentration of carbon dioxide, and hence the carbonic acid breaks down into carbon dioxide and water. Both reactions are catalyzed by carbonic anhydrase, as shown opposite.

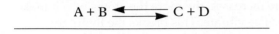

$$A + B \rightleftharpoons C + D$$

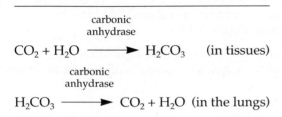

$$CO_2 + H_2O \xrightarrow{\text{carbonic anhydrase}} H_2CO_3 \quad \text{(in tissues)}$$

$$H_2CO_3 \xrightarrow{\text{carbonic anhydrase}} CO_2 + H_2O \quad \text{(in the lungs)}$$

3.2.3 Enzyme concentration

The active site of an enzyme may be used again and again. Enzymes therefore work efficiently at very low concentrations. The number of substrate molecules which an enzyme can act upon in a given time is called its **turnover number**. This varies from many millions of substrate molecules each minute, in the case of catalase, to a few hundred per minute for slow acting enzymes. Provided the temperature and other conditions are suitable for the reaction, and provided there are excess substrate molecules, the rate of a reaction is directly proportional to the enzyme concentration. If the amount of substrate is restricted it may limit the rate of reaction. The addition of further enzyme cannot increase the rate and the graph therefore tails off (Fig. 3.4).

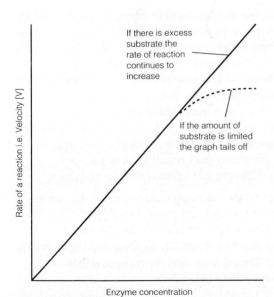

Fig. 3.4 Graph to show the effect of enzyme concentration on the rate of an enzyme-controlled reaction

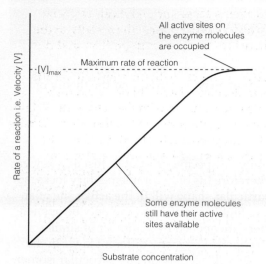

Fig. 3.5 Graph to show the effect of substrate concentration on the rate of an enzyme-controlled reaction

3.2.4 Substrate concentration

For a given amount of enzyme, the rate of an enzyme-controlled reaction increases with an increase in substrate concentration – up to a point. At low substrate concentrations, the active sites of the enzyme molecules are not all used – there simply are not enough substrate molecules to occupy them all. As the substrate concentration is increased, more and more sites come into use. A point is reached, however, where all sites are being used; increasing the substrate concentration cannot therefore increase the rate of reaction, as the amount of enzyme is the limiting factor. At this point the graph tails off (Fig. 3.5).

3.2.5 Temperature

An increase in temperature affects the rate of an enzyme-controlled reaction in two ways:

1. As the temperature increases, the kinetic energy of the substrate and enzyme molecules increases and so they move faster. The faster these molecules move, the more often they collide with one another and the greater the rate of reaction.

2. As the temperature increases, the more the atoms which make up the enzyme molecules vibrate. This breaks the hydrogen bonds and other forces which hold the molecules in their precise shape. The three-dimensional shape of the enzyme molecules is altered to such an extent that their active sites no longer fit the substrate. The enzyme is said to be **denatured** and loses its catalytic properties. (See Section 2.7.7.)

The actual effect of temperature on the rate of reaction is the combined influence of these two factors and is illustrated in Fig. 3.6.

3.2.6 pH

The precise three-dimensional molecular shape which is vital to the functioning of enzymes is partly the result of hydrogen bonding. These bonds may be broken by the concentration of hydrogen ions (H^+) present. pH is a measure of hydrogen ion concentration. It is measured on a scale of 1–14, with pH 7 being the neutral point. A pH less than 7 is acid, one greater than 7 is alkaline.

By breaking the hydrogen bonds which give enzyme molecules their shape, any change in pH can effectively denature enzymes. Each enzyme works best at a particular pH, and deviations from this optimum may result in denaturation. Fig. 3.7 illustrates the different pH optima of four enzymes.

3.2.7 Inhibition

The rate of enzyme-controlled reactions may be decreased by the presence of inhibitors. They are of two types: **reversible inhibitors** and **non-reversible inhibitors**.

Reversible inhibitors
The effect of this type of inhibitor is temporary and causes no permanent damage to the enzyme because the association of the

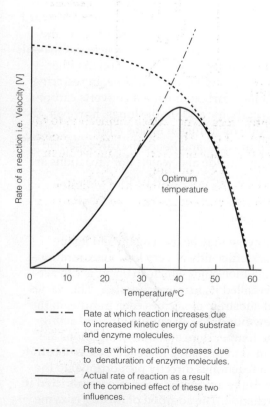

Fig. 3.6 Graph to show the effect of temperature on the rate of an enzyme-controlled reaction

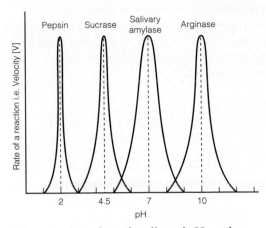

Fig. 3.7 Graph to show the effect of pH on the rate of reaction of four different enzymes

inhibitor with the enzyme is a loose one and it can easily be removed. Removal of the inhibitor restores the activity of the enzyme to normal. There are two types: **competitive** and **non-competitive**.

Competitive inhibitors compete with the substrate for the active sites of enzyme molecules. The inhibitor may have a structure which permits it to combine with the active site. While it remains bound to the active site, it prevents substrate molecules occupying them and so reduces the rate of the reaction. The same quantity of product is formed, because the substrate continues to use any enzyme molecules which are unaffected by the inhibitor. It does, however, take longer to make the products. If the concentration of the substrate is increased, less inhibition occurs. This is because, as the substrate and inhibitor are in direct competition, the greater the proportion of substrate molecules the greater their chance of finding the active sites, leaving fewer to be occupied by the inhibitor.

Malonic acid is a competitive inhibitor. It competes with succinate for the active sites of succinic dehydrogenase, an important enzyme in the Krebs cycle (Section 12.3).

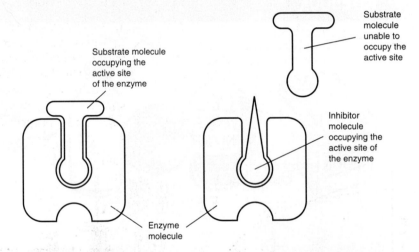

Fig. 3.8 Competitive inhibition

Non-competitive inhibitors do not attach themselves to the active site of the enzyme, but elsewhere on the enzyme molecule. They nevertheless alter the shape of the enzyme molecule in such a way that the active site can no longer properly accommodate the substrate. As the substrate and inhibitor molecules attach to different parts of the enzyme they are not

1. *Inhibitor absent –*
   The substrate attaches to the active site of the enzyme in the normal way. Reaction takes place as normal.
2. *Inhibitor present –*
   The inhibitor prevents the normal enzyme–substrate complex being formed. The reaction rate is reduced.

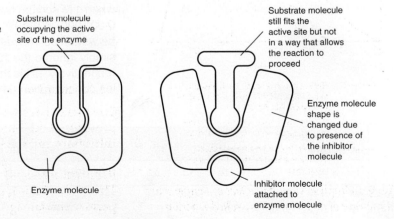

Fig. 3.9 Non-competitive inhibition

PROJECT

Many different investigations into enzyme activity can be carried out using the digestion of starch by amylase, staining with iodine/potassium iodide solution, and a colorimeter, or using starch gels with wells, for example

(a) substrate concentration
(b) enzyme concentration
(c) temperature
(d) pH.

competing for the same sites. An increase in substrate concentration will not therefore reduce the effect of the inhibitor.

Cyanide is a non-competitive inhibitor. It attaches itself to the copper prosthetic group of cytochrome oxidase, thereby inhibiting respiration (Section 12.4).

Non-reversible inhibitors

Non-reversible inhibitors leave the enzyme permanently damaged and so unable to carry out its catalytic function. Heavy metal ions such as mercury (Hg^{2+}) and silver (Ag^+) cause disulphide bonds to break. These bonds help to maintain the shape of the enzyme molecule. Once broken the enzyme molecule's structure becomes irreversibly altered with the permanent loss of its catalytic properties.

NOTEBOOK

pH

Why pH?

The term was first used by the Danish biochemist S.P.L. Sörenson when researching into the best conditions for brewing beer. Acidity is the result of free hydrogen ions (H^+) in a solution. The concentration is often very low, however. Vinegar, for example, typically has a concentration of 0.001 mol dm^{-3}. This is a rather long-winded way of expressing acid and base strength, especially when 1 M sodium hydroxide has a hydrogen ion concentration of 0.000 000 000 000 01 mol^{-3}. Sörenson appreciated that 0.001 can be written as 10^{-3} and 0.000 000 000 000 01 as 10^{-14}. He then simply ignored the 10 and the minus sign to give values of 3 and 14 respectively. pH is therefore the negative power (p) of the hydrogen ion concentration (H).

H⁺ concentration in mol dm⁻³	10^{-14}	10^{-13}	10^{-12}	10^{-11}	10^{-10}	10^{-9}	10^{-8}	10^{-7}	10^{-6}	10^{-5}	10^{-4}	10^{-3}	10^{-2}	10^{-1}
pH	14	13	12	11	10	9	8	7	6	5	4	3	2	1

3.3 Enzyme cofactors

A **cofactor** is a non-protein substance which is essential for some enzymes to function efficiently. There are three types: **activators**, **coenzymes** and **prosthetic groups**.

3.3.1 Activators

Activators are substances which are necessary for the functioning of certain enzymes. The enzyme thrombokinase, which converts prothrombin into thrombin during blood clotting, is activated by calcium (Ca^{2+}) ions. In the same way

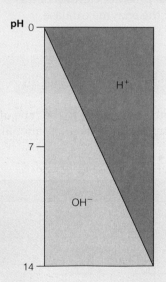

Relative concentrations of H^+ and OH^- ions at different pHs.

Why is water neutral at pH 7?

Some water molecules are always dissociated into hydrogen (H^+) and hydroxyl (OH^-) ions

$$H_2O \rightleftharpoons H^+ = OH^-$$

At 25 °C 1 dm^3 of water contains 10^{-7} moles of H^+ ions and therefore has a pH of 7. It follows from the equation above that there will also be 10^{-7} moles of OH^- ions. As the concentration of H^+ ions increases, that of OH^- ions decreases correspondingly. For example, where the concentration of H^+ ions is 10^{-5} mol dm^{-3} that of OH^- ions is 10^{-9} mol dm^{-3}. The two concentrations multiplied always give a value of 10^{-14}. Hence the pH scale is 0–14. At pH 0 almost all the ions are H^+ whereas at pH 14 they are almost entirely OH^-.

The pH scale is not linear but is logarithmic, based on a factor of 10. pH 6 = 0.000 001 mol dm^{-3} of H^+ and pH 5 = 0.000 01 mol dm^{-3} of H^+, i.e. pH 5 is 10 times more acidic than pH 6. In the same way pH 3 is 10 times more acidic than pH 4 and 100 times more so than pH 5.

The lower the pH the greater the concen–tration of H^+

Sweat is 1000× more acid than water

Water at pH 7 has H^+ concentration of 0.000 000 1 (10^{-7})

| GASTRIC JUICE pH1 | SWEAT pH4 | WATER pH7 |

salivary amylase requires the presence of chloride (Cl^-) ions before it will efficiently convert starch into maltose. It is possible that these activators assist in forming the enzyme–substrate complex by moulding either the enzyme or substrate molecule into a more suitable shape.

3.3.2 Coenzymes

Coenzymes are non-protein organic substances which are essential to the efficient functioning of some enzymes, but are not themselves bound to the enzyme. Many coenzymes are derived from vitamins, e.g. **nicotinamide adenine dinucleotide (NAD)** is derived from nicotinic acid, a member of the vitamin B complex. NAD acts as a coenzyme to dehydrogenases by acting as a hydrogen acceptor.

3.3.3 Prosthetic groups

Like coenzymes, prosthetic groups are organic molecules, but unlike them they are bound to the enzyme itself. Perhaps the best known prosthetic group is **haem**. It is a ring-shaped organic molecule with iron at its centre. Apart from its rôle as an oxygen carrier in haemoglobin, it is also the prosthetic group of the electron carrier cytochrome and of the enzyme catalase.

3.4 Classification of enzymes

Enzymes are classified into six groups according to the type of reaction they catalyse. Table 3.1 summarizes this internationally accepted classification.

TABLE 3.1 **The classification of enzymes**

Enzyme group	Type of reaction catalysed	Enzyme examples
1. Oxidoreductases	Transfer of O and H atoms between substances, i.e. all oxidation–reduction reactions	Dehydrogenases Oxidases
2. Transferases	Transfer of a chemical group from one substance to another	Transaminases Phosphorylases
3. Hydrolases	Hydrolysis reactions	Peptidases Lipases Phosphatases
4. Lyases	Addition or removal of a chemical group other than by hydrolysis	Decarboxylases
5. Isomerases	The rearrangement of groups within a molecule	Isomerases Mutases
6. Ligases	Formation of bonds between two molecules using energy derived from the breakdown of ATP	Synthetases

Each enzyme is given two names:

A **systematic** name, based on the six classification groups. These names are often long and complicated.

A **trivial** name which is shorter and easier to use.
The trivial names are derived by following three procedures:

1. Start with the name of the substrate upon which the enzyme acts, e.g. succinate.

2. Add the name of the type of reaction which it catalyses, e.g. dehydrogenation.

3. Convert the end of the last word to an -ase suffix, e.g. dehydrogenase.

The example above gives succinic dehydrogenase. Another example would be DNA polymerase. This enzyme catalyses the formation (and breakdown) of the nucleic acid DNA by polymerization. Some of the commercial uses of enzymes are considered in Sections 21.4.5.

3.5 Control of metabolic pathways

With many hundreds of reactions taking place in any single cell it is clear that a very structured system of control of metabolic pathways is essential. If the cell were merely a 'soup' of substrates, enzymes and products, the chances of particular reactants meeting would be small and the metabolic processes inefficient. In addition, different enzymes need different conditions, e.g. a particular pH, and it would be impossible to provide these in such an unstructured 'soup'. Cells contain organelles, and enzymes are often bound to these inner membranes in a precise order. This increases the chances of them coming into contact with their appropriate substrates, and leads to efficiency. The organelles may also have varying conditions to suit the specific enzymes they contain. By controlling these conditions, and the enzymes available, the cell can control the metabolic pathways within it.

Cells also make use of the enzyme's own properties to exercise control over metabolic pathways. The end-product of a pathway may inhibit the enzyme at the start **(end product inhibition)**.

```
      enzyme a     enzyme b     enzyme c     enzyme d
   A ──────────→ B ──────────→ C ──────────→ D ──────────→ E ┄┄┄┄┄┄┄┐
   └┄┄ inhibition (negative feedback) ←┄┄┄┄┄┄┄┄┄┄┄┄┄┄┄┄┄┄┄┄┄┄┄┄┄┄┘
```

In the example above, the product E acts as an inhibitor to enzyme a. If the level of product E falls, this inhibition is reduced, and so more A is converted to B, and subsequently more E is produced. If the level of E rises above normal, inhibition of enzyme a increases and so the level of E is reduced. In this way homeostatic control of E is achieved, more details of which are given in Section 18.1. The mechanism is termed **negative feedback** because the information from the end of the pathway which is fed back to the start has a negative effect, i.e. a high concentration of E reduces its own production rate.

These forms of inhibition are, for obvious reasons, reversible, i.e. they do not permanently damage the enzymes. They frequently affect the nature of an enzyme's active site by binding with the enzyme at some point on the molecule remote from the active site. Such effects are termed **allosteric** and refer to the ability of the enzyme to have more than one shape. One shape renders the enzyme active, another renders it inactive.

3.6 Questions

1. *(a)* Explain how enzyme–substrate complexes are formed. Explain how this allows enzymes to act.
(3 marks)

(b) Explain in terms of molecular shapes how the following factors affect the rate of enzyme action:
    (i) Temperature *(3 marks)*
    (ii) Competitive inhibition *(3 marks)*
    (iii) Non-competitive inhibition *(3 marks)*
(Total 12 marks)

NEAB February 1995, Paper BY1, No. 9

2. *(a)* State what you understand by each of the following terms in relation to enzymes:
    (i) Active site. *(2 marks)*
    (ii) Denaturation. *(2 marks)*

(b) In an investigation of enzyme inhibition, a student made mixtures of substrate and inhibitor in the following proportions.

Mixture	Substrate/units	Inhibitor/units
1	10	0
2	10	10
3	10	20

She added 20 cm³ of each mixture in turn to 20 cm³ of a standard enzyme solution, and measured the amount of product accumulating over a period of several minutes. The results are shown in the graph below.

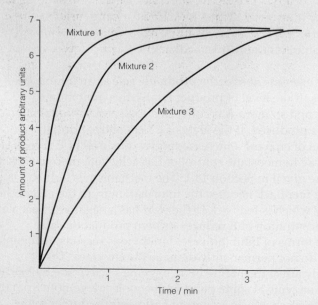

(i) What kind of enzyme inhibition is shown by these results? Explain your answer. *(3 marks)*

(ii) Draw and label on the graph curves showing the expected results if the experiment were repeated with mixtures 4 and 5 as follows.

Mixture	Substrate/units	Inhibitor/units
4	10	5
5	5	10

(4 marks)
(Total 11 marks)

ULEAC 1996 Specime Paper, B/HB1, No. 7

3. An investigation was carried out into the effect of pH on the rate of activity of a proteolytic enzyme. The results are shown in the graph.

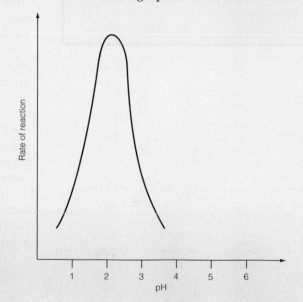

(a) In which part of the alimentary canal would you expect to find this enzyme? *(1 mark)*

(b) Explain how pH affects an enzyme molecule so as to change the rate of the reaction which it catalyses. *(3 marks)*

AEB June 1993, Paper 1, No. 10

4. Fig. 1 shows details of the region where the enzyme ribonuclease binds to its substrate RNA. Two amino acids, threonine and serine, in the ribonuclease molecule, are seen to bind to the base uracil in the RNA molecule.

(a) What name is usually given to the part of the enzyme shown? *(1 mark)*

(b) What type of bonds are shown as dotted lines in the figure? *(1 mark)*

(c) **With reference to Fig. 1** explain what is meant by enzyme specificity. *(3 marks)*

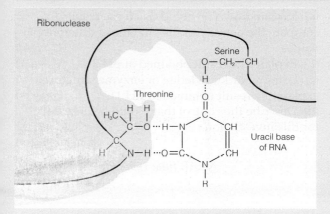

Fig. 1

(d) Fig. 2 below shows the peptide bond (cross-hatched block) between two amino acids. Complete the figure to show the end products of hydrolysis of this peptide bond by a protein-digesting enzyme. *(2 marks)*

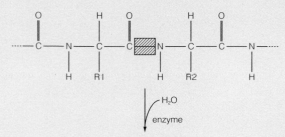

Fig. 2

(e) Select suitable symbols from those given below to construct two diagrams that show the interactions between:
  (i) an enzyme and its substrate;
  (ii) the same enzyme and a **competitive** inhibitor.

Enzymes   Substrates and inhibitors

Fig. 3

(f) Explain how a competitive inhibitor decreases the rate of an enzyme-controlled reaction. *(3 marks)*
The enzyme acetylcholinesterase is found at neuromuscular junctions. It is irreversibly inhibited by one of the poisons used in chemical weapons.
(g) (i) Explain how this inhibition affects the transmission of the nerve impulse across the synapse.
  (ii) Why is the inhalation of such a poison lethal?
                                    (5 marks)
                              (Total 15 marks)

UCLES June 1992, Paper 2, No. 2

5. Draw three simple line graphs to show the effect on the rate of enzyme activity of changes in:
    (i) pH;   *(2 marks)*
    (ii) temperature;   *(2 marks)*
    (iii) substrate concentration. *(2 marks)*

AEB June 1995, Paper 1, No. 15

6. Read through the following passage about enzymes, then write on the dotted lines the most appropriate word or words to complete the account. Enzymes are catalysts which increase the rate of chemical reactions by reducing the .... energy needed to cause the reaction to take place. Chemically, enzymes are globular .... They possess a particular region known as the ....which binds temporarily to the substrate(s). The weak chemical bonds which hold the enzyme together can be disrupted by ....and ...., thus affecting catalytic activity. .... inhibition of enzyme activity is brought about by ions of ...., which cause the enzyme molecule to precipitate and cease functioning. Other inhibitors slow down the rate of enzyme activity, because they resemble the normal substrate of the enzyme. These are known as............................... inhibitors.

(Total 8 marks)

ULEAC June 1994, Paper 1, No. 1

7. The activity of amylase can be determined experimentally by measuring the rate at which reducing sugars are formed by the hydrolysis of starch.
An experiment was carried out to investigate the effect of amylase concentration on its activity. Two solutions of amylase, A and B, of different concentrations, were incubated with a dilute starch suspension. The concentration of reducing sugars produced was measured every two minutes for fourteen minutes. The results are shown in the table below:

Time/min	Concentration of reducing sugars produced/μmol dm^{-3}	
	Amylase solution A	Amylase solution B
0	0.0	0.0
2	1.1	0.2
4	2.1	0.5
6	3.1	0.7
8	4.3	0.8
10	5.3	1.1
12	6.4	1.2
14	7.4	1.5

(a) Plot the data on graph paper.   (*5 marks*)

(b) (i) From your graph, find the mean rate of production of reducing sugars in solution A between 3 and 9 minutes. Show your working.   (*2 marks*)

(ii) Which of the two solutions contained the higher concentration of amylase? Explain your answer.   (*1 mark*)

(c) State **two** conditions which must be kept constant in this experiment and in each case explain why.   (*4 marks*)

(d) In baking, amylase is sometimes added to flour as a bread improver. Suggest why the addition of amylase may improve the quality of bread.

    (*2 marks*)

    (*Total 14 marks*)

ULEAC June 1993, Paper 1, No. 11

8. Amylase is an enzyme which breaks down starch. The effect of pH on its activity can be investigated by using a starch agar plate as shown in the diagram. Circular wells were cut into the starch agar plate using a cork borer. Six outer wells were set up, each containing the same concentration and volume of amylase, and a solution of different pH.

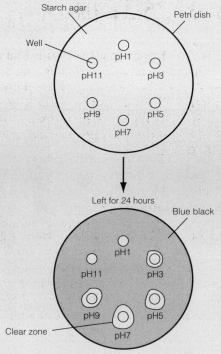

Result after plate is flooded with iodine solution then rinsed with water

(a) Explain how you could use these results to compare the activity of the enzyme at different pH values.   (*1 mark*)

(b) Explain the result obtained at pH 7.   (*1 mark*)

(c) Using your knowledge of enzyme structure, explain the result obtained at pH 11.   (*2 marks*)

(d) Describe the control that would be necessary for this investiation.   (*2 marks*)

    (*Total 6 marks*)

NEAB June 1995, Paper BY01, No. 6

4 Cellular organization

The cell is the fundamental unit of life. All organisms, whatever their type or size, are composed of cells. The modern theory of cellular organization states that:

1. All living organisms are composed of cells.

2. All new cells are derived from other cells.

3. Cells contain the hereditary material of an organism which is passed from parent to daughter cells.

4. All metabolic processes take place within cells.

4.1 Cytology – the study of cells

TABLE 4.1 **Comparison of prokaryotic and eukaryotic cells**

Prokaryotic cells	Eukaryotic cells
No distinct nucleus; only diffuse area(s) of nucleoplasm with no nuclear membrane	A distinct, membrane-bounded nucleus
No chromosomes – circular strands of DNA	Chromosomes present on which DNA is located
No membrane-bounded organelles such as chloroplasts and mitochondria	Chloroplasts and mitochondria may be present
Ribosomes are smaller	Ribosomes are larger
Flagella (if present) lack internal 9 + 2 fibril arrangement	Flagella have 9 + 2 internal fibril arrangement
No mitosis or meiosis occurs	Mitosis and / or meiosis occurs

All cells are self-contained and more or less self-sufficient units. They are surrounded by a cell membrane and have a nucleus, or a nuclear area, at some stage of their existence. They show remarkable diversity, both in structure and function. They are basically spherical in shape, although they show some variation where they are modified to suit their function. In size they normally range from 10–30 μm.

4.1.1 The structure of prokaryotic cells

Prokaryotic cells (*pro* – 'before', *karyo* – 'nucleus') were probably the first forms of life on earth. Their hereditary material, DNA, is not enclosed within a nuclear membrane. This absence of a true nucleus only occurs in two groups, the bacteria and the blue-green bacteria (Section 21.1.4). There are no membrane-bounded organelles within a prokaryotic cell, the structure of which is shown on page 48.

4.1.2 Structure of the eukaryotic cell

Eukaryotic cells (*Eu* – 'true', *karyo* – 'nucleus') probably arose a little over 1000 million years ago, nearly 2500 million years after their prokaryotic ancestors. The development of eukaryotic cells from prokaryotic ones involved considerable changes, as can be seen from Table 4.1. The essential change was the development of membrane-bounded organelles, such as mitochondria and

NOTEBOOK

Microscopy

Fig. 1 The compound light microscope

Comparison of advantages and disadvantages of the light and electron microscopes

LIGHT MICROSCOPE	ELECTRON MICROSCOPE
Advantages	**Disadvantages**
Cheap to purchase and operate	Expensive to purchase and operate
Small and portable – can be used almost anywhere	Very large and must be operated in special rooms
Unaffected by magnetic fields	Affected by magnetic fields
Preparation of material is relatively quick and simple, requiring only a little expertise	Preparation of material is lengthy and requires considerable expertise and sometimes complex equipment
Material rarely distorted by preparation	Preparation of material may distort it
Natural colour of the material can be observed	All images are in black and white
Disadvantages	**Advantages**
Magnifies objects up to 2000×	Magnifies objects over 500 000×
The depth of field is restricted	It is possible to investigate a greater depth of field

Have you ever wished you could see that little bit better – perhaps to read what someone else is writing from a distance or to recognize who exactly it is in the crowd at a football match? How frustrating it can be when you can't quite make out the print of the newspaper of the person opposite you on the train. This is how early scientists must have felt when they strained their eyes to decipher the detailed structure of organisms. How they must have rejoiced at the development of first the glass lens and then the simple light microscope.

The light microscope opened up a new world of structural detail for the biologist, revealing the variety of cell forms making up organisms. In time however, their curiosity again became thwarted as the limitations of the light microscope prevented them observing the fine detail within cells. The problem is that the wavelength of light limits the light microscope to distinguishing objects which are $0.2\ \mu m$ or further from each other. The problem could only be overcome by using a form of radiation which had a wavelength less than that of light. So in 1933 the electron microscope was developed. This instrument works on the same principles as the light microscope except that instead of light rays, with their wavelengths in the order of 500 nm, a beam of electrons of wavelengths 0.005 nm is used. This means that the electron microscope can magnify objects up to 500 000 times compared to the best light microscopes, which magnify only around 2000 times.

Whereas the light microscope uses glass lenses to focus the light rays, the electron beam of the electron microscope is focussed by means of powerful electromagnets. The image produced by the electron microscope cannot be detected directly by the naked eye. Instead, the electron beam is directed on to a screen from which black and white photographs, called **photoelectronmicrographs**, can be taken. A comparison of the radiation pathways in light and electron microscopes is given in Fig. 2.

There are two main types of electron microscope. In the **transmission electron microscope** (TEM), a beam of electrons is passed through thin, specially prepared slices of material. As the molecules in air would absorb the electrons, a vacuum has to be created within the instrument. Where electrons are absorbed by the material, and do not therefore reach the screen, the image is dark. Such areas are said to be **electron dense**. Where the electrons penetrate, the screen appears bright. These areas are termed **electron transparent**. As electrons have a very small mass, they do not easily penetrate materials and so sections need to be exceedingly thin. This sectioning creates a flat image and the natural contouring of a specimen cannot be seen. To overcome this problem, the **scanning electron microscope** (SEM) was developed. In this instrument a fine beam of electrons is passed to and fro across the specimen, beginning at one end and working across to the other. The specimen scatters many electrons, while others are absorbed. Low energy secondary electrons may be emitted by the specimen. The scattered electrons and the low energy secondary ones are amplified and transmitted to a screen. The resultant image shows holes and depressions as dark areas and ridges and extensions of the surface as bright areas. In this way the natural contouring of the material may be observed.

Electron microscope

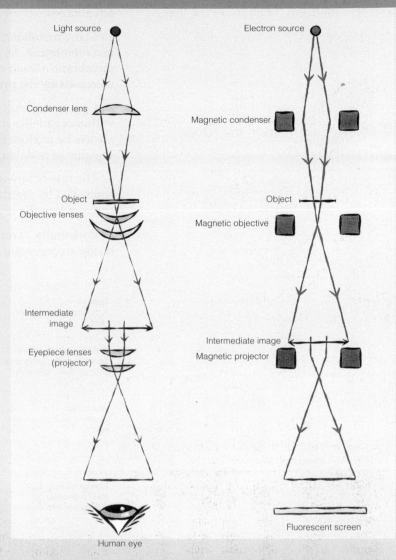

Fig. 2 Comparison of radiation pathways in light and electron microscopes

The problem with both these forms of electron microscope is that complex preparation techniques coupled with the need for a high vacuum means that not only must the material being observed be dehydrated and therefore dead, it is frequently considerably distorted; what you see may be very different from the original material. In response to this a new generation of electron microscopes has been developed – the environmental scanning electron microscope (ESEM). These microscopes allow the material on view to be kept at a low vacuum while the region around the electron gun is at a high vacuum. This is achieved by separating the microscope column into a series of chambers each with its own pressure. There is only a minute hole between chambers – wide enough to allow the tiny electron beam through. A special low voltage detector which can operate at low vacuums is used to detect the scattered electrons, secondary electrons and X-rays which provide the image.

chloroplasts, within the outer plasma membrane of the cell. The presence of membrane-bounded organelles confers four advantages:

1. Many metabolic processes involve enzymes being embedded in a membrane. As cells become larger, the proportion of membrane area to cell volume is reduced. This proportion is increased by the presence of organelle membranes.

2. Containing enzymes for a particular metabolic pathway within organelles means that the products of one reaction will always be in close proximity to the next enzyme in the sequence. The rate of metabolic reactions will thereby be increased.

3. The rate of any metabolic pathway inside an organelle can be controlled by regulating the rate at which the membrane surrounding the organelle allows the first reactant to enter.

4. Potentially harmful reactants and/or enzymes can be isolated inside an organelle so they won't damage the rest of the cell.

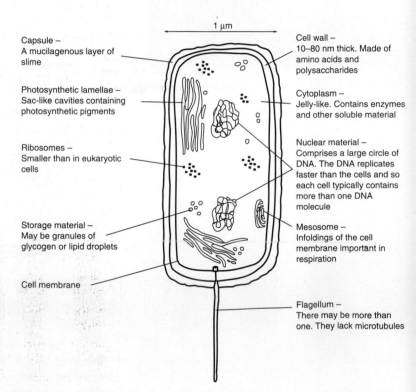

Capsule –
A mucilagenous layer of slime

Photosynthetic lamellae –
Sac-like cavities containing photosynthetic pigments

Ribosomes –
Smaller than in eukaryotic cells

Storage material –
May be granules of glycogen or lipid droplets

Cell membrane

Cell wall –
10–80 nm thick. Made of amino acids and polysaccharides

Cytoplasm –
Jelly-like. Contains enzymes and other soluble material

Nuclear material –
Comprises a large circle of DNA. The DNA replicates faster than the cells and so each cell typically contains more than one DNA molecule

Mesosome –
Infoldings of the cell membrane important in respiration

Flagellum –
There may be more than one. They lack microtubules

1 μm

Figure 4.1 Structure of the prokaryotic cell, e.g. a generalized bacterial cell

It is possible that such organelles arose as separate prokaryotic cells which developed a symbiotic relationship with larger prokaryotic ones. This would explain the existence of one membraned structure inside another, the ability of mitochondria and chloroplasts to divide themselves (self-replication) and the presence of DNA within these two organelles. Alternatively, the organelles may have arisen by invaginations of the plasma membrane which became 'pinched off' to give a separate membrane-bounded structure within the main cell. Although many variations of the eukaryotic cell exist, there are two main types, the plant cell and the animal cell. (See Figs. 4.2 and 4.3 on pages 50–1.)

4.1.3 Differences between plant and animal cells

The major differences between plant and animal cells are given in Table 4.2.

TABLE 4.2 **Differences between plant and animal cells**

Plant cells	Animal cells
Tough, slightly elastic cellulose cell wall present (in addition to the cell membrane)	Cell wall absent – only a membrane surrounds the cell
Pits and plasmodesmata present in the cell wall	No cell wall and therefore no pits or plasmodesmata
Middle lamella join cell walls of adjacent cells	Middle lamella absent – cells are joined by intercellular cement
Plastids, e.g. chloroplasts and leucoplasts, present in large numbers	Plastids absent
Mature cells normally have a large single, central vacuole filled with cell sap	Vacuoles, e.g. contractile vacuoles, if present, are small and scattered throughout the cell
Tonoplast present around vacuole	Tonoplast absent
Cytoplasm normally confined to a thin layer at the edge of the cell	Cytoplasm present throughout the cell
Nucleus at edge of the cell	Nucleus anywhere in the cell but often central
Lysosomes not normally present	Lysosomes almost always present
Centrioles absent in higher plants	Centrioles present
Cilia and flagella absent in higher plants	Cilia or flagella often present
Starch grains used for storage	Glycogen granules used for storage
Only some cells are capable of division	Almost all cells are capable of division
Few secretions are produced	A wide variety of secretions are produced

4.2   Cell ultrastructure

4.2.1 Cytoplasmic matrix

All the cell organelles are contained within a cytoplasmic matrix, sometimes called the **hyaloplasm** or **cytosol**. It is an aqueous material which is a solution or colloidal suspension of many vital cellular chemicals. These include simple ions such as sodium, phosphates and chlorides, organic molecules such as amino acids, ATP and nucleotides, and storage material such as oil

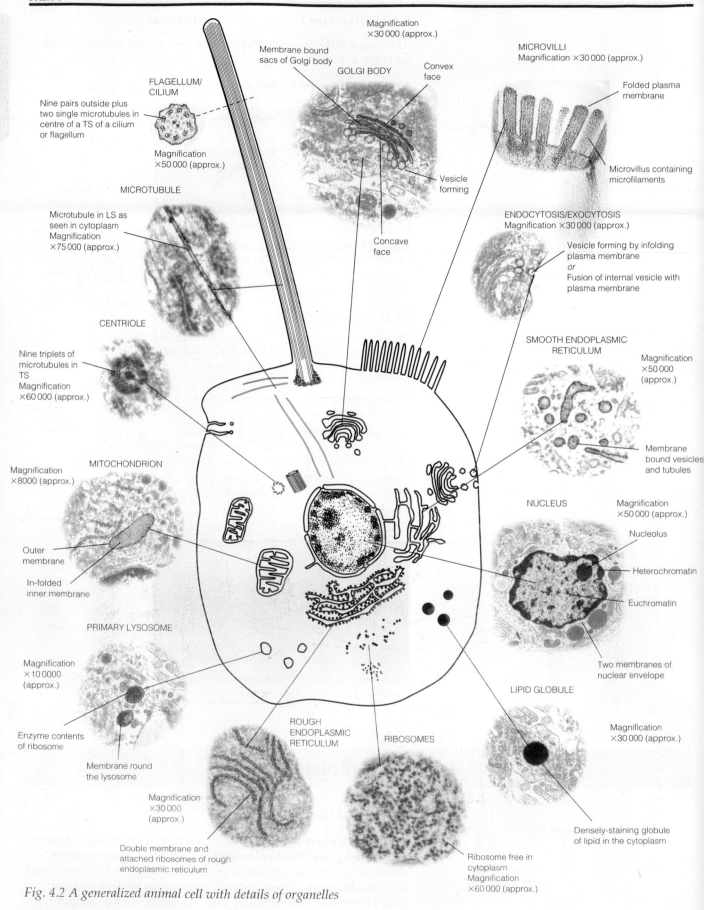

FLAGELLUM/
CILIUM

Nine pairs outside plus
two single microtubules in
centre of a TS of a cilium
or flagellum

Magnification
×50 000 (approx.)

Magnification
×30 000 (approx.)

Membrane bound
sacs of Golgi body

GOLGI BODY

Convex
face

Vesicle
forming

Concave
face

MICROVILLI
Magnification ×30 000 (approx.)

Folded plasma
membrane

Microvillus containing
microfilaments

MICROTUBULE

Microtubule in LS as
seen in cytoplasm
Magnification
×75 000 (approx.)

ENDOCYTOSIS/EXOCYTOSIS
Magnification ×30 000 (approx.)

Vesicle forming by infolding
plasma membrane
or
Fusion of internal vesicle with
plasma membrane

CENTRIOLE

Nine triplets of
microtubules in
TS
Magnification
×60 000 (approx.)

SMOOTH ENDOPLASMIC
RETICULUM

Magnification
×50 000
(approx.)

Membrane
bound vesicles
and tubules

MITOCHONDRION

Magnification
×8000 (approx.)

Outer
membrane

In-folded
inner membrane

NUCLEUS

Magnification
×50 000 (approx.)

Nucleolus

Heterochromatin

Euchromatin

Two membranes of
nuclear envelope

PRIMARY LYSOSOME

Magnification
×100 000
(approx.)

Enzyme contents
of ribosome

Membrane round
the lysosome

Magnification
×30 000
(approx.)

ROUGH
ENDOPLASMIC
RETICULUM

Double membrane and
attached ribosomes of rough
endoplasmic reticulum

RIBOSOMES

Ribosome free in
cytoplasm
Magnification
×60 000 (approx.)

LIPID GLOBULE

Magnification
×30 000 (approx.)

Densely-staining globule
of lipid in the cytoplasm

Fig. 4.2 A generalized animal cell with details of organelles

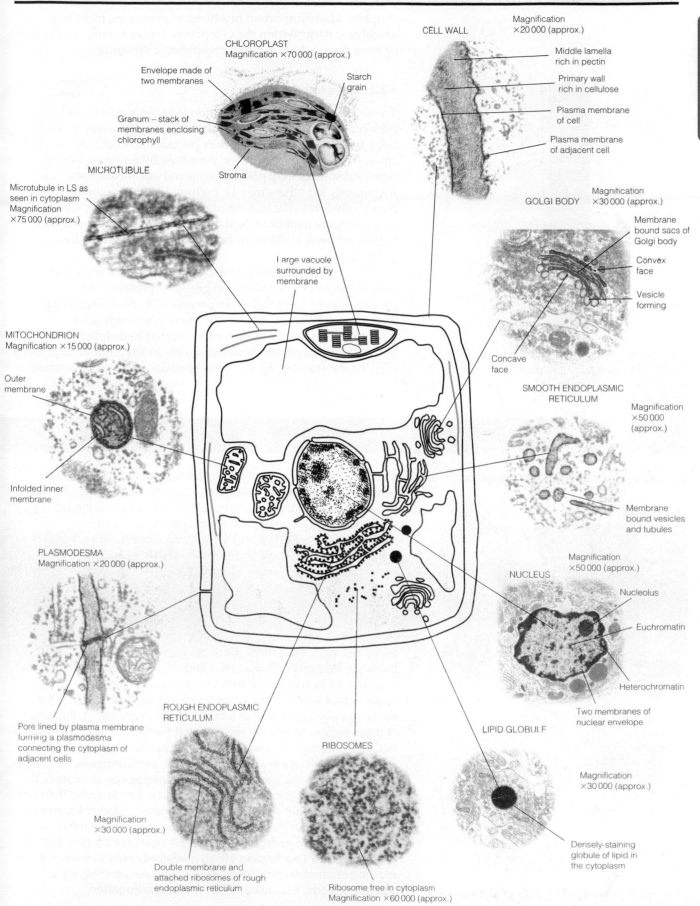

CELL WALL
Magnification
×20 000 (approx.)

Middle lamella
rich in pectin

Primary wall
rich in cellulose

Plasma membrane
of cell

Plasma membrane
of adjacent cell

CHLOROPLAST
Magnification ×70 000 (approx.)

Envelope made of
two membranes

Starch
grain

Granum – stack of
membranes enclosing
chlorophyll

Stroma

GOLGI BODY
Magnification
×30 000 (approx.)

Membrane
bound sacs of
Golgi body

Convex
face

Vesicle
forming

Concave
face

MICROTUBULE

Microtubule in LS as
seen in cytoplasm
Magnification
×75 000 (approx.)

Large vacuole
surrounded by
membrane

SMOOTH ENDOPLASMIC
RETICULUM

Magnification
×50 000
(approx.)

MITOCHONDRION
Magnification ×15 000 (approx.)

Outer
membrane

Infolded inner
membrane

Membrane
bound vesicles
and tubules

Magnification
×50 000 (approx.)

NUCLEUS

Nucleolus

Euchromatin

Heterochromatin

Two membranes of
nuclear envelope

PLASMODESMA
Magnification ×20 000 (approx.)

ROUGH ENDOPLASMIC
RETICULUM

Pore lined by plasma membrane
forming a plasmodesma
connecting the cytoplasm of
adjacent cells

RIBOSOMES

LIPID GLOBULE

Magnification
×30 000 (approx.)

Magnification
×30 000 (approx.)

Double membrane and
attached ribosomes of rough
endoplasmic reticulum

Ribosome free in cytoplasm
Magnification ×60 000 (approx.)

Densely-staining
globule of lipid in
the cytoplasm

Fig. 4.3 A generalized plant cell with detail of organelles

droplets. Many important biochemical processes, including glycolysis, occur within the cytoplasm. It is not static but capable of mass flow, which is called **cytoplasmic streaming**.

4.2.2 Cell membrane

The cell membrane's main function is to serve as a boundary between the cell and its environment. It is not, however, inert but a functional organelle. It may permanently exclude certain substances from the cell while permanently retaining others. Some substances may pass freely in and out through the membrane. Yet others may be excluded at one moment only to pass freely across the membrane on another occasion. On account of the membrane's ability to permit different substances to pass across it at different rates, it is said to be **partially permeable**.

There is little dispute that the cell membrane is made up almost entirely of two chemical groups – proteins and phospholipids. In 1972, J. J. Singer and G. L. Nicholson suggested a structure for the cell membrane. There is a bimolecular phospholipid layer with inwardly directed hydrophobic tails and a variety of protein molecules with an irregular arrangement (Fig. 4.4, on the next page). Some proteins occur on the surface of

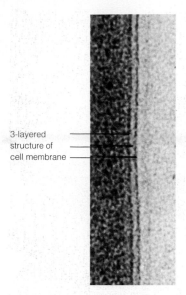

3-layered structure of cell membrane

Cell membrane (EM) ($\times 250\,000$)

NOTEBOOK

Cell fractionation and centrifugation

If you shake up particles of different sizes within a liquid such as water and leave them to settle, they separate out – the largest and heaviest at the bottom and the smallest and lightest at the top. The same principle can be applied to separate out the various components of cells. Dividing the cell into its parts (or fractions) is called **cell fractionation** and is achieved by the process of **centrifugation** using a **centrifuge**.

A centrifuge is a machine which can spin tubes containing liquid suspensions at a very high speed. The effect is to exert a force on the contents of the tube similar to, but much greater than, that of gravity. The faster the speed and the longer the time for which the tubes are spun, the greater the force. At slower speeds (less force) the larger fragments collect at the bottom of the tube and the smaller ones remain in suspension in the liquid near the top of the tube – **supernatant liquid**. If the larger fragments are removed and the supernatant recentrifuged at a faster speed (more force), the larger of these smaller fragments will collect at the bottom. By continuing in this way, smaller and smaller fragments may be recovered. As the size of any organelle is relatively constant, each organelle will tend to separate from the supernatant at a specific speed of rotation. If the suspension of cell fragments is spun at a slower speed than that required to separate out a particular organelle, all larger fragments and organelles can be collected and discarded. Spinning the supernatant at the appropriate speed will now cause a new fraction to be collected. This fraction will be a relatively pure sample of the required organelles. Since the process involves centrifuging at different speeds, it is called **differential centrifugation**.

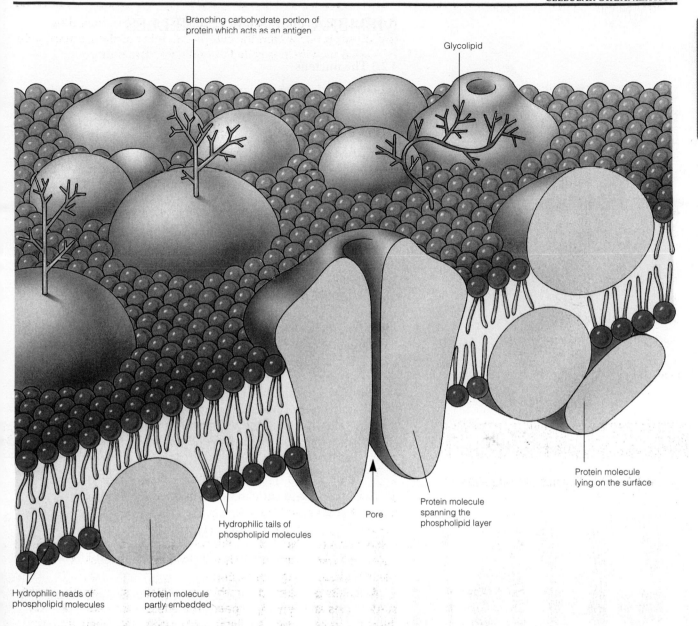

Branching carbohydrate portion of
protein which acts as an antigen

Glycolipid

Protein molecule
lying on the surface

Hydrophilic tails of
phospholipid molecules

Pore

Protein molecule
spanning the
phospholipid layer

Hydrophilic heads of
phospholipid molecules

Protein molecule
partly embedded

Fig. 4.4 The fluid-mosaic model of the cell membrane

the phospholipid layer (**peripheral** or **extrinsic proteins**) while others extend into it (**integral** or **intrinsic proteins**) and some even extend completely across (**transmembrane proteins**). Viewed from the surface, the proteins are dotted throughout the phospholipid layer in a mosaic arrangement. Other research suggests that the phospholipid layer is capable of much movement, i.e. is fluid. It was these facts which gave rise to its name, the **fluid-mosaic model**. Also present in the membrane is cholesterol which interacts with the phospholipids to make the membrane less fluid.

The proteins in the membrane have a number of functions. Apart from giving structural support they are very specific, varying from cell to cell. It is this specificity which allows cells to be recognized by other agents in the body, e.g. enzymes, hormones and antibodies. In the fluid-mosaic model it is thought probable that the proteins also assist the active transport of materials across the membrane.

MEMBRANOUS ORGANELLES

4.2.3 The nucleus

When viewed under a microscope, the most prominent feature of a cell is the nucleus. While its shape, size, position and chemical composition vary from cell to cell, its functions are always the same, namely, to control the cell's activity and to retain the organism's hereditary material, the chromosomes. It is bounded by a double membrane, the **nuclear envelope**, the outer membrane being continuous with the endoplasmic reticulum and often having ribosomes on its surface. The inner membrane has three proteins on its surface which act as anchoring points for chromosomes during interphase (see Section 6.2). It possesses many large pores (typically 3000 per nucleus) 40–100 nm in diameter, which permit the passage of large molecules, such as RNA, between it and the cytoplasm. The cytoplasm-like material within the nucleus is called **nucleoplasm**. It contains **chromatin** which is made up of coils of DNA bound to proteins. During division the chromatin condenses to form the chromosomes but these are rarely, if ever, visible in a non-dividing cell. The denser, more darkly staining areas of chromatin are called **heterochromatin**.

Within the nucleus are one or two small spherical bodies, each called a **nucleolus**. They are not distinct organelles as they are not bounded by a membrane. They manufacture ribosomal RNA, a substance in which they are especially rich, and assemble ribosomes.

The functions of a nucleus are:

1. To contain the genetic material of a cell in the form of chromosomes.

2. To act as a control centre for the activities of a cell.

3. To carry the instructions for the synthesis of proteins in the nuclear DNA.

4. To be involved in the production of ribosomes and RNA.

5. In cell division.

4.2.4 The chloroplast

Chloroplasts belong to a larger group of organelles known as **plastids**. In higher plants most chloroplasts are 5–10 μm long and are bounded by a double membrane, the **chloroplast envelope**, about 30 nm thick. While the outer membrane has a similar structure to the plasma membrane, the inner one is folded into a series of lamellae and is highly selective in what it allows in and out of the chloroplast.

Within the chloroplast envelope are two distinct regions. The **stroma** is a colourless, gelatinous matrix in which are embedded structures rather like stacks of coins in appearance. These are the **grana**. Each granum, and there may be around fifty in a chloroplast, is made up of between two and a hundred closed flattened sacs called **thylakoids**. Within these are located the photosynthetic pigments such as chlorophyll. Some thylakoids have tubular extensions which interconnect adjacent grana (Fig. 4.5).

Nucleus (EM) (×12 000 approx.)

Heterochromatin

Nuclear pore

Nuclear membrane

Nucleolus

Euchromatin

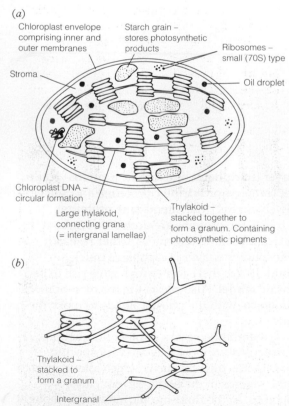

(a)

Chloroplast envelope comprising inner and outer membranes

Starch grain – stores photosynthetic products

Ribosomes – small (70S) type

Stroma

Oil droplet

Chloroplast DNA – circular formation

Large thylakoid, connecting grana (= intergranal lamellae)

Thylakoid – stacked together to form a granum. Containing photosynthetic pigments

(b)

Thylakoid – stacked to form a granum

Intergranal lamellae

Fig. 4.5 Structure of the chloroplasts

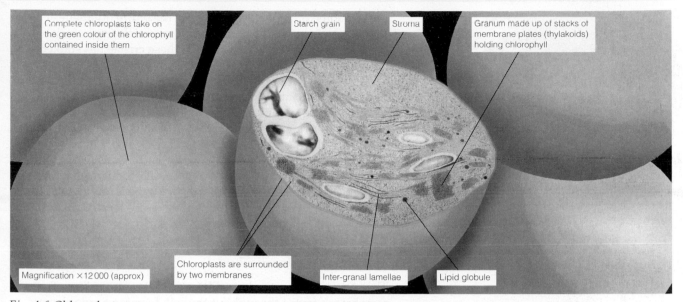

Complete chloroplasts take on the green colour of the chlorophyll contained inside them

Starch grain

Stroma

Granum made up of stacks of membrane plates (thylakoids) holding chlorophyll

Magnification ×12 000 (approx)

Chloroplasts are surrounded by two membranes

Inter-granal lamellae

Lipid globule

Fig. 4.6 Chloroplasts

Also present within the stroma are a series of starch grains which act as temporary stores for the products of photosynthesis. A number of smaller granules within the stroma readily take up osmium salts during the preparation of material for the electron microscope. They are called **osmiophilic granules** (*osmio* – 'osmium', *philo* – 'liking') but their function is not yet clear. A small amount of DNA is always present within the stroma, as are oil droplets.

4.2.5 The mitochondrion

Mitochondria are found within the cytoplasm of all eukaryotic cells, although in highly specialized cells such as mature red blood cells they may be absent. They range in shape from spherical to highly elongated and are typically 5 μm in length and 0.2 μm across. They are bounded by a double membrane, the outer of which controls the entry and exit of chemicals. The inner membrane is folded inwards, giving rise to extensions called

Fig. 4.7 Mitochondria

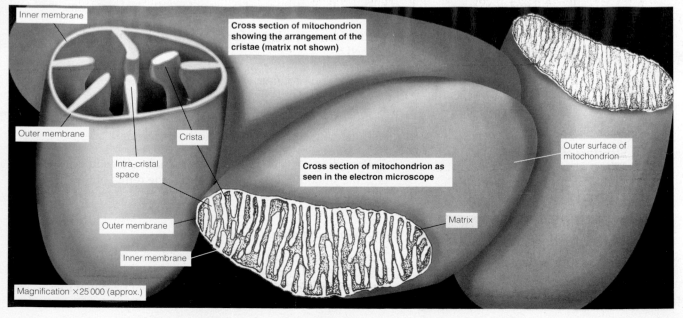

Inner membrane

Cross section of mitochondrion showing the arrangement of the cristae (matrix not shown)

Outer membrane

Crista

Intra-cristal space

Cross section of mitochondrion as seen in the electron microscope

Outer surface of mitochondrion

Outer membrane

Matrix

Inner membrane

Magnification ×25 000 (approx.)

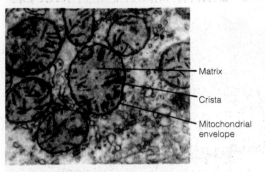

Mitochondrion (EM) (×15 000 approx.)

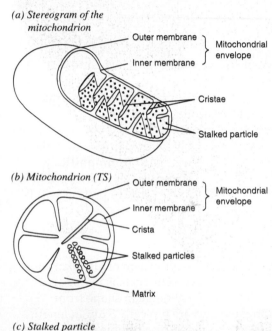

(a) Stereogram of the mitochondrion

(b) Mitochondrion (TS)

(c) Stalked particle

Fig. 4.8 Structure of a mitochondrion

cristae, some of which extend across the entire organelle. They function to increase the surface area on which respiratory processes take place. The surface of these cristae has stalked granules along its length (Fig. 4.8).

The remainder of the mitochondrion is the **matrix**. It is a semi-rigid material containing protein, lipids and traces of DNA. Electron-dense granules of 25 nm diameter also occur.

Mitochondria function as sites for certain stages of respiration, details of which are given in Section 12.4.1. The number of mitochondria in a cell therefore varies with its metabolic activity. Highly active cells may possess up to 1000. Similarly the number of cristae increases in metabolically active cells, giving weight to the proposition that respiratory enzymes are located on them.

4.2.6 Endoplasmic reticulum

The endoplasmic reticulum (ER) is an elaborate system of membranes found throughout the cell, forming a cytoplasmic skeleton. It is an extension of the outer nuclear membrane with which it is continuous. The membranes form a series of sheets which enclose flattened sacs called **cisternae** (Fig. 4.9 on page 57). Its structure varies from cell to cell and can probably change its nature rapidly; the membranes of the ER may be loosely organized or tightly packed. Where the membranes are lined with ribosomes they are called **rough endoplasmic reticulum**. The rough ER is concerned with protein synthesis (Section 5.6) and is consequently most abundant in those cells which are rapidly growing or secrete enzymes. In the same way, damage to a cell often results in increased formation of ER in order to produce the proteins necessary for the cell's repair. Where the membranes lack ribosomes they are called **smooth endoplasmic reticulum**. The smooth ER is concerned with lipid synthesis and is consequently most abundant in those cells producing lipid-related secretions, e.g. the sebaceous glands of mammalian skin and cells secreting steroids.

The functions of the ER may thus be summarized as:

1. Providing a large surface area for chemical reactions.

2. Providing a pathway for the transport of materials through the cell.

3. Producing proteins, especially enzymes (rough ER).

4. Producing lipids and steroids (smooth ER).

5. Collecting and storing synthesized material.

6. Providing a structural skeleton to maintain cellular shape (e.g. the smooth ER of a rod cell from the retina of the eye).

4.2.7 Golgi apparatus (dictyosome)

The Golgi apparatus, named after its discoverer Camillo Golgi, has a similar structure to the smooth endoplasmic reticulum but is more compact. It is composed of stacks of flattened sacs made of membranes. The sacs are fluid-filled and pinch off smaller

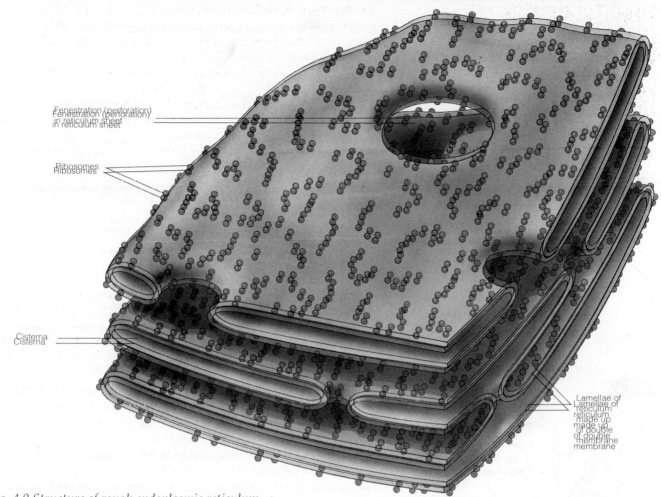

Fenestration (perforation) in reticulum sheet

Ribosomes

Cisterna

Lamellae of reticulum made up of double membrane

Fig. 4.9 Structure of rough endoplasmic reticulum

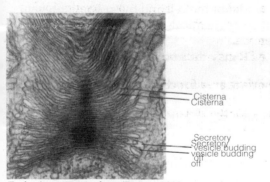

Cisterna

Secretory vesicle budding off

Endoplasmic reticulum (EM) (×9000 approx.)

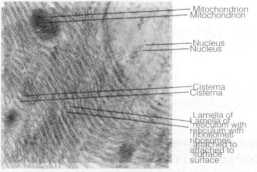

Mitochondrion

Nucleus

Cisterna

Lamella of reticulum with ribosomes attached to surface

Golgi apparatus (EM) (×30000 approx.)

membranous sacs, called **vesicles**, at their ends. There is normally only one Golgi apparatus in each animal cell but in plant cells there may be a large number of stacks known as **dictyosomes**. Its position and size varies from cell to cell but it is well developed in secretory cells and neurones and is small in muscle cells. All proteins produced by the endoplasmic reticulum are passed through the Golgi apparatus in a strict sequence. They pass first through the cis-Golgi network which returns to the ER any proteins wrongly exported by it. They then pass through the stack of cisternae which modify the proteins and lipids undergoing transport and add labels which allow them to be identified and sorted at the next stage, the trans-Golgi network. Here the proteins and lipids are sorted and sent to their final destinations. In general the Golgi acts as the cell's post office, receiving, sorting and delivering proteins and lipids. More specifically its functions include:

1. Producing glycoproteins such as mucin required in secretions, by adding the carbohydrate part to the protein.

2. Producing secretory enzymes, e.g. the digestive enzymes of the pancreas.

3. Secreting carbohydrates such as those involved in the production of new cell walls.

4. Transporting and storing lipids.

5. Forming lysosomes as described below.

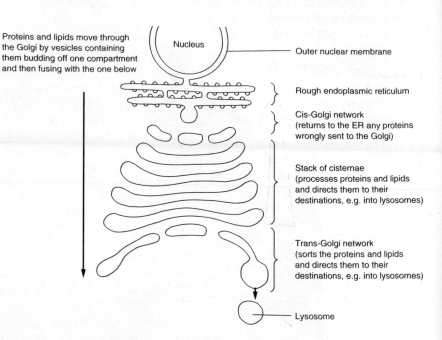

Proteins and lipids move through the Golgi by vesicles containing them budding off one compartment and then fusing with the one below

Nucleus

Outer nuclear membrane

Rough endoplasmic reticulum

Cis-Golgi network
(returns to the ER any proteins wrongly sent to the Golgi)

Stack of cisternae
(processes proteins and lipids and directs them to their destinations, e.g. into lysosomes)

Trans-Golgi network
(sorts the proteins and lipids and directs them to their destinations, e.g. into lysosomes)

Lysosome

Fig. 4.10 The Golgi apparatus and its relationship to the nucleus, endoplasmic reticulum and lysosomes

4.2.8 Lysosomes

Lysosomes (*lysis* – 'splitting', *soma* – 'body') are spherical bodies, some 0.1 to 1.0 μm in diameter. They contain around 50 enzymes, mostly hydrolases, in acid solution. They isolate these enzymes from the remainder of the cell and by so doing prevent them from acting upon other chemicals and organelles within the cell.

The functions of lysosomes are:

1. To digest material which the cell consumes from the environment. In the case of white blood cells, this may be bacteria or other harmful material. In Protozoa, it is the food which has been consumed by phagocytosis. In either case the material is broken down within the lysosome, useful chemicals are absorbed into the cytoplasm and any debris is egested by the cell by exocytosis (Fig. 4.11).

2. To digest parts of the cell, such as worn-out organelles, in a similar way to that described in **1**. This is known as **autophagy**. After the death of the cell they are responsible for its complete breakdown, a process called **autolysis** (*auto* – 'self', *lysis* – 'splitting').

3. To release their enzymes outside the cell (**exocytosis**) in order to break down other cells, e.g. in the reabsorption of tadpole tails during metamorphosis.

In view of their functions, it is hardly surprising that lysosomes are especially abundant in secretory cells and in phagocytic white blood cells.

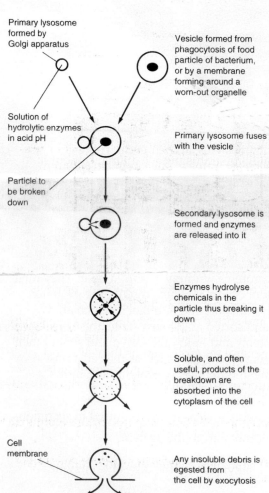

Primary lysosome formed by Golgi apparatus

Vesicle formed from phagocytosis of food particle of bacterium, or by a membrane forming around a worn-out organelle

Solution of hydrolytic enzymes in acid pH

Primary lysosome fuses with the vesicle

Particle to be broken down

Secondary lysosome is formed and enzymes are released into it

Enzymes hydrolyse chemicals in the particle thus breaking it down

Soluble, and often useful, products of the breakdown are absorbed into the cytoplasm of the cell

Cell membrane

Any insoluble debris is egested from the cell by exocytosis

Fig. 4.11 The functioning of a lysosome

NON-MEMBRANOUS STRUCTURES

4.2.9 Ribosomes

Ribosomes are small cytoplasmic granules found in all cells. They are around 20 nm in diameter in eukaryotic cells (80S type) but slightly smaller in prokaryotic ones (70S type). They may occur in groups called **polysomes** and may be associated with endoplasmic reticulum or occur freely within the cytoplasm. Despite their small size, their enormous numbers mean that they can account for up to 20% of the mass of a cell.

Ribosomes are made up of one large and one small sub-unit and comprise RNA known as **ribosomal RNA** and protein. They are important in the synthesis of proteins where they move along messenger RNA in succession (see Section 5.6).

4.2.10 Microtubules

Microtubules occur widely throughout eukaryotic cells but are not found in prokaryotic ones. They are slender, unbranched tubes 24 nm in diameter and up to several microns in length. They are made of two similar proteins **alpha-** and **beta-tubulin**, each of which comprises 450 amino acids. The arrangement of these proteins is shown in Fig. 4.13.

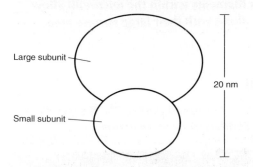

Fig. 4.12 Structure of a ribosome

Large subunit

Small subunit

20 nm

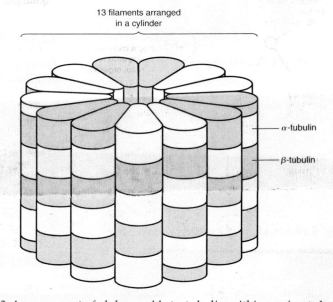

13 filaments arranged in a cylinder

α-tubulin

β-tubulin

Fig. 4.13 Arrangement of alpha- and beta-tubulin within a microtubule

The functions of microtubules are:

1. To provide an internal skeleton (**cytoskeleton**) for cells and so help determine their shape.

2. To aid transport within cells by providing routes along which materials move.

3. To form a framework along which the cellulose cell wall of plants is laid down.

4. As major components of cilia and flagella where they are grouped in a very precise way and contribute to their movement.

5. In the spindle during cell division and within the centrioles from which the spindle is formed. Here they help to draw chromosomes or chromatids to opposite poles (see Chapter 6).

4.2.11 Centrioles

Centrioles have the same basic structure as the basal bodies of cilia. They are hollow cylinders about $0.2\ \mu m$ in diameter. They arise in a distinct region of the cytoplasm known as the **centrosome**. It contains two centrioles. At cell division they migrate to opposite poles of the cell where they synthesize the microtubules of the spindle. Despite the absence of centrioles, the cells of higher plants do form spindles.

4.2.12 Microvilli

Microvilli are tiny finger-like projections about $0.6\ \mu m$ in length on the membranes of certain cells, such as those of the intestinal epithelium and the kidney tubule. They should not be confused with the much larger villi which are multicellular structures. Microvilli massed together appear similar to the bristles of a brush, hence the term **brush border** given to the edge of cells bearing microvilli. Actin filaments within the microvilli allow them to contract, which, along with their large surface area, facilitates absorption.

4.2.13 Cellulose cell wall

A cell wall is a characteristic feature of plant cells. It consists of cellulose microfibrils embedded in an amorphous polysaccharide matrix. The structure and properties of cellulose are discussed in Section 2.5.3 and the detailed structure of a cellulose microfibril is given in Fig. 4.14. The matrix is usually composed of polysaccharides, e.g. pectin or lignin. The microfibrils may be regular or irregular in arrangement.

The main functions of the cell wall is to provide support to herbaceous parts of a plant.

Microvillus

Brush order

Microvilli (EM) (×23 000 approx.)

Fig. 4.14 Structure of a cellulose microfibril

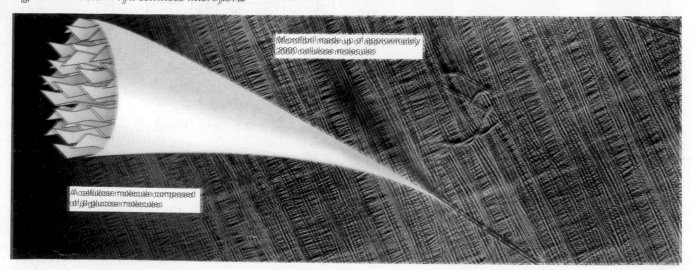

Microfibril made up of approximately 2000 cellulose molecules

A cellulose molecule composed of β glucose molecules

4.3 Movement in and out of cells

The various organelles and structures within a cell require a variety of substances in order to carry out their functions. In turn they form products, some useful and some wastes. Most of these substances must pass in and out of the cell. This they do by **diffusion**, **osmosis**, **active transport**, **phagocytosis** and **pinocytosis**.

4.3.1 Diffusion

Diffusion is the process by which a substance moves from a region of high concentration of that substance to a region of low concentration of the same substance. Diffusion occurs because the molecules of which substances are made are in random motion (kinetic theory). The process is explained in Fig. 4.15.

The rate of diffusion depends upon:

1. **The concentration gradient** – The greater the difference in concentration between two regions of a substance the greater the rate of diffusion. Organisms must therefore maintain a fresh supply of a substance to be absorbed by creating a stream over the diffusion surface. Equally, the substance, once absorbed, must be rapidly transported away.

2. **The distance over which diffusion takes place** – The shorter the distance between two regions of different concentration the greater the rate of diffusion. The rate is proportional to the reciprocal of the square of the distance (inverse square law). Any structure in an organism across which diffusion regularly takes place must therefore be thin. Cell membranes for example are only 7.5 nm thick and even epithelial layers such as those lining the alveoli of the lungs are as thin as 0.3 μm across.

3. **The area over which diffusion takes place** – The larger the surface area the greater the rate of diffusion. Diffusion surfaces frequently have structures for increasing their surface area and hence the rate at which they exchange materials. These structures include villi and microvilli.

4. **The nature of any structure across which diffusion occurs** – Diffusion frequently takes place across epithelial layers or cell membranes. Variations in their structure may affect diffusion. For example, the greater the number and size of pores in cell membranes the greater the rate of diffusion.

5. **The size and nature of the diffusing molecule** – Small molecules diffuse faster than large ones. Fat-soluble ones diffuse more rapidly through cell membranes than water-soluble ones.

1. *If 10 particles occupying the left-hand side of a closed vessel are in random motion, they will collide with each other and the sides of the vessel. Some particles from the left-hand side move to the right, but initially there are no available particles to move in the opposite direction, so the movement is in one direction only. There is a large concentration gradient and diffusion is rapid.*

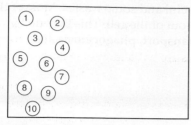

2. *After a short time the particles (still in random motion) have spread themselves more evenly. Particles can now move from right to left as well as left to right. However with a higher concentration of particles (7) on the left than on the right (3) there is a greater probability of a particle moving to the right than in the reverse direction. There is a smaller concentration gradient and diffusion is slower.*

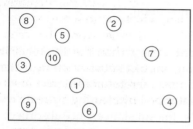

3. *Some time later, the particles will be evenly distributed throughout the vessel and the concentrations will be equal on each side. The system is in equilibrium. The particles are not however static but remain in random motion. With equal concentrations on each side, the probability of a particle moving from left to right is equal to the probability of one moving in the opposite direction. There is no concentration gradient and no net diffusion.*

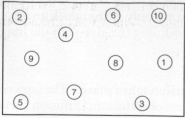

4. *At a later stage the particles remain evenly distributed and will continue to do so. Although the number of particles on each side remains the same, individual particles are continuously changing position. This situation is called* **dynamic equilibrium***.*

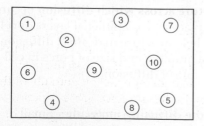

Figure 4.15 Diffusion

4.3.2 Facilitated diffusion

This special form of diffusion allows more rapid exchange. It may involve channels within a membrane which make diffusion of specific substances easier. These channels form water-filled connections across the lipid bilayer which allow water-soluble substances to move across. They are important therefore in transporting ions. The channels are selective in that they will open or close in response to certain signals such as a change in voltage or the binding of another molecule. In this way the cell can control the entry and exit of molecules and ions.

An alternative form of facilitated diffusion involves different protein molecules in the membrane called **carrier proteins**. These bind molecules to them and then change shape as a result of this binding in such a way that the molecules are released to the inside of the membrane (Fig. 4.16).

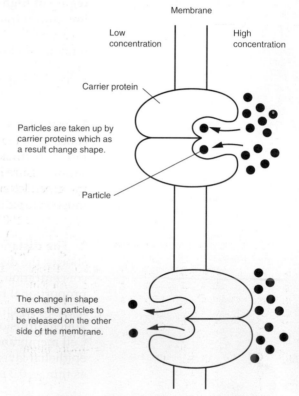

Fig. 4.16 Facilitated diffusion by carrier proteins

In all cases facilitated diffusion does not involve the use of energy (i.e. it is passive) and hence material is moved along a concentration gradient (i.e. from high to low concentration).

4.3.3 Osmosis

Osmosis is a special form of diffusion which involves the movement of solvent molecules. The solvent in biological systems is invariably water. Most cell membranes are permeable to water and certain solutes only. Such membranes are termed **partially permeable**. Osmosis in living organisms can therefore be defined as: **the passage of water from a region where it is highly concentrated to a region where its concentration is lower, through a partially permeable membrane**. The process is explained in Fig. 4.17 on page 63.

If a solution is separated from its pure solvent, as in Fig 4.17, the pressure which must be applied to stop water entering that solution, and so prevent osmosis, is called the **osmotic pressure**. The more concentrated a solution the greater is its osmotic pressure. This is a hypothetical situation and, as a solution does not actually exert a pressure under normal circumstances, the term 'osmotic potential' is preferred. As the osmotic potential is in effect the potential of a solution to pull water into it, it always has a negative value. A more concentrated solution therefore has a more positive osmotic pressure but a more negative osmotic potential.

Osmosis not only occurs when a solution is separated from its pure solvent by a partially permeable membrane but also arises when such a membrane separates two solutions of different concentrations. In this case water moves from the more dilute, or **hypotonic**, solution, to the more concentrated, or **hypertonic**, solution. When a dynamic equilibrium is established and both solutions are of equal concentration they are said to be **isotonic**.

Consider Fig. 4.18. Initially the water molecules on the right of the partially permeable membrane collide with the membrane more often than those on the left, which are to some extent impeded by the glucose molecules. In other words the water on the right has a greater potential energy than that on the left of the membrane. The greater the number of collisions the water molecules make on the membrane, the greater the pressure on it. This pressure is called the **water potential** and is represented by the greek letter psi (Ψ).

Under standard conditions of temperature and pressure (25 °C and 100 kPa) pure water is designated a water potential of zero. The addition of solute to pure water lowers its water potential because the solute molecules impede the water molecules, reducing the number of collisions they make with the membrane. It therefore exerts less pressure and has a lower water potential. Given that pure water has a water potential of zero, all solutions therefore have a lower one i.e. they have negative water potentials. The more concentrated a solution the more negative is its water potential. Water will diffuse from a region of less negative (higher) water potential to one of more negative (lower) water potential.

4.3.4 Active transport

Diffusion and osmosis are passive processes, i.e. they occur without the expenditure of energy. Some molecules are transported in and out of cells by active means, i.e. energy is required to drive the process.

The energy is necessary because molecules are transported against a **concentration gradient**, i.e. from a region of low concentration to one of a high concentration. It is thought that the process occurs through the proteins that span the membrane. These accept the molecule to be transported on one side of the membrane and, by a change in the structure of the protein, convey it to the other side (see Fig. 4.19). A good example of active transport is the **sodium–potassium pump** which exists in most cell membranes. This actively removes sodium ions from

1. *Both solvent (water) and solute (glucose) molecules are in random motion, but only solvent (water) molecules are able to cross the partially permeable membrane. This they do until their concentration is equal on both sides of the membrane.*

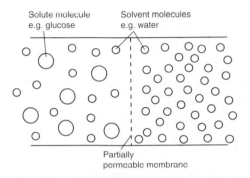

2. *Once the water molecules are evenly distributed, in theory a dynamic equilibrium should be established. However, the water molecules on the left of the membrane are impeded to some extent by the glucose molecules from crossing the membrane. With no glucose present on the right of the membrane, water molecules move more easily to the left than in reverse direction.*

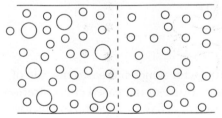

3. *A situation is reached whereby additional water molecules accumulate on the left of the membrane, until their greater concentration offsets the blocking effect of the glucose. The probability of water molecules moving in either direction is the same, and a dynamic equilibrium is established.*

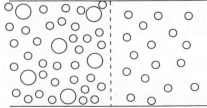

N.B.   Solution = solute + solvent
e.g.   Glucose solution = glucose powder + water

Fig. 4.17 Osmosis

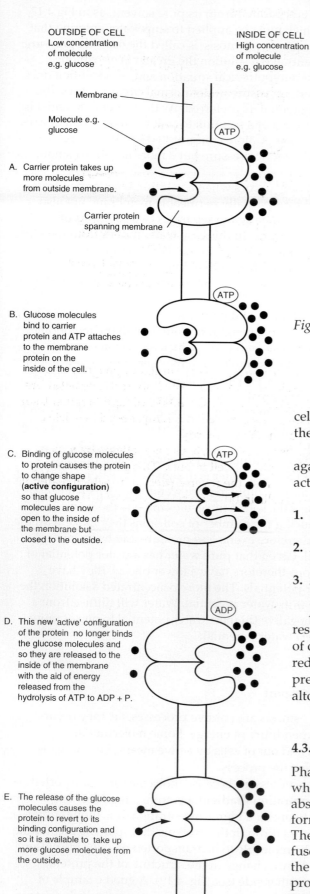

A. Carrier protein takes up more molecules from outside membrane.

B. Glucose molecules bind to carrier protein and ATP attaches to the membrane protein on the inside of the cell.

C. Binding of glucose molecules to protein causes the protein to change shape **(active configuration)** so that glucose molecules are now open to the inside of the membrane but closed to the outside.

D. This new 'active' configuration of the protein no longer binds the glucose molecules and so they are released to the inside of the membrane with the aid of energy released from the hydrolysis of ATP to ADP + P.

E. The release of the glucose molecules causes the protein to revert to its binding configuration and so it is available to take up more glucose molecules from the outside.

Fig. 4.19 Active transport

Partially permeable membrane

Net flow of molecules

○ Solute molecule, e.g. glucose

○ Water molecule

Low concentration of water molecules. Low water potential

High concentration of water molecules. High water potential

High concentration of solute molecules. High osmotic pressure

Low concentration of solute molecules. Low osmotic pressure

Fig. 4.18 Water potential and osmotic pressure

cells while actively accumulating potassium ions into them from their surroundings.

Due to the energy expenditure necessary to move molecules against a concentration gradient, cells and tissues carrying out active transport are characterized by:

1. The presence of numerous mitochondria.

2. A high concentration of ATP.

3. A high respiratory rate.

As a consequence of **3**, any factor which increases the rate of respiration, e.g. a higher temperature or increased concentration of oxygen, will increase the rate of active transport. Any factor reducing the rate of respiration or causing it to cease, e.g. the presence of cyanide, will cause active transport to slow or stop altogether.

4.3.5 Phagocytosis

Phagocytosis (*phago* – 'feeding', *cyto* – 'cell') is the process by which the cell can obtain particles which are too large to be absorbed by diffusion or active transport. The cell invaginates to form a cup-shaped depression in which the particle is contained. The depression is then pinched off to form a vacuole. Lysosomes fuse with the vacuole and their enzymes break down the particle, the useful contents of which may be absorbed (Fig. 4.20). The process only occurs in a few specialized cells (called **phagocytes**), such as white blood cells where harmful bacteria can be ingested.

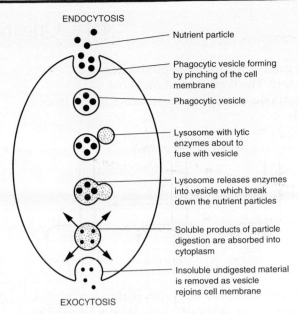

ENDOCYTOSIS

Nutrient particle

Phagocytic vesicle forming by pinching of the cell membrane

Phagocytic vesicle

Lysosome with lytic enzymes about to fuse with vesicle

Lysosome releases enzymes into vesicle which break down the nutrient particles

Soluble products of particle digestion are absorbed into cytoplasm

Insoluble undigested material is removed as vesicle rejoins cell membrane

EXOCYTOSIS

Fig. 4.20 Endocytosis and exocytosis

4.3.6 Pinocytosis

Pinocytosis or 'cell drinking' is very similar to phagocytosis except that the vesicles produced, called **pinocytic vesicles**, are smaller. The process is used for the intake of liquids rather than solids. Even smaller vesicles, called **micropinocytic vesicles**, may be pinched off in the same way.

Both pinocytosis and phagocytosis are methods by which materials are taken into the cell in bulk. This process is called **endocytosis**. By contrast, the reverse process, in which materials are removed from cells in bulk, is called **exocytosis** (Fig. 4.20).

4.4   Questions

1. Liver cells were ground to produce an homogenate. The flow chart shows how centrifugation was used to separate organelles from liver cells.

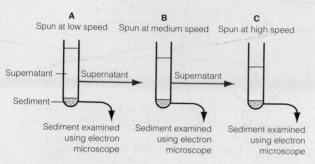

Drawings of electron micrographs of three organelles separated by the centrifugation are shown below. The drawings are **not** to the same scale.

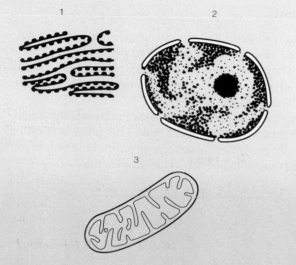

(a) Complete the table below.

Electron micrograph	Name of organelle	Centrifuge tube in which the organelle would be the main constituent of the sediment
1		
2		
3		

(2 marks)

(b) Explain why it is possible to separate the organelles in this way. *(2 marks)*

(Total 4 marks)

NEAB February 1995, Paper BY1, No. 2

2. The table refers to a liver cell, a palisade mesophyll cell and a bacterium (prokaryotic cell) and structures which may be found in them.

If the structure is present, place a tick (✓) in the appropriate box and if the structure is absent, place a cross (✗) in the appropriate box.

Structure	Liver cell	Palisade cell	Bacterium
Nuclear envelope			
Cell wall			
Microvilli			
Chloroplasts			

(Total 4 marks)

ULEAC 1996 Specimen Paper B/HB1, No. 1

3. The diagram shows structures which can be seen in most animal cells with the aid of an electron microscope.

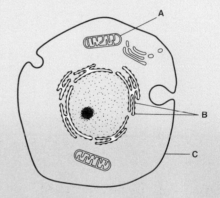

(a) Identify the parts labelled **A**, **B** and **C**.
(3 marks)

(b) What is the functional relationship between parts **A** and **B**? *(2 marks)*

(c) In each case, give **one** major way in which the structure of the following cells would differ from that of the cell shown in the diagram:
   (i) An ovum *(1 mark)*
   (ii) A cell from the first (proximal) convoluted tubule of a nephron. *(1 mark)*
(Total 7 marks)

AEB June 1993, Paper 1, No. 3

4. Write an account of the general structure of a eukaryotic cell and compare this with the structure of a prokaryotic cell.

ULEAC June 1995, Paper 1, No. 15(a)

5. (a) Compare and contrast the structure of a generalized plant and a generalized animal cell.
(8 marks)

(b) Describe how the mitochondrion is adapted to its functions. (10 marks)
(Total 18 marks)

UCLES June 1995, Paper 2, No. 8

6. The arrows in the diagram show the path followed by a protein produced in a secretory cell.

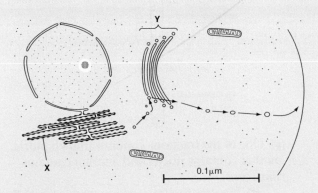

0.1μm

(a) Calculate the magnification. Show your working. (2 marks)
(b) Identify organelle X. (1 mark)
(c) With reference to the protein being produced:
(i) identify one function of organelle Y; (1 mark)
(ii) explain how the protein reaches the outside of the cell from organelle Y. (2 marks)
(Total 6 marks)

AEB June 1995, Paper 1, No. 2

7. A sample of animal tissue was treated in order to separate the cell components. A chemical analysis of the pure fractions shown in the table was carried out.

Cell Component	DNA	RNA	Protein	Phospholipid
Cell surface membrane				
Rough endoplasmic reticulum				
Mitochondria				
Nuclei				

(a) Complete the table to show the results of the analysis. Mark the box with a tick (✓) if you think that the chemical was present or with a cross (✗) if the chemical was absent. (4 marks)
(b) Describe concisely how the cell components were separated. (4 marks)
(Total 8 marks)

AEB June 1994, Paper 1, No. 2

8. The drawing below shows a leaf palisade cell as revealed by an electron microscope.

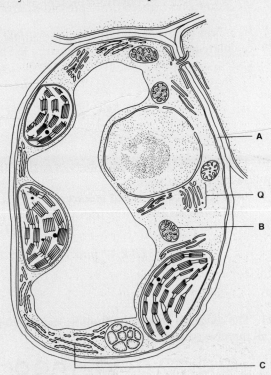

(a) Name the parts labelled A, B and C. (3 marks)
(b) (i) On the diagram, label the nuclear envelope. (1 mark)
(ii) Give one function of the nuclear envelope. (1 mark)
(c) Identify Q and describe one function. (2 marks)
(Total 7 marks)

ULEAC June 1994, Paper 1, No. 4

9. The electron micrograph below shows part of a palisade cell of a leaf.

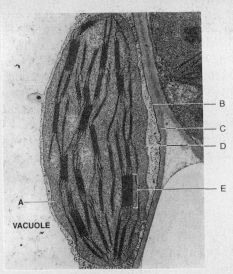

VACUOLE

(a) Name the parts labelled **A**, **B**, **C** and **D**.
(4 marks)
(b) Name **one** carbohydrate present in structure **C**.
(1 mark)
(c) Given that the magnification is ×40 000, calculate the actual length of structure **E**. Show your working. (3 marks)
(Total 8 marks)

ULEAC June 1993, Paper 1, No. 2

10. Distinguish between members of each of the following pairs of terms.
(a) Prokaryotic cell and eukaryotic cell (3 marks)
(b) Diffusion and active transport (3 marks)
(Total 6 marks)

ULEAC June 1993, Paper 1, No. 10

11. The diagram shows the fluid mosaic model of the cell membrane structure.

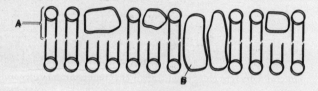

(a) Name the molecules labelled **A** and **B**.
(2 marks)
(b) Suggest **two** properties that drugs should possess if they are to enter a cell rapidly. (2 marks)
(c) Explain why an electron microscope is useful in studying cell structure. (2 marks)
(Total 6 marks)

NEAB June 1995, Paper BY01, No. 2

12. The diagram summarizes a procedure for isolating cell components. Cells, such as liver cells are homogenized (broken up) and then spun in a centrifuge at increasing speeds. At each stage the pellet is retained and the supernatant (liquid) is then centrifuged at a higher speed. Figures show centrifugal forces produced as the number of times they are greater than the force of gravity, g.

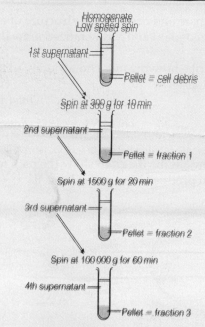

(a) One of the fractions contains mitochondria, another contains nuclei and another contains ribosomes.
(i) Identify the fraction in which each of the components is found. Write your answers in the table below.

Component	Fraction number
Mitochondria	
Nuclei	
Ribosomes	

(2 marks)
(ii) Explain the reasoning for your answer in (i). (2 marks)
(b) One of the three fractions contains the enzyme succinic dehydrogenase. The activity of this enzyme can be demonstrated using methylene blue or tetrazolium chloride (TTC) with succinic acid as the substrate.
(i) Describe a method you could use to determine which of the three fractions contains succinic dehydrogenase. (4 marks)
(ii) Which of the three fractions would show dehydrogenase activity? (1 mark)
(c) State **two** components, other than water, that would be found in the 4th supernatant. (2 marks)
(Total 11 marks)

ULEAC June 1996, Paper B/HBI, No. 7

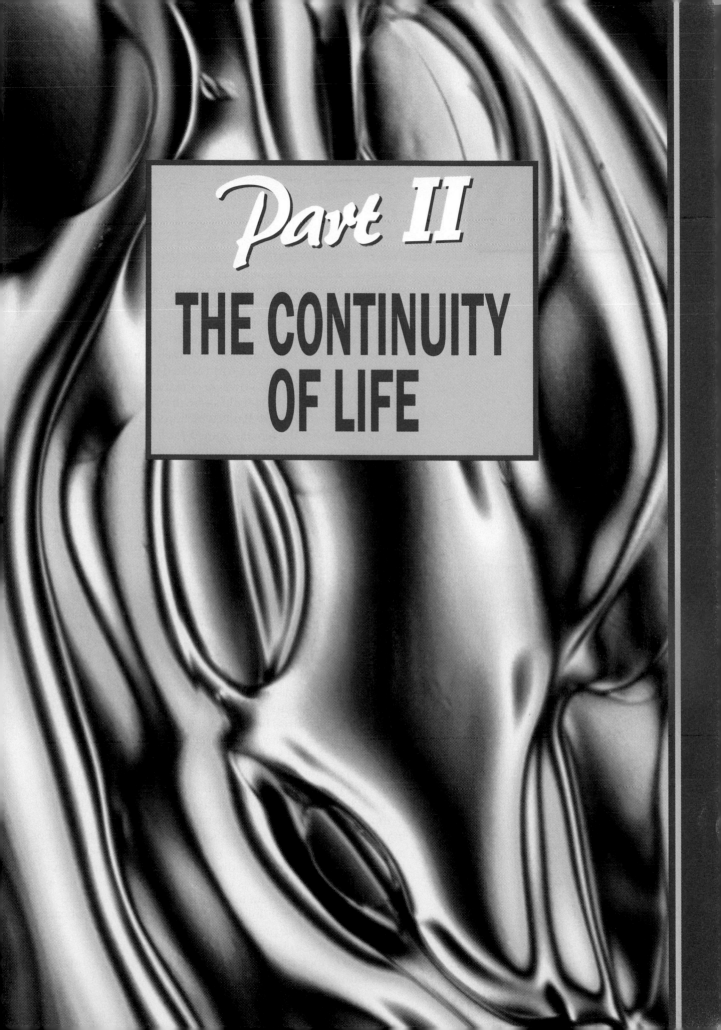

Part II
THE CONTINUITY OF LIFE

Inheritance in context

The obvious similarities between children and their parents, or sometimes their grandparents, have long been recognized. Despite many attempts to explain this phenomenon, it is only in recent years that our knowledge of the process of heredity has enabled us to understand the mechanism fully.

The fact that, in some species, both male and female are needed to produce offspring was realized from early times. The role each sex played was, however, a matter of argument. Aristotle believed that the male's semen was composed of an incomplete blend of ingredients which upon mixing with the menstrual fluid of the female, gained form and power and became the new organism. Apart from minor refinements this belief was generally accepted until the seventeenth century. When Anton van Leeuwenhoek observed sperm in human semen, the idea arose that these contained a miniature human. When these sperm were introduced into the female, one would implant in the womb and develop there, the female's rôle being nothing more than a convenient incubator. Around this period Regnier de Graaf discovered in ovaries what was later to be called the Graafian follicle. This was thought by another group of scientists to contain the miniature human, the sperm simply acting as a stimulus for its development.

The problem with both these beliefs was that it could easily be observed that any offspring tended to show characteristics of both parents rather than just one. This led, in the last century, to the idea that both parents contributed hereditary characteristics and the offspring was merely an intermediate blend of both. While closer to present thinking, it too had one flaw. Logically the offspring of a cross between a red flower and a white flower should have pink flowers and the children of a tall father and a short mother should be of medium height. It took the rediscovery of the work of Mendel at the beginning of this century to provide what is now an accepted explanation. Both parents do provide hereditary material within the sperm and ovum. The offspring therefore has two sets of genetic information – one from the mother and one from the father. For any individual characteristic, e.g. eye colour, only one of the two factors expresses itself. An individual with one factor for blue eyes and one for brown eyes will always have brown eyes. A few characters do show an intermediate state between two contrasting factors, but this is relatively rare. Only one of each pair of factors will be present in any one gamete.

Alongside these changes in the last century, another development took place. It was originally believed that new species arose spontaneously in some manner. By the end of the

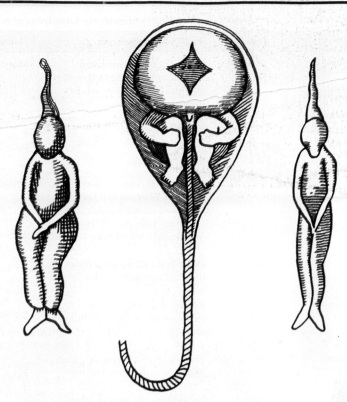

Fig. II Observers in the seventeenth century believed the human sperm contained a tiny copy of the parent – they thought they could see these down the microscope and called them homunculi

century it was more or less accepted that they were formed by adaptation of existing forms. Natural selection is considered to be the mechanism by which these changes arise and it depends upon there being much variety among individuals of a species. Without this variety and consequent selection of the types best suited to the present conditions, species could not adapt and evolve to meet the changing demands of the environment.

If this theory of evolution is accepted, then the process of inheritance must permit variety to occur. At the same time, if the offspring are to be supplied with the same genetic information as the parents, the genetic material must be extremely stable. This stability is especially important to ensure that favourable characteristics are passed on from one generation to the next. This then is the paradox of inheritance – how to reconcile the genetic stability needed to preserve useful characteristics with the genetic variability necessary for evolution. To satisfy both requirements it is necessary to have hereditary units which are in themselves exceedingly stable, which can be reassorted in an almost infinite variety of ways. The idea can be likened to a pack of playing cards. The cards themselves are stable, fixed units, but the number of different possible combinations in a typical hand of thirteen cards is immense. Imagine how much greater are the possible combinations of the thousands of hereditary units in a typical organism.

A summary of the historical events which contributed to our current understanding of heredity is given in Table II.

TABLE II **Historical review of events leading to present-day knowledge of reproduction and heredity**

Name	Date	Observation/discovery	Name	Date	Observation/discovery
Aristotle	384–322 BC	Mixing of male semen and female semen (menstrual fluid) was like blending two sets of ingredients which gave 'life'	Morgan	early 1900s	Pioneered use of *Drosophila* in genetics experiments and described linkage
General scientific belief	Up to 17th century	Simple organisms arose spontaneously out of non-living material	Garrod	1908	Postulated mutations as sources of certain hereditary diseases
van Leeuwenhoek	1677	Discovered sperm – it was generally believed that these contained miniature organisms which only developed when introduced into a female	Johannsen	1909	Coined term 'gene' as hereditary unit
			Janssens	1909	Observed chiasmata and crossing over
			Sturtevant	1913	Mapped genes on chromosomes of *Drosophila*
de Graaf	1670s	Described the ovarian follicle (later called Graafian follicle)	Muller	1920s	Observed mutagenic effect of X-rays
Lamarck	1809	Proposed theory of evolution based on inheritance of acquired characteristics	Oparin	1923	Suggested theory of origin of life
			Griffith	1928	Produced evidence suggesting that a chemical 'transforming principle' was responsible for carrying genetic information
Darwin	1859	*On the Origin of Species by Means of Natural Selection* published			
Pasteur	1864	Experimentally disproved the theory of spontaneous generation	Beadle and Tatum	1941	Produced evidence supporting the one gene, one enzyme hypothesis
Mendel	1865	Experiments on the genetics of peas and formulation of his two laws	Avery, McCarty and McCleod	1944	Showed nucleic acid to be the chemical which carried genetic information
Hertwig	1875	Witnessed fusion of nuclei during fertilization	Hershey and Chase	1952	Showed DNA to be the hereditary material
Flemming	1882	Described all stages of mitosis	Watson and Crick	1953	Formulated the detailed structure of DNA
de Vries	1900	Rediscovery of the significance of Mendel's 1865 experiment	Kornberg	1956	Produced DNA copies from single DNA template using DNA polymerase
Sutton	1902	Observed pairing of homologous chromosomes during meiosis and suggested these carried genetic information	Meselsohn and Stahl	1959	Described mechanism of semi-conservative replication in DNA
			Jacob and Monod	1961	Postulated existence of mRNA in theory on control of protein synthesis

5 DNA and the genetic code

5.1 Evidence that the nucleus contains the hereditary material

The universal occurrence of a nucleus at some stage of the life cycle of cells suggests that it performs an essential rôle. The functions of the nucleus are listed in Section 4.2.3. The fundamental rôle of the nucleus in determining the features of a cell was established by Hämmerling. Working with individual cells is normally a difficult task, not least because of their small size. Hämmerling, however, used unusually large single-celled algae belonging to the genus *Acetabularia*. Each cell is up to 5 cm in length, making the sectioning of it relatively easy.

Fig. 5.1, over the page, gives a summary of the experiments using two species of *Acetabularia*, which show the nucleus to contain the hereditary material. The experiments are based on those of Hämmerling although they incorporate some refinements made possible by modern techniques.

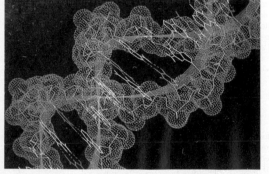

Computer representation of part of a DNA molecule

5.2 Evidence that DNA is the hereditary material

5.2.1 Chromosome analysis

With the nucleus having been shown to contain the hereditary material, attention focussed on determining the precise nature of this material. As **chromosomes** only become visible during cell division, it was hardly surprising that they quickly attracted attention. Chromosomes were shown to be made up of protein and DNA. Of the two, protein was thought a more likely candidate as it was known to be a complex molecule existing in an almost infinite number of forms – a necessary characteristic of a material which must carry an immense diversity of information. Later work showed this not to be the case and research centred on the DNA.

5.2.2 Metabolic stability of DNA

Any material which is responsible for transferring information from one generation to another must be extremely stable. If it were altered to any extent imperfect copies would be made. Unlike protein, DNA shows remarkable metabolic stability. If DNA is labelled with a radioactive isotope it can be shown that its rate of disappearance from the DNA is very slow. This suggests that, once formed, a DNA molecule undergoes little if any alteration.

METHOD	RESULTS	CONCLUSION	EXPLANATION IN LIGHT OF PRESENT KNOWLEDGE
Experiment 1 A. mediterranea is cut into two approximately equal halves Cut	The portion without the nucleus degenerates. The portion with the nucleus regenerates a new cap of the same type	The information for the regeneration of the cap is contained in, or produced by, the lower portion which contains the nucleus	The DNA in the nucleus produces mRNA which enters the cytoplasm where it provides the instructions for the formation of the enzymes needed in the production of a new cap. In the absence of a nucleus, the upper portion cannot do this
Experiment 2 A. mediterranea is cut to isolate the stalk section which does not contain the nucleus Cut Cut	A new cap is regenerated from the stalk section	The information on how to regenerate the cap is present in the stalk	As the nucleus produces a constant supply of mRNA there is sufficient in the cytoplasm of the stalk to provide instructions on how to form the enzymes necessary for the regeneration of the cap
Experiment 3 The regenerated cap from the previous experiment is again removed Cut	The stalk does not regenerate a cap for a second time	The information on how to regenerate the cap, which is contained in the stalk, must be used up and so cannot effect a second regeneration	The mRNA is broken down once its rôle in regenerating the cap is complete. It is therefore not available for the cap to be generated a second time. In the absence of a nucleus, there is no new source of mRNA
Experiment 4 The stalk of A. mediterranea is grafted onto the base portion (which contains the nucleus) of A. crenulata – a species possessing a different shaped cap Cut Cut Cut	The cap of A. crenulata is regenerated	The influence on cap regeneration of the base portion (with nucleus) is greater than the influence of the stalk portion (without the nucleus)	With the nucleus of A. crenulata present a constant supply of mRNA is available to regenerate this type of cap. The mRNA from A. mediterranea is limited to that present in the stalk when it was separated from its nucleus. The influence of the mRNA from A. crenulata is therefore greater
Experiment 5 The nucleus from a decapitated A. crenulata is removed and replaced with a transplanted nucleus from A. mediterranea Nucleus discarded Nucleus transplanted	The cap regenerated is of the A. mediterranea type	As the only part of A. mediterranea which is present is the nucleus, it alone must contain the instruction on how to regenerate the cap	The situation similar to that in experiment 4 except that it is the mRNA of A. mediterranea which is present in greater quantities, because its nucleus is present and forms a constant supply of mRNA

Fig. 5.1 Summary of experiments to show that the nucleus contains hereditary material

5.2.3 Constancy of DNA within a cell

Almost all the DNA of a cell is associated with the chromosomes in the nucleus. Small amounts do occur in cytoplasmic organelles such as mitochondria, but this represents a small proportion of the total. Analysis shows that the amount of DNA remains constant for all cells within a species except for the gametes, which have almost exactly half the usual quantity. Prior to cell division the amount of DNA per cell doubles. This is shared equally between the two daughter cells which therefore have the usual quantity. These changes are consistent with those expected of hereditary material which is being transmitted from cell to cell during division.

5.2.4 Correlation between mutagens and their effects on DNA

Mutagens are agents which cause **mutations** in living organisms. A mutation is an alteration to an organism's characteristics which is inherited. Many agents are known mutagens; they include X-rays, nitrous acid and various dyes. It can be shown that these mutagens all alter the structure of DNA in some way. A typical example is ultra-violet light of wavelength 260 nm. It both causes mutations and alters the structure of the pyrimidine bases of which DNA is made. This suggests that it is this alteration of DNA which is the source of the mutation and DNA must therefore be the hereditary material.

5.2.5 Experiments on bacterial transformation

The most convincing evidence for the genetic rôle of DNA was provided by Griffith in 1928. He experimented on the bacterium *Pneumococcus* which causes pneumonia. It exists in two forms:

1. The harmful form – a virulent (disease-causing) type which has a gelatin coat. When grown on agar it produces **shiny**, **smooth** colonies and is therefore known as the S-strain.

2. The safe form – a non-virulent (does not cause disease) type which does not have a gelatin coat. When grown on agar it produces **dull**, **rough** colonies and is therefore known as the R-strain.

Griffith's experiments may be summarized thus:

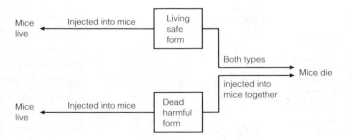

The living safe form and dead harmful form, while not causing pneumonia when injected separately, did so when injected together. The resulting dead mice were found to contain living harmful forms of *Pneumococcus*. If one discounts the improbable explanation that the dead harmful forms have been resurrected, how then could the living safe forms suddenly have acquired the ability to form a gelatin coat, produce smooth colonies and cause pneumonia? It is possible that the safe form had mutated into the harmful form, but this is unlikely. Furthermore, the experiment can be repeated with similar results and the likelihood of the same mutation arising each and every time is so improbable that it can be discounted.

If pneumonia is caused by some toxin produced by *Pneumococcus*, then the harmful type must have the ability to produce it, whereas the safe type does not. The explanation could therefore be that the dead harmful type has the information on how to make the toxin but, being dead, is unable to manufacture it. The safe type, being alive, is potentially able to make the toxin but lacks the information on how to go about it. If then the recipe for the toxin can in some way be transferred from the dead harmful to the living safe variety, the toxin can be manufactured and pneumonia will result. As the substance was able to transform one strain of *Pneumococcus* into another, it became known as the **transforming principle**.

5.2.6 Experiments to identify the transforming principle

The identity of the transforming principle was determined by Avery, McCarty and McCleod in 1944. In a series of experiments they isolated and purified different substances from the dead harmful types of *Pneumococcus*. In turn they tested the ability of each to transform living safe types into harmful ones. Purified DNA was shown to be capable of bringing about transformation, and this ability ceased when the enzyme which breaks down DNA (deoxyribonuclease) was added.

5.2.7 Transduction experiments

In 1952 Hershey and Chase performed a series of experiments involving the bacterium *Escherichia coli* and a bacteriophage (T_2 phage) which attacks it. (Details of a phage life cycle are given in Section 21.1.2.) T_2 phage transfers to *E. coli* the necessary hereditary material needed to make it manufacture new T_2 phage viruses. As the T_2 phage virus is composed of just DNA and protein, one or the other must constitute the hereditary material. Hershey and Chase carefully labelled the protein of one phage sample with radioactive sulphur (^{35}S) and the DNA of another phage sample with radioactive phosphorus (^{32}P). They then separately introduced each sample into a culture of *E. coli* bacteria. At a critical stage, when the viruses had transferred their hereditary material into the bacterial cells, the two organisms were separated mechanically and each culture of bacteria was examined for radioactivity. The culture injected with radioactive DNA contained radioactive bacteria, while that injected with radioactive protein did not. The evidence was conclusive: DNA was the hereditary material; but if further proof were needed this was provided by electron microscope studies which actually traced the movement of DNA from viruses into bacterial cells.

5.3 Nucleic acids

Adenosine monophosphate (adenylic acid)

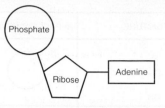

Fig. 5.2 Structure of a typical nucleotide

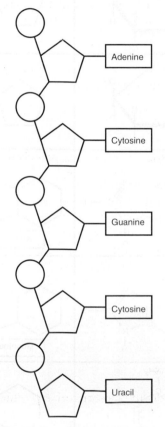

Fig. 5.3 Structure of section of polynucleotide, e.g. RNA

5.3.1 Structure of nucleotides

Individual nucleotides comprise three parts:

1. Phosphoric acid (phosphate H_3PO_4). This has the same structure in all nucleotides.

2. Pentose sugar. Two types occur, ribose ($C_5H_{10}O_5$) and deoxyribose ($C_5H_{10}O_4$).

3. Organic base. There are five different bases which are divided into two groups, described on the next page.

   (a) **Pyrimidines** – these are single rings each with six sides. Examples found in nucleic acids are: **cytosine**, **thymine** and **uracil**.

   (b) **Purines** – these are double rings comprising a six-sided and a five-sided ring. Two examples are found in nucleic acids: **adenine** and **guanine**.

The three components are combined by condensation reactions to give a nucleotide, the structure of which is shown in Fig. 5.2. By a similar condensation reaction between the sugar and phosphate groups of two nucleotides, a **dinucleotide** is formed. Continued condensation reactions lead to the formation of a **polynucleotide** (Fig. 5.3).

The main function of nucleotides is the formation of the nucleic acids **RNA** and **DNA** which play vital rôles in protein synthesis and heredity. In addition they form part of other metabolically important molecules. Table 5.1 gives some examples.

TABLE 5.1 **Biologically important molecules containing nucleotides, and their functions**

Molecule	Abbreviation	Function
Deoxyribonucleic acid	DNA	Contains the genetic information of cells
Ribonucleic acid	RNA	All three types play a vital rôle in protein synthesis
Adenosine monophosphate Adenosine diphosphate Adenosine triphosphate	AMP ADP ATP	Coenzymes important in making energy available to cells for metabolic activities, osmotic work, muscular contractions, etc.
Nicotinamide adenine dinucleotide Flavine adenine dinucleotide	NAD FAD	Electron (hydrogen) carriers important in respiration in transferring hydrogen atoms from the Krebs cycle along the respiratory chain
Nicotinamide adenine dinucleotide phosphate	NADP	Electron (hydrogen) carrier important in photosynthesis for accepting electrons from the chlorophyll molecule and making them available for the photolysis of water
Coenzyme A	CoA	Coenzyme important in respiration in combining with pyruvate to form acetyl coenzyme A and transferring the acetyl group into the Krebs cycle

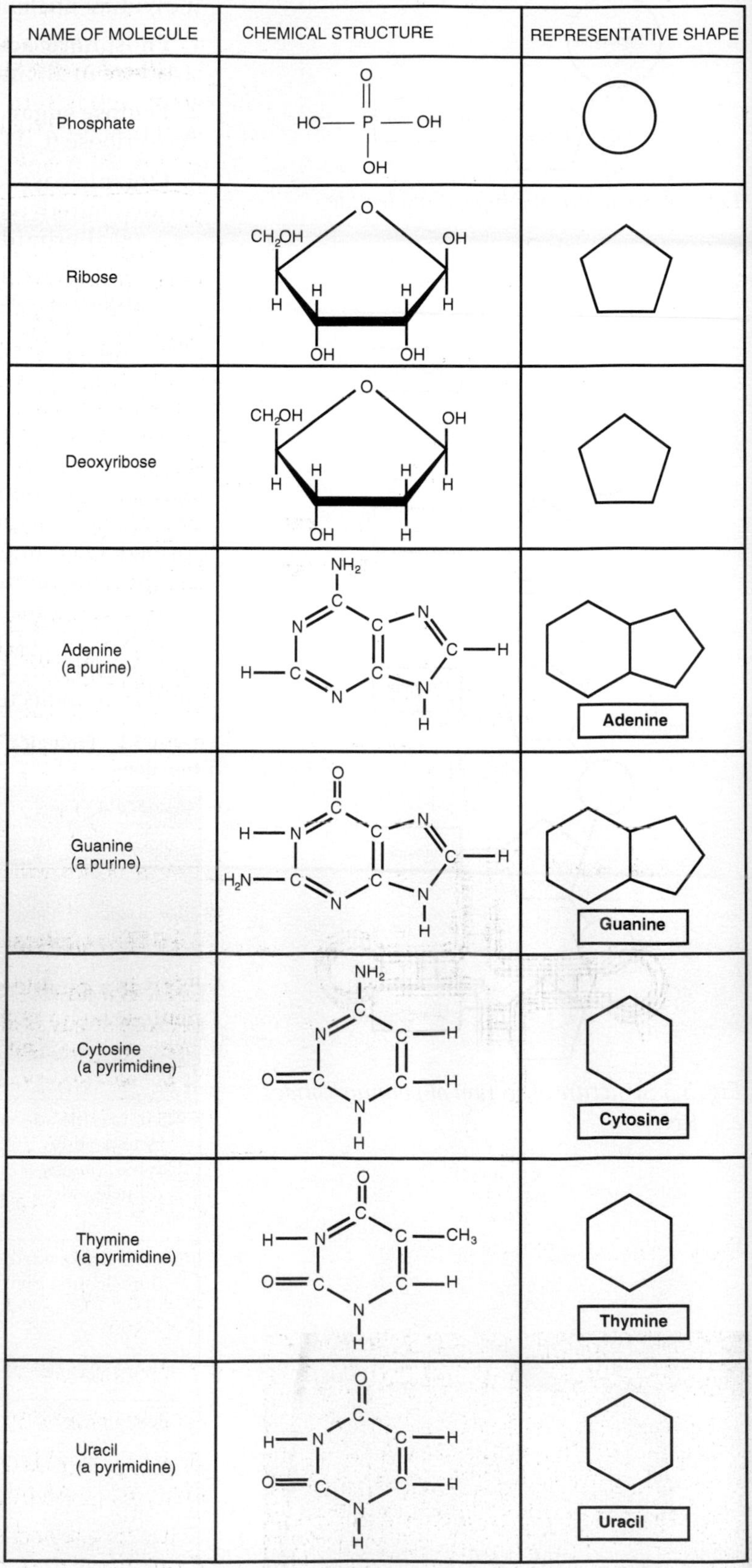

NAME OF MOLECULE	CHEMICAL STRUCTURE	REPRESENTATIVE SHAPE
Phosphate	$HO-\overset{\overset{\textstyle O}{\|}}{\underset{\underset{\textstyle OH}{\|}}{P}}-OH$	○
Ribose		(pentagon)
Deoxyribose		(pentagon)
Adenine (a purine)		Adenine
Guanine (a purine)		Guanine
Cytosine (a pyrimidine)		Cytosine
Thymine (a pyrimidine)		Thymine
Uracil (a pyrimidine)		Uracil

Fig. 5.4 Structure of molecules in a nucleotide

5.3.2 Ribonucleic acid (RNA)

RNA is a single-stranded polymer of nucleotides where the pentose sugar is always ribose and the organic bases are adenine, guanine, cytosine and uracil. Its basic structure is given in Fig. 5.3). There are three types of RNA found in cells, all of which are involved in protein synthesis.

Ribosomal RNA (rRNA) is a large, complex molecule made up of both double and single helices. Although it is manufactured by the DNA of the nucleus, it is found in the cytoplasm where it makes up more than half the mass of the ribosomes. It comprises more than half the mass of the total RNA of a cell and its base sequence is similar in all organisms.

Transfer RNA (tRNA) is a small molecule (about eighty nucleotides) comprising a single strand. Again it is manufactured by nuclear DNA. It makes up 10–15% of the cell's RNA and all types are fundamentally similar. It forms a clover-leaf shape (Fig. 5.5), with one end of the chain ending in a cytosine–cytosine–adenine sequence. It is at this point that an amino acid attaches itself. There are at least twenty types of tRNA, each one carrying a different amino acid. At an intermediate point along the chain is an important sequence of three bases, called the **anticodon**. These line up alongside the appropriate codon on the mRNA during protein synthesis (Section 5.6).

Messenger RNA (mRNA) is a long single-stranded molecule, of up to thousands of nucleotides, which is formed into a helix. Manufactured in the nucleus, it is a mirror copy of part of one strand of the DNA helix. There is hence an immense variety of types. It enters the cytoplasm where it associates with the ribosomes and acts as a template for protein synthesis (Section 5.6). It makes up less than 5% of the total cellular RNA. It is easily and quickly broken down, sometimes existing for only a matter of minutes.

5.3.3 Deoxyribonucleic acid (DNA)

DNA is a double-stranded polymer of nucleotides where the pentose sugar is always deoxyribose and the organic bases are adenine, guanine, cytosine and thymine, but never uracil. Each of these polynucleotide chains is extremely long and may contain many million nucleotide units.

By the early 1950s, information on DNA from a variety of sources had been collected, but no molecular structure had been agreed. The available facts about DNA included:

1. It is a very long, thin molecule made up of nucleotides.

2. It contains four organic bases: adenine, guanine, cytosine and thymine.

3. The amount of guanine is usually equal to that of cytosine.

4. The amount of adenine is usually equal to that of thymine.

5. It is probably in the form of a helix whose shape is maintained by hydrogen bonding.

Using the accumulated evidence, James Watson and Francis Crick in 1953 suggested a molecular structure which proved to be one of the greatest milestones in biology. They postulated a

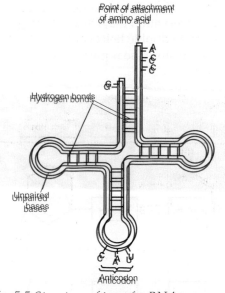

Fig. 5.5 *Structure of transfer RNA*

Point of attachment of amino acid

Hydrogen bonds

Unpaired bases

Anticodon

TABLE 5.2   **Differences between RNA and DNA**

RNA	DNA
Single polynucleotide chain	Double polynucleotide chain
Smaller molecular mass (20 000–2 000 000)	Larger molecular mass (100 000–150 000 000)
May have a single or double helix	Always a double helix
Pentose sugar is ribose	Pentose sugar is deoxyribose
Organic bases present are adenine, guanine, cytosine and uracil	Organic bases present are adenine, guanine, cytosine and thymine
Ratio of adenine and uracil to cytosine and guanine varies	Ratio of adenine and thymine to cytosine and guanine is one
Manufactured in the nucleus but found throughout the cell	Found almost entirely in the nucleus
Amount varies from cell to cell (and within a cell according to metabolic activity)	Amount is constant for all cells of a species (except gametes and spores)
Chemically less stable	Chemically very stable
May be temporary – existing for short periods only	Permanent
Three basic forms: messenger, transfer and ribosomal RNA	Only one basic form, but with an almost infinite variety within that form

double helix of two nucleotide strands, each strand being linked to the other by pairs of organic bases which are themselves joined by hydrogen bonds. The pairings are always cytosine with guanine and adenine with thymine. This was not only consistent with the known ratio of the bases in the molecule, but also allowed for an identical separation of the strands throughout the molecule, a fact shown to be the case from X-ray diffraction patterns. As the purines, adenine and guanine, are double ringed structures (Fig. 5.4) they form much longer links if paired together than the two single ringed pyrimidines, cytosine and thymine. Only by pairing one purine with one pyrimidine can a consistent separation of three rings' width be achieved. In effect, the structure is like a ladder where the deoxyribose and phosphate units form the uprights and the organic base pairings form the rungs. However, this is no ordinary ladder; instead it is twisted into a helix so that each upright winds around the other. The two chains that form the uprights run in opposite directions, i.e. are **antiparallel**. The structure of DNA is shown in Figs. 5.6 and 5.7.

The structure postulated both fitted the known facts about DNA and was consistent with its biological rôle. Its extreme length (around 2.5 billion base pairs in a typical mammalian cell) permitted a very long sequence of bases which could be almost infinitely various, thus providing an immense store of genetic information. In addition its structure allowed for its replication. The separation of the two strands would result in each half attracting its complementary nucleotide to itself. The subsequent joining of these nucleotides would form two identical DNA double helices. This fitted the observation that DNA content doubles prior to cell division. Each double helix could then enter one of the daughter cells and so restore the normal quantity of DNA.

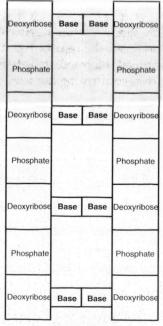

Simplified ladder
DNA structure may be likened to a ladder where alternating phosphate and deoxyribose molecules make up the 'uprights' and pairs of organic bases comprise the 'rungs'.

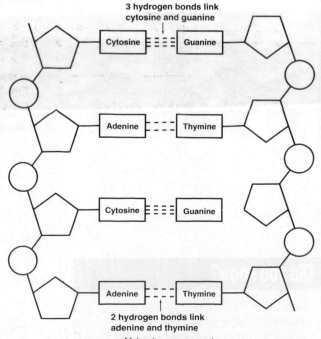

Molecular arrangement
Note the base pairings are always cytosine–guanine and adenine–thymine. This ensures a standard 'rung' length. Note also that the 'uprights' run in the opposite direction to each other (i.e. are antiparallel).

Fig. 5.6 Basic structure of DNA

5.3.4 Differences between RNA and DNA

Despite the obvious similarities between these two nucleic acids, a number of differences exist and these are listed in Table 5.2 on the previous page.

5.4 DNA replication

The uprights are composed of deoxyribose–phosphate molecules, the rungs of pairs of bases

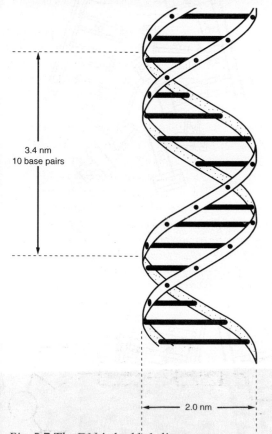

3.4 nm
10 base pairs

2.0 nm

Fig. 5.7 The DNA double helix structure

The Watson–Crick model for DNA allows for a relatively simple method by which the molecule can make exact copies of itself, something which must occur if genetic information is to be transmitted from cell to cell and from generation to generation. Replication is controlled by the enzyme DNA polymerase and an illustrated description is given in Fig. 5.9 on the next page.

Evidence for **semi-conservative replication** came from experiments by Meselsohn and Stahl. They grew successive generations of *Escherichia coli* in a medium where all the available nitrogen was in the form of the isotope ^{15}N (heavy nitrogen). In time, all the nitrogen in the DNA of *E. coli* was of the heavy nitrogen type. As DNA contains much nitrogen, the molecular weight of this DNA was measurably greater than that of DNA with normal nitrogen (^{14}N).

The *E. coli* containing the heavy DNA were then transferred into a medium containing normal nitrogen (^{14}N). Any new DNA produced would need to use this normal nitrogen in its manufacture. The question was, would the new DNA all be of the light type (contain only ^{14}N) or would it, as the semi-conservative replication theory suggests, be made up of one original strand of heavy DNA and one new strand of light DNA? In the latter case its weight would be intermediate between the heavy and light types. To answer this they allowed *E. coli* to divide once and collected all the first generation cells. The DNA from them was then extracted and its relative weight determined by special techniques involving centrifugation with caesium chloride. As the results depicted in Fig. 5.10 show, the weight was indeed intermediate between the heavy and light DNA types, thus confirming the semi-conservative replication theory.

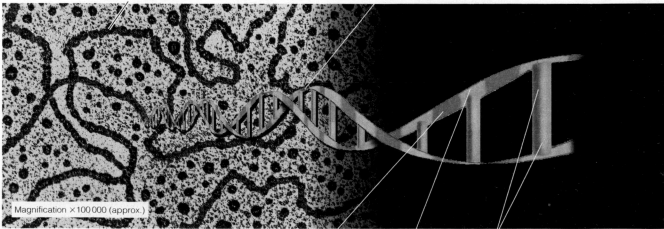

Electron micrograph of part of the long DNA molecule with associated protein molecules

Drawing of the DNA double helix without associated protein. Magnification × 13 000 000 (approx.)

Magnification × 100 000 (approx.)

Fig. 5.8 Deoxyribonucleic acid

Phosphate   Deoxyribose sugar   Complementary base pair

1. A representative portion of DNA, which is about to undergo replication, is shown.

2. DNA polymerase causes the two strands of the DNA to separate.

3. The DNA polymerase completes the splitting of the strand. Meanwhile free nucleotides are attracted to their complementary bases.

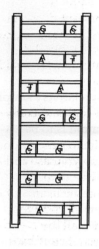

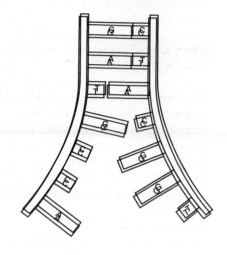

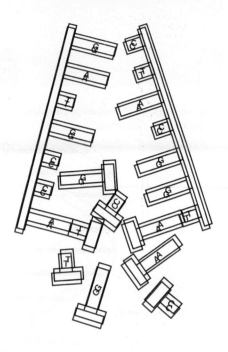

4. Once the nucleotides are lined up they join together (bottom 3 nucleotides). The remaining unpaired bases continue to attract their complementary nucleotides.

5. Finally all the nucleotides are joined to form a complete polynucleotide chain. In this way two identical strands of DNA are formed. As each strand retains half of the original DNA material, this method of replication is called the semi-conservative method.

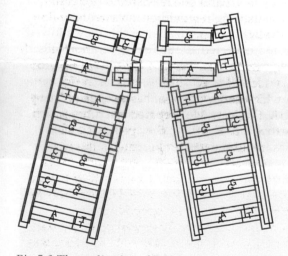

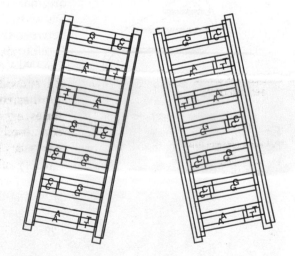

Fig 5.9 The replication of DNA

If a second generation of *E.coli* is grown from the first generation it is found to comprise half light and half intermediate weight DNA. Can you explain this?

Analysis shows that the replication of DNA takes place during interphase, shortly before cell division. Thus when the chromatids appear during prophase each has a double helix of DNA.

5.5 The genetic code

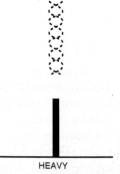

DNA extracted from *E. coli* grown in a medium containing normal nitrogen (^{14}N)

All DNA is of the 'light' type

LIGHT

DNA extracted from *E. coli* grown in a medium containing heavy nitrogen (^{15}N) and then transferred to a medium containing normal nitrogen (^{14}N)

INTERMEDIATE

DNA extracted from *E. coli* grown in a medium containing heavy nitrogen (^{15}N)

HEAVY

Relative weight of DNA as determined by centrifugation

Fig. 5.10 Interpretation of Meselsohn–Stahl experiments on semi-conservative replication of DNA

Once the structure of DNA had been elucidated and its mechanism of replication discovered, one important question remained: how exactly are the genetic instructions stored on the DNA in such a way that they can be used to mastermind the construction of new cells and organisms? Most chemicals within cells are similar regardless of the type of cell or species of organism. It is in their proteins and DNA that cells and organisms differ. It seems a reasonable starting point, therefore, to assume that the DNA in some way provides a 'code' for an organism's proteins. Moreover, most chemicals in cells are manufactured with the aid of enzymes, and all enzymes are proteins. Therefore by determining which enzymes are produced, the DNA can determine an organism's characteristics. Every species possesses different DNA and hence produces different enzymes. The DNA of different species differs not in the chemicals which it comprises, but in the sequence of base pairs along its length. This sequence must be a code that determines which proteins are manufactured.

Proteins show almost infinite variety. This variety likewise depends upon a sequence, in this instance the sequence of amino acids in the protein (Section 2.7). There are just twenty amino acids which regularly occur in proteins, and each must presumably have its own code of bases on the DNA. With only four different bases present in DNA, if each coded for a different amino acid, only four different amino acids could be coded for. Using a pair of bases, sixteen different codes are possible – still inadequate. A triplet code of bases produces sixty-four codes, more than enough to satisfy the requirements of twenty amino acids. This is called the **triplet code**.

The next problem was to determine the precise codon for each amino acid. Nirenberg devised a series of experiments towards the end of the 1950s which allowed him to break the code. He synthesized mRNA which had a triplet of bases repeated many times, e.g. GUA, GUA, GUA etc. He prepared test tubes which contained cell-free extracts of *E. coli*, i.e. they possessed all the necessary biochemical requirements for protein synthesis. Twenty tubes were set up, each with a different radioactively labelled amino acid. His synthesized mRNA was added to each tube and the presence of a polypeptide was looked for. Only in the test tube containing valine was a polypeptide found, indicating that GUA codes for valine. By repeating the process for all sixty-four possible combinations of bases, Nirenberg was able to determine which amino acid each coded for.

In some cases only the first two bases of the codon are relevant. Valine for instance is coded for by GU*, where * can be any of the four bases. Some amino acids have up to six codons. Arginine, for example, has CGU, CGC, CGA, CGG, AGA and AGG. At the other extreme, methionine, with AUG, and tryptophan, with UGG, have only one codon each. As there is more than one triplet for most amino acids it is called a **degenerate code** (a term derived from cybernetics). There are three codons UAA, UAG and UGA which are not amino acid codes. These are **stop** or **nonsense codons** and their importance is discussed in Section 5.6.4

All the codons are **universal**, i.e. they are precisely the same for all organisms.

The code is also **non-overlapping** in that each triplet is read separately. For example, CUGAGCUAG is read as CUG–AGC–UAG and not CUG–UGA–GAG–AGC etc., where each triplet overlaps the previous one, in this case by two bases. Overlapping would allow more information to be provided by a given base sequence, but it limits flexibility. Some viruses, with limited amounts of DNA, may use overlapping codes, but this is very rare.

5.6 Protein synthesis

If the triplet code on the DNA molecule determines the sequence of amino acids in a given protein, how exactly is the information transferred from the DNA, and how is the protein assembled? There are four main stages in the formation of a protein:

1. Synthesis of amino acids.

2. Transcription (formation of mRNA).

3. Amino acid activation.

4. Translation.

5.6.1 Synthesis of amino acids

In plants, the formation of amino acids occurs in mitochondria and chloroplasts in a series of stages:

(a) absorption of nitrates from the soil;

(b) reduction of these nitrates to the amino group (NH_2);

(c) combination of these amino groups with a carbohydrate skeleton (e.g. α-ketoglutarate from Krebs cycle);

(d) transfer of the amino groups from one carbohydrate skeleton to another by a process called **transamination**. In this way all twenty amino acids can be formed.

Animals usually obtain their supply from the food they ingest, although they have some capacity to synthesize their own amino acids (called **non-essential amino acids**). The remaining nine – **essential amino acids** – must be provided in the diet.

5.6.2 Transcription (formation of messenger RNA)

Transcription is the process by which a complementary mRNA copy is made of the specific region (=**cistron**) of the DNA molecule which codes for a polypeptide (about 17 base pairs). A specific region of the DNA molecule, called a cistron, unwinds. This unwinding is the result of hydrogen bonds between base pairs in the DNA double helix being broken. This exposes the bases along each strand. Each base along one strand attracts its complementary RNA nucleotide, i.e. a free guanine base on the DNA will attract an RNA nucleotide with a cytosine base. It should be remembered, however, that uracil, and not thymine, is attracted to adenine (Fig. 5.11).

A portion of DNA, called a cistron unwinds. One strand acts as a template for the formation of mRNA

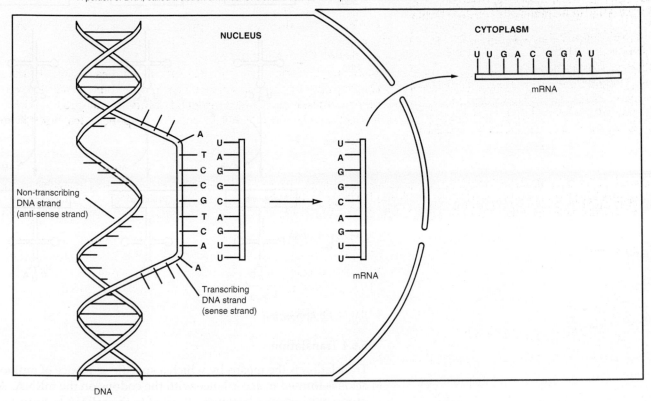

Fig. 5.11 Transcription

The enzyme **RNA polymerase** moves along the DNA adding one complementary RNA nucleotide at a time to the newly unwound portion of DNA. The region of base pairing between the DNA and the RNA is only around 12 base pairs at any one time as the DNA helix reforms behind the RNA polymerase. The DNA thus acts as a **template** against which mRNA is constructed. A number of mRNA molecules may be formed before the RNA polymerase leaves the DNA, which closes up reforming its double helix. Being too large to diffuse across the nuclear membrane, the mRNA leaves instead through the nuclear pores. In the cytoplasm it is attracted to the ribosomes. Along the mRNA is a sequence of triplet codes which have been determined by the DNA. Each triplet is called a **codon**.

5.6.3 Amino acid activation

Activation is the process by which amino acids combine with tRNA using energy from ATP. Fig. 5.5 shows the structure of a tRNA molecule. Each type of tRNA binds with a specific amino acid which means there must be at least twenty types of tRNA. Each type differs, among other things, in the composition of a triplet of bases called the **anticodon**. What all tRNA molecules have in common is a free end which terminates in the triplet CCA. It is to this free end that the individual amino acids become attached, although how each specific amino acid is specified is not known (Fig. 5.12). The tRNA molecules with attached amino acids now move towards the ribosomes.

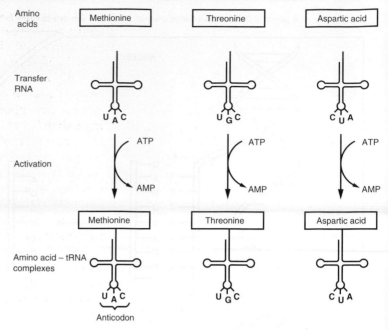

Fig. 5.12 Activation

5.6.4 Translation

Translation is the means by which a specific sequence of amino acids is formed in accordance with the codons on the mRNA. A group of ribosomes becomes attached to the mRNA to form a structure called a **polysome**. The complementary anticodon of a tRNA–amino acid complex is attracted to the first codon on the mRNA. The second codon likewise attracts its complementary anticodon. The ribosome acts as a framework which holds the

Many ribosomes may move along the mRNA at the same time, thus forming many identical polypeptides.

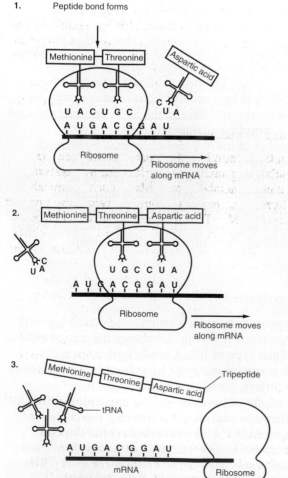

Fig. 5.13(a) Translation

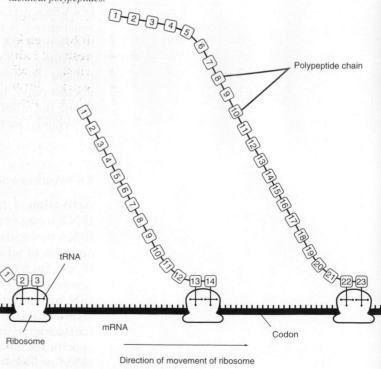

Fig. 5.13(b) Polypeptide formation

mRNA and tRNA amino acid complex together until the two amino acids form a peptide bond between each other. Once they have combined, the ribosome will move along the mRNA to hold the next codon–anticodon complex together until the third amino acid is linked with the second. In this way a polypeptide chain is assembled, by the addition of one amino acid at a time. Second and subsequent ribosomes may pass along the mRNA immediately behind the first. In this way many identical polypeptides are produced simultaneously.

Once each amino acid is linked, the tRNA which carried it to the mRNA is released back into the cytoplasm. It is again free to combine with its specific amino acid. The ribosome continues along the mRNA until it reaches one of the nonsense codes (Section 5.5) at which point the polypeptide is cast off. The process of translation is summarized in Fig. 5.13, on the previous page.

The polypeptides so formed must now be assembled into proteins. This may involve the spiralling of the polypeptide to give a secondary structure, its folding to give a tertiary structure and its combination with other polypeptides and/or prosthetic groups to give a quaternary structure (see Fig. 2.13).

5.7 Genetic engineering

Perhaps the most significant scientific advance in recent years has been the development of technology which allows genes to be manipulated, altered and transferred from organism to organism – even to transform DNA itself. This has enabled us to use rapidly reproducing organisms such as bacteria as chemical factories producing useful, often life-saving, substances. The list of these substances expands almost daily and includes hormones, antibiotics, interferon and vitamins. Details of the production of some of these chemicals are given in Section 21.5.

5.7.1 Recombinant DNA technology

It has been known that a number of human diseases are the result of individuals being unable to produce for themselves chemicals which have a metabolic role. Many such chemicals, e.g. insulin and thyroxine, are proteins and therefore the product of a specific portion of DNA. The treatment of such deficiencies had previously been to extract the missing chemical from either an animal or human donor. This has presented problems. While the animal extracts may function effectively, subtle chemical differences in their composition have been detected by the human immune system, which has responded by producing antibodies which destroy the extract. Even chemically compatible extracts from human donors present a risk of infection from other diseases, as the transmission of the HIV virus to haemophiliacs illustrates only too well. Whether from animals or humans, the cost of such extracts is considerable.

It follows that there are advantages in producing large quantities of 'pure' chemicals from non-human sources. As a result, methods have been devised for isolating the portion of human DNA responsible for the production of insulin and combining it with bacterial DNA in such a way that the microorganism will continually produce the substance. This DNA, which results from the combination of fragments from two different organisms, is called **recombinant DNA**.

5.7.2 Techniques used to manipulate DNA

The manipulation of DNA involves three main techniques, each using a specific enzyme or group of enzymes:

1. Cutting of DNA into small sections using restriction endonucleases

These enzymes are used to cut DNA between specific base sequences which the enzyme recognizes. For example, *Hae* III nuclease recognizes a four base-pair sequence and cuts it as shown by the arrow:

```
G   G ↑ C   C ⎫
            ⎬  four complementary base-pairs
C   C ↓ G   G ⎭  on DNA double helix
```

The *Hind* III nuclease however recognizes a six base-pair sequence, cutting it as shown by the arrow below:

```
A ↑ A   G   C   T   T ⎫
                      ⎬  six complementary base-
T   T   C   G   A ↓ A ⎭  pairs on DNA double helix
```

As any sequence of four base-pairs is likely to occur more frequently than a six base-pair sequence, the nucleases recognizing four base-pairs cut DNA into smaller sections than those recognizing six base-pairs. The latter group are, however, more useful as the longer sections they produce are more likely to contain an intact gene.

2. Production of copies of DNA using either plasmids or reverse transcriptase

In bacterial cells there are small circular loops of DNA called **plasmids**. Plasmids are distinct from the larger circular portions of DNA which make up the bacterial chromosome. Bacteria replicate their plasmid DNA so that a single cell contains many copies. If a portion of DNA from, say, a human cell, is inserted into a plasmid and it is reintroduced into the bacterial cell, replication of the plasmid will result in up to 200 identical copies of the human DNA being made. A population of bacteria containing this human DNA can now be grown to provide a permanent source of it. By repeating the process for other DNA portions, a complete library of human DNA can be maintained. Geneticists can then select as required, any gene (a portion of DNA) they require for further investigation or use, in much the same way as a book is selected from a conventional library. Selection is, however, more complex requiring the use of DNA probes or specific antibodies. This collection of genetic information is called a **genome library**.

A second method of duplicating particular portions of DNA is appropriate where the protein for which it codes is synthesized in a specific organ. Thyroxine, for example, is produced in the thyroid gland and therefore cells from this gland would be expected to contain a relatively large amount of messenger RNA which codes for thyroxine. Reverse transcriptase (Section 21.1.3) can be used to synthesize DNA, called **copy DNA (cDNA)**, from the mRNA in thyroid cells. A large proportion of the cDNA produced is likely to code for thyroxine and it can be isolated using the techniques described in Section 5.7.3.

3. Joining together portions of DNA using DNA ligase

The recombination of pieces of DNA, e.g. the addition of cDNA into bacterial plasmid DNA, is carried out with the aid of the enzyme **DNA ligase**.

5.7.3 Gene cloning

The techniques described in the previous section are utilized in the process of gene cloning in which multiple copies of a specific gene are produced which may then be used to manufacture large quantities of valuable products.

Manufacture involves the following stages:

1. Identification of the required gene.

2. Isolation of that gene.

3. Insertion of the gene into a vector.

4. Insertion of the vector into a host cell.

5. Multiplication of the host cell.

6. Synthesis of the required product by the host cell.

7. Separation of the product from the host cell.

8. Purification of the product.

Figure 5.14 on the next page illustrates how gene cloning is used in the production of insulin. The bacteria produced in this way can be grown in industrial fermenters using a specific nutrient medium under strictly controlled conditions. The bacteria may then be collected and the insulin extracted from them by suitable means. Alternatively, it is possible to engineer bacteria which secrete the insulin and this can be extracted from the medium which is periodically drawn off. Details of these, and other, fermentation techniques are given in Chapter 21.

5.7.4 Applications of genetic engineering

The techniques illustrated above may be utilized to manufacture a range of materials which can be used to treat diseases and disorders. In addition to insulin, human growth hormone is now produced by bacteria in sufficient quantity to allow all children in this country requiring it to be treated. Among other hormones being produced in this manner are erythropoietin, which controls red blood cell production and calcitonin which regulates the levels of calcium in the blood. Much research is taking place into the production of antibiotics and vaccines through recombinant DNA technology and already interferon, a chemical produced in response to viral infection, is in production.

A form of abnormal haemoglobin is produced by a defective gene causing a disease called **thalassaemia**. It is likely that genetic engineering will provide a cure for the disease, by the transference of a normal gene for haemoglobin into patients afflicted by the disease.

The scope of recombinant DNA technology is not restricted to the field of medicine. In agriculture, it is now possible to transfer

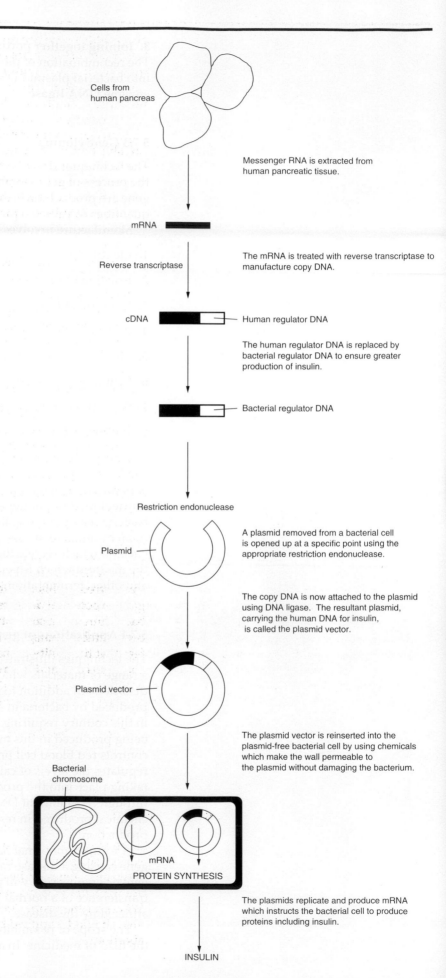

Cells from
human pancreas

Messenger RNA is extracted from
human pancreatic tissue.

mRNA

Reverse transcriptase

The mRNA is treated with reverse transcriptase to
manufacture copy DNA.

cDNA — Human regulator DNA

The human regulator DNA is replaced by
bacterial regulator DNA to ensure greater
production of insulin.

— Bacterial regulator DNA

Restriction endonuclease

Plasmid

A plasmid removed from a bacterial cell
is opened up at a specific point using the
appropriate restriction endonuclease.

The copy DNA is now attached to the plasmid
using DNA ligase. The resultant plasmid,
carrying the human DNA for insulin,
is called the plasmid vector.

Plasmid vector

The plasmid vector is reinserted into the
plasmid-free bacterial cell by using chemicals
which make the wall permeable to
the plasmid without damaging the bacterium.

Bacterial
chromosome

mRNA

PROTEIN SYNTHESIS

The plasmids replicate and produce mRNA
which instructs the bacterial cell to produce
proteins including insulin.

*Fig. 5.14 Use of plasmid vector in gene
cloning*

INSULIN

genes which produce toxins with insecticidal properties from bacteria to higher plants such as potatoes and cotton. In this way these plants have 'built-in' resistance to certain insect pests. The saving in time and money by not having to spray such crops regularly with insecticides is obvious, to say nothing of avoiding killing harmless or beneficial insect species which inevitably happens however carefully spraying is carried out. It may prove possible to transfer genes from nitrogen-fixing bacteria to cereal crops, to enable them to fix their own nitrogen. There would then be less need to apply expensive nitrogen fertilizers thus reducing the pollution problems of 'run-off' (Section 14.7).

There would seem to be no end of possibilities – transfer of genes conferring resistance to all manner of diseases, development of plants with more efficient rates of photosynthesis, the control of weeds and the development of oil-digesting bacteria to clear up oil spillages are just some of the potential uses of recombinant DNA technology. There are however ethical as well as practical problems to be overcome before many of these ideas can be brought to fruition. Some of these problems are discussed in the following section.

5.7.5 Implications of genetic engineering

The benefits of genetic engineering are obvious but it is not without its hazards. It is impossible to predict with complete accuracy what the ecological consequences might be of releasing genetically engineered organisms into the environment. It is always possible that the delicate balance that exists in any habitat may be irretrievably damaged by the introduction of organisms with new gene combinations. It is also possible that organisms designed for use in one environment may escape to others with harmful consequences. We know that viruses can transfer genes from one organism to another. Advantageous genes added to our domestic animals or crop plants may be transferred in this way to their competitors making them even greater potential dangers. The escape of a single pathogenic bacterium into a susceptible population could result in considerable damage to a species. Perhaps more sinister is the fear that the ability to manipulate genes could allow human characteristics and behaviour to be modified. In the wrong hands this could be used by individuals, groups or governments in order to achieve certain goals, control opposition or gain ultimate power.

Even without these dangers there are still ethical issues which arise from the development of recombinant DNA technology. Is it right to replace a 'defective' gene with a 'normal' one? Is the answer the same for a gene which causes the bearer pain, as it is where the gene has a merely cosmetic effect? Who decides what is 'defective' and what is 'normal'? A 'defective' gene may actually confer some other advantage, e.g. sickle-cell gene (Section 8.5.3). Is there a danger that we shall in time reduce the variety so essential to evolution, by the progressive removal of unwanted genes or, by combining genes from different species, are we actually increasing variety and favouring evolution? Where a gene probe detects a fatal abnormality, what criteria, if any, should be applied before deciding whether to carry out an abortion?

Cystic fibrosis and gene therapy

One person in 2000 in Britain suffers from cystic fibrosis. CF patients produce mucus secretions which are too viscous. Thick, sticky mucus blocks the pancreatic duct and prevents pancreatic enzymes from reaching the duodenum and clogging up of the lungs leads to recurrent infections.

The long arm of chromosome 7 carries the CFTR (cystic fibrosis transmembrane conductance regulator) gene which codes for a protein which is essential for chloride transport. Everyone has two copies of this gene in every cell, one from the mother and one from the father. As long as one copy of the CFTR gene works correctly chloride transport is adequate but if two defective genes are present CF results.

Microbiologists have succeeded in isolating and cloning the CFTR gene and have found that 70% of its mutations consist of the same change to the normal DNA sequence. CFTR is a big gene, covering 250 000 base pairs of DNA and the commonest mutation is a small deletion in which three nucleotides are missing. After transcription and translation the CFTR gene lacks one amino acid, phenylalanine number 508, in the protein chain. People who have at least one chromosome bearing this mutation can be identified in the laboratory. This is done by using a blood sample or shed cells in a mouthwash to collect a DNA sample. DNA polymerase is used to make many copies of a 50 base-pair segment of both CFTR genes. The copies are then run on an electrophoretic gel (see Notebook page 24) in which small fragments move faster than big ones. If either of the CFTR genes has the three-base deletion it will move more quickly.

This test is quick and easy. A series of other, more expensive, tests would enable another 20% of CF carriers to be identified. But once a carrier for CF, or any other genetic disease, has been identified is it possible to replace the mutant gene with a normal version of the gene? Gene therapy is now becoming a realistic possibility, although there are many medical and ethical problems to be solved.

In **germ-line therapy** the approach could be to repair the gene in a fertilized egg so that the repaired gene would be

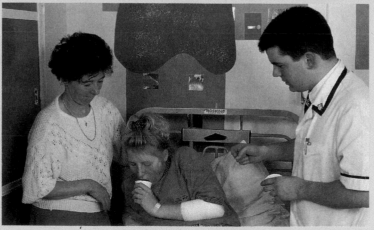

Cystic fibrosis patient coughing up mucus following treatment to loosen it

copied into each daughter cell at mitosis. In this way the mutant gene will not only have been eliminated from the person receiving treatment, but also from all his or her offspring. This raises the ethical question of whether we have the right to alter the genes of future generations and following the report of the Warnock committee such germ-line therapy is prohibited in Britain.

Research now centres on a different approach: **somatic cell gene therapy**. Although the mutated gene occurs in every cell of the patient's body, somatic cell gene therapy would target just the affected tissues, for example:

the lungs in cystic fibrosis;

the muscles in Duchenne muscular dystrophy;

blood cells or their precursors (reticulocytes in the bone marrow) in β – thalassaemia.

These tissues are fully differentiated and will eventually die so treatments may have to be repeated as the treated cells die and are replaced. It has not yet been possible to isolate and treat the undifferentiated stem cells which give rise to the mature tissues. It is relatively easy to introduce large molecules of DNA into a cell nucleus using a fine glass needle or by subjecting cells in a test tube to an electric pulse which causes temporary holes in the plasma membrane and induces them to take up DNA. DNA can also be carried into the cell by a suitable virus.

There are two types of genetic disease: those due to loss of function and those due to gain of function. Gain-of-function diseases are normally dominant and the mutated gene which causes them is doing something positively bad. Such a gene would need to be removed or neutralized and this is proving a very difficult task. On the other hand gene supplementation is providing a possible treatment for loss-of-function diseases and the approach looks promising for CF sufferers. It is hoped that an aerosol inhaler could be used to restore the missing gene to the lung epithelia. This would leave patients with their digestive problems but would solve the problem of congested and infected lungs.

An example of successful treatment by gene supplementation is in Severe Combined Immunodeficiency Disease (SCID). The gene coding for adenosine deaminase is mutated and homozygotes are unable to deaminate adenosine. This leads to the death of lymphocytes and sufferers have no immunity at all. Since 1990 two affected children have had some of their lymphocyte precursor cells infected with a special virus carrying the missing gene. The treatment is repeated every month or so to replace the lymphocytes as they die and the two children now attend normal schools.

For many Mendelian recessive disorders in which the damage is confined to an accessible tissue, gene therapy by gene supplementation looks a promising way forward. Even cancer, where mutations are confined to tumour cells, may be a candidate for gene therapy in the future.

FOCUS

Transgenic animals

While it is possible to clone plants from any differentiated plant cell, the same is not true of animals. It is however possible to mix together cells from two different embryos, such as a sheep and a goat, to produce a chimaera, in this example called a geep.

The problem with chimaeras is that no-one can predict which cells will form which part of the animal. A more precise method of producing desired characteristics is to augment traditional animal breeding by genetic engineering to make transgenic animals.

For a brief time following the fusion of a sperm and an ovum the cell contains two pronuclei. Cloned DNA (Section 5.8.3) can be injected into one of these and in some cases it will integrate into one or more of the chromosomes. The manipulated offspring are then transferred to a foster mother and the resulting offspring screened for the presence of the introduced gene. A more recent approach which allows the gene to be positioned more precisely involves transferring the DNA into embryonic stem cells (cells from embryos prior to implantation). These cells can be grown indefinitely in a test tube and can be monitored to see if they produce the desired protein before they are injected into a normal embryo and transferred to a foster mother.

Genetic engineering may be used to improve animal health. For example, genes responsible for resistance to a particular disease could be introduced into otherwise vulnerable animals. Transgenic animals may also be used to produce rare and expensive proteins for use in human medicine. The genes coding for certain proteins may be expressed in a sheep's mammary glands and the protein recovered from the milk. Researchers have managed to insert the gene for a blood clotting protein known as factor IX alongside the regulator of the lactoglobulin gene which encodes for one of the proteins in sheep's milk. The transgenic ewes now produce factor IX in their milk and it can be used to treat one type of haemophilia. Some people suffer congenital emphysema (page 365) because they are unable to make a protein known as ATT (alpha-1-antitrypsin). This protein can also be extracted from the milk of transgenic ewes.

In transgenic animals the 'foreign' DNA has become stably integrated into the animal's own genome so that it can be passed from generation to generation, effectively giving rise to a new strain of the animal.

This transgenic ram has had a human gene incorporated into its DNA. This gene for the production of the protein alpha-1-antitrypsin (ATT) is inherited by the ram's offspring and the protein is secreted in the ewe's milk

It is inevitable that we shall remain inquisitive about the world in which we live and, in particular, about ourselves. Scientific research will therefore continue. The challenge is to develop regulations and safeguards within moral boundaries which permit genetic engineering to be used in a safe and effective way to the benefit of both individuals in particular and humans in general.

5.8 Gene therapy – Its benefits and hazards

Gene therapy offers the promise of a cure to certain diseases, but at the same time raises many ethical issues about its use.

Benefits

Treatment of single-gene disorders, e.g. cystic fibrosis – see Focus on pages 94–96)

Supply of missing molecules, e.g. insulin – Gene therapy can be used to supply the genes which control the synthesis of insulin, permitting patients to manufacture their own rather than being dependent on injecting it.

Cancer treatment – Cancer occurs when the division of cells is out of control. Gene therapy can be used in some instances to rid the body of cancer cells without damage to the normal cells.

Prevention of heart disease – Blood cholesterol levels can be lowered by the introduction of a gene for the low-density lipoprotein (LDL) receptor in the liver. This causes the liver to take up more LDLs, most of which are cholesterol. The blood cholesterol level therefore falls reducing the risk of a heart attack.

Treatment of infectious diseases, e.g. AIDS – Gene therapy is being used to try to stimulate the body's response to HIV infection.

Hazards

In the long-term gene therapy is likely to complement rather than replace other forms of treatment. The use of somatic gene therapy raises few ethical problems as the introduced genes are not passed on to the next generation and there is therefore no attempt to alter the course of human evolution. Germ-line therapy however does interfere with inheritance. Such potential manipulation of future generations is held by many to be unacceptable and is therefore prohibited in Britain at present. Even with somatic gene therapy the question arises as to how far we should extend its use. While most people would not argue with treating cystic fibrosis or cancers in this way, is it acceptable to use gene therapy for cosmetic purposes such as altering height, hair texture or eye colour?

5.9 Genetic fingerprinting

The pattern of dermal ridges and furrows which constitute the fingerprint not only persist unchanged throughout our lives, but are also unique to each one of us (identical twins excepted). For this reason they have long been used to help solve crimes by comparing the fingerprint pattern of the suspect with the impressions left, as a result of the furrow's oily secretions, at the scene of the crime. To this well-tried and successful forensic technique has now been added another – **genetic fingerprinting**.

While having nothing to do with either fingers or printing, the technique is equally, if not more, successful in identifying individuals from 'information' they provide. This 'information' is contained in a spot of blood, a sample of skin, a few sperm – in fact almost any cell of the body.

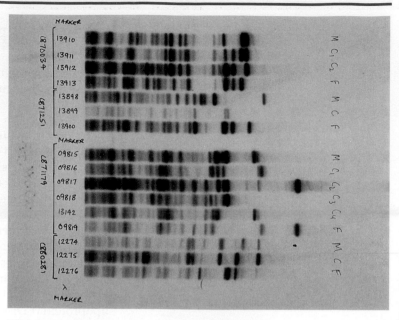

DNA fingerprint

The technique, developed by Alec Jeffreys of Leicester University, takes around six days and involves the following stages:

1. The DNA is separated from the sample.

2. Restriction endonucleases are used to cut the DNA into sections.

3. The DNA fragments are separated in an agarose gel using electrophoresis.

4. The fragments are transferred to a nitrocellulose (or nylon) membrane – a process called **Southern Blotting** after its inventor, Professor Southern.

5. Radioactive DNA probes (**gene probes**) are used to bind to specific portions of the fragments known as the core sequences.

6. The portions of the DNA not bound to the radioactive probes are washed off.

7. The remaining DNA still attached to the nylon membrane is placed next to a sheet of X-ray film.

8. The radioactive probes on this DNA expose the film, revealing a pattern of light and dark bands when it is developed. The pattern makes up the genetic fingerprint.

The patterns, like fingerprints, are unique to each individual (except identical twins) and remain unchanged throughout life. Unlike fingerprints, however, the pattern is inherited from both parents. The scope for genetic fingerprinting, therefore, extends beyond catching criminals, it can also be used in paternity suits for example (Section 7.5.1). To do this, white blood cells are taken from the mother and the possible father. From the pattern of bands of the child are subtracted those bands which correspond to the mother's bands. If the man is truly the parent, he must possess all the remaining bands in the child's genetic fingerprint.

As sperm contain DNA, they too can be used to provide a genetic fingerprint, leading to a remarkably accurate method of determining guilt, or otherwise, of an accused rapist. The method has also been successfully applied in immigration cases where the relationship of an immigrant to someone already resident in a country, is in dispute. Confirming the pedigree of animals, detecting some inherited diseases and monitoring bone-marrow transplants are other applications of the technique.

Despite the fact that we are, as yet, unclear as to what exactly the dark bands of the genetic fingerprint represent, the chances of two individuals (other than identical twins) having identical patterns is so small, that the technique is widely used and its results accepted as accurate.

5.10   Questions

1. (a) Suggest why it is important that there are many different types of restriction endonuclease enzymes available to genetic engineers.   (*2 marks*)
People suffering from haemophilia need treatment with the blood-clotting protein, factor VIII, because they are genetically unable to produce their own. Factor VIII used to be extracted from human blood but a genetically engineered kind has just been made available. An artificial version of the human gene has been produced which codes for the same sequence of 2338 amino acids that is present in natural factor VIII. This is inserted into hamster kidney cells which are grown in large fermenters. The cells secrete large amounts of factor VIII into the surrounding fluid.

(b) (i) Why was it necessary to know the amino acid sequence of factor VIII before an artificial version of the human gene could be produced?
          (*1 mark*)

(ii) What is the minimum number of nucleotides which must be present in the gene for factor VIII?   (*1 mark*)

(c) Suggest **one** advantage of the use of genetically engineered factor VIII over that extracted from blood.   (*1 mark*)
          (*Total 5 marks*)

NEAB February 1995, Paper BY2, No. 4

2. Read through the following passage on gene technology (genetic engineering), then write on the dotted lines the most appropriate word or words to complete the passage.

The isolation of specific genes during a genetic engineering process involves forming eukaryotic DNA fragments. These fragments are formed using .... enzymes which make staggered cuts in the DNA within specific base sequences. This leaves single-stranded 'sticky ends' at each end. The same enzyme is used to open up a circular loop of bacterial DNA which acts as a .... for the eukaryotic DNA. The complementary sticky ends of the bacterial DNA are joined to the DNA fragment using another enzyme called. .... DNA fragments can also be made from......................... template. Reverse transcriptase is used to produce a single strand of DNA and the enzyme .... catalyses the formation of a double helix. Finally new DNA is introduced into host .... cells. These can then be cloned on an industrial scale and large amounts of protein harvested. An example of a protein currently manufactured using this technique is.. .   (*Total 7 marks*)

ULEAC 1996, Specimen Paper B/HB1, No. 4

3. The diagram shows the sequence of bases on one strand of a short length of DNA.

C G A C C C C A G

This sequence should be read from left to right.
(a) Give:
(i) the base sequence that will be produced as a result of transcription of the complete length of DNA shown in the diagram   (*2 marks*)
(ii) the three bases of the tRNA which will correspond to the sequence of bases shown in the box on the diagram.   (*1 mark*)
The table shows some DNA base sequences and the amino acids for which they code.

DNA base sequence	Amino acid
ACC	Tryptophan
CAG	Valine
CCA	Glycine
CCC	Glycine
CGA	Glycine
CGA	Alanine
GAC	Leucine

As a result of a mutation, the first base in the length of DNA shown in the diagram is lost (deleted).
(b) (i) Use the table to identify the first two amino acids for which the mutated DNA codes.
          (*1 mark*)

(ii) Explain why mutations involving the deletion of a base may have greater effects than those involving substitution of one base for another.   (*2 marks*)
          (*Total 6 marks*)

NEAB February 1995, Paper BY2, No. 1

4. In some genetic engineering processes a synthetic gene is inserted into a bacterial host. This process is shown in the diagram at the top of the next page.
(a) i) What term is used to describe the function of the plasmid in this process?   (*1 mark*)
(ii) Name the type of enzyme used at Q to cleave (cut) the DNA.   (*1 mark*)

(b) Genetically engineered human insulin is now used in the treatment of diabetes. State **three** advantages of the use of this type of insulin.

          (*3 marks*)

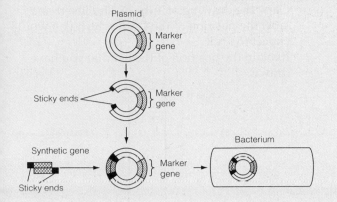

(Total 5 marks)

ULEAC 1996 Specimen Paper B/HB4A, No. 4

5. The table shows the DNA triplet codes for a number of amino acid molecules.

Amino acid	DNA triplet code	mRNA codon
Alanine	CGG	
Asparagine	CTG	
Isoleucine	TAG	
Leucine	GAG	
Valine	CAG	

(a) Complete the table to show the mRNA codons which would be formed by each of these DNA triplet codes. (2 marks)

(b) (i) A fault in the DNA molecules later causes the nucleotides with thymine to be substituted by nucleotides with guanine.

Which **two** DNA triplet codes would have been affected by this fault?

(1 mark)

(ii) If protein synthesis were now to take place, name the amino acid which would be specified by each of the faulty triplet codes. (1 mark)

(Total 4 marks)

AEB June 1993, Paper 1, No. 8

6. The diagram represents a small part of a DNA molecule.

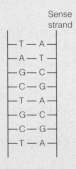

Sense strand

```
T — A
A — T
G — C
C — G
T — A
G — C
C — G
T — A
```

Draw a similar diagram to show how the genetic information in this piece of DNA is:

(a) replicated; (1 mark)

(b) transcribed as mRNA. (2 marks)

(Total 3 marks)

AEB June 1992, Paper 1, No. 10

7. Read through the following account of protein synthesis, then write on the dotted lines the most appropriate word or words to complete the account.

During protein synthesis amino acids are linked by .... to form .... This process occurs at the ribosomes. The function of the ribosome is to hold the .... in such a way that its .... can be recognized and paired with the complementary .... on the t-RNA. The molecules manufactured by ribosomes situated on the .... of the cell may be converted by glycoproteins in the ....

(Total 7 marks)

ULEAC June 1995, Paper 1, No. 3

8. Fig. 1 shows an enzyme-producing cell from the pancreas that has been treated briefly with

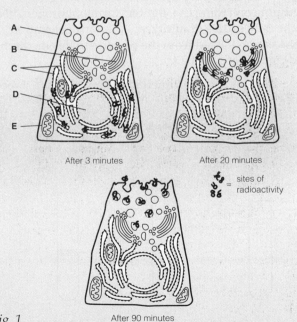

Fig. 1

radioactive-labelled amino acids at time zero and then incubated in a non-radioactive medium with the same amino acids for various times. When the cell is placed next to a photographic emulsion (autoradiography), the developed photographs show the sites of the radioactivity.

(a) Label parts **A** to **E**. (5 marks)

(b) Explain what has happened to the amino acids during the following periods:
- (i) 0–3 mins;
- (ii) 3–20 mins;
- (iii) 20–90 mins. (5 marks)

(*Total 10 marks*)

UCLES June 1993, Paper 2, No. 1

9. In experiments to determine the way DNA replicates, the bacterium *Escherichia coli* (*E. coli*) is often grown in a medium rich in nitrogen. Nitrogen can exist in two forms. Normally it occurs as ^{14}N, but it also occurs as a 'heavier' form, called ^{15}N.

In one experiment, some of the bacteria were grown in a medium containing the 'light' form of nitrogen, ^{14}N. In addition, bacteria were grown in a medium containing the 'heavy' form of nitrogen, ^{15}N, for several generations, so that all the DNA in the bacteria was labelled with ^{15}N.

Samples of bacteria were removed from both cultures, the DNA was extracted and then centrifuged. The band of heavier DNA settled lower in the centrifuge tube (Tube **B**) than the band of lighter DNA (Tube **A**).

The remaining bacteria which had been grown in 'heavy' nitrogen were then transferred to a growth medium containing the 'lighter' form of nitrogen, ^{14}N, as the only source of nitrogen. After one generation, DNA was extracted from the bacteria in this medium and centrifuged (Tube **C**).

The results of the experiments are shown in the three tubes below.

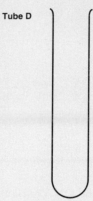

Tube A
Centrifuged DNA from *E. coli* grown in ^{14}N medium

Tube B
Centrifuged DNA from *E. coli* grown in ^{15}N medium

Tube C
Centrifuged DNA from *E. coli* labelled with ^{15}N and grown in ^{14}N medium for one generation

Band of 'light' DNA

Band of DNA after one generation

Band of 'heavy' DNA

(a) (i) Describe how the position of the DNA band in Tube **C** compares with that in Tubes **A** and **B**. (1 mark)
(ii) Explain the difference in the position of the bands of DNA in Tube **B** and Tube **C**. (3 marks)
(iii) In another experiment, *E. coli* labelled with ^{15}N was grown in ^{14}N for two generations before the DNA was extracted and centrifuged.

Copy the drawing of Tube **D**, and insert and label the position of the DNA which you would expect to find.
Explain the position of the band(s) you have drawn. (3 marks)

Tube D

(b) The mRNA codons for three amino acids are:
alanine = GCG   tyrosine = UAC
valine = GUG

Draw the section of a double-stranded DNA molecule to show the sequence of bases necessary to code for these three amino acids in the order given above. Show clearly which is the complementary strand. (3 marks)

(c) DNA molecules contain all the information that a cell requires to synthesise proteins. One of the stages of protein synthesis is shown in the diagram below.

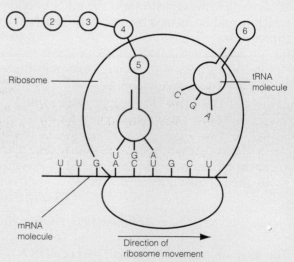

(i) What name is given to this stage of protein synthesis? (1 mark)
(ii) How was the mRNA shown in the diagram formed? (3 marks)
(iii) What is the sequence of the tRNA anticodon bases linking to the mRNA codon for amino acid 4 in the diagram? (1 mark)
(iv) Amino acid 1 has the formula, NH_2, CHR^1, COOH
Amino acid 2 has the formula, NH_2, CHR^2, COOH

Show the structure of the dipeptide formed when the two amino acids combine. Name the type of reaction involved when two amino acids form a dipeptide. (*3 marks*)

(*d*) Briefly explain how proteins function in the body:
  (i) as buffers;
  (ii) in blood coagulation. (*6 marks*)
(*Total 24 marks*)

AEB June 1994, Paper 2, No. 3

10. Write an essay on the genetic code and protein synthesis. (*30 marks*)

ULEAC June 1994, Paper 1, No. 1(a)

11. Scientists have shown that kidney beans are resistant to cowpea weevils and adzuki bean weevils, two of the most serious pests of African and Asian pulses (vegetables related to peas and beans). This is because the beans produce a protein that inhibits one of the weevils' digestive enzymes. Weevils that eat the pulses soon starve to death. The researchers have identified the gene that produces the inhibitor and removed it from the kidney bean DNA. They inserted the gene that produces the inhibitor into the DNA of a bacterium called *Agrobacterium tumefaciens*. Using this bacterium they have been able to add the inhibitor gene to peas. They hope soon to be able to add the gene to African and Asian pulses.

(*a*) Describe how scientists could:
  (i) remove the gene that produces the inhibitor from kidney beans. (*2 marks*)
  (ii) insert this gene into the DNA of a bacterium. (*2 marks*)
(*b*) The DNA in the bacterium is able to replicate to produce many copies of itself for insertion into pea cells.
Describe the structure of a DNA molecule and explain how this structure enables the molecule to replicate itself. (*8 marks*)
(*Total 12 marks*)

NEAB June 1995, Paper BY02, No. 8

12. (*a*) Give a brief account of the structure of DNA. (*5 marks*)
(*b*) Review briefly the evidence that DNA is the hereditary material. (*3 marks*)
(*c*) Explain **in outline** how the information contained within the DNA molecule is transcribed and translated into specific protein production by cells. (*10 marks*)

UCLES June 1993, Paper 2, No. 5

13. The diagram shows how a genetically modified organism may be produced by inserting a gene from a human into a bacterium.

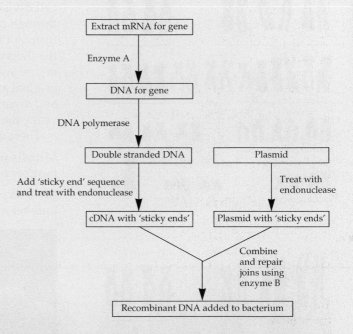

(*a*) Name enzymes A and B. (*2 marks*)
(*b*) Describe how treating plasmids with endonuclease produces sticky ends and explain their importance. (*3 marks*)
(*c*) Suggest **one** way in which genetically modified organisms may be used. (*1 mark*)
(*Total 6 marks*)

ULEAC June 1996, Paper B/HB1, No. 3

103

6

Cell division

Modern cell theory, as described in Chapter 4, states that 'all new cells are derived from other cells'. The process involved is **cell division**. All 10^{14} cells which comprise a human are derived, through cell division, from the single zygote formed by the fusion of two gametes. These gametes in turn were derived from the division of certain parental cells. It follows that all cells in all organisms have been formed from successive divisions of some original ancestral cell. The remarkable thing is that, while cells and organisms have diversified considerably over millions of years, the process of cell division has remained much the same.

There are two basic types:

Mitosis which results in all daughter cells having the same number of chromosomes as the parent.

Meiosis which results in the daughter cells having only half the number of chromosomes found in the parent cell.

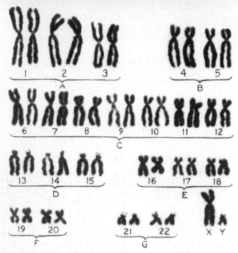

Human karyotypes (male and female)

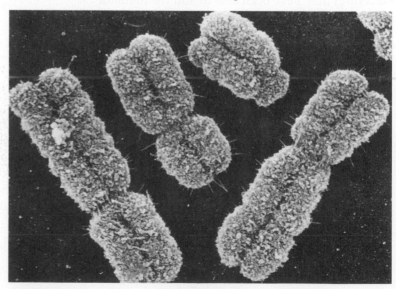

Scanning electron micrograph (SEM) of a group of human chromosomes

6.1 Chromosomes

6.1.1 Chromosome structure

Chromosomes carry the hereditary material DNA (15%). In addition they are made up of protein (70%) and RNA (10%). Individual chromosomes are not visible in a non-dividing (resting) cell, but the chromosomal material can be seen,

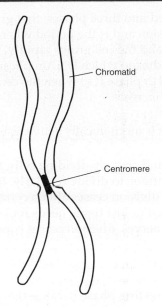

Fig. 6.1 *Structure of a chromosome*

especially if stained. This material is called **chromatin**. It is only at the onset of cell division that individual chromosomes become visible. They appear as long, thin threads between 0.25 μm and 50 μm in length. Each chromosome is seen to consist of two threads called **chromatids** joined at a point called the **centromere** (Fig. 6.1). Chromosomes vary in shape and size, both within and between species.

6.1.2 Chromosome number

The number of chromosomes varies from one species to another but is always the same for normal individuals of one species. Table 6.1 gives some idea of the range of chromosome number in different species. It can be seen that the numbers are not related to either the size of the organism or to its evolutionary status; indeed it is quite without significance.

Although the chromosome number of a cell varies from two to 300 or more, the majority of organisms have between ten and forty chromosomes in each of their cells. With well over one million different species, it follows that many share the same chromosome number, twenty-four being the most common.

TABLE 6.1 **The chromosome number of a range of species**

Species	Chromosome number
Certain roundworms	2
Crocus (*Crocus balansae*)	6
Fruit fly (*Drosophila melanogaster*)	8
Onion (*Allium cepa*)	16
Maize (*Zea mays*)	20
Locust (*Locusta migratoria*)	24
Lily (*Lilium longiflorum*)	24
Tomato (*Solanum lycopersicum*)	24
Cat (*Felis cattus*)	38
Mouse (*Mus musculus*)	40
Human (*Homo sapiens*)	46
Potato (*Solanum tuberosum*)	48
Horse (*Equus caballus*)	64
Dog (*Canis familiaris*)	78
Certain Protozoa	300+

6.2   Mitosis

Dividing cells undergo a regular pattern of events, known as the **cell cycle**. This cycle may be divided into two basic parts:

Interphase – when the cell undergoes a period of intense chemical activity. The amount of DNA is doubled during this

Nuclear division, or mitosis, typically occupies 5–10% of the total cycle. The cycle may take as little as 20 minutes in a bacterial cell, although it typically takes 8–24 hours.

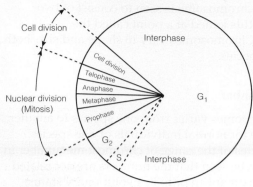

Fig. 6.2 The cell cycle

period. Interphase is divided into three phases: first growth phase (G_1) follows cell division and is the period where most cell organelles are synthesized and the cell grows rapidly. The synthesis (S) phase is next, during which DNA replication occurs and finally the second growth phase (G_2) when the centrioles replicate and energy stores increase.

Mitosis – when the nucleus is mechanically active as it divides.

In single-celled organisms and actively dividing cells, the cycle is continuous, i.e. the cells continue to divide regularly. In some cells, like those of the liver, division ceases after a certain time and only resumes if damaged or lost tissue needs replacing. In specialized tissues, such as nerves, division ceases completely once the cells are mature.

Interphase
Although often termed the **resting phase** because the chromosomes are not visible, interphase is in fact a period of considerable metabolic activity. It is during this phase that the DNA content of the cell is doubled. Duplication of the cell organelles also takes places at this time.

Prophase
The chromosomes become visible as long, thin tangled threads. Gradually they shorten and thicken, and each is seen to comprise two chromatids joined at the centromere. With the exception of higher plant cells which lack them, the centrioles migrate to opposite ends or **poles** of the cell. From each centriole, microtubules develop and form a star-shaped structure called an **aster**. Some of these microtubules, called **spindle fibres**, span the cell from pole to pole. Collectively they form the **spindle**. The nucleolus disappears and finally the nuclear envelope disintegrates, leaving the chromosomes within the cytoplasm of the cell.

Metaphase
The chromosomes arrange themselves at the centre or **equator** of the spindle, and become attached to certain spindle fibres at the centromere. Contraction of these fibres draws the individual chromatids slightly apart.

Anaphase
The centromeres split and further shortening of the spindle fibres causes the two chromatids of each chromosome to separate and migrate to opposite poles. The shortening of the spindle fibres is due to the progressive removal of the **tubulin** molecules of which they are made. The energy for this process is provided by mitochondria which are observed to collect around the spindle fibres.

Telophase
The chromatids reach their respective poles and a new nuclear envelope forms around each group. The chromatids uncoil and lengthen, thus becoming invisible again. The spindle fibres disintegrate and a nucleolus reforms in each new nucleus.

PROJECT

1. Examine longitudinal sections of bean root using a microscope. Locate the area just behind the tip of the root where mitosis is occurring.

2. Count the number of cells at interphase and at the various phases of mitosis and from this data determine the relative time taken for each phase.

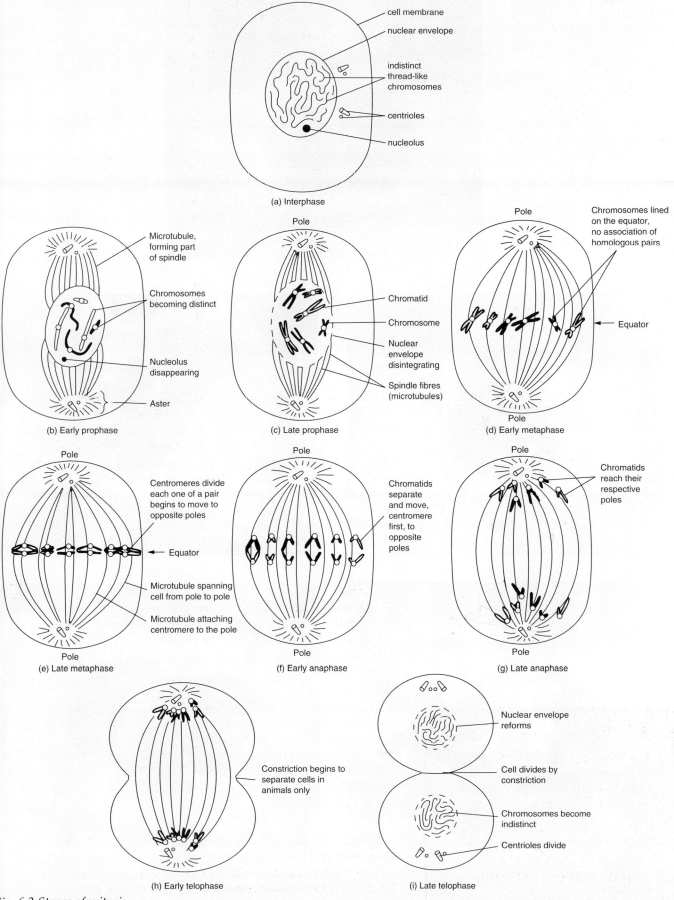

Fig. 6.3 Stages of mitosis

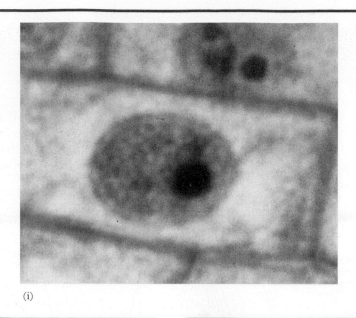

(i)

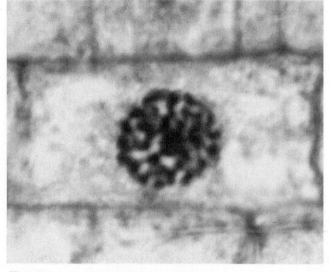

(ii)

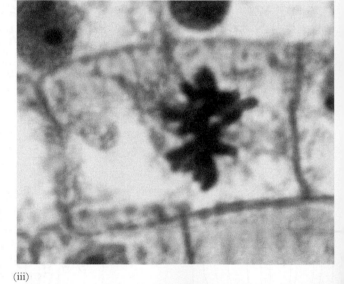

(iii)

(iv)

(v)

The main stages of mitosis (×500 approx.):
(i) interphase
(ii) prophase – chromosomes become visible

(iii) metaphase – chromosomes line up on the equator
(iv) anaphase – chromatids migrate to opposite poles
(v) telophase – daughter nuclei form at opposite poles

6.3 Meiosis (reduction division)

Meiosis involves one division of the chromosomes followed by two divisions of the nucleus and cell. The result is that the number of chromosomes in each cell is reduced by half. The **diploid (2n)** parent cell gives rise to **four haploid (n)** daughter cells. Meiosis occurs in the formation of gametes, sperm and ova, in animals, and in the production of spores in most plants.

Meiosis comprises two divisions:

1. **First meiotic division** – similar to mitosis except for a highly modified prophase stage.

2. **Second meiotic division** – a typically mitotic division.

The process is continuous but for convenience is divided into the same stages as mitosis. The symbols I and II indicate the first and second meiotic divisions respectively.

Interphase
The cell is in the non-dividing condition during which it replicates its DNA and organelles.

Prophase I
Organisms have two sets of chromosomes, one derived from each parent. Any two chromosomes which determine the same characteristics, e.g. eye colour, blood groups, etc., are called an **homologous pair**. Although each chromosome of a pair determines the same characteristics, they need not be identical. For instance, while one of the pair may code for blue eyes, the other may code for brown eyes.

Prophase I of meiosis is similar to prophase in mitosis, in that the chromosomes become visible, shorten and fatten, but differs in that they associate in their homologous pairs. They come together by a process termed **synapsis** and each pair is called a **bivalent**.

Each chromosome of the pair is seen to comprise two chromatids. These chromatids wrap around each other. The chromatids of the pair partially repel one another although they remain joined at certain points called **chiasmata** (singular – **chiasma**). It is at these points that chromatids may break and recombine with a different chromatid. This swapping of portions of chromatids is termed **crossing over**. The chromatids continue to repel one another although at this stage they still remain attached at the chiasmata. The nucleolus disappears and the nuclear envelope breaks down. Where present, the centrioles migrate to the poles and the spindle forms.

Metaphase I
The bivalents arrange themselves on the equator of the cell with each of a pair of homologous chromosomes orientated to opposite poles. This arrangement is completely random relative to the orientation of other bivalents. The genetic significance of

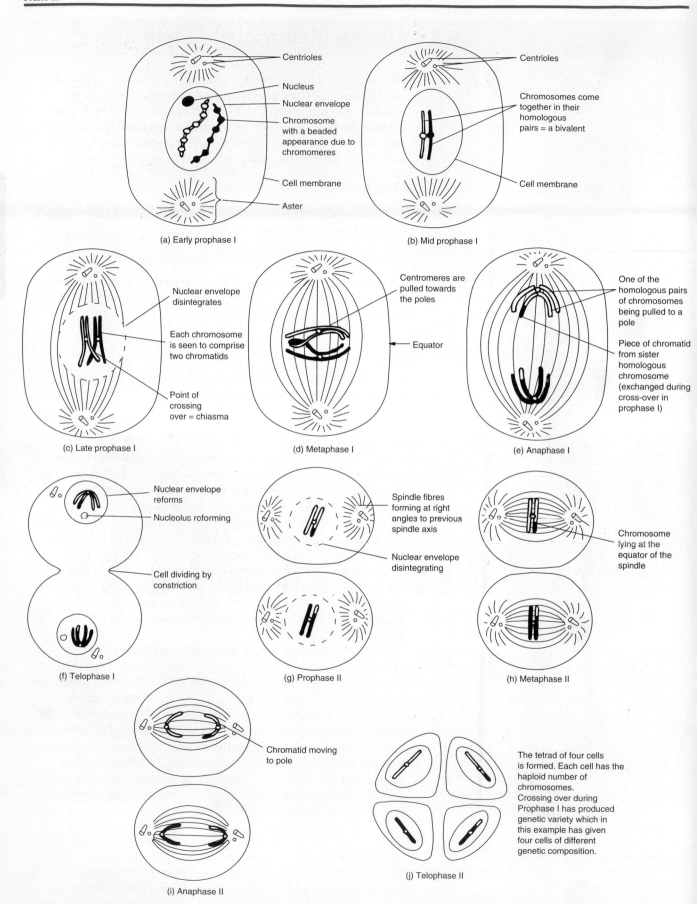

Fig. 6.4 Stages of meiosis (only one pair of chromosomes shown)

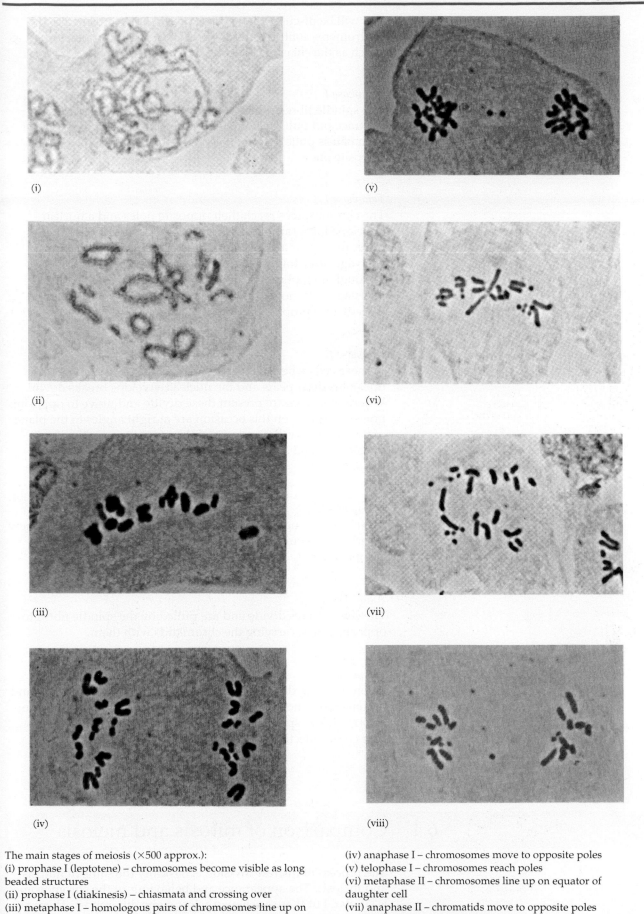

The main stages of meiosis (×500 approx.):
(i) prophase I (leptotene) – chromosomes become visible as long beaded structures
(ii) prophase I (diakinesis) – chiasmata and crossing over
(iii) metaphase I – homologous pairs of chromosomes line up on equator
(iv) anaphase I – chromosomes move to opposite poles
(v) telophase I – chromosomes reach poles
(vi) metaphase II – chromosomes line up on equator of daughter cell
(vii) anaphase II – chromatids move to opposite poles
(viii) telophase II – chromatids reach opposite poles

this will be discussed later. The spindle fibres attached to the centromeres contract slightly, pulling the chromosomes apart as much as the chiasmata allow.

Anaphase I

The spindle fibres, which are attached to the centromeres, contract and pull the homologous chromosomes apart. One of each pair is pulled to one pole, its sister chromosome to the opposite one.

Telophase I

The chromosomes reach their opposite poles and a nuclear envelope forms around each group. In most cells the spindle fibres disappear and the chromatids uncoil. Cell division, or **cleavage**, may follow. The nucleus may enter interphase although no replication of the DNA takes place. In some cells this stage does not occur and the cell passes from anaphase I directly into prophase II.

Prophase II

In those cells where telophase and interphase take place, the nucleolus disappears and the nuclear envelope breaks down. Where centrioles are present these divide and move to opposite poles. The poles on this occasion are at right angles to the plane of the previous cell division and therefore the spindle fibres develop at right angles to the spindle axis of the first meiotic division.

Metaphase II

The chromosomes arrange themselves on the equator of the new spindle. The spindle fibres attach to the centromere of each chromosome.

Anaphase II

The centromeres divide and are pulled by the spindle fibres to opposite poles, carrying the chromatids with them.

Telophase II

Upon reaching their opposite poles, the chromatids unwind and become indistinct. The nuclear envelope and the nucleolus are reformed. The spindle disappears and the cells divide to give four cells, collectively called a **tetrad**.

6.4   Comparison of mitosis and meiosis

The process of nuclear division is basically the same in mitosis and meiosis. The appearance and behaviour of the chromosomes is similar, but there are nevertheless some differences. These are listed in Table 6.2.

6.5   The significance of cell division

TABLE 6.2   **Differences between mitosis and meiosis**

Mitosis	Meiosis
A single division of the chromosomes and the nucleus	A single division of the chromosomes but a double division of the nucleus
The number of chromosomes remains the same	The number of chromosomes is halved
Homologous chromosomes do not associate	Homologous chromosomes associate to form bivalents in prophase I
Chiasmata are never formed	Chiasmata may be formed
Crossing over never occurs	Crossing over may occur
Daughter cells are identical to parent cells (in the absence of mutations)	Daughter cells are genetically different from parental ones
Two daughter cells are formed	Four daughter cells are formed, although in females only one is usually functional
Chromosomes shorten and thicken	Chromosomes coil but remain longer than in mitosis
Chromosomes form a single row at the equator of the spindle	Chromosomes form a double row at the equator of the spindle during metaphase I
Chromatids move to opposite poles	Chromosomes move to opposite poles during the first meiotic division

6.5.1 Significance of mitosis

The significance of mitosis is its ability to produce daughter cells which are exact copies of the parental cell. It is important in three ways.

(a) Growth

If a tissue is to extend by growth it is important that the new cells are identical to the existing cells. Cell division must therefore be by mitosis.

(b) Repair

Damaged cells must be replaced by exact copies of the originals if the repair is to return a tissue to its former condition. Mitosis is the means by which this is achieved.

(c) Asexual reproduction

If a species is successful in colonizing a particular habitat, there is little advantage, in the short term, in producing offspring which differ from the parents, because these may be less successful. It is better to establish quickly a colony of individuals which are similar to the parents. In simple animals and most plants this is achieved by mitotic divisions. See 'Focus' on Micropropagation.

6.5.2 Significance of meiosis

The long-term survival of a species depends on its ability to adapt to a constantly changing environment. It should also be able to colonize a range of new environments. To achieve both these aims it is necessary for offspring to be different from their parents as well as different from each other.

There are three ways in which this variety is brought about with the aid of meiosis.

(a) Production and fusion of haploid gametes

Variety of offspring is increased by mixing the genotype of one parent with that of the other. This is the basis of the sexual process in organisms. It involves the production of special sex cells, called gametes, which fuse together to produce a new organism. Each gamete must contain half the number of chromosomes of the adult if the chromosome number is not to double at each generation. It is therefore essential that meiosis, which halves the number of chromosomes in daughter cells, occurs at some stage in the life cycle of a sexually reproducing organism. Meiosis is thus instrumental in permitting variety in organisms, and giving them the potential to evolve.

(b) The creation of genetic variety by the random distribution of chromosomes during metaphase I

When the pairs of homologous chromosomes arrange themselves on the equator of the spindle during metaphase I of meiosis, they do so randomly. Although each one of the pair determines the same general features, they differ in the detail of these features. The random distribution and consequent independent assortment of these chromosomes produces new genetic combinations. A simple example is shown in Fig. 6.5.

In arrangement 1, the two pairs of homologous chromosomes orientate themselves on the equator in such a way that the chromosome carrying the allele for brown eyes and the one carrying the allele for blood group A migrate to the same pole. The alleles for blue eyes and blood group B migrate to the opposite pole. Cell 1 therefore carries the alleles for brown eyes and blood group A while cell 2 carries the ones for blue eyes and blood group B.

In arrangement 2, the left hand homologous pair of chromosomes is shown orientated the opposite way around. As this orientation is random this arrangement is equally as likely as the first one. The result of this different arrangement is that cell 3 carries the alleles for blue eyes and blood group A whereas cell 4 carries ones for brown eyes and blood group B.

All four resultant cells are different from one another. With more homologous pairs the number of possible combinations becomes enormous. A human, with 23 such pairs, has the potential for $2^{23} = 8\,388\,608$ combinations.

(c) The creation of genetic variety by crossing over between homologous chromosomes

During prophase I of meiosis, equivalent portions of homologous chromosomes may be exchanged. In this way new genetic combinations are produced and linked genes separated.

The variety which meiosis brings about is essential to the process of evolution. By providing a varied stock of individuals it permits the natural selection of those best suited to the existing conditions and so ensures that species constantly change and adapt when these conditions alter. This is the main significance of meiosis.

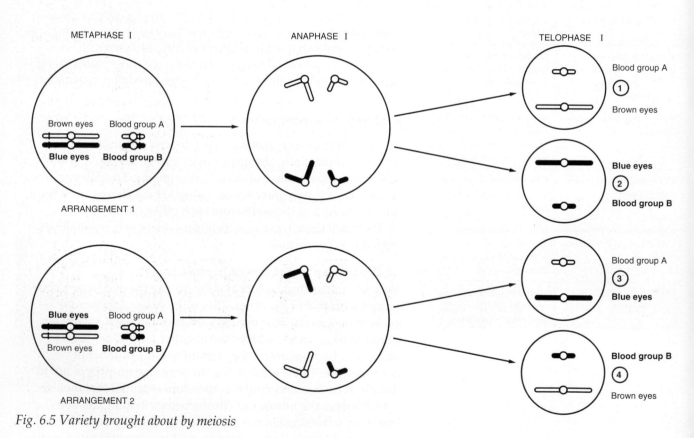

Fig. 6.5 Variety brought about by meiosis

Micropropagation

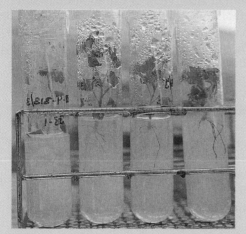

Micropropagation of plants in growing medium

Plant cells are totipotent, that is any differentiated plant cell has the potential to give rise to all the different cells of an adult plant. This is the basis of the tissue culture techniques which form the basis of micropropagation.

Stock plants are kept as pathogen- and pest-free as possible and small pieces are cut (excised) from them. These explants may be pieces of stem tissue, with nodes, flower buds, leaves or tiny sections of shoot tip meristems. The surfaces of the explants are sterilized by using solutions such as dilute sodium hypochlorite and, in aseptic conditions, are transferred to a culture vessel containing nutrients and growth regulators. The medium is usually solidified using a gelling agent, such as agar, to provide a firm matrix for the growing shoots. The vessels are then incubated for 3–9 weeks at 15–30 °C with light for 10–14 hours per day. The new shoots that develop are removed from the explant and subcultured on a new medium. This process is repeated every few weeks so that a few explants can give rise to millions of plants within one year. The composition of medium used varies for different varieties. Tissue culture plants must be acclimatized in special greenhouses until they reach marketable size.

Micropropagation is now widely used as an alternative to conventional propagation of many horticultural species (for pot plants, cut flowers and ornamental bulbs) and some agricultural crops such as potatoes and sugar beet. Tissue culture allows the rapid production of large numbers of genetically identical plants, can be used for plant species which are difficult to propagate by traditional methods, helps to eliminate plant diseases, overcomes seasonal restrictions and enables cold storage of large numbers of plants in a small space.

However, there are also some problems. Plants propagated in this way may be genetically unstable or infertile, their chromosomes being structurally altered or their chromosome numbers being unusual. When oil palms produced by micropropagation were introduced to Malaysia in the 1970s they turned out to be sterile. This problem has now been overcome and most oil palms are the result of micropropagation techniques. It is a technology which requires sterile conditions and a well trained labour force and so costs are higher than with traditional propagation methods.

FOCUS

Cancer

Superficially cancer seems to be a range of diseases in which tumours arise at different sites, grow at different rates and may be benign or lethal. However, in all cancers a population of cells multiplies in an unregulated manner independent of normal control mechanisms. Most cancers are believed to arise from single cells which transform from a normal into a malignant state. If the abnormal cell is not recognized and destroyed by the immune system it multiplies into a small mass and then into a large primary tumour with its own blood supply. Primary tumours can be managed and the patients are often cured. The more usual causes of death are the effects of secondary tumours, or metastases, in distant organs. Transport within the lymph duct will give rise to metastases in lymph nodes adjacent to the primary tumour while transport within the blood may give rise to more distant secondaries.

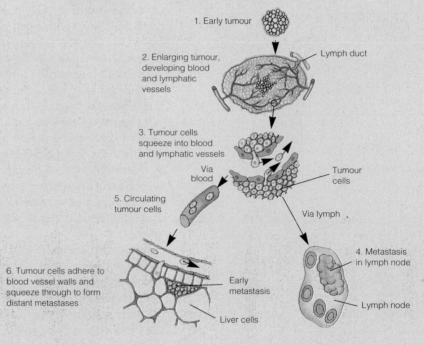

The early development and spread of secondary tumour

Cancers can occur at any age but overall incidence rises rapidly with age and they are a more prevalent cause of death in men than in women. Cancers which are clearly age-related are carcinomas of the gut, skin, urinary tract and some leukaemias. In breast cancer the incidence rises steeply up to menopause and then declines; cervical cancer peaks in the 30s.

It has been suggested that the cumulative effect of carcinogens in the environment may account for cancers whose incidence increases with age. The pattern of breast cancer suggests a hormonal link and cervical cancer correlates with sexual behaviour, age at which intercourse began and possibly the number of sexual partners.

As a cause of death today, cancer is second only to diseases of the circulatory system and in terms of working years lost it

FOCUS continued

exceeds all other diseases. In the Western world the commonest forms of cancer are those of the lung, breast, skin, gut and prostate gland. In men the greatest killer is lung cancer while in women it is breast cancer. There are, however, considerable national variations. Skin cancer is 200 times more prevalent in parts of Australia than in India – possibly linked to the long exposure of Caucasian skin to sunlight. Stomach cancer is 30 times more common in Japan than in parts of Britain – possibly due to dietary or genetic effects.

The transformation of a normal cell into a cancerous one may be brought about by exposure to certain chemicals, by radiation or by the action of retroviruses (see Section 5.2.2). Chemical carcinogens fall into several classes which include polycyclic hydrocarbons, nitrosamines, aromatics, amines and others. The first of these classes is found in soot and cigarette smoke. It has been estimated that 25–30% of environmentally associated cancers can be attributed to smoking and it is now the main cause of lung cancer which kills over 40 000 people a year in Britain.

Carcinogenic transformation may also be brought about by exposure to radiation, the most damaging being short wavelengths – X-rays, gamma rays and some ultra-violet rays. Ultra-violet rays do not penetrate beyond superficial layers of the skin but they are responsible for a significant number of skin cancers.

Some cancers, including Burkitt's lymphoma and AIDS-related Kaposi's sarcoma have been linked to viruses, namely EB virus and HIV-I respectively, but in general it is now recognized that the relationship involves certain cancer-causing genes termed oncogenes rather than the viruses themselves.

If cancer cannot be prevented then early detection and diagnosis can at least improve the likelihood of a cure. Progress in this field has been rapid and now relies on specific biochemical and chemical reagents as well as sophisticated instruments such as ultrasound, computer tomography (CT) scanning and magnetic resonance imaging (MRI).

Once diagnosed, the choice of therapy will depend on the nature, site and extent of the tumours but may include surgery, radiotherapy, the use of drugs or immunotherapy. Surgery remains a major weapon in the fight against cancer although it is often used in association with radio- or chemotherapy. Radiotherapy has been used in cancer treatments for many years although many tumours respond poorly, especially those with low internal oxygen levels. There are many classes of anti-cancer drugs in use but the search still goes on for derivatives which retain their activity but have reduced toxicity.

It is generally accepted that the immune system plays an important role in preventing cancer and research is now centred on finding suitable molecules to stimulate the immune reaction. Such substances include interferons and interleukins, both produced by genetically engineered bacteria.

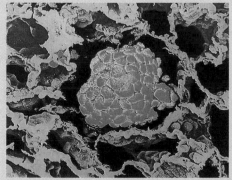

Scanning electron micrograph (SEM) of a bronchial carcinoma (lung tumour) filling an alveolus

6.6   Questions

1. The diagrams show stages of cell division. Only one pair of homologous chromosomes is shown.

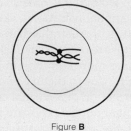

Figure **A**   Figure **B**

(a) Identify the type of cell division shown.
(1 mark)
(b) Name the stage of cell division shown in:
Figure **A**;
Figure **B**.   *(2 marks)*
(c) With reference to the process shown in Figure **A**:
(i) describe what is happening to the chromosomes;   *(1 mark)*
(ii) explain the biological significance of the process.   *(1 mark)*
(d) Describe how a chromosome mutation could occur during this type of cell division.   *(1 mark)*
(Total 6 marks)

AEB June 1992, Paper 1, No. 13

2. Describe what is meant by each of the following terms.
(a) Mitosis   *(3 marks)*
(b) Meiosis   *(3 marks)*
(c) Autosomal linkage   *(3 marks)*
(Total 9 marks)

ULEAC June 1995, Paper 1, No. 8

3. Fig. 1 represents a stage of meiosis in an animal cell.

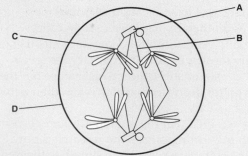

Fig. 1

(a) Name the structures labelled **A** to **D**.   *(4 marks)*
(b) Name the stage of division shown in Fig. 1.
(1 mark)

Fig. 2 shows homologous chromosomes undergoing meiosis.

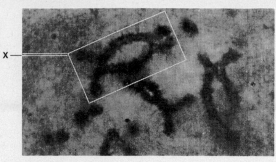

Fig. 2

(c) Draw and label a diagram to explain what has happened to the pair of chromosomes labelled **X** in Fig. 2.   *(3 marks)*
Fig. 3 shows the four homologous pairs of chromosomes of the male fruit fly *Drosophila melanogaster*.

(d) Crossing over does not occur in male fruit flies. How many genotypes would be possible in the sperm of this fruit fly? Explain your answer.
(2 marks)
(Total 10 marks)

UCLES June 1995, Paper 2, No. 1

4. Describe **four** events that occur to a single chromosome between the end of interphase and the end of prophase I in meiosis.   *(4 ×1 mark)*

AEB June 1995, Paper 1, No, 18

5. The drawing shows animal cells in different stages of mitosis.

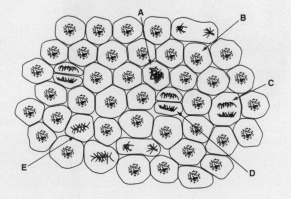

(a) Using only the letters in the diagram, list the cells in the correct sequence, beginning with the cell in the earliest stage. *(1 mark)*

(b) (i) Describe what is happening to the genetic material in cell **B**. *(1 mark)*

(ii) How are the events you have described in (i) being brought about? *(3 marks)*

(c) Explain why the cells produced by mitosis are genetically identical. *(3 marks)*

(Total 8 marks)

AEB June 1994, Paper 1, No. 9

6. (a) State **two** differences between the process of mitosis and that of meiosis. *(2 marks)*

(b) Explain how meiosis gives rise to genetic variation. *(3 marks)*

(c) Explain why if two organisms heterozygous for one pair of alleles are crossed, the theoretical ratio of offspring phenotypes is 3 : 1. *(2 marks)*

(Total 7 marks)

ULEAC June 1993, Paper 1, No. 6

7. The graph shows the changes in the incidence of some forms of cancer in the United States over the period 1973 to 1990.

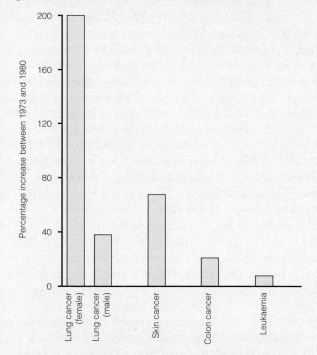

(a) Describe **three** characteristic features of tumours. *(3 marks)*

(b) For any **three** of the cancers on this graph, describe and explain how possible risk factors might have led to the change in incidence over this period of time. *(6 marks)*

(c) Suggest ways in which the death rate from cancer of **either** the breast **or** the cervix might be reduced. *(3 marks)*

(Total 12 marks)

NEAB June 1995, Paper BY08, No. 9

8. (a) Explain **two** ways in which meiosis contributes to genetic variation. *(4 marks)*

(b) The bar chart shows the amount of DNA present in one cell of an organism at different stages of mitosis.

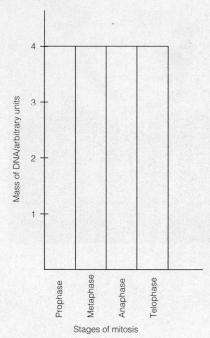

How many units of DNA would you expect to be present in one cell of this organism

(i) during the first division of meiosis;

(ii) in one of the gametes formed as a result of meiosis? *(2 marks)*

(Total 6 marks)

NEAB June 1996, Biology Paper I, No. 13

7   Heredity and genetics

Gregor Mendel

It has been estimated that all the ova from which the present human population was derived could be contained within a five-litre vessel. All the sperm which fertilized these ova could be contained within a thimble. Put another way, all the information necessary to produce in excess of 5 000 000 000 different humans can be stored within this relatively tiny volume. Indeed, we now know that the genetic information itself occupies only a small proportion of the ovum. Imagine the space occupied if all the characteristics of every living human being were printed in book form (see 'Did You Know?' on p. 86). Whatever else it may be, the genetic information is remarkably condensed. In Chapter 5 we described the chemical nature of this genetic information, namely DNA. In this chapter we shall concern ourselves with the means by which it is transmitted from generation to generation.

Genetics is a fundamental and increasingly important branch of biology. Humans have unknowingly used genetic principles in the breeding of animals and plants for many thousands of years. An understanding of the underlying genetic principles is, however, fairly recent. In fact the term genetics was first used only at the beginning of this century. The understanding of the chemical foundations of heredity and genetics came even more recently with the discovery of the structure of DNA by Watson and Crick in 1953.

Observation of individuals of the same species shows them all to be recognizably similar. This is **heredity**. Closer inspection reveals minor differences by which each individual can be distinguished. This is **variation**.

The genetic composition of an organism is called the **genotype**. This often sets limits within which individual characteristics may vary. Such variation may be due to the effect of environmental influences, e.g. the genotype may determine a light-coloured skin, but the precise colour of any part of the skin will depend upon the extent to which it is exposed to sunlight. The **phenotype**, or set of characteristics, of an individual is therefore determined by the interaction between the genotype and the environment. Any change in the genotype is called a **mutation** and may be inherited. Any change in the phenotype only is called a **modification** and it is not inherited.

7.1   Mendel and the laws of inheritance

Gregor Mendel (1822–84) was an Austrian monk and teacher. He studied the process of heredity in selected features of the garden pea *Pisum sativum*. He was not the first scientist to study heredity, but he was the first to obtain sufficiently numerous, accurate and detailed data upon which sound scientific conclusions could be based. Partly by design and partly by luck, Mendel made a suitable choice of characteristics for study. He isolated pea plants which were **pure-breeding**. That is, when bred with each other, they produced consistently the same characteristics over many generations. He referred to each character as a **trait**. He chose traits which had two contrasting features, e.g. he chose stem length, which could be either long or short and flower colour which could be red or white. It must be remembered that Mendel began his ten-year-long experiments in 1856, when the nature of chromosomes and genes was yet to be discovered.

7.1.1 Monohybrid inheritance (Mendel's Law of Segregation)

Monohybrid inheritance refers to the inheritance of a single character only. One trait which Mendel studied was the shape of the seed produced by his pea plants. This showed two contrasting forms, round and wrinkled. When he crossed plants which were pure-breeding for round seed with ones pure-breeding for wrinkled seed, all the resulting plants produced round seed. The first generation of a cross is referred to as the **first filial generation (F_1)**. When individuals of the F_1 generation were intercrossed the resulting **second filial generation (F_2)** produced 7324 seeds, 5474 of which were round and 1850 wrinkled. This is a ratio of $2.96 : 1$.

In all his crosses, Mendel found that one of the contrasting features of a pair was not represented in the F_1 generation. This feature reappeared in the F_2 generation where it was consistently outnumbered 3 to 1 by the contrasting feature.

The significance of these findings was that the F_1 seeds were not intermediate between the two parental types, i.e. partly wrinkled, partly smooth. This shows that there was no blending or mixing of the features. It also indicated that as only one of the features expressed itself in the F_1, this feature was **dominant** to the other. The feature which does not express itself in the F_1 is said to be **recessive**. In the example given, round is dominant and wrinkled is recessive.

In interpreting his results, Mendel concluded that the features were passed on from one generation to the next via the gametes. The parents he decided must possess two pieces of information about each character. However, only one of these pieces of information was found in an individual gamete. On the basis of this he formulated his first law, the **Law of Segregation**, which states:

The characteristics of an organism are determined by internal factors which occur in pairs. Only one of a pair of such factors can be represented in a single gamete.

We know that Mendel's 'factors' are specific portions of a chromosome called **genes**. We also know that the process which produces gametes with only one of each pair of factors is meiosis. On the basis of his results, Mendel had effectively predicted the existence of genes and meiosis.

7.1.2 Representing genetic crosses

Genetic crosses are usually represented in a form of shorthand. There is more than one system of this shorthand, but the following one has been adopted here because it is both quick and less liable to errors, especially under the pressures of an examination.

TABLE 7.1

Instruction	Reason/notes	Example [round and wrinkled seed]
Choose a single letter to represent each characteristic	An easy form of shorthand. In some conventional genetic crosses, e.g. in *Drosophila*, there are set symbols, some of which use two letters	
Choose the first letter of one of the contrasting features	When more than one character is considered at one time such a logical choice means it is easy to identify which letter refers to which character	Choose either R (round) or W (wrinkled)
If possible, choose the letter in which the upper and lower case forms differ in shape as well as size	If the upper and lower case forms differ it is almost impossible to confuse them regardless of their size	Choose R, because the upper case form (R) differs in shape from the lower case form (r), whereas W and w differ only in size, and are more likely to be confused.
Let the upper case letter represent the dominant feature and the lower case letter the recessive one. Never use two different letters where one character is dominant. Always state clearly what feature each symbol represents	The dominant and recessive features can easily be identified. Do *not* use two different letters as this indicates incomplete dominance or codominance	Let R = round and r = wrinkled Do *not* use R for round and W for wrinkled
Represent the parents with the appropriate pairs of letters. Label them clearly as 'parents' and state their phenotypes	This makes it clear to the reader which the symbols refer to	Round seed Wrinkled seed Parents RR v rr
State the gametes produced by each parent. Label them clearly, and encircle them. Indicate that meiosis has occurred	This explains why the gametes only possess one of the two parental factors. Encircling them reinforces the idea that they are separate	meiosis meiosis ↓ ↓ Gametes Ⓡ ⓡ
Use a type of chequerboard or matrix, called a **Punnett square**, to show the results of the random crossing of the gametes. Label male and female gametes even though this may not affect the results	This method is less liable to error than drawing lines between the gametes and the offspring. Labelling the sexes is a good habit to acquire – it has considerable relevance in certain types of crosses, e.g. sex-linked crosses	♂ gametes ♀ gametes Ⓡ Ⓡ ⓡ Rr Rr ⓡ Rr Rr
State the phenotype of each different genotype and indicate the numbers of each type. Always put the upper case (dominant) letter first when writing out the genotype.	Always putting the dominant feature first can reduce errors in cases where it is not possible to avoid using symbols with the upper and lower case letters of the same shape	All offspring are plants producing round seed (Rr)

NB Always carry out the above procedures in their entirety. Once you have practised a number of crosses, it is all too easy to miss out stages or explanations. Not only does this lead to errors, it often makes your explanations impossible for others to follow. *You* may understand what you are doing, but if the reader cannot follow it, it isn't much use, neither will it bring full credit in an examination.

7.1.3 Genetic representation of the monohybrid cross

Using the principles outlined in Table 7.1, the full genetic explanation of one of Mendel's experiments is shown below.

Let R = allele for round seed
 r = allele for wrinkled seed

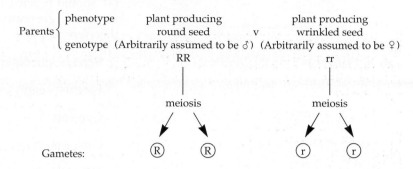

Parents {
phenotype   plant producing   plant producing
          round seed   v   wrinkled seed
genotype (Arbitrarily assumed to be ♂) (Arbitrarily assumed to be ♀)
          RR   rr
}

meiosis   meiosis

Gametes: (R)   (R)   (r)   (r)

F$_1$ generation:

		♂ gametes	
♀ gametes		(R)	(R)
	(r)	Rr	Rr
	(r)	Rr	Rr

All offspring are plants producing round seed (Rr)

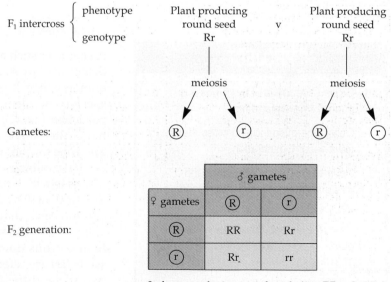

F$_1$ intercross {
phenotype   Plant producing   Plant producing
          round seed   v   round seed
genotype   Rr   Rr
}

meiosis   meiosis

Gametes: (R)   (r)   (R)   (r)

F$_2$ generation:

		♂ gametes	
♀ gametes		(R)	(r)
	(R)	RR	Rr
	(r)	Rr	rr

3 plants producing round seeds (1 × RR + 2 × Rr)
1 plant producing wrinkled seeds (rr)

Mendel's actual results gave a ratio of 2.96 : 1, a very good approximation to the 3 : 1 ratio which the theory suggests should be achieved. Any discrepancy is due to statistical error. Such errors are inevitable. Imagine for instance tossing a coin ten times – it should in theory come down heads five times and tails five times. More often than not, some other ratio is achieved in practice. The actual results are rarely exactly the same as predicted by the theory. The larger the sample, the more nearly the results approximate to the theoretical value. This was an essential aspect of Mendel's experiments. Probably because he was trained partly as a mathematician, he appreciated the need to collect large numbers of offspring if he was to draw meaningful conclusions from his experiments.

The use of 'F$_1$ generation' should be limited to the offspring of homozygous parents. Similarly, 'F$_2$ generation' should refer only to the offspring of the F$_1$ generation. In all other cases 'offspring (1)' should replace 'F$_1$ generation', and 'offspring (2)' should replace 'F$_2$ generation'. The complete set of headings in order therefore will be:

Parents: phenotypes

Parents: genotypes

Gametes

Offspring (1) genotypes

Offspring (1) phenotypes

Gametes

Offspring (2) genotypes

Offspring (2) phenotypes

Whether the variation from an expected ratio is the result of statistical chance or not can be tested for mathematically using the chi-squared test. Details of this are given in Section 8.3.

7.1.4 Genes and alleles

A character such as the shape of the seed coat in peas is determined by a single gene. The gene is therefore the basic unit of inheritance. It is a region of the chromosome or, more specifically, a length of the DNA molecule, which has a particular function. Each gene may have two, or occasionally more, alternative forms. Each form of the gene is called an **allele**. The gene for the shape of the seed coat in peas has two alleles, one determining round shape, the other wrinkled. The position of a gene within a DNA molecule is called the **locus**. When two identical alleles occur together at the same locus on a chromosome, they are said to be **homozygous**, e.g. when two alleles for round seeds occur together (RR) they are said to be **homozygous dominant**. Similarly, the two alleles for wrinkled seeds (rr) are referred to as **homozygous recessive**. Where the two alleles differ (Rr) they are termed **heterozygous**.

7.1.5 Dihybrid inheritance (Mendel's Law of Independent Assortment)

Dihybrid inheritance refers to the simultaneous inheritance of two characters. In one of his experiments Mendel investigated the inheritance of seed shape (round v. wrinkled) and seed colour (green v. yellow) at the same time. He knew from his monohybrid crosses that round seeds were dominant to wrinkled ones and yellow seeds were dominant to green. He chose to cross plants with both dominant features (round and

PROJECT

1. Cross *Drosophila* of two types e.g. normal × vestigial wing.

2. Collect the offspring and cross them to get a second generation.

3. Count the numbers of normal and vestigial winged flies in the second generation.

4. Using the χ^2 test, determine if your numbers agree with the Mendelian ratio of 3 : 1.

yellow) with ones that were recessive for both (wrinkled and green). The F_1 generation yielded plants all of which produced round, yellow seeds – hardly surprising as these are the two dominant features.

Mendel planted the F_1 seeds, raised the plants and allowed them to self-pollinate. He then collected the seeds. Of the 556 seeds produced, the majority, 315, possessed the two dominant features – round and yellow. The smallest group, 32, possessed the two recessive features – wrinkled and green. The remaining 209 seeds were of types not previously found. They combined one dominant and one recessive feature; 108 were round (dominant) and green (recessive) and 101 were wrinkled (recessive) and yellow (dominant). At first inspection these results may appear to contradict those obtained in the monohybrid cross, but as Table 7.2 shows, the ratio of dominant to recessive for each feature is still 3 : 1, as expected.

TABLE 7.2 **Results of Mendel's dihybrid cross**

Parents: round, yellow seeds v. wrinkled, green seeds

F_1 generation: all round, yellow seeds

F_2 generation:

		Seed shape			
		Round	Wrinkled	Total	Approx. ratio
Seed colour	Yellow	315	101	416	3 yellow
	Green	108	32	140	1 green
	Total	423	133		
	Approx. ratio	3 round	1 wrinkled		

Approx. ratio: round, yellow   round, green   wrinkled, yellow   wrinkled, green
          (2 dominants) (dominant + recessive) (recessive + dominant) (2 recessives)
               9   :   3   :   3   :   1

The significance of these findings was that as the features of seed shape and colour had each produced a 3 : 1 ratio (dominant : recessive), the two features had behaved completely independently of one another. The presence of one had not affected the behaviour of the other. On the basis of these findings, Mendel formulated his second law, the Law of Independent Assortment, which states:

Each of a pair of contrasted characters may be combined with either of another pair.

With our present knowledge of genetics the law could now be rewritten as:

Each member of an allelic pair may combine randomly with either of another pair.

PROJECT

1. From Table 7.2 we find that:
   315 seeds were round and yellow
   108 were round and green
   101 were wrinkled and yellow
   32 were wrinkled and green.

   Using the χ^2 test, find out if these figures agree with the Mendelian ratio of 9 : 3 : 3 : 1. Look up other numbers counted by Mendel and do the same.

2. Carry out dihybrid crosses, for example with *Drosophila*, count the F_2 offspring and find out if the numbers agree with Mendel's 9 : 3 : 3 : 1 ratio.

7.1.6 Genetic representation of the dihybrid cross

Using the principles outlined in Table 7.1, the full genetic explanation of this dihybrid cross is shown below.

Let R = allele for round seed
r = allele for wrinkled seed
G = allele for yellow seed
g = allele for green seed

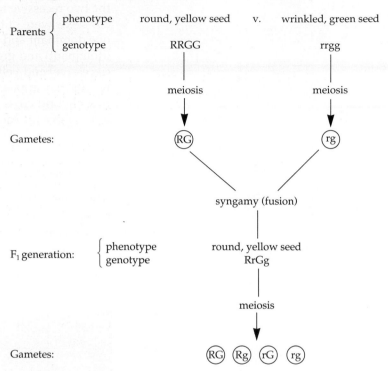

Parents
{
phenotype   round, yellow seed   v.   wrinkled, green seed

genotype   RRGG   rrgg
}

meiosis   meiosis

Gametes: RG   rg

syngamy (fusion)

F_1 generation:
{
phenotype   round, yellow seed
genotype   RrGg
}

meiosis

Gametes: RG   Rg   rG   rg

As the plants are self-pollinated the male and female gametes are of the same types. The offspring of this cross may therefore be represented in the following Punnett square.

♀ gametes	♂ gametes			
	RG	Rg	rG	rg
RG	RRGG	RRGg	RrGG	RrGg
Rg	RRGg	RRgg	RrGg	Rrgg
rG	RrGG	RrGg	rrGG	rrGg
rg	RrGg	Rrgg	rrGg	rrgg

In the following list, '–' represents either the dominant or recessive allele.

                                        Total

R–G– = round, yellow seed   9 (315)

R–gg = round, green seed   3 (108)

rrG– = wrinkled, yellow seed   3 (101)

rrgg = wrinkled, green seed   1 (32)

Allowing for statistical error, Mendel's results (shown in brackets) were a reasonable approximation to the expected 9:3:3:1 ratio.

7.2 The test cross

One common genetic problem is that an organism which shows a dominant character can have two possible genotypes. For example, a plant producing seeds with round coats could either be homozygous dominant (RR) or heterozygous (Rr). The appearance of the seeds (phenotype) is identical in both cases. It is often necessary, however, to determine the genotype accurately. This may be achieved by crossing the organism of unknown genotype with one whose genotype is accurately known. One genotype which can be positively identified from its phenotype alone is one which shows the recessive feature. In the case of the seed coat, any pea seed with a wrinkled coat must have the genotype rr. By crossing the dominant character, the unknown genotype can be identified. To take the above example:

Let R = allele for round seeds
  r = allele for wrinkled seeds

If the plant producing round seed has the genotype RR:

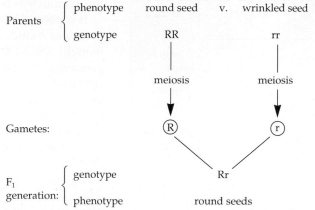

The only possible offspring are plants which produce round seeds.

If the plant producing round seeds has the genotype Rr:

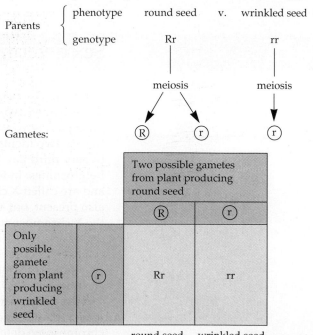

TABLE 7.3 Dihybrid backcross

Possible genotypes of plant producing round, yellow seeds	Possible gametes	Genotypes of offspring crossed with plant producing wrinkled, green seeds (gamete = rg)	Phenotype (type of seeds produced)
RRGG	RG	RrGg	All round and yellow
RrGG	RG	RrGg	$\frac{1}{2}$ round and yellow
	rG	rrGg	$\frac{1}{2}$ wrinkled and yellow
RRGg	RG	RrGg	$\frac{1}{2}$ round and yellow
	Rg	Rrgg	$\frac{1}{2}$ round and green
RrGg	RG	RrGg	$\frac{1}{4}$ round and yellow
	Rg	Rrgg	$\frac{1}{4}$ round and green
	rG	rrGg	$\frac{1}{4}$ wrinkled and yellow
	rg	rrgg	$\frac{1}{4}$ wrinkled and green

The offspring comprise equal numbers of plants producing round seeds and ones producing wrinkled seeds.

If some of the plants produce seeds with wrinkled coats (rr), then the unknown genotype must be Rr. An exact 1:1 ratio as above is not often achieved in practice, but this is unimportant as the presence of a single plant producing wrinkled seeds is proof enough (the possibility of a mutation must be discounted as it is highly unlikely and totally unpredictable). Such a plant with its rr genotype could only be produced if both parents donated an r gamete. The only way a plant which produces round seed can donate such a gamete is if it is heterozygous (Rr).

If all the offspring of our test cross were plants producing round seed, then no definite conclusions could be drawn, since both parental genotypes (Rr and RR) are capable of producing such offspring. However, provided a large number of offspring are produced, the absence of ones producing wrinkled seeds would strongly indicate that the unknown genotype was RR. Had it been Rr, half the offspring should have produced wrinkled seeds. While it would be theoretically possible for no wrinkled seeds to arise, this would be highly improbable where the sample was large.

It is possible to perform a dihybrid test cross. A plant which produces round, yellow seeds has four possible genotypes, namely: RRGG, RrGG, RRGg and RrGg. To determine the genotype of such a plant, it must be crossed with one producing wrinkled, green seeds. Such a plant has only one possible genotype, rrgg, and produces only one type of gamete, namely rg. The outcome of each of the crosses is shown in Table 7.3.

From the table it can be seen that the unknown genotypes can be identified from the results of the test cross as follows. If the offspring contain at least one plant producing wrinkled, yellow seeds, the unknown genotype is RrGG; if round, green seeds it is RRGg, and if wrinkled, green seeds it is RrGg. If the number of offspring is large and *all* produce round, yellow seeds it is highly probable that the genotype is RRGG.

7.3 Sex determination

In humans there are twenty-three pairs of chromosomes. Of these, twenty-two pairs are identical in both sexes. The twenty-third pair, however, is different in the male from the female. The twenty-two identical pairs are called **autosomes** whereas the twenty-third pair are referred to as **sex chromosomes** or **heterosomes**. In females, the two sex chromosomes are identical and are called **X chromosomes**. In males, an X chromosome is also present, but the other of the pair is smaller in size and called the **Y chromosome**. Unlike other features of an organism, sex is determined by chromosomes rather than genes.

Humans of the genotype XXY arise from time to time and are phenotypically male, while genotypes with just one X chromosome (XO) are phenotypically female. This suggests that it is the presence of the Y chromosome which makes a human male; in its absence the sex is female. How then does the Y chromosome determine maleness? The Y chromosome possesses several copies of a **testicular differentiating gene** which codes for the production of a substance which causes the undifferentiated gonads to become testes. In the absence of this gene and hence this substance, the gonads develop into ovaries.

It can be seen that in humans the female produces gametes which all contain an X chromosome and are therefore the same. She is called the **homogametic sex** ('same gametes'). The male, however, produces gametes of two genetic types: one which contains an X chromosome, the other a Y chromosome. The male is called the **heterogametic sex** ('different gametes').

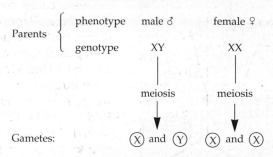

Offspring	♂ gametes	
♀ gametes	X	Y
X	XX	XY
X	XX	XY

Sex ratio   1 female : 1 male

7.4   Linkage

For just twenty-three pairs of chromosomes to determine the many thousands of different human characteristics, it follows that each chromosome must possess many different genes. Any two genes which occur on the same chromosome are said to be **linked**. All the genes on a single chromosome form a **linkage group**.

Under normal circumstances, all the linked genes remain together during cell division and so pass into the gamete, and hence the offspring, together. They do not therefore segregate in accordance with Mendel's Law of Independent Assortment. Fig. 7.1 shows the different gametes produced if a pair of genes A and B are linked rather than on separate chromosomes.

7.4.1 Crossing over and recombination

It is known that genes for flower colour and fruit colour in tomatoes are on the same chromosome. Plants with yellow flowers bear red fruit, those with white flowers bear yellow fruit. If the two types are crossed, the following results are obtained.

Let R = allele for red fruit (dominant) and
    r = allele for yellow fruit (recessive)
   W = allele for yellow flowers (dominant) and
   w = allele for white flowers (recessive)

If genes A and B occur on the same chromosome i.e. are linked

Only one homologous pair is needed to accommodate all four alleles

Possible types of gamete

If genes A and B occur on separate chromosomes i.e. are not linked

Two homologous pairs are needed to accommodate all four alleles

According to Mendel's Law of Independent Assortment, any one of a pair of contrasted characters may combine with any of another pair. There are thus four different possible types of gamete

Fig. 7.1 Comparison of gametes produced by an organism heterozygous for two genes A and B, when they are linked and not linked.

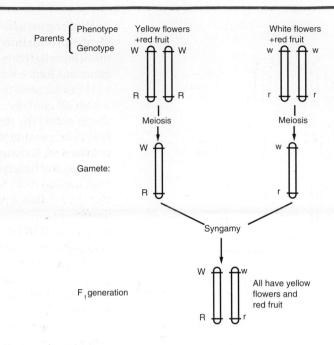

If the F$_1$ generation is intercrossed (i.e. self-pollinated), the following results would be expected:

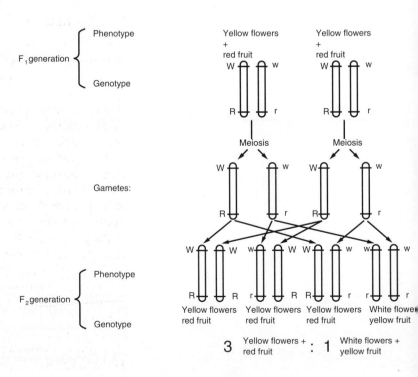

When the actual cross is performed, however, the following results are typical if 100 F$_2$ plants are produced:

Yellow flowers and red fruit	68
Yellow flowers and yellow fruit	7
White flowers and red fruit	7
White flowers and yellow fruit	18

F₁ generation   Phenotype   Yellow flower
red fruit

Genotype

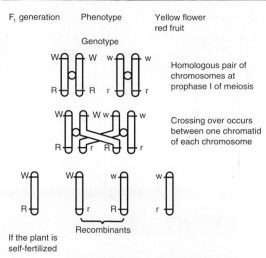

Homologous pair of
chromosomes at
prophase I of meiosis

Crossing over occurs
between one chromatid
of each chromosome

Recombinants

If the plant is
self-fertilized

F₂ generation:	♂ gametes			
♀ gametes	WR	Wr	wR	wr
WR	WWRR	WWRr	WwRR	WwRr
Wr	WWRr	WWrr	WwRr	Wwrr
wR	WwRR	WwRr	wwRR	wwRr
wr	WwRr	Wwrr	wwRr	wwrr

New combinations WWrr and Wwrr (yellow flowers, yellow fruit)
wwRR and wwRr (white flowers, red fruit)

What then is the explanation? Could it be that the two characters are not linked, but occur on separate chromosomes? If this were so, it would be a normal dihybrid cross, and a 9:3:3:1 ratio should be found. For 100 plants this would mean a 56:19:19:6 distribution. This is sufficiently different from the actual ratio of 68:7:7:18 which was obtained for it to be discounted. For the answer, we have to go back to Section 6.3 and the events in prophase I of meiosis. During this stage portions of the chromatids of homologous chromosomes were exchanged in the process called crossing over. Could this be the explanation as to how the two unexpected phenotypes (yellow flowers/yellow fruit and white flowers/red fruit) came about? To find out, let us consider the same F₁ intercross as before but assume that in one parent crossing over took place and this plant was subsequently self-pollinated (see opposite).

The new combinations are thus the result of crossing over in prophase I of meiosis. These new combinations are called **recombinants**. As shown, this cross produces a 9:3:3:1 ratio. However, in practice, crossing over will not always occur between the two genes. In some cases it may not occur at all; in others it may occur in such a way that the two genes are not separated. In these circumstances the only gametes are WR and wr. For this reason plants with yellow flowers and red fruit, and those with white flowers and yellow fruit, occur in greater numbers than expected.

7.4.2 Sex linkage

Sex linkage refers to the carrying of genes on the sex chromosomes. These genes determine body characters and have nothing to do with sex. The X chromosome carries many such genes, the Y chromosome has very few. Features linked on the Y chromosome will only arise in the heterogametic (XY) sex, i.e. males in humans. Features linked on the X chromosome may arise in either sex.

Two well known sex-linked genes in humans are those causing haemophilia and red–green colour-blindness. Both are linked to the X chromosome and both occur almost exclusively in males. For the condition to arise in females requires the double recessive state and as the recessive allele is relatively rare in the population this is unlikely to occur. In females the recessive allele is normally masked by the appropriate dominant allele which occurs on the other X chromosome. These heterozygous females are not themselves affected but are capable of passing the recessive allele to their offspring. For this reason such females are termed **carriers**. When the recessive allele occurs in males it expresses itself because the Y chromosome cannot carry any corresponding dominant allele. The inheritance of red–green colour-blindness is illustrated below.

Normal sight is dominant over red–green colour-blindness. Therefore let B represent the allele for normal sight and b represent the allele for colour-blindness

As this gene is carried on the X chromosome, its alleles are represented as X^B and X^b respectively. In humans the male is the heterogametic sex (XY) and the female is the homogametic sex (XX).

PROJECT

The Ishihara test can be used to find out if someone is red-green colour-blind

1. Use this test to find out how much more common is the incidence of red–green colour-blindness in boys than in girls.

2. Are there any who are colour-blind in one eye and not in the other?

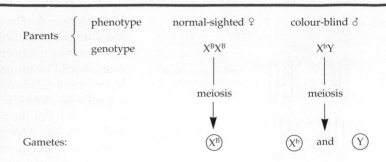

Parents { phenotype   normal-sighted ♀   colour-blind ♂

genotype $X^B X^B$ $X^b Y$

meiosis   meiosis

Gametes: X^B X^b and Y

♀ gametes	♂ gametes	
	X^b	Y
X^B	$X^B X^b$	$X^B Y$

50% normal-sighted carrier ♀ ($X^B X^b$)
50% normal-sighted ♂ ($X^B Y$)

F_1 intercross { phenotype   normal-sighted carrier ♀   normal-sighted ♂

genotype $X^B X^b$ $X^B Y$

meiosis   meiosis

Gametes: X^B X^b X^B Y

F_2 generation:

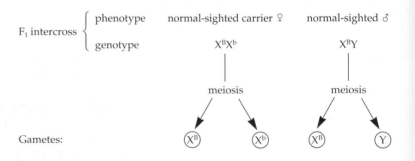

♀ gametes	♂ gametes	
	X^B	Y
X^B	$X^B X^B$	$X^B Y$
X^b	$X^B X^b$	$X^b Y$

25% normal-sighted ♀ ($X^B X^B$)   25% normal-sighted ♂ ($X^B Y$)
25% normal-sighted carrier ♀ ($X^B X^b$)   25% colour-blind ♂ ($X^b Y$)

Did you know?

One person in 20 is colour-blind

A study of the crosses reveals that the recessive gene causing colour-blindness is exchanged from one sex to the other at each generation. The father passes it to his daughters, who thus become carriers. The daughters in turn may pass it to their sons, who are thus colour-blind. This pattern of inheritance is perhaps more obvious when viewed another way. As the male is XY, his Y chromosome must have been inherited from his father as the mother does not possess a Y chromosome. The X chromosome and hence colour-blindness must therefore have been inherited from the mother. The colour-blind male can only donate his X chromosome to his daughters as it is bound to fuse with another

X chromosome – the only type the mother produces. Colour-blind females can only arise from a cross between a carrier female and a colour-blind male. As both types are rare in the population, the chance of this happening is very small indeed. Even then, there is only a one in four chance of any single child of such a cross being a colour-blind female.

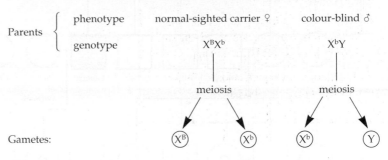

Parents $\left\{\begin{array}{l}\text{phenotype} \\ \text{genotype}\end{array}\right.$ normal-sighted carrier ♀ $\qquad$ colour-blind ♂

$X^B X^b$ $\qquad\qquad$ $X^b Y$

meiosis $\qquad$ meiosis

Gametes: X^B $\qquad$ X^b $\qquad$ X^b $\qquad$ Y

Offspring genotypes:

♀ gametes	♂ gametes	
	X^b	Y
X^B	$X^B X^b$	$X^B Y$
X^b	$X^b X^b$	$X^b Y$

25% normal-sighted carrier ♀ ($X^B X^b$) $\qquad$ 25% colour-blind ♂ ($X^b Y$)
25% normal-sighted ♂ ($X^B Y$) $\qquad$ 25% colour-blind ♀ ($X^b X^b$)

The inheritance of haemophilia follows a similar pattern to that of colour-blindness. Haemophilia is the inability of the blood to clot leading to slow and persistent bleeding, especially in the joints. Unlike colour-blindness it is potentially lethal. For this reason, the recessive allele causing it is even rarer in the population. Haemophiliac females are thus highly improbable, and in any case are unlikely to have children as the onset of menstruation at puberty is often fatal. Haemophilia is the result of an individual being unable to produce one of the many clotting factors, namely **factor 8** or **anti-haemophiliac globulin (AHG)** (see Focus on p. 96). The extraction of this factor from donated blood now permits haemophiliacs to lead near-normal lives, although they still run the same risk of conveying the disease to their children.

Any mutant recessive allele, such as that causing haemophilia, is normally rapidly diluted among the many normal alleles in a population. Its expression is thus a rare event. If, however, there is close breeding between members of a family in which a mutant gene exists, the chances of it expressing itself are enhanced. This accounts for the higher than normal occurrence of the haemophiliac gene among members of various European royal families. The origin of this particular gene can be traced back to England's Queen Victoria, who had a haemophiliac son, Leopold Duke of Albany. Prior to this there was no history of the gene among the royal family, although it existed elsewhere in the population. In order to marry someone of similar status, members of the European royal families were limited in their choice of partners and tended to marry within a relatively small circle. In effect, the gene pool was very restricted. As a result

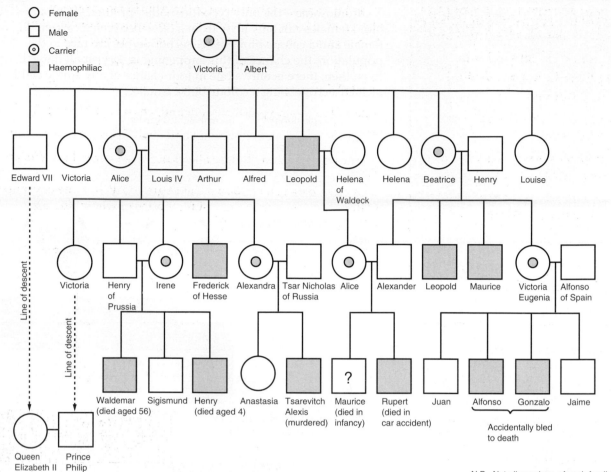

Fig. 7.2 Transmission of haemophilia from Queen Victoria

N.B. Not all members of each family are shown.

there was a disproportionately large number of haemophiliacs in these families. Fig. 7.2 traces the inheritance of this gene. The present English royal family is unaffected, as it is descended from Edward VII who did not inherit the haemophilia gene. The chart also illustrates another method of representing sex-linked crosses.

It is unusual to find dominant mutant genes linked to the X chromosome in humans, but one example is the congenital absence of incisor teeth. These conditions occur in both sexes but are more common in females as they have two X chromosomes. Genes linked to the Y chromosome are very rare, but hairy ear rims are an example.

7.5   Allelic interaction

Up to now we have looked at inheritance in a straightforward way – the black and white of genetics so to speak. We now turn our attention to the less straightforward situations – the many shades of grey which exist when alleles interact in different ways.

7.5.1 Multiple alleles

All examples so far studied have involved a gene having two alternative alleles. We now look at a situation where a gene has more than two possible alleles.

PROJECT

Surveys can be carried out among your fellow students to find, for example:

1. The relationships between skin, hair and eye colour.

2. The proportions of tongue-rollers and non-rollers; ear-lobe types, etc.

3. If there are any correlations in laterality studies, for example, between handedness and
   (a) eye dominance
   (b) arm folding
   (c) volumes of hands
   (d) lengths of fingers, etc.

TABLE 7.4 **Possible genotypes of blood groups in the ABO system**

Blood group	Possible genotypes
A	I^AI^A or I^AI^O
B	I^BI^B or I^BI^O
AB	I^AI^B
O	I^OI^O

In humans the inheritance of the ABO blood groups is determined by a gene I which has three different alleles. Any two of these can occur at a single locus at any one time.

Allele A causes production of antigen A on red blood cells.

Allele B causes production of antigen B on red blood cells.

Allele O causes no production of antigens on red blood cells.

Alleles A and B are codominant and allele O is recessive to both.

The transmission of these alleles occurs in normal Mendelian fashion.

A cross between an individual of group AB and one of group O therefore gives rise to individuals none of whom possess either parental blood group.

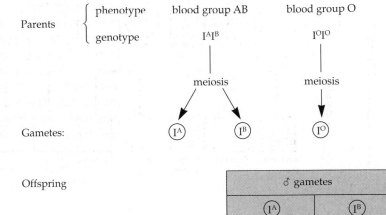

50% blood group A (I^AI^O)
50% blood group B (I^BI^O)

A cross between certain individuals of blood group A and certain individuals of blood group B may produce offspring with any one of the four blood groups.

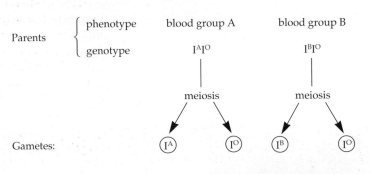

25% blood group A (I^AI^O)   25% blood group AB (I^AI^B)
25% blood group B (I^BI^O)   25% blood group O (I^OI^O)

135

Paternity suits

Although blood groups cannot prove who is the father of a child, it is possible to use their inheritance to show that an individual could not possibly be the father. Imagine a mother who is blood group B having a child of blood group O. She claims the father is a man whose blood group is found to be AB. As the child is group O its only possible genotype is $I^O I^O$. It must therefore have inherited one I^O allele from each parent. The mother, if $I^B I^O$, could donate such an allele. The man with blood group AB can only have the genotype $I^A I^B$. He is unable to donate an I^O allele and cannot therefore be the father.

7.5.2 Pleiotropy

We have looked at situations so far where an allele determines one character. Sometimes however an allele may affect more than one character. Such an allele is termed **pleiotropic**. An example was given on page 94 where the allele for cystic fibrosis caused the production of especially viscous mucus. One effect was the blockage of the pancreatic duct leading to poor digestion as a result of the pancreatic enzymes not being able to enter the duodenum. These enzymes may therefore accumulate in the pancreas, so digesting its cells including the Islets of Langerhans which produce insulin. Unable to produce insulin the patient suffers diabetes – a second effect of the allele. The viscous mucus also blocks alveoli and bronchioles, leading to breathing problems – a third effect.

7.6   Gene interaction

We have examined how alleles at a single locus (i.e. the alleles of a single gene) may interact and we have called this 'allelic interaction'. Sometimes the alleles of more than one gene (i.e. at more than one locus) interact. This we call **gene interaction**, although in practice it is still the alleles of these genes which are influencing each other.

7.6.1 Simple interaction

This occurs where a group of genes or a **gene complex** act together to determine a single character. An example in humans is the inheritance of skin pigmentation which is controlled by two genes A and B. An individual with the genotype AABB produces darkly pigmented skin whereas an individual with the genotype aabb has white unpigmented skin. A mating between these two types produces an intermediate skin colour (genotype AaBb). In the F_2 generation skin colour varies from dark (AABB) through dark brown (AABb or AaBB), half-coloured (AAbb or AaBb or aaBB), light brown (Aabb or aaBb) to white (aabb).

7.7 Questions

1. Pituitary dwarfism is an inherited condition in humans in which affected individuals have very short limbs. The allele for pituitary dwarfism, d, is recessive to the allele for normal limbs, D, and its locus is situated on the X-chromosome. The family tree shows part of one affected family.

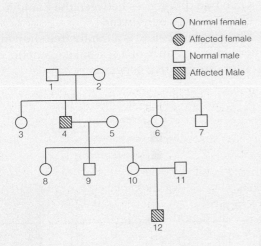

(a) Identify and explain **one** piece of evidence from this family tree to show that the allele for pituitary dwarfism is recessive to the allele for normal length limbs. *(2 marks)*

(b) Explain why the genotype of:
  (i) individual 10 must be X^DX^d; *(1 mark)*
  (ii) individual 11 must be X^DY; *(1 mark)*

(c) As their son showed pituitary dwarfism, individuals 10 and 11 consulted a genetic counsellor before the woman became pregnant again.

  (i) What prediction would have been made about the probability of the couple's next child showing pituitary dwarfism? *(1 mark)*

  (ii) Complete the genetic diagram below to explain your answer.

Individual 10   Individual 11
Parental phenotypes ....
Parental genotypes ....
Gametes ....

Offspring genotypes...
Offspring phenotypes ....
(3 marks)
(Total 8 marks)

NEAB February 1995, Paper BY2, No. 5

2. (a) Describe the process by which blood clots when the body is wounded. *(4 marks)*

(b) Haemophilia is an inherited condition in which the blood fails to clot readily. One type of haemophilia is determined by the presence of a recessive allele of a blood-clotting gene on the X chromosome.

  (i) What is a gene? *(1 mark)*

  (ii) Suggest how the location of this blood-clotting gene might explain the fact that more males than females suffer from this type of haemophilia. *(3 marks)*

The diagram shows the inheritance of haemophilia in the members of one family.

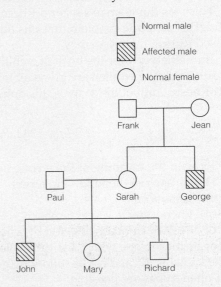

Use the symbols X^H to represent the normal allele for blood clotting and X^h to represent the defective allele.

(c) Giving an explanation for your answer in each case, what is the genotype of each of the following members of the family:
  (i) Sarah;
  (ii) Richard? *(4 marks)*

(d) What is the probability of Mary possessing a defective allele for blood-clotting? Explain your answer. *(3 marks)*

(e) Before modern medical techniques existed, haemophilia was a potentially lethal condition. Suggest why the allele for haemophilia has survived in human populations. *(3 marks)*

(f) At present, some haemophiliacs are treated with donated blood products which supply the missing protein which will enable the blood to clot.

  (i) Suggest **one** disadvantage of obtaining the missing protein from this source. *(1 mark)*

(ii) Suggest how microorganisms can be made to produce proteins such as this by the process of genetic engineering. (5 marks)
(Total 24 marks)

AEB June 1993, Paper 2, No. 3

3. A woman of blood group A Rhesus-negative claimed that a man whose blood group was B and Rhesus-positive was the father of her child. The child's blood group was O and Rhesus positive.

(a) Give the possible ABO and Rhesus genotypes of the:
   (i) woman; (1 mark)
   (ii) man; (1 mark)
   (iii) child. (1 mark)
(b) Could the man have been the father of the child? Explain your answer. (2 marks)
(c) This was the woman's second Rhesus-positive child. Describe **one** problem that this might have caused during the pregnancy. (2 marks)
(d) Immediately after the birth of a child most Rhesus-negative women are given an injection of anti-Rhesus antibodies. Why is this done? (1 mark)
(Total 8 marks)

AEB June 1992, Paper 1, No. 3

4. (a) Explain the meaning of the term *gene*. (3 marks)
(b) Define each of the following terms.
   (i) Genotype (1 mark)
   (ii) Phenotype (1 mark)
(c) Coat colour in rats is affected by a number of genes including one which has three alleles at the same locus, **R**, **R**^{h} and **r**. The following genotypes and phenotypes are possible.

Genotype	Phenotype
RR, R R^h**, Rr**	Full colour
R^h **R**^{h}	Siamese (white with coloured extremities)
R^h **r**	Himalayan (white with coloured extremities, less colour than a Siamese)
rr	White

A breeder buys a rat that has a full coat colour, but he is unsure whether the genotype is **RR** or **R R**^{h}. Explain the simplest way in which he could determine the genotype of this rat. (5 marks)
(d) Coat colour is affected by a second gene which has two alleles. The dominant allele, **A**, gives a brown coat and the recessive allele, **a**, gives a black coat. In a rat with full colour all the fur is brown or black; in a Siamese or Himalayan rat only the extremities are coloured brown or black.
   (i) A rat with genotype **AA RR** is crossed with a rat of genotype **aa R**^{h} **R**^{h}, what will be the genotype of the offspring? (1 mark)

(ii) These offspring are allowed to interbreed. Draw a genetic diagram to show the results of this cross. (4 marks)
(iii) What would be the expected phenotypic ratio in the offspring from the cross in (ii)? (1 mark)
(Total 16 marks)

ULEAC June 1995, Paper 1, No. 13

5. (a) Give **two** differences between the X and Y chromosomes of humans. (2 marks)
(b) The diagram below is a family tree showing the pattern of inheritance of a sex-linked genetic disorder through five generations.

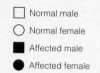

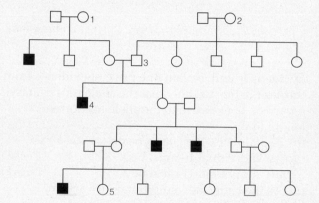

(i) Identify **two** features of the inheritance of this disorder that are characteristic of sex-linked inheritance. (2 marks)
(ii) The disorder is caused by a recessive allele of a single gene. Using the symbol **A** to represent the normal allele and **a** to represent the recessive allele, write down the most likely genotypes of individuals 1, 2, 3 and 4. (4 marks)
(c) Individual 5 is engaged to be married. Her future partner comes from a family with no history of this genetic disorder. They plan to have several children.
   (i) If individual 5's first child is a boy, what is the probability that he will have the disorder? (1 mark)
   (ii) If individual 5's first child is a girl, what is the probability that she will have the disorder? (1 mark)
(d) The diagram overleaf shows a small part of the same family tree, involving individuals 1 and 3. If this disorder had been caused by a dominant allele rather than a recessive allele, the pattern of inheritance would be different.

Using information in the complete tree, in the space provided, re-draw this part of the tree to show this different pattern of inheritance.

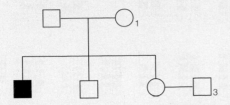

(4 marks)
(Total 14 marks)

ULEAC June 1995, Paper 3, No. 8

6. (a) Distinguish between the terms *genotype* and *phenotype* (3 marks)
  (b) Explain the meaning of the following:
   (i) 'segregation of factors' (Mendel's 1st law);
   (ii) 'independent assortment of factors' (Mendel's 2nd law) (4 marks)

The fruit fly, *Drosophila*, has the same arrangement of sex chromosomes as humans (two X chromosomes in the female and one X and one Y chromosome in the male). In this insect, the inheritance of eye colour is sex-linked. The normal red eye colour is dominant to white eye colour.

If a homozygous red-eyed female $X^R X^R$ and a white-eyed male $X^r Y$ are mated, all the offspring (F_1) are red-eyed. When the latter are intercrossed, their offspring (F_2) produce an average ratio of 2 red-eyed females to 1 red-eyed male to 1 white-eyed male.
  (c) Draw diagrams to illustrate the genetic basis of the crosses from the parents to the F_1 and then from the F_1 to F_2. (6 marks)
  (d) What would be the result of a cross between a red-eyed male and a white-eyed female? (3 marks)
  (e) (i) State **two** examples of sex linkage in humans.
   (ii) Explain why it is more difficult to study inheritance in humans rather than fruit flies. (5 marks)
(Total 21 marks)

UCLES June 1992, Paper 2, No. 3

7. Read through the passage and answer the questions that follow.

Phenylketonuria (PKU) is an inherited disease caused by a recessive allele. Sufferers lack the enzyme phenylalanine hydroxylase in the liver and are, therefore, unable to oxidize the amino acid phenylalanine to tyrosine. Consequently, phenylalanine and toxic derivatives build up in the blood. Affected children are phenotypically normal at birth, but the production of toxins soon results in severe mental subnormality.

In 1963, Guthrie and Susi developed a sensitive test for one of the toxins, phenylpyruvic acid. The test requires only a small blood sample and is used for detecting PKU in newborn infants.
  (a) PKU is an inherited disease caused by the lack of a particular enzyme. What is the connection between a gene and an enzyme? (2 marks)
  (b) Explain how the lack of just one enzyme can have such profound consequences for the development of a child. (2 marks)
  (c) The figure shows a family pedigree for PKU.

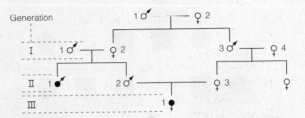

Key

♂ = male

♀ = female

Shaded symbols = PKU sufferer

   (i) What is the evidence from the pedigree in the figure above that the gene for PKU is recessive?
   (ii) What is the evidence from the pedigree that the gene for PKU is not on the X chromosome?
   (iii) The individual III-1 has PKU and is the offspring of a marriage between first cousins II-2 and II-3. Explain why genetic counsellors usually advise against such marriages among families with a known history of genetic disease.
   (iv) What is the probability that the next child of II-2 and II-3 will have PKU? (7 marks)
  (d) The frequency of carriers (heterozygotes) for PKU in the general population is about 2%. Is genetic counselling likely to be successful in removing the gene for PKU from the human population? Explain your answer. (3 marks)
  (e) Explain how it is possible for a PKU child to remain healthy while in its mother's womb. (3 marks)
  (f) State **two** of the likely benefits of ensuring that all newborn babies are tested for PKU. (2 marks)
  (g) PKU infants are placed on a diet containing protein with relatively little phenylalanine, to prevent phenylalanine from accumulating. Explain why this amino acid is not removed entirely from the diet of a PKU patient. (2 marks)

(h) The amino acid tyrosine is used by the thyroid gland to make thyroxine. Describe and explain the effects that a lack of tyrosine would have on a child's development.

(*4 marks*)
(*Total 25 marks*)

UCLES June 1992, Paper 3 (Option 3), No. 1

8 *(a)* The pedigree shows the inheritance of ellipsocytosis, a condition which causes oval erythrocytes in humans. Only those with the dominant allele (E) are affected. The Rhesus phenotype caused by the presence of the dominant allele (R) is also shown.

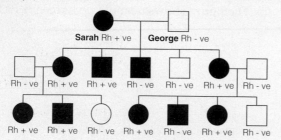

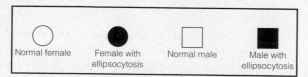

(i) Assuming that the gene for ellipsocytosis and the gene for the Rhesus factor are found on the same chromosome. Draw a fully labelled genetic diagram of the cross between Sarah and George. (*6 marks*)

(ii) What evidence is there, in the data provided, that the genes for ellipsocytosis and the Rhesus factor are linked on the same chromosome? (*2 marks*)

(iii) Is there any evidence, in the data, that either of the genes is sex-linked? Explain your answer. (*2 marks*)

(iv) One form of ellipsocytosis can produce harmful effects. A man and his father suffer from this form of the disease, but the man's mother was normal. The man has married a normal woman.

Assuming that the harmful allele can be detected in a fetus, what advice might be given to the couple who are worried about having an affected baby? (*2 marks*)

(b) The diagram at the top of the next column shows the karyotype of an individual affected by Klinefelter's syndrome.

(i) Giving your reasons indicate the gender of this individual. (*1 mark*)

(ii) What is this **type** of chromosomal mutation called? Suggest how it could arise during gametogenesis. (*3 marks*)

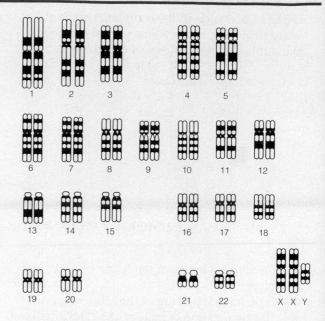

(iii) Some males have an XYY genotype. Such males are usually fertile. If such a man married and had children by a normal female, what possible genotypes could arise in their offspring? Your answer should include a labelled genetic diagram to explain this.

(*4 marks*)

(c) Explain how the *gene* mutation which causes sickle cell anaemia could give rise to changes in the gene pool. (*4 marks*)
(*Total 12 marks*)

AEB June 1995, Paper 2, No. 3

9. Write an essay on the involvement of chromosomes and genes in the production of different genotypes and phenotypes. (*30 marks*)

ULEAC June 1994, Paper 1, No. 15(b)

10. Familial hypophosphataemia is a sex-linked condition caused by a dominant allele on the X chromosome. The pedigree of a family with this condition is shown in the diagram below.

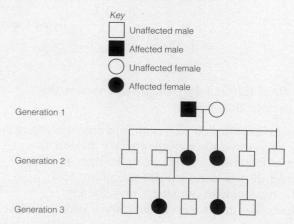

(a) What is meant by the term *sex linkage*?

(2 marks)

(b) Explain why none of the males in generation 2 suffers from hypophosphataemia. (2 marks)

(c) If person **A** were to have another son, what is the probability that this son would suffer from hypophosphataemia? Give a reason for your answer. (2 marks)

(Total 6 marks)

ULEAC June 1994, Paper 3, No. 3

11. The ABO blood group is governed by a set of three multiple alleles, I^A, I^B and I^O. I^A and I^B are codominant, I^O is recessive. Another blood group system is known as the MN system. The MN blood groups are governed by a pair of codominant alleles giving three possible blood groups, M, MN and N.

a) A man of blood group B married a woman of unknown ABO blood group. They had three children. One of the children had blood group A, one had blood group AB and one had blood group O.

   (i) State the genotypes of the parents and given an explanation for your answer.

(5 marks)

   (ii) Draw a genetic diagram to show the inheritance of ABO blood groups in this family.

(2 marks)

(b) In another family, the man is accusing his wife of infidelity. Their first and second children, whom they both claim, are of blood groups O and AB respectively. The third child, whom the man disclaims, is blood group B.

Can this information be used to support the man's accusation that the third child is not his? Give the reasoning for your answer. (4 marks)

(c) Another test was carried out using the MN blood group system. In the test, it was found that the third child was blood group M. The man was blood group N.

Explain why this shows that the man is unlikely to be the child's father. (4 marks)

(Total 15 marks)

ULEAC June 1993, Paper 1, No. 12

12. The diagram shows the inheritance of cystic fibrosis among the members of a family.

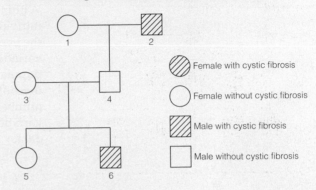

Female with cystic fibrosis

Female without cystic fibrosis

Male with cystic fibrosis

Male without cystic fibrosis

(a) Explain the evidence from this diagram that the allele for cystic fibrosis is recessive. (2 marks)

(b) What is the probability that the next child born to individuals 3 and 4 will

   (i) possess the cystic fibrosis allele; (1 mark)

   (ii) show the condition of cystic fibrosis?

(1 mark)

(c) Explain why possession of the cystic fibrosis alleles results in the formation of thick mucus in the lungs. (2 marks)

(Total 6 marks)

NEAB June 1995, Paper BY08, No. 7

8 Genetic change and variation

Within any given population there are variations among individual organisms. It is this variation which forms the basis of the evolutionary theory of Darwin. There are two basic forms of variation: **continuous variation**, where the individuals in a population show a gradation from one extreme to the other, and **discontinuous (discrete) variation**, where there is a limited number of distinct forms within the population. Any study of variation inevitably involves the collection of large quantities of data.

8.1 Methods of recording variation

The investigation of variation within a population may involve recording the number of individuals which possess a particular feature, e.g. black hair. On the other hand, it may involve recording the number of individuals which fall within a set range of values, e.g. those weighing between 1 kg and 10 kg. What is being measured in both cases is the **frequency distribution**. This may be presented in a number of ways. To illustrate each method the same set of data is used throughout (Table 8.1), although it is not really suitable for some methods of presentation.

8.1.1 Table of data

Tabulation is the simplest means of presenting data. It is a useful method of recording information initially but is less useful for demonstrating the relationship between two variables.

8.1.2 Line graph

A graph typically has two axes, each of which measures a variable. One variable has fixed values which are selected by the experimenter. This is called the **independent variable**. The other variable is the measurement taken and as such is not selected by the experimenter. This is called the **dependent variable**. In Table 8.1, 'height' is the independent variable and 'frequency' the dependent variable. The values of the independent variable are plotted along the horizontal axis (also known as the x axis or abscissa) and the values of the dependent variable are plotted along the vertical axis (also known as the y axis or ordinate). The

TABLE 8.1 **Frequency of heights (measured to the nearest 2 cm) of a sample of humans**

Height/cm	Frequency
140	0
142	1
144	1
146	6
148	23
150	48
152	90
154	175
156	261
158	352
160	393
162	462
164	458
166	443
168	413
170	264
172	177
174	97
176	63
178	46
180	17
182	7
184	4
186	0
188	1
190	0

corresponding values of the two variables can be plotted as points on the graph known as **coordinates**. These points may then be joined to give a line or smooth curve, as in Fig. 8.1.

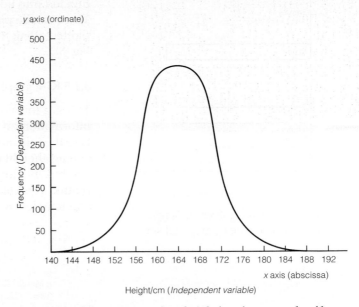

Fig. 8.1 *Graph of frequency against height/cm for a sample of humans*

8.1.3 Histogram

Axes are drawn in much the same way as for a line graph. The values for the independent variable on the *x* axis are, however, normally reduced, often by grouping the data into convenient classes. For example, the twenty-six values for height used on the line graph may be reduced to ten by grouping the heights into sets of 5 cm, e.g. 140–145, 145–150 etc. Instead of plotting points, vertical columns are drawn. The method is illustrated in Fig. 8.2.

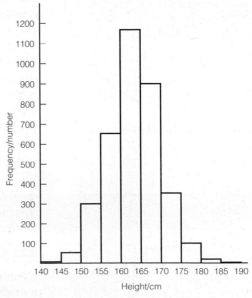

Fig. 8.2 *Histogram showing height frequencies in a sample human population*

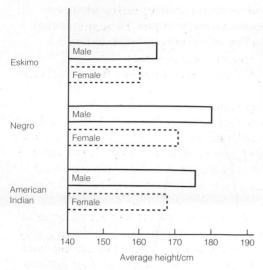

Fig. 8.3 Bar graph showing average height variation according to racial group and sex

8.1.4 Bar graph

This is similar to a histogram except that a non-numerical value is plotted on the y axis. Let us suppose the sample population is divided into non-numerical sets such as racial groups and sex. These can be plotted along the y axis, with average height being plotted along the x axis. The resultant bar graph is shown in Fig. 8.3.

8.1.5 Kite graph

This is a form of bar graph, which gives more detailed information on the frequency of a non-numerical variable. To take the information given in Fig. 8.3, it simply reveals the average height of each group and not the frequency at different heights. In a kite graph, the frequency of particular heights is plotted vertically for certain non-numerical variables, e.g. males and females. A kite graph is shown in Fig. 8.4.

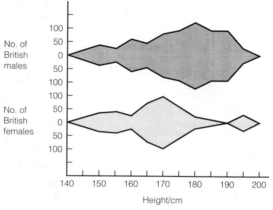

Fig. 8.4 Kite graphs to show the height frequency for British males and females in the population sample

8.1.6 Pie chart

Pie charts are a simple and clearly visible means of showing how a whole sample is divided up into specified parts. A circle (the pie) represents the whole and it is subdivided into different sized sections according to the relative proportions of each constituent part. To be effective the pie chart should not be divided into a large number of portions, nor should it be used when it is necessary to read off precise information from the chart. It is simply a means of giving an idea of relative proportions. Fig. 8.5 shows a pie chart depicting the proportions of our sample which fall within broad height ranges.

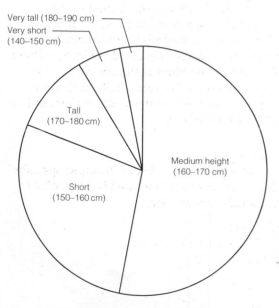

Fig. 8.5 Pie chart to show the relative proportions of five height categories in a population sample

8.2 Types of variation

8.2.1 Continuous variation

Certain characteristics within a population vary only very marginally between one individual and the next. This results in a gradation from one extreme to the other, called continuous variation. The height and weight of organisms are two

PROJECT

Determine the distribution of characteristics of your fellow students. The list is endless, but examples would be:

(a) heights and weights of males and females of different ages
(b) lengths of middle fingers
(c) sizes of feet
(d) lengths or widths of ears etc.

characteristics which show such a gradation. If a frequency distribution for such a characteristic is plotted, a bell-shaped graph similar to that in Fig. 8.1 is obtained. This is called a **normal distribution curve** or **Gaussian curve** (after the mathematician Fredrick Gauss). It is discussed further in Section 8.2.2.

Characteristics which show continuous variation are controlled not by one, but by the combined effect of a number of genes, called **polygenes**. Thus any character which results from the interaction of many genes is called a **polygenic character**. The effect of an individual gene is small, but their combined effect is marked. The random assortment of the genes during prophase I of meiosis ensures that individuals possess a range of genes from any polygenic complex. Where a group of genes all favouring the development of a tall individual combine, a very tall individual results. A combination of genes favouring small size results in a very short individual. These extremes are rare because it is probable that an individual will possess genes from both extremes. The combined effect of these genes produces individuals of intermediate height.

8.2.2 The normal distribution (Gaussian) curve

Fig. 8.6 shows a normal distribution curve; its bell-shape is typical for a feature which shows continuous variation, e.g. height in humans. The graph is symmetrical about a central value. Occasionally the curve is shifted slightly to one side. This is called a skewed distribution and is illustrated in Fig. 8.7. There are three main terms used in association with normal distribution curves, whether skewed or not. To illustrate these terms let us consider the values given in the table for the number of children in eleven different families.

The mean (arithmetic mean)
This is the average of a group of values. In our example opposite this is found by totalling the number of children in all families and dividing it by the number of families.

Total children in all families
$$= 0+1+1+1+2+2+3+4+6+6+7 = 33$$
Total number of families A–K = 11

Mean = $33 \div 11 = 3$

The mode
This is the single value of a group which occurs most often. In our example more families have one child than any other number. The mode is therefore equal to 1.

The median
This is the central or middle value of a set of values. In our example the values are already arranged in ascending order of the number of children in each family. There are eleven families. The sixth family in the series (family F) is therefore the middle family of the group. There are five families (A–E) with the same number or fewer children, and five families (G–K) with more children. As family F has two children the median is 2.

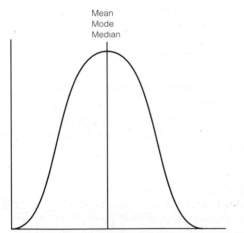

Mean
Mode
Median

Fig. 8.6 A normal distribution curve where the mean, mode and median have the same value

Family	Number of children
A	0
B	1
C	1
D	1
E	2
F	2
G	3
H	4
I	6
J	6
K	7

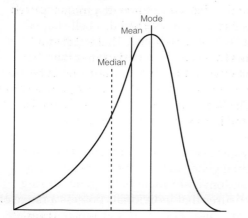

Fig. 8.7 A skewed distribution where the mean, mode and median have different values

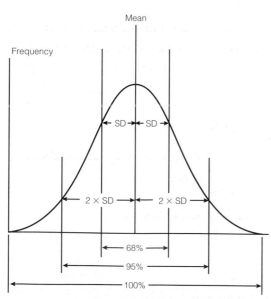

Fig. 8.8 The normal distribution curve showing the values for standard deviation

Fig 8.6 shows a typical symmetrical normal distribution curve in which the mean and mode (and often the median) have the same value.

Fig 8.7 shows a skewed distribution in which the mean, mode and median all have different values.

The mean height of a sample population gives a good indication of its relative height compared to other sample populations. It does not, however, give any indication of the distribution of height within the sample. Indeed, the mean can be misleading. A population made up of individuals who were either 140 or 180 cm tall would have a mean of 160 cm, and yet no single individual would be anywhere near this height. It is therefore useful to have a value which gives an indication of the range of height either side of the mean. This value is called the **standard deviation (SD)**. It is calculated as follows:

$$SD = \sqrt{\frac{\Sigma d^2}{n}}$$

Σ = the sum of
d = difference between each value in the sample and the mean
n = the total number of values in the sample

How then does the standard deviation provide information on the range within a sample? Let us suppose the mean height of a sample human population is 170 cm and its standard deviation is ±10 cm. This means that over two thirds (68%) of the sample have heights which are within 10 cm of 170 cm, i.e. 68% of the sample have heights between 160 cm and 180 cm. Furthermore we can say that 95% of the sample lie within two standard deviations of the mean. In our example two standard deviations = 2 × 10 = 20 cm. In other words, 95% of the sample have heights between 150 cm and 190 cm. Fig. 8.8 illustrates these values.

8.2.3 Discontinuous (discrete) variation

Certain features of individuals in a population do not show a gradation between extremes but instead fall into a limited number of distinct forms. There are no intermediate types. For example, humans may be separated into distinct sets according to their blood groups. In the ABO system there are just four groups: A, B, AB and O. Unlike continuous variation, which is controlled by many genes (polygenes), a feature which exhibits discontinuous variation is normally controlled by a single gene. This gene may have two or more alleles. Features exhibiting discontinuous variation are normally represented on histograms, bar graphs or pie charts.

8.3   The chi-squared test

Imagine tossing a coin 100 times. It is reasonable to expect it to land heads on 50 occasions and tails on 50 occasions. In practice it would be unusual if these results were obtained (try it if you like!). If it lands heads 55 times and tails only 45 times, does this mean the coin is weighted or biased in some way, or is it purely a chance deviation from the expected result?

The **chi-squared test** is the means by which the statistical validity of results such as these can be tested. It measures the extent of any deviation between the expected and observed results. This measure of deviation is called the **chi-squared value** and is represented by the Greek letter chi, shown squared, i.e. χ^2. To calculate this value the following equation is used:

$$\chi^2 = \sum \frac{d^2}{x}$$

where $\sum$ = the sum of

d = difference between observed and expected results (the deviation)

x = the expected result

Using our example of the coin tossed 100 times, we can calculate the chi-squared value. We must first calculate the deviation from the expected number of times the coin should land heads:

Expected number of heads in 100 tosses of the coin $(x) = 50$

Actual number of heads in 100 tosses of the coin $= 55$

Deviation (d) $\quad 5$

Therefore $\dfrac{d^2}{x} = \dfrac{5^2}{50} = \dfrac{25}{50} = 0.5$

We then make the same calculation for the coin landing tails.

Expected number of tails in 100 tosses of the coin $\quad (x) = 50$

Actual number of tails in 100 tosses of the coin $= 45$

Deviation (d) $\quad 5$

Therefore $\dfrac{d^2}{x} = \dfrac{5^2}{50} = \dfrac{25}{50} = 0.5$

The chi-squared value can now be calculated by adding these values:

Therefore $\chi^2 = 0.5 + 0.5 = 1.0$.

The whole calculation can be summarized thus:

$$\chi^2 = \sum \frac{d^2}{x}$$

$$\chi^2 = \overset{\text{Heads}}{\left[\frac{(55-50)^2}{50}\right]} + \overset{\text{Tails}}{\left[\frac{(50-45)^2}{50}\right]}$$

$$= \left[\frac{(5)^2}{50}\right] + \left[\frac{(5)^2}{50}\right]$$

$$= \frac{1}{2} + \frac{1}{2}$$

$$= 1.0$$

To find out whether this value is significant or not we need to use a chi-squared table, part of which is given in Table 8.2. Before trying to read these tables it is necessary to decide how

TABLE 8.2   **Part of a χ^2 table (based on Fisher)**

Degrees of freedom	Number of classes	χ^2							
1	2	0.00	0.10	0.45	1.32	2.71	3.84	5.41	6.64
2	3	0.02	0.58	1.39	2.77	4.61	5.99	7.82	9.21
3	4	0.12	1.21	2.37	4.11	6.25	7.82	9.84	11.34
4	5	0.30	1.92	3.36	5.39	7.78	9.49	11.67	13.28
5	6	0.55	2.67	4.35	6.63	9.24	11.07	13.39	15.09
Probability that deviation is due to chance alone		0.99 (99%)	0.75 (75%)	0.50 (50%)	0.25 (25%)	0.10 (10%)	0.05 (5%)	0.02 (2%)	0.01 (1%)

many **classes of results** there are in the investigation being carried out. In our case there are two classes of results, 'heads' and 'tails'. This corresponds to one degree of freedom. We now look along the row showing 2 classes (i.e. one degree of freedom) for our calculated value of 1.0. This lies between the values of 0.45 and 1.32 on the table. Looking down this column we see that this corresponds to a probability between 0.50 (50%) and 0.25 (25%). This means that the probability that chance alone could have produced the deviation is between 0.50 (50%) and 0.25 (25%). If this probability is greater than 0.05 (5%), the deviation is said to be **not significant**. In other words the deviation is due to chance. If the deviation is less than 0.05 (5%), the deviation is said to be **significant**. In other words, some factor other than chance is affecting the results. In our example the value is greater than 0.05 (5%) and so we assume the deviation is due to chance. Had we obtained 60 heads and 40 tails, a chi-squared value of slightly less than 0.05 (5%) would be obtained, in which case we would question the validity of the results and assume the coin might be weighted or biased in some way.

8.4   The *t*-test

While the chi-squared test can be used to test the statistical significance of discontinuous (discrete) variables the *t*-test is used to test the statistical significance of continuous variables (see Section 8.2). It therefore has less application in genetics and far more in other areas of biology such as ecology. It is nevertheless dealt with here because of its statistical nature and the use it makes of standard deviations. The *t*-test is used when a sample size is relatively small, e.g. under 30 readings/figures. The mean and standard deviation of these small samples are prone to error since a single 'extreme' reading will have a disproportionate effect. The *t*-test accounts for this error. For the *t*-test to be of use the data used have to conform to certain conditions; namely:

1. They must be related to one another.
2. They must be normally distributed (section 8.2.2).
3. They must have similar variances.
4. The sample size must be small.

TABLE 8.3 Yield of wheat for fertilizers 1 and 2

	Number of tonnes of wheat per plot	
	Fertilizer 1	Fertilizer 2
	5	4
	9	3
	11	6
	9	7
	10	5
	7	3
	5	3
	8	5
Total:	64	36
No. of plots:	8	8
Mean:	8	4.5

The *t*-test can be expressed as:

$$t = \frac{\overline{x}_1 - \overline{x}_2}{\sqrt{\dfrac{s_1^2}{n_1} + \dfrac{s_2^2}{n_2}}}$$

where $\overline{x}$ = mean of observations
n = number of observations (sample size)
s = standard deviation
(The suffixes 1 and 2 refer to samples 1 and 2 respectively.)

To take an example. A farmer wishes to decide which of two fertilizers gives the best crop yield for her crop of wheat. She divides one of her fields into 16 plots, 8 of which she treats with fertilizer 1 and eight with fertilizer 2. The number of tonnes of wheat obtained from each plot is given in Table 8.3.

The first stage of the *t*-test is to calculate the standard deviation for each sample (see Section 8.2.2). To do this we must calculate:

1. The mean of each sample (see Table 8.4)
2. The deviation of each reading from the mean (see Table 8.4)
3. The square of this deviation and the sum of the squares (see Table 8.4)

TABLE 8.4

Fertilizer 1			Fertilizer 2		
Observation (x)	Deviation from the mean ($x - \overline{x}_1$)	Square of the deviation ($x - \overline{x}_1$)^2	Observation (x)	Deviation from the mean ($x - \overline{x}_2$)	Square of the deviation ($x - \overline{x}_2$)^2
5	−3	9	4	−0.5	0.25
9	+1	1	3	−1.5	2.25
11	+3	9	6	+1.5	2.25
9	+1	1	7	+2.5	6.25
10	+2	4	5	+0.5	0.25
7	−1	1	3	−1.5	2.25
5	−3	9	3	−1.5	2.25
8	0	0	5	+0.5	0.25
Sum of squares of deviation:		34	Sum of squares of deviation:		16
Standard deviation $\sqrt{\dfrac{\Sigma(x - \overline{x}_1)^2}{n-1}}$		$\sqrt{\dfrac{34}{7}} = 2.2$	Standard deviation $\sqrt{\dfrac{\Sigma(x - \overline{x}_2)^2}{n-1}}$		$\sqrt{\dfrac{16}{7}} = 1.51$

To obtain the standard deviation, we saw in Section 8.2.2 that we divide the sum of the squares of deviation, $\Sigma(x - \overline{x})^2$ by the number of values in the sample (n) and then take the square root. However, it has been shown that when we use deviations from a sample mean, rather than a population mean, a better estimate of variance is given by dividing by $n - 1$ rather than n.

Thence we can now substitute in the equation:

$$t = \frac{\bar{x}_1 - \bar{x}_2}{\sqrt{\dfrac{s_1^2}{n_1} + \dfrac{s_2^2}{n_2}}}$$

$$t = \frac{8 - 4.5}{\sqrt{\dfrac{2.2^2}{8} + \dfrac{1.51^2}{8}}}$$

$$= \frac{3.5}{\sqrt{\dfrac{4.84}{8} + \dfrac{2.28}{8}}}$$

$$= \frac{3.5}{\sqrt{0.61 + 0.29}}$$

$$= \frac{3.5}{\sqrt{0.9}}$$

$$= \frac{3.5}{0.95}$$

$$= \mathbf{3.68}$$

Finally, to discover whether our value of 3.68 indicates whether the different readings are significant, or merely due to chance, we need to look up 3.68 on a statistical table called the t-table, part of which is reproduced as Table 8.5 To do this we need to know the degrees of freedom. This is calculated according to the formula:

degrees of freedom $(v) = (n_1 + n_2) - 2$
in our example: $\quad v = (8 + 8) - 2$
$\quad\quad\quad = 14.$

We now find that looking along the row for 14 degrees of freedom, our value of 3.68 lies between 2.98 and 4.14 which corresponds to a probability value of 0.01 and 0.001. This refers to the probability that chance alone is the reason for the difference between our two sets of data. In our example the probability that the different wheat yields when using our two fertilizers was pure chance was between one in one hundred ($p = 0.01$) and one in one thousand ($p = 0.001$). In other words it is more than 99% certain that the different yields were the result of differences in the two fertilizers (assuming all other factors in the experiment were constant).

8.5 Origins of variation

Variation may be due to the effect of the environment on an organism. For example, the action of sunlight on a light-coloured skin may result in its becoming darker. Such changes have little evolutionary significance as they are not passed from one generation to the next. Much more important to evolution are the inherited forms of variation which result from genetic changes. These genetic changes may be the result of the normal and frequent reshuffling of genes which occurs during sexual reproduction, or as a consequence of mutations.

TABLE 8.5

Degrees of freedom	Rejection level probabilities				
	$p = 0.1$	$p = 0.05$	$p = 0.02$	$p = 0.01$	$p = 0.001$
1	6.31	12.71	31.82	63.66	636.62
2	2.92	4.30	6.97	9.93	31.60
3	2.35	3.18	4.54	5.84	12.94
4	2.13	2.78	3.75	4.60	8.61
5	2.02	2.57	3.37	4.03	6.86
6	1.94	2.45	3.14	3.71	5.96
7	1.90	2.37	3.00	3.50	5.41
8	1.86	2.31	2.90	3.36	5.04
9	1.83	2.26	2.82	3.25	4.78
10	1.81	2.23	2.76	3.17	4.59
11	1.80	2.20	2.72	3.11	4.44
12	1.78	2.18	2.68	3.06	4.32
13	1.77	2.16	2.65	3.01	4.22
14	1.76	2.15	2.62	2.98	4.14
15	1.75	2.13	2.60	2.95	4.07
16	1.75	2.12	2.58	2.92	4.02
17	1.74	2.11	2.57	2.90	3.97
18	1.73	2.10	2.55	2.88	3.92
19	1.73	2.09	2.54	2.86	3.88
20	1.73	2.09	2.53	2.85	3.85
21	1.72	2.08	2.52	2.83	3.82
22	1.72	2.07	2.51	2.82	3.79
23	1.71	2.07	2.50	2.81	3.77
24	1.71	2.06	2.49	2.80	3.75
25	1.71	2.06	2.49	2.79	3.73
26	1.71	2.06	2.48	2.78	3.71
27	1.70	2.05	2.47	2.77	3.69
28	1.70	2.05	2.47	2.76	3.67
29	1.70	2.05	2.46	2.76	3.66
30	1.70	2.04	2.46	2.75	3.65
40	1.68	2.02	2.42	2.70	3.55
60	1.67	2.00	2.39	2.66	3.46
			fairly confident	very confident	almost certain

← Results not significant i.e. is more and more likely to be due to chance

Results increasingly significant i.e. more and more likely that the difference is **not** pure chance →

8.5.1 Environmental effects

We saw in the previous chapter that the final appearance of an organism (phenotype) is the result of its genotype and the effect of the environment upon it. If organisms of identical genotype are subject to different environmental influences, they show considerable variety. If one of a pair of genetically identical twins were to be raised on a diet deficient in some essential component for growth, e.g. calcium, it would be unlikely to attain the height of the other twin if he/she had been raised on a complete diet. Because environmental influences are themselves very various, and because they often form gradations, e.g. temperature, light intensity, they are largely responsible for continuous variation within a population.

8.5.2 Reshuffling of genes

The sexual process in organisms has three inbuilt methods of creating variety:

1. The mixing of two different parental genotypes where cross-fertilization occurs.

2. The random distribution of chromosomes during metaphase I of meiosis.

3. The crossing over between homologous chromosomes during prophase I of meiosis.

These changes, which were dealt with in more detail in Section 6.5.2, do not bring about major changes in features but rather create new combinations of existing features.

Mutations
Any change in the structure or the amount of DNA of an organism is called a **mutation**. Most mutations occur in somatic (body) cells and are not passed from one generation to the next. Only those mutations which occur in the formation of gametes can be inherited. These mutations produce sudden and distinct differences between individuals. They are therefore the basis of discontinuous variation.

8.5.3 Changes in gene structure (point mutations)

A change in the structure of DNA which occurs at a single locus on a chromosome is called a **gene mutation** or **point mutation**. In Section 5.5 we saw that the genetic code, which ultimately determines an organism's characteristics, is made up of a specific sequence of nucleotides on the DNA molecule. Any change to one or more of these nucleotides, or any rearrangement of the sequence, will produce the wrong sequence of amino acids in the protein it makes. As this protein is often an enzyme, it may result in it having a different molecular shape and hence prevent it catalysing its reaction. The result will be that the end product of that reaction cannot be formed. This may have a profound effect on the organism. For example, a gene mutation may result

Human variability

Variability in behaviour and appearance is characteristic of all living organisms as their environment varies, and it is probably no greater in humans than it is in many other species. All humans, except identical twins, vary because they carry different genetic material as well as showing variations due to their environment. Environmental influences are seen to have their greatest effect as we move across the world to areas separated from each other by oceans or mountain ranges. On the basis of adaptations to the different climates we recognise more or less distinct **geographical races**. Because the distinctions between races are not clear cut and because there is gene flow between them, there are many ways of classifying races. A typical classification based on human visible variation is as follows:

- **Caucasoid** – from northern Europe to northern Africa. Skin largely depigmented; hair fine and wavy or straight; narrow face and prominent narrow nose.
- **Negroid** – from sub-Saharan Africa. Skin pigment is dense; hair woolly; short face with broad nose and thick lips.
- **Mongoloid** – found in much of Asia, parts of the Pacific and in the Americas. Skin brown to light; hair coarse and sparse on face and body; face broad and flat with internal skin fold on eyelids.
- **Australoid** – the Aboriginals of Australia and Polynesia. Skin is dark; hair commonly blond in children and dark in adults; head long and narrow with prominent brow ridges and projecting jaw.

Although human populations have clearly adjusted to their physical environment in various ways, little is known about the adaptive significance of many of these differences. Skin colour is best understood since melanin screens the dermis from the harmful effects of solar ultra-violet radiation. This may have favoured the dark pigmentation of negroids and the fair skin of Europeans, who need some exposure to ultra-violet so that vitamin D can be generated and rickets avoided. Nose shape is also associated with climate since a narrow nose may better moisten and warm the cold air before it reaches the lungs.

Not surprisingly most racial differences are 'skin deep'. It is after all the skin which acts as an interface between the body and the environment. The frequency of particular blood groups varies in different parts of the world but blood groups are not affected by the environment, they are genetically determined. Their only use in the study of races is to give us some idea of the relatedness and migration or isolation of human populations in the past, but the picture is not clear. In fact most of the variation in blood groups is between individuals within populations rather than between the 'races' of humankind. Although the significance of the observation is not understood, there does appear to be a correlation between particular blood groups and susceptibility to certain diseases. For example group A individuals seem most liable to stomach cancer and pernicious anaemia, while those of group O are more susceptible to gastric and duodenal ulcers. It is important to remember that this description of human variability is based on features which are, on the whole, trivial. Humans are in fact all broadly similar, related biologically and with a shared ancestry and history.

Did you know?

The name 'malaria' comes from the Italian 'mal aria' meaning 'bad air'. Until the 20th century most people thought malaria was caused by bad air in the mist arising in marshes.

TABLE 8.6

Message on telegram	Equivalent form of gene mutation	Likely result of receiving the message
Meet station 2100 hours today	Normal	Individuals meet as arranged
Meet Met station 2100 hours today	Duplication	Individuals arrive at correct time, one at the prearranged station, the other at the nearest station on the Metropolitan line (or London police station)
Met station 2100 hours today	Deletion	
Meet bus station 2100 hours today	Addition	Individuals arrive on time but one at the bus station, the other at the prearranged station
Meet station 1200 hours today	Inversion	Individuals arrive at correct place – but 9 hours apart
Meet station 1100 hours today	Substitution	Individuals arrive at correct place but 12 hours apart
Meet sat on it 2100 hours today	Inversion (including translocation	Message incomprehensible

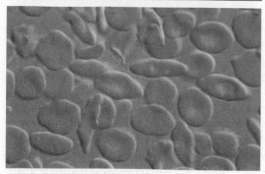

Blood with sickle cells

in the absence of pigments such as melanin. The person will be unpigmented, i.e. an albino. There are many forms of gene mutation.

1. **Duplication** – a portion of a nucleotide chain becomes repeated.

2. **Addition (insertion)** – an extra nucleotide sequence becomes inserted in the chain.

3. **Deletion** – a portion of the nucleotide chain is removed from the sequence.

4. **Inversion** – a nucleotide sequence becomes separated from the chain. It rejoins in its original position, only inverted. The nucleotide sequence of this portion is therefore reversed.

5. **Substitution** – one of the nucleotides is replaced by another which has a different organic base.

To illustrate these different types, let us imagine each nucleotide is equivalent to a letter of the alphabet. The sequence of nucleotides therefore makes up a sentence or groups of sentences which can be understood by the cell's chemical machinery as the instructions for making specific proteins. If a mutation results in the instructions being incomprehensible, the cell will be unable to make the appropriate protein. In most cases this will result in the death of the cell or organism at an early stage. Sometimes, however, the mutation will result in inaccurate, and yet comprehensible, instructions being given. A protein may well be produced, but it is the wrong one. The defect may create some phenotypic change, but not of sufficient importance to cause the death of the organism.

Imagine a telegram to confirm the details of an earlier arrangement to meet at a pre-arranged station. If we alter just one or two letters each time, either the message may be totally incomprehensible or it may be understood by the receiver but not in the way intended by the sender. Table 8.6, gives some examples.

A gene mutation in the gene producing haemoglobin results in a defect called **sickle-cell anaemia**. The replacement of just one base in the DNA molecule results in the wrong amino acid being incorporated into two of the polypeptide chains which make up the haemoglobin molecule. The abnormal haemoglobin causes red blood cells to become sickle-shaped, resulting in anaemia and possible death. The detailed events are illustrated in Fig. 8.9.

The mutant gene causing sickle-cell anaemia is codominant. In the homozygous state, the individual suffers the disease and frequently dies. In the heterozygous state, the individual has 30–40% sickle cells, the rest being normal. This is called the sickle-cell trait. These individuals suffer less severe anaemia and rarely die from the condition. As they still suffer some disability, it might be expected that the disease would be very rare, if not completely eliminated, by natural selection. In parts of Africa, however, it is very common. The reason is that the malarial parasite, *Plasmodium*, cannot easily invade sickle cells. Individuals with either sickle-cell condition are therefore more resistant to severe attacks of malaria. In the homozygous condition, this resistance is insufficient to offset the considerable disadvantage of having sickle-cell anaemia. In the heterozygous condition (sickle-cell trait), however, the advantage of being resistant to severe malarial attacks outweighs the disadvantage of the mild anaemia the individual suffers. In malarial regions of the world the mutant gene is selected in favour of the one producing normal haemoglobin. Outside malarial regions, there is no advantage in being resistant to malaria, and the disadvantage of suffering anaemia results in selection *against* the mutant gene.

One relatively common gene mutation in European countries causes **cystic fibrosis**, which is the result of a recessive gene. Further details of this disorder are given on pages 94–5.

Dominant gene mutations are rarer but include **Huntington's disease**. This is characterized by involuntary muscular movement and progressive mental deterioration. The mutant gene is so rare (around 1 in 100 000 people carry it) that it occurs almost exclusively in the heterozygous state.

8.5.4 Changes in whole sets of chromosomes

Sometimes organisms occur that have additional whole sets of chromosomes. Instead of having a haploid set in the sex cells and a diploid set in the body cells, they have several complete sets. This is known as **polyploidy**. Where three sets of chromosomes are present, the organism is said to be **triploid**. With four sets, it is said to be **tetraploid**.

Polyploidy can arise in several different ways. If gametes are produced which are diploid and these self-fertilize, a tetraploid is produced. If instead the diploid gamete fuses with a normal haploid gamete, a triploid results. Polyploidy can also occur when whole sets of chromosomes double after fertilization.

Tetraploid organisms have two complete sets of homologous chromosomes and can therefore form homologous pairings during gamete production by meiosis. Triploids, however, cannot form complete homologous pairings and are usually sterile. They can only be propagated by asexual means. The type of polyploidy whereby the increase in sets of chromosomes occurs within the same species is called **autopolyploidy**. The actual number of chromosomes in an autopolyploid is always an exact multiple of its haploid number. Autopolyploidy can be induced by a chemical called **colchicine** which is extracted from certain crocus corms. Colchicine inhibits spindle formation and so prevents chromosomes separating during anaphase.

Sometimes hybrids can be formed by combining sets of chromosomes from species with different chromosome numbers. These hybrids are ordinarily sterile because the total number of chromosomes does not allow full homologous pairing to take place. If, however, the hybrid has a chromosome number which is a multiple of the original chromosome number, a new fertile species is formed. The species of wheat used today to make bread was formed in this way. The basic haploid number of wild grasses is seven. A tetraploid with 28 chromosomes called emmer wheat was accidentally cross-fertilized with a wild grass with 14 chromosomes. The resultant wheat with 42

1. *The DNA molecule which codes for the beta amino acid chain in haemoglobin has a mutation whereby the base adenine replaces thymine.*

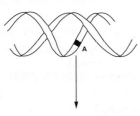

2. *The mRNA produced has the triplet codon GUA (for amino acid valine) rather than GAA (for amino acid glutamic acid).*

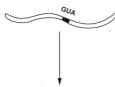

3. *The beta amino acid chain produced has one glutamic acid molecule replaced by a valine molecule.*

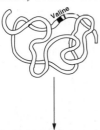

4. *The haemoglobin molecule containing the abnormal beta chains forms abnormal long fibres when the oxygen level of the blood is low. This haemoglobin is called haemoglobin-S.*

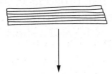

5. *Haemoglobin-S causes the shape of the red blood cell to become crescent (sickle) shaped.*

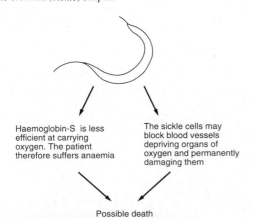

Haemoglobin-S is less efficient at carrying oxygen. The patient therefore suffers anaemia

The sickle cells may block blood vessels depriving organs of oxygen and permanently damaging them

Possible death

Fig. 8.9 Sequence of events whereby a gene mutation causes sickle-cell anaemia

chromosomes is today the main cultivated variety. Having a chromosome number which is a multiple of the original haploid number of 7, is fertile. This form of polyploidy is called **allopolyploidy**.

Polyploidy is rare in animals, but relatively common in plants. Almost half of all flowering plants (angiosperms) are polyploids, including many important food plants. Wheat, coffee, bananas, sugar cane, apples and tomatoes all have polyploid forms. The polyploid varieties often have some advantage. Tetraploid apples, for example, form larger fruits and tetraploid tomatoes produce more vitamin C.

8.5.5 Changes in chromosome number

Sometimes it is an individual chromosome, rather than a whole set, which fails to separate during anaphase. If, for example, in humans one of the 23 pairs of homologous chromosomes fails to segregate during meiosis, one of the gametes produced will contain 22 chromosomes and the other 24, rather than 23 each. This is known as **non-disjunction** and is often lethal. The condition where an organism possesses an additional chromosome is represented as $2n + 1$; where one is missing, $2n - 1$. Where two additional chromosomes are present it is represented as $2n + 2$ etc.

One frequent consequence of non-disjunction in humans is **Down's syndrome** (mongolism). In this case the 21st chromosome fails to segregate and the gamete produced possesses 24 chromosomes. The fusion of this gamete with a normal one with 23 chromosomes results in the offspring having 47 ($2n + 1$) chromosomes. Non-disjunction does occur with other chromosomes but these normally result in the fetus aborting or the child dying soon after birth. The 21st chromosome is relatively small, and the offspring is therefore able to survive. Down's syndrome children have disabilities of varying magnitude. Typically they have a flat, broad face, squint eyes with a skin fold in the inner corner and a furrowed and protruding tongue. They have a low IQ and a short life expectancy.

Non-disjunction in the case of Down's syndrome appears to occur in the production of ova rather than sperm. Its incidence is related to the age of the mother. The chance of a teenage mother having a Down's syndrome child is only one in many thousands. A forty-year-old mother has a one in a hundred chance and by forty-five the risk is three times greater. The risk is unaffected by the age of the father.

Sometimes non-disjunction of the sex chromosomes occurs. In some instances the X chromosomes fail to separate at anaphase during the production of an ovum (oogenesis). The ovum therefore contains two X chromosomes rather than one. On fertilizing with a sperm carrying an X-chromosome the offspring will have an XXX genotype. Such individuals are usually normal females in other respects although some fail to menstruate and are sterile. On fertilizing with a sperm containing a Y chromosome the resultant offspring will have an XXY genotype. This condition is known as **Klinefelter's syndrome** which also arises if non-disjunction occurs more than once during oogenesis giving rise to ova with 3 or even 4 X-chromosomes. The

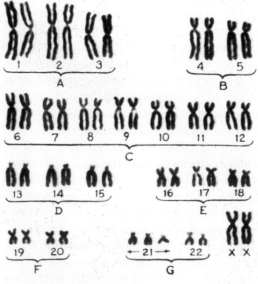

Karyotype of Down's syndrome

individuals with Klinefelter's syndrome may therefore have genotypes of XXY, XXXY or XXXXY. They are phenotypically male but have small testes, produce no sperm in the ejaculate, may develop small breasts and are taller than average. The greater the number of Xs in the genotype, the more marked is the condition. The fact that these individuals are male indicates that the presence of the Y-chromosome is the cause of maleness.

It follows that if non-disjunction leads to some ova bearing two X-chromosomes, others must possess no X-chromosome at all. If such an ovum is fertilized by a Y sperm, the resultant YO type zygote does not develop further, indicating that the X-chromosome possesses genes which are essential to life. If fertilized by a sperm carrying an X-chromosome, the XO type zygote develops further but may not survive pregnancy; those that do, develop into females with **Turner's Syndrome**. These individuals are born with a very broad neck due to a fold of skin on either side. They do not develop secondary sexual characteristics at puberty and so remain sexually immature and sterile.

8.5.6 Changes in chromosome structure

During meiosis it is normal for homologous pairs of chromosomes to form chiasmata. The chromatids break at these points and rejoin with the corresponding portion of chromatid on its homologous partner. It is not surprising that from time to time mistakes arise during this process. Indeed, it is remarkable that these chromosome mutations do not occur more frequently. There are four types:

1. **Deletion** – a portion of a chromosome is lost (Fig. 8.10a). As this involves the loss of genes, it can have a significant effect on an organism's development, often proving lethal.

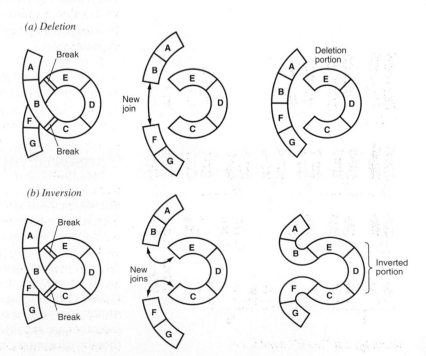

Fig. 8.10 Diagrams illustrating the four types of chromosome mutation

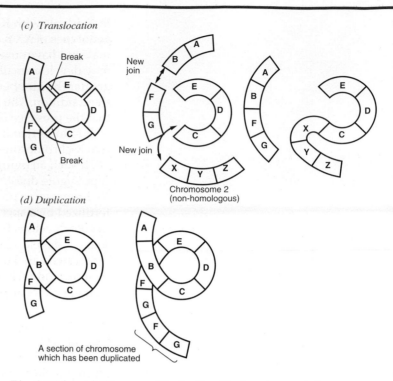

(c) Translocation

(d) Duplication

A section of chromosome which has been duplicated

Fig. 8.10 (cont.) Diagrams illustrating the four types of chromosome mutation

2. Inversion – a portion of chromosome becomes deleted, but becomes reattached in an inverted position. The sequence of genes on this portion are therefore reversed (Fig. 8.10b). The overall genotype is unchanged, but the phenotype may be altered. This indicates that the sequence of genes on the chromosome is important.

3. Translocation – a portion of chromosome becomes deleted and rejoins at a different point on the same chromosome or with a different chromosome (Fig. 8.10c). The latter is equivalent to crossing over except that it occurs between non-homologous chromosomes.

4. Duplication – a portion of chromosome is doubled, resulting in repetition of a gene sequence (Fig. 8.10d).

8.6 Causes of mutations

Mutations occur continually. There is a natural mutation rate which varies from one species to another. In general, organisms with shorter life cycles, and therefore more frequent meiosis, show a greater rate of mutation. A typical rate of mutation is 1 or 2 new mutations per 100 000 genes per generation.

This natural mutation rate can be increased artificially by certain chemicals or energy sources. Any agent which induces mutations is called a **mutagen**. Most forms of high energy radiation are capable of altering the structure of DNA and thereby causing mutations. These include ultra-violet light,

X-rays and gamma rays. High energy particles such as α and β particles and neutrons are even more dangerous mutagens.

A number of chemicals also cause mutations. We saw in Section 8.5.4 that colchicine inhibits spindle formation and so causes polyploidy. Other chemical mutagens include formaldehyde, nitrous acid and mustard gas.

8.7 Genetic screening and counselling

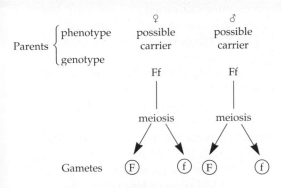

25% normal children
50% normal children, but carriers of the gene
25% children with cystic fibrosis

As our knowledge of inheritance has increased, more and more disabilities have been found to have genetic origins. Some of these disabilities cannot be predicted with complete accuracy. In Down's syndrome, for example, it is impossible to give a precise prediction of its occurrence for any individual. The risk for a mother of a particular age can, however, be calculated. Other disabilities like haemophilia, cystic fibrosis, some forms of muscular dystrophy and Huntington's disease can be predicted fairly accurately, provided enough information on the history of the disease in the family is known.

8.7.1 Genetic counselling

Genetic counselling has developed in order to research the family history of inherited disease and to advise parents on the likelihood of it arising in their children. Imagine a mother, whose family has a history of cystic fibrosis. If she herself is unaffected but possesses the gene, she can only be heterozygous for the condition. Suppose she wishes to produce children by a man with no history of the disease in his family. It must be assumed that he does not carry the gene for the disease and therefore none of the children will suffer from it, although they may be carriers. If, on the other hand, the potential father's family has a history of the disease, it is possible he too carries the gene. As we see from the genetic diagram opposite, it is possible to advise the parents that there is a one in four chance of their children being affected. The gene for cystic fibrosis is recessive and autosomal (i.e. not sex-linked).

On the basis of this advice the parents can choose whether or not to have children. With a very detailed knowledge of the disease in each of the parent's families it may even be possible to establish for certain whether they are carriers or not. It is now possible to carry out tests to establish with some accuracy whether an individual is heterozygous for the gene, and so to make precise predictions about the likelihood of having a child with cystic fibrosis (see Focus on p. 94). The advantages of genetic counselling are fairly clear: individuals, in fuller knowledge of the facts, can make informed decisions on whether to have children or terminate a pregnancy. Indeed it may seem, at a superficial level, that it can be nothing but advantageous to know the probability of producing children with a genetic disorder. This view perhaps disguises the momentous decisions which individuals have to make. Does one not have children rather than risk offspring that may be handicapped? What if the risk is only 50%, 25% or 10%? Where does one draw the line? If

FOCUS

Screening in early pregnancy

Screening is usually offered when a family has a history of an inherited disorder or when the mother is comparatively old and is therefore more likely to give birth to a child with Down's syndrome.

Amniocentesis is carried out from 10 weeks' gestation. A small quantity of amniotic fluid is taken through a hypodermic needle and the fetal cells contained in it are separated from the liquid by centrifugation. The cells are then cultured and their chromosomes examined.

Chorionic villus sampling is also carried out after 10 weeks' gestation. A sample of cells is taken from the chorion, the developing placenta, using a plastic catheter inserted through the vagina under ultrasound guidance. Preliminary results can be obtained within a day but the procedure is thought to increase the risk of miscarriage by about 4% (compared to a 1% increased risk with amniocentesis).

Coelocentesis is a new, relatively untried technique which involves the removal of cells from the coelomic cavity surrounding the amniotic sac. It can be carried out before 10 weeks' gestation and is thought to present less risk to the unborn child.

parents discover as a result of counselling that their children have Huntington's Disease (which is lethal but only displays symptoms in middle age) when and how does one break such news to them? To tell them as soon as they are old enough to understand might seem appropriate but what happens when they apply for work or an insurance policy? If they declare the fact, they may risk refusal but not to do so could nullify the post or policy. If they are left in ignorance they could hardly be penalized for not declaring what they did not know. But what if they applied for a job where their condition might put others at risk? Could one let them go ahead, however innocently? The effects of the same disorder can vary widely – some living in distress and dependent on others, some leading independent and happy lives. In these circumstances the decision as to whether to have children or not, or to terminate a pregnancy or not, is an unenviable one. Genetic Counselling has its disadvantages too.

8.7.2 Genetic screening

What then of the parents who have children knowing that there is a greater than usual possibility of them inheriting a genetic defect? Is there any means of establishing whether a child is affected, before it is born? The answer is yes, for some defects at least. Doctors can now diagnose certain genetic defects in a fetus, by studying samples of cells taken from the amniotic fluid which surrounds the fetus. In a process called **amniocentesis**. Certain genetic defects such as Down's syndrome can be detected directly as the additional chromosomes are easily seen. Biochemical tests on the cells, or even the amniotic fluid (which contains much fetal urine), may reveal other genetic defects. On the basis of these tests the parents can decide whether or not to have the pregnancy terminated. Details of the processes are given in the Focus on 'Screening in early pregnancy' on p. 160.

8.7.3 Gene tracking

Gene tracking has proved a useful aid in genetic counselling. It is first necessary to find out on which chromosome a defective gene is located, something achieved through mapping chromosomes. The technique of making selected crosses of pure-breeding parents and collecting thousands of F_1 offspring in order to determine cross-over values and hence map chromosomes, may be appropriate with *Drosophila*, but can hardly be used with humans. Instead the inheritance of other, easily distinguished features such as blood groups, are traced in families to act as **genetic markers**. Study of the correlation between certain blood group alleles and the occurrence of a genetic disease can determine whether or not the gene for the disease is on the same chromosome as that for blood groups. If one genetic marker is not linked to the disease in question another must be tried and so on until the one which shows linkage with the disease is found. Linked markers are then used to work out whether or not someone carries a disease – this is the process of gene tracking.

8.8   Population genetics

To a geneticist, a population is an interbreeding group of organisms. In theory, any individual in the population is capable of breeding with any other. In other words, the genes of any individual organism are capable of being combined with the genes of any other. The genes of a population are therefore freely interchangeable. The total of all the alleles of all the genes in a population is called the **gene pool**. Within the gene pool the number of times any one allele occurs is referred to as its frequency.

8.8.1 Heterozygotes as reservoirs of genetic variation (the Hardy–Weinberg principle)

If one looks at a particular characteristic in a population, it is apparent that the dominant form expresses itself more often than the recessive one. In almost all human populations, for example, brown eyes occur more frequently than blue. It might be thought, therefore, that in time the dominant form would predominate to the point where the recessive type disappeared from the population completely. The proportion of dominant and recessive alleles of a particular gene remains the same, however. It is not altered by interbreeding. This phenomenon is known as the **Hardy–Weinberg principle**. It is a mathematical law which depends on four conditions being met:

1. No mutations arise.

2. The population is isolated, i.e. there is no flow of genes into, or out of, the population.

3. There is no natural selection.

4. The population is large and mating is random.

FOCUS

Gene probes and tracking Huntington's disease

Huntington's disease is a rare, inherited neuropsychiatric disorder resulting from a dominant form of a gene. Individuals with the disease lead a normal healthy life until they reach their 40s or 50s, when they experience personality changes and loss of control of movement. The condition worsens resulting in death within 15 years of its onset. At present there is no cure and the only treatment is to relieve the symptoms.

As it is inherited, Huntington's disease runs in families and as it is caused by a dominant form of the gene there is a strong risk of offspring acquiring it from an affected parent – a 50% chance if the other parent is unaffected. Such offspring live in agonizing uncertainty, never knowing whether they will, in middle age, develop the disease. As if this wasn't enough they have the added burden of deciding whether to have children, knowing they too may well be affected. Therefore, to be able to tell at an early age whether or not they carry the gene might relieve the anxiety altogether, or at least, allow them to plan for the inevitable.

Gene tracking, as outlined in Section 18.7.3 has made detection possible. DNA can be broken up into fragments using restriction endonuclease enzymes (see Section 5.7.2). Fragments can then be detected using a **gene probe**. A gene probe is a radioactive section of DNA or RNA which has a sequence of bases which complement another fragment of DNA. These fragments of DNA can be separated using gel electrophoresis and then the probe can be added to each one separately. Only the fragment with the exact complementary sequence of bases will take up the radioactive probe. We can detect which one this is by placing each fragment next to X-ray sensitive film – a process called **autoradiography**. Only the fragment bearing the radioactive probe will cause exposure of the film.

In 1983 this technique finally discovered a fragment of DNA on human chromosome 4 which was almost always found in sufferers of Huntington's disease. This was not the actual gene causing the condition (this has so far proved elusive) but one very close to it on the chromosome. Anyone with this form of the gene had a 95% chance of having the gene for Huntington's disease also. There was just a 5% chance that crossing over between chromosomes during meiosis (see Section 6.3) might have separated the two closely linked genes during gametogenesis. More recent work has revealed a marker gene which is even closer to the Huntington's disease gene and this allows us to be 98% accurate in our prediction rather than 95%.

While these conditions are probably never met in a natural population, the Hardy–Weinberg principle nonetheless forms a basis for the study of gene frequencies.

To help understand the principle, consider a gene which has a dominant allele A and a recessive one a.

Let p = the frequency of allele A and
q = the frequency of allele a

In diploid individuals these alleles occur in the combinations given opposite.

1st allele	2nd allele	Frequency
A	A	$p \times p = p^2$
A	a	$p \times q$
a	A	$q \times p$ $\Big\}$ $2pq$
a	a	$q \times q = q^2$

As the homozygous dominant (AA) combination is 1/4 of the total possible genotypes, there is a 1/4 (25%) chance of a single individual being of this type. Similarly, the chance of it being homozygous recessive (aa) is 1/4 (25%) whereas there is a 1/2 (50%) chance of it being heterozygous. There is a 1/1 (100%) chance of it being any one of these three types. In other words:

homozygous dominant (1/4) + heterozygous 1/2) + homozygous recessive (1/4) = 1.0 (100%)

thus   AA + 2Aa + aa = 1.0 (100%)

and p^2 + $2pq$ + q^2 − 1.0 (100%)

The Hardy–Weinberg principle is expressed as:

$$p^2 + 2pq + q^2 = 1.0$$

(where p and q represent the respective frequencies of the dominant and recessive alleles of any particular gene).

The formula can be used to calculate the frequency of any allele in the population. For example, imagine that a particular mental defect is the result of a recessive allele. If the number of babies born with the defect is one in 25 000, the frequency of the allele can be calculated as follows:

The defect will only express itself in individuals who are homozygous recessive. Therefore the frequency of these individuals (q^2) = 1/25 000 or 0.000 04.
The frequency of the allele (q) is therefore $\sqrt{0.000\,04}$
$$= 0.0063 \text{ approx.}$$
As the frequency of both alleles must be 1.0, i.e. $p + q = 1.0$, then the frequency of the dominant allele (p) can be calculated.

$$p + q = 1.0$$
$$\therefore p = 1.0 - q$$
$$\therefore p = 1.0 - 0.0063$$
$$\therefore p = 0.9937$$

The frequency of heterozygotes can now be calculated.

From the Hardy–Weinberg formula, the frequency of heterozygotes is $2pq$, i.e. $2 \times 0.9937 \times 0.0063 = 0.0125$.

In other words, 125 in 10 000 (or 313 in 25 000) are carriers (heterozygotes) of the allele.

This means that in a population of 25 000 individuals, just one individual will suffer the defect but around 313 will carry the allele. The heterozygotes are acting as a reservoir of the allele, maintaining it in the gene pool. As these heterozygotes are normal, they are not specifically selected against, and so the allele remains. Even if the defective individuals are selectively removed, the frequency of the allele will hardly be affected. In our population of 25 000, there is one individual who has two recessive alleles and 313 with one recessive allele – a total of 315. The removal of the defective individual will reduce the number of alleles in the population by just 2, to 313. Even with the removal of all defective individuals it would take thousands of years just to halve the allele's frequency.

Occasionally, as in sickle cell anaemia (Section 8.5.3), the heterozygote individuals have a selective advantage. This is known as **heterozygote superiority**.

8.9   Questions

1. Rats and mice are common pests. Warfarin was developed as a poison to control rats and was very effective when first used in 1950.

Resistance to warfarin was first reported in British rats in 1958 and is now extremely common. Warfarin resistance in rats is determined by a single gene with two alleles W^S and W^R. Rats with the genotypes listed below have the characteristics shown.

W^SW^S Normal rats susceptible to warfarin

W^SW^R Rats resistant to warfarin needing slightly more vitamin K than usual for full health

W^RW^R Rats resistant to warfarin but requiring very large amounts of vitamin K. They rarely survive.

(*a*) Explain why:

(i) there was a high frequency of W^S alleles in the British population of wild rats before 1950;
(*1 mark*)

(ii) the frequency of W^R alleles in the wild rat population rose rapidly from 1958.   (*2 marks*)

(*b*) Explain what would be likely to happen to the frequency of W^R alleles if warfarin were no longer used.   (*2 marks*)

(*c*) Mice show continuous variation in their resistance to warfarin. What does this suggest about the genetic basis of warfarin resistance in mice?   (*1 mark*)

In humans, deaths from conditions where blood clots form inside blood vessels occur frequently in adults over the age of fifty. These conditions may be treated successfully with warfarin. However, some people possess a dominant allele which gives resistance to warfarin.

(*d*) Why would you not expect this allele to change in frequency?   (*2 marks*)

(*Total 8 marks*)

NEAB February 1995, Paper BY2, No. 6

2. The typical form of the European Swallow-tail butterfly has yellow patches on its wings, but in a rare variety called *nigra* these areas are shaded black.
A cross between a typical male and a *nigra* female produced 14 typical offspring and 6 *nigra*.

(*a*) As a first hypothesis to explain this result, it was suggested that the *nigra* variety is caused by a recessive allele of a single gene which is not sex-linked.

(i) On the basis of this hypothesis, a 1 : 1 ratio would be expected in the offspring.
Construct a genetic diagram to show the genotypes of the parents of this cross, and to show how this ratio could be obtained.

Use the letters **N** and **n** to represent the two alleles of the gene.   (*3 marks*)

(ii) The table below gives the expected numbers (E) of each phenotype on the basis of this hypothesis, and the differences between the observed and expected numbers ($O{-}E$).

Phenotype	Observed number O	Expected number E	Difference $O{-}E$
Typical	14	10	4
Nigra	6	10	4

Using the formula below, calculate the value of chi-squared (χ^2). Show your working.

$$\chi^2 = \Sigma \frac{(O-E)^2}{E}$$

(*3 marks*)

(iii) Probability levels (P) corresponding to some values of χ^2 in this case are shown below.

χ^2	0.004	2.71	3.85	6.63
$P(\%)$	95	10	5	1

What does your calculated value for χ^2 indicate in relation to this particular cross?   (*1 mark*)

(*b*) A second hypothesis was suggested, in which the *nigra* variety is produced by interaction between two unlinked genes, **A** and **B**. One of the genes has alleles **A** and **a** and the other gene has alleles **B** and **b**. The *nigra* phenotype is seen only in individuals that are homozygous for the **a** allele and *either* homozygous *or* heterozygous for the **B** allele (either **aaBB** or **aaBb**).

This second hypothesis suggested that the genotypes of the original parents in the above cross were as follows.

The typical parent **AaBb**
The nigra parent **aaBb**

Construct a genetic diagram to show the genotype and phenotype ratios expected from the cross on the basis of the second hypothesis.   (*4 marks*)

(*c*) Comparison of the observed results with those expected from the second hypothesis gives a value for χ^2 of 0.48.

Compare this with the value calculated for this first hypothesis and suggest which hypothesis has the greater probability of being correct. Justify your answer.   (*2 marks*)

(*Total 13 marks*)

ULEAC 1996, Specimen Paper Syn AHBio, No. 2

3. It has been suggested that, in humans, certain eye colours and hair colours are often inherited together. The table below shows the observed numberc (O) and the expected numbers (E) for each combination of eye and hair colour found in a sample of 130 British men.

Eye colour	Hair colour						Observed totals
	Fair		Brown		Black		
	O	E	O	E	O	E	
Blue	65	53.3	26	32.0	8	13.7	99
Brown	5	16.7	16	10.0	10	4.3	31
Observed totals	70		42		18		130

The null hypothesis states that there is no link between the inheritance of eye colour and hair colour.

(a) (i) Test the null hypothesis by means of a χ^2 test.
Fill in the values of (O–E) and (O–E)^2 in the following table.

Combination of eye colour and hair colour	(O–E)	(O–E)^2
Blue eyes with fair hair		
Blue eyes with brown hair		
Blue eyes with black hair		
Brown eyes with fair hair		
Brown eyes with brown hair		
Brown eyes with black hair		

(2 marks)

(ii) Use the formula given below to calculate the value of χ^2. Show your working.

$$\chi^2 = \Sigma \frac{(O-E)^2}{E}$$ (2 marks)

(iii) How many degrees of freedom are shown in this investigation? Explain how you arrived at your answer. (2 marks)

(b) For this number of degrees of freedom, χ^2 values corresponding to important values of P are as follows.

Value of P	0.990	0.95	0.05	0.01	0.001
Value of χ^2	0.020	0.103	5.991	9.210	13.820

What conclusions can be drawn from this χ^2 test concerning the inheritance of eye colour and hair colour? (3 marks)

(Total 9 marks)

ULEAC 1996, Specimen Paper Syn AHBio, No. 1

4. Of four hundred people inoculated with a vaccine against a particular disease, 38 people later developed the disease. Among a control unvaccinated group of four hundred people, 80 developed the disease. A χ^2 (chi-square) test was used to test the hypothesis that there was no difference between the results in the vaccinated and the control group.

(a) Complete the table to show observed and expected results, O–E, $(O-E)^2$ and $\frac{(O-E)^2}{E}$ values in each column.

	Developed the disease	Did NOT develop the disease
Observed result (O) (vaccinated group)		
Expected result if vaccine ineffective (E) (unvaccinated group)		
O–E		
$(O-E)^2$		
$\frac{(O-E)^2}{E}$		

(2 marks)

(b) Calculate the value of χ^2 given that:

$$\chi^2 = \Sigma \frac{(O-E)^2}{E}$$ (1 mark)

(c) How many degrees of freedom are there in this χ^2 test? (1 mark)

(d) Use the probability table below to decide whether the vaccine had a significant effect. Explain your answer.

Degrees of freedom	Probability value					
	.99	.95	0.1	0.05	0.01	0.001
1	.0001	.0039	2.71	3.84	6.63	10.83
2	.020	.103	4.61	5.99	9.21	13.82
3	.115	.352	6.25	7.81	11.34	16.27
4	.297	.711	7.78	9.49	13.28	18.47

(1 mark)
(Total 5 marks)

AEB June 1992, Paper 1, No. 9

5. Human haemoglobin is built from four polypeptide chains (2 α-chains and 2 β-chains) consisting altogether of approximately 600 amino acids. A haem group is bound to each chain. A genetic variant of the normal (type A) haemoglobin is referred to as haemoglobin S. People possessing the alleles for haemoglobin S in the homozygous condidion suffer from sickle cell anaemia. The sequence of amino acids from 1 to 8 in the β-polypeptide chains differs between the two variants as follows .
Haemoglobin A:
valine–histidine–leucine–threonine–proline–glutamic acid–glutamic acid–lysine

Haemoglobin S:
valine–histidine–leucine–threonine–proline–valine–glutamic acid–lysine

(a) (i) How many **different** amino acids are likely to be present within the 600 amino acids that make up the molecule of haemoglobin? Explain your answer.

(ii) What term is used to describe the type of structure whereby four polypeptide chains are bound into the single protein molecule of haemoglobin? (*3 marks*)

(b) What is the physiological significance of the haem group bound to each of the polypeptide chains? (*1 mark*)

(c) What general term is given to the process by which genetic variants of haemoglobin are produced? (*1 mark*)

(d) Explain, **in general terms**, how the mRNA for haemoglobin S would differ from the mRNA for haemoglobin A. (*3 marks*)

Individuals that are heterozygous for the sickle cell gene have a mixture of normal and abnormal haemoglobins in their red cells. The red cells do not normally undergo 'sickling' but can be made to do so when the amount of oxygen in the blood is reduced.

(e) Using this information, devise a single test which you could use to identify heterozygotes in the population. (*3 marks*)

(f) What is the probability of a couple, both of whom are heterozygous for the sickle cell gene, having a child who suffers from sickle cell anaemia? Explain your answer by means of a genetic diagram. (*2 marks*)

(*Total 13 marks*)

UCLES June 1993, Paper 2, No. 4

6. (a) Suggest a genetic explanation for the fact that:
   (i) human height is a continuous variable; (*1 mark*)

   (ii) eyelash length is a discontinuous variable. (*1 mark*)

   Table 1 shows the distribution of the total number of ridges on the fingers of identical male twin pairs. Table 2 shows similar data for non-identical male twin pairs.

TABLE 1 **Identical male twin pair**

		Number of ridges on fingers of second twin					
		0–49	50–99	100–149	150–199	200–249	250–299
Number of ridges on fingers of first twin	0–49	4	2				
	50–99	2	48	4			
	100–149		4	88	11		
	150–199			11	68	4	
	200–249				4	8	
	250–299						2

TABLE 2 **Non-identical male twin pairs**

		Number of ridges on fingers of second twin					
		0–49	50–99	100–149	150–199	200–249	250–299
Number of ridges on fingers of first twin	0–49	2	1	3	1		
	50–99	1	16	15	8		
	100–149	3	15	38	18	3	
	150–199	1	8	18	28	6	
	200–249			3	6	2	1
	250–299					1	

(b) Use the evidence from the tables to explain the fact that the total number of ridges on fingers is influenced by:
   (i) genetic factors (*2 marks*)

   (ii) environmental factors. (*2 marks*)

(*Total 6 marks*)

NEAB June 1995, Paper BY09, No. 4

7. The allele for normal haemoglobin, Hb^A, and the allele for sickle-cell haemoglobin, Hb^S, are codominant.

(a) Explain the meaning of the terms:
   (i) allele; (*1 mark*)

   (ii) codominant. (*1 mark*)

(b) What is the probability that two heterozygotes will have a child who is homozygous for the sickle-cell condition? (*1 mark*)

(c) In some Afican populations 20% of people are heterozygous for the sickle-cell allele. Explain why, in these African populations:
   (i) many individuals with the genotype $Hb^A Hb^A$ do not survive: (*1 mark*)

   (ii) the heterozygotes have a selective advantage over individuals with genotype. $Hb^S Hb^S$. (*1 mark*)

(d) In the descendants of people taken from these African populations to the United States 200 years ago, the frequency of people who are heterozygous for the sickle-cell allele is now much lower. Suggest an explanation for this. (*2 marks*)

(*Total 7 marks*)

NEAB June 1995, Paper BY09, No. 2

8. Albino mice are completely white because they cannot produce coat pigment. They cannot produce this pigment because of a gene mutation that affects the formation of an enzyme in the metabolic pathway that produces the pigment. The enzyme produced by the mutant gene does not function effectively.

(a) (i) Explain what is meant by gene mutation. (*1 mark*)

   (ii) Explain how a gene mutation could result in a change in the amino acid sequence in the enzyme produced by the coat-pigment gene. (*4 marks*)

(b) Explain why mice which are heterozygous for this mutant gene are never albinos. *(2 marks)*

(Total 7 marks)

NEAB June 1995, Paper BY02, No.4

9. Caffeine is a drug which affects synaptic transmission. It is commonly ingested as a component of tea, coffee or soft drinks.

A student measured the reaction times of eight people before and after they had ingested caffeine. The table shows the reaction times to an aural stimulus of eight people, firstly without caffeine, and then one hour after ingesting 80 mg of caffeine.

Person	Reaction time/ms		Difference in reaction time x	x^2
	Caffeine intake Zero	Caffeine intake 80 mg		
A	285	270	15	225
B	315	285	30	900
C	255	245	10	100
D	305	345	−40	1600
E	340	285	55	3025
F	275	255	20	400
G	315	280	35	1225
H	267	245	22	484
Mean	**294.63**	**276.25**	$\Sigma x = 147$	$\Sigma x^2 =$

(Adapted from Foster, *J. Biol. Ed.* (1989))

Carry out a *t*-test to determine whether the difference in reaction times afteb caffeine ingestion is significant at the 5 per cent level.

Use the formula given below.

$$t = \frac{\overline{x}\sqrt{n}}{s}$$

where $\overline{x}$ is the mean of the difference in reaction time.

n is the number of people tested

s is found from the formula

$$s = \sqrt{\frac{\Sigma x^2 - \frac{(\Sigma x)^2}{n}}{n-1}}$$

(a) (i) Calcelate the values of Σx^2

and $\frac{(\Sigma x)^2}{n}$. *(2 marks)*

(ii) Use your values from (i) to calculate the value of *s*. Show your working. *(2 marks)*

(iii) Use the information in the table and your value from (a) (ii) to calculate the value of *t*. *(2 marks)*

(b) A stadistical table showed that significance at the 5 per cent level with 7 degrees of freedom required a *t*-value of at least 2.365.

What does this tell you about the effects of caffeine ingestion on reaction time in this investigation? *(1 mark)*

(Total 7 markc)

ULEAC June 1993, Paper 3, No. 6

10. The graphs show the distribution of ear length in a variety of the corn, and the length of the horn on the head of males of a species of beetle.

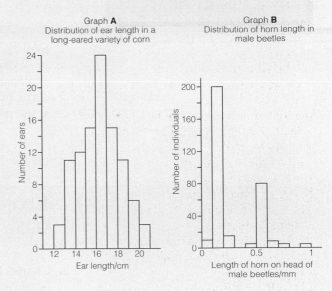

Graph **A**
Distribution of ear length in a long-eared variety of corn

Graph **B**
Distribution of horn length in male beetles

(a) What type of graphic is shown by graph **A**? *(1 mark)*

(b) Variation can be caused by genetic and environmental factors. Use your knowledge of the causes of genetic variation to explain the pattern of variation in

(i) ear length in corn;

(ii) horn length in beetles. *(2 marks)*

(c) Studies of twins are sometimes used to determine whether human characteristics are controlled mainly by genetic or by environmental factors. The table shows mean differences in certain physical characteristics between pairs of twins.

Mean difference in	Identical twins reared together	Non-identical same-sex twins reared together	Identical twins reared apart
Height	1.7	4.4	1.8
Mass/kg	2.0	4.9	4.8
Head width/mm	2.8	4.2	2.9

From these data, in which of these characteristics is variation controlled mainly by differences in (i) genotype and (ii) environment? Explain your answers. *(4 marks)*

(Total 7 marks)

NEAB June 1996, Biology Paper I, No. 16

9 Evolution

Evolution is the process by which new species are formed from pre-existing ones over a period of time. It is not the only explanation of the origins of the many species which exist on earth, but it is the one generally accepted by the scientific world at the present time.

9.1 Evolution through natural selection (Darwin/Wallace)

Charles Darwin (1809–1882) became the naturalist on HMS *Beagle* which sailed in 1832 to South America and Australasia. On the voyage he had an excellent opportunity to examine a wide variety of living plants and animals and his knowledge of geology was invaluable for studying fossils he came across. He was struck by the remarkable likeness between the fossils he found and present-day organisms. At the same time he observed the differences in certain characters that occurred when otherwise similar animals lived in different environments. He noted such differences between the organisms of different continents and between the east and west coast of South America. What impressed him most were the distinct variations between the species which inhabited different islands in a small group 580 miles off the coast of Ecuador. These were the Galapagos Islands. In particular he studied the finches which inhabited each of the islands. While they all had a general resemblance to those on the mainland of Ecuador, they nevertheless differed in certain respects, such as the shape of their beaks. He considered that originally a few finches had strayed from the mainland to these volcanic islands, shortly after their formation. Encountering, as they did, a range of different foods, each type of finch developed a beak which was adapted to suit their diet. Following the five-year voyage, Darwin set about developing his views on the mechanism by which these changes occurred.

Quite independently of Darwin, Alfred Wallace had drawn his own conclusions on the mechanism of evolution. Wallace sent Darwin a copy of this theory and Darwin realized that they were in essence the same as his own. As a result, they jointly presented their findings to the Linnaean Society in 1858. A year later Darwin published his book *On the Origin of Species by Means*

Charles Darwin

of Natural Selection and the Preservation of Favoured Races in the Struggle for Life. The essential features of the theory Darwin put forward are:

1. Overproduction of offspring
All organisms produce large numbers of offspring which, if they survived, would lead to a geometric increase in the size of any population.

2. Constancy of numbers
Despite the tendency to increase numbers due to overproduction of offspring, most populations actually maintain relatively constant numbers. The majority of offspring must therefore die, before they are able to reproduce.

3. Struggle for existence
Darwin deduced on the basis of **1** and **2** that members of the species were constantly competing with each other in an effort to survive. In this struggle for existence only a few would live long enough to breed.

4. Variation among offspring
The sexually produced offspring of any species show individual variations (Section 8.5) so that generally no two offspring are identical.

5. Survival of the fittest by natural selection
Among the variety of offspring there will be some better able to withstand the prevailing conditions than others. That is, some will be better adapted ('fitter') to survive in the struggle for existence. These types are more likely to survive long enough to breed.

6. Like produces like
Those which survive to breed are likely to produce offspring similar to themselves. The advantageous characteristics which gave them the edge in the struggle for existence are likely to be passed on to the next generation.

7. Formation of new species
Individuals lacking favourable characteristics are less likely to survive long enough to breed. Over many generations their numbers will decline. The individuals with favourable characteristics will breed, with consequent increase in their numbers. The inheritance of one small variation will not, by itself, produce a new species. However, the development of a number of variations in a particular direction over many generations will gradually lead to the evolution of a new species.

9.2   Natural selection

The evolutionary theory of Darwin and Wallace is based on the mechanism of natural selection. Let us look more closely at exactly how this process operates.

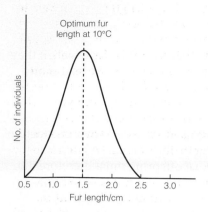

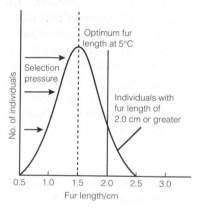

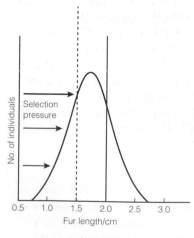

Selection is the process by which organisms that are better adapted to their environment survive and breed, while those less well adapted fail to do so. The better adapted organisms are more likely to pass their characteristics to succeeding generations. Every organism is therefore subjected to a process of selection, based upon its suitability for survival given the conditions which exist at the time. The organism's environment exerts a **selection pressure**. The intensity and direction of this pressure varies in both time and space. Selection pressure determines the spread of any allele within the gene pool.

9.2.1 Types of selection

There are three types of selection which operate in a population of a given species.

Directional selection
When environmental conditions change, there is a selection pressure on a species causing it to adapt to the new conditions. Within a population there will be a range of individuals in respect of any one character. The continuous variation among individuals forms a normal distribution curve, with a mean which represents the optimum for the existing conditions. When these conditions change, so does the optimum necessary for survival. A few individuals will possess the new optimum and by selection these in time will predominate. The mean for this particular character will have shifted. An example is illustrated in Fig. 9.1.

In human evolution the climate has acted as a selection agent bringing about directional selection. Warmer conditions have gradually resulted in greater skin pigmentation (to protect against the UV rays of the sun), a longer, thinner body shape (to dissipate heat more easily), and a broader nose as exemplified by negroid races. Colder conditions have gradually resulted in lighter skin colour, a shorter, more squat body and a narrower nose (to warm and moisten cold air more effectively) as exemplified by Inuit (Eskimo) groups.

Stabilizing selection
This occurs in all populations and tends to eliminate the extremes within a group. In this way it reduces the variability of a population and so reduces the opportunity for evolutionary change.

In a population of a particular mammal fur length shows continuous variation.

1. When the average environmental temperature is 10 °C, the optimum fur length is 1.5 cm. This then represents the mean fur length of the population.

2. A few individuals in the population already have a fur length of 2.0 cm or greater. If the average environmental temperature falls to 5 °C these individuals are better insulated and so are more likely to survive to breed. There is a selection pressure favouring individuals with longer fur.

3. The selection pressure causes a shift in the mean fur length towards longer fur over a number of generations. The selection pressure continues.

4. Over further generations the shift in the mean fur length continues until it reaches 2.0 cm – the optimum length for the prevailing average environmental temperature of 5 °C. The selection pressure now ceases.

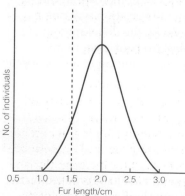

Fig. 9.1 Directional selection

In our earlier example, we see that at 10 °C there was an optimum coat length of 1.5 cm. Individuals within the population, however, had a range of coat lengths from 0.5 cm to 3.0 cm. Under normal climatic circumstances the average temperature will vary from one year to the next. In a warm year with an average temperature of 15 °C the individuals with shorter fur may be at an advantage as they can lose heat more quickly. In these years the numbers of individuals with short fur increase at the expense of those with long fur. In cold years, the reverse is true and individuals with long fur increase at the expense of their companions with shorter coats. The periodic fluctuations in environmental temperature thus help to maintain individuals with very long and very short fur.

Imagine that the average environmental temperature was 10 °C every year and there were no fluctuations. Without the warmer years to give them an advantage in the competition with others in the population, the individuals with short hair would decline in numbers. Likewise the absence of colder years would reduce the number of long-haired individuals. The mean fur length would remain at 1.5 cm but the distribution curve would show a much narrower range of lengths (Fig. 9.2). One human example of stabilizing selection is body weight at birth. Most babies are around 3.6 kg with those who are smaller or larger having a higher death rate.

Disruptive selection
Although much less common, this form of selection is important in achieving evolutionary change. Disruptive selection may occur when an environmental factor takes a number of distinct forms. To take our hypothetical example, suppose the environmental temperature alternated between 5 °C in the winter and 15 °C in the summer, with no intermediate temperatures occurring. These conditions would favour the development of two distinct phenotypes within the population: one with a fur length of 2.0 cm (the optimum of an environmental temperature of 5 °C); the other with a fur length of 1.0 cm (optimum length at 15 °C). (Fig. 9.3)

9.2.2 Polymorphism

Polymorphism (*poly* – 'many', *morph* – 'form') is the word used to describe the presence of clear-cut, genetically determined differences between large groups in the same population. One well known example is the A B O blood grouping system found in human populations; another is the colour and banding patterns which arise in certain species of land snail.

Polymorphism in the land snail (Cepaea nemoralis)
The shells of the land snail *Cepaea nemoralis* have a variety of distinct colours including yellow, pink and brown. The snail shells may also be marked with dark bands, ranging in number from 1 to 5. Colour and banding are both genetically determined.

The snail is an important source of food for the song thrush. The thrush uses rocks as anvils upon which to smash the shells to enable them to eat the soft parts within. Examination of the smashed shells reveals that the proportions of each type differ

1. *Initially there is a wide range of fur length about the mean of 1.5 cm. The fur lengths of less than 1.0 cm or greater than 2.0 cm in individuals, are maintained by rapid breeding in years when the average temperature is much warmer or colder than normal.*

2. *When the average environmental temperature is consistently around 10°C with little annual variation, individuals with very long or very short hair are eliminated from the population over a number of generations.*

1.
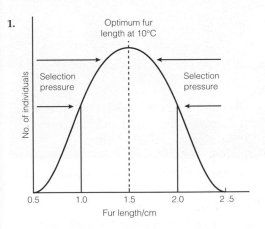

2.
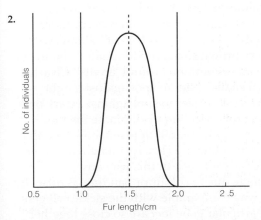

Fig. 9.2 Stabilizing selection

1. *When there is a wide range of temperatures throughout the year, there is continuous variation in fur length around a mean of 1.5 cm.*

2. *Where the summer temperature is static around 15°C and the winter temperature is static around 5°C, individuals with two distinct fur lengths predominate: 1.0 cm types which are active in summer and 2.0 cm types which are active in winter.*

3. *After many generations two distinct sub-populations are formed.*

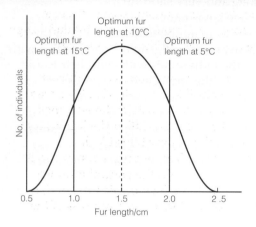

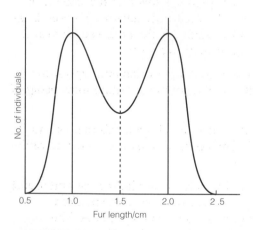

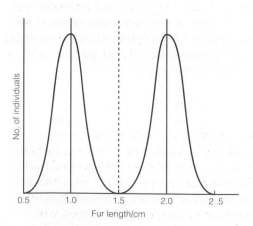

Fig. 9.3 Disruptive selection

according to the habitat around. Where the surrounding area is relatively uniform, e.g. grassland, the proportion of banded shells is greater among those smashed by thrushes. Where the surrounding area is less uniform, e.g. hedgerows, the proportion of unbanded shells is greater. How can we interpret these results?

It must be assumed that on uniform backgrounds, banded shells are more conspicuous and so more easily seen by predators such as thrushes. These shells form a disproportionately large number of smashed shells found around 'anvils' in this type of habitat. In less uniform backgrounds, bands on the shells tend to break up the shape of the animal, thus providing a form of disruptive camouflage. By contrast, the unbanded ones are not camouflaged. Being more conspicuous these forms are more frequently captured by thrushes and are consequently more common around nearby 'anvils'. As a result of this selection, the variety of snail shell commonly found around any anvil is correspondingly rare in the surrounding habitat.

Colour varieties (variously striped and unstriped) of white-lipped snail (*Cepaea hortensis*)

In a similar way, there is a correlation between shell colour and the predominant colour of the habitat background. Where the habitat is light in colour yellow-shelled snails are most common in the area, but remains of brown ones occur more frequently around 'anvils'. The reverse is true of habitats with dark backgrounds where brown snails predominate overall, but remains of yellows are more common around 'anvils'. Clearly the thrushes find brown snails easier to spot against a light background and yellow snails easier to spot against a dark one. In time one might expect this selection to eliminate the more conspicuous variety from any habitat. It appears, however, that the genes for colour and banding are closely linked with other genes which may confer advantages. In this way any evolutionary disadvantage due to colour or banding, is offset by these advantages, in a way comparable with the sickle cell gene (Section 8.5.3). When particular gene loci are so close together that crossing over almost never separates them, then these genes

Peppered moth (*Biston betularia*) – normal and melanic forms on charred tree trunk (top) and on birch trunk (above)

effectively act as a single unit. This unit is called a **super-gene** and is the possible explanation for the continued existence of certain polymorphic forms of *Cepaea* in particular habitats.

Polymorphism in the peppered moth (Biston betularia) (*Industrial melanism*)

Another example of polymorphism occurs in the peppered moth *Biston betularia*. It existed only in its natural light form until the middle of the last century. Around this time a melanic (black) variety arose as a result of a mutation. These mutants had doubtless occurred before (one existed in a collection made before 1819) but they were highly conspicuous against the light background of lichen-covered trees and rocks on which they normally rest. As a result, the black mutants were subject to greater predation from insect-eating birds, e.g. robins and hedge sparrows, than were the better camouflaged, normal light forms.

When in 1848 a melanic form of the peppered moth was captured in Manchester, most buildings, walls and trees were blackened by the soot of 50 years of industrial development. The sulphur dioxide in smoke emissions killed the lichens that formerly covered trees and walls. Against this black background the melanic form was less, not more conspicuous than the light natural form. As a result, the natural form was taken by birds more frequently than the melanic form and, by 1895, 98% of Manchester's population of the moth was of the melanic type.

Dr H.B.D. Kettlewell attempted to show that this change in gene frequency was the result of natural selection. He bred large stocks of both varieties of the moth. He then marked them and released them in equal numbers in two areas:

1. Birmingham (an area where soot pollution and high sulphur dioxide levels had resulted in 90% of the existing moths being of the melanic form).

2. Rural Dorset (where the absence of high levels of soot and sulphur dioxide meant lichen-covered trees and no record of the melanic form of the moth).

He recaptured samples of the moths using light traps and found that in polluted Birmingham over twice as many marked melanic moths were recaptured as normal light ones. The reverse was true for unpolluted Dorset where the normal light form was recaptured with twice the frequency of the melanic type.

Further studies have confirmed the findings that the melanic form has a selection advantage over the lighter form in industrial areas. In non-polluted areas the selection advantage lies with the lighter form.

9.2.3 Drug resistance

Following the production of antibiotics in the 1940s, it was noticed that certain bacterial cells developed resistance to these drugs, i.e. the antibiotics failed to kill them in the normal way. Experiments showed that this was not a cumulative tolerance to the drug, but the result of chance mutation. This mutation in some way allowed the bacteria to survive in the presence of drugs like penicillin, e.g. by producing an enzyme to break it

PROJECT

The land snail *Cepaea nemoralis* possesses a shell with or without black bands

1. Collect data on land snails from two different localities, for example from a beech-wood and from under hedges, or from an oak-wood and from grassland.

2. Score the numbers of banded and unbanded snails from the two localities.

3. Analyse the data and suggest a hypothesis to explain the results.

Any species of plant can exhibit polymorphism

Select examples of a particular species from two different localities and find out how they differ, for example, in

(a) height
(b) branching
(c) leaf shape
(d) numbers and colours of flowers, etc.

down. In the presence of penicillin non-resistant forms are destroyed. There is a selection pressure favouring the resistant types. The greater the quantity and frequency of penicillin use, the greater the selection pressure. The medical implications are obvious. Already the usefulness of many antibiotics has been destroyed by bacterial resistance to them. By 1950, the majority of staphylococcal infections were already penicillin-resistant.

The problem has been made more acute by the recent discovery that resistance can be transmitted between species. This means that disease-causing bacteria can become resistant to a given antibiotic even before the antibiotic is used against them. As a result, certain staphylococci are resistant to all major antibiotics.

9.3 Artificial selection

Humans have cultivated plants and kept animals for about 10 000 years. Over much of this time they have bred them selectively. There have been two basic methods, each with a particular aim:

1. Inbreeding – When, by chance, a variety of plant or animal arose which possessed some useful character, it was bred with its close relatives in the hope of retaining the character for future generations. Inbreeding is still widely practised today, especially with dogs and cats.

One problem with inbreeding is that it increases the danger of a harmful recessive gene expressing itself, because there is greater risk of a double recessive individual arising (Section 7.1.4). As a result, inbreeding is not usually carried out indefinitely but new genes are introduced by outbreeding with other stock. While this makes consistent qualities harder to achieve, it can lead to stronger, healthier offspring. Crop improvements of cereals such as wheat can be carried out in this way.

2. Outbreeding – This is carried out in order to improve existing varieties. Where two individuals of a species each have their own beneficial feature they are often bred together in order to combine the two. A racehorse breeder, for example, might cross a fast mare with a strong stallion in the hope of attaining a strong, fast foal. Outbreeding frequently produces tougher individuals with a better chance of survival, especially where many generations of inbreeding have taken place. This is known as **hybrid vigour**. Programmes of crop improvement using this method include the breeding of maize plants.

Extreme examples of outbreeding occur when individuals of different species are mated. Only rarely is this successful. When it is, the resulting offspring are normally sterile. These sterile hybrids may still be useful. Mules, produced from a cross between a horse and a donkey, have strength and endurance which make them useful beasts of burden.

The improvement of the human race by the selection or elimination of specific characters is called **eugenics**. To some, the idea of such selection is offensive but, as we saw in Section 8.7, genetic counselling is now fairly commonplace. Provided the

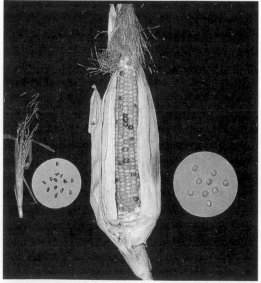

Selective breeding of corn. Note the small cob and seeds of the wild type (left) compared to the modern variety (right)

individuals involved remain free to make their own choice about whether to have children, many see no harm in providing them with statistical information which might help them reach a decision.

9.4 Isolation mechanisms

Within a population of one species there are groups of individuals which breed with one another. Each of these breeding sub-units is called a **deme**. Although individuals within the deme breed with each other most of the time, it is still possible for them to breed with individuals of separate demes. There therefore remains a single gene pool. If demes become separated in some way, the flow of genes between them may cease. Each deme may then evolve along separate lines. The two demes may become so different that, even if reunited, they would be incapable of successfully breeding with each other. They would thus become separate species each with its own gene pool. The process by which species are formed is called **speciation** and depends on groups within a population becoming isolated in some way. There are three main forms of isolation:

9.4.1 Allopatric speciation

Allopatric speciation occurs as the result of two populations becoming geographically isolated. Any physical barrier which prevents two groups of the same species from meeting must prevent them interbreeding. Such barriers include mountain ranges, deserts, oceans, rivers, etc. The effectiveness of any barrier varies from species to species. A small stream may separate two groups of woodlice, whereas the whole of the Pacific Ocean may fail to isolate some species of birds. A region of water may separate groups of terrestrial organisms, whereas land may isolate aquatic ones. The environmental conditions on either side of a barrier frequently differ. This leads to the group on each side adapting to suit its own environment – a process called **adaptive radiation**.

Imagine, for example, that climatic changes resulted in two areas becoming separated from one another by an area of arid grassland. A possible sequence of events which could lead to a new species being formed under these conditions is illustrated in Fig. 9.4.

9.4.2 Sympatric speciation

Sympatric speciation occurs when organisms inhabiting the same area become reproductively isolated into two groups for reasons other than geographical barriers. Such reasons might include:

1. **The genitalia of the two groups may be incompatible (mechanical isolation)** – It may be physically impossible for the penis of a male mammal to enter the female's vagina.

2. **The gametes may be prevented from meeting** – In animals, the sperm may not survive in the female's reproductive tract or, in plants, the pollen tube may fail to grow.

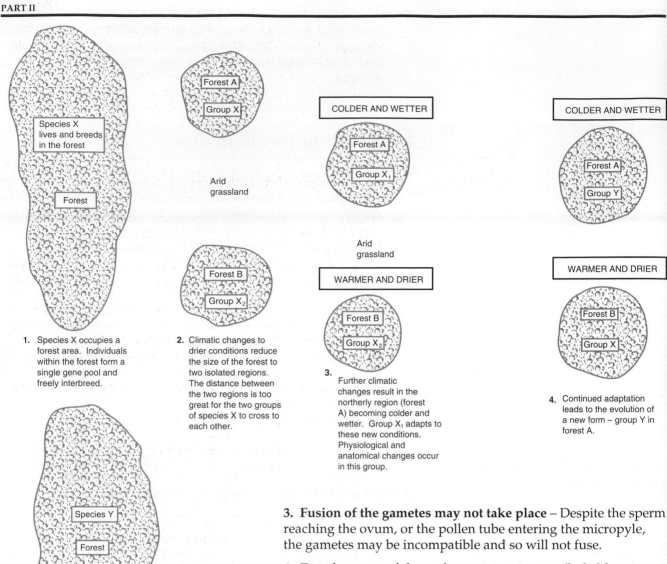

1. Species X occupies a forest area. Individuals within the forest form a single gene pool and freely interbreed.

2. Climatic changes to drier conditions reduce the size of the forest to two isolated regions. The distance between the two regions is too great for the two groups of species X to cross to each other.

3. Further climatic changes result in the northerly region (forest A) becoming colder and wetter. Group X_1 adapts to these new conditions. Physiological and anatomical changes occur in this group.

4. Continued adaptation leads to the evolution of a new form – group Y in forest A.

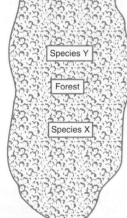

5. A return to the original climatic conditions results in regrowth of forest. Forests A and B are merged and groups X and Y are reunited. The two groups are no longer capable of interbreeding. They are now two species X and Y each with its own gene pool.

Fig. 9.4 Speciation due to geographical isolation

3. Fusion of the gametes may not take place – Despite the sperm reaching the ovum, or the pollen tube entering the micropyle, the gametes may be incompatible and so will not fuse.

4. Development of the embryo may not occur (hybrid inviability) – Despite fertilization taking place, further development may not occur, or fatal abnormalities may arise during early growth.

5. Polyploidy (hybrid sterility) – When individuals of different species breed, the sets of chromosomes from each parent are obviously different. These sets are unable to pair up during meiosis and so the offspring cannot produce gametes. For example, the cross between a horse (2n = 60) and an ass (2n = 66) results in a mule (2n = 63). It is impossible for 63 chromosomes to pair up during meiosis. More details of polyploidy are given in Section 8.5.

6. Behavioural isolation – Before copulation can take place, many animals undergo elaborate courtship behaviour. This behaviour is often stimulated by the colour and markings on members of the opposite sex, the call of a mate or particular actions of a partner. Small differences in any of these may prevent mating. If a female stickleback does not make an appropriate response to actions of the male, he ceases to court her. The beak shape in many of Darwin's finches in the Galapagos Islands is the only feature which distinguishes the species. Individuals will only mate with partners having a similar beak to themselves. The song of a bird or the call of a frog must be exact if it is to elicit the appropriate breeding response from the opposite sex. The timing of courtship behaviour and gamete production is also important. If the breeding season of two groups (demes) does not coincide, they cannot breed. Different flowering times in plants may mean that cross-pollination is impossible. These are both examples of **seasonal isolation**.

9.5 Humans as primates

Humans are classified with lemurs, monkeys and apes in the order Primate. This subdivision of the vertebrate class Mammalia is a difficult one to define, but there are some common trends in their evolution which have led to their being grouped together. These trends include:

- separate ulna and radius allowing the wrist to be turned
- possession of nails instead of claws allowing for the development of sensitive pads on the fingertips
- shortening of the snout and decreasing dependence on the sense of smell
- tendency for the eyes to be on the front of the head allowing for binocular vision
- greater development of the brain
- prolonged gestation period
- prolonged postnatal development allowing for increased potential for learning.

Fig. 9.5 Simplified classification of the order Primate

Order Primate

Suborder Prosimii
- long snout and wet noses
- eyes tend to be directed sideways
- nails (except claws on 2nd digit)
- seasonal breeding
- no fovea
  e.g. lemurs
       lorises
       tarsiers

Suborder Anthropoidea
(monkeys and apes)
- short snout and dry noses
- eyes forward facing
- nails on all digits
- breed all year
- fovea

Superfamily Ceboidea
(New World monkeys)
- tails
- nostrils face sideways
- first digit not fully opposable
- ischial callosities absent
  e.g. marmosets
       spider monkey

Superfamily Cercopithecoidea
(Old World monkeys)
- most have tails
- nostrils face downwards
- first digit not fully opposable on hand and foot
- ischial callosities present
  e.g. rhesus monkeys
       baboons

Superfamily Hominoidea
(Apes)
- no tails
- nostrils face downwards
- first digit not fully opposable on hand
- ischial callosities absent

Family Hylobatidae
- cannot walk bipedally
- do not knuckle walk
  e.g. gibbon

Family Pongidae
- cannot balance well on two legs
- knuckle walk
  e.g. orang-utan
       chimpanzee
       gorilla

Family Hominidae
- balance fully on two legs
- do not knuckle walk
- large brain
- sparse body hair
- speech
  e.g. humans

9.5.1 Arboreal adaptations of primates

There are approximately 200 species of living primates, almost all of which spend most of their time in trees in tropical and subtropical forests. Many of the features which distinguish primates from other mammals may be considered as adaptations to an arboreal existence. This is most apparent in the anatomy of the hands and feet. The thumb is separated from the four fingers and in all non-human primates the big (great) toe is separated by a cleft from the other toes. These manipulative hands and feet are ideal for grasping tree branches. The loss of claws to be replaced by nails and sensitive fingertips and toetips has been interpreted as a way of making the fingers and toes more pliant in clinging to the bark of trees. It has also been argued that a tree dweller cannot rely on the sense of smell to search for food and mates but instead the visual sense becomes more important. Having eyes set close together and both pointing forwards favours the binocular vision required to judge distances when jumping from branch to branch. A corresponding development takes place in the regions of the brain receiving input from the eyes, fingers and toes and those areas which control precise movements of the limbs.

Some tree-dwelling animals, such as squirrels and birds, rely on producing large numbers of offspring to offset the loss by predation. Primates have adopted a different strategy and are unusual among mammals for producing few offspring at a time, for their relatively long gestation period and for their long infant-mother relationship. The long childhood period is an adaptation to behaviour patterns based on learning and the parents are often supported by living in family groups or larger troops.

9.5.2 Prosimians

The prosimians ('before the monkeys') are generally considered to show more primitive features than other primates and are distinguished from them largely by what they lack. Compared with monkeys and apes prosimians do not have short snouts, large brains, fused frontal bones, a fused joint in the centre of the lower jaw, and a post-orbital plate behind the eyes. There are fossil representatives but present-day forms include the lorises and bushbabies of Asia and Africa, the lemurs of Madagascar and the tarsiers of Indonesia. Most prosimians are nocturnal but the lemurs, isolated from competition in Madagascar, are largely diurnal. They have a well-developed sense of smell with a long snout and a wet nose like that of a dog. They live in large social groups occupying home ranges, or territories, of varying sizes. The olfactory communication on which prosimians rely is relatively slow and cannot transmit complex information; however it does persist and is useful in marking territorial boundaries. In common with other primates, prosimians have flattened nails supporting their sensitive finger and toe tips but they also retain a grooming claw on the second toe.

The tarsier is intermediate in form between the majority of the prosimians and the anthropoids having a shorter snout and a reduced dependence on the sense of smell.

Ring-tailed lemur. This prosimian has a long snout and grasping hands and feet

Prosimians

Anthropoids

Unfused
frontal bones

Larger, more forward facing eyes

Fused frontal bones

Small
upper incisors
separated
by a cleft

Unfused
midline joint
in the lower jaw

Lower jaw fused in midline

Postorbital bar (no closure)

Long
snout

Postorbital closure

Reduced
snout

Larger, more rounded braincase

Grooming claw

Fur

Fig. 9.6 The main distinctions between prosimians and anthropoids

9.5.3 New World Monkeys

The New World monkeys of South America are sometimes referred to as the *platyrrhines* or broad-nosed monkeys. They are thought to have evolved about 50 million years ago from lemur-like animals which were then widely distributed over Europe and North America. The New World monkeys are a diverse group including the tiny marmosets and tamarins, the medium-sized capuchin and squirrel monkeys and the larger spider monkeys. The most familiar New World monkey is the spider monkey whose prehensile tail serves almost as a fifth limb in locomotion and manipulation, its tip being covered with fingerprint ridges. In form and behaviour these platyrrhine monkeys show similarities with Old World monkeys and gibbons, even though their origins are entirely different.

9.5.4 Old World Monkeys

The narrow-nosed or *catarrhine* primates of the Old World are divided into two main groups: the Old World monkeys (Cercopithecoidea) and the apes (Hominoidea).

The Cercopithecoidea are tailed quadrupedal monkeys with two notable features. They have calloused buttock-like skin pads called **ischial callosities** which support their weight when they sit down and they have highly specialized teeth. Compared with

Squirrel monkey

Baboon. The narrow thorax of this grassland monkey is evident

hominoids the Old World Monkeys have molars with higher and more pointed cusps, connected by sharp shearing crests. The front premolar is like an elongated blade against which the dagger-like upper canine is sharpened. These adaptations make the cercopithecoids efficient leaf-eaters and fearsome fighters. The leaf-monkeys are such highly specialized leaf-eaters that they have evolved stomachs with multiple subdivisions rather like those of a cow. Other Old World monkeys are principally fruit-eaters but many eat a variety of food ranging from seeds to baby antelope.

Although the leaf-monkeys retain an arboreal existence in the high forest canopy other Old World monkeys, such as baboons and the Patas monkeys live mainly in grassland savannah areas. The vertebral column and limb bones are adapted for this terrestrial way of life. The thorax is narrow and there is a reduced ability to spread the arms caused by a re-orientation of the shoulder blades and shoulder joints. These features are especially evident in the fast-running Patas monkeys. The terrestrial habit of the baboon is also apparent in its shortened fingers and strong fully opposable thumbs.

9.5.5 Hominoids

There are two groups of non-human hominoids, or apes: the gibbons (family Hylobatidae) and the great apes (family Pongidae) which includes the chimpanzees, gorillas and orangutans. They all have elongated arms and fingers and resemble humans in having a broad thorax, reduction in the length of the vertebral column between the rib cage and the pelvis, and extremely flexible shoulders, elbows and wrists.

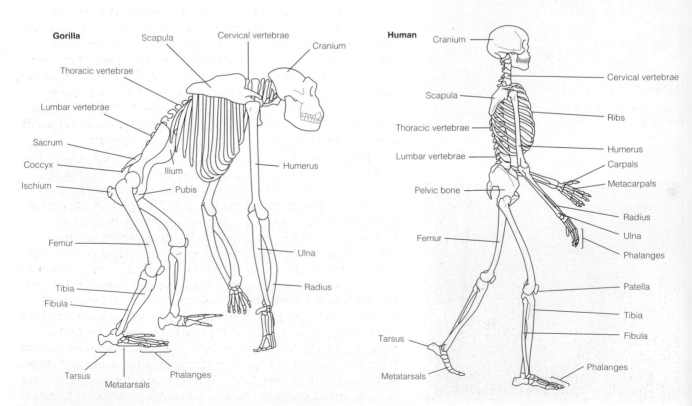

Fig. 9.7 Comparison of the skeletons of two hominoids: the knuckle-walking gorilla and a bipedal human

The value of these arboreal adaptations is particularly apparent in the gibbon which moves by swinging under branches with its arms, a method of locomotion known as **brachiation**. The tail, no longer needed for balance, is reduced to a vestige. The larger hominoids are less gibbon-like in their activity because of their greater mass. Orang-utans do brachiate but also use their hind limbs to support their weight when clambering through trees. Gorillas, with adult males reaching 200 kg, spend most of their time on or near the ground. The hands of gorillas and chimpanzees show arboreal and terrestial features. Although they have long fingers for grasping branches they fold them into their palms when walking on the ground and support their weight on the thickly padded areas at the back of their knuckles.

The stable social groups formed by the higher primates are important for animals whose young have a prolonged period of dependence on the adults. To primates, grooming is far more than a form of hygiene. It is part of the dominance ritual, it reduces tensions within the group and it appears to be an enjoyable pastime. Most of the grooming is done by females; dominant males get the most grooming and give the least. For young primates childhood play is an opportunity for learning, protected by the social group. Learned behaviour among primates means that the group as a whole has more knowledge and experience than its individual members.

The mountain gorillas of Rwanda were studied extensively by Dian Fossey from 1967 until her death in 1985. Most of the gorillas she studied lived in groups of 5 to 20, each group led by a powerful silverback male. His dominance over the group is absolute, but generally amiable. Although the groups spend much of their time eating and lying in the sun the males can become aggressive when the group is threatened or during reproductive rivalry. Males reaching full maturity can form their own family groups only by kidnapping females from other groups or usurping the dominant silverback male in their own group. The take-over of a group from an ageing male can involve fights between rival young males during which some older females and often the youngest infants may be killed. The new dominant male will then mate with the young females who will rear his progeny rather than those of his predecessor.

Chimpanzees have also been extensively studied in the wild and from both chimpanzees and gorillas we may be able to develop insights into human social behaviour. Males form the core of chimpanzee social groups and although they are ranked in a dominance hierarchy, aggression between them is rare. Females share the home range of the males but seldom have much contact with them unless they are sexually receptive. For most of the time lone females forage with their young. The main diet of chimpanzees comprises fruit, vegetation and birds' eggs but some males are hunters. They actively search for and kill monkeys and young baboons and occasionally share the carcass with others, regardless of their place in the hierarchy. Males regularly patrol the borders of their range and may seek out and fight neighbouring troops. They frequently use sticks and stones as weapons which they throw. Chimpanzees also exhibit the use of tools, using stones to crack nuts and sticks to extract termites from holes.

The gorilla supports its weight on thickly padded knuckles

Chimpanzee. The elongated fingers are clearly visible

9.6   Evidence for human evolution

It is important to realize that we are faced with many difficulties when trying to sort out fact from fiction in the evolution of mankind. When Darwin published his theory of evolution scientists knew only two fossils relevant to the search for our ancestors: an extinct ape and an early type of *Homo sapiens* called Neanderthal man. In a ten-year period about a century later over 600 near-human bones were unearthed in East Africa. When examining anatomical similarities in, say, humans and chimpanzees, it is difficult to assess how much they reflect an adjustment to the specialized lifestyle of the organism and how much they indicate a common ancestry. Modern science has provided us with more than the ability to examine anatomy and fossils. We can now employ various molecular and immunological techniques to study relatedness together with a variety of methods to produce a time scale for human evolution, but we must still be wary of making sweeping conclusions from limited evidence.

In 1932 G.E. Lewis discovered, in what is now Pakistan, jaw fragments with four teeth. The age of the fragments was uncertain, but probably lay between 8 and 10 million years ago. The creature was called *Ramapithecus* and it was supposed to be neither ape nor human, but something between the two. In the 1980s following the discovery of more fossils and after more than 50 years of being considered a proto-human, *Ramapithecus* was assigned to a group ancestral to the orang-utans which bore no close relationship to our own lineage. Before these new discoveries it was widely believed that *Ramapithecus* was a possible ancestor of the Hominidae and that humans most probably evolved in Asia, rather than in Africa as now generally accepted.

9.6.1 Comparative anatomy

We can test relationships between species by looking for characteristics that are similar in different species because they have been inherited from a common ancestor. Such similarities are called **homologies**. The more homologous characters that two species share the more closely related they are. We can look for similarities in the bones, teeth and soft parts of the body between ourselves and other living apes and try to decide which apes are our closest relatives – the gibbons, the orang-utans, the gorillas or the chimpanzees. Evidence suggests that the gibbons and the orang-utans are not as closely related to us as chimpanzees and gorillas are. For example, humans, gorillas and chimpanzees all have a frontal sinus (a cavity in the skull, just above the eye). Gibbons, orang-utans and other primates do not have a true frontal sinus. Comparative anatomy does not enable us to determine whether chimpanzees or gorillas are our closest relatives.

The possible relationships can be represented by simple branching diagrams called **cladograms** as shown in Fig. 9.8.

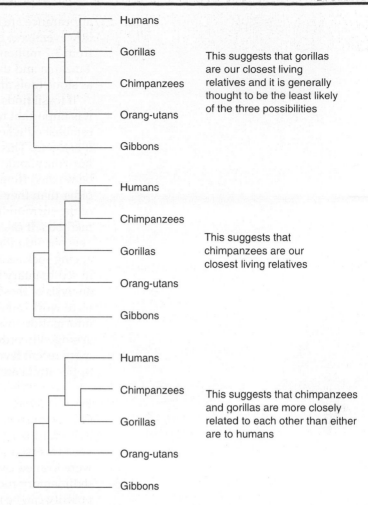

Fig. 9.8 Cladograms of humans, gorillas, chimpanzees, orang-utans and gibbons

9.6.2 Fossils and geochronology

All fossil records are very incomplete and that of primates is no exception: far more forms must have lived than are represented as fossils. In addition the record is geographically imbalanced with few examples from the Oligocene period (around 23–35 million years ago) in Africa, even though there is good reason to suppose it was a major centre of primate evolution. Human fossils are rare for a number of reasons. Humans existed in small numbers, reproduced slowly and lived a relatively long time. They often lived and died in the open where their bones could be gnawed by scavengers or decomposed. It was only when bones and teeth were buried rapidly in lake sediments, pools of mud or under volcanic ash that there was any chance of them being fossilized. Bone, by dry mass, is 35% protein and 65% mineral. Buried bones are subject to decay and the degeneration of the protein component can give an indication of the bone's age. In basic soils or lava the calcium content of the bone may be added to or it may be replaced by substances such as silica making the fossilized bone a heavy replica of the original. Fossilised bones may be crushed or distorted by earth movements or the mass of the overlying strata.

It is important to realize that no fossils have been found of the soft parts of early humans and so any representations of their appearance are based solely on informed reconstructions. We do, however, have other traces of our ancestors. Fossilized footprints from 3.7 million years ago have been found at Laetoli in Tanzania and there have been numerous finds of artefacts such as stone tools and pottery.

If fossil finds are to be of value in studying human evolution it is important to be able to age them. It should first be established whether a fossil is the same age as the rock in which it is found. This is not always easy but the bones at one level, or horizon, should be similar in chemical composition. Fossils may be washed from one horizon to a lower one and hence appear older than they actually are. The next step is to calculate the age of the surrounding rock using relative and/or absolute dating methods. If calculated ages are to be believed it is important to get concordant results with a number of methods. The science of ageing rocks is known as **geochronology**. Most fossils are found in sedimentary rocks deposited in layers known as strata. The analysis of these layers is known as **stratigraphy** and it permits us to work out a rough picture of past earth history. From this information fossils found in different rock structures can be arranged in order of age. The deepest strata are the oldest and more recent levels are laid down above them. Thus fossils in the upper strata are relatively younger than those in the lower strata.

Relative dating

The magnetic field of the earth runs from pole to pole. At irregular intervals in geological time the polarity of this field has been reversed. A record of the magnetic field present when rocks were formed can be preserved in iron-rich minerals within sedimentary rocks or lavas. The pattern of changes in the earth's polarity can be measured using a magnetometer and the results compared with a known palaeomagnetic polarity time scale.

Another relative method of dating depends on the fact that at any one time a particular organism is likely to have been widespread. For example in the Great Rift Valley of East Africa wild pig fossils are abundant and if they can be aged in one area it is likely that similar fossils, and bones of other animals found with them, found elsewhere, will be of a similar age.

Absolute dating

It is rarely possible to date fossil bones with any precision and so it is usually the geological material with which they are found which is examined. The process starts with an attempt to order past events and to link fossils to particular strata in the stratigraphic column. During the past 50 years many techniques have been devised for measuring the age of rocks and minerals but primate palaeontologists are mainly interested in those methods which are applicable to the past 70 million years. Three methods will be looked at which depend on the radioactive decay of one element or another. Decay is independent of temperature, pressure and prevailing chemical conditions and can be a very reliable method of dating.

Radiocarbon dating. Carbon 14 (^{14}C) is an unstable form of carbon. A certain proportion of ^{14}C exists in the atmosphere and, as CO_2, is absorbed and incorporated into the bodies of plants as carbohydrates. Animals absorb ^{14}C by eating the plants. Thereafter the ^{14}C disintegrates at a known rate – the half-life –

and the extent of this disintegration can be measured and related to the amount of ^{14}C remaining. ^{14}C has a half-life of only 5730 years and therefore measurements of the age of carbon compounds will cover a relatively short period. The method is most useful between 500 and 40 000 years ago. Errors occur because the level of ^{14}C in the atmosphere is not constant and also because samples can easily be contaminated by modern organic compounds.

Potassium–argon dating has been of great importance in primate palaeontology mainly because many important fossil sites in East Africa are in an area where volcanic activity was widespread. The radioactive potassium 40 (^{40}K) breaks down into argon gas at a known, constant rate. Because ^{40}K is found in volcanic ash potassium–argon dating can be used to date fossils found in, or between layers of, volcanic rock. The decay starts as the lava or ash cools and it takes 1265 million years for half the ^{40}K in a sample to decay into argon. Since argon is produced extremely slowly the method cannot be used with great accuracy for dates of less than 0.5 million years.

Fission-track dating methods are used mainly as a cross-check on dates established by the potassium–argon method and the same volcanic samples are normally used. The rare radioactive element uranium 238 splits spontaneously to create a tiny area of disruption within a crystal. This area of disruption is known as a track. Since the rate of spontaneous fission is known, microscopic examination of crystals to determine the track density, can give an estimate of age.

9.6.3 Comparative physiology and biochemistry

Morphological studies alone do not enable us to form a definitive picture of the relationship between humans and other higher primates. However, over 80 years ago the immunological properties of various primate proteins began to be investigated to provide evidence of evolutionary relationships.

Protein immunology
When serum albumin from animal A is injected into animal B the latter forms antibodies against it. These antibodies are specific to the proteins found in animal A. If the serum from animal B (which contains the antibodies) is mixed with serum from animal C, the antibodies will combine with their specific proteins. This causes a precipitate to form. If animal C has the same proteins as animal A there will be a maximum precipitation (100%). If animal C has fewer similar proteins, the amount of precipitation will be less. In other words, the more closely related any two animals are, the more similar are their proteins and the more precipitation occurs.

The results on the next page appear to indicate that chimpanzees and gorillas are very closely related to each other and that they are our nearest living relatives, probably sharing a common ancestor about 5 million years ago.

Amino acid sequencing
The sequences of amino acids present in fibrinopeptides, haemoglobins and myoglobins in various primates have been

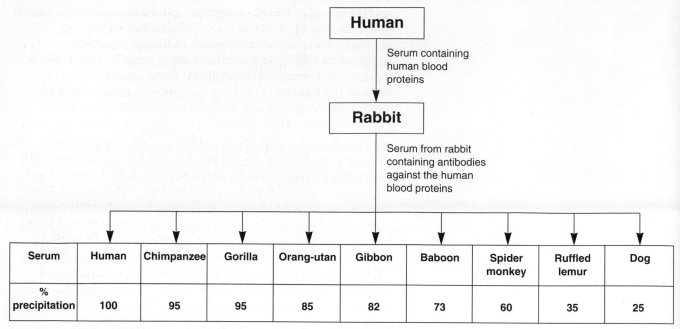

Fig. 9.9 *Immunological studies of relatedness*

studied in order to throw more light on primate evolution. The results of studies on β and α haemoglobin sequences are shown in Table 9.1. In this table four numbered positions on the β-chain and three on the α-chain have been investigated; each letter in the table represents a different amino acid.

TABLE 9.1 **Seven positions of β and α haemoglobin sequences showing differences among primates**

Primate	$\beta80$	$\beta87$	$\beta104$	$\beta125$	$\alpha12$	$\alpha23$	$\alpha113$
Human	N	T	R	P	A	E	L
Chimpanzee	N	T	R	P	A	E	L
Gorilla	N	T	*K*	P	A	*D*	L
Orang-utan	N	*K*	R	*Q*	*T*	*D*	L
Gibbon	*D*	*K*	R	*Q*	*T*	*D*	*H*
Lemur	N	*Q*	*T*	*A*	*T*	E	*H*

This shows that the amino acid sequences for the chimpanzee and the human are identical, the gorilla differs by two amino acids and the orang-utan by four. This would seem to indicate that humans are more closely related to chimpanzees than to gorillas, but studies of other amino acid sequences do not always support this view.

DNA–DNA hybridization
Changes in the DNA sequences of each generation are small but the net change over time is cumulative. Genetic divergence is therefore directly related to time. Since the early 1960s we have been able to measure genetic change between living organisms using the DNA–DNA hybridization technique. In outline this method depends on the fact that complementary base pairs in DNA are held together by hydrogen bonds. If the two chains of

the helix are separated they will recombine because they have complementary bases. If single strands of DNA from one organism are mixed with single strands from another there may be areas along the strands where the bases are complementary and duplexes will form. The more similar the chains, the more stable the duplexes will be and the higher the temperature that will be needed to separate them.

The difference in separation, or melting, temperature is often calculated as the temperature at which half the single-copy DNA sequences are in the duplex form and half have dissociated into single strands. This is called the T_{50H} (the temperature at 50 per cent hybridization). The difference in this parameter (the ΔT_{50H}) between the two species is an indicator of how much their sequences have diverged since they shared a common ancestor. DNA–DNA hybridization techniques indicate the following relationships between hominoid primates:

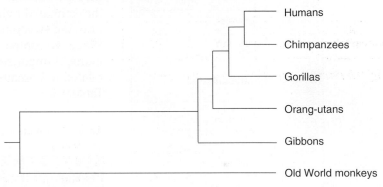

9.7 Evolution of hominoids

The earliest fossil evidence of primates is from over 60 million years ago with squirrel-like prosimians such as *Presiadapsis*. The first anthropoids were discovered in the Oligocene deposits at Fayum near Cairo where there are many primate remains such as *Apidium*, an arboreal animal resembling a squirrel monkey. *Apidium* is thought to mark the divergence between Old World and New World monkeys. Later in the Oligocene period, about 30 million years ago the Old World monkeys were beginning to show signs of their present diversity with some lightly built animals such as *Propliopithecus*. The Miocene beds of East Africa and Europe contain a range of fossils from about 25–10 million years ago. These include a forest-dwelling knuckle-walker called *Dryopithecus*, similar to a modern chimpanzee.

From about 15 million years ago in the Miocene and on into the Pliocene there was a gradual but highly significant climate change. Rainfall became less reliable and rain forests gave way to more open deciduous woodlands able to tolerate drier conditions. More plants flowered and fruited seasonally and animals evolved which were more suited to the new environments. Two groups of fossil apes, the **sivapithecines** and the smaller **ramapithecines** lived between 14 million and 8 million years ago. For many years these were thought to be ancestors of modern humans, but it is now generally accepted

TABLE 9.2 **The geological time scale**

Time	Era		Period
0.01	CENOZOIC	Quaternary	Holocene
2			Pleistocene
5.1		Tertiary	Pliocene
24.6			Miocene
38			Oligocene
65			Eocene
144	MESOZOIC		Cretaceous
213			Jurassic
248			Triassic
286	PALAEOZOIC		Permian
360			Carboniferous
408			Devonian
438			Silurian
505			Ordovician
590			Cambrian

Millions of years ago

that they are more closely related to present-day orang-utans. Most people now agree that the first man-apes were the **australopithecines** which lived between 5 million and 1.2 million years ago and that *Homo* arose in Africa 2.4 million years ago. When studying the evolution of *Homo* a number of trends become apparent: an increase in brain size, a decrease in tooth size, a change in skull shape and thickness and changes in behaviour.

9.7.1 Australopithecines

The first fragments of an australopithecine skull were found in 1924 at Taung, South Africa. Since then there have been numerous finds in many parts of East Africa, but especially along the Great Rift Valley. Numerous though these finds are they are only thought to represent between 0.02 and 0.000 02% of the estimated living population and we must be wary of drawing sweeping conclusions from our observations of them. When we compare australopithecine skulls with those of orang-utans, chimpanzees and humans they appear to be more closely related to humans and chimpanzees than to orang-utans. (See Table 9.3.)

TABLE 9.3 **Comparison of skulls of australopithecines with those of chimpanzees, humans and orang-utans**

Feature	Australopithecine Chimpanzee Human	Orang-utan
Frontal sinus	Present	Absent
Eye sockets	Wide and set apart	Tall and close together
Nose	Broad with stepped floor	Narrow with smooth floor
Second incisor	Nearly same size as first	Much smaller than first

However, if we are going to consider australopithecines as possible ancestors of ourselves we would expect them to have some features in common with humans, but which are not shared with chimpanzees (or gorillas). These features might include the possession of two cusps on each premolar tooth, walking upright and having a large brain. Australopithecines do have two cusps on their premolars, and the fragments of skeleton found support the idea that they walked upright on two legs. The evidence for the latter is as follows.

1. The backbone meets the skull towards the middle, so the head is quite well balanced on the backbone.
2. The neck muscles would have been quite small and attached low down on the skull.

These features resemble humans; gorilla skulls meet the backbone towards the back and the neck muscles are large and attached high on the skull.

3. The hip bones are short and broad.

Gorillas have long narrow hip bones to reflect the different size of the walking muscles.

4. The femur has a long neck and the shaft is long and only slightly curved.

5. The toes are short and the big toe points forwards.

In gorillas the toes are very long and the big toe sticks out at the side.

Although we believe australopithecines to have walked on two legs they probably stooped more than modern humans and did not stride along in the same way. This is indicated by the fact that their hip bones were more at the back of the body, rather than the side, and the head of the femur was flattened, not rounded.

The most well known australopithecine skeleton is that found at Hadar, Ethiopia in 1974 and nicknamed 'Lucy'. 'Lucy' is known as the Hadar australopithecine or *Australopithecus afarensis*. The remains of two other types have also been found: the **robust australopithecines** *Australopithecus robustus* and *A. boisei* and the **gracile australopithecines** *A. africanus*. Each of the australopithecines has special features which could link it to human beings: robust australopithecines have a similar pattern of tooth eruption; gracile australopithecines have a similar domed sloping forehead and Hadar australopithecines have their cheek bones in the same relative position. We do not, as yet, have enough evidence to decide which is our closest relative.

Fossil evidence shows that australopithecines probably existed for at least 3 million years and may have lived in grassland or at the edge of woodland. The structure of their teeth indicates that they are likely to have eaten vegetables and fruits, possibly with hard outer shells which needed crushing. We can speculate that they may have foraged during the day and then sheltered in caves or trees at night, possibly in multimale groups or as single males with a harem. There is no evidence for them making tools although they may have used objects such as sticks in a way similar to modern chimpanzees.

Fig. 9.10 Comparison of the skulls of a chimpanzee and a modern human with the skull of an australopithecine

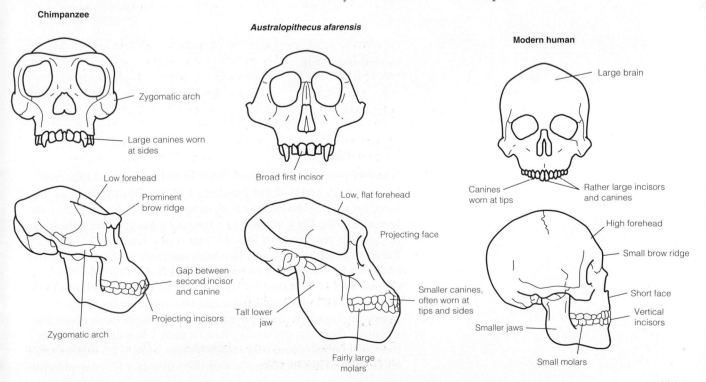

Chimpanzee

Zygomatic arch

Large canines worn at sides

Low forehead

Prominent brow ridge

Gap between second incisor and canine

Projecting incisors

Zygomatic arch

Australopithecus afarensis

Broad first incisor

Low, flat forehead

Projecting face

Tall lower jaw

Smaller canines, often worn at tips and sides

Fairly large molars

Modern human

Large brain

Canines worn at tips

Rather large incisors and canines

High forehead

Small brow ridge

Short face

Vertical incisors

Smaller jaws

Small molars

Walking on two legs

Humans are the only bipedal primates and there are many theories for the emergence of this unique pattern of locomotion. The argument that bipedalism evolved in conjunction with the use of stone tools is not supported by the fossil record. Another suggestion is that bipedalism frees the hands so that food and water can be carried from distant foraging sites back to the home base. It has even been proposed that walking upright increases the chance of evaporative cooling in a hot climate and prevents an enlarged brain from overheating. Whatever the reasons for its acquisition bipedalism has resulted in some unique human adaptations of the skeleton for taking the weight on the hind legs and balancing on one leg only as each stride is taken.

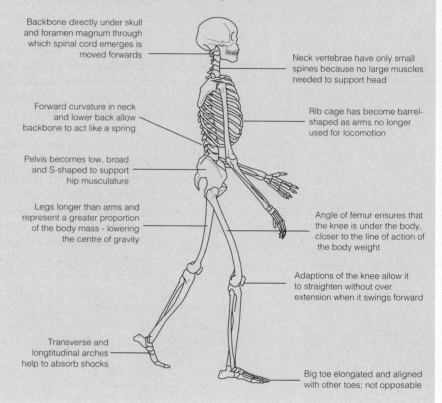

Backbone directly under skull and foramen magnum through which spinal cord emerges is moved forwards

Neck vertebrae have only small spines because no large muscles needed to support head

Forward curvature in neck and lower back allow backbone to act like a spring

Rib cage has become barrel-shaped as arms no longer used for locomotion

Pelvis becomes low, broad and S-shaped to support hip musculature

Legs longer than arms and represent a greater proportion of the body mass - lowering the centre of gravity

Angle of femur ensures that the knee is under the body, closer to the line of action of the body weight

Adaptions of the knee allow it to straighten without over extension when it swings forward

Transverse and longtitudinal arches help to absorb shocks

Big toe elongated and aligned with other toes; not opposable

9.7.2 *Homo habilis*

Another group of organisms thought to be our fossil relatives lived in East Africa about 2 million to 1.5 million years ago. They have been called **habilines** and were probably the first animals to make tools. They appear to have had a range of morphology or possibly two more or less distinct types: small and large. Like the australopithecines and like humans their premolars had two cusps and the structure of the skeleton shows that they walked on two legs. It is likely that they were more closely related to humans than to australopithecines because they had larger brains and made tools. Consequently they have been given the scientific name *Homo habilis* ('handy man'). It is apparent from the fossil bones found that *H. habilis* was only 1–1.5 metres tall and weighed about 40 kg – about the same as a 12-year-old child.

TABLE 9.4 **Some distinguishing features of the genus *Homo***

Feature	Description
Brain	Large in relation to body size. Volume normally exceeds 700 cm^3
Cranium	Large, to house enlarged brain
Nose	Prominent with bony ridge around nasal opening and bony spine in centre of nasal opening
Skull shape	Short (possibly associated with change in shape of throat and development of larynx)
Lower jaw	Bone is thin and often has a distinct prominence forming a chin
Teeth	Generally small and slow to erupt compared with apes
Behaviour	Development of: • food sharing • manipulative skills • speech and language • extended childhood • pair bonding

Brain casts made from the fossil crania show a brain volume of between 500 and 800 cm^3 which is large for an organism of that size and linked to the learning required to make tools. These casts also suggest that the left hemisphere frontal, parietal and temporal lobes already had speech centre developments to a greater extent than in modern apes. Although speech would only have been rudimentary it would have been an important cohesive force in a social group. Some progress towards smaller teeth and a lighter lower jaw is seen but these developments were not marked. The pelvis was larger than in australopithecines and this has been associated with the birth of babies with larger brains (and therefore heads).

The ability to make and use tools not only needs a brain capable of learning and one able to co-ordinate quite precise movements; it also needs a dextrous hand. *Homo habilis* had modern hand bones with fingers slightly incurved and a thumb only a little shorter than ours. The hominid would not have had a precise grip but a prehensile power grip quite adequate for making and using stone tools.

The oldest known stone tools are dated to the Palaeolithic period more than 2 million years ago from sites in Ethiopia, Kenya, Malawi and Zaire. However, the site which has yielded most tools is the Olduvai Gorge in Tanzania where the oldest finds are 1.9 million years old. Tools from Olduvai and other early African sites vary in form and are known as the **Oldowan industry**. The stone tools are all very simple and based on the single idea that a sharp edge can be produced by knocking a flake off a cobble by using another stone, called a hammerstone. The habilines made knife-like tools as well as choppers and scrapers, often from igneous basalt rock. This simple technology would have significantly expanded the variety of food available to them as flesh could have been scraped from scavenged carcasses and marrow extracted from bones. There is speculation as to whether *H. habilis* hunted prey or merely scavenged but it is thought that food could have been carried by these fully bipedal hominids and possibly shared at a home base. Water may also have been carried in animal skins or ostrich egg shells.

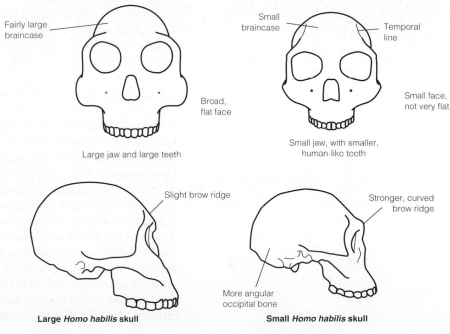

Fig. 9.11 Reconstructions of large and small Homo habilis *skulls*

191

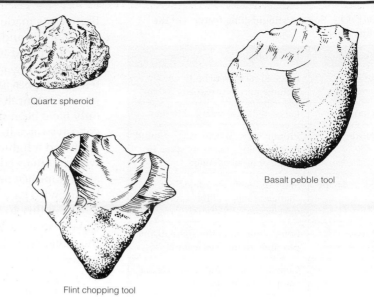

Quartz spheroid

Basalt pebble tool

Flint chopping tool

Fig. 9.12 Oldowan stone tools

It is envisaged that if *H. habilis* lived in social groups with a more or less settled home base this, together with some pair bonding, would have allowed infants an extended childhood with the opportunity for learning. This structured society would have had a greater survival value for the group as a whole.

9.7.3 *Homo erectus*

About 1.8 million years ago a new type of early human appeared in East Africa, a type that was to persist in Africa for over a million years and become the first human type to move out of Africa to Asia and Europe. *Homo erectus* stood 1.5–1.8 metres tall and had a skeleton which closely resembled that of modern humans, although the outer cortex of the bone was consistently thicker. However, the skull was quite different from our own in many respects. It was thick and low-domed with a flattened cranium enclosing a brain with a volume of between 700 and 1250 cm^3. The brow ridges were massive and the whole skull was elongated anterio-posteriorly with a thick bump in the occipital region at the back. The teeth and jaws were relatively large and these features, together with the large processes for the attachment of chewing muscles, suggest that the diet was less refined than that of modern man. Although the head was held upright its articulation with the backbone was not right under the cranium's centre of gravity and so large neck muscles were inserted on the back of the skull. Peking (Beijing) Man, Java man and Heidelburg man are all examples of fossil *H. erectus* specimens.

Huge cultural changes took place from 1.5–0.5 million years ago: the design and manufacture of stone tools developed further, speech probably became more important and early man learnt to use fire. The earliest true hand axes appear with *H. erectus* at Olduvai 1.6 million years ago but the 'industry' is named **Acheulian culture** after finds in France dated to 0.2 million years ago. The Acheulian hand axe has two flat sides and two cutting edges leading to a point. Such **bifaces** are difficult to make and imply that the design was 'held in the mind' before

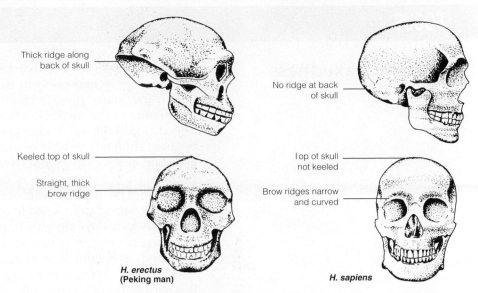

Thick ridge along
back of skull

No ridge at back
of skull

Keeled top of skull

Top of skull
not keeled

Straight, thick
brow ridge

Brow ridges narrow
and curved

H. erectus
(Peking man)

H. sapiens

Fig. 9.13 Comparison of the skulls of Homo erectus *and* Homo sapiens

being impressed on the stone. In addition to axes the Acheulian tool-kit comprised scrapers, chisels, cleavers, awls, anvils and hammerstones.

As well as gathering fruits *H. erectus* ate meat. Animals may have been hunted and killed or efficiently scavenged – we shall never be sure which. However, the protein provided by increased meat eating was important for fetal and infant brain development. *H. erectus* would certainly have been more intelligent than *H. habilis*, able to learn more about his environment and communicate with other members of the social group. *H. erectus* was also the first hominid to make use of fire. Evidence of fire hearths have been found in the caves at Zhoukoudian near Beijing and dated to be 0.5 million years old. Fire would have provided warmth, been used to frighten predators and, for the first time, to cook food which softened it and killed pathogens. Fire would certainly have been important for hominids moving from the warmth of East Africa northwards into Europe and Asia but it may also have assumed some symbolic significance.

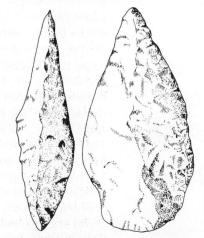

Two views of an early Acheulian hand axe

Late Acheulian hand axe

Fig. 9.14 Acheulian tool-kit

Human nakedness

When the human lineage diverged from that of the great apes our ancestors were possibly as hairy as those animals are now. But, by the time of *Homo erectus* their hair had probably grown less dense and the sweat glands in the skin more numerous. This change differentiates humans from other primates because, although we have as many hair roots, our hair is fine and short and we have more sweat glands than any other primate. There are a number of theories to account for these changes but the most plausible concerns our ancestors' change of habitat from forest to open savannah. Early hominids were daytime scavengers (or possibly hunters) and they were in danger of over-heating in the hot African grasslands. It became an evolutionary advantage to have a large number of very active sweat glands to cool the skin, but this only works efficiently if the air can blow over the skin surface. It was therefore a further selective advantage to reduce the covering of hair – except on the head where it protected the brain from the direct heating effect of the sun. Further protection from the sun's harmful ultra-violet rays would be afforded by having dark skin.

Although the loss of hair and development of extra sweat glands allowed early humans to exert themselves in tropical sunlight for longer than apes and monkeys it was at a cost. Sweating causes enormous losses of water and salts which need constant replenishment and this must have put some restrictions on the home range of early hominids.

Early modern human

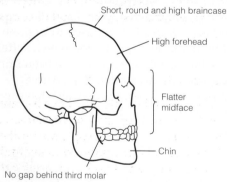

Neanderthal

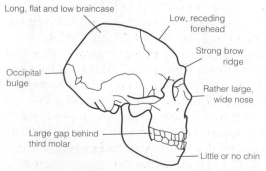

Fig. 9.15 Comparison of the skull of a Neanderthal and an early modern human

9.7.4 Neanderthal man

Remains of Neanderthal man were first discovered in the Neander Valley, Germany in 1856 but fossils have since been unearthed in Britain, France, Russia and Israel. None have been found in Africa. The Neanderthals are often regarded as a subspecies of *Homo sapiens*, *H. sapiens neanderthalensis*, but are now increasingly treated as a distinct species, *Homo neanderthalensis*. They lived 150 000–30 000 years ago and were of stocky build, well adapted to cope with the ice ages of the period. The Neanderthals were highly evolved humans in many respects, but were probably not our direct ancestors. They were about 1.5–1.7 metres tall and weighed about 65 kg. The skull was heavily built with a marked brow ridge and prominent nose and cheek bones. The cranium enclosed a large brain of between 1200 and 1750 cm^3 – at least as large as ours, but of a different shape. The front teeth were large and may have been used as a clamp for tool-making and skin processing, as well as for eating.

The technology of the Neanderthals was that of the middle Palaeolithic period and shows a refinement of the flake-orientated tool-kits of their ancestors. Many examples have been found at Le Moustier, France, giving rise to the term **Mousterian flake culture**. Previous stone tools were made by knocking pieces off a core of stone; the core remaining became the final implement. Neanderthals used silicate minerals such as flint and obsidian, and the flakes which they struck off the core were refined into fine tools with razor-sharp edges. Most of these tools were still held in the hand, and shafts are extremely rare. The muscular build of the Neanderthals ensured the efficiency of these flake tools. Their hands held them in a powerful grip aided by large joint surfaces and fingertips and two equal length bones in the thumb which increased the strength of the power grip.

The Neanderthals spread over much of Europe and Asia where the climate was like that of present-day tundra areas. Many bones have been found in caves which probably served as their home base, although they may also have constructed tents of skins. Their success was only possible because they were able to keep warm. As well as being of stocky build, rather like the present-day Inuit, Neanderthals had large nasal cavities which would have conserved heat and moisture in the freezing air. They possibly dressed in animal skins which were probably tied on, no evidence being found of needles. Most importantly they had fire, without which they could not have colonized such inhospitable areas. They would have been dependent on seasonal migrations of animals for their meat which they may also have preserved by drying, smoking or freezing. As well as hunting they would have gathered fruits and other plant material.

Neanderthals were probably the first people to have ceremonies for their dead, evidence having been found at a number of sites, such as Teshik-Tash in Russia. Here the body of a Neanderthal child was placed in a shallow pit, pairs of goats' horns were placed in a circle round it and a fire was lit alongside. Ceremonies like these reflect a complex social structure with formal ritual and an awareness of the possibility of future life.

However, after about 40 000 years' domination of Europe the Neanderthal people suddenly disappeared. How they died out we shall never know but maybe it was the result of competition with early modern man.

9.7.5 Early modern man

The disappearance of the Neanderthals may have had much to do with the appearance in Europe of early modern man, *Homo sapiens sapiens* (or just *H. sapiens*). These people are unlikely to have evolved from Neanderthals who showed many highly specialized features, nor is there any fossil evidence for them originating from archaic predecessors in Asia. The only place where transitional fossils have been found is in Africa and genetic evidence indicates that all living people are closely related and share a recent common ancestor who probably lived in Africa. This has been termed the **'Out of Africa'** model.

The spread of modern humans into Europe probably occurred about 40 000 years ago and fossil evidence of them found at Cro-Magnon, France in 1868 has given rise to their familiar name **'Cro-Magnons'**. They also spread to Asia and from there into Australia and America where regional differences in physique and culture rapidly developed. The first modern humans looked very different from the Neanderthals with their less prominent brow ridges, higher, shorter and more rounded skulls, shorter lower jaws and a bony chin and a taller less robust skeleton.

While Neanderthals are associated with a Middle Palaeolithic culture, Cro-Magnons are invariably associated with Upper Palaeolithic industries. The latter are much more varied and contain many blade tools some of which were specialized for the working of bone, antler and ivory, materials available to, but rarely used by, the Neanderthals. Upper Palaeolithic tools were made by knocking long flakes off a central core, often using indirect percussion by using a hammerstone on an antler fine punch. This method could produce a large number of blades in a short time. It is estimated that a kilogram flint core would yield 50 blades with a total cutting edge of 25 metres; an efficiency ten times that of the Acheulian cultures. These long flakes were used to make knives, saws and chisels and smaller microliths were used to tip arrows and harpoons. This range of tools made the Cro-Magnons into efficient hunters of large animals such as deer, horses and mammoths. In order to kill these animals, they must have lived and hunted in large organized groups. Each group would probably have had a leader and the work of hunting, making traps, building shelters and caring for children would have been divided amongst the members of the group. Clothes and tents were made from animal skins stitched together using bone needles. There is also evidence for the first time of basketry which would have greatly eased the gathering of fruits and vegetables as well as their storage. In Japan hunter-gatherers dependent on the sea started to use pottery vessels for collection and storage.

Individuals in these complex social groups would almost certainly have communicated by means of a language and these hunters of the last Ice Age used symbols too. They made simple musical instruments like bone whistles, carved female figures out of stone or moulded them out of clay and they produced magnificent cave paintings of the animals they hunted. Although cave art was widespread the most famous sites are at Lascaux in France and Altamira in Spain. Four colours were available to Palaeolithic artists red, yellow and brown from iron oxide and black from manganese dioxide. Experiments suggest that the pigments were fixed to the rock surface with water and that they were applied by fingers, brushes, pads or spraying. Many figures are drawn on easily accessible surfaces but some would have required ladders or scaffolding. Some stone lamps have been found but burning torches were probably used as well. Although there have been many attempts to explain Palaeolithic art and sculpture no single explanation can suffice for a culture spanning 20 000 years and a vast area of the world.

Upper Palaeolithic people were concerned with death as well as life, and their treatment of the dead was careful and thoughtful. The bodies were often sprinkled with red ochre and were placed in graves dug in the ashes of previously occupied living sites. A grave of two boys excavated in Russia in the 1960s shows that they were both dressed in clothes decorated with ivory beads and that they wore ivory bracelets and rings. An assortment of ivory and bone weapons was found with them.

We know that Cro-Magnons led a complex social life but there are details of it that we shall never discover. However, their ability to exploit a variety of environments led to a great growth in their numbers and, some 12 000 years ago, they had laid the foundation for the emergence of a modern human culture with agriculture, domestication, writing and even politics.

Altamira cave painting

9.8 Development of farming

Towards the end of the Pleistocene era, about 14 000 years ago the climate began to change and the ice of the last Ice Age began to melt. The people of the time continued their nomadic hunter–gatherer way of life eating a varied diet and suffering from very few infectious diseases. They used a variety of tools developed from those of their predecessors, tools which would later be modified into agricultural implements.

As the ice sheets retreated further the people tended to lead less nomadic lives, hunting game in relatively small forest territories. The milder climate favoured the evolution of cereal plants and their grains were gathered together with many other edible plant foods. This period in our history is sometimes referred to as the **Mesolithic** or Middle Stone Age, although it is not clearly defined. Then, about 12 000 to 9000 years ago, in a few areas of the world, some people began to cultivate cereal and root crops and to live in settled communities. Their technology was still based on the use of stone tools and this period is called the **Neolithic** or New Stone Age. It was the beginning of the first **Agricultural Revolution**. Within a few thousand years agriculture had spread throughout the world, almost reaching its present geographical limits. At the same time the domestication of animals began, at first for food but later to pull carts and ploughs.

All this began to increase the food supply leading to surpluses which could be traded between groups of people living in different areas. As societies became larger and more settled they became subject to new health problems. There were periods of famine and starvation, unsanitary conditions caused the spread of diseases and parasites and rivalries were set up within and between groups. Human populations continued to expand and, although their impact on the environment was slight at first, it became more severe as they started to clear forests to create new fields and, much later, to build towns, industrial developments and modern communications networks.

9.8.1 Domestication of plants

In regions of the Middle East, near Jericho, evidence has been found of a culture that existed between 11 000 BC and 8000 BC. Although the Natufians of this period were not farmers, archaeological remains show us that they had made important progress towards being so. These people gathered the grain of the wild **einkorn wheat** and the natural tetraploid hybrid **emmer wheat** using sickles made of antlers and microlith blades. Experiments have shown that they would have collected enough in three weeks to provide a family with their carbohydrate needs for a year. Pestles and mortars and storage bins have been found in the ground near the hut sites indicating that processing and storage took place. The Natufians therefore carried out two of the four generally accepted components of farming: they **harvested** and **conserved** but did not yet undertake **propagation** or **husbandry**.

We shall never know why people started to plant and tend crops. Perhaps it was in response to a food shortage as

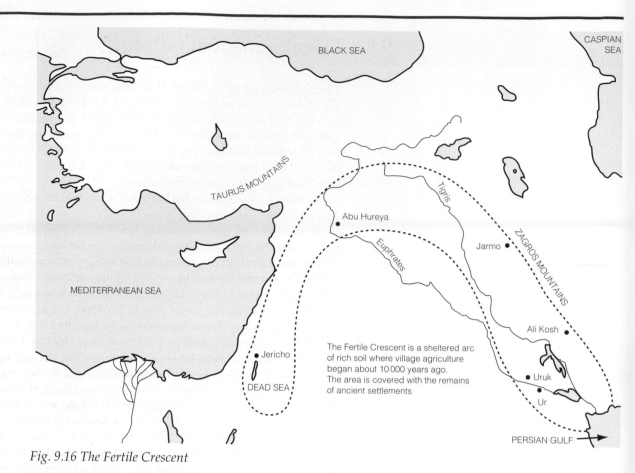

On the map: BLACK SEA, CASPIAN SEA, TAURUS MOUNTAINS, Tigris, ZAGROS MOUNTAINS, Abu Hureya, Jarmo, Euphrates, Ali Kosh, MEDITERRANEAN SEA, Uruk, Jericho, Ur, DEAD SEA, PERSIAN GULF

The Fertile Crescent is a sheltered arc of rich soil where village agriculture began about 10 000 years ago. The area is covered with the remains of ancient settlements

Fig. 9.16 The Fertile Crescent

populations increased. Perhaps as populations expanded some people moved to new areas, taking with them the food plants on which they had depended. Whatever the stimulus, farming started to develop in several different parts of the world, notably in the **Fertile Crescent**. This region is south of the Taurus and Zagros Mountains in what is now parts of Iran, Iraq, Turkey, Syria, Jordan, Israel and Lebanon. The Fertile Crescent provided us with cultivated wheat, barley, various legumes, grapes, melons and nuts such as almonds.

The Americas were the homeland of three types of crop of major importance: maize, potatoes and manioc. Rice is thought to be native to most lowland regions of South East Asia. Early farmers would have cultivated plants which were native to their area, palatable, easy to grow and harvest and which could be stored successfully. However, there is also evidence of cultural preferences and some of the plants which have become most widespread, like maize and wheat, may not be the most nutritionally valuable or suited to the conditions in which they are now found. The most important domesticated plants are the cereal grasses whose grains provide a concentrated source of carbohydrates and other nutrients and which can be stored. Wild cereal grasses have small seeds with firmly attached covers called **bracts** and **glumes** and a hairy process called an **awn**. The seeds are borne on a brittle stalk, or **rachis**, which breaks easily when the seeds ripen so that they can be dispersed as the awn becomes attached to a mammal's fur. Cultivated cereals have lost many of these features. The rachis is less brittle, so that harvesting can take place without the loss of the grain; the glumes and awls are only loosely attached, so that they can be removed by winnowing and the grains are both larger and more numerous. In wild cereals a very small proportion of plants have a tough rachis as a result of a genetic mutation. When early farmers reaped their wheat or barley they would lose some normal seeds but all those on a tough rachis would be collected. When the seeds were sown tough-rachis mutations would be passed on and when the numbers with this mutation rose significantly the farmers may have positively selected seeds of this more favourable variety for sowing.

Wheat

The wild form of wheat found in the Fertile Crescent gathered by the Natufians around 8000 BC had a chromosome number of 14 and is known as 'einkorn' wheat; its scientific name is *Triticum monococcum*. Cultivated 'einkorn' is a low-yielding species, still grown as a crop in Turkey and other parts of Europe. Tetraploid wheats, with 28 chromosomes, developed when the diploid 'einkorn' wheat hybridized with a wild goat grass, *Aegilops* spp. These wheats are known as 'emmer' wheats and they are still grown in the Balkans, North East India and Ethiopia. The natural tetraploid wheat, in its wild form *T. dicoccoides*, was gathered by the Natufians as early as 11 000 BC. Hexaploid wheats, with a chromosome number of 42, have arisen by the hybridization of emmer wheat with another goat grass *Aegilops squarrosa*, followed by chromosome doubling. The first evidence we have of these hexaploid wheats is from about 5500 BC in the Middle East but *T. aestivum* has given rise to all our modern bread wheats.

Barley

Barley was domesticated between 7000 and 6000 BC in the Near East. It is tolerant of a wide range of conditions and was at one time as important as wheat. Selective breeding has given rise to varieties with six rows of grains on each rachis instead of the two found on wild varieties, increasing the yield.

We can only speculate on whether the development of agricultural techniques brought with it a rapid increase in population or whether the increase in population came first, bringing with it pressures for more food and therefore the development of agriculture. Whatever the order of events, the two factors would have a positive feedback effect on each other, leading to a rapid change in population and culture. Once the cultivation of crops and living in settled communities had begun they needed to continue. Crops needed tending and harvesting and food stores had to be protected. As the community grew, craft specialization would emerge as potters, textile-makers, basket-makers and tool-makers would trade their skills for food and other items. Small village settlements soon grew into towns. The most ancient city known to us is Jericho, first built about 10 000 years ago, no doubt on the site of a smaller settlement. Jericho, like many of the great early cities was in an area of rich agricultural land, where productivity was greatest – reflecting the foundation on which these communities were built.

!Kung people of the Kalahari

Until recently small groups of people in Africa followed a hunter–gatherer way of life similar to that of our Palaeolithic ancestors. The !Kung San, or Bushmen, of the Kalahari Desert in South West Africa have been the subject of numerous demographic studies and tentative conclusions have been drawn from them concerning the survival strategies of early hominids. However, we must be wary, after all their very survival into the twentieth century as hunter–gatherers makes them unusual! The !Kung are also found in a particularly inhospitable habitat with low rainfall and few mammals to hunt. Palaeolithic hunter–gatherers are unlikely to have chosen such a place in which to live but would have been found where there was more water, and more animals, in areas now occupied by settled farming communities. However, the studies have provided us with some interesting information. !Kung tend to live in bands of up to 50 people, but more usually around 25. Bands may exchange members or split to form new bands. From time to time groups of up to 500 meet for periods of hunting or ritual. The present density of hunter–gatherer communities is 0.1–1 person per square kilometre but higher in favourable areas such as riverbanks or coasts. On the whole it is likely that hunter–gatherer societies both now and in the past suffered less from infectious diseases than people in settled communities and they may also have suffered less from famine since their nomadic existence exploited varied environments.

For !Kung women the average interval between births is 4 years, twice that of preindustrial Europe and longer than in peasant populations in developing countries. Frequent births would cause difficulties with a nomadic life but the low birth rate may actually be due to a prolonged period of lactation or, possibly, a low body weight suppressing successful ovulation. There are now almost no !Kung following the hunter–gatherer way of life. For many years they have been exploited by other people and most of their land is now farms, settlements and game parks. A few rely on subsistence farming and herding but many work as farm hands or live on government hand-outs.

9.8.2 Domestication of animals

Domestication takes place when animals become incorporated into the social structure of a human group. This incorporation implies ownership of the animal and a control over its reproduction. When domesticated animals are reproductively isolated from the wild population changes appear in them over successive generations and artificial selection may result in the dominance of characters selected for economic, cultural or aesthetic reasons. This will eventually lead to the evolution of new and distinct breeds.

It is possible to tame many mammals and it is envisaged that even our late Pleistocene ancestors may have kept young animals as companions, possibly if the mother had been hunted and killed. Wolves (*Canis lupus*) are sociable animals and it is quite easy to imagine their taming and eventual evolution into dogs (*Canis familiaris*). The earliest evidence of dogs is from Natufian sites in Israel, dated to be about 12 000 years ago. These dogs would possibly have had roles as hunting partners and watchdogs as well as companions; in North America they were used to pull loads.

Herding, or pastoralism, may develop with animals that are at an early stage of domestication and with those that are fully domesticated. Early herding of goats and sheep probably began with our Neolithic ancestors in western Asia who kept some of the animals close to their homesteads, isolated from their wild relatives in the mountains. Although these animals would have provided a convenient source of meat, without the need to go out hunting, they would also provide milk and wool. The animals, together with planted cereals, enabled many Neolithic communities to thrive as their environment became increasingly arid and the number of wild mammals decreased. The possession of large flocks of goats and sheep also became a symbol of status in the community. The domestication of sheep and goats has been dated to about 9000 years ago. The goats are all descended from the scimitar-horned species of western Asia (*Capra aegagrus*) and the sheep from the Asiatic mouflon (*Ovis orientalis*).

A domesticated animal may be considered to be one that is kept for the economic profit of a community. The people control its food, territory and reproduction, keeping it isolated from its wild relatives. Natural and artificial selection over many generations will result in an animal that looks very different from its wild type, although it may still be able to interbreed with it. There are four main effects of domestication which are common to a large number of mammals:

1. **Reduction in body size** – Small animals are easier to handle and to house and so this feature is probably the result of artificial selection. This trend may not continue throughout the domestication of a breed.

2. **Changes in outward appearance** – Initially features which distinguished between domesticated and wild animals may have been selected for so that an owner could recognize his herd. Selection might also have occured for reasons of status or aesthetics. Animals with short, or no, horns may have been chosen for ease of handling.

3. **Changes in internal anatomy and physiology** – It is in the skull that change is most obvious as the face is shortened and the teeth become more crowded. The brain size may be reduced as the sense organs become less acute. Breeding periods change, often becoming more frequent and the number of offspring produced increases. In cattle, fat is deposited throughout the muscle whereas in wild bovids it is concentrated under the skin and around the kidneys.

4. **Behaviour** – Our domesticated animals, with the exception of the cat, have all been derived from wild species which are sociable rather than solitary. This has made domestication easier and means that many of the behaviour patterns seen

are similar to those of the wild ancestor. Behavioural changes that have occurred tend to result in the retention of juvenile traits which make the animals more 'trusting' and affectionate.

The domestication of cattle began in Asia about 8000 years ago, their initial value probably being for religious rites or as draught animals rather than as food. We have our first evidence of them being used for milk production in Egypt and Mesopotamia about 6000 years ago. Cattle have evolved from the aurochs or wild ox (*Bos primigenius*) that lived in Europe and western Asia until they became extinct in the seventh century AD. Two distinct forms of cattle exist today, probably derived from different subspecies of the aurochs. The humped form (*Bos indicus*), or zebu, is common in Asia and parts of Africa where it is used to pull ploughs, rather than for meat. The zebu-type is well adapted to tropical and subtropical climates. The humpless form (*Bos taurus*), which may be shorthorned or longhorned, occurs throughout Europe, northern Africa and northern Asia, being bred mainly for milk and meat. Over the years cattle have provided us with many products: meat and dairy produce, clothing from the hide, candles from the fat and weapons and ornaments from the bones and horns. The dung is used as a manure and also to make building bricks.

Although the keeping of farm animals for food and transport has provided the foundation on which civilizations have been built, the intensification of farming and settlement of nomadic pastoralists has led to severe overgrazing. In addition the domestication of both plants and animals has led to the elimination of many wild varieties. The loss of biodiversity is accelerated by modern farming practices in which there is no need for an organism to adapt to local conditions.

9.9   Questions

1. (*a*) Give **two** differences between the members of each of the following pairs.

(i) Old World and New World monkeys

(2 marks)

(ii) Old World monkeys and apes   *(2 marks)*

The diagrams show the skeletons of a gibbon (anthropoid ape) and a human drawn to the same scale.

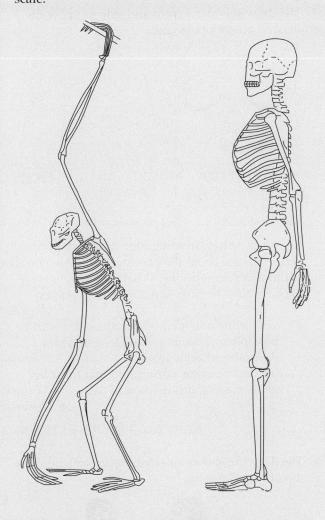

The lengths of the forelimb and backbone of each organism, measured from the diagram, are given in the table below.

Organism	Length of forelimb/mm	Length of backbone/mm
Gibbon	72	37
Human	54	51

(i) The ratio of the length of the forelimb to the length of the backbone is 1.95 : 1 in the gibbon. Calculate the ratio of the length of the forelimb to the length of the backbone for the human. Show your working.   *(2 marks)*

(ii) Suggest a reason for the different relative lengths of the forelimb in gibbons and humans.

(2 marks)

(*c*) Comment on differences, shown in the diagrams, in the skeletons of gibbons and humans with respect to:

(i) the pelvis;   *(2 marks)*

(ii) the hind limb.   *(2 marks)*

(Total 12 marks)

ULEAC 1996, Specimen Paper HB2, No. 6

2. (*a*) The diagrams below show the side views and rear views of the skulls of two subspecies of *Homo sapiens*.

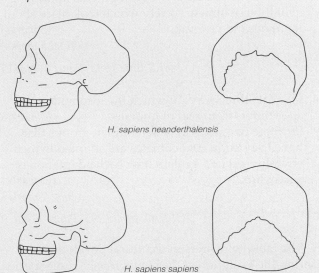

H. sapiens neanderthalensis

H. sapiens sapiens

State **three** visible differences shown by the skulls of these two subspecies.   *(3 marks)*

(*b*) Describe **one** method by which fossilized skeletons can be dated.   *(2 marks)*

(Total 5 marks)

ULEAC 1996, Specimen Paper HB2, No. 1

3. Individuals of *Homo habilis* were no more than 1.5 m tall, walked upright, had small brow-ridges, flat noses and projecting jaws. They lived in East and South Africa and South-east Asia. They made stone tools and built simple shelters. They collected plant foods and scavenged from the carcasses of animals killed by large carnivores. Brain size was approximately 725 cm³.

Individuals of *Homo erectus* grew to about 1.8 m tall, walked upright, had heavi brow-ridges, flat faces and projecting jaws. They lived in Africa, South-east and East Asia and throughout Europe. They made hand-axes, choppers and spears and built huts and stone hearths. They ate seeds and fruits and meat from large carcasses. Brain size was approximately 850 cm³. Individuals of *Homo sapiens neanderthalensis* grew, to about 1.65 m tall, walked upright, had heavy brow-ridges and projecting midfaces. They lived throughout Europe and the Middle East and made specialized stone and wooden tools and clothing; they lived in caves and huts. They ate seeds, fruit, roots and large prey. Brain size was approximately 1500 cm³.

(*a*) Indicate approximately how long ago each species lived.   *(1 mark)*

(*b*) Although these species may not have been the direct ancestors of modern humans, they show certain trends in the evolution towards modern humans. Use information given above and your own knowledge to describe **two** such trends.

     (2 marks)

(*c*) Describe **two** further developments in the evolution of human society which took place about ten thousand years ago.   *(2 marks)*

     (Total 5 marks)

AEB June 1993, Paper 1, No. 15

4. (*a*) State **three** ways in which the locomotion of apes differs from that of humans.   *(3 marks)*

(*b*) State **two** ways in which human groups that have evolved in cold climates are adapted to their environment and explain how each adaptation is successful.   *(4 marks)*

     (Total 7 marks)

ULEAC June 1995, Paper 1, No. 9

5. The table below refers to cultural developments during the evolution of the genus *Homo*. Three species of *Homo* are listed in the table.

If the statement is correct, place a tick (✔) in the appropriate box and if the statement is incorrect, place a cross (✘) in the appropriate box.

Statement	*H. habilis*	*H. erectus*	*H. sapiens*
Use of fire			
Food sharing			
Oldowan (pebble tool) culture present			
Acheulian (hand-axe) culture present			
Tools made by striking flakes from a core			
Production of cave art			
Development of speech			

     (Total 7 marks)

ULEAC June 1995, Paper 1, No. 5

6. **Either**

(*a*) Give an account of inherited variation within the human species and discuss the possible relationship between variation and the environment during human evolution.   *(30 marks)*

Or

(*b*) Discuss the social and cultural changes which took place in the development of the genus *Homo* during the palaeolithic period.   *(30 marks)*

ULEAC June 1993, Paper 1, No. 15(a) and (b)

7. The drawings show front and side views of the skull of an australopithecine.

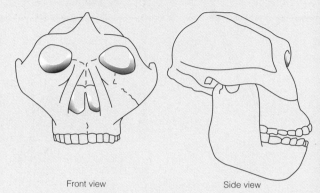

Front view   Side view

(*a*) Describe how investigation of this skull could give evidence about the posture, brain size and diet of this australopithecine. What conclusions were likely to have been drawn about these points?

     (8 marks)

(*b*) (i) Outline **one** method by which it would be possible to determine how long ago this Australopithecine lived.   *(3 marks)*

(ii) Describe **one** assumption that must be made in using this method of dating.   *(1 mark)*

     (Total 12 marks)

NEAB June 1995, Paper BY09, No. 8

8. The drawing shows an artist's reconstruction of a group of early humans.

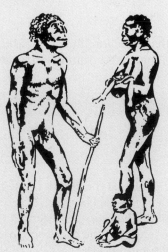

Illustrating your answer with reference to this drawing, explain what is meant by:

(a) sex differences; *(2 marks)*
(b) gender-appropriate behaviour: *(2 marks)*
(c) innate infant reflex. *(2 marks)*

(Total 6 marks)

NEAB June 1995, Paper BY09, No. 6

9. The shift from gathering wild grain to cultivating early varieties of cereals involved selection for favourable characteristics such as the strength of the rachis holding the individual grains. The drawing shows the position of the rachis and individual grains in a typical cereal.

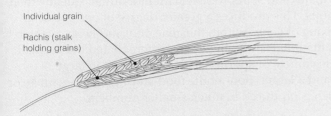

Individual grain

Rachis (stalk holding grains)

(a) (i) Give **one** advantage to the early farmers of a rachis that did not break easily. *(1 mark)*
(ii) How did the activities of these early farmers lead to the development of cereal plants with a stronger rachis? *(2 marks)*
(b) Suggest **two** ways in which the change from hunting and gathering to simple agriculture may have influenced the development of human communities. *(2 marks)*

The table gives some details of different varieties of wheat.

Variety	Year introduced	Mean stem length/cm	Mean grain yield/ tonnes hectare^{-1}
Little Jos	1908	142	5.22
Capelle Desprez	1953	110	5.86
Maris Huntsman	1972	106	6.54
Hobbit	1977	84	7.30
Norman	1980	80	7.57

(c) Suggest **two** ways in which the change in stem length that has taken place in these varieties of wheat might have contributed to an increase in yield. *(2 marks)*

(Total 7 marks)

NEAB June 1995, Paper BY09, No. 5

10. The table summmarizes the distance between the different members of a wild gorilla group observed when its members were resting.

Category of first resting animal	Category of second resting animal	Number of instances in which the distance apart was between				
		0–5 metres	6–10 metres	11–15 metres	16–20 metres	over 20 metres
Adult male	Immature male	0	3	3	0	4
Adult male	Adult female	12	9	4	2	0
Adult male	Juvenile	21	13	7	1	2
Adult female	Immature male	0	1	7	1	2
Adult female	Adult female	8	3	2	1	0
Adult female	Juvenile	32	17	0	1	1
Immature male	Juvenile	0	11	7	12	3
Juvenile	Juvenile	22	10	2	0	1

(a) Explain why it was important that the observer remained out of sight while these observations were made. *(1 mark)*
(b) From your knowledge of the structure of wild gorilla groups, suggest why there are no figures for the distance between adult males. *(1 mark)*
(c) (i) What do the data show about the distance between immature males and other gorillas? *(1 mark)*
(ii) Explain the importance of this to the social life of the gorilla group. *(1 mark)*
(d) (i) What do the data show about the distance between juveniles and other gorillas? *(1 mark)*
(ii) Explain the importance of this to the social life of the gorilla group? *(1 mark)*

(Total 6 marks)

NEAB June 1995, Paper BY09, No. 1

11. Give an account of human evolution over the past five million years.

AEB June 1994, Paper 2, No. 5(a)

10 Reproduction, development and growth

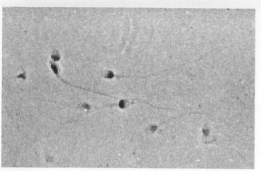

Sperm (× 600 approx.)

One major advantage of sexual reproduction is the genetic variety it creates, and that the extent of this variety is greater the more diverse the parental genotypes are. Animals, with their capacity for locomotion, are able to move far afield in their search for mates and so reproduce with individuals outside their family groups. This produces a greater degree of outbreeding, greater mixing of genes within the gene pool and hence greater variety. In mammals the gametes are differentiated into a small motile male gamete or **sperm** which is produced in large numbers, and a larger, non-motile food-storing female gamete or **ovum** which is produced in much smaller numbers.

10.1 Gametogenesis

Gametogenesis is the formation of gametes. In the case of sperm production it is called **spermatogenesis** and where eggs are formed it is called **oogenesis**. Both types involve a multiplication phase, a growth phase and a maturation phase as depicted in Fig. 10.1 on the next page.

The organs which produce gametes are called **gonads** and are of two types: the ovaries which produce ova and the testes which produce sperm. In humans, the reproductive and excretory systems are closely associated with one another; in such cases they are often represented together as the urinogenital system.

10.2 Human male reproductive system

The male gonads, the **testes**, develop in the abdominal cavity and descend into an external sac, the **scrotum**, prior to birth. The optimum temperature for sperm development is around 35°C, about 2°C below normal human body temperature. The testes can be kept at this temperature by the contraction and relaxation of muscle in the scrotal wall. When the temperature of the testes exceeds 35°C the muscles relax, holding them away from the body to assist cooling. In colder conditions the muscles contract to bring the testes as close to the abdominal cavity as is necessary to maintain them at the optimum temperature. Each testis is suspended by a spermatic cord composed of the sperm

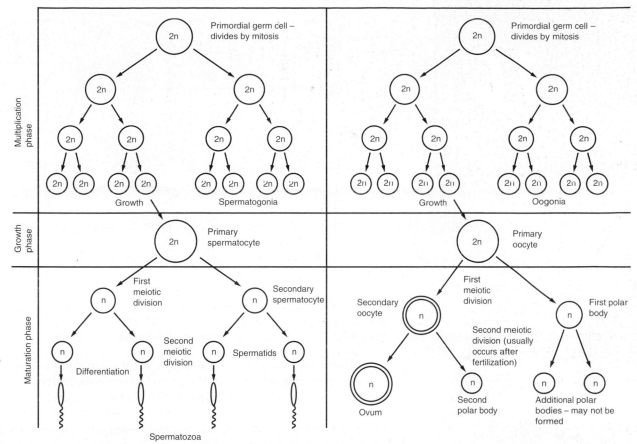

Fig. 10.1(a) Spermatogenesis – formation of sperm

Fig. 10.1(b) Oogenesis – formation of ova

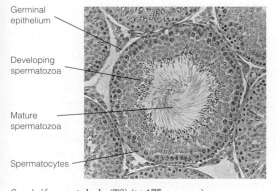

Germinal epithelium

Developing spermatozoa

Mature spermatozoa

Spermatocytes

Seminiferous tubule (TS) (× 175 approx.)

duct or vas deferens, spermatic artery and vein, lymph vessels and nerves, bound together by connective tissue. A single testis is surrounded by a fibrous coat and is separated internally by septa into a series of lobules (Fig. 10.5).

Within each lobule are convoluted **seminiferous tubules**, the total length of which is over 1 km. Between the tubules are the **interstitial cells** which secrete the hormone **testosterone**. Each seminiferous tubule is lined by **germinal epithelium** which, by a series of divisions, gives rise to sperm, a process taking 8–9 weeks (Fig. 10.6).

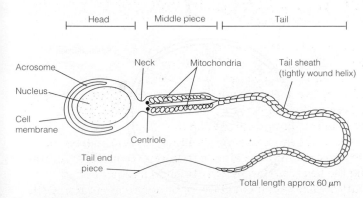

Head   Middle piece   Tail

Acrosome

Nucleus

Cell membrane

Neck

Mitochondria

Centriole

Tail sheath (tightly wound helix)

Tail end piece

Total length approx 60 µm

Fig. 10.2(a) Human spermatozoan based on electron micrograph

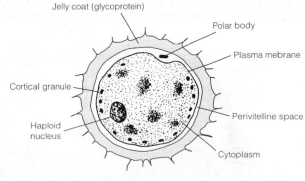

Jelly coat (glycoprotein)

Polar body

Plasma mebrane

Cortical granule

Haploid nucleus

Perivitelline space

Cytoplasm

Fig. 10.2(b) Human egg cell approx 120 µm in diameter

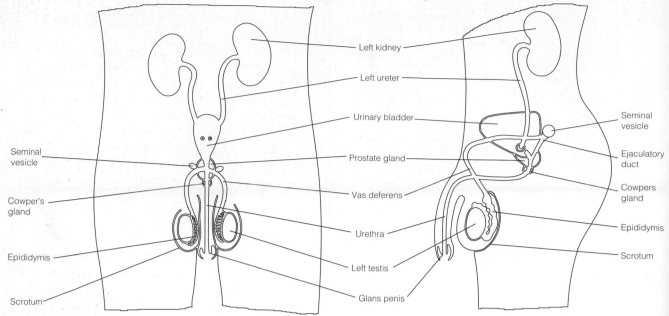

Fig. 10.3 Male urinogenital system (simplified) – front view

Male urinogenital system – side view

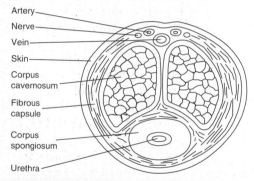

Fig. 10.4 Penis (TS)

Did you know?

During his lifetime one male human may produce as many as 12 000 000 000 000 (1.2×10^{13}) sperm.

The seminiferous tubules merge to form small ducts called the **vasa efferentia**, which in turn join up to form a six-metre-long coiled tube called the **epididymis**. The sperm are stored here, gaining motility over a period of 18 hours. From the epididymis leads another muscular tube, the **vas deferens**, which carries the sperm towards the urethra. Before it joins the urethra it combines with the duct leading from the **seminal vesicle**, forming the **ejaculatory duct**. The seminal vesicles produce a mucus secretion which aids sperm mobility. The ejaculatory duct then passes through the **prostate gland** which produces an alkaline secretion that neutralizes the acidity of any urine in the urethra as well as aiding sperm mobility. Below the prostate gland is a pair of **Cowper's glands** which secrete a sticky fluid into the urethra. The resultant combination of sperm and secretions is called **semen**. The semen passes along the **urethra**, a muscular tube running through the **penis**. The penis comprises three cylindrical masses of spongy tissue covered by an elastic skin (Fig. 10.4).

The end of the penis is expanded to form the **glans penis**, a sensitive region covered by loose retractable skin, the **prepuce** or **foreskin**. The foreskin is sometimes removed surgically, for medical or religious reasons, in a small operation called circumcision.

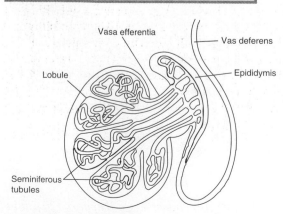

Fig. 10.5 Testis (LS)

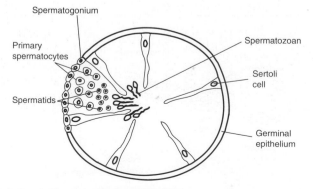

Fig. 10.6 Seminiferous tubule ×500 (TS)

Prostate cancer – the Cinderella of cancers

After lung cancer, prostate cancer is the biggest cancer killer of men in the Western World. In 1992, in Britain it claimed nearly 10 000 lives, four times as many as cervical cancer. In the United States more than 100 000 new cases are diagnosed annually and the death toll each year is 33 000. While men may develop prostate tumours in their forties, the symptoms develop much later, if at all. An increased incidence of the disease has been linked to the increase in average age of the male population, improved rates of detection and, possibly, poorly understood effects such as diet. Black North Americans have the highest incidence (about 100 cases per 10 000 men) and the Far East has the lowest – about 6 cases per 10 000. The fact that this pattern is similar to the one for heart disease suggests that a western-style diet may be one risk factor. Some forms of prostate cancer seem to run in families and research is being directed towards identifying the genes which may provide hope of a diagnostic test in the future.

The prostate gland is found just below the bladder, around the urethra and it has a tendency to enlarge in old age – possibly under the influence of testosterone. This enlargement causes the gland to constrict the urethra making it difficult to pass urine. Such an enlargement, or hypertrophy, of the prostate gland may be benign but if it is malignant the prognosis is poor. About 75% of prostate cancers detected have already spread to the lymph nodes and bones. Of the cases diagnosed in Britain each year only about one third of patients are alive 5 years later.

In the US and Germany men over the age of 45 are advised to have an annual rectal examination and blood test. The basis of this test is the relatively high level of **prostate specific antigen (PSA)** which occurs if a tumour is present. Although screening reduces the incidence of prostate cancer many argue that it is not economical for what is, after all, a disease of old age. In fact many men not only remain oblivious of their tumours but go on to die of unrelated causes. Neither is there any consensus on how best to treat prostate cancer. Most specialists favour surgical removal of the gland together with the seminal vesicles or radiotherapy if the carcinoma is detected relatively early. If it reaches a more advanced stage, oestrogen may be used to slow down or reverse growth. In the United States researchers are investigating the possibility of inhibiting an enzyme called 5-alpha-reductase. This is the enzyme which converts testosterone to dihydrotestosterone, a hormone believed to encourage prostate tumours to grow.

Perhaps in the future more money will be spent on research into one of the most deadly diseases facing ageing men.

10.3   Human female reproductive system

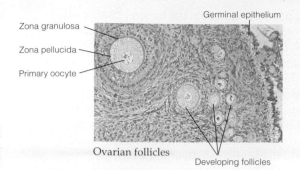

Zona granulosa
Zona pellucida
Primary oocyte
Germinal epithelium
Ovarian follicles
Developing follicles

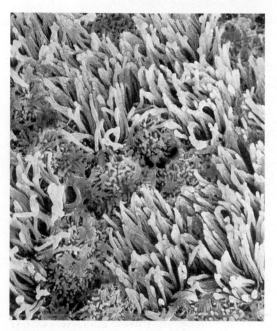

SEM of epithelium of Fallopian tube

The female gonads, the **ovaries**, lie suspended in the abdominal cavity by the ovarian ligaments. The external coat is made up of **germinal epithelium** which begins to divide to form ova while the female is still a fetus. At birth around 400 000 cells have reached prophase of the first meiotic division and are called **primary oocytes**. Each month after puberty, one of these cells completes its development into an ovum. As each cell takes some time to complete this change, the ovary consists of a number of oocytes at various stages of development. These oocytes lie in a region of fibrous tissue, the stroma, which fills the rest of the ovary. The largest and most mature of the cells are called **Graafian follicles** which are fluid-filled sacs each containing a secondary oocyte. A mature Graafian follicle can reach a diameter greater than 1 cm before it releases its ovum. Once the ovum is released the empty follicle develops into a yellow body called the **corpus luteum** (Fig. 10.8).

Close to the ovary is the funnel-shaped opening of the **oviduct** or **Fallopian tube**. The opening has fringe-like edges called **fimbriae**. The oviducts are about 10 cm long and have a muscular wall lined with a mucus-secreting layer of ciliated epithelium. They open into the **uterus**, or womb, which is a pear-shaped body about 5 cm wide and 8 cm in length, held in position by ligaments joined to the pelvic girdle. It has walls of unstriated muscle and is lined internally by a mucus membrane called the **endometrium**. The uterus opens into the **vagina** through a ring of muscle, the **cervix**. The vagina has a wall of unstriated muscle with an inner mucus membrane lined by stratified epithelium. The vagina opens to the outside through the **vulva**, a collective name for the external genital organs. These consist of two outer folds of skin, the **labia majora**, covering two inner, more delicate folds, the **labia minora**. Anterior to the vaginal opening is a small body of erectile tissue, the **clitoris**, which is homologous to the penis of the male. Between the vaginal opening and the clitoris is the opening of the urethra.

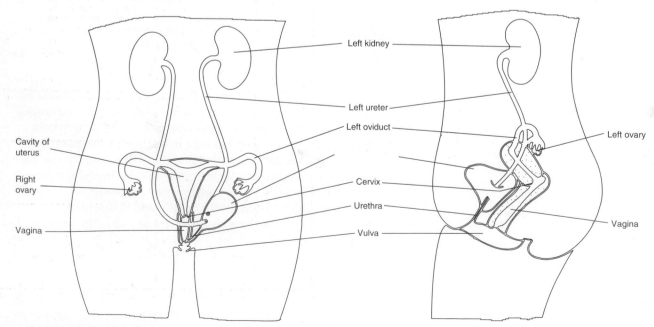

Left kidney
Left ureter
Left oviduct
Left ovary
Cavity of uterus
Right ovary
Cervix
Urethra
Vagina
Vulva
Vagina

Fig. 10.7 Female urinogenital system – front view

Female urinogenital system – side view

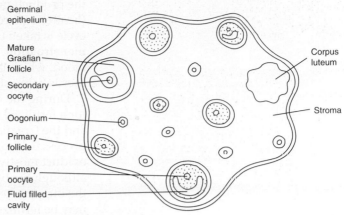

Fig. 10.8 Section through ovary

10.4　The menstrual cycle

In human females the onset of the first menstrual cycle is called
menarche and represents the start of puberty. This takes place
around the age of 12 years although the age varies widely
between individuals. The menstrual cycle, which lasts about 28
days, continues until the **menopause** at the age of 45–50 years.
The events of the cycle are controlled by hormones to ensure that

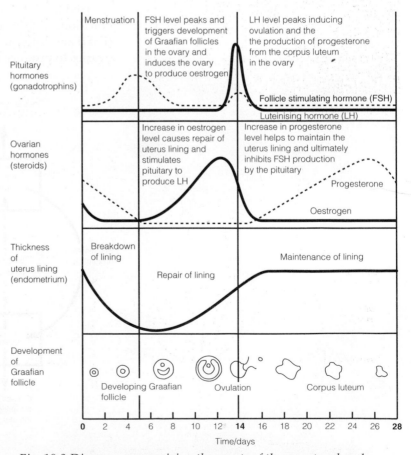

Fig. 10.9 Diagram summarizing the events of the menstrual cycle

the production of an ovum is synchronized with the readiness of the uterus to receive it, should it be fertilized. The start of the cycle is taken to be the initial discharge of blood known as **menstruation**, as this event can be easily identified. This flow of blood, which lasts about five days, is due to the lining of the uterus being shed, along with a little blood.

During the following days the lining regenerates in readiness for a fertilized ovum. By day 14 it has thickened considerably and the Graafian follicle releases its ovum into the oviduct, the process being called **ovulation**. The ovum is moved down the oviduct mostly by muscular contractions of the oviduct wall, although the beating of the cilia may also assist. The journey to the uterus takes about three days during which time the ovum may be fertilized. If it is not, the ovum quickly dies and passes out via the vagina. The uterine lining is maintained for some time but finally breaks down again about 28 days after the start of the cycle.

10.4.1 Hormonal control of the menstrual cycle

The control of the menstrual cycle is an excellent example of hormone interaction. The action of one hormone is used to stimulate or inhibit the production of another. There are four hormones involved, two produced by the anterior lobe of the pituitary gland at the base of the brain, and two produced by the ovaries. The production of the hormones from the ovaries is stimulated by the pituitary hormones. These hormones are thus referred to as the gonadotrophic hormones. The two gonadotrophic hormones are **follicle stimulating hormone (FSH)** and **luteinizing hormone (LH)**. These stimulate the ovaries to produce **oestrogen** and **progesterone** respectively.

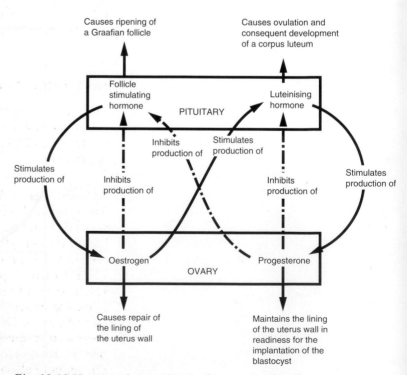

Fig. 10.10 Hormone interaction in the menstrual cycle

The functions of these hormones are as follows:

Follicle stimulating hormone
1. Causes Graafian follicles to develop in the ovary.

2. Stimulates the ovary to produce oestrogen.

Oestrogen
1. Causes repair of the uterus lining following menstruation.

2. Stimulates the pituitary to produce luteinizing hormone.

Luteinizing hormone
1. Causes ovulation to take place.

2. Stimulates the ovary to produce progesterone from the corpus luteum.

Progesterone
1. Causes the uterus lining to be maintained in readiness for the blastocyst (young embryo).

2. Inhibits production of FSH by the pituitary.

The hormones are produced in the following sequence: FSH, oestrogen, LH, progesterone. Progesterone at the end of the sequence inhibits the production of FSH. In turn, the production of the other hormones stops, including progesterone itself. The absence of progesterone now means that the inhibition of FSH ceases and so oestrogen production commences again. In turn, all the other hormones are produced. This alternate switching on and off of the hormones produces a cycle of events – the menstrual cycle. At the end of their fertile period, **the menopause**, women often experience a number of symptoms which can sometimes be relieved by the use of **hormone replacement therapy (HRT)** details of which are given in the Focus on p. 496.

10.4.2 Artificial control of the menstrual cycle

The artificial control of the menstrual cycle has two main purposes: firstly as a contraceptive device by preventing ovulation and secondly as a fertility device by stimulating ovulation.

The contraceptive Pill
The Pill contains both oestrogen and progesterone and when taken daily it maintains high levels of these hormones in the blood. These high levels inhibit the production of the gonadotrophic hormones from the pituitary, and the absence of LH in particular prevents ovulation. The Pill is normally taken for 21 consecutive days followed by a period of 7 days without it, during which the uterus lining breaks down and a menstrual period occurs. The 'morning after' Pill contains the synthetic oestrogen, diethylstibestrol which is thought to prevent implantation of the fertilized ovum if it is present. Both types of Pill are very effective forms of contraception. These and other methods of contraception are reviewed in Table 10.1 overleaf.

TABLE 10.1 Birth control

Method	How it works	Effectiveness	Advantages	Disadvantages
Sterilization	**Male (vasectomy)** – The vasa deferentia (the ducts carrying sperm from the testes to the urethra) are cut and tied off	100%	No artificial appliance is involved. Once the operation has been performed there is no further cost	Irreversible in normal circumstances
	Female (tubal ligation) – The oviducts are cut and tied off			
Prevention of ovulation	**Oral contraceptive** – Contains artificial oestrogen and progesterone	99%	Very reliable if taken regularly	A slightly higher than normal risk of thrombosis. Occasional side effects e.g. nausea, breast tenderness and water retention
	Injection contraceptive (e.g. Depo-provera) – Injection given by doctor about every 3 months	100%	Almost totally reliable	Hormonal surge on injection may produce side-effects e.g. irregular menstrual bleeding
	Implant contraceptive (e.g. Norplant) – Implant placed under the skin which releases artificial oestrogen and progesterone	100%	Almost totally reliable. Each implant lasts 5 years	Can cause irregular menstrual bleeding
Prevention of implantation	**Morning-after Pill** – Contains high level of oestrogen. Taken orally	Not widely used but probably 99–100%	Can be used after rather than before intercourse	High dose of oestrogen can produce side-effects. Not suitable for regular use
	Intra-Uterine Device (loop, coil) – A device usually made of plastic and/or copper which is inserted into the womb by a doctor and which prevents implantation	99–100%	Once fitted, no further action is required except for annual check-ups	Possible menstrual discomfort. The device may be displaced or rejected. Must be inserted by a trained practitioner. Only really suitable for women who have had children
	Intra-vaginal ring – Ring shaped device which releases artificial progesterone. Placed in vagina	Very reliable	Very reliable	Long term health effects yet to be assessed
Barriers which prevent sperm reaching an egg	**Female (diaphragm, cap)** – A dome-shaped sheet of thin rubber with a thicker spring rim which is inserted into the vagina, over the cervix. Best used with spermicide	Very reliable	Reliable. Available for use by all women	Must be inserted prior to intercourse and should be removed 8–24 hours after intercourse. Initial fitting must be by a trained practitioner
	Female (condom) – Sheath of thin rubber with two springy rings. Smaller inserted into vagina, larger remains outside	Very reliable	Readily available, quite easy to fit. Gives some protection against sexually transmitted diseases	May reduce enjoyment of intercourse
	Male (condom, sheath) – a sheath of thin rubber unrolled onto the erect penis prior to intercourse. Semen is collected in teat at the tip. Best used with a spermicide.	Very reliable	Easily available, no fitting or instruction by others needed. Available for use by all men. Gives some protection against sexually transmitted disease including AIDS	May reduce the sensitivity of the penis and so interfere with enjoyment
	Spermicide – Cream, jelly or foam inserted into vagina. Only effective with a mechanical barrier. Kills sperm	Not reliable alone	Easy to obtain and simple to use	Not effective on its own. May occasionally cause irritation
Natural method	**Rhythm method** – Refraining from intercourse during those times in the menstrual cycle when conception is most likely	Variable – not very reliable	No appliance required. Only acceptable method to some religious groups	Not reliable. Restricts times when intercourse can take place. Unsuitable for women with irregular cycles

Premenstrual syndrome

The natural fluctuation in sex hormone levels during the menstrual cycle produces a wide range of side effects especially in the days leading up to the menstrual period. Over a hundred such effects have been identified, ranging from breast tenderness, bloating due to water retention, headache and pelvic·pain through to irritability, depression, clumsiness and a craving for sweet foods. Such is the range of symptoms that the term pre-menstrual tension (PMT) is misleading and PMS is now preferred. It is estimated that 70% of fertile women suffer from PMS to a varying degree. A variety of drugs may be used to alleviate the symptoms but longer term treatment often involves providing oestrogen in patch, pill or implant form.

Fertility drugs

A fertility drug may induce ovulation in one of two ways:

1. It may provide gonadotrophins such as FSH which stimulate the development of Graafian follicles.

2. It may provide some chemical which inhibits the natural production of oestrogen. As oestrogen normally inhibits FSH production, the level of FSH increases and Graafian follicles develop.

Fertility drugs frequently result in multiple births.

10.5   Male sex hormones

Although male humans do not have a sexual cycle similar to that of females, they nonetheless produce some gonadotrophic hormones from the anterior lobe of the pituitary gland. Follicle stimulating hormone (FSH) stimulates sperm development. Luteinizing hormone (LH) stimulates the interstitial cells between the seminiferous tubules of the testis to produce **testosterone**. For this reason, in the male, LH is often called **interstitial cell stimulating hormone (ICSH)**. Testosterone is the most important of a group of male hormones or **androgens**. It is first produced in the fetus, where it controls the development of the male reproductive organs. An increase in production takes place at puberty and causes an enlargement of the reproductive organs and the development of the secondary sex characteristics. Removal of the testes (castration) prevents these changes taking place. It was used in the past as a rather drastic means of preventing choirboys' voices from breaking. Castration of animals is still practised in order to help fatten them and make the meat less tough. (See Fig. 10.11 for details of the control of male sex hormones.)

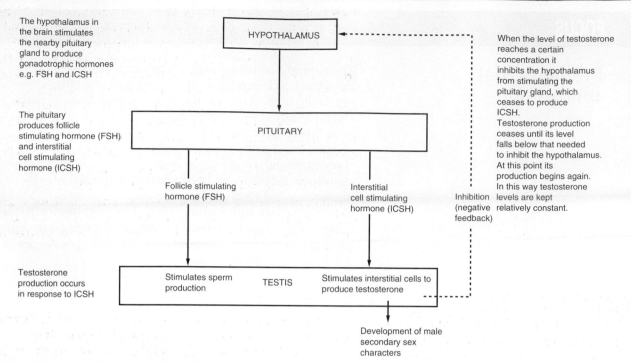

The hypothalamus in the brain stimulates the nearby pituitary gland to produce gonadotrophic hormones e.g. FSH and ICSH

HYPOTHALAMUS

When the level of testosterone reaches a certain concentration it inhibits the hypothalamus from stimulating the pituitary gland, which ceases to produce ICSH.
Testosterone production ceases until its level falls below that needed to inhibit the hypothalamus. At this point its production begins again. In this way testosterone levels are kept relatively constant.

The pituitary produces follicle stimulating hormone (FSH) and interstitial cell stimulating hormone (ICSH)

PITUITARY

Follicle stimulating hormone (FSH)

Interstitial cell stimulating hormone (ICSH)

Inhibition (negative feedback)

Testosterone production occurs in response to ICSH

Stimulates sperm production

TESTIS

Stimulates interstitial cells to produce testosterone

Development of male secondary sex characters

Fig. 10.11 Control of male hormone production

10.6 Fertilization and development

10.6.1 Courtship

In many species it is necessary for both partners to follow a specific pattern of behaviour before mating can occur. Courtship behaviour as it is called is developed in sexually mature individuals. In this way matings between sexually immature individuals, which cannot produce offspring, are avoided. This ensures that any pairing has a good chance of producing offspring. On reaching sexual maturity many species develop easily recognizable features which are sexually attractive to a potential partner. These are referred to as the **secondary sex characteristics**. In humans, secondary sex characteristics include the growth of pubic hair in both sexes, increased musculature, growth of facial hair and deepening of the voice in males and development of the breasts and broadening of the hips in females.

10.6.2 Mating

Under a variety of erotic conditions the blood supply to the genital regions increases. In females the process is slower than in males and results in the clitoris and labia becoming swollen with blood. At the same time the walls of the vagina secrete a lubricating fluid which assists the penetration of the penis. The fluid also neutralizes the acidity of the vagina which would otherwise kill the sperm. In males the increased blood supply results in the spongy tissues of the penis becoming swollen with blood, making it hard and erect. In this condition it more easily enters the vagina. By repeated thrusting of the penis within the vagina the sensory cells in the glans penis are stimulated. This leads to reflex contractions of muscles in the epididymis and vas deferens. The sperm are thus moved by peristalsis along the vas deferens and into the urethra. Here they mix with the secretions from the seminal vesicles, prostate and Cowper's glands. The resultant semen is forced out of the penis by powerful contractions of the urethra, a process called **ejaculation**. This is accompanied by **orgasm**, a sensation of extreme pleasure as a result of physiological and emotional release. The female orgasm is similarly intense resulting from the contraction of the muscles of the vagina and uterus although there is no associated expulsion of fluid. The process of mating, also known as **copulation** or **coitus**, results in internal fertilization and is an adaptation to life on land. The sperm, which require a liquid environment in which to swim, are never exposed to the drying effect of air.

Did you know?

Wild boar produce 0.5 l of semen in a single ejaculation.

10.6.3 Semen

In humans, each ejaculation consists of approximately $5\,cm^3$ of semen. While it contains around 500 million sperm they comprise only a tiny percentage of the total volume, the majority being made up of the fluids secreted by the seminal vesicles, prostate and Cowper's glands. The semen therefore contains:

1. **Sperm**.

2. **Sugars** which nourish the sperm and help to make them mobile.

3. **Mucus** which forms a semi-viscous fluid in which the sperm swim.

4. **Alkaline chemicals** which neutralize the acid conditions encountered in the urethra and vagina, which could otherwise kill the sperm.

5. **Prostaglandins**, hormones which help sperm reach the ovum by causing muscular contractions of the uterus and oviducts.

10.6.4 Fertilization

The force of ejaculation of the semen from the penis is sufficient to propel some sperm through the cervix into the uterus, with the remainder being deposited at the top of the vagina. The sperm swim up through the uterus and into the oviducts by the lashing movements of their tails. The speed with which they reach the top of the oviducts indicates that muscular contractions of the uterus and oviduct are also involved. The egg or ovum released from the Graafian follicle of the ovary is metabolically inactive and dies within 24 hours unless fertilized. The ovum is surrounded by up to 2000 **cumulus cells** which aid its movement towards the uterus by giving the cilia which line the oviduct a large mass to 'grip'. The cumulus cells may also provide nutrients to the ovum. As the journey to the uterus takes three days in humans, it follows that fertilization must take place in the top third of the oviduct if the ovum is still to be alive when the sperm reaches it. There is no evidence that the ovum attracts

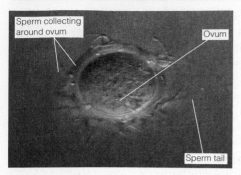

Sperm collecting around ovum

Ovum

Sperm tail

Sperm fertilizing ovum

the sperm in any way; their meeting would appear to be largely a matter of chance. Of the 500 million sperm in the ejaculate only a few hundred reach the ovum, and only one actually fertilizes it.

The fertilized ovum is called a **zygote**. The fertilizing sperm firstly releases **acrosin**, a trypsin-like enzyme, from the acrosome. This softens the plasma membrane which covers the ovum. Inversion of the acrosome results in a fine needle-like filament developing at the tip of the sperm and this pierces the already softened portion of the plasma membrane. An immediate set of changes occurs which thickens the membrane and so ensures that no other sperm can penetrate the egg. This is essential to prevent a 'multinucleate' fertilized egg; such cells normally degenerate after a few divisions. The thickened membrane is now called the **fertilization membrane**. The sperm discards its tail, and the head and middle piece enter the cytoplasm. The second meiotic division of the ovum nucleus normally occurs immediately following the penetration of the sperm. The sperm and ovum nuclei fuse, restoring the diploid state. A spindle forms, the two sets of chromosomes line up and the cell undergoes mitotic division at once.

If the ovum is not fertilized it quickly dies and in humans the lining of the uterus is later shed to give the menstrual flow.

10.6.5 Causes of infertility and its cures

There are a number of reasons why a couple may have difficulty conceiving a baby:

1. **Blocked oviducts** – These may prevent ova and sperm meeting, in which case an operation may be undertaken to unblock the tubes or *in vitro* fertilization can be attempted.

2. **An irregular menstrual cycle** – This may make the chance of fertilization remote and hormone treatment necessary to regularize the cycle.

3. **Incorrect frequency and/or timing of intercourse** may make conception unlikely and couples may need to be counselled on the most appropriate time (the middle of the menstrual cycle) to have sexual intercourse in order to increase the possibility of fertilization.

4. **Non-production of ova** – This affects a few females making it impossible for them to contribute genetically to their offspring. Adoption or the use of a donated ovum from another female for in vitro fertilization are the possible alternatives. Artificial insemination of a surrogate mother with the potential father's sperm is another option.

5. **Non-production of sperm** – Some men produce no sperm, or so few that there is little realistic prospect of conception. Donated semen from another male can be used to artificially inseminate the woman.

6. **Impotence** – Some men are unable to erect the penis and/or ejaculate semen. The cause is often psychological, or the result of prolonged drug or alcohol abuse. In these cases counselling and guidance can sometimes remedy the problem. In other

FOCUS

In vitro fertilization and test tube babies

After first being achieved in rabbits in 1959, *in vitro* fertilization or IVF, was successfully performed between human sperm and ova by Drs Edwards, Bavister and Steptoe ten years later. The development of these zygotes and their successful transfer into the uterus of the mother, called **embryo transfer** or **ET**, took a number of years but finally, in 1978, the first test tube baby was born.

The success of this technique owes as much to the development of a suitable medium in which the sperm, ova and embryo can survive and grow, as to the clinical techniques of obtaining ova and implanting the embryo. Such a medium must have not only a pH, osmotic potential and ionic concentration similar to that of blood, but also contain the patient's serum as a source of protein and other macromolecules. Glucose, lactate and pyruvate are other essential components.

The process begins with a fertility drug being administered to the potential mother to increase her ova production. Around six of these are collected using a fine needle, via the vagina. Some 100 000 sperm, collected from the potential father's semen sample by centrifugation, are added to the ova in a Petri dish. When the embryos are two days old a few are transferred into the mother's uterus where, if all goes well, one will develop normally. More than one is used to guard against some not implanting successfully.

A major cause of infertility is blocked oviducts which therefore prevent ova and sperm meeting in natural circumstances. IVF has solved this problem in some cases, allowing both parents to contribute genetically to the offspring and almost all embryo development to take place inside the natural mother. IVF clinics are now common throughout the UK and despite their low success rate, at 10%, make a major contribution to providing otherwise childless couples with much wanted children. For those with other forms of infertility the technique is unsuitable.

cases an implant may be used which can be pumped up as required. Alternatively an injection of a drug at the base of the penis will raise blood pressure within it and so create an erection.

Some of the above causes of infertility may be the result of certain diseases or infections. Sexually transmitted diseases such as gonorrhoea can cause sterility, especially in females; mumps, if contracted in adult life, sometimes makes males infertile. Even when conception occurs, a few women are not able to sustain the pregnancy because either the embryo does not implant in the uterus lining, or having implanted, it is later miscarried. For some, the solution is to use *in vitro* fertilization (see Focus above) but rather than implant the embryo into the natural mother, it is transferred to a different female. The process whereby one woman carries a fertilized egg for another through to birth, is known as **surrogacy**.

Surrogate motherhood, *in vitro* fertilization and artificial insemination all raise complex legal and moral issues. Should the surrogate mother or sperm donor have any legal rights over the offspring they helped produce? To what extent should the natural mother be able to influence the behaviour of the surrogate mother during pregnancy – should she be able to insist on abstinence from smoking or drinking, both of which could damage the fetus? What details, if any, should a potential mother be entitled to know about the donor of the sperm to be used in artificial insemination? Should the excess embryos which result from in vitro fertilization be used for the purposes of medical research? These are just a few of the issues which have been raised by recent scientific research into the causes of, and cures for, infertility.

10.6.6 Implantation, growth and development

Following fertilization, the zygote divides (cleavage) mitotically until a hollow ball of cells, the **blastocyst**, is produced. It takes three days to reach the uterus and a further three or four days to become implanted in the lining of the uterus. The outer layer of cells of the blastocyst, called the **trophoblast**, develops into the embryonic membranes, the **chorion** and the **amnion**. The chorion develops villi which grow into the surrounding uterine tissue from which they absorb nutrients. These villi form part of the **placenta** which is connected to the fetus by the **umbilical cord**.

After fertilization, the nucleus of the zygote divides mitotically followed by cleavage of the cytoplasm. In this way a series of smaller and smaller cells called **blastomeres** are formed. These divisions continue, resulting after 5–6 days, in an embryonic structure called the blastocyst. While these events take place the structure has been travelling down the oviduct towards the uterus and it is at about this stage that it implants in the uterus lining. There is a cavity at the centre of the blastocyst called the blastocoel. Over the next 7 or 8 days the blastocyst develops an inner mass of cells which forms the embryo and an outer layer, called the **trophoblast**.

The trophoblast develops into the embryonic membranes, the **chorion** and the **amnion**. The amnion develops as a membrane around the fetus. It is made up of two layers and produces the amniotic fluid during the early stages of development. Urine from the fetus is added to this until its total volume reaches around one litre at birth. Other material is excreted by the fetus into the fluid and it is analysis of this and discarded skin which allows genetic and other abnormalities to be detected before birth (see Focus on page 160). The fetus drinks the amniotic fluid from about the middle of its gestation period until birth. Wastes are absorbed by the fetal gut into its blood and are passed to the maternal blood via the placenta. The amniotic fluid provides protection for the fetus as it cushions it from physical damage.

The chorion develops villi which grow into the surrounding uterine tissue from which they absorb nutrients. These villi form part of the placenta which is connected to the fetus by the umbilical cord. The cells of the embryo become organized into an outer **ectoderm** and an inner **endoderm**. Spaces which form in the ectoderm will become the amniotic cavity.

A thickening called the **primitive streak** appears on the embryo 14–15 days after fertilization and ectodermal cells in this position move down to fill the cavity between the endoderm and ectoderm. These cells then form the intermediate layer called the **mesoderm**. The three layers so formed are called the **germ layers**.

The cells of the germ layer continue to divide and become differentiated (see Table 10.2). The mesoderm forms a **notochord** which will become the vertebral column. The ectoderm becomes thickened down the length of the embryo and folds inward to form the **neural tube** which later develops into the nerve cord, the anterior part of which expands to form the brain. The gut increases in length and becomes folded and gradually all other major organs such as the heart develop.

TABLE 10.2

Germ layer	Tissue/organ formed during development
Ectoderm	Skin Jaws Nerves and central nervous system
Mesoderm	Striated muscle/smooth muscle Connective tissue (bone, cartilage, blood) Heart, blood system Kidney and excretory system Reproductive system Eyes
Endoderm	Alimentary canal Lining of gut, bladder and lungs Liver, pancreas and thyroid glands Germinative epithelium

10.6.7 The placenta

The chorionic villi will develop about 14 days after fertilization and represent the beginning of the placenta. It rapidly develops into a disc of tissue covering 20% of the uterus. The capillaries of the mother and fetus come into close contact without actually combining.

10.6.8 Functions of the placenta

1. It allows exchange of materials between the mother and fetus without the two bloods mixing. This is necessary as the fetal blood may be different from that of the mother due to the influence of the father's genes. If incompatible bloods mix they agglutinate (clot), causing blockage in vital organs such as the kidney, possibly resulting in death.

2. Oxygen, water, amino acids, glucose, essential minerals, etc. are transferred from maternal to fetal blood to nourish the developing fetus.

3. Carbon dioxide, urea and other wastes are transferred from fetal to maternal blood to allow their excretion by the mother and prevent harmful accumulation in the fetus.

4. It allows certain maternal antibodies to pass into the fetus, providing it with some immunity against disease. Such immunity is termed **passive natural immunity** as, while the antibodies are naturally produced, they are not formed by the fetus itself. The immunity only lasts for a few months after birth

Did you know?

The longest pregnancy of any mammal is that of the Asiatic elephant with an average of 609 days and maximum of 760 days.

Embryo experimentation and its implications

Embryos developed from *in vitro* fertilization can be used to achieve a successful pregnancy. The process however, usually produces more embryos than are needed for implantation and it is these surplus embryos which some scientists wish to use for research designed to improve our knowledge, for example about disease. Opponents argue that such research is improper because it leads to the death of the embryos which they believe have a similar status to any fully developed human being. They argue that human life commences when a sperm fertilizes an egg and to attempt to distinguish any later point in development where it becomes human is artificial. Those supporting embryo research contest that there are many benefits from the work including improving ways of detecting genetic disorders and in the treatment of infertility. They believe that the alleviation of suffering that could follow is justification enough for research on human embryos.

In 1982 the Government set up a committee of inquiry under the now Baroness Warnock to 'consider recent and potential developments in medicine and science related to human fertilization and embryology'. One initial task was to define what is meant by an embryo. The committee chose to regard the six weeks immediately following fertilization as the embryonic stage. Others prefer to use the first eight weeks after fertilization as their definition, with the first two weeks being regarded as the 'pro-embryo' stage. The committee recommended that there should be a legal time limit after which it would be a criminal offence to use an embryo for research purposes. This limit the government proposed should be the point at which a feature called 'the primitive streak' appeared or 14 days after fertilization, whichever is earlier. Embryo research is now permitted in Britain only under licence from the Statutory Licensing Authority.

The committee also addressed concerns over the possible developments in human embryo research such as cloning, manipulation of the genetic make-up of an embryo and keeping of embryos for progressively longer periods in the laboratory. As a result the government has legislated against such activities unless Parliament specifically makes exceptions should this be felt appropriate in the future. The transfer of human embryos into the uterus of other species is also prohibited as is any process which involves fusing human embryo cells with those of a different species to produce a hybrid organism (chimera).

although this period may be extended by antibodies provided in the mother's milk.

5. It protects the fetus by preventing certain pathogens (disease-causing organisms) and their toxins from crossing the placenta. This protection is by no means complete. Notable exceptions include toxins of the rubella (German measles) virus which can cross the placenta causing physical and mental damage to the fetus, and the HIV virus which can also pass into the fetus.

The chorionic villi present a large surface area for the exchange of materials by diffusion across the chorionic membrane. In some mammals the maternal and fetal bloods flow in opposite directions. This counter-current flow leads to more efficient exchange.

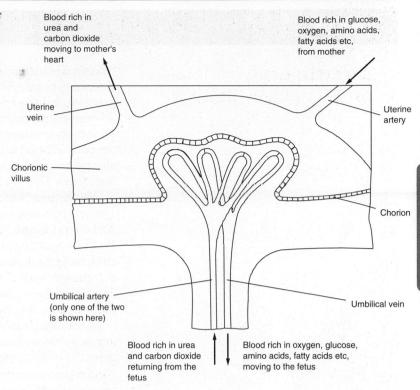

Fig. 10.12 *The mammalian placenta*

6. In a similar way it acts as a barrier to those maternal hormones and other chemicals in the mother's blood which could adversely affect fetal development. Again the protection is not complete and substances like nicotine, alcohol and heroin can all enter the fetus causing lasting damage.

7. As the two blood systems are not directly connected, the placenta permits them to operate at different pressures without harm to mother or fetus.

8. As the pregnancy progresses the placenta increasingly takes over the role of hormone production. In particular it produces progesterone which prevents ovulation and menstruation. It also secretes **human choriogonadotrophin** (HCG), a hormone whose presence in the urine of pregnant women is the basis of most pregnancy tests (see Focus on page 385).

10.6.9 Birth (parturition)

During pregnancy the placenta continues to produce progesterone and small amounts of oestrogen. The amount of progesterone decreases during pregnancy while oestrogen increases. These changes help to trigger the onset of birth. As the end of the gestation period nears, the posterior lobe of the pituitary produces the hormone **oxytocin** which causes the uterus to contract. These contractions increase in force and frequency during labour.

Abortion

Abortion is the premature termination of a pregnancy before the embryo/fetus is capable of surviving. It may be a natural process, perhaps the result of some genetic abnormality preventing normal development of the fetus e.g. the absence of an X chromosome (see page 156) or failure to implant properly. This is called **spontaneous abortion**. Abortion may also be brought on artificially by the use of suction or hormones. This is called **induced abortion**.

Abortion by suction takes place under general anaesthetic. The cervix is stretched open and the contents of the uterus are sucked out through the vagina by machine. This is only feasible when the fetus/embryo is small as, even with stretching, the aperture of the cervix is small. The alternative is the introduction into the uterus of prostaglandins contained in a fluid. These cause dilation of the cervix and contraction of the uterus wall and so expel the fetus/embryo.

In Britain, abortion is not available on demand: it is only permitted in certain circumstances and where two doctors agree. The circumstances are where continuing the pregnancy would cause greater damage to the woman's mental or physical health than if the pregnancy were terminated, or if there is a strong likelihood of severe handicap in the expected child. Abortion can also be legal if the two doctors agree that there is a risk to the health of the woman's existing children as a result of continuing the pregnancy.

Modern medical expertise has meant that premature babies can be kept alive at earlier stages of their development. As a result a recent amendment to the 1967 Abortion Act reduced the time limit for a legal termination from 28 weeks to 24 weeks.

Those in favour of abortion point out that prior to the 1967 Act almost 100 women a year died from having illegal 'back-street' abortions and many more were seriously injured; since the Act there have been almost no such deaths. They argue that there have always been abortions and always will be, and so it is better to make it safe and honest rather than potentially harmful and illegal. They also argue that the rights of the baby have to be weighed against those of the mother who might otherwise suffer physical or psychological harm and who is, in any case, better suited than anyone to decide whether to have the child or not. It is each woman's right to decide her own fertility and as no method of contraception is foolproof, abortion will still be necessary. The birth of a handicapped child, they point out, can place an intolerable burden on the parents and may cause suffering to the child. Unwanted children, they feel, may well be neglected or even abandoned, and may create problems for society. Supporters of abortion say that in certain circumstances, e.g. rape resulting in pregnancy, abortion is the only practical and humane solution.

Arguments against abortion centre on the sanctity of life which many opponents argue begins at conception. To destroy the embryo/fetus after this time they consider to be 'murder'. They point out that fewer than 10% of abortions are carried out for reasons of fetal handicap, the majority being for social reasons. In any case, new methods (e.g. chorionic villus sampling) of detecting abnormalities allows, in some cases, remedial measures to be undertaken while the fetus is still in the womb. Abortion, they contest, is the easy way out and more should be done to improve the quality of life rather than taking it away. Handicapped people can often lead happy, creative and fulfilling lives and any aborted fetus may have had the potential to be a great artist, scientist or world leader and hence of great value to mankind. When abortions go wrong they can leave physical and psychological scars.

The process of birth can be divided into three stages:

1. The dilation of the cervix, resulting in loss of the cervical plug ('the show') and the rupture of the embryonic membranes ('breaking of the waters').

2. The expulsion of the fetus.

3. The expulsion of the placenta ('afterbirth') which is eaten by most mammals.

10.6.10 Lactation

During pregnancy the hormones progesterone and oestrogen cause the development of lactiferous (milk) glands within the mammary glands. Following birth, the anterior lobe of the pituitary gland produces the hormone **prolactin** which causes the lactiferous glands to begin milk production. Suckling by the offspring causes the reflex expulsion of this milk from the nipple of the mammary glands. The first formed milk, called **colostrum**, is mildly laxative and helps the baby expel the bile which has accumulated in the intestines during fetal life. As well as essential nutrients, the milk contains antibodies which give some passive immunity to the newly born.

10.7   Growth

10.7.1 Measurement of growth

Growth is estimated by measuring some parameter (variable) over a period of time. The parameter chosen depends upon the organism whose growth is to be measured. It may be appropriate to measure the weight of a mouse; but this method would be impractical for an oak tree. Mass and length are most often used, but these may be misleading. A bush for example, while not increasing in height, may continue to grow in size by spreading sideways. Area or volume give a more accurate

FOCUS

Drugs across the placenta

Drugs taken by a pregnant woman can cross the placenta if their molecules are small enough. The effect they have on the fetus depends on the nature of the drug, the dose taken and the stage of pregnancy. Obviously the best way to avoid damaging the unborn child is to avoid all drugs but this may not be possible if a serious condition needs treatment. The effects of a few legal and illegal drugs on the development of the fetus will be considered.

Tetracyclines: When given in early pregnancy these antibiotics may cause cataracts and bone abnormalities. Later on they are stored in the bones and also in the teeth where they cause yellow staining.

Cytotoxic drugs: These drugs are used in the treatment of cancers but they must be avoided during pregnancy because of their effect on dividing cells.

Aspirin: This rarely causes any harm but large doses towards the end of pregnancy interfere with the production of prostaglandins and thus delay the onset and progress of labour.

Cannabis and LSD: Both these drugs may cause growth retardation and LSD causes chromosome damage.

Opiates: Babies whose mothers are addicted to heroin become addicted in the uterus. They suffer withdrawal symptoms and growth retardation and may die of their addiction.

Alcohol: Alcohol abuse may lead to mid-term abortion and premature labour. Babies may be retarded both physically and mentally. Approximately one unit of alcohol (half a pint of beer or a glass of wine) taken daily during pregnancy can reduce fetal growth by 1% and the risk of developmental problems rises by 1.5%. In severe cases fetal alcohol syndrome develops whose symptoms include mental retardation, heart lesions and a small head.

Nicotine: Smoke contains many substances which cross the placenta and damage the fetus. Even passive smoking causes an alteration in the heart rate and breathing pattern of the fetus and the constriction of blood vessels in the placenta leads to slower growth. Smoking leads to an increased risk of spontaneous abortion, congenital abnormalities, still birth and mental and physical retardation in later childhood.

indication of growth but are often impractical to measure. The measurement of mass has its problems. If an organism takes in a large amount of water its mass may increase markedly, and yet such a temporary increase could not be considered as growth. For this reason two types of mass are recognized:

1. Fresh mass – This is the mass of the organism under normal conditions. It is easy to measure and doing so involves no damage to the organism. It may, however, be inaccurate due to temporary fluctuations in water content.

FOCUS

Infections across the placenta

The most significant infections which cross the placenta to affect the fetus are rubella and syphilis.

Rubella: If the rubella virus is contracted during the first 12 weeks of pregnancy the risk of having a child with a congenital abnormality is between 5 and 12 times greater. Growth of the early fetal organs may be disorganized leading to possible damage of the eyes, ears, heart and other organs.

Syphilis: The bacterium *Treponema pallidum* which causes syphilis can only cross the placenta after the twentieth week of pregnancy but it causes either death in the uterus or the birth of a child with congenital syphilis.

Babies are unable to manufacture **antibodies** in the uterus or for about 6 weeks after birth. Immunity to many diseases is transferred to them by the passage of the mother's antibodies across the placenta. However, the antibodies to tuberculosis and whooping cough cannot cross the placenta and young babies require protection against these two diseases.

PROJECT

Investigations on fellow students, for example:

(a) Do finger and toe nails grow at the same rate?
(b) Is there any correlation between foot-size and height?
(c) Is there any difference in the lengths of the fingers of the right and left hands?
(d) Does red hair grow more quickly than black/blond hair?
(e) How does the growth of boys and girls at various ages differ?
(f) Do we get smaller as the day progresses?

Did you know?

The fastest growing mammal is the blue whale. Its mass increases from 1 mg to 26 tonnes in less than 2 years.

2. Dry weight – This involves removing all water by drying, before weighing. It is difficult to carry out and permanently destroys the organisms involved, but does give an accurate measure of growth.

10.7.2 Growth patterns

When any parameter of growth is measured against set intervals of time, **a growth curve** is produced. For many populations, organisms or organs, this curve is S-shaped and is called a **sigmoid curve**. It represents slow growth at first, because there are so few cells initially that even when they are dividing rapidly the actual increase in size is small.

As the number of cells becomes greater the size increases more quickly because there are more cells carrying out division. There is a limit to this rapid phase of growth. This limit may be imposed by the genotype of the individual, which specifies a certain maximum size, or any external factors, such as shortage of food. Whatever the cause, the growth rate decreases until it ceases altogether. At this point cells are still dividing, but only at a rate which replaces those which have died. The size of the organism therefore remains constant.

While the sigmoid curve forms the basis of most growth curves, it may be modified in certain circumstances. In humans, for example, there are two phases of rapid growth; one during the early years of life, the other during adolescence. Between these two phases there is a period of relatively slow growth. The growth curve therefore resembles two sigmoid curves, one on top of the other.

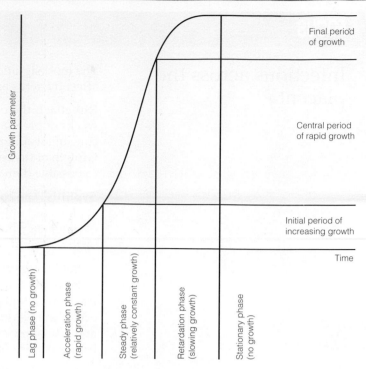

Fig. 10.13 The sigmoid growth curve

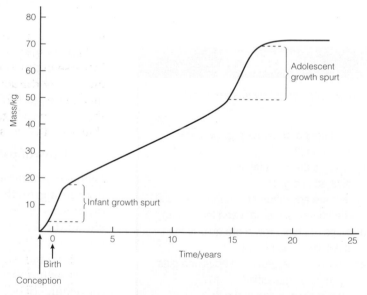

Fig. 10.14 Human growth curve

Certain organs of a human grow at the same rate as the organism as a whole. This is called **isometric growth**. Other organs grow at a different rate from the entire being. This is called **allometric growth**.

In humans, organs often exhibit allometric growth. Lymph tissue, which produces white blood cells to fight infection, grows rapidly in early life when the risk of disease is greater as immunity has not yet been acquired. By adult life the mass of lymph tissues is less than half of what it was in early adolescence. The reproductive organs grow very little in early life but develop rapidly with the onset of sexual maturity at puberty. Fig. 10.15 illustrates allometric growth in some human organs.

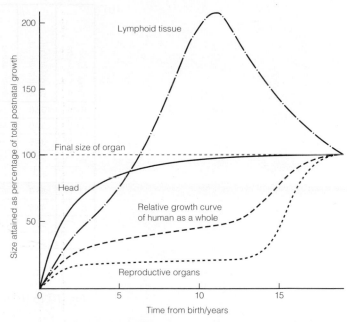

Fig. 10.15 *Allometric growth as shown by human organs and tissues*

10.7.3 Rate of growth

The actual growth of a human is the cumulative increase in size over a period of time. If we look at the growth by weight of a human during adolescence we obtain a growth curve as shown in Figure 10.16 (a). The rate of growth is a measure of size increase over a series of equal time intervals. If instead of measuring the actual weight of the female we measure the increase in weight over each one year period, a set of results like that shown in Fig. 10.16 (b) is obtained. These produce a bell-shaped graph as shown.

(a)

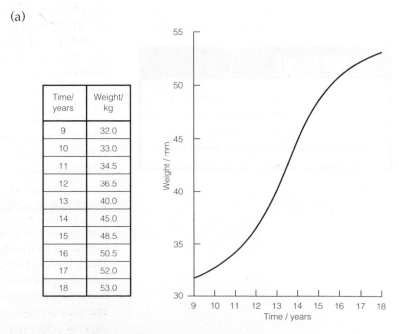

Time/ years	Weight/ kg
9	32.0
10	33.0
11	34.5
12	36.5
13	40.0
14	45.0
15	48.5
16	50.5
17	52.0
18	53.0

Fig. 10.16(a) *Actual growth curve of a human*

(b)

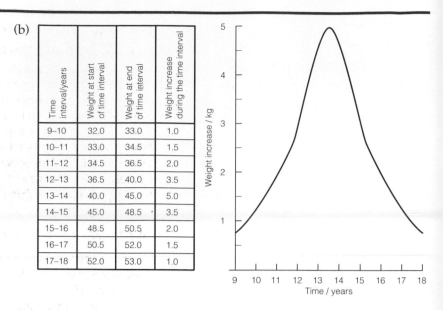

Time interval/years	Weight at start of time interval	Weight at end of time interval	Weight increase during the time interval
9–10	32.0	33.0	1.0
10–11	33.0	34.5	1.5
11–12	34.5	36.5	2.0
12–13	36.5	40.0	3.5
13–14	40.0	45.0	5.0
14–15	45.0	48.5	3.5
15–16	48.5	50.5	2.0
16–17	50.5	52.0	1.5
17–18	52.0	53.0	1.0

Fig. 10.16 (b) Rate of growth curve of a human

10.8 Ageing and senescence

Human body systems normally reach their peak of efficiency during the early years of adulthood. As a person ages the functioning of these systems declines although the mechanisms of this ageing are not well understood. It may be that deterioration of body systems is the result of cells no longer being able to divide. Some human cell types are known to be unable to divide more than about 50 times in total which means that in older people they are not replaced and the tissue hence degenerates. The differences in the rate at which various people age might then be the result of differences in an individual's cell reproductive capacity. Disease, injury and nutrition may all affect the rate of cell division and hence the rate of ageing. Other theories of ageing include the action of 'ageing' viruses over a period of time and the body's own immune system acting on an individual's body tissues. Other scientists believe that ageing is predetermined by certain genes and a gene has been discovered which causes **Werner's Syndrome**, a condition which causes premature ageing to people in their twenties most of whom die by the age of 50.

10.8.1 Effects of ageing

The outward appearance of ageing in humans is evident in wrinkling of the skin which becomes thin, dry and less elastic. There is also thinning and loss of hair (especially in men) and the loss of pigmentation causing greying of the hair. Inwardly the body systems are also undergoing changes causing such general effects as a reduction in the basal metabolic rate (BMR) and overall reduction in mass (up to 10% between the ages of 65 and 90 years). More specific effects to particular systems are detailed below.

Did you know?

The average life span in Britain since the beginning of the century has increased from 48 to 72 years for men and from 52 to 77 years for women.

10.8.2 Ageing of the skeletal system

As bones age their edges become less distinct and develop various extensions and spurs. Where this occurs around joints, movement may become restricted and painful. Changes in the calcification of bone can result in them becoming more porous leading to **osteoporosis** more details of which are given in Section 20.3. These changes can also result in the shortening of bones which explains why elderly people may become shorter. Osteoporosis makes bones more brittle and hence more easily broken. The cartilage at the ends of bones also degenerates leading to **osteoarthritis** (see Section 22.4.3).

10.8.3 Ageing of the nervous system

After the age of 30 years, the rate at which nerve impulses are conducted gradually diminishes until at an age of 80 years they are around 15% slower. As a result there is a gradual decline in the response time to stimuli and the performance of the sense organs.

In the eyes there is often an increase in pressure known as glaucoma and this is a frequent cause of blindness. The lens of the eye hardens and so is less able to change shape to allow focusing on objects close to the eye. This leads to increasing farsightedness (**presbyopia**) in people over the age of 45 years. The lens and cornea also become more opaque, a condition known as **cataract** which leads to a gradual loss of sight. **Senile macular degeneration (SMD)** is the main cause of blindness in the UK. It is the degeneration of the main focusing area of the retina making it impossible to see detail. SMD is often caused by haemorrhageing of small abnormal blood vessels in the retina.

In the ears, the sensory hair cells of the cochlea degenerate leading to reduced hearing especially of high frequency sound. The loss of elasticity as a result of senescence that is common in many tissues, also affects the eardrum which is consequently less efficient at transmitting sound waves leading to further loss of hearing. This may be exacerbated by some fusion of the three ear ossicles.

The sense of taste also diminishes as taste buds become replaced by connective tissue with around 40% of them being lost between the ages of 30 and 75 years.

The gradual loss of brain cells can reduce the total mass of the brain by 10% between the ages of 30 and 90 years.

10.8.4 Ageing of the reproductive system

While many men and women remain sexually active throughout their lives their fertility nevertheless declines. Men can remain fertile into their eighties although their sperm count diminishes. Women on the other hand cease to release ova, usually some time between the ages of 45 and 50 years. This is called the menopause and results from a decrease in the production of gonadotrophins from the pituitary gland (see Section 10.4). As a result menstrual periods cease, the vagina wall thins and hot flushes and night sweats may be experienced; changes in oestrogen levels at this time can also cause osteoporosis. These symptoms of the menopause may be offset by the use of **hormone replacement therapy (HRT)** which is discussed in the Focus on p. 496.

> ## Did you know?
>
> Cataract operations in the UK rose from 38 000 in 1978 to 60 000 in 1990.

There may also be changes in sexual responses as one ages. The desire for sex may decline and men may experience greater difficulty in achieving and maintaining an erection while women may produce less mucus to lubricate the vagina.

10.8.5 Effects of ageing on the respiratory system

The calcification of the cartilage which accompanies old age affects the cartilage which fixes the ribs to the sternum. As this hardens, it is more difficult to expand and contract the rib cage during breathing. The rib cage remains in the expanded position causing the chest to assume a more barrel shape and making breathing increasingly difficult. A person's vital capacity (see Section 15.4) may be reduced by as much as 50% as a consequence of this change and the reduced muscular strength of the intercostal muscles. The lining membrane of the alveoli thickens with age decreasing the diffusion of oxygen across it by up to 50% in a 75-year-old compared with a 30-year-old.

10.8.6 Effects of ageing on the circulatory system

With age, deposits of fat build up in the walls of blood vessels reducing the rate of blood flow through them. This condition, known as **atherosclerosis**, is described in the Focus on cholesterol on page 21. The vessel may ultimately become completely blocked. If this is in an artery leading to the heart muscle or the brain, a heart attack or stroke may occur. Hardening of the walls of blood vessels, known as **arteriosclerosis**, increases with age and often leads to increased blood pressure – **hypertension** – possibly resulting in heart attack or stroke (see Focus on page 401). The decline in the strength of cardiac muscle means that around 30% less blood is pumped in a given time by a 90-year-old than by someone aged 30 years.

10.8.7 Effects of ageing on the excretory system

As the efficiency of the circulatory system diminishes so does that of the kidney which depends on an efficient blood supply in order to function effectively. Add to this, the 50% reduction in the number of nephrons that occurs between the ages of 30 and 75 years, and it is hardly surprising that the renal filtration rate may have diminished by more than half in old age. The loss of muscle strength may affect the bladder so that it cannot be fully emptied and so urination needs to be more frequent. Loss of strength and control of the urinary sphincter can lead to incontinence, a condition which affects 7% of men and 12% of women over the age of 65 years.

Did you know?

Over the last 30 years the number of people in the UK living beyond 85 years has more than doubled from 300 000 to 650 000.

10.9 Questions

1. Either

(a) (i) Compare the structure of a human egg and sperm. *(10 marks)*

(ii) Describe and explain the means by which a sperm travels within a woman's body to reach an egg, and the process of fertilisation. *(10 marks)*

(iii) Why are more sperms produced than eggs? *(3 marks)*

Or

(b) (i) Explain how contraception may be achieved and discuss the advantages and disadvantages of the methods you describe. *(17 marks)*

(ii) Discuss the bio-social implications of carrying out abortions. *(6 marks)*

(Total 23 marks)

UCLES June 1992, Paper 3 (Option 3), Nos. 3(a) and 3(b)

2. Either

(a) (i) Describe the structure of the human placenta. *(8 marks)*

(ii) Explain how materials are transferred across the placenta. *(4 marks)*

(iii) Discuss the importance of pre-natal care for the healthy development of the embryo. *(6 marks)*

Or

(b) (i) Explain the importance of the hypothalamus and pituitary gland in the control of the menstrual and ovarian cycles. *(8 marks)*

(ii) Explain the hormonal basis of the contraceptive pill. *(4 marks)*

(iii) Discuss the advantages and disadvantages of the contraceptive pill as a means of birth control. *(6 marks)*

(Total 18 marks)

UCLES June 1995, Paper 3 (Option 3), Nos. 3(a) and 3(b)

3. Either

(a) Discuss the biological and the social consequences of treating human infertility by artificial insemination, surrogacy and *in vitro* fertilization. *(30 marks)*

Or

(b) Discuss the roles of hormones in human reproduction. *(30 marks)*

ULEAC June 1993, Paper 3, Nos. 9(a) and 9(b)

4.

The graph shows changes in certain reproductive hormone levels during pregnancy. All the hormones have an effect on the uterus.

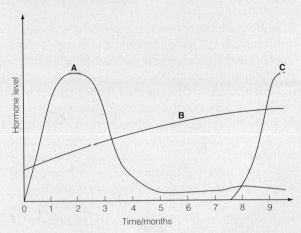

(a) Name the hormones **A** and **B** shown on the graph. *(2 marks)*

(b) Using information on the graph describe and explain the effect of hormone **C** on the uterus. *(2 marks)*

(c) Name **one** hormone involved in lactation and describe its function. *(2 marks)*

(Total 6 marks)

AEB June 1995, Paper 1, No. 8

5.

The graph shows changes in the levels of two female sex hormones involved in controlling the menstrual cycle.

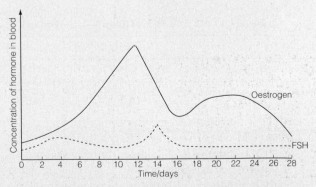

(a) (i) What is the main function of FSH? *(1 mark)*

(ii) Describe the effect of oestrogen on the level of FSH during days 4 to 10 of this cycle. *(1 mark)*

(b) Use the information in the graph to explain **one** way in which oral contraceptives might act to prevent fertilization taking place. *(2 marks)*

(c) In a study of a large sample of women fitted with an intra-uterine device (IUD), the mean menstrual blood loss was 90 cm³. The mean menstrual blood loss in a control group was 41 cm³. In the light of these findings, suggest what dietary advice should be given to a woman using an IUD.

(2 marks)

(Total 6 marks)

NEAB June 1995, Paper BY09, No. 3

6. Read through the following account of stages in embryonic development then write on the dotted lines the most appropriate word or words to complete the account.

Fertilisation occurs in the oviduct (Fallopian tube) and is followed by mitotic cell divisions. These divisions of the fertilized egg occur during the stage known as .... and result in the formation of a ...., which implants in the wall of the uterus. The embryo soon develops a series of membranes, the first of which called the .... probably serves no useful function. Outgrowths from the embryonic coelom then develop and soon surround the embryo forming two membranes. The inner membrane, the ...., will secrete fluid to protect the developing embryo. The outer membrane or .... forms an absorbing surface by developing outgrowths called villi. The .... is the last membrane to develop resulting in the formation of the placenta and umbilical cord.

(Total 6 marks)

ULEAC June 1995, Paper 3, No. 2

7. (a) A variety of factors may affect a woman's ability to ovulate. The table shows data relating to two groups of 18-year-old women.

Factor	Group 1	Group 2
Ovulation	Normal	Absent
Mean water: dry mass ratio	1.08 : 1	1.33 : 1
Mean lean mass: fat mass ratio	2.5 : 1	4.0 : 1

Use these data to explain why the following 18-year-old women might stop ovulating:
(i) a woman who has recently followed a weight-reduction diet; (2 marks)
(ii) a female body-builder at her peak level of competitive performance. (2 marks)

The four graphs at the top of the next column show the plasma levels of four hormones involved in the control of the human menstrual cycle. The plasma hormone levels were plotted over an interval of 30 days.

The days are numbered in either direction from the peak level of secretion of luteinising hormone.

(b) Explain, with reference to the graphs, the role of each of the hormones in controlling the timing of the events of the menstrual cycle. (8 marks)

(c) (i) If the woman were to become pregnant during the next cycle, on which day of the cycle might implantation take place? Use the graphs to help explain your answer. (3 marks)
(ii) What effect would this have on the other hormones involved? (2 marks)

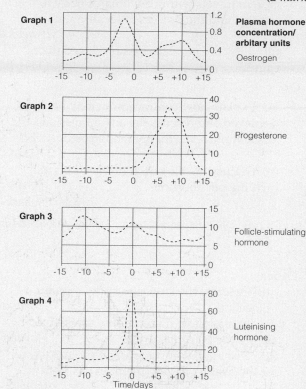

(d) **Graph 5** shows the level of secretion of one of the two pituitary hormones secreted by a woman who had been trying for two years, without success, to conceive a child.

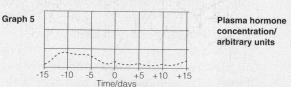

(i) Identify the hormone shown in the graph and suggest why the woman's fertility was affected.
Suggest what medical treatment might be given to deal with this effect (3 marks)
(ii) Artificial forms of some of the hormones shown in the graphs are used to make various types of the contraceptive (birth control) pill. The combined pill contains synthetic progesterone, as the drug progestogen, together with synthetic oestrogen.
Explain the mode of action of the combined contraceptive pill. (4 marks)

(Total 24 marks)

AEB June 1994, Paper 2, No. 2

8. The diagram below shows a section of a human ovary.

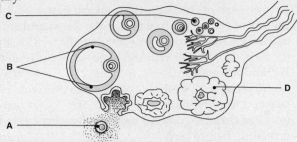

(a) Name the structures labelled **A**, **B**, **C** and **D**.
(*4 marks*)

(b) Name the type of cell division which gave rise to structure **C**. (*1 mark*)

(c) State **one** function of structure **D**. (*1 mark*)

(d) Name the hormone, secreted by the pituitary gland, which is responsible for the development of structure **B**. (*1 mark*)

(*Total 7 marks*)

ULEAC June 1994, Paper 3, No. 1

9. The graph shows the mean body mass of human males and females from birth to eighteen years of age.

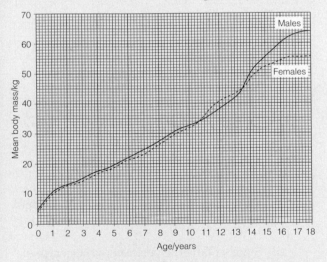

(a) (i) For how long is the mean body mass of females greater than that of males? (*1 mark*)

(ii) Explain why this difference occurs. (*1 mark*)

(b) (i) During which **two** separate one-year periods does the mass of males increase faster than at any other times? (*1 mark*)

(ii) Calculate which of these **two** periods shows the greater, relative growth rate. Show your working. (*3 marks*)

(*Total 6 marks*)

AEB June 1994, Paper 1, No. 15

10. Human chorionic gonadotrophin (HCG) is produced by the developing chorion and is present in the blood of pregnant women in high concentration.

During pregnancy, the concentration of HCG and progesterone can be monitored by taking blood samples. The figure shows the hormone concentrations and placental mass during the 40 weeks gestation period.

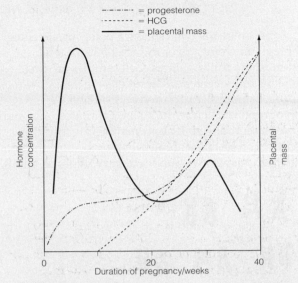

(a) (i) With reference to the figure describe the relationship between the concentration of HCG and progesterone during the first 20 weeks of pregnancy.

(ii) Suggest an explanation for the relationship you have described. (*4 marks*)

(b) Why is there a close parallel between the level of progesterone and placental mass from weeks 20–40? (*2 marks*)

(c) Describe **two** ways in which progesterone is important during pregnancy. (*2 marks*)

(d) Oxytocin is released from the posterior lobe of the maternal pituitary gland as a result of the reflex initiated as the cervix is dilated during labour.

(i) Suggest **one** mechanism by which a stimulus from the fetus results in the release of oxytocin by the mother's pituitary gland.

(ii) Outline the process of birth that will follow once the fetal head has entered the cervix.
(*4 marks*)

(e) Twins occur in about 1% of human births; about 75% of twins are non-identical and about 25% identical.

(i) State **two** methods by which the presence of twins could be detected in the womb.

(ii) Twins occasionally differ in mass at birth by as much as a factor of two. Suggest **two** reasons for this.

(iii) Suggest **two** reasons why twins are relatively uncommon in humans.

(iv) In non-identical twins, the combination of a girl and a boy is about twice as common as having either two girls or two boys. Explain why this is so.

(v) Suggest, giving examples, why identical twins are so useful in studies of the effects of the environment on growth and health

(13 marks)

(Total 25 marks)

UCLES June 1992, Paper 3 (Option 3), No. 2

11. Some antenatal clinics have a policy of screening all pregnant women over the age of 35 for fetal chromosome abnormalities. Cell samples are first taken by amniocentesis. These cells are then grown in culture, osmotically ruptured and stained. A photograph is taken of the stained chromosomes and a karyotype produced. If abnormalities are found, a decision can be taken about whether to abort the fetus. The figure shows two abnormal karyotypes, **A** and **B**.

(a) Explain why the cells need to be grown in culture before staining. (1 mark)

(b) For each of the karyotypes in the figure, state the sex of the individual and name the syndrome caused by the chromosome abnormality. (2 marks)

(c) Explain how the chromosome set of individual **B** could have arisen. (2 marks)

(d) Explain why women over the age of 35 are selected for screening. (2 marks)

(e) Give **three** arguments **against** the use of genetic screening before birth. (3 marks)

(f) (i) Explain why phenylketonuria cannot be detected from a karyotype. (2 marks)

(ii) Explain how phenylketonuria can be treated. (2 marks)

(Total 14 marks)

UCLES June 1995, Paper 3 (Option 3), No. 2

12. The diagram shows the relative proportions of a human female from two months after conception to an adult.

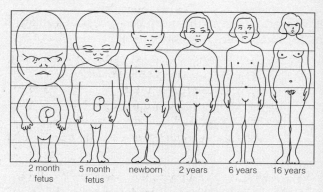

(a) On graph paper **sketch** the curves of the relative length of (i) the head and (ii) the leg for the stages shown in the diagram. (3 marks)

(b) (i) How does the centre of gravity of the body move as the newborn baby grows to an adult? (1 mark)

(ii) Suggest how the position of the centre of gravity would affect the two year old learning to walk. (1 mark)

(Total 5 marks)

AEB June 1995, Paper 1, No. 14

13. Read through the passage and answer the questions that follow.

The technique of *in vitro* fertilization (IVF) was developed to overcome female infertility. About one-third of such cases are due to diseased or damaged Fallopian tubes, so that although eggs are produced by the ovaries, conception does not occur. In the technique of IVF, a woman takes hormonal drugs that cause her ovaries to produce several mature eggs in one menstrual cycle. These eggs are then collected and fertilized in the laboratory. A day later the eggs are checked to see if fertilization has been successful. The embryos are then cultured for a further day or two and then implanted into the woman when they are at the 4- or 8-cell stage.

A biopsy can be performed before implantation to determine the sex of the embryo. This is possible since only males carry both X and Y chromosomes. A hole is cut in the glycoprotein coat that surrounds the embryo and one or two cells removed. A DNA probe is used to detect a region of the Y chromosome. This technique has been used successfully with those women at risk of giving birth to sons suffering from inherited sex-linked diseases, such as Duchenne muscular dystrophy which is caused by the recessive allele of a gene carried on the X chromosome.

(a) Describe how eggs which are to be fertilized *in vitro* are collected from the ovaries. (3 marks)

(b) Explain why IVF clinics rarely implant more than three embryos at a time. (2 marks)

(c) (i) What is the advantage of performing embryo biopsy in the case of families with a history of Duchenne muscular dystrophy?
(ii) State **one** ethical objection to the process of embryo biopsy.
(iii) Describe **one** method of prenatal diagnosis in which the sex of an embryo can be determined after implantation. (9 marks)

(d) Explain why the techniques of IVF and embryo biopsy cannot be used to eradicate totally sex-linked diseases like Duchenne muscular dystrophy. (3 marks)

The overall success rate of IVF is low. In spite of the fact that 70–80% of eggs are fertilized, only about 10% of women entering IVF programmes have pregnancies which reach full term. An alternative method to overcome infertility is gamete intra-Fallopian transfer (GIFT). Eggs and sperm are collected in the same way as in IVF, but they are introduced directly into the woman's Fallopian tube. This technique is both cheaper and more successful than IVF.

(e) (i) State **one** reason why GIFT is not a suitable method for overcoming all forms of female infertility.

(ii) Explain why GIFT is a cheaper form of treatment than IVF. (3 marks)

(f) Discuss briefly the medical and ethical reasons for regulating IVF, GIFT and research on embryos. (5 marks)

(Total 25 marks)

UCLES June 1992, Paper 3 (Option 1), No. 1

14. *When the Pill gets under your skin*

When news of a new contraceptive method reached British women in 1993, family planning organizations were flooded with enquiries. The contraceptive is an implant called Norplant. Not everyone, however, is thrilled by Norplant. Organizations around the world are concerned that it might be used as a method of social control.

Norplant delivers in a new way. It consists of six capsules, each 34 millimetres long. Each capsule contains 38 milligrams of a synthetic progesterone hormone. This hormone thickens the mucus produced by the cervix (neck) of the uterus. It also inhibits the production of LH (luteinizing hormone).

A health worker inserts the contraceptive capsules through an incision on the inside of the upper arm and they remain under the skin for five years, steadily releasing progesterone into the bloodstream.

(Adapted from an article in the *New Scientist*)

(a) Suggest how the thickening of the mucus produced by the neck of the uterus might help to prevent conception. (1 mark)

(b) (i) Describe the role of LH in the menstrual cycle and then explain how the inhibition of LH production prevents conception. (5 marks)

(ii) Hormone levels are often affected by negative feedback processes. Explain as fully as you can what is meant by negative feedback. (2 marks)

(c) Suggest and explain the advantages and disadvantages of using Norplant as a contraceptive. (4 marks)

(Total 12 marks)

NEAB February 1995, Paper BY1, No. 8

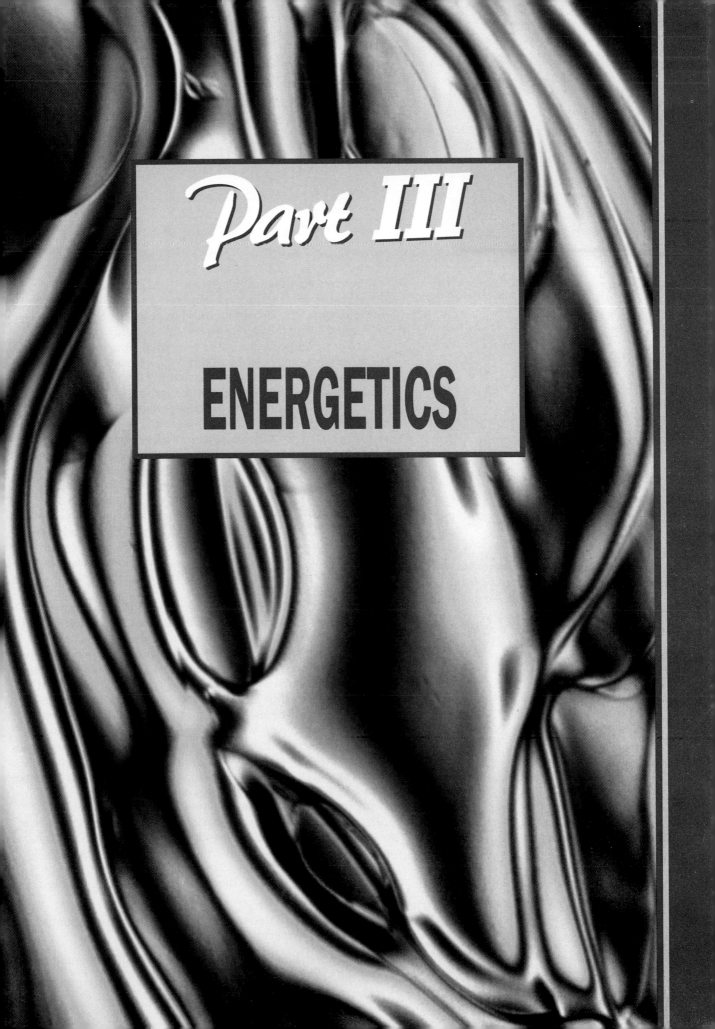

Part III

ENERGETICS

Energy and organisms

Energy is defined as the 'capacity to do work'. It exists in a number of different forms: heat, light, electrical, magnetic, chemical, atomic, mechanical and sound. The laws which apply to energy conversions are the **laws of thermodynamics**.

The first law of thermodynamics states: **energy cannot be created or destroyed but may be converted from one form into another**. Energy may also be stored. Water in a lake high up on a mountain is an example of stored energy. The energy it possesses is called **potential energy**. If the water is released from the lake it begins to flow downhill, and the energy of its motion is called **kinetic energy**. The stream of moving water may be used to drive a turbine which produces electricity (hydroelectric power). The kinetic energy is thus converted to electricity. This electricity may in turn be converted into light (light bulb), heat (electric fire/cooker), sound (CD or cassette player) etc. During these changes not all the energy is converted into its intended form; some is lost as heat. By 'lost' we mean the energy is no longer available to do useful work because it is distributed evenly. Energy which is available to do work under conditions of constant temperature and pressure is called **free energy**. Reactions which liberate energy are termed **exothermic**, those which absorb free energy are termed **endothermic**.

The second law of thermodynamics states: **all natural processes tend to proceed in a direction which increases the randomness or disorder of a system**. The degree of randomness is called **entropy**. A highly ordered system has low entropy whereas a disordered one, with its high degree of randomness, has high entropy. We have seen that entropy and free energy are inversely related. Systems with high entropy have little free energy, those with low entropy have more free energy. We also saw that the ability of living systems to maintain low entropy is what distinguishes them from non-living systems. The fact that living systems can decrease their entropy does not mean that they fail to obey the second law of thermodynamics. The reason that they are able to reduce their entropy is that they take in useful energy from their surroundings and release it in a less useful form. While the organism's entropy decreases, that of its surroundings increases to an even greater extent. The organism and its environment represent one system, the total entropy of which increases. The second law of thermodynamics is therefore not violated.

There are three stages to the flow of energy through living systems:

1. The conversion of the sun's light energy to chemical energy by plants during photosynthesis.

2. The conversion of the chemical energy from photosynthesis into ATP – the form in which cells can utilize it.

3. The utilization of ATP by cells in order to perform useful work.

The chemical reactions which occur within organisms are collectively known as **metabolism**. They are of two types:

1. The build-up of complex compounds from simple ones. These synthetic reactions are collectively known as **anabolism**.

2. The breakdown of complex compounds into simple ones. Such reactions are collectively known as **catabolism**.

A typical chemical reaction may be represented as:

$$A \rightarrow B + C$$

In this case A represents the **substrate** and B and C are the **products**. If the entropy of C and B is greater than A then the reaction will proceed naturally in the direction shown. A reaction which involves an increase in entropy is said to be **spontaneous**. The free energy of the products is less than that of the substrate. The word spontaneous could be misleading because the reaction is not instantaneous. Before any chemical reaction can proceed it must initially be activated, i.e. its energy must be increased. The energy required is called the **activation energy**. Once provided, the activation energy allows the products to be formed with a consequent loss of free energy and increase in entropy (Fig. III). Chemical reactions are reversible and therefore C and B can be synthesized into A. Such a reaction is not, however, spontaneous and requires an external source of energy if it is to proceed. Most biological processes are in fact a cycle of reversible reactions. Photosynthesis and respiration, for example, are basically the same reaction going in opposite directions.

$$\text{Energy} + 6CO_2 + 6H_2O \underset{\text{respiration}}{\overset{\text{photosynthesis}}{\rightleftarrows}} C_6H_{12}O_6 + 6O_2$$

As there is inevitably some loss of free energy in the form of heat each time the reaction is reversed, the process cannot continue without a substantial input of energy from outside the organisms. The ultimate source of this energy is the light radiation of the sun. The way in which organisms obtain their energy for metabolic and other processes is probably more important in determining their design than any other single factor. The fundamental differences between plants and animals are a result of their modes of nutrition.

Plants obtain their energy from the sun and use it to combine carbon dioxide and water in the synthesis of organic molecules. As the raw materials are readily available almost everywhere, there is no necessity for plants to move to obtain their nutrients. Indeed, in order to obtain sufficient light plants need to have a large surface area. They therefore need to be as large as possible in order to compete with other plants for light. For this reason many plants are large. Locomotion for these plants would not only be difficult and slow, it would also be very energy-consuming. Plants therefore do not exhibit locomotion.

Animals obtain their energy from complex organic compounds. These occur in other organisms which must be sought. Most animals therefore exhibit locomotion in order to obtain their food. To help animals move from place to place they have developed a wide range of locomotory mechanisms. They are therefore more complex, and variable, in their design than plants. In carrying out locomotion, animals require a complex nervous system to coordinate their actions and a range of sense organs to help them to manoeuvre and to locate food.

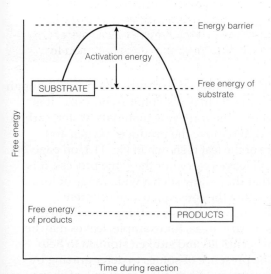

Fig. III Concept of activation energy

11 Nutrition

In this chapter we shall learn how, through the process of photosynthesis, plants convert the light energy of the sun into the chemical energy of food which humans then digest to release the energy necessary for their own vital activities.

11.1 Photosynthesis

We have seen that living systems differ from non-living ones in their ability to replace lost energy from the environment and so maintain themselves in an ordered condition (low entropy). Photosynthesis is the means by which this energy is initially obtained by living systems. All life is directly or indirectly dependent on this most fundamental process in living organisms. It provides part of the air we breathe, the food we eat and the fossil fuels we burn.

Photosynthesis is important because:

1. It is the means by which the sun's energy is captured by plants for use by all organisms.

2. It provides a source of complex organic molecules for other organisms.

3. It releases oxygen for use by aerobic organisms.

11.2 Leaf structure

The leaf is the main photosynthetic structure of a plant, although stems, sepals and other parts may also photosynthesize. It is adapted to bring together the three raw materials, water, carbon dioxide and light, and to remove the products oxygen and glucose. The structure of the leaf is shown in Fig. 11.1, on page 244.

Considering that all leaves carry out the same process, it is perhaps surprising that they show such a wide range of form. This range of form is often the consequence of different environmental conditions which have nothing directly to do with photosynthesis. In dry areas, for example, leaves may be small in size with thick cuticles and sunken stomata to help reduce water loss. The presence of spines to deter grazing by herbivores is not uncommon. Other differences in leaf shape are a result of the plant living in a sunny or shady situation.

Did you know?

Leaves of the Raphia palm found in tropical forests can be 22 metres long.

The equation for photosynthesis may be summarized as:

$$6CO_2 + 6H_2O + sunlight \xrightarrow{chlorophyll} C_6H_{12}O_6 + 6O_2$$

$$carbon\ dioxide + water + sunlight \xrightarrow{chlorophyll} glucose + oxygen$$

$$gas + liquid + energy \xrightarrow{chlorophyll} liquid + gas\ (solution\ in\ water)$$

The adaptations of the leaf to photosynthesis are therefore:

1. To obtain energy (sunlight).

2. To obtain and remove gases (carbon dioxide and oxygen).

3. To obtain and remove liquids (water and sugar solution).

11.2.1 Adaptations for obtaining energy (sunlight)

As sunlight is the energy source which drives the photosynthetic process, it is often the factor which determines the rate of photosynthesis. To ensure its efficient absorption the leaf shows many adaptations:

1. **Phototropism** causes shoots to grow towards the light in order to allow the attached leaves to receive maximum illumination.

2. **Etiolation** causes rapid elongation of shoots which are in the dark, to ensure that the leaves are brought up into the light as soon as possible.

3. **Leaves arrange themselves into a mosaic**, i.e. they are arranged on the plant in a way that minimizes overlapping and so reduces the degree of shading of one leaf by another.

4. **Leaves have a large surface area** to capture as much sunlight as possible. They are held at an angle perpendicular to the sun during the day to expose the maximum area to the light. Some plants, e.g. the compass plant, actually 'track' the sun by moving their leaves so they constantly face it during the day.

5. **Leaves are thin** – If they were thicker, the upper layers would filter out all the light and the lower layers would not then photosynthesize.

6. **The cuticle and epidermis are transparent** to allow light through to the photosynthetic mesophyll beneath.

7. **The palisade mesophyll cells are packed with chloroplasts** and arranged with their long axes perpendicular to the surface. Although there are some air spaces between them, they still form a continuous layer which traps most of the incoming light. In some plants this layer is more than one cell thick.

8. **The chloroplasts within the mesophyll cells can move** – This allows them to arrange themselves into the best positions within a cell for the efficient absorption of light.

9. **The chloroplasts hold chlorophyll in a structured way** – The chlorophyll within a chloroplast is contained within the grana, where it is arranged on the sides of a series of unit membranes. The ordered arrangement not only presents the maximum

(a)

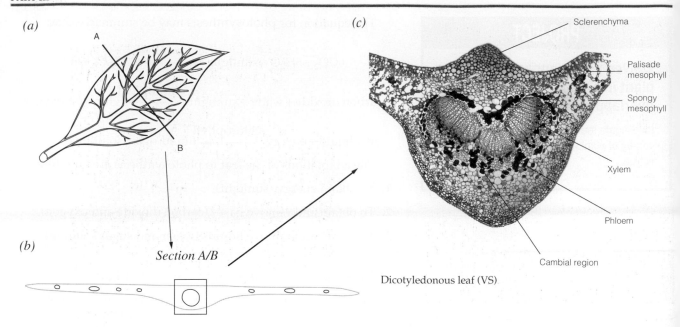

(b)

Section A/B

(c)

Sclerenchyma

Palisade mesophyll

Spongy mesophyll

Xylem

Phloem

Cambial region

Dicotyledonous leaf (VS)

(d) *Dicotyledonous leaf (VS) (×40 approx.)*

(e) *Palisade cell*

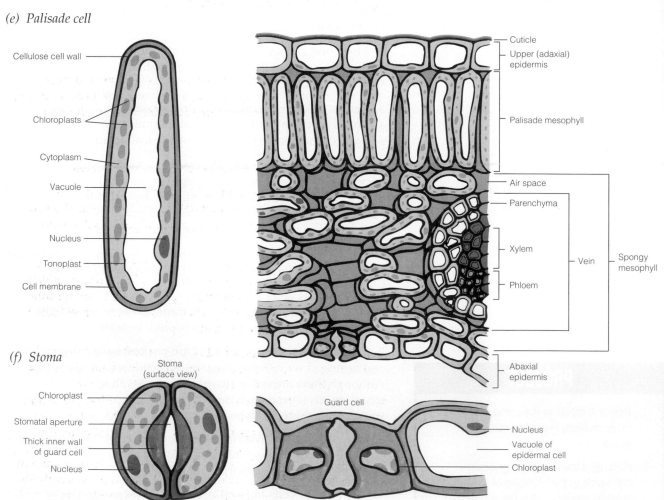

Cellulose cell wall

Chloroplasts

Cytoplasm

Vacuole

Nucleus

Tonoplast

Cell membrane

Cuticle

Upper (adaxial) epidermis

Palisade mesophyll

Air space

Parenchyma

Xylem

Phloem

Vein

Spongy mesophyll

Abaxial epidermis

(f) *Stoma*

Stoma (surface view)

Chloroplast

Stomatal aperture

Thick inner wall of guard cell

Nucleus

Guard cell

Nucleus

Vacuole of epidermal cell

Chloroplast

Fig. 11.1 The structure of the leaf (continued on next page)

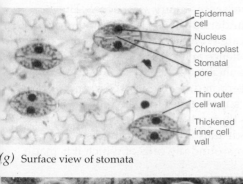

Epidermal cell
Nucleus
Chloroplast
Stomatal pore
Thin outer cell wall
Thickened inner cell wall

(g) Surface view of stomata

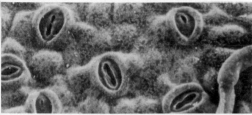

Stomata in surface view (scanning EM) (× 600 approx.)

(h)

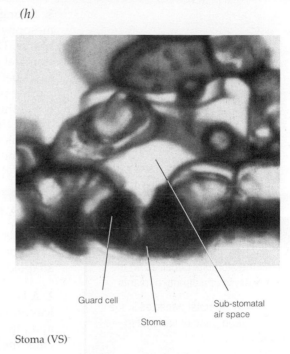

Guard cell

Stoma

Sub-stomatal air space

Stoma (VS)

Fig. 11.1 The structure of the leaf (continued)

amount of chlorophyll to the light but also brings it in close proximity to other pigments and substances which are necessary for its functioning. The structure of a chloroplast is shown in Fig. 4.5, Section 4.2.4.

11.2.2 Adaptations for obtaining and removing gases

As gases diffuse relatively rapidly, the leaf has no special transport mechanism for carbon dioxide and oxygen. The leaf does, however, show a number of adaptations which ensure rapid diffusion of these gases:

1. **Numerous stomata** are present in the epidermis of leaves. There may be tens of thousands per cm^2 of leaf surface, which itself represents a very considerable area. Stomata are minute pores in the epidermis which, when open, permit unrestricted diffusion into and out of the leaf.

2. **Stomata can be opened and closed** – Plants need to be relatively impermeable to gases in order to prevent water loss, and yet they need the free entry of carbon dioxide for photosynthesis. To overcome this problem, they have stomatal pores which are bounded by two **guard cells**. Alterations in the turgidity of these cells open and close the stomatal pore, thus controlling the uptake of carbon dioxide and the loss of water. Stomata open in conditions which favour photosynthesis and at this time some water loss is unavoidable. When photosynthesis cannot take place, e.g. at night, they close, thus reducing considerably the loss of water. At times of considerable water loss, the stomata may close anyway, regardless of the demands for carbon dioxide.

3. Spongy mesophyll possesses many airspaces – The mesophyll layer on the underside of the leaf has many air spaces. These communicate with the palisade layer and the stomatal pores. There is hence an uninterrupted diffusion of gases between the atmosphere and the palisade mesophyll. During photosynthesis carbon dioxide diffuses in and oxygen out of this layer. The air spaces avoid the need for these gases to diffuse through the cells themselves, a process which would be much slower. The palisade mesophyll also possesses air spaces to permit rapid diffusion around the cells of which it is made.

11.2.3 Adaptations for obtaining and removing liquids

As water is a liquid raw material for photosynthesis and as the sugar produced is carried away in solution, the leaf has to be adapted for the efficient transport of liquids.

1. A large central midrib is possessed by most dicotyledonous leaves. This contains a large vascular bundle comprising xylem and phloem tissue. The xylem permits water and mineral salts to enter the leaf and the phloem carries away sugar solution, usually in the form of sucrose.

2. A network of small veins is found throughout the leaf. These ensure that no cell is ever far from a xylem vessel or phloem sieve tube, and hence all cells have a constant supply of water for photosynthesis and a means of removing the sugars they produce. The xylem, and any sclerenchyma associated with the vascular bundle, also provide a framework of support for the leaf, helping it to present maximum surface area to the light.

PROJECT

1. Estimate the stomatal densities on the lower epidermis of a variety of plants.

2. Find out if the stomatal densities in the white and green parts of variegated leaves differ.

3. Determine if there are any differences in stomatal densities of leaves collected randomly from a tree.

11.3 Mechanism of photosynthesis

The overall equation for photosynthesis is:

$$6CO_2 + 6H_2O \xrightarrow[\text{chlorophyll}]{\text{sunlight}} C_6H_{12}O_6 + 6O_2$$

carbon dioxide + water $\longrightarrow$ glucose + oxygen

Photosynthesis is essentially a process of energy transduction. Light energy is firstly converted into electrical energy and finally into chemical energy. It has three main phases:

1. Light harvesting. Light energy is captured by the plant using a mixture of pigments including chlorophyll.

2. The light dependent stage (photolysis) in which a flow of electrons results from the effect of light on chlorophyll and so causes the splitting of water into hydrogen ions and oxygen.

3. The light independent stage during which these hydrogen ions are used in the **reduction of carbon dioxide** and hence the manufacture of sugars.

11.3.1 Light harvesting

Within the thylakoid membranes of the chloroplast, chlorophyll molecules are arranged along with their accessory pigments into groups of several hundred molecules. Each group is called an **antenna complex**. Special proteins associated with these pigments help to funnel photons of light entering the chloroplast on to special molecules of chlorophyll *a*, known as the **reaction centre chlorophyll molecule**. On striking this molecule an electron in its orbit is raised to a higher energy level, thus initiating a flow of electrons.

There are two types of reaction centre which differ in both their chlorophylls and their functions. These are known as **photosystem I (PSI)** and **photosystem II (PSII)**.

11.3.2 Light dependent stage (photolysis)

The light dependent stage of photosynthesis occurs in the thylakoids of the chloroplasts and involves the splitting of water by light – **photolysis of water**. In the process, ADP is converted to ATP. This addition of phosphate is termed **phosphorylation** and as light is involved it is called **photophosphorylation**. These processes are brought about by two photochemical systems which are summarized in Figs. 11.2 and 11.3.

In the process summarized in Fig. 11.3, electrons from chlorophyll are passed into the light independent reaction via $NADPH + H^+$. They are replaced by electrons from another source – the water molecule. The same electrons are *not* recycled back into the chlorophyll. This method of ATP production is thus called **non-cyclic photophosphorylation**. It is alternatively called the **Z-scheme** because the zig-zag route of the electrons in the diagram resembles a Z on its side.

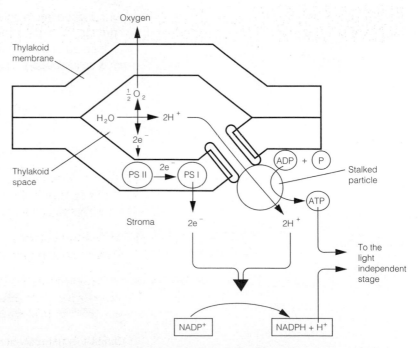

Fig. 11.2 Summary of the events of the light dependent stage and their locations within the chloroplast

1. *Light energy is trapped in photosystem II and boosts electrons to a higher energy level.*
2. *The electrons are received by an electron acceptor.*
3. *The electrons are passed from the electron acceptor along a series of electron carriers to photosystem I. The energy lost by the electrons is captured by converting ADP to ATP. Light energy has thereby been converted to chemical energy.*
4. *Light energy absorbed by photosystem I boosts the electrons to an even higher energy level.*
5. *The electrons are received by another electron acceptor.*
6. *The electrons which have been removed from the chlorophyll are replaced by pulling in other electrons from a water molecule.*
7. *The loss of electrons from the water molecule causes it to dissociate into protons and oxygen gas.*
8. *The protons from the water molecule combine with the electrons from the second electron acceptor and these reduce **nicotinamide adenine dinucleotide phosphate**.*
9. *Some electrons from the second acceptor may pass back to the chlorophyll molecule by the electron carrier system, yielding ATP as they do so. This process is called **cyclic photophosphorylation**.*

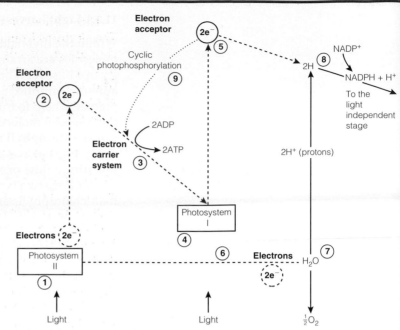

Fig. 11.3 *Summary of the light dependent stage of photosynthesis*

NOTEBOOK

Chromatography

Chromatography is a means of separating one type of molecule from another. It involves moving the mixture, normally as a liquid or a gas, over a stationary phase embedded in cellulose or silica. The separation may depend on a range of chemical and physical properties of the molecules such as solubility and molecular mass.

Essentially there are two basic ways of carrying out the separation. **Paper chromatography** is often used in schools and colleges to separate photosynthetic pigments, sugars or amino acids. The mixture is 'spotted' near one end of a paper strip and then dipped into a solvent which moves up the paper by capillarity, carrying the molecules with it.

Instead of using paper a thin layer of silica may be formed on an inert solid support. This is called **thin layer chromatography**.

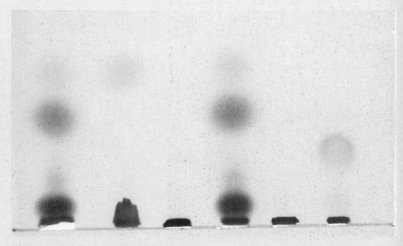

Chromatography plate at end of run

There is a second method by which ATP can be generated. The electrons from the pigment system may return to the chlorophyll directly, via the electron carrier system, forming ATP in the process. Such electrons are recycled, harnessing energy from light and generating ATP. This is called **cyclic photophosphorylation** and involves only photosystem I. No reduced NADP is produced during cyclic photophosphorylation.

11.3.3 The light independent stage

The light independent stage of photosynthesis occurs in the stroma of the chloroplasts and it takes place whether or not light is present. The details of this stage were analysed by Melvin Calvin and his co-workers and the process is often called the **Calvin cycle** (Figs. 11.4 and 11.5). It is basically the reduction of carbon dioxide using the reduced nicotinamide adenine dinucleotide phosphate (NADPH + H$^+$) and ATP from the light dependent reaction. The carbon dioxide is initially fixed by combining it with a 5-carbon compound – **ribulose bisphosphate** with the aid of an enzyme called **ribulose bisphosphate carboxylase oxygenase** – thankfully abbreviated to **RUBISCO**.

Column chromatography

The second, more commonly used method involves the mobile phase flowing over a supporting matrix held in a glass or metal tube. This is known as **column chromatography**. There have been many recent advances in the development of new matrices so that the liquid can now be pumped through under high pressure and very small fractions can be separated in miniature columns.

If chromatography is to be a really useful biochemical tool it is necessary to link separation to detection. This may be simply on the basis of colour, as with photosynthetic pigments.

Proteins, peptides and nucleic acids can be detected by their ability to absorb light in the ultra-violet region of the spectrum. Other molecules, such as amino acids, are colourless but can be made to form coloured derivatives if treated with particular chemicals, e.g. ninhydrin causes amino acids to form purple derivatives.

In paper chromatography the identification of a particular molecule is usually made on the basis of the distance travelled by the substance in relation to the distance moved by the solvent. Each molecule can then be referred to by its R_f value (retardation factor) expressed as:

$$\frac{\text{Distance travelled by a compound}}{\text{Distance travelled by solvent front}}$$

If a mixture of radioactive compounds is separated the molecules can be detected by their emission of radioactivity. This was the basis of Calvin's work on the light independent stages of photosynthesis (above).

1. *Carbon dioxide diffuses into the leaf through the stomata and dissolves in the moisture on the walls of the palisade cells. It diffuses through the cell membrane, cytoplasm and chloroplast membrane into the stroma of the chloroplast.*

2. *The carbon dioxide combines with a 5-carbon compound called **ribulose bisphosphate** to form an unstable 6-carbon intermediate.*

3. *The 6-carbon intermediate breaks down into two molecules of the 3-carbon **glycerate 3-phosphate (GP)**.*

4. *Some of the ATP produced during the light dependent stage is used to help convert GP into **triose phosphate** (glyceraldehyde 3-phosphate – GALP).*

5. *The reduced nicotinamide adenine dinucleotide phosphate (NADPH + H⁺) from the light dependent reaction is necessary for the reduction of the GP to triose phosphate. NADP⁺ is regenerated and this returns to the light dependent stage to accept more hydrogen.*

6. *Pairs of triose phosphate molecules are combined to produce an intermediate hexose sugar.*

7. *The hexose sugar is polymerized to form starch which is stored by the plant.*

8. *Not all triose phosphate is combined to form starch. A portion of it is used to regenerate the original carbon dioxide acceptor, ribulose bisphosphate. Five molecules of the 3-carbon triose phosphate can regenerate three molecules of the 5-carbon ribulose bisphosphate. More of the ATP from the light dependent stage needed to provide the energy for this conversion.*

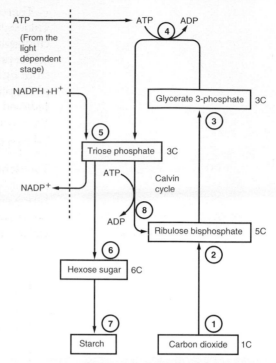

Fig. 11.4 *Summary of the light independent stage of photosynthesis*

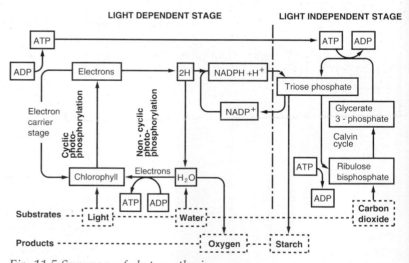

Fig. 11.5 *Summary of photosynthesis*

11.4 Factors affecting photosynthesis

The rate of photosynthesis is affected by a number of factors, the level of which determine the yield of material by a plant. Before reviewing these factors it is necessary to understand the principle of limiting factors.

11.4.1 Concept of limiting factors

In 1905, F. F. Blackman, a British plant physiologist, measured the rate of photosynthesis under varying conditions of light and carbon dioxide supply. As a result of his work he formulated the **principle of limiting factors**. It states: **At any given moment, the rate of a physiological process is limited by the one factor which is in shortest supply, and by that factor alone**.

In other words, it is the factor which is nearest its minimum value which determines the rate of a reaction. Any change in the level of this factor, called the **limiting factor**, will affect the rate of the reaction. Changes in the level of other factors have no effect. To take an extreme example, photosynthesis cannot proceed in the dark because the absence of light limits the process. The supply of light will alter the rate of photosynthesis – more light, more photosynthesis. If, however, more carbon dioxide or a higher temperature is supplied to a plant in the dark, there will be no change in the rate of photosynthesis. Light is the limiting factor, therefore only a change in its level can affect the rate.

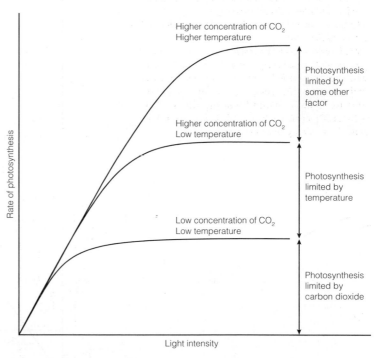

Fig. 11.6 The concept of limiting factors as illustrated by the levels of different conditions on the rate of photosynthesis

If the amount of light given to a plant is increased, the rate of photosynthesis increases up to a point and then tails off. At this point some other factor, such as the concentration of carbon dioxide, is in short supply and so limits the rate. An increase in carbon dioxide concentration again increases the amount of photosynthesis until some further factor, e.g. temperature, limits the process. These changes are illustrated in Fig. 11.6.

11.4.2 Effect of light intensity on the rate of photosynthesis

The rate of photosynthesis is often measured by the amount of carbon dioxide absorbed or oxygen evolved by a plant. These forms of measurement do not, however, give an absolute measure of photosynthesis because oxygen is absorbed and carbon dioxide is evolved as a result of cellular respiration. As light intensity is increased, photosynthesis begins, and some carbon dioxide from respiration is utilized in photosynthesis and so less is evolved.

With a continuing increase in light intensity a point is reached where carbon dioxide is neither evolved nor absorbed. At this point the carbon dioxide produced in respiration exactly balances that being used in photosynthesis. This is the **compensation point**. Further increases in light intensity result in a proportional increase in the rate of photosynthesis until **light saturation** is reached. Beyond this point further increases in light intensity have no effect on the rate of photosynthesis. If, however, more carbon dioxide is made available to the plant further increases in light intensity do increase the rate of photosynthesis until light saturation is again reached, only this time at a higher light intensity. At this point the carbon dioxide concentration, or possibly some new factor such as temperature, is limiting the process. These relationships are represented graphically in Fig. 11.7.

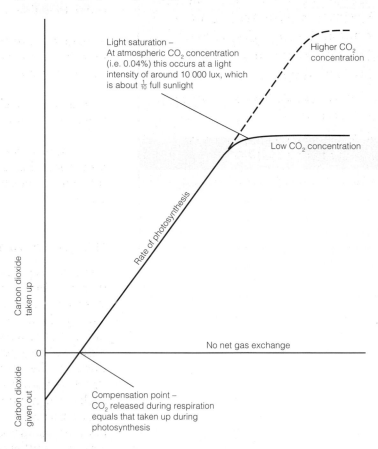

Fig. 11.7 Graph showing the effect of light intensity on the rate of photosynthesis, as measured by the amount of CO_2 exchanged

11.5 Digestion in humans

Details of the molecular structure of the components of the human diet are given in Chapter 2 while matters relating to a balanced diet and its effects on health are discussed in Chapter 23. Digestion in humans takes place along a muscular tube which measures around 10 m in length in adults. Associated with it are a variety of secretory glands, some of which are embedded in the wall of the alimentary canal, others are separate from it but connected to it by a duct.

PROJECT

Right-handed people find it easier to brush the teeth on the left so that more teeth on the right suffer from dental caries. The opposite is true for left-handed people.

1. Tidy up this statement into a testable hypothesis.

2. Test your hypothesis using fellow students as 'subjects'.

11.5.1 Digestion in the mouth

Mechanical breakdown of food begins in the mouth or **buccal cavity**. Humans are omnivores and hence have an unspecialized diet of mixed animal and plant origin. Their teeth reflect this lack of specialization, all types being present and developed to a similar extent. Apart from assisting speech, the tongue also manipulates the food during chewing and so ensures it is well mixed with **saliva** produced from three pairs of **salivary glands** (Fig. 11.8). Around 1.0–1.5 dm^3 of saliva are produced daily. Saliva contains:

1. **Water** – Over 99% of saliva is water.

2. **Salivary amylase** – A digestive enzyme which hydrolyses starch to maltose.

3. **Mineral salts** (e.g. sodium hydrogencarbonate) – This helps to maintain a pH of around 6.5–7.5 which is the optimum for the action of salivary amylase.

4. **Mucin** – A sticky material which helps to bind food particles together and lubricate them to assist swallowing.

Taste buds on the tongue allow food to be selected – unpleasant tasting food being rejected. The thoroughly chewed food is rolled into a **bolus** and passed to the back of the mouth for swallowing.

11.5.2 Swallowing and peristalsis

The bolus is pushed by the tongue to the back of the mouth and then into the **pharynx** where the **oesophagus** (leading to the stomach) meets with the trachea (which leads to the lungs). A variety of reflexes ensure that food when swallowed passes down the oesophagus and not the trachea. One such reflex is the closure of the opening into the larynx (which leads to the trachea). This opening, called the **glottis**, is covered by a structure known as the **epiglottis** when food is passed to the back of the mouth. The opening to the nasal cavity is closed by the **soft palate**. In this way, which is illustrated in Fig. 11.8, the bolus enters the oesophagus, a muscular tube lined with stratified epithelium and mucus glands. Lubricated by the mucus secreted by these glands, the bolus passes to the stomach by means of a wave of muscular contraction which causes constriction of the oesophagus behind the bolus. As this constriction passes along the oesophagus it pushes the bolus before it, down to the stomach. This process, which continues throughout the alimentary canal, is called **peristalsis**.

11.5.3 Digestion in the stomach

The stomach is roughly J-shaped, situated below the diaphragm. It is a muscular sac with a folded inner layer called the **gastric mucosa**. Embedded in this is a series of **gastric pits** which are lined with secretory cells (Fig. 11.9). These produce **gastric juice** which contains:

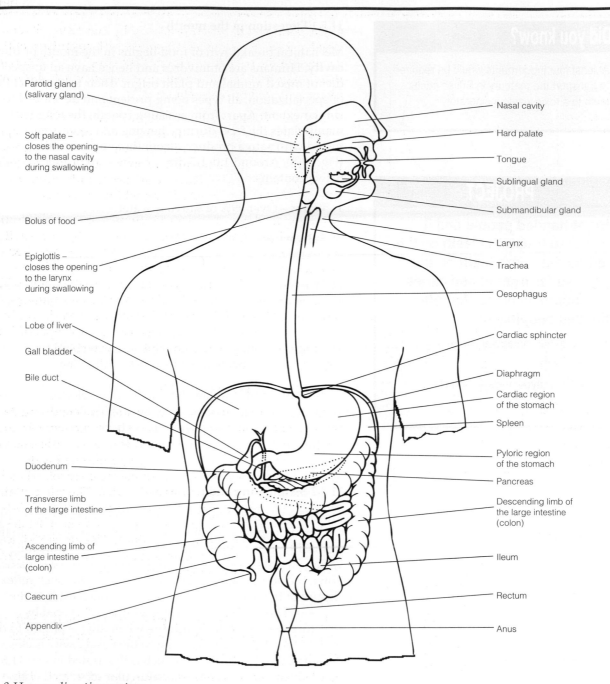

Fig. 11.8 Human digestive system

Labels (clockwise from top left):

- Parotid gland (salivary gland)
- Soft palate – closes the opening to the nasal cavity during swallowing
- Bolus of food
- Epiglottis – closes the opening to the larynx during swallowing
- Lobe of liver
- Gall bladder
- Bile duct
- Duodenum
- Transverse limb of the large intestine
- Ascending limb of large intestine (colon)
- Caecum
- Appendix
- Nasal cavity
- Hard palate
- Tongue
- Sublingual gland
- Submandibular gland
- Larynx
- Trachea
- Oesophagus
- Cardiac sphincter
- Diaphragm
- Cardiac region of the stomach
- Spleen
- Pyloric region of the stomach
- Pancreas
- Descending limb of the large intestine (colon)
- Ileum
- Rectum
- Anus

1. Water – The bulk of the secretion is water in which are dissolved the other constituents.

2. Hydrochloric acid – This is produced by **oxyntic cells** and with the water forms a dilute solution giving gastric juice its pH of around 2.0. It helps to kill bacteria brought in with the food and activates the enzymes pepsinogen and prorennin. It also initiates the hydrolysis of sucrose and nucleoproteins.

3. Pepsinogen – This is produced by the **zymogen** or **chief cells** in an inactive form to prevent it from hydrolysing the proteins of the cells producing it. Once in the stomach it is activated to **pepsin** by hydrochloric acid. Pepsin is an endopeptidase which hydrolyses protein into polypeptides.

(a) Entire stomach

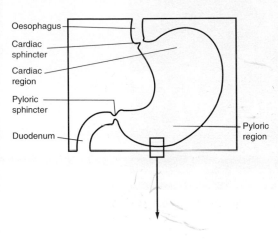

(b) Part of the stomach wall

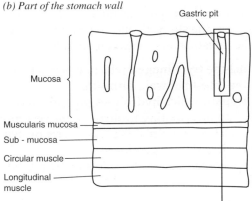

(c) Detail of gastric gland

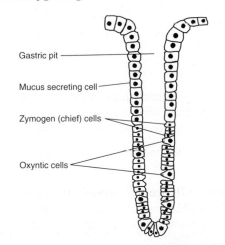

Fig. 11.9 Structure of the human stomach

4. Prorennin – This too is produced by zymogen cells and is an inactive form of **rennin**, an enzyme which coagulates milk by converting the soluble **caseinogen** into the insoluble **casein**. It is therefore especially important in young mammals. Prorennin, too, is activated by hydrochloric acid.

5. Mucus – This is produced by **goblet cells** and forms a protective layer on the stomach wall, thus preventing pepsin and hydrochloric acid from breaking down the gastric mucosa (i.e. prevents autolysis). If the protection is not effective and the gastric juice attacks the mucosa, an ulcer results. Mucus also helps lubricate movement of food within the stomach.

During its stay in the stomach, food is thoroughly churned and mixed with gastric juice by periodic contractions of the muscular stomach wall. In this way a creamy fluid called **chyme** is produced. Relaxation of the pyloric sphincter and contraction of the stomach allow the chyme to enter the duodenum. The chyme from any one meal is released gradually over a period of 3–4 hours. This enables the small intestine to work on a little material at a time and provides a continuous supply of food for absorption throughout the period between meals.

11.5.4 Digestion in the small intestine

In humans the small intestine is over 6 m in length and its coils fill much of the lower abdominal cavity. It consists of two main parts: the much shorter **duodenum** where most digestion occurs and the longer **ileum** which is largely concerned with absorption. The walls of the small intestine are folded and possess finger-like projections called **villi**. The villi contain fibres of smooth muscle and regularly contract and relax. This helps to mix the food with the enzyme secretions and keep fresh supplies in contact with the villi, for absorption. The digestive juices which operate in the small intestine come from three sources: the liver, the pancreas and the intestinal wall.

Bile juice
Bile juice is a complex green fluid produced by the liver. It contains no enzymes but possesses two other substances important to digestion.

1. Mineral salts (e.g. sodium hydrogencarbonate) – These help to neutralize the acid chyme from the stomach and so create a more neutral pH for the enzymes of the small intestine to work in.

2. Bile salts – sodium and potassium glycocholate and taurocholate – They **emulsify** lipids, breaking them down into minute droplets. This is a physical, not a chemical change, which provides a greater surface area for pancreatic lipase to work on.

The liver performs other functions, some associated with digestion, and these are detailed in Section 18.3.2.

Pancreatic juice
The pancreas is situated below the stomach and is unusual in that it produces both an exocrine secretion, the pancreatic juice, and an endocrine secretion, the hormone insulin. (See Focus on p. 448.) Pancreatic juice, in addition to water, contains:

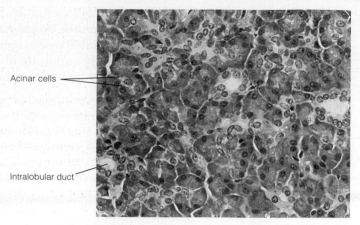

Acinar cells

Intralobular duct

Cellular structure of pancreas showing intralobular ducts

1. Mineral salts (e.g. sodium hydrogencarbonate) – Help to neutralize acid chyme from the stomach and so provide a more neutral pH in which the intestinal enzymes can operate.

2. Proteases – These include **trypsinogen** which, when activated by enterokinase from the intestinal wall, forms the endopeptidase called **trypsin** which hydrolyses proteins into peptides. Trypsin also activates another protease in the secretion, chymotrypsinogen into **chymotrypsin**; this too converts proteins into peptides. Also present is the exopeptidase called **carboxypeptidase** which converts peptides into smaller peptides and some amino acids.

3. Pancreatic amylase – Completes the hydrolysis of starch to maltose which began in the mouth.

4. Lipase – Breaks down fats into fatty acids and monoglycerides (glycerol + one fatty acid) by hydrolysis.

5. Nuclease – Converts nucleic acids into their constituent nucleotides.

Intestinal juice (succus entericus)
The mucus and sodium hydrogencarbonate in intestinal juice are made by coiled **Brunner's glands** whereas the enzymes are produced by the breakdown (lysis) of cells at the tips of the villi.

1. Mucus – Helps to lubricate the intestinal walls and prevent autolysis.

2. Mineral salts (e.g. sodium hydrogencarbonate) – Produced by the Brunner's glands in order to neutralize the acid chyme from the stomach and so provide a more suitable pH for the action of enzymes in the intestine.

3. Proteases (erepsin) – These include the exopeptidase called **aminopeptidase**, which converts peptides into smaller peptides and amino acids, and **dipeptidase**, which hydrolyses dipeptides into amino acids.

4. Enterokinase – A non-digestive enzyme which activates the trypsinogen produced by the pancreas.

5. Nucleotidase – Converts nucleotides into pentose sugars, phosphoric acid and organic bases.

FOCUS

Lactose intolerance and galactosaemia

In early life humans feed exclusively on milk, whether breast milk or a substitute formulated from the milk of other mammals such as a cow. Milk contains the disaccharide lactose as its main sugar and so young babies produce the enzyme lactase to digest it into its component monosaccharides, glucose and galactose, which are readily absorbed in the intestines.

Lactose is not a component of other food and our distant ancestors did not drink milk as adults. As a consequence the production of lactose was unnecessary and wasteful in adult life and so humans have evolved a system whereby the gene for lactase production is normally switched off in late childhood. Only in those areas where milk continues to be consumed by adults is the production of lactase continued. These areas include much of Europe and some populations of West Africa such as the Fulani who keep cattle whose milk they use to supplement their diet. Elsewhere the adult population is unable to digest lactose: a condition known as **lactose intolerance**.

Lactose intolerance in infants is rare but can be life-threatening. These infants cannot produce lactase and so cannot obtain their glucose from lactose digestion. One remedy is to feed these babies a milk substitute made from soy or other plants where sugars are in the form of glucose rather than lactose.

Another problem arises in babies who suffer from **galactosaemia**. About one in every 40 000 babies suffer from this inherited condition which prevents them producing the enzyme **galactose transferase (GALT)**. This enzyme converts the galactose absorbed into the bloodstream from lactose digestion into glucose, which is then used as an energy source. Without the enzyme, galactose accumulates causing sickness. Once again the remedy is a lactose-free diet.

6. **Carbohydrases** – These include **amylase**, which helps complete the hydrolysis of starch to maltose; **maltase**, which hydrolyses maltose to glucose; **lactase**, which hydrolyses the milk sugar lactose into glucose and galactose; and **sucrase**, which hydrolyses sucrose into glucose and fructose.

11.5.5 Absorption and assimilation

Digestion results in the formation of relatively small, soluble molecules which, provided there is a concentration gradient, could be absorbed into the body through the intestinal wall by diffusion. This, however, would be slow and wasteful and in any case, if the epithelial lining were permeable to molecules such as glucose, it could just as easily result in it diffusing out of the body when the concentration in the intestines was too low. For these reasons most substances are absorbed by **active transport** (Section 4.3.4) which only allows inward movement. Efficient uptake is often dependent on the presence of other factors. For

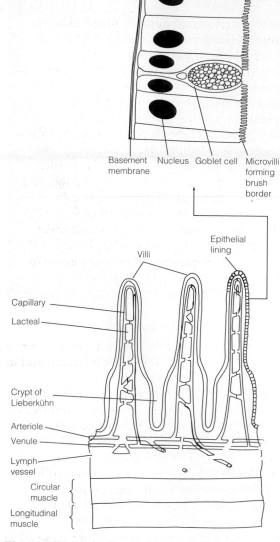

Fig. 11.10 Intestinal wall showing villi (LS)

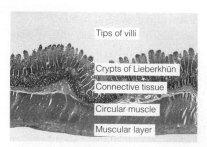

TS ileum showing villi

Did you know?

Folds, villi and microvilli increase the internal surface area of the intestine from about 4 m² to 250 m² – greater than the area of a tennis court.

example, glucose and amino acid absorption appear to be linked to the movement of sodium ions across the membranes of epithelial cells; calcium ion absorption requires the presence of vitamin D.

Efficient absorption is also dependent on a large surface area being available. The wall of the ileum achieves this in four ways:

1. It is very long – almost 6 m in humans and up to 45 m in cattle.

2. Its walls are folded (**folds of Kerkring**) to provide large internal projections.

3. The folds themselves have numerous tiny finger-like projections called **villi** (Fig. 11.10).

4. The epithelial cells lining the villi are covered with minute projections about 0.6 μm in length, called **microvilli** (not to be confused with cilia). These collectively form a **brush border**.

Sugars, amino acids and other water-soluble materials such as minerals enter the blood capillaries of the villi. From here they enter arterioles which later merge to form the hepatic portal vein which carries blood to the liver. In general, the level of different absorbed foods in the hepatic portal vein varies, depending on the type of food eaten and the interval since ingestion. It is the main role of the liver to regulate these variations by storing excess where the level of a substance is above normal and by releasing its store when its level in the hepatic portal vein is low. For this reason, blood from the intestines is sent to the liver for homeostatic regulation before it passes to other organs where fluctuations in blood composition could be damaging. The liver is also able to break down any harmful substances absorbed, a process called **detoxification**. The fatty acids and glycerol from lipid digestion enter the epithelial cells lining the villi where they recombine into lipids. These then enter the lacteals rather than the blood capillaries. From here they are transported in the lymph vessels before later joining the venous system of the blood near the heart.

The passage of food from the ileum into the large intestine or colon is controlled by the **ileo-caecal valve**. The caecum in humans is little more than a slight expansion between the small and large intestine and the appendix is a small blind-ending sac leading from the caecum. In humans neither structure performs any important digestive function but they are of considerable importance to herbivorous mammals.

11.5.6 Water reabsorption in the large intestine

Most of the water drunk by humans is absorbed by the stomach. The large intestine or **colon** is partly responsible for reabsorbing the water from digestive secretions. With the gastric and intestinal juices each producing up to 3 dm³ (litre) of secretion every day and the saliva, pancreatic and bile juices each adding a further 1.5 dm³ the total volume of digestive secretions may exceed 10 dm³. As most of this volume is water, it follows that the body cannot afford to allow it simply to pass out with the faeces. While most water is absorbed in the ileum, the large

Oral rehydration therapy

Many gastro-intestinal infections such as dysentry and diarrhoea cause excessive peristalsis. As a result the contents of the intestines are removed too quickly for normal reabsorption of water to take place in the colon. The patient rapidly dehydrates, sometimes to such a degree that his/her life is threatened. This is especially the case with infants – indeed diarrhoea is one of the leading causes of infant mortality in developing countries. Not only water is lost with such infections but certain nutrients and salts also.

A simple treatment, **oral rehydration therapy**, is cheaply available and much effort is now being expended in educating mothers about its benefits to their children. A solution of sugar and salt of a specific concentration is given to the patient by mouth. This replaces the nutrients, salt and water lost in the diarrhoeal fluid. The solution must be given regularly and in large amounts throughout the duration of the illness to be effective.

intestine plays an important role in reabsorbing the remainder. In doing so it changes the consistency of the faeces from liquid to semi-solid.

Within the large intestine live a huge population of bacteria, such as *Escherichia coli*, which in humans synthesize a number of vitamins including biotin and vitamin K. Deficiency of these vitamins is therefore rare, although orally administered antibiotics may destroy most of the bacteria and so create a temporary shortage. The vitamins produced are absorbed by the wall of the large intestine with water and some mineral salts. This wall is folded to increase the surface area available for absorption. Excess calcium and iron salts are actively transported from the blood into the large intestine for removal with the faeces.

11.5.7 Elimination (egestion)

The semi-solid faeces consist of a small quantity of indigestible food (fibre) but mostly comprise the residual material from the bile juice and other secretions, cells sloughed off the intestinal wall, a little water and immense numbers of bacteria. The wall of the large intestine produces mucus which, in addition to lubricating the movement of the faeces, helps to bind them together. After 24–36 hours in the large intestine the faeces pass to the rectum for temporary storage before they are removed through the anus, a process known as **defecation**. Control of this removal is by two sphincters around the **anus**, the opening of the rectum to the outside.

As much of the material making up the faeces is not the result of metabolic reactions within the body, it is said to be eliminated or egested rather than excreted. However, cholesterol and bile pigments from the breakdown of haemoglobin are metabolic products and are therefore excretory.

11.6 Nervous and hormonal control of secretions

The production of a digestive secretion must be timed to coincide with the presence of food in the appropriate region of the gut. In mammals the production of digestive secretions is under both nervous and hormonal control.

Nervous stimulation occurs even before the food reaches the mouth. The sight, smell or even the mere thought of food is sufficient to cause the salivary glands to produce saliva. This response is a conditioned reflex and is explained more fully in Section 19.7.3. Once in the mouth, contact of food with the tongue causes it to transmit nervous impulses to the brain. The brain in turn sends impulses which stimulate the salivary glands to secrete saliva. This is an unconditioned reflex response. At the same time the brain stimulates the stomach wall to secrete gastric juice, a response reinforced by nervous impulses transmitted as the food is swallowed. The stomach is thus prepared to digest the food even before it reaches it. Once initiated, the response will continue for up to an hour. The stretching of the stomach due to the presence of food within it stimulates production of gastric juice after this time.

Hormonal control of secretions begins with the presence of food in the stomach. This stimulates the stomach wall to produce a hormone called **gastrin** which passes into the bloodstream. Gastrin continues to stimulate the production of gastric juice for up to four hours. Because fat digestion takes longer and requires less acidic conditions, its presence in the stomach initiates the production of **enterogasterone** from the stomach wall. This hormone reduces the churning motions of the stomach and decreases the flow of the acid gastric juice. As stomach ulcers are irritated by gastric juice, sufferers are often urged to drink milk. Being rich in fat, it reduces the production of gastric juice.

When food leaves the stomach and enters the duodenum, it stimulates the production of two hormones from the duodenal wall. **Secretin**, via the bloodstream, travels to the liver where it causes the production of bile and to the pancreas, where it stimulates the secretion of mineral salts. **Cholecystokinin-pancreozymin** causes the gall bladder to contract (releasing the bile juice into the duodenum) and stimulates the pancreas to secrete its enzymes.

TABLE 11.1   **Summary of digestion**

Organ/ secretion	Production induced by	Site of action	pH of secretion	Contents	Effect
Salivary glands produce saliva	Visual or olfactory expectation and reflex stimulation	Mouth	About neutral	Salivary amylase	Amylose(starch) → maltose
				Mineral salts	Produce optimum pH for amylase action
				Mucin	Binds food particles into a bolus
Gastric glands in stomach wall produce gastric juice	Presence of food in mouth and swallowing. Presence of food in stomach. Hormones – gastrin and enterogasterone from stomach wall	Stomach	Very acid	Pepsin(ogen)	Proteins → peptides
				(Pro)rennin	Caseinogen → casein
				Hydrochloric acid	Activates pepsinogen and prorennin. Produces optimum pH for action of these enzymes
				Mucus	Lubrication and prevention of autolysis
Liver produces bile juice	Secretion stimulates production of bile and cholecystokinin causes it to be released	Duodenum	Neutral	Bile salts	Emulsify fats
				Mineral salts	Neutralize acid chyme
				Bile pigments	Excretory products from breakdown of haemoglobin
				Cholesterol	Excretory product
Pancreas produces pancreatic juice	Secretion stimulates production of mineral salts and pancreozymin production of enzymes	Duodenum	Neutral	Trypsin (ogen)	Protein → peptides + amino acids activates chymotrypsinogen
				Chymotrypsin (ogen)	Peptides → smaller peptides + amino acids
				Carboxypeptidase	Peptides → smaller peptides + amino acids
				Amylase	Amylose (starch) → maltose
				Lipase	Fats → fatty acids + glycerol
				Nuclease	Nucleic acids → nucleotides
				Mineral salts	Neutralize acid chyme
Wall of small intestine produces intestinal juice (succus entericus)	Presence of food stimulates the intestinal lining	Duodenum and ileum	Alkaline	Aminopeptidase	Peptides → amino acids
				Dipeptidase	Dipeptides → amino acids
				Enterokinase	Activates trypsinogen
				Nucleotidase	Nucleotides → organic base + pentose sugar + phosphate
				Maltase	Maltose → glucose
				Lactase	Lactose → glucose + galactose
				Sucrase	Sucrose → glucose + fructose
				Mineral salts	Neutralize acid chyme

11.7   Questions

1. The following information refers to the gene that codes for the enzyme lactase which digests lactose. The sugar lactose accounts for about 7 or 8 per cent of human milk. Human babies are born with the enzyme lactase, which hydrolyses lactose into the monosaccharides glucose and galactose in the small intestine. When the child is about four years old, the infant lactase gene is switched off and the adult gene is switched on.

Only white American and European populations appear to have an adult lactase gene. Most other populations, including some Africans, Chinese and Thais for example, are lactose intolerant and show a range of symptoms, including digestive upsets and skin rashes, when milk is consumed. Adults who are lactose intolerant can usually eat yogurt and other fermented milk products without any ill effects. The figure shows the percentage of individuals intolerant to lactose in a number of populations.

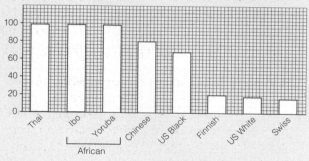

Evidence suggests that originally most humans were lactose intolerant. Milk was probably not included in the adult diet until about 10 000 years ago when goats, cattle, sheep and reindeer were first domesticated.

(a) (i) Write a word equation for the effect of lactase on lactose.

(ii) Name the type of chemical bond which is broken by lactase. *(2 marks)*

(b) Suggest why lactose intolerant adults may be able to eat some fermented milk products without ill effect. *(2 marks)*

(c) Using the information in the figure, state the percentage of the population who are lactose tolerant amongst

(i) Swiss

(ii) Thais *(1 mark)*

(d) (i) Suggest an explanation for the difference in lactose intolerance between the African populations and the Finnish and Swiss populations.

(ii) Suggest why there is a difference between the two US populations shown in the figure.

(5 marks)

(Total 10 marks)

UCLES June 1994, Paper 2, No. 2

2. The diagram shows part of the light independent reaction of photosynthesis.

(a) In which part of the chloroplast does this series of reactions take place? *(1 mark)*

(b) Name the compound labelled **X** on the diagram. *(1 mark)*

(c) Name the **two** compounds, labelled **Y** and **Z** on the diagram, which are necessary for the reduction of glycerate 3-phosphate to carbohydrate.

(2 marks)

(d) Give **one** possible fate of the glycerate 3-phosphate other than being converted into carbohydrate. *(1 mark)*

(Total 5 marks)

NEAB February 1995, Paper BY1, No. 6

3. The drawing shows a section through the wall of the human small intestine.

(a) Use guidelines and the appropriate letter to label:

(i) X – a villus;

(ii) Y – muscle responsible for bringing about peristalsis. *(2 marks)*

(b) Complete the table which gives the action of two of the digestive enzymes which are produced in the small intestine.

Enzyme	Substrate	Product(s)
Exopeptidase		
Maltase		

(2 marks)

(c) The goblet cells in the epithelium of the small intestine produce mucus. Suggest **one** function of this mucus. *(1 mark)*

(d) Explain how the following features of the cells which line the small intestine help the efficient absorption of the products of digestion.
   (i) microvilli: *(1 mark)*
   (ii) large numbers of mitochrondria. *(2 marks)*
   (Total 8 marks)

NEAB February 1995, Paper BY3, No. 1

4. The graph shows the rate of photosynthesis of tomato plants under different environmental conditions.

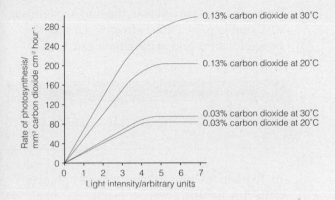

(a) (i) How is the carbon dioxide content of the air in a glasshouse usually increased? *(1 mark)*
   (ii) Use the graph to help explain the environmental conditions under which it might be profitable to increase the carbon dioxide content of the air in the glasshouse in which the tomatoes were growing. *(3 marks)*

The table shows some effects of doubling the quantity of carbon dioxide in the air on plants growing in glasshouses.

Plant	Percentage increase in total dry biomass
Tomato	40
Lettuce	37
Weeds	34

(b) What is the advantage of giving these figures:
   (i) as percentages; *(1 mark)*
   (ii) in terms of *dry* mass? *(1 mark)*
(c) Increasing the percentage of carbon dioxide to crops may not be economically sensible as the supply of other substances would also have to be increased. Using information in the table to help, suggest **two** such substances that would have to be increased. Give an explanation for your answer in **each** case. *(2 marks)*
   (Total 8 marks)

NEAB June 1995, Paper BY07, No. 7

5. The diagram below shows a longitudinal section of part of the ileum wall.

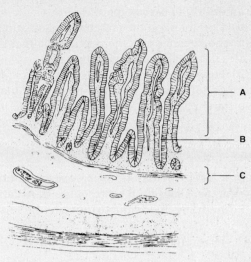

(a) Name the structures labelled **A**, **B** and **C**. *(3 marks)*
(b) Describe **one** way in which the structure of the ileum is adapted to the function it performs. *(2 marks)*
   (Total 5 marks)

ULEAC 1996, Specimen Paper HB2, No. 3

6. The diagram below shows a short peptide. The side chains of the different amino acids are represented by filled shapes. The diagram also shows the specific sites at which the peptide chain is broken during digestion in the human gut by three digestive enzymes, trypsin, chymotrypsin and carboxypeptidase.

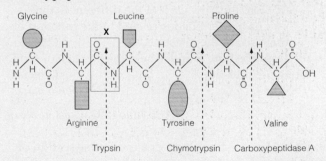

(a) (i) Name the chemical bond which is broken by the action of these enzymes. *(1 mark)*
   (ii) Name the type of chemical reaction by which the bonds are broken. *(1 mark)*
   (iii) In the space below, re-draw the part of the chain enclosed in the box marked **X** to shows its appearance after the action of trypsin. *(3 marks)*
(b) Trypsin and chymotrypsin are described as *endopeptidases* because they catalyse the breaking of bonds within the peptide chain. Carboxypeptidase A is described as an *exopeptidase* because it catalyses the breaking of a bond at one end of the peptide chain.

(i) Comment on the fact that trypsin and chymotrypsin are secreted into the gut anteriorly to carboxypeptidase A.   (3 marks)

(ii) Comment on the fact that trypsin and chymotrypsin break the peptide chain at the sites indicated, but not at other sites.   (3 marks)

(iii) How does the effect of trypsin on peptides and proteins differ from the effect of amylase on starch?   (3 marks)

(Total 14 marks)

ULEAC 1996, Specimen Paper A HBIO, No. 4

7. Diagram **A** represents a transverse section through the oesophagus. Diagram **B** represents a transverse section through the duodenum (drawn to the same scale).

Diagram **A**   Diagram **B**

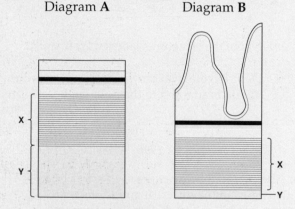

(a) (i) Give **two** differences, visible in the diagrams, between the transverse section of the oesophagus and the transverse section of the duodenum.   (2 marks)

(ii) Explain how each of the differences that you have identified is related to the function of that area of the intestine.   (2 marks)

(b) Describe how **X** and **Y** help the passage of food along the intestine.   (2 marks)

(Total 6 marks)

AEB June 1993, Paper 1, No. 9

8. The diagram shows part of a transverse section of human duodenum.

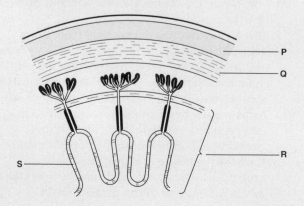

(a) Identify layer **R**.   (1 mark)

(b) (i) What type of muscle is found in layers **P** and **Q**?   (1 mark)

(ii) What is the name given to the gut movement caused by rhythmic contractions of muscle layer **Q**?   (1 mark)

(c) Describe **one** hormonal relationship between the contents of the stomach and feature **S**.   (1 mark)

(Total 4 marks)

AEB June 1992, Paper 1, No. 1

9. (a) Describe the process of peristalsis in the gut.   (3 marks)

(b) There are two sphincters in the human stomach.

(i) Complete the table below by naming the **two** sphincters and stating their exact positions.

	Name of sphincter	Position
1		
2		

(2 marks)

(ii) Explain the importance of these sphincters in the functioning of the stomach.   (3 marks)

(Total 8 marks)

ULEAC June 1995, Paper 1, No. 4

10. Gastrin is a hormone which stimulates acid secretion into the stomach.

During a hospital investigation into the effect of this hormone, the gastric juice was collected from two patients, **A** and **B**. The stomach contents were completely removed every 30 minutes for four hours, and the amount of hydrochloric acid present in each sample was measured. Both patients were given an identical injection of the hormone gastrin immediately after removing the first sample. The graph at the top of the next page shows the amount hydrochloric acid in millimoles secreted in each 30-minute period of the test. The total amount of hydrochloric acid secreted in the four-hour period in patient **A** was 342 millimoles and in patient **B** was 169 millimoles.

(a) Describe the roles of hydrochloric acid in the stomach in the process of digestion.   (3 marks)

(b) (i) Comment on the differences shown by the two patients in their secretion of hydrochloric acid.   (3 marks)

(ii) Express the peak acid secretion of patient **A** as a percentage of patient **B**. Show your working.   (2 marks)

(iii) Gastric secretion could have been stimulated by giving the patients a meal. Suggest why a gastrin injection was used instead.   (2 marks)

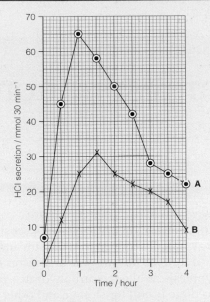

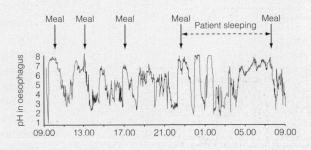

Comment on the relative effectiveness of bile and pancreatic juice in neutralizing the acid chyme.

(*3 marks*)
(*Total 15 marks*)

ULEAC June 1993, Paper 1, No. 13

11. One kind of 'heartburn' is caused when the acid contents of the stomach pass up into the oesophagus, a condition called acid-reflux. To find out if acid-reflux was the cause of the patient's 'heartburn', a pH probe was inserted into the oesophagus and pH levels in the oesophagus were recorded over a period of 24 hours. The patient was asked to record the times at which drinks were taken during the 24-hour period. The graph shows the results of this investigation.

(*c*) Stomach ulcers are caused by erosion of the mucosa, which of the two patients is most likely to develop stomach ulcers? Explain your answer.

(*2 marks*)

(*d*) The stomach acids are neutralized by hydrogencarbonate ions in the duodenum when the chyme passes through the pyloric sphincter. The diagram below shows the ionic composition of pancreatic juice and bile. About 500 cm³ of pancreatic juice and 500 cm³ of bile are released per day.

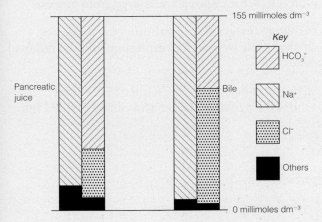

(*a*) Suggest how the stomach contents are normally prevented from passing into the oesophagus.

(*2 marks*)

(*b*) (i) Describe the relationship between taking a meal and the pH in the oesophagus. (*1 mark*)
(ii) Suggest why the pH in the oesophagus was very low between 02.00 and 04.00, but high between 05.00 and 07.00. (*2 marks*)

(*c*) The secretion of acid by the stomach is partly controlled by the hormone gastrin.
(i) Describe the general characteristics of hormones (*3 marks*)
(ii) Describe the role of gastrin in the control of gastric secretions. (*4 marks*)
(*Total 12 marks*)

NEAB June 1995, Paper BY03, No. 7

Cellular respiration

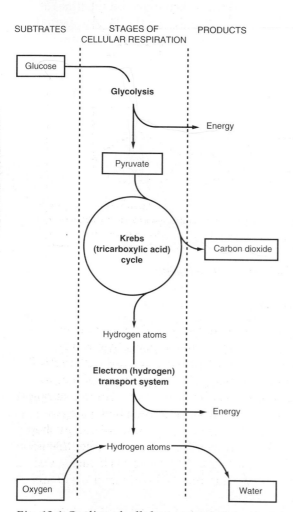

SUBTRATES   STAGES OF   PRODUCTS
              CELLULAR RESPIRATION

Glucose

Glycolysis

→ Energy

Pyruvate

**Krebs
(tricarboxylic acid)
cycle**

→ Carbon dioxide

Hydrogen atoms

**Electron (hydrogen)
transport system**

→ Energy

Hydrogen atoms

Oxygen   Water

Fig. 12.1 Outline of cellular respiration

In Chapter 11 we saw that living systems require a constant supply of energy to maintain low entropy and so ensure their survival. This energy initially comes from the sun and is captured in chemical form by autotrophic organisms during the process of photosynthesis. While the carbohydrates, fats and proteins so produced are useful for storage and other purposes, they cannot be directly used by cells to provide the required energy. The conversion of these chemicals into forms like adenosine triphosphate, which can be utilized by cells, occurs during respiration.

Whatever form the food of an organism initially takes, it is converted into carbohydrate, usually the hexose sugar glucose, before being respired. Most respiration is the oxidation of this glucose to carbon dioxide and water with the release of energy, and the process can be conveniently divided into two parts:

1. **Cellular (internal or tissue) respiration** – the metabolic processes within cells which release the energy from glucose.

2. **Gaseous exchange (external respiration)** – the processes involved in obtaining the oxygen for respiration and the removal of gaseous wastes.

Gaseous exchange is dealt with in Chapter 15. Cellular respiration is the subject of this chapter and can be divided into three stages:

1. Glycolysis

2. Krebs (tricarboxylic acid) cycle

3. Electron (hydrogen) transport system.

The relationship of these stages in cellular respiration is outlined in Fig. 12.1.

12.1   Adenosine triphosphate (ATP)

Adenosine triphosphate (ATP) is the short-term energy store of all cells. It is easily transported and is therefore the universal energy carrier.

12.1.1 Structure of ATP

ATP is formed from the nucleotide adenosine monophosphate (Fig. 12.2) by the addition of two further phosphate molecules. Its structure is shown in Fig. 12.2.

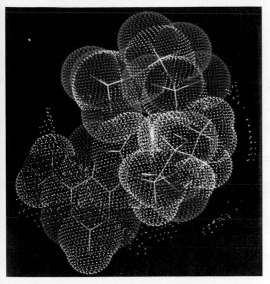

Computer graphics representation of ATP

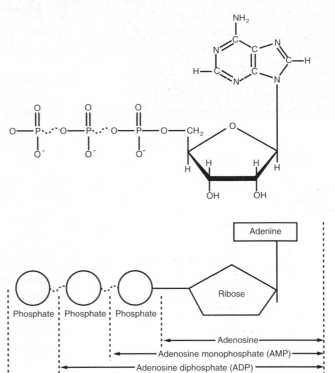

Fig. 12.2 Structure of adenosine triphosphate

12.1.2 Importance of ATP

The hydrolysis of ATP to ADP is catalyzed by the enzyme ATP-ase and the removal of the terminal phosphate yields 30.6 kJ mol^{-1} of free energy. Further hydrolysis of ADP to AMP yields a similar quantity of energy, but the removal of the last phosphate produces less than half this quantity. For this reason the last two phosphate bonds are often termed high energy bonds on account of the relatively large quantity of energy they yield on hydrolysis. This is misleading in that it implies that all the energy is stored in these bonds. The energy is in fact stored in the molecule as a whole, although the breaking of the bonds initiates its release.

AMP and ADP may be reconverted to ATP by the addition of phosphate molecules in a process called **phosphorylation**, of which there are two main forms:

1. Photosynthetic phosphorylation – occurs during photosynthesis in chlorophyll-containing cells (Chapter 11).

2. Oxidative phosphorylation – occurs during cellular respiration in all aerobic cells.

The addition of each phosphate molecule requires 30.6 kJ of energy. If the energy released from any reaction is less than this, it cannot be stored as ATP and is lost as heat. The importance of ATP is therefore as a means of transferring free energy from energy-rich compounds to cellular reactions requiring it. While not the only substance to transfer energy in this way, it is by far the most abundant and hence the most important.

12.1.3 Uses of ATP

A metabolically active cell may require up to two million ATP molecules every second. ATP is the source of energy for:

1. **Anabolic processes** – It provides the energy needed to build up macromolecules from their component units, e.g.
    – polysaccharide synthesis from monosaccharides
    – protein synthesis from amino acids
    – DNA replication.

2. **Movement** – It provides the energy for many forms of cellular movement including:
    – muscle contraction
    – ciliary action
    – spindle action in cell division.

3. **Active transport** – It provides the energy necessary to move materials against a concentration gradient, e.g. ion pumps.

4. **Secretion** – It is needed to form the vesicles necessary in the secretion of cell products.

5. **Activation of chemicals** – It makes chemicals more reactive, enabling them to react more readily, e.g. the phosphorylation of glucose at the start of glycolysis.

12.2   Glycolysis

Glycolysis (*glyco* – 'sugar'; *lyso* – 'breakdown') is the breakdown of a hexose sugar, usually glucose, into two molecules of the three-carbon compound **pyruvate (pyruvic acid)**. It occurs in all cells; in anaerobic organisms it is the only stage of respiration. Initially the glucose is insufficiently reactive and so it is phosphorylated prior to being split into two triose sugar molecules. These molecules yield some hydrogen atoms which may be used to give energy (ATP) before being converted into pyruvate. During its formation, the ATP used in phosphorylating the glucose is regenerated. Glycolysis takes place in the cytoplasm of the cell and its main stages are outlined opposite.

Each glucose molecule produces two molecules of glycerate 3-phosphate and there is therefore a pair of every subsequent molecule for each glucose molecule. The energy yield is a net gain of two molecules of ATP (Stage 7). The two pairs of hydrogen atoms produced (Stage 5) may yield a further six ATPs (see Section 12.4), giving an overall total of eight ATPs.

Stages of glycolysis

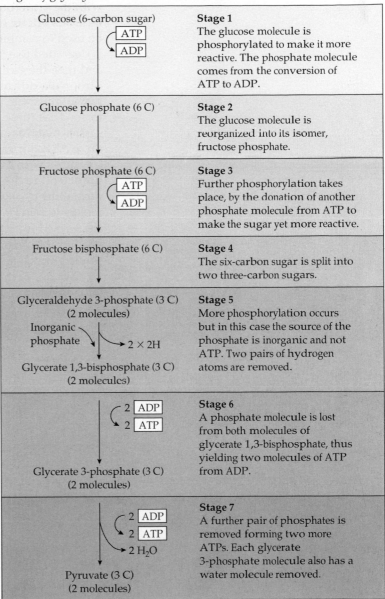

	Stage 1
Glucose (6-carbon sugar) → ATP/ADP	The glucose molecule is phosphorylated to make it more reactive. The phosphate molecule comes from the conversion of ATP to ADP.
Glucose phosphate (6 C)	**Stage 2** The glucose molecule is reorganized into its isomer, fructose phosphate.
Fructose phosphate (6 C) → ATP/ADP	**Stage 3** Further phosphorylation takes place, by the donation of another phosphate molecule from ATP to make the sugar yet more reactive.
Fructose bisphosphate (6 C)	**Stage 4** The six-carbon sugar is split into two three-carbon sugars.
Glyceraldehyde 3-phosphate (3 C) (2 molecules) — Inorganic phosphate → 2 × 2H — Glycerate 1,3-bisphosphate (3 C) (2 molecules)	**Stage 5** More phosphorylation occurs but in this case the source of the phosphate is inorganic and not ATP. Two pairs of hydrogen atoms are removed.
2 ADP → 2 ATP — Glycerate 3-phosphate (3 C) (2 molecules)	**Stage 6** A phosphate molecule is lost from both molecules of glycerate 1,3-bisphosphate, thus yielding two molecules of ATP from ADP.
2 ADP → 2 ATP → 2 H_2O — Pyruvate (3 C) (2 molecules)	**Stage 7** A further pair of phosphates is removed forming two more ATPs. Each glycerate 3-phosphate molecule also has a water molecule removed.

12.3 Krebs (tricarboxylic acid) cycle

Although glycolysis releases a little of the energy from the glucose molecule, the majority still remains 'locked-up' in the pyruvate. These molecules enter the mitochondria and, in the presence of oxygen, are broken down to carbon dioxide and hydrogen atoms. The process is called the **Krebs cycle**, after its discoverer Hans Krebs. There are a number of alternative names, notably the **tricarboxylic acid cycle (TCA cycle)** and **citric acid cycle**. While the carbon dioxide produced is removed as a waste product, the hydrogen atoms are oxidized to water in order to yield a substantial amount of free energy. Before pyruvate enters the Krebs cycle it combines with a compound called coenzyme A to form **acetyl coenzyme A**. In the process, a molecule of carbon dioxide and a pair of hydrogen atoms are removed. The 2-carbon

269

acetyl coenzyme A now enters the Krebs cycle by combining with the 4-carbon **oxaloacetate (oxaloacetic acid)** to give the 6-carbon **citrate (citric acid)**. Coenzyme A is reformed and may be used to combine with a further pyruvate molecule. The citrate is degraded to a 5-carbon α-**ketoglutarate (α-ketoglutaric acid)** and then the 4-carbon oxaloacetate by the progressive loss of two carbon dioxide molecules, thus completing the cycle. For each turn of the cycle, a total of four pairs of hydrogen atoms are also formed. Of these, three pairs are combined with the hydrogen carrier **nicotinamide adenine dinucleotide (NAD)** and yield three ATPs for each pair of hydrogen atoms. The remaining pair combines with a different hydrogen carrier, **flavine adenine dinucleotide (FAD)** and yields only two ATPs. In addition, each turn of the cycle produces sufficient energy to form a single molecule of ATP. It must be remembered that all these products are formed from a single pyruvate molecule of which two are produced from each glucose molecule. The total yields from a single glucose molecule are thus double those stated. The significance of this will become apparent when considering the total quantity of energy released (Section 12.6).

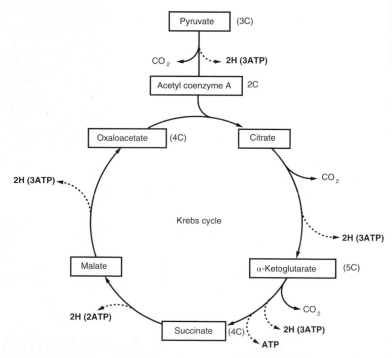

Fig. 12.3 Summary of Krebs cycle

12.3.1 Importance of Krebs cycle

The Krebs cycle plays an important rôle in the biochemistry of a cell for three main reasons:

1. It brings about the degradation of macromolecules – The 3-carbon pyruvate is broken down to carbon dioxide.

2. It provides the reducing power for the electron (hydrogen) transport system – It produces pairs of hydrogen atoms which are ultimately the source of metabolic energy for the cell.

3. It is an interconversion centre – It is a valuable source of intermediate compounds used in the manufacture of other substances, e.g. fatty acids, amino acids, chlorophyll.

12.4 Electron transport system

The electron transport system is the means by which the energy, in the form of hydrogen atoms, from the Krebs cycle, is converted to ATP. The hydrogen atoms attached to the hydrogen carriers NAD and FAD are transferred to a chain of other carriers at progressively lower energy levels. As the hydrogens pass from one carrier to the next, the energy released is harnessed to produce ATP. The series of carriers is termed the **respiratory chain**. The carriers in the chain include **NAD**, **flavoproteins**, **coenzyme Q** and iron-containing proteins called **cytochromes**. Initially hydrogen atoms are passed along the chain, but these later split into their protons and electrons, and only the electrons pass from carrier to carrier. For this reason, the pathway can be called the electron, or hydrogen, transport system. At the end of the chain the protons and electrons recombine, and the hydrogen atoms created link with oxygen to form water. This formation of ATP through the oxidation of the hydrogen atoms is called **oxidative phosphorylation**. It occurs in the mitochondria.

The role of oxygen is to act as the final acceptor of the hydrogen atoms. While it only performs this function at the end of the many stages in respiration, it is nevertheless vital as it drives the whole process. In its absence, only the anaerobic glycolysis stage can continue. The transfer of hydrogen atoms to oxygen is catalyzed by the enzyme **cytochrome oxidase**. This enzyme is inhibited by cyanide, so preventing the removal of hydrogen atoms at the end of the respiratory chain. In these circumstances the hydrogen atoms accumulate and aerobic respiration ceases, making cyanide a most effective respiratory inhibitor.

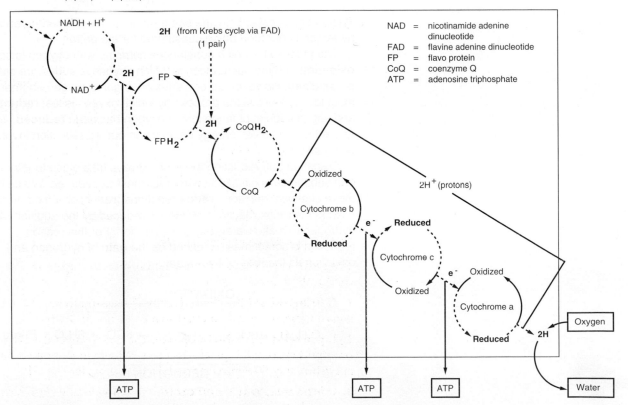

Fig. 12.4 Summary of the electron transport system

12.4.1 Mitochondria and oxidative phosphorylation

Mitochondria are present in all eukaryotic cells where they are the main sites of respiratory activity. Highly active cells, requiring much energy, characteristically have numerous large mitochondria packed with cristae. Such cells include:

Liver cells – Energy is required to drive the large and varied number of biochemical reactions taking place there.

Striated muscle cells – Energy is needed for muscle contraction, especially where this is rapid, e.g. flight muscle of insects.

Sperm tails – These provide energy to propel the sperm.

Nerve cells – Mitochondria are especially numerous adjacent to synapses where they provide the energy needed for the production and release of transmitter substances.

NOTEBOOK

Oxidation, reduction and energy

Many everyday processes such as burning, rusting and respiration are the result of substances combining with oxygen. These reactions also release energy. Fuel in a car engine for example, petrol (made almost entirely of hydrogen and carbon) is mixed with air in the carburettor, the oxygen of which combines with the petrol to form oxides of both hydrogen and carbon when ignited by a spark. The reaction is **exothermic**, i.e. it releases much energy, which is used to propel the car.

Hydrocarbon + Oxygen ⟶ Carbon dioxide + Water + Energy
(Petrol)   (From   (Oxide of   (Oxide of
           air)   carbon)   hydrogen)

Respiration is essentially the same process with the carbon and hydrogen in our food being substituted for the petrol.

The process by which substances combine with oxygen is called **oxidation** and the substances to which oxygen is added are said to be **oxidized**. However, as one substance gains oxygen another must lose it. We call the process by which oxygen is lost **reduction** and say that the substance losing oxygen has been **reduced**. Just as oxidation involves energy being given out, so reduction involves it being taken in.

Oxidation and reduction therefore always take place together; as one substance is oxidized so another must be reduced. We call these chemical reactions **redox** reactions (**red**uction + **ox**idation).

In many redox reactions oxygen is reduced by the addition of hydrogen to make water, e.g. in respiration. For this reason reduction is sometimes described as the **gain** of hydrogen and oxidation as the **loss** of hydrogen.

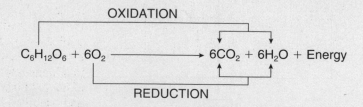

$$C_6H_{12}O_6 + 6O_2 \longrightarrow 6CO_2 + 6H_2O + \text{Energy}$$

Intestinal epithelial cells – Many mitochondria occur beneath the microvilli on these cells to provide energy for the absorption of digested food by active transport.

We saw in Section 4.2.5 that mitochondria have an inner membrane which is folded to form cristae in order to increase its surface-area. The cristae are lined with stalked particles. Within the inner mitochondrial membrane there appears to be a mechanism which actively transports protons (H^+) from the matrix into the space between the inner and outer membranes of the organelle. This creates an electrochemical gradient of hydrogen ions across the inner membrane. According to the **chemi-osmotic theory** put forward by the British biochemist Peter Mitchell, in 1961, it is the energy of this 'charged' membrane which is used to synthesize ATP. Basically the

A closer investigation of redox reactions shows that when a substance is oxidized it **loses electrons** and when it is reduced it **gains electrons**. This is the modern definition of the two processes.

	Reduction	Oxidation
Oxygen	lost	gained
Hydrogen	gained	lost
Electrons	gained	lost
Energy	absorbed	released

We can now see a pattern emerging which is helpful when considering the biochemical reactions of metabolism. The build up or synthesis of substances (**anabolism**) involves the reduction of molecules and hence an intake of energy, whereas the breakdown or degradation of substances (**catabolism**) involves the oxidation of molecules and a consequent release of energy. How then does this help our understanding of biological molecules? Clearly substances rich in hydrogen or electrons have more to lose, i.e. they can more easily become oxidized and since oxidation involves the release of energy these substances are more 'energy rich'. Conversely substances rich in oxygen are more likely to be reduced – a process involving the absorption of energy. From the point of view of our food, molecules with much hydrogen and little oxygen have the greatest potential to provide energy. So which foods are these? Let us consider two types: fats and carbohydrates. Typical examples are given in the table, left.

While the ratio of hydrogen to carbon is about 2:1 in both cases, there is proportionally more oxygen in the carbohydrates. This is because they comprise many H—C—OH groups whereas fats have H—C—H groups. In other words the carbohydrates are already partially oxidized and therefore can undergo less further oxidation than fats. Since oxidation releases energy, carbohydrates have less to release – typically 17 kJ per gram compared to 38 kJ for one gram of fat. In terms of energy then, it is the relative amount of hydrogen and oxygen a food molecule contains which is important; the carbon simply acts as a 'skeleton' to which these atoms are attached.

Typical fat	Typical carbohydrate
Stearic acid	Glucose
Formula: $C_{17}H_{35}COOH$	Formula: $C_6H_{12}O_6$

hydrogen atoms are picked up by NAD in the matrix and later split into protons and electrons. The protons enter the space between the inner and outer membrane of the mitochondrion while the electrons pass along the cytochromes located within the inner membrane. The protons flow back to the matrix via the stalked granules due to their high concentration in the intermembrane space. This flow acts as the driving force to combine ADP with inorganic phosphate and so synthesize ATP. ATP-ase associated with the stalked granules catalyzes this reaction. These protons then recombine in the matrix with the electrons and the hydrogen atoms so formed then combine with oxygen to form water.

In addition to carrying out oxidative phosphorylation, the mitochondria perform the reactions of the Krebs cycle. The enzymes for these reactions are mostly found within the matrix, with a few, like succinic dehydrogenase, attached to the inner mitochondrial membrane.

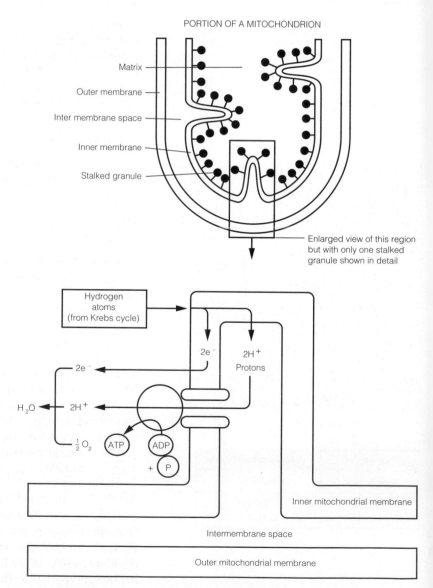

Fig. 12.5 The synthesis of ATP according to the chemi-osmotic theory of Mitchell

12.5 Anaerobic respiration (anaerobiosis)

Present thinking suggests that life originated in an atmosphere without oxygen and the first forms of life were therefore anaerobic. Many organisms today are also anaerobic; indeed, some find oxygen toxic. These forms are termed **obligate anaerobes**. Most anaerobic organisms will, however, respire aerobically in the presence of oxygen, only resorting to anaerobiosis in its absence. These forms are **facultative anaerobes**. The cells of almost all organisms are capable of carrying out anaerobic respiration, for a short time at least. From what we have so far learnt it is clear that, in the absence of oxygen, the Krebs cycle and electron transport system cannot operate. Only glycolysis can take place. This yields a little ATP directly (two molecules for each glucose molecule) and a total of two pairs of hydrogen ions. In the previous section we saw that these hydrogen ions possess much free energy. In the absence of oxygen, however, this energy cannot be released. Nevertheless, these hydrogen ions must be removed if glycolysis is to continue. They are accepted by the pyruvate formed at the end of glycolysis, to give either ethanol (alcohol) or lactate, in a process called **fermentation**. Neither process yields any additional energy; both are merely mechanisms for 'mopping-up' the hydrogen ions.

12.5.1 Alcoholic fermentation

In alcoholic fermentation the pyruvate from glycolysis is first converted to ethanal (acetaldehyde) through the removal of a carbon dioxide molecule.

$$CH_3COCOOH \longrightarrow CH_3CHO + CO_2$$
pyruvate $\qquad$ ethanal $\qquad$ carbon dioxide

The ethanal then combines with the hydrogen ions, which are transported by the hydrogen carrier NAD, to form the alcohol, ethanol.

$$NADH + H^+ \qquad NAD^+$$
$$CH_3CHO \longrightarrow CH_3CH_2OH$$
ethanal $\qquad\qquad\qquad$ ethanol

This form of fermentation occurs in yeast, where the alcohol produced may accumulate in the medium around the cells until its concentration rises to a level which prevents further fermentation, and so kills the yeast. The ethanol cannot be further broken down to yield additional energy.

The overall equation is:

$$C_6H_{12}O_6 \longrightarrow 2CH_3CH_2OH + 2CO_2$$
glucose $\qquad\qquad$ ethanol $\qquad\qquad$ carbon dioxide

Under anaerobic conditions, e.g. waterlogging of plant roots, the cells of higher plants may temporarily undergo this form of fermentation. Alcoholic fermentation is of considerable economic importance to humans. It is the basis of the brewing industry, where the ethanol is the important product, and of the baking industry, where the carbon dioxide is of greater value (Section 21.4).

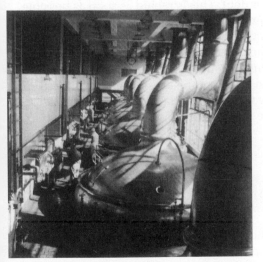

An industrial fermenter

12.5.2 Lactate fermentation

In lactate fermentation the pyruvate from glycolysis accepts the hydrogen atoms from NADH + H$^+$ directly.

$$\text{CH}_3\text{COCOOH} \xrightarrow{\text{NADH + H}^+ \quad \text{NAD}^+} \text{CH}_3\text{CHOHCOOH}$$

pyruvate   lactate
                                            (2-hydroxypropanoic acid)

Unlike alcoholic fermentation, the lactate can be further broken down, should oxygen be made available again, thus releasing its remaining energy. Alternatively it may be resynthesized into carbohydrate, or excreted.

This form of fermentation is common in animals. Clearly any mechanism which allows an animal to withstand short periods without oxygen (anoxia) has great survival value. Animals living in environments of fluctuating oxygen levels, such as a pond or river, may benefit from the temporary use of it, as might a baby in the period during and immediately following birth. A more common occurrence of lactate fermentation is in a muscle during strenuous exercise. During this period, the circulatory system may be incapable of supplying the muscle with its oxygen requirements. Lactate fermentation not only yields a little energy, but removes the pyruvate which would otherwise accumulate. Instead lactate accumulates, and while this in time will cause cramp and so prevent the muscle operating, tissues have a relatively high tolerance to it.

In the process of lactate fermentation, the organism accumulates an **oxygen debt**. This is repaid as soon as possible after the activity, by continued deep and rapid breathing following the exertion. The oxygen absorbed is used to oxidize the lactate to carbon dioxide and water, thereby removing it, and at the same time replenishing the depleted stores of ATP and oxygen in the tissue. In some organisms such as parasitic worms, where the food supply is abundant, the lactate is simply excreted, obviating the need to repay an oxygen debt.

12.6   Comparison of energy yields

Let us now compare the total quantity of ATP produced by the aerobic and anaerobic pathways.

Aerobic respiration
The ATP is derived from two sources: directly by phosphorylation of ADP and indirectly by oxidative phosphorylation using the hydrogen ions generated during glucose breakdown.

The figures given represent the yield for each pyruvate molecule which subsequently enters the Krebs (TCA) cycle. As there are two pyruvate molecules formed for each glucose molecule (Section 12.3), all these figures must be doubled (×2) to give the quantities formed per glucose molecule.

The energy yield for each molecule of NADH + H$^+$ is three ATPs whereas for FADH$_2$ it is only two ATPs (Section 12.4).

TABLE 12.1 **ATP yield during aerobic respiration of one molecule of glucose**

Respiratory process	Number of reduced hydrogen carrier molecules formed	Number of ATP molecules formed from reduced hydrogen carriers	Number of ATP molecules formed directly	Total number of ATP molecules
Glycolysis (glucose → pyruvate)	$2 \times (NADH + H^+)$	$2 \times 3 = 6$	2	8
pyruvate → acetyl CoA	$1 \times (NADH + H^+)(\times 2)$	$2 \times 3 = 6$	0	6
Krebs (TCA) cycle	$3 \times (NADH + H^+)(\times 2)$ $1 \times FADH_2 (\times 2)$	$6 \times 3 = 18$ $2 \times 2 = 4$	$1(\times 2)$	24
		Total ATP =		38

The total of thirty-eight ATPs produced represents the maximum possible yield; the actual yield may be different depending upon the conditions in any one cell at the time. For example, the two $NADH + H^+$ may enter the mitochondria in two different, indirect ways. Depending on the route taken, they may yield only four ATPs, rather than six ATPs as shown in Table 12.1.

Each ATP molecule will yield 30.6 kJ of energy. The total energy available from aerobic respiration is $38 \times 30.6 = 1162.8$ kJ. Compared to the total energy available from the complete oxidation of glucose of 2880 kJ, this represents an efficiency of slightly over 40%. This may not appear very remarkable, but it compares very favourably with machines – the efficiency of a car engine is around 25%.

Anaerobic respiration
We have seen in the previous section that only glycolysis occurs during anaerobiosis and that the $NADH + H^+$ it yields is not available for oxidative phosphorylation. The total energy released is therefore restricted to the two ATPs formed directly. With each providing 30.6 kJ of energy, the total yield is a mere 61.2 kJ. Compared to the 2880 kJ potentially available from a molecule of glucose, the process is a little over 2% efficient. It must, however, be borne in mind that in lactate fermentation all is not lost, and the lactate may be reconverted to pyruvate by the liver, and so enter the Krebs cycle, thus releasing its remaining energy.

12.7 Respiratory quotients

The **respiratory quotient (RQ)** is a measure of the ratio of carbon dioxide evolved by an organism to the oxygen consumed, over a certain period.

$$RQ = \frac{CO_2 \text{ evolved}}{O_2 \text{ consumed}}$$

For a hexose sugar like glucose, the equation for its complete oxidation is:

$$C_6H_{12}O_6 + 6O_2 \longrightarrow 6CO_2 + 6H_2O$$

The RQ is hence: $\dfrac{6CO_2}{6O_2} = 1.0$

In fats, the ratio of oxygen to carbon is far smaller than in a carbohydrate. A fat therefore requires a greater quantity of oxygen for its complete oxidation and thus has a RQ less than one.

$$C_{18}H_{36}O_2 + 26O_2 \longrightarrow 18CO_2 + 18H_2O$$
stearic acid

$$RQ = \frac{18CO_2}{26O_2} = 0.7$$

The composition of proteins is too varied for them to give the same RQ, but most have values around 0.9.

Organisms rarely, if ever, respire a single food substance, nor are substances always completely oxidized. Experimental RQ values therefore do not give the exact nature of the material being respired. Most resting animals have RQs between 0.8 and 0.9. With protein only respired during starvation, this must be taken to indicate a mixture of fat and carbohydrate as the respiratory substrates.

12.8   Questions

1. The diagram below shows some of the stages in cell respiration.

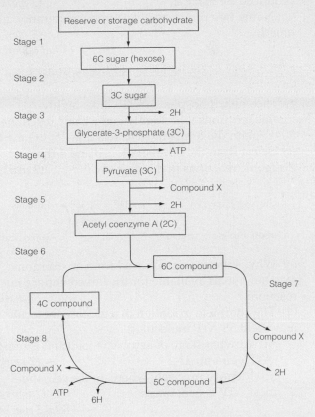

(a) What respiratory substrate would be used in a liver cell?   (1 mark)
(b) State in which part of a cell Stage & occurs.
                                                            (1 mark)
(c) Identify compound **X**, removed at stages 5, 7 and 8.   (1 mark)
(d) Describe what happens to the hydrogen atoms removed at Stages 3, 5, 7 and 8.   (2 marks)
                                              (Total 5 marks)

ULEAC 1996, Specimen Paper B/HB2, No. 3

2. The diagram at the top of the next column shows **three** stages in respiration.
(a) Name each stage **A**, **B** and **C**.   (3 marks)
(b) (i) What is substance **X**?   (1 mark)
   (ii) What happens to the pyruvate if substance **X** is not available?   (1 mark)
(c) The respiratory system in a cell was poisoned so that electron transport was uncoupled from ATP production. Suggest what would be likely to happen to:
   (i) the rate of ATP production;   (1 mark)
   (ii) the energy released.   (1 mark)
                                              (Total 7 marks)

AEB June 1993, Paper 1, No. 13

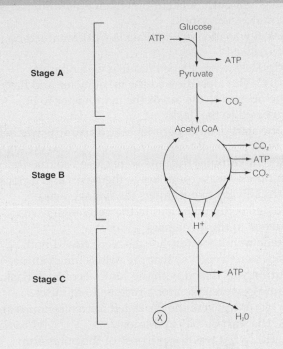

3. (a) (i) Outline how glucose is broken down to pyruvate in respiration in a muscle cell. Details of individual chemical reactions are not required.   (3 marks)
   (ii) Describe what happens to the pyruvate in anaerobic conditions.   (2 marks)
(b) (i) Show that, under aerobic conditions, the respiratory quotient for glucose is 1.0.
                                                            (2 marks)
   (ii) If the respiratory quotient is 0.75, and negligible protein is being respired, what can you deduce about the respiratory substrate?
                                                            (2 marks)
(c) Describe how a molecule of oxygen:
   (i) moves from an alveolus in the lung to the blood;   (2 marks)
   (ii) is transported in the blood.   (3 marks)
(d) The diagram shows part of a Gilson respirometer.

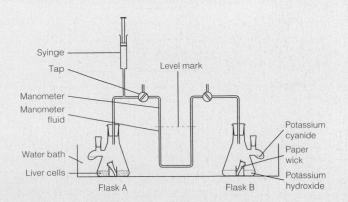

Flask **A** contained living liver cells in a buffered nutrient medium. The side arm contained 1% potassium cyanide solution which is an inhibitor of respiratory enzymes.

Flask **B** was identical to Flask **A** but contained no liver cells.

Both flasks were suspended in a water bath at 37.0 °C. The taps allowed the manometer and flasks to be opened to the air, or the manometer to be connected to the flasks.

At the start of an experiment the apparatus was set up with the flasks and manometer open to the air. After ten minutes the taps were closed so that the manometer was connected to the flasks and a clock started. Every two minutes the syringe was adjusted so that the fluid in the manometer was returned to the level mark.

Sixteen minutes after the taps were closed both flasks were tipped so that the potassium cyanide solution was mixed with the contents of each flask. Readings were taken for a further 16 minutes.

(i) Why were the flasks left for ten minutes at the start of the experiment? *(1 mark)*

(ii) What was the purpose of the potassium hydroxide in each flask? *(1 mark)*

(iii) Precisely what was being measured by this apparatus? *(1 mark)*

(iv) Describe how Flask **B** acted as a control. *(1 mark)*

(v) Sketch a graph to show the volume of gas added from the syringe against time from the time when the taps were closed and the clock started. *(3 marks)*

(vi) Indicate **three** ways in which the experiment would need to be modified if the apparatus were to be used to measure photosynthesis. *(3 marks)*

(Total 24 marks)

AEB June 1992, Paper 2, No. 1

4. The diagram below shows some of the stages of anaerobic respiration in a yeast cell.

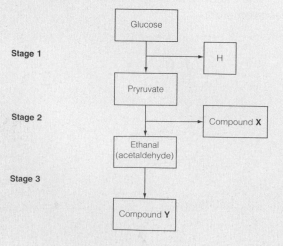

(a) (i) Identify compound **X**, produced at Stage 2. *(1 mark)*

(ii) Identify compound **Y**, produced at Stage 3. *(1 mark)*

(b) State what happens to the hydrogen atoms produced by Stage 1. *(2 marks)*

(c) Name **two** products of anaerobic respiration in muscle. *(2 marks)*

(Total 6 marks)

ULEAC June 1995, Paper 1, No. 1

5. Adenosine triphosphate (ATP) links highly exergonic reactions with highly endergonic reactions.

(a) Explain the term *exergonic* reaction. *(1 mark)*

(b) Select from the numbers 1, 2, 3 and 4 the exergonic reactions in the diagram. *(2 marks)*

$$\text{Glucose + oxygen} \quad \underset{\text{Carbon dioxide + water}}{\overset{\text{Glucose + oxygen}}{1}} \quad \underset{\text{ATP}}{\overset{\text{ADP + Pi}}{2}} \quad 3 \quad \underset{\text{Amino acids}}{\overset{\text{Proteins}}{4}}$$

(c) Why is the energy released from an exergonic reaction not **all** available for the linked endergonic reaction? *(1 mark)*

(d) The complete oxidation of a glucose molecule may yield 38 ATP molecules.

(i) At what stage of aerobic respiration is most ATP generated? *(1 mark)*

(ii) Identify precisely where, in the cell, the most ATP is generated. *(2 marks)*

(Total 7 marks)

AEB June 1995, Paper 1, No. 7

6. The diagram below summarizes stages in the complete aerobic breakdown of one molecule of glucose.

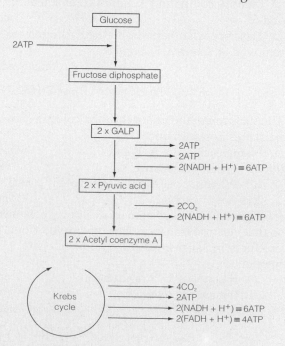

(a) Comment on the use of ATP in the conversion of glucose to fructose diphosphate. *(1 mark)*

(b) ATP can provide approximately 30.7 kJ mole^{-1} of usable energy. When glucose is completely oxidized to carbon dioxide and water in a calorimeter the total energy yield is 2880 kJ mole^{-1}.

(i) Calculate the net energy by ATP during the complete aerobic breakdown of 1 mole of glucose. Show your working. *(2 marks)*

(ii) Calculate the percentage efficiency of the energy capture. *(1 mark)*

(iii) What happens to the energy which is not captured in ATP? *(1 mark)*

(c) Explain why, when conditions are anaerobic, the net yield of ATP is only 2 moles of ATP per mole of glucose oxidized in actively working skeletal muscle. *(3 marks)*

(Total 8 marks)

ULEAC June 1994, Paper 1, No. 9

7. The diagram summarizes the process of aerobic respiration.

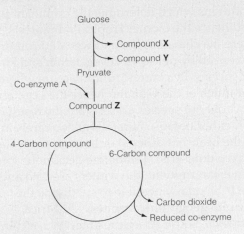

Glucose
Compound **X**
Compound **Y**
Pryuvate
Co-enzyme A
Compound **Z**
4-Carbon compound
6-Carbon compound
Carbon dioxide
Reduced co-enzyme

(a) Name:
(i) compound **X**;
(ii) compound **Y**;
(iii) compound **Z**. *(3 marks)*

(b) Explain how oxidative phosphorylation produces ATP. *(3 marks)*

(Total 6 marks)

NEAB June 1995, Paper BY01, No. 3

8. Read through the following passage about respiration, then write on the lines the most appropriate word or words to complete the account.

Respiration is the process by which organisms can release energy from organic compounds. In living cells, ... respiration can be divided into several stages. Glycolysis takes place in the .... of the cell. Glycolysis produces the compound .... which enters the next stage, the .... cycle. This compound is broken down releasing .... and .... and energy in the form of heat and ATP.

(Total 6 marks)

ULEAC June 1996, Paper B/HB1, No. 4

13

Energy and the ecosystem

Organisms live within a relatively narrow sphere over the earth's surface; it is less than 20 km thick, extending about 8 km above sea level and 10 km below it. The total volume of this thin film of land, water and air around the earth's surface is called the **biosphere**. It consists of two major divisions, the aquatic and terrestrial environments, with the aquatic environment being subdivided into freshwater, marine and estuarine. The terrestrial portion of the biosphere is subdivided into **biomes** which are determined by the dominant plants found there. It is, of course, largely climatic conditions which determine the dominant plant type of a region, and hence the biome. Tropical rain forests, for example, occur where the climate is hot and wet all through the year and are characterized by dense, lush vegetation and an immense variety of species. By contrast tundra occurs where the ground is frozen for much of the year and hence the vegetation is sparse with little variety of species. Deserts are the result of a lack of usable water, either because rain falls all too rarely and soon evaporates in the heat (hot deserts) or because the water is permanently frozen (cold deserts). Temperate deciduous forests occur where the rain is intermittent, the winters are cold and the summers are warm. It is equally possible to subdivide the terrestrial biosphere into **geographical zones**, e.g. Africa, Australia, North America, South America, Antarctica, etc. In this case the divisions are made by barriers like oceans or mountain ranges.

A biome can be further divided into **zones** which consist of a series of small areas called **habitats**. Examples of habitats include a rocky shore, a freshwater pond and a beech wood.

Within each habitat there are **populations** of individuals which collectively form a **community** (see Section 13.6). An individual member of the community is usually confined to a particular region of the habitat, called the **microhabitat**. The position any species occupies within its habitat is referred to as its **ecological niche**. It represents more than a physical area within the habitat as it includes an organism's behaviour and interactions with its living and non-living environment. No two species can occupy the same ecological niche.

The inter-relationship of the living (**biotic**) and non-living (**abiotic**) elements in any biological system is called the **ecosystem**. There are two major factors within an ecosystem:

1. The flow of energy through the system.

2. The cycling of matter within the system.

It is feasible to consider the biosphere as a single ecosystem because, in theory at least, energy flows through it and nutrients may be recycled within it. However, in practice there are much smaller units which are more or less self-contained in terms of energy and matter. A freshwater pond, for example, has its own community of plants to capture the solar energy necessary to supply all organisms within the habitat, and matter such as nitrogen and phosphorus is recycled within the pond with little or no loss or gain between it and other habitats. It is often easier to consider these smaller units as single ecosystems.

13.1 Energy flow through the ecosystem

The study of the flow of energy through the ecosystem is known as **ecological energetics**. All the energy utilized by living organisms is ultimately derived from the sun but as little as 1% of its total radiant energy is actually captured by green plants for distribution throughout the ecosystem. This relatively small amount is nonetheless sufficient to support all life on earth. It may at first glance appear inefficient, but it must be remembered that factors other than light intensity often limit photosynthesis – carbon dioxide, temperature, water and mineral availability, to name a few.

13.1.1 Food chains

Because green plants manufacture sugars from simple raw materials utilizing solar energy, they are called **primary producers**. All are autotrophic and they include some bacteria as well as green plants.

Organisms that are unable to utilize light energy for the synthesis of food must obtain it by consuming other organisms. These are heterotrophs and include all animals as well as fungi and some bacteria. If they feed off the primary producers they are called **primary consumers**. These are typically herbivores but also include plant parasites.

Some heterotrophs, the carnivores, feed on other heterotrophs. These are called **secondary consumers** if they feed on a herbivore, and **tertiary consumers** if they feed on other carnivores. There is hence a type of feeding hierarchy with the primary producers at the bottom and the consumers at the top. The energy is therefore passed along a chain of organisms, known as a **food chain**. Each feeding level in the chain is called a **trophic level**. Only a small proportion of the available energy is transferred from one trophic level to the next. Much energy is lost as heat during the respiratory processes of each organism in the chain. It is this loss of energy at each stage which limits the length of food chains. It is rare for this reason to find chains with more than six different trophic levels.

On the death of the producers and consumers, some energy remains locked up in the complex organic compounds of which they are made. This is utilized by further groups of organisms which break down these complex materials into simple components again and in doing so contribute to the recycling of nutrients. The majority of this work is achieved by the saprobiontic fungi and bacteria, called **decomposers**, and to a lesser extent by certain animals called **detritivores**. The trophic relationships of these groups are shown on Fig. 13.1 below.

Trophic efficiency

This is the percentage of the energy at one trophic level which is incorporated into the next trophic level. The values differ from one ecosystem to another with some of the highest values, around 40%, occurring in oceanic food chains. At the other extreme values under 1% have been calculated for small mammals at the top of food chains, e.g. the shrew.

A classic piece of research carried out by Odum at Silver Springs in Florida provided the following figures for trophic efficiency:

Photosynthesis – 1.2%
Primary consumers (herbivores) – 15.9%
Secondary consumers (1st level carnivores) – 4.5%
Tertiary consumers (2nd level carnivores) – 6.7%.

13.1.2 Food webs

With rare exceptions, the diet of an individual is not restricted to a single food. Most animals feed on many different types. In the same way, an individual is normally a potential meal for many different species. The idea of a food chain as a sequence of species which feed exclusively off the individuals below them in the series is clearly oversimplified. Individual food chains interconnect in an intricate and complex way. A single species may form part of many different chains, not always occupying the same trophic level in each chain. Fig. 13.2 gives an example of a simplified food web for a woodland habitat.

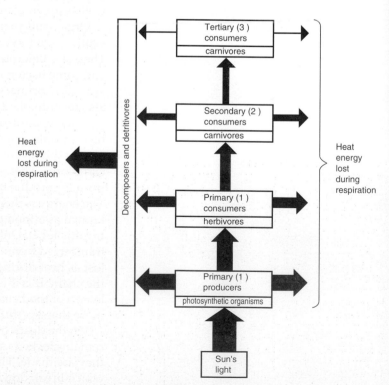

Fig. 13.1 Energy flow through different trophic levels of a food chain

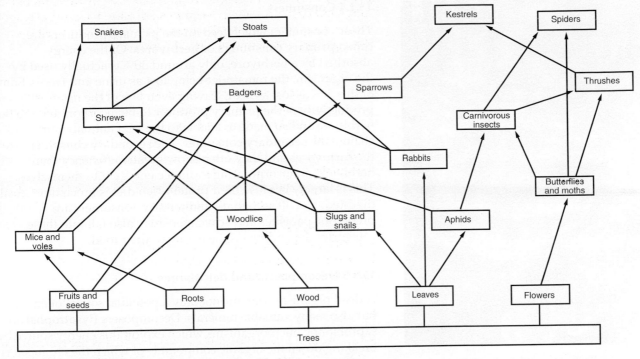

Fig. 13.2 Simplified food web based on a woodland habitat

13.1.3 Primary producers

It is the role of the photosynthetic organisms which make up the primary producers to manufacture organic substances using light, water and carbon dioxide. The rate at which they produce this organic food per unit area, per unit time, is called **gross primary productivity**. Not all this food is stored; around 20% is utilized by the plant, mainly during respiration. The remainder is called **net primary productivity**. It is this food which is available to the next link in the food chain, namely the primary consumers (herbivores). The net primary productivity depends upon climatic and other factors which affect photosynthesis. It is reduced in certain conditions such as cold, drought, absence of essential minerals, low light intensity, etc. The type of primary producer varies from habitat to habitat and some examples are given in Table 13.1.

TABLE 13.1   **Trophic levels of a food chain in each of 5 different habitats**

	Habitat				
Trophic level	**Grassland**	**Woodland**	**Freshwater pond**	**Rocky marine shore**	**Ocean**
Quaternary consumers (3° carnivores)	Mammal e.g. stoat	Bird e.g. thrush	Large fish e.g. pike	Bird e.g. gull	Marine mammal e.g. seal
Tertiary consumers (2° carnivores)	Reptile e.g. grass snake	Arachnid e.g. spider	Small fish e.g. stickleback	Crustacean e.g. crab	Large fish e.g. herring
Secondary consumers (1° carnivores)	Amphibian e.g. toad	Carnivorous insect e.g. ladybird	Annelid e.g. leech	Carnivorous mollusc e.g. whelk	Small fish e.g. sand eel larvae
Primary consumers (herbivores)	Insect larva e.g. caterpillar	Herbivorous insect e.g. aphid	Mollusc e.g. freshwater snail	Herbivorous mollusc e.g. limpet	Zooplankton e.g. copepods
Primary producers (e.g. photosynthetic organisms)	Grass e.g. *Festuca*	Tree e.g. oak leaves	Aquatic plant e.g. *Elodea*	Seaweed e.g. sea lettuce	Phytoplankton e.g. diatom

Saprobiontic fungi are important decomposers of wood

13.1.4 Consumers

Those consumers which feed on the primary producers are called **primary consumers** or **herbivores**. Of the energy absorbed by a herbivore, only around 30% is actually used by the organism, the remainder being lost as urine and faeces. Some of this 30% is lost as heat, leaving even less of the net productivity of the primary producer to be incorporated into the herbivore and so made available to the next animal in the food chain – the **secondary consumer**. The secondary consumers are the **carnivores** and they often show greater efficiency than herbivores in incorporating available energy into themselves. This is largely because their protein-rich diet is much more easily digested. Not all secondary and tertiary consumers are predators; parasites and scavengers may also fall into these categories depending on the nature of their food.

13.1.5 Decomposers and detritivores

A dead organism contains not only a potential source of energy but also many valuable minerals. Decomposers **(lysotrophs)** are saprobiontic microorganisms which exploit this energy source by breaking down the organic compounds of which the organism is made. In so doing they release valuable nutrients like carbon, nitrogen and phosphorus which may then be recycled (Section 13.2). Apart from dead organisms they also decompose the organic chemicals in urine, faeces and other wastes.

    Detritus is the organic debris from decomposing plants and animals and is normally in the form of small fragments. It forms the diet of a group of animals called **detritivores**. They usually differ from decomposers in being larger and in digesting food internally rather than externally. Examples of detritivores include earthworms, woodlice, maggots, dog whelks and sea cucumbers.

13.1.6 Ecological pyramids

Pyramids of numbers

If a bar diagram is drawn to indicate the relative numbers of individuals at each trophic level in a food chain, a diagram similar to that shown in Fig. 13.3(a) is produced. The length of each bar gives a measure of the relative numbers of each organism. The overall shape is roughly that of a pyramid, with primary producers outnumbering the primary consumers which in turn outnumber secondary consumers. Accepting that there is inevitably some loss when energy is transferred from one trophic level to the next in a food chain, it follows that to support an individual at one level requires more energy from the individual at the level below to compensate for this loss. In most instances this can only be achieved by having more individuals at the lower level (Fig. 13.3(a)).

    The use of pyramids of numbers has drawbacks, however:

1. All organisms are equated, regardless of their size. An oak tree is counted as one individual in the same way as an aphid.

2. No account is made for juveniles and other immature forms of a species whose diet and energy requirements may differ from those of the adult.

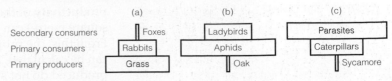

Fig 13.3 Pyramids of numbers

3. The numbers of some individuals are so great that it is impossible to represent them accurately on the same scale as other species in the food chain. For example, millions of blackfly may feed on a single rose-bush and this relationship cannot be effectively drawn to scale on a pyramid of numbers.

These problems may create some different shaped 'pyramids'. Take for example the food chain:

oak tree → aphid → ladybird

The pyramid of numbers produced is illustrated in Fig. 13.3(b). It clearly bulges in the middle.

The food chain:

sycamore → caterpillar → protozoan parasites (of the caterpillar)

produces a complete inversion of the pyramid as illustrated in Fig. 13.3(c).

These difficulties are partly overcome by the use of a pyramid of biomass, instead of one of numbers.

Pyramids of biomass
To overcome some of the problems of using pyramids of numbers, the dry mass of all the organisms at each trophic level may instead be estimated. The relative biomass is represented by bars of proportionate length. While this method is an improvement, it too has its drawbacks:

1. It is impossible to measure exactly the biomass of all individuals in a population. A small sample is normally taken and measured. This sample may not be representative.

2. The time at which a sample is taken may affect the result. Figures for a deciduous tree in summer may be very different from those in winter. What the sample measures is only the amount of material present at a particular instant. This is called the **standing crop** and gives no indication of total productivity. A young tree, for example, is the result of the accumulation of many years' growth, but it may not yet have seeded and produced offspring. A diatom, itself much smaller than the tree, may however have produced many times the tree's biomass in the same period of time. Such anomalies can occasionally lead to inverted pyramids of biomass, e.g. in oceans at certain times of the year zooplankton biomass exceeds phytoplankton biomass, although over the year as a whole the reverse is true.

Pyramids of energy
An energy pyramid overcomes the main drawbacks of the other forms of ecological pyramid. Here the bar is drawn in proportion to the total energy utilized at each trophic level. The total

productivity of the primary producers of a given area (e.g. one square metre) can be measured for a given period (e.g. one year). From this, the proportion of it utilized by the primary consumer can be calculated, and so on up the food chain. The pyramids produced do not show any anomalies, but obtaining the necessary data can be a complex and difficult affair. Once again the unifying nature of energy in ecology is apparent.

13.2   The cycling of nutrients

Energy exists in a number of forms, only some of which can be utilized by living organisms. In an ecosystem, energy is obtained almost entirely as light and this is converted to chemical energy which then passes along the food chain. During chemical reactions in living organisms some of this energy is lost as heat – 'lost', because heat is a form of energy which is dissipated to the environment and cannot be re-used by organisms. It is exactly because this heat cannot be recycled that energy flows through ecosystems in one direction only. Like energy, minerals such as carbon, nitrogen and phosphorus exist in different forms. Unlike energy in ecosystems, these forms can be continuously recycled and so used repeatedly by organisms. Most nutrient or mineral cycles have two components:

1. **A geological component** – This includes rock and other deposits in the oceans and the atmosphere. These form the major reservoirs of the mineral.

2. **A biological component** – This includes those organisms which in some way help to convert one form of the mineral into another and so recycle it. It therefore includes the producers, the consumers and especially the decomposers.

13.2.1 The carbon cycle

Despite containing less than 0.04% carbon dioxide, the atmosphere acts as the major pool of carbon. The turnover of this carbon dioxide is considerable. It is removed from the air by the photosynthetic activities of green plants and returned as a result of the respiration of all organisms. This may lead to short-term fluctuations in the proportions of oxygen and carbon dioxide in the atmosphere. For example the concentration of CO_2 varies daily, being up to 40 parts per million (ppm) higher at night, and seasonally – it is around 16 ppm lower in summer than in winter. These differences are accounted for by changes in the rate of photosynthesis. Overall however there is a long-term global balance between the two gases. Heterotrophic organisms (animals and fungi) obtain their carbon by eating plants, directly or indirectly. At times in the past, large quantities of dead organisms accumulated in anaerobic conditions and so were prevented from decaying. In time they formed coal, oil and other fossil fuels. The combustion of these fuels returns more carbon dioxide to the atmosphere and has resulted in a rise in its level from an estimated 265 parts per million (ppm) in 1600 to 315 ppm

Did you know?

In hectare of good farm soil there can be up to 2 tonnes of bacteria, algae and protozoa, 2 tonnes of fungi, 1 tonne of arthropods and 1 tonne of earthworms.

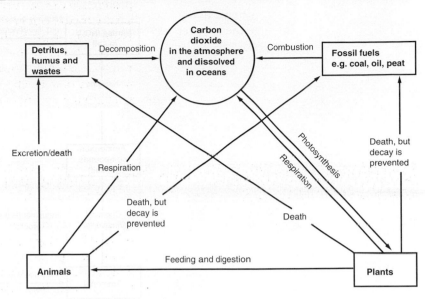

Fig. 13.4 The carbon cycle

in 1958 and to 350 ppm today. Another factor contributing to a rise in atmospheric carbon dioxide has been the clearance of forests. As net users of carbon dioxide trees make a major contribution to the reduction of atmospheric carbon dioxide, especially in tropical rain forests where wet, hot conditions throughout the year favour rapid photosynthesis. It has been estimated that removal of these trees has produced 30% of the increase in atmospheric carbon dioxide which, as a 'greenhouse gas', contributes to global warming (see Section 14.6.3).

13.2.2 The nitrogen cycle

In Chapter 2 (Table 2.1) we saw the range of biologically important chemicals which contain nitrogen, and it is clear from these just how essential a mineral it is to all organisms. Although the atmosphere contains 78% nitrogen, very few organisms can use this gaseous nitrogen directly. Instead they depend upon soil minerals, especially nitrates, as their source of nitrogen. The supply of these nitrates is variable, not least because they are soluble and therefore easily leached from the soil. For this reason a deficiency of nitrates is often the limiting factor to plant growth, and hence the size of the ecosystem it supports. Surrounded by an atmosphere abundant in nitrogen, the growth of many plants is stunted by a lack of it. This is the main reason that it is commonly applied in the form of artificial fertilizers.

Deforestation, especially of tropical rain forests, has also led to nitrate deficiency. With the trees gone there has been large scale erosion due to the high rainfall in these areas washing away the soil. Previously the trees not only acted as a canopy preventing the rain beating directly on the soil, but they also absorbed much of the water which otherwise washes off the surface taking the soil with it. Their roots, in addition, helped to bind the soil particles together. The combination of soil erosion and leaching of nitrates in these areas has impoverished the land making it unfit for vegetation.

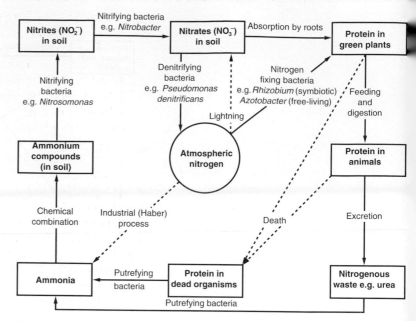

Fig. 13.5 *The nitrogen cycle*

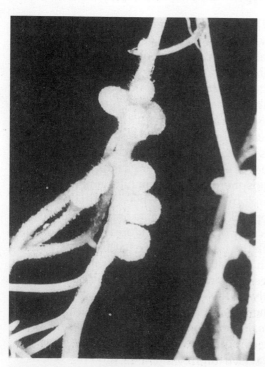

Legume with root nodules

Nitrification

This is the name given to the series of reactions involved in the oxidation of ammonia to nitrates. The process is carried out in two stages:

1. The oxidation of ammonia or ammonium compounds to nitrites by free-living bacteria e.g. *Nitrosomonas*.

$$\underset{\text{ammonia}}{2NH_3} + \underset{\text{oxygen}}{3O_2} \longrightarrow \underset{\text{nitrite}}{2NO_2^-} + \underset{\text{hydrogen ions}}{2H^+} + \underset{\text{water}}{2H_2O}$$

2. The oxidation of the nitrite by other free-living bacteria e.g. *Nitrobacter* and *Nitrococcus*.

$$\underset{\text{nitrite}}{2NO_2^-} + \underset{\text{oxygen}}{O_2} \longrightarrow \underset{\text{nitrate}}{2NO_3^-}$$

In both cases these chemosynthetic bacteria carry out these processes as a means of obtaining their respiratory energy.

Denitrification

This is the process by which nitrate in the soil is converted into gaseous nitrogen, and thereby made unavailable to the majority of plants. It is carried out by anaerobic bacteria like *Pseudomonas denitrificans* and *Thiobacillus denitrificans*. The necessary anaerobic conditions are more likely in waterlogged soil. Where this occurs, denitrifying bacteria thrive and by converting nitrates to atmospheric nitrogen they reduce soil fertility. It is to avoid this that farmers and gardeners plough or dig up their land in order to improve drainage and aeration, so avoiding anaerobic conditions.

Nitrogen fixation

Nitrogen fixation is the opposite to denitrification in that it converts gaseous nitrogen into a form in which it can be utilized by plants, usually organic nitrogen-containing chemicals. It is carried out by both free-living organisms and organisms living in symbiotic association with leguminous plants.

Free-living **nitrogen-fixing bacteria** include *Azotobacter* and *Clostridium* and **nitrogen-fixing blue-green bacteria** include *Nostoc*. Both types reduce gaseous nitrogen to ammonia which they then use to manufacture their amino acids. Around 90% of the total nitrogen fixation is carried out by free-living microorganisms such as these and they make a worthwhile contribution to soil fertility.

Symbiotic nitrogen-fixing bacteria like *Rhizobium* live mostly in association with leguminous plants such as beans, peas and clover although a few types associate with non-leguminous species. They live in special swollen areas on roots, known as **root nodules**. The raising of an appropriate leguminous crop as part of a crop rotation scheme has long been used as a means of improving soil fertility. The crop fixes nitrogen during its growth and may later be ploughed into the soil so that its decay can slowly release much needed nitrogen for use by later crops.

13.3 Ecological factors and their effects on distribution

An organism's environment may be divided into two main parts: the non-living or **abiotic** component and the living or **biotic** component. They work both separately and jointly to influence the distribution and behaviour of organisms in the ecosystem. To help consider these influences we shall examine both components although, for convenience, the abiotic portion will be divided into **climatic** factors and **edaphic** (soil) factors.

13.3.1 Edaphic factors

Soil possesses both living and non-living components. The living portion comprises plant roots and an immense population of microorganisms and small animals. The non-living portion includes particles ranging in size from boulders to fine clay. In addition, there are minerals, water, organic matter and gases. Soil is the result of the weathering of rock which takes two forms:

1. Physical weathering – the mechanical breakdown of rock as a result of the action of water, frost, ice, wind and other rocks.

2. Chemical weathering – the chemical breakdown as a result of water, acids, alkalis and minerals attacking certain rock types.

The general appearance of a soil seen in vertical section and called a **soil profile** is given in Fig. 13.6.

We have seen that the nature of any ecosystem is dependent upon the type of primary producer and its productivity. Both these factors are, in turn, largely determined by the properties of the soil on which the producer grows. The factors which determine a soil's properties are briefly described overleaf.

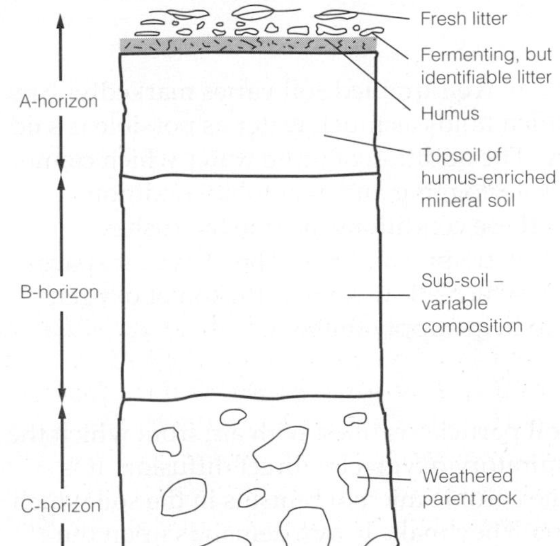

Did you know?

It can take 500 years of weathering to turn rock into 2 cm of top soil.

Fig. 13.6 A generalized soil profile

A-horizon
— Fresh litter
— Fermenting, but identifiable litter
— Humus
— Topsoil of humus-enriched mineral soil

B-horizon
— Sub-soil – variable composition

C-horizon
— Weathered parent rock

D-horizon
— Parent rock

TABLE 13.2   **Classification of soil particles according to size**

Particle size (diameter in mm)	Particle type
2.00–0.200	Coarse sand
0.20–0.020	Fine sand
0.02–0.002	Silt
<0.002	Clay

TABLE 13.3   **A comparison of clay and sandy soils**

Clay soil	Sandy soil
Particle size is less than 0.002 mm (2 μm)	Particle size from 0.02 mm to 2.0 mm
Small air spaces between particles giving poor aeration	Large air spaces between particles giving good aeration
Poor drainage; soil easily compacted	Good drainage; soil not compacted
Good water retention leading to possible waterlogging	Poor water retention and no waterlogging
Being a wet soil, evaporation of water causes it to be cold	Less water evaporation and therefore warmer
Particles attract many mineral ions and so nutrient content is high	Minerals are easily leached and so mineral content is low
Particles aggregate together to form clods, making the soil heavy and difficult to work	Particles remain separate, making the soil light and easy to work

Did you know?

The number of dormant seeds found in 2.4 ha of soil at Rothampstead Horticultural Research Centre was 300 million.

Particle size and nature

The size of the constituent mineral particles of soil probably affects its properties, and hence the type of plant which grows on it, more than any other single factor. Soils are classified according to the size of their particles as shown in Table 13.2.

The **texture** of a soil is determined by the relative proportions of sand, silt and clay particles and this affects the agricultural potential of a soil. A clay soil, with its many tiny particles, has the advantage over a sandy soil, with its coarse particles, in holding water more readily and being less likely to have its minerals leached. On the other hand, it may easily become compacted, reducing its air content; it is slower to drain, colder and more difficult to work, especially when wet. A fuller comparison of clay and sandy soils is given in Table 13.3.

The nature of the particles as well as their size affects soil properties. Sand and silt are mainly silica (SiO_2) which is inert. Clay particles, however, have negative charges and these react with minerals in the soil, especially cations. This helps to prevent these nutrient minerals from being leached.

Organic (humus) content

This includes all dead plant and animal material as well as some animal waste products. Dead animals, leaves, twigs, roots and faeces are broken down by the decomposers and detritivores into a black, amorphous material called **humus**. It has a complicated and variable chemical make-up and is often acidic. It acts rather like a sponge in retaining water and in this way improves the structure of sandy soils. It is equally beneficial to a clay soil where it helps to lighten it by breaking up the clods and thereby improving aeration and drainage. Its slow breakdown releases valuable minerals in both types of soil. This breakdown is carried out by aerobic decomposers and thereby ceases in waterlogged conditions due to the lack of oxygen. In these circumstances the partly decomposed detritus accumulates as **peat**.

Water content

The water content of any well-drained soil varies markedly. Any freely drained soil which holds as much water as possible is said to be at **field capacity**. The addition of more water which cannot drain away leads to waterlogging and anaerobic conditions. Plants able to tolerate these conditions include the rushes (*Juncus* spp.), sedges (*Carex* spp.) and rice. They have air spaces among the root tissues which allow some diffusion of oxygen from the aerial parts to help supply the roots.

Air content

The space between soil particles is filled with air, from which the roots obtain their respiratory oxygen by direct diffusion. It is equally essential to the aerobic microorganisms in the soil which decompose the humus. They make heavy demands upon the available oxygen and may create anaerobic conditions.

Mineral content

A wide variety of minerals is necessary to support healthy plant growth. Different species make different mineral demands and therefore the distribution of plants depends to some extent on the mineral balance of a particular soil. Some plants have particular nutrient requirements; the desert shrub, *Atriplex*, for example, requires sodium, a mineral not essential to most species.

Biotic content

Soils contain vast numbers of living organisms. They include bacteria, fungi and algae as well as animals like protozoans, nematodes, earthworms, insects and burrowing mammals. Bacteria and fungi carry out decomposition, while burrowing animals such as earthworms improve drainage and aeration by forming air passages in the soil. Earthworms also improve fertility by their thorough mixing of the soil which helps to bring leached minerals from lower layers within reach of plant roots. They may improve the humus content through their practice of pulling leaves into their burrows. By passing soil through their bodies they may make its texture finer.

pH

The pH of a soil influences its physical properties and the availability of certain minerals to plants. Plants such as heathers, azaleas and camelias grow best in acid soils, while dog's mercury and stonewort prefer alkaline ones. Species which are tolerant to extremes of pH can become dominant in certain areas because competing species find it hard to survive in these extreme conditions. The dominance of heathers on upland moors is, in part, due to their ability to withstand very low soil pH. Most plants, however, grow best in an optimum pH close to neutral.

Temperature

All chemical and biological activities of a soil are influenced by temperature. The temperature of a soil may be different from that of the air above it. Evaporation of water from a soil may cool it to below that of the air whereas solar radiation may raise it above air temperature. Germination and growth depend on suitable temperatures and the optimum varies from species to species. The activity of soil organisms is likewise affected by changes in temperature, earthworms becoming dormant at low temperatures, for example.

Topography

Three features of topography may influence the distribution of organisms:

1. **Aspect** (slope) – South-facing slopes receive more sunlight, and are therefore warmer than north-facing ones (in the northern hemisphere).

2. **Inclination** (steepness) – Water drains more readily from steep slopes and these therefore dry more quickly than ones with a shallower gradient.

3. **Altitude** (height) – At higher altitudes the temperature is lower, the wind speed is greater and there is more rainfall.

13.3.2 Climatic factors

The world's major biomes are largely differentiated on the basis of climate. From the warm, humid tropical rain forest to the cold arctic tundra it is the prevailing weather conditions which determine the predominant flora and hence its attendant fauna.

Tropical rain forest

Tundra

Each climatic zone has its own community of plants and animals which are suited to the conditions. The adaptations of plants and animals to these conditions are dealt with elsewhere in this book and what follows is merely a general review of the major climatic variables within ecosystems.

Light

As the ultimate source of energy for ecosystems, light is a fundamental necessity. Light is not only needed for photosynthesis, however. It plays a role in such photoperiodic behaviour as flowering in plants, and reproduction, hibernation and migration in animals. There are three aspects to light – its wavelength, its intensity and its duration. The influence of these on photosynthesis is dealt with in Chapter 11.

Temperature

Just as the sun is the only source of light for an ecosystem, so it is the main source of heat. The temperature range within which life exists is relatively small. At low temperatures ice crystals may form within cells, causing physical disruption, and at high temperatures enzymes are denatured. Fluctuation in environmental temperature is more extreme in terrestrial habitats than aquatic ones because the high heat capacity of water effectively buffers the temperature changes in aquatic habitats. The actual temperature of any habitat may differ in time according to the season and time of day, and in space according to latitude, slope, degree of shading or exposure, etc.

Water

Water is essential to all life and its availability determines the distribution of terrestrial organisms. The adaptations of terrestrial organisms to conserve water are discussed in Chapter 17. Even aquatic organisms do not escape problems of water shortage. In saline conditions water may be withdrawn from organisms osmotically, thus necessitating adaptations to conserve it. The salinity of water is a major factor in determining the distribution of aquatic organisms. Some fish, e.g. roach and perch, live exclusively in fresh water; others, like cod and herring, are entirely marine. A few fish, like salmon and eels, are capable of tolerating both extremes during their life.

Air and water currents

Air movements may affect organisms indirectly, for example by evaporative cooling or by a change in humidity. They may also affect them directly by determining their shape; the development of branches and roots of trees in exposed situations is an example. Wind is an important mechanism for dispersing seeds and spores. In the same way that the air currents determine the distribution of certain species in terrestrial habitats, so too do water currents in aquatic ones.

Humidity

Humidity has a major bearing on the rate of transpiration in plants and so affects their distribution. Although to a lesser degree, it affects the distribution of some animals by affecting the rate of evaporation from their bodies.

13.3.3 Biotic factors

Relationships between organisms are obviously varied and complex and are detailed throughout the book, but a brief outline of a few major biotic factors which affect organisms' distribution is given below.

Competition

Organisms compete with each other for food, water, light, minerals, shelter and a mate. They compete not only with members of other species – **interspecific competition** – but also with members of their own species – **intraspecific competition**. Where two species occupy the same ecological niche, the interspecific competition leads to the extinction of one or the other – the **competitive exclusion principle**.

Predation

The distribution of a species is determined by the presence or absence of its prey and/or predators. The predator–prey relationship is an important aspect in determining population size.

Antibiosis

Organisms sometimes produce chemicals which repel other organisms. These may be directed against members of their own species. Many mammals, for example, use chemicals to mark their territories, with the intention of deterring other members of the species from entering. Some ants produce a type of external hormone called a **pheromone** when they are in danger and, in sufficient concentrations, this warns off other members of the species. The chemicals may also be directed against different species. Many fungi, e.g. *Penicillium*, produce **antibiotics** to prevent bacterial growth in their vicinity.

Dispersal

Many organisms depend upon another species to disperse them. Plants in particular use a wide variety of animal species to disperse their seeds.

Pollination

Angiosperms utilize insects to transfer their pollen from one member of a species to another, and a highly complex form of interdependence between these two groups has developed.

Mimicry

Many organisms, for a variety of reasons, seek to resemble other living organisms. Warning mimicry is used by certain flies which resemble wasps. Potential predators are warned off the harmless flies, fearing they may be stung.

Human influence

Humans influence the distribution of other organisms more than any other single species. As hunters, fishers, farmers, developers and polluters, to name a few activities, they dictate which organisms grow where. Some aspects of these influences are considered in Chapter 14.

Hoverfly mimicking a wasp

13.3.4 Species diversity index

The number and range of different species found in an ecosystem is called its **species diversity**. A measure of species diversity is helpful when considering the interaction of the edaphic, climatic and biotic factors which influence an ecosystem. In general, a stable ecosystem has a wide range of different species each with a similar population size. A less stable ecosystem, i.e. one which is under stress due to pollution or extreme climatic conditions, has just a few species with very large populations.

One method of measuring species diversity is the **Simpson index**. It is most often used to estimate plant diversity and involves counting the numbers of each type found in a given area. The diversity is then calculated using the formula:

$$D = \frac{N(N-1)}{\Sigma n(n-1)}$$

where D = diversity index
N = total number of plants
n = total number of species
Σ = sum of.

13.4   Sampling methods

PROJECT

Use quadrats to investigate the distribution of plant or animal species in two different localities, for example:

(a) sheltered and exposed rocky shores
(b) different types of wood
(c) grazed and ungrazed grassland, etc.

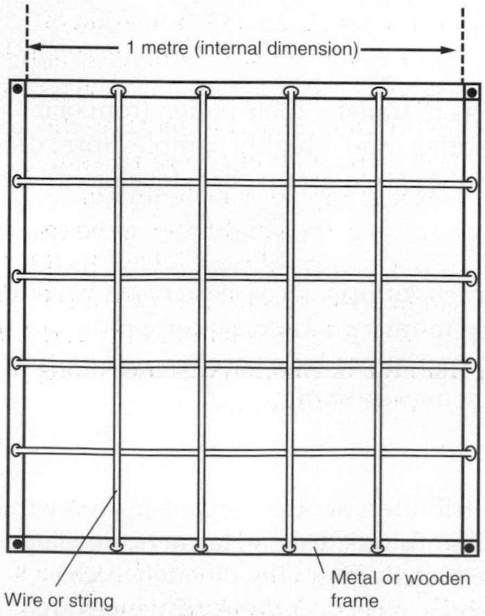

It is virtually impossible to identify and count every organism in a habitat. For this reason only small sections of the habitat are usually studied in detail. Provided these are representative of an area as a whole, any conclusions drawn from the findings will be valid. There are four basic sampling techniques.

13.4.1 Quadrats

A quadrat (Fig. 13.7) is a sturdily built wooden frame, often designed so it can be folded to make it more compact for storage and transport. It is placed on the ground and the species present within the frame are identified and their abundance recorded. Where the species are small and/or densely packed, one or more of the smaller squares within the frame may be used rather than the quadrat as a whole.

Sampling with a quadrat may be random or systematic. **Random sampling** can be as simple as throwing a quadrat over one's shoulder and counting the species within it wherever it falls. Even with the best of intentions it is difficult not to introduce an element of personal bias using this method. A better form of random sampling is to lay out two long tape measures at right angles to each other, along two sides of the study area. Using random numbers generated on a computer or certain calculators, a series of coordinates can be obtained. The quadrat is placed at the intersection of each pair of coordinates and the species within it recorded. **Systematic sampling** involves placing the quadrat at regular intervals, for example, along a transect. It is sometimes necessary to sample the same area over many years in order to investigate seasonal changes or monitor ecological succession. In these circumstances a

1 metre (internal dimension)

Wire or string

Metal or wooden frame

Fig. 13.7 A quadrat frame

PROJECT

Use transects to investigate the distribution of plant or animal species, for example:

(a) down a seashore
(b) from the middle to the edge of a small wood
(c) across sand dunes
(d) across a peat bog
(e) across a path in grassland, etc.

Using a quadrat along a belt transect

rectangular area of ground may be marked out by boundary stakes which are connected by rope. This is known as a **permanent quadrat**.

13.4.2 Point frames

A point frame, or point quadrat (Fig. 13.8), consists of vertical legs across which is fixed a horizontal bar with small holes along it. A long metal pin, resembling a knitting needle, is placed in each of the holes in turn. Each time the pin touches a species, it is recorded. The point frame is especially useful where there is dense vegetation as it can sample at many different levels.

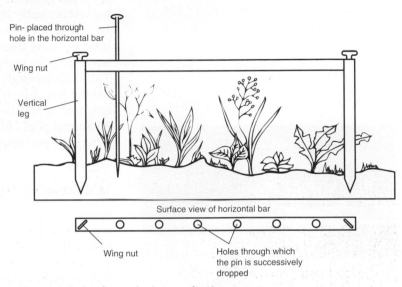

Fig. 13.8 Point frame (point quadrat)

13.4.3 Line transect

A line transect is used so that systematic sampling of an area can be carried out. A string or tape is stretched out along the ground in a straight line. A record is made of the organisms touching or covering the line all along its length, or at regular intervals. This technique is particularly useful where there is a transition of flora and/or fauna across an area, down a sea shore for example. If there is any appreciable height change along the transect, it is advisable to construct a profile of the transect to indicate the changes in level. This is especially important where vertical height is a major factor in determining the distribution of species. On a sea shore, for example, the height above the sea affects the duration of time any point is submerged by the tide. This has a considerable bearing on the species that can survive at that level. So, the distribution of species is related to the vertical height on the shore rather than the horizontal distance along it. This form of transect is called a **profile transect**.

13.4.4 Belt transect

A belt transect is a strip, usually a metre wide, marked by putting a second line transect parallel to the other. The species between the lines are carefully recorded, working a metre at a time. Another method is to use a frame quadrat in conjunction with a single line transect. In this case the quadrat is laid down alongside the line transect and the species within it recorded. It is then moved its own length along the line and the process repeated. This gives a record of species in a continuous belt, but the quadrat may also be used at regular intervals, e.g. every 5 m, along the line.

13.5 Estimating population size

To count accurately every individual of any species within a habitat is clearly impractical, and yet much applied ecology requires information on the size of animal and plant populations. It is necessary therefore to use sampling techniques in particular ways in order to make estimates of the size of any population. The exact methods used depend not only on the nature of the habitat but also on the organism involved. Whereas, for example, it may be useful to know the number of individuals in an animal population, this may be misleading for a plant species, where the percentage cover may be more relevant.

13.5.1 Using quadrats

By sampling an area using quadrats and counting the number of individuals within each quadrat, it is possible to estimate the total number of individuals within the area. If, for example, an area of 1000 m² is studied and 100 quadrats, each 1 m², are sampled, it follows that a total of 100 m² of the area has been sampled. This represents one tenth of the total. The total number of individuals of a species in all 100 quadrats must therefore be multiplied by ten to give an estimate of the total population of that species in the area. The use of quadrats in estimating population size is largely confined to plants and sessile, or very slow-moving animals. Faster-moving animals would simply disperse upon being disturbed.

13.5.2 Capture–recapture techniques

The capture–recapture method of estimating the size of a population is useful for mobile animals which can be tagged or in some other way marked. A known number of animals are caught, clearly marked and then released into the population again. Some time later, a given number of individuals is collected randomly and the number of marked individuals recorded. The size of the population is calculated on the assumption that the proportion of marked to unmarked individuals in this second sample is the same as the proportion of marked to unmarked individuals in the population as a whole. This, of course, assumes that the marked individuals released from the first sample distribute themselves evenly among the remainder of the population and have sufficient time to do so. This may not be the case, due to deaths, migrations and other factors. Another problem is that while the tag or label may not itself be toxic, it often renders the individual more conspicuous and so more liable to predation. In this case the number of marked individuals surviving long enough to be recaptured is

Quadrat in use

PROJECT

Use the Lincoln index to estimate the population size of any particular animal, for example:

(a) woodlice in leaf and bark litter
(b) isopods or amphipods under stones on the upper shore, etc.

reduced and the size of the population will consequently be over-estimated. The population size can be estimated using the calculation below:

$$\text{Estimated size of population} = \frac{\text{Total number of individuals in the first sample} \times \text{Total number of individuals in the second sample}}{\text{Number of marked individuals recaptured}}$$

The estimate calculated is called the **Lincoln index**.

The method can be used on a variety of animals; arthropods may be marked on their backs with non-toxic dabs of paint, fish can have tags attached to their opercula, mammals may have tags clipped to their ears and birds can have their legs ringed.

13.6   Populations and communities

Organisms live, not in isolation, but as part of populations and communities.

A **population** is a group of individuals of the same species, all occupying a particular area at the same time.

A **community** comprises all the plants and animals which occupy a particular area. Communities therefore consist of a number of populations.

13.6.1 Population growth

Provided the birth rate exceeds the death rate, a population will grow in size. If only a few individuals are present initially, the rate of growth will be very slow. This is called the **lag phase**. As numbers increase, more individuals become available for reproduction and the population grows at an ever increasing rate, provided no factor limits growth. This is called the **exponential phase**. Growth cannot continue indefinitely because

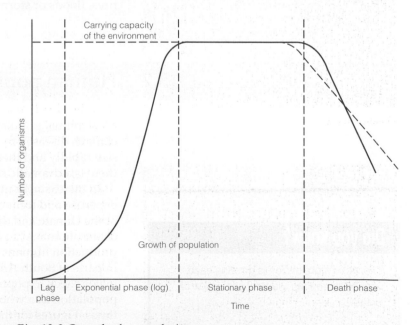

Fig. 13.9 Growth of a population

there is a limit to the number of individuals any area can support. This limit is called the **carrying capacity** of the area. Beyond this point certain factors limit further population growth. The size of the population may then stabilize at a particular level. This is called the **stationary phase**. The high population level may, however, cause the carrying capacity of the environment to decline. In these circumstances the population level falls. This is called the **death phase**.

The factors which limit the growth of a particular population are collectively called the **environmental resistance**. Such factors include predation, disease, the availability of light, food, water, oxygen and shelter, the accumulation of toxic waste and even the size of the population itself.

13.6.2 Density-dependent growth

In this type of growth a population reaches a certain size and then remains stable. It is referred to as density-dependent because the size (or density) of the population affects its growth rate. Typical density-dependent factors are food availability and toxic waste accumulation. In a small population, little food is used up and only small amounts of waste are produced. The population can continue to grow. At high population densities the availability of food is reduced and toxic wastes build up. These cause the growth of the population to slow, and eventually stabilize at a particular level.

13.6.3 Density-independent growth

In this type of growth a population increases until some factor causes a sudden reduction in its size. Its effect is the same regardless of the size of the population, i.e. it is independent of the population density. A typical density-independent factor is temperature. A sudden fall in temperature may kill large numbers of organisms regardless of whether the population is large or small at the time. Environmental catastrophes such as fires, floods or storms are other density-independent factors.

13.7   Human populations

Most animal populations are kept in check by food availability, climate, disease or predators. Populations frequently increase in size rapidly and then undergo a sudden 'crash' during which there is a dramatic reduction in numbers.

In increasingly more regions of the world human knowledge, expertise and technology are succeeding in reducing the impact of the climate and disease. As the top organism in many food chains, humans have little to fear from predators. Even in food production humans have made considerable advances, although in parts of South America, Asia and Africa famine remains a major check to population growth. As a result, the human population as a whole has grown virtually unchecked in recent times. Figures for the past rate of increase in human populations can only be estimated, but it seems probable that prior to 1600 it

Did you know?

The world's population is growing each year by more than the total population of Britain.

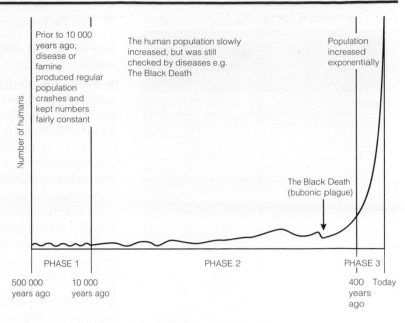

Fig. 13.10 The growth of the human population

had taken around 2000 years to double the world's population. By 1850, it had doubled again. It took just 80 years to complete the next doubling in 1939 and a mere 50 years to double again. At present the world population increases by about 1 500 000 every week, equivalent to about 150 people every minute.

In 1798, Thomas Robert Malthus, an English economist, published an essay on population in which he suggested that while the world's food supply would increase arithmetically, the human population would do so geometrically. The so-called **Malthusian principle** suggested famine as the inevitable consequence of this state of affairs. The predictions of Malthus have so far not been realized owing largely to the greatly improved means of agricultural production which have yielded more food than Malthus could have anticipated possible in 1798. Despite these agricultural advances, much of the world's population is still undernourished, and it is inconceivable that agricultural advancements can continue indefinately to increase food production. War, famine or disease will inevitably curb further increases in population unless humans reduce their birth rate by appropriate forms of birth control.

13.7.1 Factors affecting the size of human populations

The basic factors which affect the size of the world human population are the **birth rate** and the **death rate**. The balance between these two will determine whether the world population is stable, increases or decreases. The population of a given town or country is further affected by **migrations** which occur when people move from one population to take up residence in another. Migrations involve immigration and emigration. **Immigration** occurs when individuals join the population from outside and **emigration** occurs when individuals depart.

The birth rate of different countries in 1990 is given in Table 13.4.

TABLE 13.4   The birth rate of seven countries for 1990.

Country	Birth rate (measured as no. of births to all mothers of child bearing age)
England	1.8
United States of America	2.0
North Korea	2.7
Sri Lanka	3.4
Mexico	4.6
Bangladesh	6.5
Kenya	8.0

Did you know?

Britain's population is expected to add between 110 000 and 128 000 people, or a town about the size of Chester, every year.

13.7.2   Factors affecting birth rates

There are many factors which influence the birth rate of a country:

1. **Economic conditions** – Generally countries with low per capita income have higher birth rates. The reasons may be poorer education (especially about health and birth control) or the need to have more children to ensure that some at least survive to look after the parents in old age (countries with lower per capita income tend to have higher death rates). Another reason may be to improve the finances of the family because in these countries children start earning or producing goods at an early age. In Bangladesh many have more than 'paid off' the parents' investment in their upbringing by the age of 10, whereas in Britain children may be into their twenties before they begin work and the cost of upbringing is therefore a deterrent to having large families.

2. **Social pressures and traditions** – In some countries having a large family improves one's social standing. In others the need for a male heir is still paramount leading to further births until one (or more) is produced.

3. **Cultural and religious background** – Some cultures encourage larger families and some religions, e.g. Roman Catholicism are opposed to artificial birth control.

4. **Political factors** – Governments may bring pressures to bear in order to influence population size. Many European countrys' policies of providing 'family allowance' are seen as a form of encouragement to have children. In India there are financial incentives for men to be sterilized in order to reduce the birth rate, whereas in China a second child may bring swingeing financial penalties in the form of increased taxation and reduced housing allowances.

5. **Birth control and abortion** – The extent to which either or both of these are practised has a major bearing on the birth rate. More discussion of these takes place in Chapter 10.

13.7.3   Factors affecting death rates

1. **Age profile of the population** – The greater the proportion of older people in a population the higher the death rate is likely to be. This explains why developed countries often have a higher death rate than developing ones. In Central America for example, where there is a high proportion of young people in the population, the death rate is lower than in Britain and most of Europe.

2. **Health care** – Access to medical care and health education is an important factor in reducing the death rate.

3. **Life-expectancy at birth** – This is related to the degree of economic and technological development of a country. The occupants of Europe, the USA and Japan can expect to live for over 75 years while those of India and Peru have a life expectancy of under 50 years.

4. **Natural disasters** – Major disasters such as a long-term drought can cause famine and a resulting high death rate for the

population affected. Disease epidemics can also have an impact on the death rate the extent of which will depend on the extent of medical care and resources available to combat them.

5. War – The deaths during wars tend to be of younger males and may therefore lead not only to a short-term increase in the death rate but also a longer term reduction in population size. It has been estimated for example that in the recent Bosnian war around 200 000 children under the age of 16, most of them male, either died or disappeared.

13.7.4 Factors affecting migrations

Migrations can be classified as voluntary and involuntary. **Voluntary migrations** frequently occur for economic reasons with people moving to secure work promotion or for social reasons such as marriage. **Involuntary migrations** may result from a need to escape war, other conflicts, a harsh climate or disaster. They may also be the result of political persecution or discrimination.

13.7.5 Population pyramids

Population pyramids are a graphical means of displaying the age and gender structure of a given population. They are made up of a series of stacked bars which represent the percentage of males and females in each age group. As the resulting figures are always two-dimensional and sometimes wider at the apex than the base, the word 'pyramid' is something of a misnomer. Care needs to be taken in interpreting the graphs as the x-axis can represent the total numbers in a population, the percentage of the total population in a group or the percentage of the male and female population in a group. These pyramids give useful information of the demographic trends of different populations. Fig. 13.11 for example shows these populations: one stable, one increasing in numbers and the other declining in numbers.

The population pyramids for a developed country and a developing country are often markedly different (see Fig 13.12). For a developed country such as Japan the bars are relatively short at the base indicating a low birth rate, they get smaller towards the base indicating a declining birth rate and the bars are of fairly equal length throughout the pyramid – indicating a low death rate. By contrast the pyramid for Kenya is wide at the base (high birth rate), gets markedly wider towards the base (increasing birth rate) and is much narrower towards the apex (higher death rate).

13.7.6 Changes in the population of the British Isles

The population of Britain remained relatively constant until around the middle of the fourteenth century. There were fluctuations as a result of famine and disease up to this time but there was little overall increase in size. The population was relatively small, estimated at between one and a half and two million. The arrival of the Black Death, however, dramatically cut the population (see Focus on page 305). Thereafter there was a slow, but perceptible rise to around 7 million in 1750 when the industrial revolution began. The use of fossil fuels to

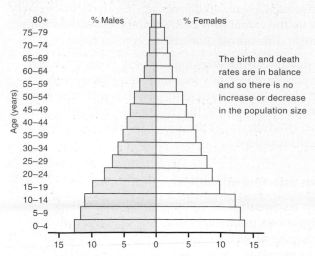

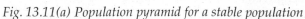

The birth and death rates are in balance and so there is no increase or decrease in the population size

Fig. 13.11(a) Population pyramid for a stable population

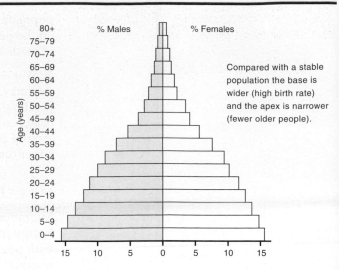

Compared with a stable population the base is wider (high birth rate) and the apex is narrower (fewer older people).

Fig. 13.11(b) Population pyramid for an increasing population

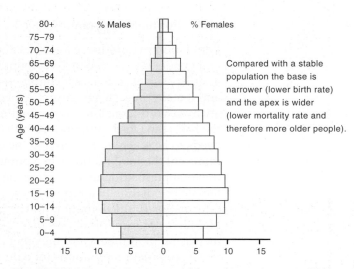

Compared with a stable population the base is narrower (lower birth rate) and the apex is wider (lower mortality rate and therefore more older people).

Fig. 13.11(c) Population pyramid for a decreasing population

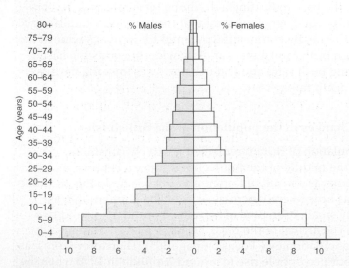

Fig. 13.12(a) Population pyramid for Kenya (1981)

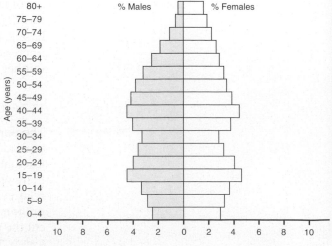

Fig. 13.12(b) Population pyramid for Japan (1990)

The Black Death

The plague bacillus (*Pasteurella pestis*) may be transmitted either indirectly by rat fleas as **bubonic plague**, or directly as **pneumonic plague**. This allows it to sustain itself when host population densities are low and to spread rapidly when they are high. The invention of the mould-board plough allowed top soil to be broken up each year and removed the burrows of rodents such as rats. This may have forced the black rat (*Rattus rattus*) into closer contact with human populations where it fed on human refuse and lived in thatched roofs. Ship-borne rats were responsible for the introduction of the plague bacillus into Europe during the middle of the fourteenth century. The original focus of plague was in Myanmar (formerly Burma) from where it spread to China causing an estimated 50% drop in the population between 1200 and 1400. From China it spread across the caravan routes to the Crimea from where plague-infected rats boarded ships and spread it to the whole of Europe and the Near East. Plague caused such a devastating epidemic that it became known as the Black Death. Between 1346 and 1350 it is estimated to have reduced the population of Europe by 25 to 40%. Plague reappeared in London as the Great Plague of 1665. This was followed by the Great Fire of 1666 after which thatched roofs were replaced by slates, reducing the contact between humans and rat fleas carrying plague.

Irish potato famine

During the 1840s farmers in Ireland were extremely poor, paying high rents to absentee landlords in England. Their principal food source was the potato and each person consumed a large amount each day. Long periods of cold wet weather in the mid 1840s caused the potatoes to rot in the ground, infected by late blight caused by the fungus *Phytophthora infestans*. The farmers had little food and no potatoes to sell and so they could not pay their rent and were evicted from the land. Between 1845 and 1847 the population of Ireland was reduced by about two and a half million people: one million starved and one and a half million emigrated to the United States.

Potato blight has also been blamed for reducing the morale of the Germans at the end of World War One. During the 1880s a complex mixture of copper sulphate and lime, called Bordeaux mixture, was developed to protect the potatoes. In 1916 late blight struck in Germany but the military would not release the copper needed for the Bordeaux mixture. As a result the harvest was severely reduced and many farmers starved.

manufacture a range of produce and to improve transport helped to provide food and materials which enabled people in Britain to live longer. With the later development of better housing, sanitation and medical care, the death rate was reduced drastically and the population increased exponentially, reaching 55 million in the 1970s. With some fluctuations, birth rates generally increased over this period but the effect on the overall population was minor compared with the reduction in death rate. Birth rates have tended to fall since the 1970s and the population of Britain is beginning to stabilize. This is in contrast to the population of the world which continues to rise (see Fig. 13.10). In the same way that Britain's population trend has recently differed from that of the remainder of the world, so even within Britain there have been individual variations, none more so than the population of Ireland which dropped by 8 million between 1840 and 1940. The Irish potato famine (see Focus on page 305) in the 1840s was responsible for deaths, emigration and retarded economic growth in the country which led to the dramatic reduction.

13.7.7 Implications of world population trends

The effects of population trends differ according to whether the population is increasing or decreasing.

Where a population is increasing the main concern is that the consumption of resources, including food, will outstrip the supply. Some predictions suggest that even if consumption remains constant rather than increases, without major new discoveries of resources the current world industrial and economic system faces ultimate collapse. Even if new resources were to be found to satisfy the increased demand, the fear is that the pollution from the utilization of these resources would actually hasten disaster rather than delay it.

Increasing population may lead to famine, water shortage and disease, all of which bring political unrest as populations migrate across borders and increase the pressure on the resources and systems of adjacent countries. Such unrest and difficulties have recently been witnessed in Ethiopia.

Where a population is decreasing one major economic problem is that an ever-increasing retired older population is dependent upon a smaller and smaller number of younger working individuals to provide the income to support them. The distribution of older residents is uneven, with many moving to warmer areas or coastal regions in their retirement and this may place a disproportionate need for old people's homes, health care and transport in these districts. These problems in relation to Europe are discussed in the Focus 'A grey future for Europe' on page 307.

Did you know?

There are more cars in Britain today than there were people in 1871.

A grey future for Europe

In March of 1996 the European Commission produced a report which attempted to view Europe in 2025. It predicted a 50% increase in people aged over 60 giving a likely total of 113 500 000 pensioners in the European Union – almost one third of the total population. By contrast they predicted a decline in the number of working people with 13 000 000 fewer 20 to 59 year olds. An 11% decrease in the under-20's was also envisaged. It is likely that in the United Kingdom there will be around a 44% increase in over-60's with almost a 3% decrease in the working population.

The report warned that the labour market will have to change to meet different demands, especially in the areas of education, housing, health, transport and leisure. How will a younger generation which is diminishing in numbers be able to produce sufficient resources for an ever-expanding older generation? How will it be able to finance its elders pensions?

The report added that social and family life would be increasingly dominated by the needs of older people. It warned that the decline of the family unit might make it more difficult for the elderly to be cared for within the family. The report also predicted that increasing numbers of older people would head for the coastal districts of the warmer south of Europe. Whereas these demographic changes were originally the result of reduced infant mortality, recent changes have principally been due to falling mortality at advanced ages and a lower rate of reproduction in most areas of Europe.

13.8 Questions

1. (a) Define the following ecological terms:
   (i) ecosystem;
   (ii) community;
   (iii) niche. *(9 marks)*
   (b) Construct a food chain with **four** trophic levels and explain fully how energy flows through this chain. *(9 marks)*
   (Total 18 marks)

   UCLES June 1993, Paper 2, No. 7

2. (a) Discuss the consequences of the Black Death, Irish Potato famine and the Industrial Revolution on the population of the British Isles. *(10 marks)*
   (b) Suggest why many human populations are still increasing despite the effects of disease and starvation. *(8 marks)*
   (Total 18 marks)

   UCLES June 1994, Paper 3, No. 3(b)

3. In an investigation to measure the size of a grasshopper population in a field, 30 grasshoppers were captured and marked with a small dot of paint before being released. The next day, 24 grasshoppers were captured using the same technique and of these, 6 were found to be marked with the paint dot.
   (a) Suggest a suitable technique for capturing grasshoppers. *(1 mark)*
   (b) Estimate the size of the grasshopper population in the field. Show your working. *(2 marks)*
   (c) Give **three** assumptions which must be made when estimating population size using the capture and recapture method. *(3 marks)*
   (Total 6 marks)

   NEAB June 1995, Paper BY05, No. 4

4. Give an account of the factors which influence the size of human populations. *(10 marks)*

   ULEAC 1996, Specimen Paper HB2, No. 8

5. During succession there is a change in species composition of a community. There are also changes in species diversity, stability of the ecosystem, and in gross and net production until a climax community is reached.
   (a) Explain what is meant by a climax community. *(1 mark)*
   (b) Explain **each** of the following changes which occur during succession.
   (i) Species diversity increases. *(1 mark)*
   (ii) Gross production increases. *(1 mark)*
   (iii) Stability of the ecosystem increases. *(2 marks)*

(c) Give **two** reasons why farmland in the UK does **not** reach a climax community. *(2 marks)*
(d) Describe the techniques that you would have used in this investigation to compare the vegetation before and after myxomatosis was introduced *(5 marks)*
(Total 12 marks)

NEAB June 1995, Paper BY05, No. 6

6. The figure shows how the net primary productivity of the marine alga *Halosphaera viridis*, as measured by net oxygen evolution, varies in relation to depth in sea water at 20 °C.

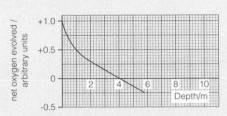

(a) (i) Describe the relationship between net oxygen evolution and depth in *H. viridis* at 20 °C.
   (ii) Account for the relationship you have described. *(4 marks)*
(b) (i) What is meant by the term *net primary productivity*?
   (ii) Why can net oxygen evolution be used to measure net primary productivity? *(4 marks)*
(c) Indicate the position of the compensation point by making a cross on or copy of the curve in the figure. Explain the reasons for your choice of position. *(2 marks)*
(d) The net primary productivity of marine algae is greater around estuaries. Suggest how a human activity might be responsible for this increase. *(4 marks)*
(Total 14 marks)

UCLES June 1994, Paper 2, No. 3

7. The diagram at the top of the next page shows the flow of energy through a woodland ecosystem. The units are megajoules per hectare per year.
   (a) Which animals are eaten by great tits? *(1 mark)*
   (b) Only 25% of the energy taken in by spiders is passed on to other animals. Describe what happens to the other 75% of the energy. *(3 marks)*
   (c) Calculate the percentage of the energy taken in by great tits which is passed on to other animals. *(1 mark)*

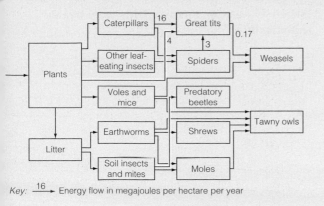

Key: $\xrightarrow{16}$ Energy flow in megajoules per hectare per year

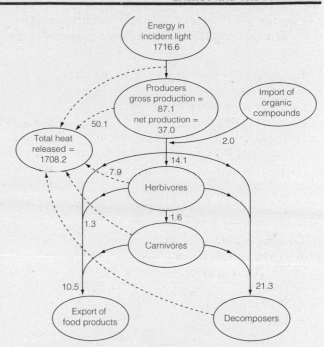

(d) Shrews are mammals, spiders are arthropods. Why do shrews pass on a much lower percentage of energy they take in than spiders do? *(1 mark)*

(Total 6 marks)

NEAB February 1995, Paper BY1, No. 5

8. The diagram below shows the energy flow for part of a large pond. All values are given in $kJ\,m^{-2}\,yr^{-1}$.

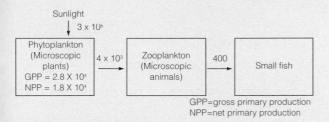

GPP=gross primary production
NPP=net primary production

(a) Name the trophic levels to which each of the following belong.
   (i) zooplankton;   *(1 mark)*
   (ii) small fish.   *(1 mark)*
(b) (i) Calculate the percentage energy from sunlight which is fixed as GPP by phytoplankton. Show your working. *(2 marks)*
   (ii) Suggest **two** reasons why not all of the incident sunlight is utilized in photosynthesis.
                            (2 marks)

(Total 6 marks)

ULEAC June 1993, Paper 1, No. 4

9. The diagram at the top of the next column shows the energy flow through a food-producing ecosystem. All figures are in $MJ\,m^{-2}\,year^{-1}$.
(a) (i) By what process is the energy in incident light converted to energy in organic molecules by the producers? *(1 mark)*
   (ii) Approximately what percentage of the energy in incident light is converted to energy in organic molecules by the producers?
                            (1 mark)
   (iii) What is meant by *net production* of the producers? *(1 mark)*

(b) With the help of the figures in the diagram explain why the export of food must be mainly in the form of producers. *(2 marks)*
(c) Give **one** example of a way in which humans might import organic compounds into this community. *(1 mark)*

(Total 6 marks)

AEB June 1992, Paper 1, No. 11

10. Carbon dioxide labelled with ^{14}C, a radioactive isotope of carbon, was supplied to a greenhouse crop of lettuce. It was later found that slugs inhabiting the greenhouse were producing labelled carbon dioxide ($^{14}CO_2$) as a waste product.
(a) Name a compound in which the ^{14}C may enter the slugs. *(1 mark)*
(b) By means of labelled arrows between the boxes, construct a flow diagram to show the processes involved in the recycling of the labelled carbon (^{14}C) in the greenhouse.

$^{14}CO_2$

DECOMPOSERS   LETTUCE

SLUGS

(3 marks)

The figure below shows the flow of energy through two different ecosystems. The arrow represents loss of energy.

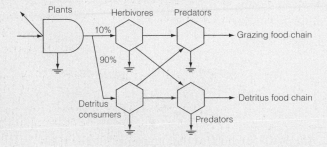

Ecosystem **A**

Ecosystem **B**

© Odum, *Ecology*, reproduced by permission of
Holt, Rhinehart & Winston, 1975

(c) For each labelled arrow (**W**, **X**, **Y**, **Z**), name a **different** process accounting for the transfer of energy. *(4 marks)*

(d) Suggest a reason for the different proportions of energy flowing through the detritus food chains in the ecosystems **A** and **B**. *(2 marks)*

(Total 10 marks)

UCLES June 1995, Paper 2, No. 3

11. *(a)* The diagram shows some of the processes in the nitrogen cycle.

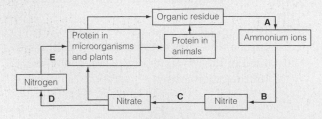

Microorganisms are involved in the stages labelled **A–E**.
Give the letter of **one** stage which involves:
   (i) nitrifying bacteria;
   (ii) denitrifying bacteria;
   (iii) nitrogen-fixing bacteria;
   (iv) saprophytic fungi. *(4 marks)*

(b) The graph shows the nitrate content at different depths in two similar fields. One field was mown and the grass removed; the other was grazed by

sheep. Otherwise the two fields were treated identically.

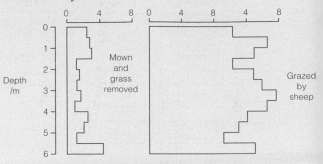

Suggest an explanation for the different nitrate 'profiles' in the two fields. *(2 marks)*

(Total 6 marks)

NEAB February 1995, Paper BY1, No. 3

12. The graph shows the United Kingdom birth rates and death rates during part of this century. (Units for the birth rate and death rate have not been provided.)

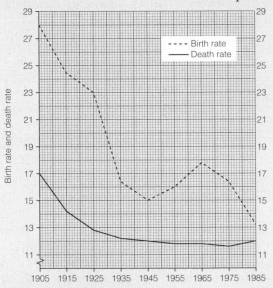

(a) In what units would the birth rate and death rate have been provided? *(2 marks)*

(b) Assuming that immigration and emigration were negligible, during which ten-year period was there the greatest change in the size of the population? Give a reason for your answer. *(2 marks)*

(c) Suggest how the birth rates and death rates between 1945 and 1985 affected the age composition of the population in 1985. Use the graph to explain your answer. *(2 marks)*

(Total 6 marks)

AEB June 1995, Paper 1, No. 4

13. Table 1 shows the natural increase in population, and the effects of migration, on the populations of England and Wales, Scotland and Northern Ireland. All figures given in the table are in thousands.

Years	Population at beginning of period	Natural increase: excess of births over deaths	Net gain (+) or net loss (−) by migration
England and Wales			
1901–11	32 528	4 044	−501
1921–31	37 887	2 236	−170
1941–51	43 758	1 957	+387
1961–71	46 196	2 720	+230
Scotland			
1901–11	4 472	543	−254
1921–31	4 882	352	−392
1941–51	5 096	339	−282
1961–71	5 184	340	−300
Northern Ireland			
1901–11	1 237	79	−65
1921–31	1 257	81	−58
1941–51	1 280	158	−67
1961–71	1 455	87	−35

TABLE 1

(a) (i) Complete the table below by stating the actual increase or decrease of the populations of England and Wales for the years 1901–11 and 1961–71.

Country	Actual increase or decrease (thousands)	
	1901–11	1961–71
England and Wales		
Scotland	289	40
Northern Ireland	14	52

(ii) Calculate the percentage change in the population of the United Kingdom (England and Wales, Scotland and Northern Ireland) for the period 1961–71. (Show your working.)
(4 marks)

(b) Summarize **four** trends revealed by the data in Table 1. (4 marks)

(c) Comment on the social consequences of population increase in the United Kingdom.
(5 marks)

Population pyramids for France and Kenya for the years 1969 and 1970, respectively, are shown in the following figure.

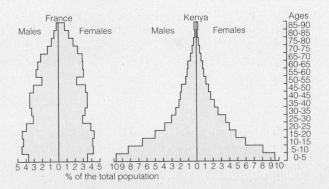

(d) Describe the population structure of the two countries as depicted in the figure. (4 marks)

(e) With reference to the population pyramid for France in the figure, state the advantages of showing males and females separately in a population pyramid. (3 marks)

(f) Account for the shape of the pyramid for the Kenyan population. (3 marks)

The structure of the population of many Caribbean countries broadly resembles that shown for Kenya in the figure. As a result of large scale unemployment (estimated to be as much as 30% in Jamaica in the mid 1970s), many people of working age migrated to Canada, the United States and Europe.

(g) Suggest **two** possible effects of this migration on the population structure of Caribbean countries such as Jamaica. (2 marks)
(Total 25 marks)

UCLES June 1992, Paper 3 (Option 4), No. 2

14. The graph shows changes in birth rate and in death rate at various stages in the human demographic transition.

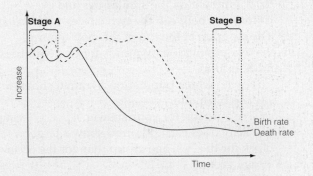

(a) Using specific examples to illustrate your answer, describe the importance of disease and food supply at Stage **A**. (6 marks)

(b) What are the main ways in which the structure of the population differs in Stages **A** and **B**?
(6 marks)
(Total 12 marks)

NEAB June 1995, Paper BY09, No. 9

15. A comparison was made of the fertility rates of women who married between the ages of 20 and 22 and those who delayed marriage until between the ages of 30 and 32.

The fertility rate is the mean number of children born to each woman in a population.

The data were taken from a contemporary population with controlled fertility and are summarized in the table on the next page.

| Age | Fertility rate | |
	Women married between ages 20 and 22 years	Women married between ages 30 and 32 years
22	0.43	–
24	0.36	–
26	0.26	–
28	0.18	–
30	0.16	–
32	0.12	0.27
34	0.10	0.21
36	0.08	0.08
38	0.06	0.06
40	0.05	0.04
42	0.04	0.03

Adapted from L Henry, *Population Analysis and Models* (Arnold, 1976)

(a) Plot the data on graph paper.   (*5 marks*)

(b) (i) Suggest what is meant by the term *controlled fertility*. (*1 mark*)

(ii) Comment on the similarities and differences between the two curves.   (*4 marks*)

(c) The diagram at the top of the next column shows two population pyramids for two countries, **A** and **B**, in 1983.

(i) State which population pyramid shows a rising birth rate.

Give a reason for your answer.   (*2 marks*)

(ii) Why does each pyramid show a larger block for the 70+ age group than for the 65 to 69 age group?   (*1 mark*)

(iii) Comment on the birth rate in country **B** between 1953 and 1973.   (*2 marks*)

(*Total 15 marks*)

ULEAC June 1995, Paper 1, No. 11

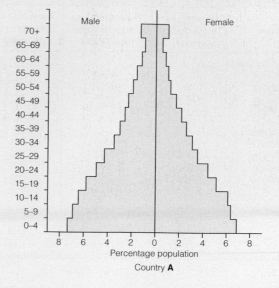

Country **A**

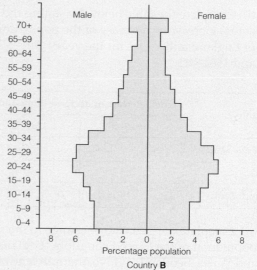

Country **B**

14 Human activities and the ecosystem

The effect of human activities on the environment is proportional to the size of the human population. As we saw in Section 13.7, the size of the human population has been rising exponentially and is presently increasing at the rate of one and a half million people each week, equivalent to 150 people per minute. The reasons for this increase are many but include more intensive forms of food production and better medical care. The latter has given many individuals a greater life expectancy and, more importantly, reduced child mortality. Reducing the mortality of individuals who have passed child-bearing age has little significance on the population, but reducing mortality among children means more people reach sexual maturity and so are able to produce offspring. The effect of this on the population is significant.

14.1 Exploitation of natural resources

Prior to the industrial revolution, the energy expended in the production of food by humans and their beasts of burden came from the food itself. Much of the crop therefore went into producing the next one. With the industrial revolution came machines which carried out ploughing, sowing, harvesting, etc. Instead of food, these machines used fossil fuels like coal, and more recently oil, as energy sources. A very much smaller proportion of the crop harvested was therefore needed to produce the next one. More food was left and a larger population could be supported. This partly explains the exponential rise in the size of the human population since the industrial revolution. The use of fertilizers, pesticides and better crops are other significant factors.

Humans are dependent for their survival on the earth's resources, and these take two forms: renewable and non-renewable.

14.1.1 Renewable resources

Renewable resources, as the name suggests, can be replaced. They are things which grow, and are materials based on plants or animals, e.g. trees and fish. They are not, however, produced in limitless quantities and their supply is ultimately exhausted if the rate at which they are removed exceeds that at which they have been produced. Renewable resources have a **sustainable yield**. This means that the amount removed (yield) is equal to, or

FOCUS

Desertification

Grazing in a desertified area

Desertification is the term used to describe severe land degradation which turns semi-arid areas into deserts. There are many possible causes but they normally involve climatic changes and/or an increase in the human population above the carrying capacity (Section 13.6.1) of the land. Extended periods of drought make plant regeneration difficult and bare soils are exposed to erosion. Increased human populations put additional pressures on the vegetation as shrubs and trees are cut for fuel and the land is overgrazed. The further loss of ground vegetation allows wind erosion to remove the soil and makes replanting difficult. Little can be done to combat these problems in the short term if there is not adequate water, although there is evidence of recovery in the longer term. In the more favourable semi-arid areas with sufficient water, skilful engineering schemes and a thorough knowledge of plant nutrition and soil structure have enabled some tree planting programmes to be successful in halting the spread of desertification.

Effect of irrigation from the Nile

less than, the rate of production. If the trees in a forest take 100 years to mature, then one hundredth of the forest may be felled each year without the forest becoming smaller. A sustainable yield can be taken indefinitely.

Whilst wood is a renewable resource, its production is not without ecological problems. Trees grow relatively slowly and so give a small yield for a given area of land. For this reason, it is not economic to use fertile farmland for their cultivation. Instead, poorer quality land typical of upland areas is often used. As conifers grow more rapidly, these softwood species are more often cultivated than indigenous hardwoods such as elm, oak, ash and beech. Large areas in Scotland, Wales and the Lake District have become **afforested**. The trees are often grown in rows and many square miles are covered by the same species. Not only does this arrangement have an unnatural appearance, but the density of the trees permits little, if anything, to grow

Deforestation

Early humans removed trees to make fires and shelters, but being nomadic they did not remain in one place long enough to have a significant effect. When they moved on the natural environment recovered. They did use fire and where this accidently got out of hand larger areas of forest may have been destroyed. Fire may also have been used to flush out prey delibrately to allow it to be captured. In these ways humans may have created some grasslands at the expense of forests, but their total impact was small.

In time humans domesticated animals such as sheep, cattle, llamas and alpacas, all of which required large areas of grassland to graze. To extend the grasslands humans deliberately burnt large areas of trees leading to greater deforestation. Clearance of forest, especially rain forests, has accelerated in recent times both as a means of opening up land for cultivating crops and for sale of hardwood timber. Probably 14% of the earth's surface was covered with rainforest when humans first evolved – now less than half this remains.

The removal of large areas of forest breaks the natural nutrient cycle. The soil is exposed to both the torrential rain and the fierce heat of the sun common in tropical regions. The wind further increases evaporation and minerals are left on the surface as the water evaporates; leaving an impervious crystalline layer – the **laterite** crust. This increases water run-off when it rains and the soil is rapidly eroded making it useless for agriculture and, as a result of changed soil chemistry, for the regeneration of the forest.

Deforestation has a number of other detrimental effects. Firstly it may cause irreversible climatic changes as the burning of forests releases huge quantities of carbon dioxide which trap heat radiation from the earth causing global warming (see Section 14.6.3 on the greenhouse effect). This causes a rise in sea level as a result of the combined effect of the thermal expansion of oceans and the melting of the polar ice-caps; a further climatic effect results from water running off the soil surface rather than being transpired from the leaves of the trees. This absence of atmospheric water reduces rainfall causing prolonged periods of drought and making desertification more likely (see Focus on page 314).

Perhaps the most significant effect of deforestation is the loss of potentially beneficial species. About half of all known species of living things inhabit the tropical rain forests – yet more have still to be discovered. Destruction of the rain forest leads to the extinction of many species and a consequent reduction in biodiversity. These species may have possessed a number of unique chemicals and genes which might have had undiscovered benefits for mankind.

The solutions to the problems of deforestation include:
1. Finding alternative sources of revenue from forests, e.g. nuts, fruits, latex and medical compounds for countries with rain forest so that their dependence on income from timber is reduced.

2. Rescheduling of these countries' debts to the developed nations so that there is less need to destroy the forests in order to provide the income to repay the debts.
3. Reducing these financial debts to developed nations, e.g. by agreeing to offset debt repayments where the money is used to conserve and protect the environment.
4. Controlled removal of timber and planned replanting so that only a sustainable yield is harvested.
5. Reduction of damage caused in the removal of timber.
6. The managed conservation of virgin rain forest with its potential to earn income from limited tourism.

Rows of larch planted on a hillside

beneath them and the forest floor is a barren place. There is little diversity of animal life within these forests. The demand for wood, not only for construction but also for paper, necessitates this intensive form of wood production.

Another renewable resource is fish, more details of which are given in Section 14.2.1.

14.1.2 Non-renewable resources

These are resources which, for all practical purposes, are not replaced as they are used. Minerals such as iron and fuels like coal and oil are non-renewable. There is a fixed quantity of these resources on the planet and in time they will be exhausted. Oil and natural gas supplies are unlikely to last more than 50 years, although much depends upon the rate at which they are burned.

Mineral and ore extraction have been carried out for a considerable time with important metals such as iron, copper, lead, tin and aluminium being mined. In theory these metals can be recycled, but in practice this is often difficult or impossible.

Fossil fuels are continually being formed, but the process is so slow compared to their rate of consumption that for all practical purposes they may be considered as a non-renewable resource. Over 80% of the world's consumption of fossil fuels occurs in developed countries, where only 25% of its population lives. The burning of fossil fuels produces a range of pollutants and even their extraction is not without its hazards. As the supply of these fuels is becoming rapidly depleted, humans have sought alternative energy sources. Nuclear power is a potentially long-term supplier of energy, but it has inherent dangers as the accident at Chernobyl in Russia in April 1986 illustrated. It is therefore treated by the public with some suspicion. Attempts continue to be made to harness wind, wave and solar energy effectively. In the end it could be **biological fuels** that humans may have to look to to supply their growing energy needs. The energy content of the organic matter produced annually by photosynthesis exceeds annual human energy consumption by 200 times. The main end-product of this photosynthesis is cellulose, most of which is unused by humans. Some of it can be burnt as wood or straw to provide heat or electricity. Much can

Did you know?

Four out of five new aluminium cans are dumped on the landscape.

FOCUS

Oil as a fossil fuel

Oil is a major fossil fuel whose demand has slowly and inexorably increased over the years; it now exceeds 30 million barrels a day. Japan, Europe and the USA are the major consumers of oil.

While oil produces less particulate pollution than coal when burnt, it usually yields more sulphur dioxide, a major atmospheric pollutant (see Section 14.6.2). It is therefore a major contributor to acid rain and the greenhouse effect. In particular, as the raw material from which petroleum fuel is distilled, it causes much urban pollution when burnt by the internal combustion engine.

Oil's main advantage as a fossil fuel is that, being liquid, it is easily transported either by pipeline or supertanker. This property however is a distinct disadvantage when oil leaks as it rapidly spreads over a wide area. Such tanker disasters as the *Exxon Valdez* (Alaska 1989), *Braer* (Shetland, 1992) and *Sea Empress* (Milford Haven, 1996) testify to this.

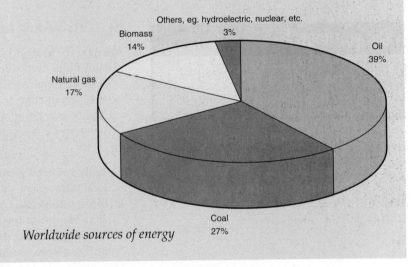

Worldwide sources of energy

Part of the Chernobyl nuclear reactor after the explosion in April 1986

be converted to other fuels like methane (CH_4), methanol (CH_3OH), ethanol (C_2H_5OH) and other gases. These processes need not use valuable food resources; the energy may be obtained from plants with no food value or from the discarded parts of food plants, estimated to total 20 million tonnes dry mass year^{-1} in the UK alone. The gasohol programme in Brazil, where sugar cane wastes are used to produce a motor vehicle fuel, is an example of this (Section 21.6.1). Wastes such as animal manure (45 million tonnes dry mass year^{-1} in the UK), human sewage (6 million tonnes dry mass year^{-1} in the UK) and other domestic and industrial wastes (30 million tonnes dry mass year^{-1} in the UK) could be converted to useful fuels like methane by biogas digesters (Section 21.6.1). These conversions can be carried out by bacteria, often as part of fermentation reactions. The day may not be far away when large industrial plants convert these wastes into useful fuels and energy forms and where crops cultivated entirely for conversion to fuels are commonplace.

14.2   Food production systems

To feed a growing world population adequately, mankind has both harvested organisms from natural ecosystems and created artificial ones. Food production systems may be classified according to the level of intensity.

Extensive food production occurs over a wide area where the area of land is large enough for the overall return from the whole of the system to be important rather than the return per unit area. While yields may not be large, the system may still be profitable because the labour requirement is low. Where the amount of capital needed to run the system is low, e.g. the Amazon Basin the output is usually small, but where the capital input is high, e.g. Canadian prairies, the output can be large.

Intensive food production involves concentrating activity in a small area. This occurs either where the labour requirement is high but the capital investment is low, e.g. the Ganges valley, or where the labour requirement is low and the capital investment is high. In both cases the yield per unit area is high.

14.2.1 Harvesting from natural ecosystems – fish

We saw in Section 14.1.1 that renewable resources all have a sustainable yield which, if exceeded, can result in the resource becoming exhausted. Where man takes a food crop from a natural ecosystem it is therefore essential that the process is carefully managed so that the populations of organisms in that ecosystem are adequately maintained. In general this is achieved by:

1. Only removing certain varieties/ages/sizes of the organism, i.e. being selective about what is taken.
2. Only removing a set quantity or **quota** of the organism - this may require international agreement to be effective;
3. Avoiding taking organisms during the breeding season and/or from breeding areas.

An example of an organism harvested from natural ecosystems is the fish. For the most part humans remove them from the seas with no attempt to replace stocks by breeding - replenishment being left to nature. As the seas have long been considered as a common resource for all, there has, in the past, been little attempt to control the amount of fish removed by each country. This lack of control presented almost no problems while fishing was carried out by small boats working locally; its impact on stocks was negligible because only a sustainable yield was removed. Modern fishing methods, however, involve large factory ships, capable of travelling thousands of miles and catching huge hauls of fish, which can be processed and frozen on board. Sonar equipment, echo sounders and even helicopters may be used in locating shoals. These methods have lead to **over-fishing**, with sustainable yields being exceeded and hence stocks depleted.

In an attempt to rectify the situation and preserve the dwindling fish stocks a series of controls have been introduced. There are some international agreements on the quotas of fish which each country can take. These are however, often bitterly

Thirty-tonne catch of fish by deep-sea trawler

disputed and are not easy to enforce. Regulations on **net sizes** restrict the size of the mesh that fishermen can use. By use of larger mesh sizes smaller, younger fish escape capture and therefore survive to sexual maturity. These fish can then spawn, thus ensuring replenishment of the stock. **Close seasons** have been introduced so that no fishing takes place during the breeding period. **Exclusion zones** have been designated, in which no fishing is permitted. These zones are often the areas in which fish regularly breed. These methods are designed to give the fish a better opportunity to breed undisturbed and so produce adequate stocks for the future. One species to have suffered from over-fishing is the North Sea herring whose numbers have become so depleted that fishing them is potentially uneconomic.

14.2.2 Fish farming – the trout

As the populations of wild fish have diminished over the past 30 to 40 years, there has been an expansion of the intensive rearing of fish under controlled conditions. While this has not yet reached the degree of domestication and intensification we see in other animals such as cattle, pigs and poultry, the practice of fish farming or **aquaculture** is on the increase and now produces over 10% of all fish harvested worldwide. This figure does however include shellfish, which make up half the amount, as well as true fish!

In Britain one fish now frequently raised in fish farms is the trout. Female trout are **stripped** of their eggs by hand and these eggs are then fertilized by the sperm from the male trout stripped in the same way. The fertilized eggs are kept in an incubator in which temperature, light and oxygen levels are controlled. Before they hatch, the developing eggs are moved from the hatchery to troughs at the fish farm. The fish are provided with food until they weigh around 5 g, at which point they are transferred to ponds for 'growing on'. As these are fed by natural rivers, any deterioration in the river water quality, e.g. change in pH, presence of pollutants, fall in oxygen level, can be fatal to the fish. It is not normally economic to heat these ponds, but other factors such as food, oxygen levels and pH are carefully controlled. The feed must be high in protein and it is often derived from cheap marine fish which are not directly used for human consumption. In this way a cheap, unpalatable fish can be converted into high quality edible ones.

14.2.3 Intensive cultivation of plants – wheat

Farming of crops which are intensively cultivated often exhibits the following features:

1. There is a high degree of mechanization and hence it is **not** labour intensive.
2. A large yield is obtained from a small area of land.
3. Genetically selected (and sometimes engineered) varieties of plant are used.
4. There is considerable use of fertilizers.
5. Pesticides are used to control unwanted species.
6. Crops are often grown as a monoculture.
7. The same crop is grown on the same area of land each year, i.e. there is continuous cropping rather than crop rotation.

Wheat is an example of a cereal crop which is intensively cultivated. To grow well, wheat needs a relatively low temperature for the seed to germinate, followed by a period of warm, bright weather for its main growth and ripening. Such conditions occur in the temperate regions of the world. Wheat's requirement for rainfall of up to 750 mm each year is also satisfied by a temperate climate such as that of North America and northern Europe. A heavy to medium, well-drained, loamy soil containing lime is also an advantage.

There are two classes of wheat. **Winter wheats** are sown in the autumn and develop before the onset of winter which temporarily checks its growth before it is renewed in the spring. Harvesting takes place during late spring and summer. Winter wheat is hardy and requires the cold of winter to initiate flowering and hence the production of a crop. **Spring wheats** are sown in early spring and mature quickly – some in as little as 90 days. They generally produce a smaller yield than winter wheats.

Land has traditionally been ploughed prior to sowing of wheat, often incorporating the remains of any previous crop. Of late, the practice of **direct drilling** has been operated. Here the remains of the previous crop is destroyed by a non-persistant herbicide such as paraquat and the seed is sown into the unploughed earth by a special drill capable of penetrating it. Energy, and hence money, is saved by not having to plough.

Once growing, the wheat has to be protected from competition from weeds and this is usually achieved by use of selective weedkillers which destroy broad-leaved species leaving narrow-leaved ones such as wheat relatively unaffected. Wheat can be affected by a variety of fungal diseases such as rusts (caused by *Puccinia* spp.), mildews (*Erysiphe* spp.), smuts (*Tilletia* spp.) and damping off disease (*Fusarium* spp.). As wheat is mostly grown as a monoculture, such diseases can spread rapidly destroying the whole crop. Fungicides may be used to control them but with resistance to these developing in many fungal pathogens, attention has turned to developing genetic varieties of wheat which are resistant to these diseases. Fertilizers rich in nitrogen, phosphates and potassium are added to the soil to ensure high yields.

Harvesting takes place in dry conditions by use of large combine harvesters which cut, thresh and then pour the grain into a waiting truck or trailer – all in one operation. This high degree of mechanisation allows rapid and economic harvesting. The grain can then be stored under controlled temperature and humidity conditions.

The economically efficient growing and harvesting of wheat is highly dependent upon fossil fuels such as oil which is used, as petrol or diesel oil, to drive the machinery used in ploughing, sowing, spreading of fertilizers and pesticides, harvesting and transporting the grain. In the past these processes were carried out by humans and various domesticated animals such as the horse. A considerable amount of the yield had to be kept to feed both species with the result that less was available for sale, and hence consumption by others. With the energy now obtained from fossil fuels, almost the whole of the crop goes onto the market to feed others.

Did you know?

Between 1945 and 1995 oil used by farmers in the USA increased four-fold and crop yields increased three-fold.

14.2.4 Intensive rearing of animals, e.g. pigs

Pigs are intensively reared for their meat which is either eaten soon after slaughter or is preserved by freezing salting and/or smoking to give ham, gammon and bacon, which can be kept longer before being consumed. The pig has proved a useful animal for the mass production of meat because it can:

1. Be reared intensively in small areas or extensively ranging free over a larger region.
2. Eat a diverse mixture of foods, from specialized feed to scavenging roots etc. for itself.
3. Produce 10 or more young in a single litter.
4. Have two litters each year.
5. Grow rapidly in a short period of time.
6. Tolerate a wide range of habits and environments.
7. Have its meat preserved in a variety of different ways and stored for some time before consumption.

Free range pigs are usually kept in fields with small huts for shelter and they forage for their own food as well as having their diet supplemented by that provided by the farmer. Most pigs in the UK are however intensively reared in special housing units. These units are heated and a specially prepared diet is provided. The disadvantage of raising pigs in this way is that proximity may result in any infections that arise spreading rapidly to the whole group. Respiratory illnesses are particularly common in the closed, humid conditions. For this reason the pigs are often given antibiotics to prevent or control such infections. Another problem is the disposal of waste and in large units the pigs may be kept on slats through which the faeces and urine drop to be mechanically removed from beneath.

The process of birth of a pig is known as **farrowing** and the young piglet is at risk from being crushed by its mother, the **sow**. For this reason the sow is often contained in a crate, or by a horizontal bar, to prevent her injuring her young. In the confined space, the piglets are prone to fight by biting one another and so the piglets may have their canine teeth clipped and their tails cut back to avoid damage. Injections of iron are given to prevent anaemia. The temperature, light and ventilation need to be carefully controlled to increase the piglets' chances of survival.

The suckling pigs are also fed dry food continuously so that they can consume as much as they want and to encourage them to wean quickly. Then the sow may resume her oestrous cycle and be fertilized by the boar, so producing another litter as soon as possible. Male pigs which are not required for breeding purposes are sometimes castrated by their second week to ensure that they are more docile and the meat is more tender without the unpleasant taint that otherwise results.

Modern production from pigs is designed to be economically efficient through the use of fossil fuels as a source of energy rather than human labour which is more expensive. Accordingly the removal of wastes is carried out mechanically. It is also more economic to use fossil fuels to heat the pig housing units than to leave the animals to roam free. This may seem illogical, but an animal left outside in all weathers and temperatures will lose much of the energy in the food it eats in maintaining its body temperature. More food is needed to increase the weight of a pig by a given amount than would be the case for an animal kept in the warmer controlled conditions of a pig unit. Provided the cost of fossil fuels needed to heat such a unit is less than the additional feed to rear a free range pig to the same weight, the units are more economical. Such calculations are dependent on the volatile price of oil and other fossil fuels and the situation can rapidly change, making free-range methods more economic. There is also a growing consumer preference for free-range produce as well as public concern about the methods used in the intensive rearing of pigs, especially the use of sow crates. Between them these forces are persuading an increasing number of farmers to consider free range rearing of pigs as an economic alternative.

14.2.5 Genetic techniques in agriculture and horticulture

We have seen that food production within ecosystems can be maintained at a high level by the intensive farming of organisms such as wheat, fish and pigs. Genetic understanding is used to augment the processes that have been described in three main ways, namely by:

1. Selective breeding.
2. Genetic engineering.
3. The production of genetically identical organisms.

Selective breeding is discussed in Section 9.3 and genetic engineering in Section 5.7.

The production of identical crop organisms allows the beneficial features of one individual to be replicated perfectly thus giving a consistent product. Organisms produced by this means are called **clones** and while their production has certain advantages their widespread use may greatly reduce the number of alleles in a population of a species and so reduce the potential for exploiting variation through selective breeding.

In plants, genetically identical offspring are produced naturally by a process known as **vegetative propagation**. In general it entails the separation of a part of the parent plant which then develops into an individual. Almost any part – root, stem, leaf or bud – may serve the purpose. They are often highly specialized for the task and bear little resemblance to the original plant organ from which they evolved. Potatoes, an example of a crop produced by vegetative means, are in fact the modified stem of the potato plant. The artificial production of genetically identical plants is achieved by **micropropagation** (see Focus on page 115).

In mammals, cloning involves splitting apart the cells of an embryo at an early stage of development when all cells are still identical. Each individual cell can then be implanted into the uterus of a female of the species to continue its development.

14.2.6 Artificial control of reproduction by hormones

Modern mass food production makes considerable use of hormones and growth substances in controlling both the reproduction and growth of organisms.

Plant growth substances are chemicals produced in plants which accelerate, inhibit, or otherwise modify growth. There are five groups of growth substances generally recognized: **auxins**, **gibberellins**, **cytokinins**, **abscisic acid** and **ethene**. The commercial applications of these are described in the Focus on the following page.

Commercial applications of synthetic growth regulators

As the main function of plant hormones is to control growth, it is hardly surprising that they, or rather their synthetic derivatives, have been extensively used in crop production.

Synthetic auxins such as 2,4-dichlorophenoxyacetic acid (2,4-D) and 2,4,5-trichlorophenoxyacetic acid (2,4,5-T) are used as **selective weedkillers**. When sprayed on crops, they have a more significant effect on broad-leaved (dicotyledonous) plants than on narrow-leaved (monocotyledonous) ones. They so completely disrupt the growth of broad-leaved plants that they die, while narrow-leaved ones at most suffer a temporary reduction in growth. As cereal crops are narrow-leaved and most of their competing weeds are broad-leaved, the application of these hormone weedkillers is of much commercial value. They are also extensively used domestically for controlling weeds in lawns. Other details of these weedkillers are given in Section 14.2.8. Another synthetic auxin, naphthaleneacetic acid (NNA), is used to increase fruit yields. If sprayed on trees, it helps the fruit to set naturally, or in some species causes them to set without the initial stimulus of fertilization (parthenocarpy). This usually results in seedless fruits which may be a commercial advantage. Gibberellins extracted from fungal cultures are used commercially in the same way.

Auxins are the active constituent of rooting powders. The development of roots is initiated when the ends of cuttings are dipped in these compounds. Cytokinins will delay leaf senescence. They are therefore sometimes used commercially to keep the leaves of crops, like lettuce, fresh and free from yellowing after they have been picked. Both gibberellins and cytokinins are sometimes applied to seeds to help break dormancy and so initiate rapid germination. The longer a seed remains ungerminated in the soil, the more vulnerable it is to being eaten, e.g. by birds.

Abscisic acid may be sprayed on fruit crops to induce the fruits to fall so they can be harvested together. Ethene is applied to tomatoes and citrus fruits in order to stimulate ripening.

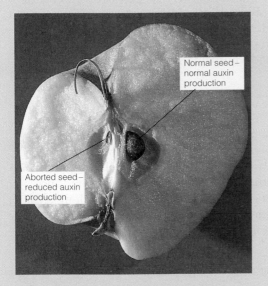

Normal seed – normal auxin production

Aborted seed – reduced auxin production

Apple sectioned to show effects of auxin production

Synthetic animal hormones are used in food production in a number of ways. Growth hormones may be given to animals to increase meat production and reproductive hormones can be used to produce embryos for transplantation or to increase milk production, e.g. in cows (see Focus on page 324).

14.2.7 Use of fertilizers in food production

In natural systems the minerals which a plant removes from the soil during its growth are returned to the soil when the plant is broken down on its death. As the plant is normally broken down at, or around, the place where it grew, the nutrient level of the soil remains stable. Where crops are concerned, the plants are removed and transported to destinations a long way, possibly thousands of miles, from their point of origin. While the nutrients are ultimately released on the breakdown of the urine, faeces and dead remains of the consumer of the plant, these are rarely returned directly to the land. To maintain the nutrient levels of the soil, **inorganic fertilizers** are spread on the land. These comprise largely the three elements, nitrogen, phosphorus

FOCUS

BST

The hormone bovine somatotrophin (BST) controls lactation in cows by increasing the number of cells in the mammary glands. When the genetically engineered version is injected into the animals, their milk production can increase by up to 20%. The use of BST was approved by the US Food and Drug Administration (FDA) in November 1993 who declared milk produced from cows given the artificial hormone to be indistinguishable from other milk. Its use is banned in Europe.

Opponents are concerned because the incidence of mastitis among cows given the hormone is 79% higher than normal. They fear that this will lead farmers to use more antibiotics which could stay in the milk and eventually reduce the effectiveness of antibiotics against bacteria that affect humans. Opposition groups have threatened to boycott the milk but the FDA has ruled that it need not carry special labels and neither can other milk simply be declared 'hormone-free'. The introduction of such genetically engineered products without the implementation of strict labelling regulations concerns a number of 'pure food' campaign groups.

Did you know?

World phosphate use has been rising by 4% a year since 1950 and if this growth continues known reserves will be exhausted by 2050.

and potassium in some form and are dervied from minerals mined in various regions of the world. **Organic fertilizers** comprise the dead and decaying remains of plants or animals. Research suggests that a combination of both organic and inorganic fertilizers gives the greatest yield in the long term.

The advantages and disadvantages of organic and inorganic fertilizers are given in Table 14.1.

TABLE 14.1 **The advantages and disadvantages of using organic and inorganic fertilizers**

	ADVANTAGES	DISADVANTAGES
Organic	• Supply all the necessary nutrients for growth • Increase water retention of the soil. • Maintain the air content of the soil both directly and by encouraging earthworms • Effective over a long period • Improve the crumb structure of the soil • Improve drainage and so help prevent waterlogging	• Not easily obtained • Bulky and therefore expensive to transport and apply • Slow acting and therefore not effective in a single season • Difficult to handle • Relatively expensive
Inorganic	• Relatively light and therefore easy to transport and apply • Quick acting • Easy to handle • Relatively cheap • Easily obtained	• Do not improve the physical characteristics of the soil • Can be easily removed by leaching • Need to be regularly applied • Run-off can cause pollution of water courses

The polluting effects caused by the run-off of inorganic fertilizers is dealt with in section 14.7.2.

14.2.8 Use of pesticides in food production

It is difficult to define what exactly is a 'pest', but it is generally accepted to be an organism which is in competition with humans for food or soil space, or is potentially hazardous to health. It may even be an organism which is simply a nuisance and so causes annoyance. Pesticides are poisonous chemicals which kill pests, and they are named after the pests they destroy; hence insecticides kill insects, fungicides kill moulds and other fungi, rodenticides kill rodents such as rats and mice, and herbicides kill weeds. Unlike other pollutants, where their poisonous nature is an unfortunate and unwanted property, pesticides are quite deliberately produced and dispersed in order to exploit their toxicity.

An ideal pesticide should have the following properties:

1. It should be **specific**, in that it is toxic only to the organisms at which it is directed and harmless to all others.

2. It should **not persist** but be unstable enough to break down into harmless substances. It is therefore temporary and has no long-term effect.

3. It should **not accumulate** either in specific parts of an organism or as it passes along food chains.

Pesticides have been used for some time. A mixture of copper sulphate and lime, called Bordeaux mixture, was used over 100 years ago to control fungal diseases of vines. The problem is that in an attempt to produce food more economically and control human disease, pesticides have been used in large amounts in most regions of the world. A summary of some major pesticides is given in Table 14.2.

TABLE 14.2 **Some major pesticides**

Name of pesticide	Type of pesticide	Additional information
Inorganic pesticides Calomel (mercuric chloride)	Fungicide	Used for dusting seeds to control transmission of fungal diseases
Copper compounds (e.g. copper sulphate)	Fungicide and algicide	One of the first pesticides ever used was Bordeaux mixture (copper sulphate + lime)
Sodium chlorate	Herbicide	Used to clear paths of weeds. Persistent, although not very poisonous
Organic pesticides Organo-phosphorus compounds (e.g. malathion and parathion)	Insecticides	Although very toxic they are not persistent and therefore not harmful to other animals if used responsibly. May kill useful insects such as bees, however
Organo-chlorine compounds (e.g. DDT, BHC, dieldrin, aldrin)	Insecticides	DDT is fairly persistent and accumulates in fatty tissue as well as along food chains. Aldrin may persist for more than 10 years. Resistance to them is now common. Most kill by inhibiting the action of cholinesterase
Hormones (e.g. 2,4-D, 2,4,5-T)	Herbicides	Selective weedkillers which kill broad-leaved species. Stimulate auxin production and so disrupt plant growth. May contain a dangerous impurity – dioxin

Weed control. Sugar beet crop in which weeds on the right have been controlled by chemicals and those on the left are untreated

Did you know?

British gardeners spread, on average, more than £1m worth of pesticides a week.

Most pesticides are not persistent. Warfarin, for example, readily kills any rodent which eats it, but as it is quickly broken down inside the rodent's body, it is harmless to anything which eats the corpse, e.g. maggots. Some pesticides, dichlorodiphenyl-trichlorethane (DDT), for example, are unfortunately persistent. First synthesized in 1874, its insecticidal properties were not appreciated until 1939. It was used extensively during the Second World War, in which it played a vital role in controlling lice, fleas and other carriers of disease. It was subsequently used in killing mosquitoes and so helped control malaria. Not only is DDT persistent, it also accumulates along food chains. If, for example, garden plants are sprayed with it in order to control greenfly, some of the flies will survive despite absorbing the DDT. These may then be eaten by tits who further concentrate the chemical in their bodies, especially in the fat tissues where it accumulates. If a number of tits, each containing DDT, are consumed by a predator, e.g. a sparrowhawk, the DDT builds up in high enough concentrations to kill the bird. Even where the concentrations are not sufficient to kill, they may still cause harm. It is known that DDT can alter the behaviour of birds, sometimes preventing them building proper nests. It may cause them to become infertile and can result in the egg shells being so thin that they break when the parent bird sits on them during incubation. In Britain these effects led to a marked decline in the 1950s and 60s of populations of peregrine falcons, sparrowhawks, golden eagles and other predatory birds. As a consequence, Britain, along with many other countries, restricted the use of DDT with the result that populations of these birds have now recovered.

Owing to the persistence of DDT, it remains in the environment despite the death of the organism containing it. With over one million tonnes of the chemical having already been used it now occurs in all parts of the globe and is found in almost all animals. Indeed, many humans contain more DDT than is permitted by many countries in food for human consumption.

With such widespread use of DDT, it is not surprising that selection pressure has resulted in insect varieties which are able to break it down and so render it useless. The development of **resistance** is now common among insect disease vectors like mosquitoes, and has set back prospects of eradicating malaria.

Herbicides make up 40% of the world's total pesticide production, and in developed countries the figure exceeds 60%. Some herbicides like paraquat kill all vegetation. While paraquat is highly poisonous it is rapidly broken down by bacteria and rendered harmless. Other weedkillers are selective, destroying broad-leaved plants (mostly dicotyledons) but not narrow-leaved ones (mostly monocotyledons). As most cereal crops are narrow-leaved and the weeds that compete with them are broad-leaved, such selective weedkillers are extensively used. They are similar to the plant's natural hormones, auxins, and as such are quickly broken down and rendered harmless. The two best known examples are 2,4-dichlorophenoxyacetic acid (2,4-D) and 2,4,5-trichlorophenoxyacetic acid (2,4,5-T). In the production of 2,4,5-T an impurity called **dioxin** is formed. Dioxin is one of the most toxic compounds known, a single gram being sufficient to kill in excess of 5000 humans. Even in minute quantities it may cause cancer, a skin disorder called chloracne and abnormalities in unborn babies. The chemical gained notoriety when used as a defoliant by the US army during the Vietnam war in the 1970s. It was a constituent of 'Agent Orange', 50 million dm³ (litres) of which were sprayed over jungle areas to cause the leaves to drop so that enemy camps could be revealed. The dioxin produced physical and mental defects in children born in the area, as well as in those born to American servicemen working in the region. In 1976, an accident at a factory in Seveso, Italy, resulted in the release of dioxin into the atmosphere. Despite evacuation of the area, thousands of people suffered with chloracne, miscarriages, cancer and fetal abnormalities.

14.2.9 Biological Control

The effect of the predator–prey relationship in regulating populations has been exploited by humans as a method of controlling various pests. Biological control is a means of managing populations of organisms which compete for human food or damage the health of humans or livestock. The aim is to bring the population of a pest down to a tolerable level by use of its natural enemies. A beneficial organism (the **agent**) is deployed against an undesirable one (the **target**). A typical situation is where a natural predator of a harmful organism is introduced in order to reduce its numbers to a level where they are no longer harmful. The aim is not to eradicate the pest; indeed, this could be counter-productive. If the pest was reduced to such an extent that it no longer provided an adequate food source for the predator, then the predator in its turn would be eradicated. The few remaining pests could then increase their population rapidly, in the absence of the controlling agent. The ideal situation is where the controlling agent and the pest exist in balance with one another, but at a level where the pest has no major detrimental effect.

TABLE 14.3   **Some examples of biological control**

Target (pest)	Harmful effects of pest	Control agent	Method of action
Scale insect (*Icerya*)	Kills citrus fruit trees	Ladybird (*Rodolia*)	Ladybird uses scale insect as a food source
Codling moth (*Crypto-phlebia*)	Ruins orange crop	African wasp (*Tricho-gamatoidea*)	Wasp parasitizes moth eggs
Mosquito (*Anopheles*)	Vector of malarial parasite (*Plasmo-dium*)	Hydra (*Chloro-hydra*)	Hydra is a predator of mosquito larvae
Snail (*Biomphal-aria*)	Vector of *Schistosoma* which causes bilharzia	Snail (*Marisa*)	Control agent snail is predatory on the snail vector
Prickly pear (*Opuntia*)	Makes land difficult to farm by restricting access	Cochineal insect (*Dactylo-pius*)	*Opuntia* is a food source for the insect
Larvae of many butterflies and moths	Consume the foliage of many economic-ally important plants	Bacterium (HD-1 strain of *Bacillus thuringien-sis*)	Bacterium parasitizes the larvae of moths and butterflies

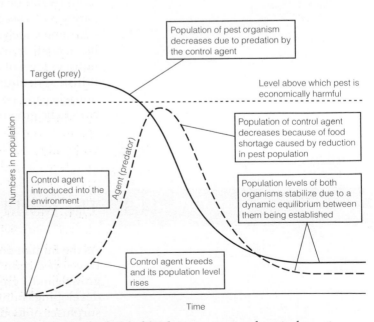

Fig. 14.1 *General relationships between pest and control agent populations in biological control*

Biological control was originally used against insect and weed pests of economically important crops. In more recent times its use has broadened to include medically important pests such as snails and even vertebrate pests. In the same way the type of controlling agent has become more diverse and the following are now employed: bacteria, viruses, fungi, protozoans, nematodes, insects and even amphibians and birds. These agents are sometimes used in combination. Certain nematodes carry bacteria which are deadly to many insects and their larvae. These nematodes have been nicknamed 'biological exocets' because of their ability to seek out their insect larvae hosts. The nematodes enter the insects' bodies releasing a fatal cargo of bacteria. Insects controlled in this way include the black vine weevil. Table 14.3 lists some examples of biological control.

One interesting and unusual form of biological control takes place in Australia. Cattle dung there presents a problem because two major pests, the bush fly and buffalo fly, lay their eggs in it. In addition, the dung carries the eggs of worms which parasitize the cattle. The indigenous dung beetles which are adapted to coping with the fibrous wastes of marsupials are ineffective in burying the soft dung of cattle. The introduction of an African species of dung beetle, which bury the dung within forty-eight hours, has been effective in controlling the flies. By burying the dung before the flies can mature, or before the parasitic worm can develop and reinfect cattle, they have controlled the populations of these pests.

14.2.10 Crop rotation

The principle of crop rotation is based on the fact that different crops remove different minerals from the soil and each has its own diseases and pests which may remain dormant in the soil for some years. By growing a different crop on a particular area of land each year, soil fertility may be maintained and the risk of disease reduced. A typical rotation might involve four different crops over four years, e.g. wheat, root crop (such as turnip), barley and a seed crop comprising grass and clover. As clover is a legume which is able to take nitrogen from the air and incorporate it into the soil as nitrate, this crop improves the nutrient level of the soil. Crop rotations are rare in modern British agriculture, which uses fertilizers to maintain soil nutrients and pesticides to reduce disease, thus allowing one crop to be grown continuously.

14.3　The world food problem

As the human population has increased so has the need for food. Developed countries have had a slower rate of population growth and a greater increase in food production than the developing countries over the past 40 years. This has led to surpluses of food in developed countries and deficits in developing ones. The problem is therefore not only one of food production but also of distribution.

14.3.1 Increasing food production in developing countries

High yielding plant varieties – High yielding plant varieties (HYVs) were first developed in Mexico with the production of hybrid varieties of wheat and maize. These varieties were more resistant to disease and climatic conditions and produced more seed. Together these factors doubled the yield of maize and trebled those of wheat. The IR-8 variety of rice, later developed in the Philippines, produced a six-fold increase in yields, but as Table 14.4 shows the use of HYVs has its problems too.

TABLE 14.4   **Beneficial and adverse effects of high yielding varieties of plants**

Beneficial	Adverse
Yields are increased up to four-fold	To obtain high yields large quantities of fertilizers are needed
Varieties can withstand wind and other climatic conditions better	They are less adapted to drought and irrigation is often required
Being shorter, the plants do not fall over as they mature and are more easily harvested	With shorter stems, less straw is produced for use as bedding or thatching
They ripen more quickly allowing more than one crop to be gathered in a season	They are more susceptible to weeds and disease and other pests and hence require large quantities of pesticides to control them
They can be grown in a wider range of environments	Being hybrid varieties new seed rather than that from the crop, is needed each year
	The food yield is sometimes not as palatable

Use of fertilizers – Replenishment of soil nutrients removed when harvesting crops is important to any variety of plant but the high yielding ones even more so. In addition many infertile soils may be brought back into agricultural production through the use of fertilizers, especially those which might naturally have been fertilized by the floodwater and silt from rivers such as the Nile, but which modern irrigation schemes have now prevented. One problem with using fertilizers has been the pollution caused by run-off (see Section 14.7.2).

Use of pesticides – These have contributed to greater production by diminishing or erradicating disease-causing and competing organisms such as fungi and weeds. High yielding varieties, being more vulnerable to disease, require pesticide use to be especially effective.

Increased mechanization and use of technology – Machinery, often highly automated has been used to plough, sow and harvest crops, to control feeding, light and temperature in intensive animal rearing systems, to manufacture and apply pesticides and fertilizers, to transport and store crops under controlled conditions and to maintain irrigation and effluent systems. The energy, coming as it does, from fossil fuels has reduced labour overheads and hence increased the proportion of the crop available for market.

Our disappearing soil

The soil available for agriculture is diminishing. Apart from land which is used to accommodate our ever-expanding cities extra is lost as a consequence of pollution. Much more disappears as a result of poor management of farmland or its wasteful use. Badly designed irrigation schemes have increased salt levels of some soils to the point where they can no longer support plant growth. Water extracted from rivers and lakes has lowered their levels to such an extent that the surrounding land has been turned into deserts. The Aral Sea in the former USSR is a case in point.

Perhaps the biggest pollution problem is that of soil erosion. It is estimated that each year 75 billion tonnes of soil worldwide are either washed or blown away. In parts of Jamaica up to 400 tonnes are lost from each hectare of land each year. Even in the UK the average figure is 17 tonnes per hectare per year .

Crop rotation and intercropping – Crop rotation can help maintain the fertility of the soil and protect crops from disease (see Section 14.2.10). Intercropping is based on a similar principle, with two or more crops being grown together, but frequently harvested at different times. Not only can two yields be taken from the same space but, if one crop is a leguminous plant, the nitrogen content of the soil will be improved. There may also be some natural control of weeds as little soil space remains for these to establish themselves.

Increasing the amount of productive land e.g. by irrigation – Some land in developing countries has been brought into food production by irrigation, fertilization, reclamation or drainage schemes. Paradoxically, areas which are very fertile and so highly productive are becoming densely populated with the result that the land is being taken out of production because it is needed for houses, industry and roads.

14.3.2 Food surpluses and redistribution

Farming in developed countries has used fertilizers, pesticides and mechanization to increase productivity. To ensure a rich harvest of food, governments have offered tax incentives to farmers, paid subsidies to them and guaranteed a minimum price for their produce (see Figs. 14.2 and 14.3). So successful have these methods been that there has been overproduction of certain foods in Europe and North America. As prices are guaranteed it is not possible to let the lack of demand for the produce force down the price to a level which developing countries can afford. Instead the food is held in stores colloquially known as 'mountains' or 'lakes' depending on their consistency.

The cost of storage alone is vast – nearly £1 million per day in 1986 to store excess European butter. To reduce the surplus in the short term the EEC sold the butter cheaply to less well-off groups in the community as well as to countries such as the, then, USSR. In the longer term it reduced milk production by

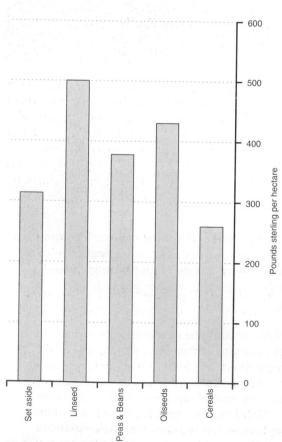

Fig. 14.2 Subsidies for crop growing (1995)

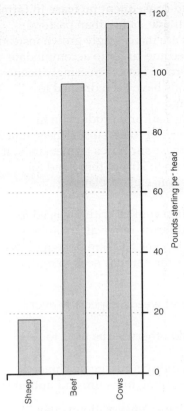

Pounds sterling per head

Fig. 14.3 Subsidies for livestock (1995)

nearly 10% in three years. These remedial actions were not without their own problems: the sale of butter to the USSR – a country many saw as a potential enemy – was politically unpopular and reducing milk production put dairy farmers out of work and led to the slaughter of some 5 million cattle. The action was at least effective with a 1 400 000 tonne butter mountain in 1986 being reduced to 500 000 tonnes in 1989. Beef mountains and wine lakes have been similarly reduced with cereal production being cut back by paying farmers to leave potentially productive land idle – a scheme known as **set-aside** (£340 per hectare in 1995).

With surpluses in some countries and deficits in others, the solution would seem a simple one of redistribution. While the problem of transporting vast amounts of food is not insuperable, the cultural, political and economic barriers are far harder to overcome.

Even at highly subsidized rates, the cost of importing food is beyond the financial means of many developing countries; they therefore borrow money from developed countries to pay for it. To repay this debt they often grow crops with a high value abroad and export them for currency – **cash crops**. In doing so they use land which might otherwise produce food for their own population. As they are producing less home-grown food their dependency on importing it from the developed nations increases thus exacerbating the problem, especially as the more of the cash crop they produce the more the price falls.

14.4 The impact of agriculture on the environment

We all need to eat to live and with an ever increasing population the need to produce sufficient food to meet the growing needs of the world's population has led to intensification of agricultural practices as described in the earlier sections of this chapter. Land is artificially prevented from reaching its climax vegetation through regular grazing, ploughing and the use of fertilizers and pesticides. In the United Kingdom agricultural food production has been doubled over the last 40 years. This has been achieved in a number of ways:

1. Improved strains of plant and animal species – Through artificial selection and genetic engineering the productivity of most crop plants and livestock animals has been increased.

2. Greater use of fertilizers and pesticides – There has been almost a ten-fold increase in the use of artificial fertilizers over the past 50 years.

3. Increased mechanization and use of biotechnology – There have been major technological advances in machines used to sow, fertilize, harvest and transport crops as well as advances in the use of technology in controlling the harvesting and the conditions under which crops are stored. Animals are often reared under the optimum conditions for growth which are carefully controlled. There has been a consequent reduction in the number of farm labourers employed.

Did you know?

Satellites show that 10 000 km of hedgerow disappeared between 1990 and 1993 in Britain.

Farmland with small fields and many hedgerows

Large area of arable land without hedgerows

4. Changes in farm practices and consequent increase in farm size – There has been a trend to arable, rather than pastoral, farming. Sugar beet and oilseeds are increasingly grown instead of turnips and rye. Fields have become larger to accommodate modern machinery and so hedgerows have increasingly been removed. Wetland areas and ponds have been drained to increase the area of productive land.

Such has been the success of agricultural production in Europe that there are now surpluses of foods such as beef, dairy products and cereals. To reduce these surpluses farmers may, if they choose, be paid to **set-aside** up to 20% of their land for purposes other than food production, e.g. for planting woodland.

The demands of agriculture often conflict with the need for conservation. One example is **hedgerow removal**. It has been estimated that each year in the UK some 8000 km of hedgerows are removed. On the one hand the farmer may seek to remove hedges because:

1. They harbour pests, diseases and weeds, especially over winter.
2. They take up space which could otherwise be used to cultivate a crop.
3. They impede use of and accessibility for large machinery.
4. They reduce crop yields by absorbing moisture and nutrients.

On the other hand the hedges have conservation value:

1. They are a habitat for a rich and diverse variety of plant and animal species.
2. They produce food for many birds and other animals which do not actually live in the hedgerows.
3. They act as corridors along which many species move and disperse themselves.
4. They act as wind-breaks, often preventing soil erosion by the wind.
5. They add diversity and interest to the landscape.

14.5 Pollution

Pollution is a difficult term to define. It has its origins in the Latin word *polluere* which means 'contamination of any feature of the environment'. Any definition of pollution should take account of the fact that:

1. It is not merely the addition of a substance to the environment but its addition at a rate faster than the environment can accommodate it. There are natural levels of chemicals such as arsenic and mercury in the environment, but only if these levels exceed certain critical values can they be considered pollutants.

2. Pollutants are not only chemicals; forms of energy like heat, sound, α-particles, β-particles and X-rays may also be pollutants.

3. To be a pollutant, a material has to be potentially harmful to life. In other words, some harmful effect must be recognized.

Using the above criteria, it is arguable that there is such a thing as natural pollution. We know for example that sulphur dioxide, one product of the combustion of fossil fuels, is a pollutant, and yet 70% of the world's sulphur dioxide is the result of volcanic activity. To avoid 'natural pollution' some scientists like to add a fourth criterion, namely that pollution is only the result of human activities.

14.6   Air pollution

Air pollution from a coking plant

The layer of air which supports life extends about 8 km above the earth's surface and is known as the **troposphere**. While there may be small localized variations in the levels of gases in air, its composition overall remains remarkably constant. Almost all air pollutants are gases added to this mixture. Air pollution has existed since humans first used fire but it is only since the industrial revolution in the nineteenth century that its effects have become significant. Almost all air pollution is the result of burning fossil fuels, either in the home, by industry or in the internal combustion engine.

14.6.1 Smoke

Smoke is tiny particles of soot (carbon) suspended in the air, which are produced as a result of burning fossil fuels, particularly coal and oil. It has a number of harmful effects:

1. When breathed in, smoke may blacken the alveoli, causing damage to their delicate epithelial linings. It also aggravates respiratory ailments, e.g. bronchitis.

2. While it remains suspended in the air, it can reduce the light intensity at ground level. This may lower the overall rate of photosynthesis.

3. Deposits of smoke, or more particularly soot and ash, may coat plant leaves, reducing photosynthesis by preventing the light penetrating or by blocking stomata.

4. Smoke, soot and ash become deposited on clothes, cars and buildings. These are costly to clean.

14.6.2 Sulphur dioxide

Fossil fuels contain between 1 and 4% sulphur and as a result around 30 million tonnes of sulphur dioxide is emitted from the chimneys of Europe each year. Much of this combines readily with other chemicals like water and ammonia and is quickly deposited. It may increase soil fertility in areas where sulphates are deficient, or even help to control diseases such as blackspot of roses by acting as a fungicide. Nevertheless its effects, especially in high concentrations, are largely harmful:

1. It causes irritation of the respiratory system and damage to the epithelial lining of the alveoli. It can also irritate the conjunctiva of the eye.

TABLE 14.5   **Tolerance of moss and lichen species to sulphur dioxide**

Annual average sulphur dioxide concentration in $\mu g\,m^{-3}$	Species tolerant and therefore able to survive
Greater than 60	*Lecanora conizaeoides* (lichen) *Lecanora dispersa* (lichen) *Ceratodon purpureus* (moss) *Funaria hygrometrica* (moss)
Less than 60	*Parmelia saxatilis* (lichen) *Parmelia fulginosa* (lichen)
Less than 45	*Grimma pulvinata* (lichen) *Hypnum cupressiforme* (moss)

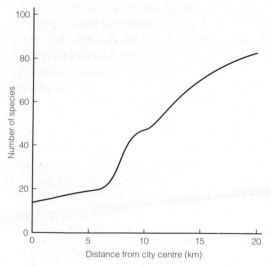

Fig. 14.4 *Number of lichen species as one moves from the centre of Newcastle upon Tyne*

TABLE 14.6 **Sources of acidifying gases**

Source	Percentage contribution	
	Nitrogen oxides	Sulphur dioxide
Motor vehicles	45	1
Power stations	37	71
Industry	12	19
Domestic	3	5
Other sources	3	4

PROJECT

The fungus *Rhytisma acerinum* forms black spots on sycamore leaves

Find out if this fungus is an air pollution indicator by comparing its incidence at varying distances from the centre of a town.

2. It reduces the growth of many plants, e.g. barley, wheat, lettuce, while others such as lichens may be killed.

The tolerance of lichen and moss species to sulphur dioxide is very variable and makes them useful **indicator species** for measuring sulphur dioxide pollution. Table 14.5 shows the tolerance of some mosses and lichen species to sulphur dioxide.

As one moves from the centre of a major industrial city like Newcastle upon Tyne, the concentration of sulphur dioxide falls rapidly. At the same time the number of species of lichen and moss increases. In the centre only the most tolerant species are found, whereas on the outskirts less tolerant ones also occur (Fig. 14.4). Using Table 14.5, we can see that if an area of a city possesses *Lecanora dispersa* and *Funaria hygrometrica* but none of the other species, then the levels of sulphur dioxide must exceed $60 \, \mu g \, m^{-3}$.

If all species in the table are present, the sulphur dioxide level must be less than $45 \, \mu g \, m^{-3}$.

Much of the sulphur dioxide released into the atmosphere returns to earth as gas or minute particles (dry deposition) but about one third dissolves in rain water. The sulphur dioxide and water combine to form sulphurous and sulphuric acids. The rain therefore has a low pH and is known as **acid rain**. The oxides of nitrogen are other pollutants which contribute to acid rain. Indeed, while the contribution of sulphur dioxide has diminished due to the industrial recession, that from nitrogen oxides has increased due to the increase in motor vehicle use. Table 14.6 shows the relative amounts of acidifying gases from different sources. Due to the prevailing winds, much of the sulphur dioxide from Europe, including that from Britain, is carried over Scandinavia. It is here that acid rain causes the greatest problems. Coniferous trees are particularly vulnerable and considerable damage has been caused to some forests. Lakes in the region are extremely acid and many species within them have been killed, largely as a result of the accumulation of aluminium leached from soils as a result of acid rain. This affects aquatic organisms' gills and their osmoregulatory mechanisms. Many countries have committed themselves to reducing the level of sulphur dioxide emissions, largely through changing to 'cleaner' fuels such as natural gas or by fitting desulphurization units to remove sulphur dioxide from the flue gases at power stations.

14.6.3 Carbon dioxide

Carbon dioxide is formed during the respiration of organisms, and by the burning of fossil fuels. That produced as a result of respiration is taken up by plants during photosynthesis, ensuring it does not accumulate. The additional carbon dioxide produced in the burning of fossil fuels has caused a rise in atmospheric carbon dioxide concentration. Scientists believe that this change in air composition prevents more of the sun's heat escaping from the earth, much in the way the glass in a greenhouse does. They argue that the rise in temperature that this so-called **greenhouse effect** produces will cause expansion of the oceans and the gradual melting of the polar ice caps with a consequent rise in sea level. This would in turn cause flooding of low-lying land, upon which, as it happens, many of the world's capital cities lie. The greenhouse effect is neither new, nor all bad. Indeed it is its influence which maintains the earth's surface at an average of 15 °C rather than −18 °C which would be the case in the absence of greenhouse gases. The problem lies in the additional greenhouse gases which have been released over the past 200 years. While water vapour, methane and nitrogen oxides are all greenhouse gases, it is the influence of carbon dioxide that has been most significant in contributing to global warming. Estimates of the warming which is attributable to carbon dioxides vary from 50–70%. While the other greenhouse gases are present in much lower concentrations than carbon dioxide they are much more efficient at absorbing infra-red radiation and hence have a potentially greater influence on the greenhouse effect. Carbon dioxide however remains the greatest influence, not just because of its higher concentration but also the fact that it remains in the atmosphere longer – on average each molecule remains for 100 years, compared to 10 years for methane and a few months for carbon monoxide.

14.6.4 Carbon monoxide

Carbon monoxide occurs in exhaust emissions from cars and other vehicles. It is poisonous on account of having an affinity for haemoglobin some 250 times greater than that of oxygen. Upon combining with haemoglobin, it forms a stable compound which is not released and prevents oxygen combining with it. Continued inhalation leads to death as all haemoglobin becomes combined with carbon monoxide, leaving none to transport oxygen. In small concentrations it may cause dizziness and headache. Even on busy roads levels of carbon monoxide rarely exceed 4%, and it does not accumulate due to the action of certain bacteria and algae which break it down, according to the equation:

$$4CO + 4H_2O \rightarrow 4CO_2 + 8H^+ + 8e^-$$

carbon   water   carbon   protons   electrons
monoxide   dioxide

Cigarette smoking is known to increase the carbon monoxide concentration of the blood; up to 10% of a smoker's haemoglobin may be combined with carbon monoxide at any one time.

14.6.5 Nitrogen oxides

Nitrogen oxides, like nitrogen dioxide, are produced by the burning of fuel in car engines and emitted as exhaust. In themselves they are poisonous, but more importantly they contribute to the formation of **photochemical smog**. Under certain climatic conditions pollutants become trapped close to the ground. The action of sunlight on the nitrogen oxides in these pollutants causes them to be converted to **peroxyacyl nitrates (PAN)**. These compounds are much more dangerous, causing damage to vegetation, and eye and lung irritation in humans.

Photochemical smog in Rio de Janeiro

14.6.6 Lead

The toxicity of lead has been known for some time. It has long been used in making water pipes and water obtained through these may be contaminated with it. As lead is not easily absorbed from the intestines this does not present a major health hazard. Much more dangerous is the lead absorbed from the air by the lungs. Most lead in the air is emitted from car exhausts. **Tetraethyl lead (TEL)** is added to petrol as an **anti-knock** agent to help it burn more evenly in car engines. Each year in Britain alone, around 50 000 tonnes of lead are added to the atmosphere in this way. While much of this is deposited close to roads, that which remains in the atmosphere and is absorbed by the lungs could have the following adverse effects:

1. Digestive problems, e.g. intestinal colic.
2. Impairing the functioning of the kidney.
3. Nervous problems, including convulsions.
4. Brain damage and mental retardation in children.

Anti-knock agents which do not contain lead exist and in some countries legislation permits only this type. The British Government has made price incentives on unleaded fuel, but latest research shows unleaded fuel may contain higher levels of benzene – a pollutant more harmful than lead.

14.6.7 Control of air pollution

On 9 December 1952, foggy conditions developed over London. Being very cold, most houses kept fires burning, with coal as the major fuel. The smoke from these fires mixed with the fog and was unable to disperse, resulting in a smog which persisted for four days. During this period some 4000 more people died than would be expected at this time of the year. Most of these additional deaths were due to respiratory disorders. These alarming consequences of smog prompted the government to seek ways of controlling smoke emissions from chimneys. This led ultimately to the **Clean Air Act** of 1956. Among other things this created smokeless zones, in which only smoke-free fuels could be burned. Grants were made available to assist with the cost of having fires converted to take these smokeless fuels. For many years now most cities have been smokeless and the smogs, once a common feature of winter, no longer occur.

Other methods of controlling air pollution include the use of non-lead anti-knock agents and the removal of pollutants such as sulphur dioxide before smoke is emitted from chimneys. The latter is achieved by passing the smoke through a spray of water in which much of the sulphur dioxide dissolves. The use of electric cars is a further means of limiting air pollution.

14.6.8 Ozone depletion

Between 15 and 40 kilometres above the earth is a layer of ozone which is formed by the effect of ultra-violet radiation on oxygen molecules. In this way, a large amount of the potentially harmful ultra-violet radiation is absorbed and so prevented from reaching the earth's surface. There is evidence that this beneficial ozone layer is being damaged by atmospheric pollution to the

TABLE 14.7 **Estimated relative importance of various gases to the greenhouse effect**

Gas	% contribution
Carbon dioxide	71
CFCs	10
Methane	9
Carbon monoxide	7
Oxides of nitrogen	3

point where a hole in it has appeared over the Antarctic and possibly the Arctic too.

A number of pollutants can affect the ozone layer, the **chlorofluorocarbons (CFCs)** being the best known. CFCs are used in refrigerators, as propellants in aerosol sprays, and make up the bubbles in many plastic foams, e.g. expanded polystyrene. They are remarkably inert and therefore reach the upper stratosphere unchanged. Along with other ozone depleting gases such as **nitrous oxide** (NO), CFCs are contributing to global warming – the so-called 'greenhouse effect' (Section 14.6.3). In addition, the ultra-violet radiation causes skin cancer: an increase in the incidence of this disease is already evident.

14.7 Water pollution

Pure water rarely, if ever, exists naturally. Rain water picks up additives as it passes through the air, not least sulphur dioxide (Section 14.6.2). Even where there is little air pollution, chlorides and other substances are found in rain water. As water flows from tributaries into rivers it increasingly picks up minerals, organic matter and silt. If not the result of human activities, these may be considered as natural additives and therefore not pollutants. For domestic use alone, each individual in Britain uses an average of 150 litres of water each day.

14.7.1 Sewage and its disposal

Sewage is quite simply anything which passes down sewers. It has two main origins: from industry and from the home (domestic). Domestic effluent is 95–99% water, the remainder being organic matter. In itself, the organic material is harmless, but it acts as a food source for many saprobiontic organisms, especially bacteria. Where oxygen is available, aerobic saprobionts decompose the organic material – a process called **putrefaction** – and in so doing use up oxygen. This creates a **biochemical oxygen demand (BOD).**

Where sewage is deposited untreated into relatively small volumes of water, i.e. rivers and lakes rather than the oceans, the BOD may be great enough to remove entirely the dissolved oxygen. This causes the death of all aerobic species, including fish, leaving only anaerobic ones. The BOD is offset by new oxygen being dissolved, and in fast-moving, shallow, turbulent streams this is sufficient to prevent anaerobic conditions. Unfortunately many centres of population are situated near river estuaries where the waters are slower moving, deeper and less turbulent. The amount of oxygen dissolving is much less and so any untreated sewage added to these waters quickly results in them becoming anaerobic. With only around $5\,cm^3$ of dissolved oxygen in each dm^3 (litre) of fresh water, every individual human produces enough organic matter each day to remove the oxygen from $9000\,dm^3$ of water. Where untreated sewage enters a river it creates a BOD which gradually decreases further downstream as

Outlet pipe discharging sewage on to a beach

organic material is decomposed. Part of this sewage is combined nitrogen; each human produces 8 g of this daily, mostly in the form of urea and uric acid. This combined nitrogen is converted to ammonia by bacteria. While the ammonia may be toxic, its effects are temporary, as nitrifying bacteria rapidly oxidize it to nitrates. These relationships are illustrated in Fig. 14.5.

The chemical and physical changes brought about by sewage are accompanied by changes in the fauna and flora of the water. Where the level of organic material is high, saprobiontic bacteria concentrations, including filamentous bacteria known as **sewage fungus**, increase as they feed on the sewage. The algal levels initially fall, possibly due to the sewage reducing the amount of light which penetrates the water. Further down stream the algal levels rise above normal because the bacterial breakdown of the sewage releases many minerals, including nitrates. These minerals, which previously limited algal growth, now allow it to flourish. As the minerals are used up, algal population levels return to normal.

The population levels of animal species vary according to the level of oxygen in the water. Most tolerant of low oxygen levels are worms of the genus *Tubifex* whose haemoglobin has a particularly high affinity for oxygen which it obtains even at

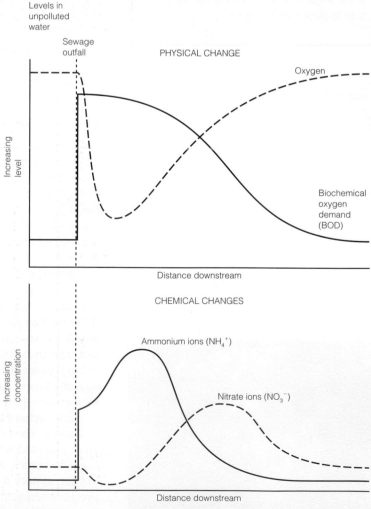

Fig. 14.5 Physical and chemical changes in a river due to sewage effluent

very low concentrations. These worms can therefore survive close to a sewage outfall; indeed, as other species cannot survive there, *Tubifex* are free from competitors and predators and so their numbers increase greatly.

Further down stream, as oxygen levels rise, other species such as the larvae of the midge *Chironomus* are also able to tolerate low oxygen levels. These compete with *Tubifex* for the small amount of available oxygen, and the worm population is reduced as a consequence. A continuing rise in oxygen level further from the outfall results in the appearance of species like the water louse, *Asellus*. Its presence adds to the competition, causing reduction in the populations of *Tubifex* and *Chironomus*. Finally, as the sewage is completely decomposed, oxygen levels in the water return to normal and clean-water species, like the freshwater shrimp, *Gammarus*, are present again. The ecological equilibrium is restored and population levels return to those found above the outfall. These changes in fauna and flora are illustrated in Fig. 14.6.

These organisms act as indicator species for polluted water. Where repeated additions of sewage occur at different points along the river, the water may be anaerobic for much of its length. In addition to the death of aerobic species, these conditions can result in the build-up of ammonia and hydrogen sulphide from anaerobic decomposition of sewage. These chemicals are toxic and result in an almost lifeless river. This was the situation with most large British rivers until the introduction

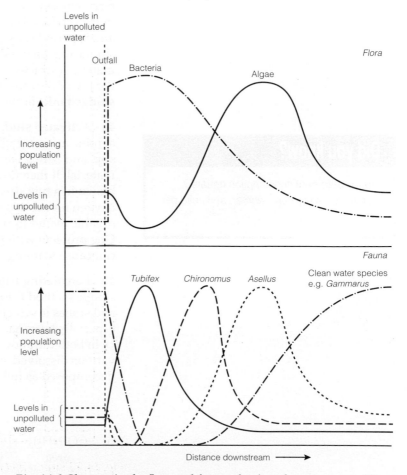

Fig. 14.6 Changes in the flora and fauna of a river due to sewage effluent

Sewage treatment works – primary sedimentation

of **sewage treatment works**. These works not only remove organic material but also potentially dangerous pathogenic organisms such as those causing cholera and typhoid.

The process of sewage treatment is outlined in Fig. 14.7 on page 341. It consists of a series of stages:

1. Screening – Large pieces of debris are filtered off to prevent them blocking pipes and equipment in the treatment works. This filtering is performed by a screen of metal rods, about 2 cm apart. The debris which is trapped on the screen is periodically scraped off and either buried or broken up into smaller pieces ready to undergo normal sewage treatment. Alternatively, the sewage enters a machine called a comminuter which reduces all the sewage into pieces small enough to enter the treatment works without risk of blockage.

2. Detritus removal – The sewage enters a tank or channel in which the rate of flow is reduced sufficiently to allow heavy inorganic material such as grit to deposit out. The lighter organic matter is, however, carried along in the water flow. The material that settles out is called **detritus** and can be dumped without further treatment.

3. Primary sedimentation – The sewage flows into large tanks which have a conical shaped base with a central exit pipe. The flow across these tanks is very slow, and may take several days. Fine silt and sand along with any organic material settle out and become deposited at the bottom of these tanks. The addition of ferric chloride, which causes flocculation, assists sedimentation in these tanks. The material which settles out is called **sludge** and is periodically pumped from the bottom of the tank to sludge digestion tanks. The sewage which has had most solid material extracted is now known as **effluent**. It is removed from the top of the sedimentation tanks and either enters **activated sludge tanks** or passes through **percolating filters**.

4a. Activated sludge method – The effluent is inoculated with aerobic microorganisms including *Zoogloea* spp., *Nitrosomonas* spp. and *Nitrobacter* spp. which break down dissolved organic material. It then flows into long channels through which air is blown in a fine stream of bubbles from the bottom. This provides oxygen for aerobic microorganisms rapidly to decompose the organic matter into carbon dioxide and some nitrogen oxides. One problem with this method is that detergents in the sewage can cause foaming.

4b. Percolating filter method – The alternative to the activated sludge method is to spray the effluent on to beds of sand, clinker and stones in which live a large variety of aerobic organisms, especially bacteria.

In both the above processes microorganisms oxidize the various dissolved substances. Urea for example may be decomposed as follows:

$$\text{(i)} \quad \underset{\text{urea}}{CO(NH_2)_2} + \underset{\text{water}}{H_2O} \xrightarrow{\underset{\substack{\text{producing}\\\text{urease}}}{\text{bacteria}}} \underset{\text{ammonia}}{2NH_3} + \underset{\substack{\text{carbon}\\\text{dioxide}}}{CO_2}$$

(ii)

$$2NH_3 + 3O_2 \xrightarrow{\text{Nitrosomonas}} 2NO_2^- + 2H^+ + H_2O$$

ammonia   oxygen   nitrite   hydrogen   water
                                                                  ions

(iii)

$$2NO_2^- + O_2 \xrightarrow{\text{Nitrobacter}} 2NO_3^-$$

nitrite   oxygen   nitrate

5. **Final (humus) sedimentation** – The effluent from the sludge tanks or percolating filters contains a large number of microorganisms. It therefore passes into further sedimentation tanks to allow these organisms to settle out. The sediment, known as **humus**, is then passed into the sludge treatment tanks.

6. **Fine filters** – These remove any suspended particles in the effluent which may then be safely discharged into rivers.

7. **Sludge digestion** – The sludge and humus are pumped into large covered tanks where they are hydrolysed by anaerobic microorganisms such as *Clostridium* spp. and *Methanobacterium* spp. into simpler compounds, leaving gases such as methane, and a digested sludge.

8. **Use of methane for generating power** – The methane produced during sludge digestion is usually collected and used as a fuel to drive turbines in a power-house. The electricity generated can be used to power the equipment and lights at the sewage works, making them, in some cases, self-sufficient in energy.

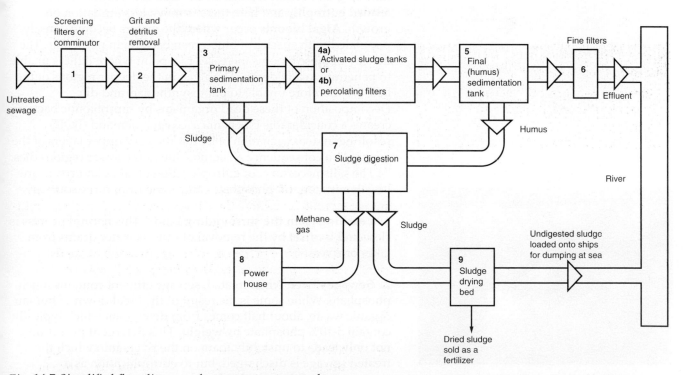

Fig. 14.7 Simplified flow diagram of a sewage treatment plant

9. Sludge drying beds – The sludge is led off into large tanks where its water content is reduced by air-drying. The resultant semi-solid material may either be loaded on to ships for dumping at sea or sold as fertilizer.

The removal of solid material during sewage treatment is highly efficient, being reduced from $400\,mg\,dm^{-3}$ in untreated sewage to $10\,mg\,dm^{-3}$ once treated. Similarly, the amount of organic carbon is reduced from $250\,mg\,dm^{-3}$ to $20\,mg\,dm^{-3}$. Ninety-nine per cent of complex chemicals like the pesticide DDT are also removed. Potential pollutants such as zinc, copper and phosphates may only be 50% removed. The phosphates are a particular problem as they are widely used as water softeners in detergents and are therefore present in high concentrations in sewage. Up to 95% of these phosphates can be removed by precipitating them out of solution by the addition of calcium carbonate or ammonium iron(III) sulphate. Most pathogenic organisms are removed by sewage treatment although *Salmonella paratyphi* (causes paratyphoid) and *Enteramoeba histolytica* (causes dysentery) may survive in small numbers. The eggs of worm parasites like *Ascaris* and *Taenia* have also been found in sewage works' effluent.

14.7.2 Eutrophication by sewage and fertilizer

Eutrophication is a natural process during which the concentration of salts builds up in bodies of water. It occurs largely in lakes and the lower reaches of rivers, and the salts normally accumulate until an equilibrium is reached where they are exactly counterbalanced by the rate at which they are removed. Lakes and rivers with low salt concentrations are termed **oligotrophic** and the salts are frequently the factor limiting plant growth. Waters with high concentrations are termed **eutrophic** and here there is much less limitation on growth. **Algal blooms** occur where the waters become densely populated with species of blue-green bacteria in particular. The density of these blooms increases to a point where light is unable to penetrate to any depth. The algae in the deeper regions of the lake are therefore unable to photosynthesize, and die. Decomposition of these dead organisms by saprobiontic bacteria creates a considerable biochemical oxygen demand (BOD) resulting in deoxygenation of all but the very upper layers of the water. As a consequence all aerobic life in the lower regions dies.

The salts necessary for eutrophication of lakes and rivers are largely nitrates and phosphates and come from three sources:

1. Leaching from the surrounding land – This natural process is slow and is offset by the removal of salts as water drains from lakes or rivers.

2. Sewage - Even when treated, sewage effluent contains much phosphate. While some is the result of the breakdown of human organic waste, about half comes from detergents which typically contain 5-10% phosphate by weight. This **detergent pollution** not only leads to unsightly foam on the rivers into which the treated sewage is discharged, but to eutrophication as a consequence of the soluble phosphate. Solutions to the problem

Cormorant killed by the *Braer* oil spill

include the use of detergents with a much lower phosphate concentration and removal of phosphate as part of sewage treatment (Section 14.7.1).

3. Fertilizers – An increasing quantity of inorganic fertilizer is now applied to farmland to increase crop yield. A major constituent of these fertilizers is nitrate. As this is highly soluble it is readily leached and quickly runs off into lakes and rivers.

14.7.3 Oil

The effects of oil pollution are localized, but nonetheless serious. Oil is readily broken down by bacteria, especially when thoroughly dispersed. Most oil pollution is either the result of illegal washing at sea of storage tanks of oil tankers or accidental spillage. The first major oil pollution incident in Great Britain occurred in 1967 when the *Torrey Canyon* went aground off Land's End. It released 120 000 tonnes of crude oil which was washed up on many Cornish beaches. Sea birds are particularly at risk because the oil coats their feathers, preventing them from flying; it also reduces their insulatory properties, causing death by hypothermia. The *Torrey Canyon* incident alone is estimated to have killed 100 000 birds. On shores, the oil coats seaweed, preventing photosynthesis, and covers the gills of shellfish, interfering with feeding and respiration. The effects are, however, temporary and shores commonly recover within two years. Detergents, used to disperse oil, can increase the ecological damage as they are toxic. With larger 'super-tankers', the potential danger from oil pollution is increased. The wrecking of the *Amoco Cadiz* off the Brittany coast in 1978 with the release of 200 000 tonnes of crude oil made the *Torrey Canyon* incident appear small by comparison. In 1989 *Exxon Valdez* spilt 38 000 tonnes in Prince William Sound, Alaska in 1993 the *Braer* spilt 84 000 tonnes in the Shetlands, and in 1996, 70 000 tonnes were lost from the *Sea Empress* in Milford Haven. The long-term effects of these spills in such environmentally sensitive areas are yet to be seen.

14.7.4 Thermal pollution

All organisms live within a relatively narrow range of temperature. Wide fluctuations in temperature occur more often in terrestrial environments as the high specific heat of water buffers temperature changes. For this reason aquatic organisms are less tolerant of temperature fluctuations. Most thermal pollution of water is the result of electricity generation in power-stations. The steam used to drive the turbines in these stations is condensed back to water in large cooling towers. The water used in the cooling process is consequently warmed, being discharged at a temperature some 10–15 °C higher than when removed from the river. Although warmer water normally contains less dissolved oxygen, the spraying of water in cooling towers increases its surface area and thereby actually increases its oxygen content. The main effect of thermal pollution is to alter the ecological balance of a river by favouring warm-water species at the expense of cold-water ones. Coarse fish such as roach and perch may, for example, replace salmon and trout.

14.8   Conservation

There has been a growing interest in conservation as a result of increasing pressures placed upon the natural environment, the widespread loss of natural habitats and the growing numbers of extinct and endangered species. As early as 1872, the Yellowstone National Park in the USA was established in order to protect a particularly valuable natural environment. Australia (1886) and New Zealand (1894) established national parks soon after. It was not until 1949 that the first national park in Britain was established, but prior to that many societies such as the Royal Society for the Protection of Birds (1889) and the National Trust (1895) had been set up to promote conservation. There are now a large number of agencies responsible for conservation in one form or another. These include international groups like the World Wide Fund for Nature, large national bodies such as the Department of the Environment (DoE), Nature Conservancy Council (NCC), and the National Trust (NT); commercial organizations like the water authorities and the Forestry Commission; charitable groups like the Royal Society for the Protection of Birds (RSPB) as well as County Trusts for Nature Conservation and Farming and Wildlife Advisory Groups. The main impetus for conservation has come as a result of the pressures created by an ever-increasing human population – likely to be 6000 million before the end of the century.

There is, more often than not, a conflict between the needs of a country to produce enough food to feed its inhabitants and the need to conserve natural habitats; this can be illustrated by the use of nitrogen-containing fertilizers. There is no doubt that the use of chemical fertilizers containing nitrogen increases the crop yield from a given area of land and so helps to feed the populus. Equally there is no doubt that some of this fertilizer runs off into watercourses causing eutrophication (see Section 14.7.2). Conservationists argue that there are viable non-polluting alternatives to the use of chemical fertilizers. For example crop rotation or intercropping which uses nitrogen-fixing leguminous species will improve the nitrogen content of soils. Alternatively organic manures, which release their nitrogen too slowly to create pollution problems, could be used. These manures can be added to the surface in a thick enough layer to prevent weed growth – a process called **mulching** - and by so doing prevent additional loss of nitrogen from the soil into the weeds.

Conservation is more than preservation. The latter seeks to maintain individuals, populations and ecosystems in their current state without the capacity for change. Conservation however, seeks, not to keep things as they are indefinitely, but rather to allow them to evolve naturally, much as they may have done without our presence. Why conserve at all? There are two basic reasons. Ethically many feel mankind has a duty to allow all species, most of which have occupied the earth far longer, to continue to exist in the same balance that existed before human evolution. Economically the long-term productivity of natural ecosystems is greater if they are maintained in their naturally balanced state; the richness and variety are not only aesthetically pleasing but retain the potential to provide natural products to satisfy not only mankind's present needs but also solutions to problems we have yet to encounter.

14.8.1 Endangered species

Many species have become **extinct**, i.e. they have not been definitely located in the wild during the past 50 years. Others are **endangered**, i.e. they are likely to become extinct if the factors causing their numbers to decline continue to operate. At least 25 000 plant species are considered to be endangered.

There are a number of reasons why organisms become endangered:

1. **Natural selection** – It is, and always has been, part of the normal process of evolution that organisms which are genetically better adapted replace ones less well adapted.

2. **Habitat destruction** – Humans exploit many natural habitats, destroying them in the process. Timber cutting destroys forests and endangers species like the orang-utan. Industrial and agricultural development threaten many plant species of the Amazon forest. Clearing of river banks destroys the natural habitat of the otter, and modern farming methods remove hedgerows and drain wetlands, endangering the species which live and breed there. Maintaining the diversity of organisms in a habitat is important as species may have economic importance outside their habitat, e.g. pollinating insects. They may also possess undiscovered chemicals and/or genes with future medicinal or other importance.

3. **Competition from humans and their animals** – Where a species is restricted to a small area, e.g. the giant tortoises in the Galapagos Islands, they are often unable to compete with the influx of humans and their animals. Because their habitat is restricted, in this case by water, they cannot escape.

4. **Hunting and collecting** – Humans hunt tigers for sport, crocodiles for their skins, oryx as trophies, elephants for ivory, whales for oil and rhinoceros for their horn. Other organisms are collected for the pet trade, e.g. tamarins and parrots; and for research purposes, e.g. frogs. These are in addition to the numerous species hunted purely as food.

5. **Destroyed by humans as being a health risk** – Many species are persecuted because they carry diseases of domesticated species, e.g. badgers (tuberculosis of cattle) and eland (various cattle diseases).

6. **Pollution** – Oil pollution threatens some rare species of sea birds. The build-up of certain insecticides along food chains endangers predatory birds like the peregrine falcon and the golden eagle (Section 14.2.8).

14.8.2 Conservation methods

To combat the pressures listed above a number of conservation techniques are used:

1. **Development of national parks and nature reserves** – These are habitats legally safeguarded and patrolled by wardens. They may preserve a vulnerable food source, e.g. in China areas of bamboo forest are protected to help conserve the giant panda. In Africa game parks help to conserve endangered species such as the African elephant. Efforts are being made to conserve the

Heather moorland in Dartmoor National Park, Devon

FOCUS

Coppicing

Coppiced trees

Coppicing is an ancient technique for obtaining long, flexible lengths of wood of small diameter. Traditionally these were used to make fences known as **hurdles**, in furniture making, buildings or just as firewood. The technique relies upon the fact that if a tree, even a mature one, is cut back near to the ground, many new shoots will develop from the remaining stump. If allowed to grow for a few years, these new stems can be harvested. The length of time they are permitted to grow depends on the species involved and the purpose to which the wood is to be put. Varieties of tree involved include ash, oak, hazel, lime and hornbeam.

Coppicing provides a good example of taking a sustainable yield because the stems quickly regrow in readiness for the next harvest. It is also an excellent conservation technique in the management of deciduous woodland, because coppicing provides a variety of habitats, especially when done in conjunction with the maintenance of larger trees around. In this way areas of woodland are opened up to more light than would be the case if all trees were permitted to reach maturity. Plants which would normally only grow on the periphery of the wood can now thrive within it, attracting as they do associated insects, and birds. The coppices themselves prove excellent nesting sites for birds such as nightingales, dunnocks and nuthatches.

dwindling areas of tropical rainforest. Planning authorities have greater powers to control developments and activities within these areas.

2. **Planned land use** – On a smaller scale, specific areas of land may be set aside for a designated use. The types of activities permitted on the land are carefully controlled by legislation. Such areas include Green Belts, Areas of Outstanding Natural Beauty, Sites of Special Scientific Interest, and country parks. Some places are designated as Environmentally Sensitive Areas (ESAs) and farmers or other landowners may be compensated for restricting activities which might conflict with conserving the natural habitats in the region.

3. **Legal protection for endangered species** – It is illegal to collect or kill certain species, e.g. the koala in Australia. In Britain, the Wildlife and Countryside Act gives legal protection to many plants and animals. Even legislation such as the Clean Air Act, may indirectly protect some species from extinction. Despite stiff penalties, such laws are violated because of the difficulty of enforcing them.

4. **Commercial farming** – The development of farms which produce sought-after goods, e.g. mink farming, deer farming, may produce enough material to satisfy the market and so remove the necessity to kill these animals in the wild.

5. **Breeding in zoos and botanical gardens** – Endangered species may be bred in the protected environment of a zoo and

Conservation of grasslands

Much of Britain is prevented from reaching its natural woodland climax vegetation type as a result of agricultural practices such as mowing and grazing. Together these maintain a grassland vegetation. Traditionally these grasslands were grazed by animals such as sheep and/or were mowed annually for hay. The fertility of the soil was maintained by the addition of animal manure with little, or no, chemical fertilizers or pesticides used. A rich and diverse flora of meadow plants resulted, partly because the overall fertility of the soil was relatively low and partly as a result of the meadow being cropped very close to the ground. Intensive farming and with it the use of herbicides, fertilizers and machine cutting rather than grazing has led to higher productivity but a much reduced diversity of species because a few grass varieties are favoured.

The conservation of species-rich grassland meadows is best achieved by grazing sheep on them because they leave a very short turf which favours a range of small perennial herbs rather than grasses. The trampling by the sheep also encourages the new plant arrivals because it creates bare patches of disturbed ground on which they can establish themselves. The lower soil fertility as a result of natural manuring rather than artificial fertilizers also favours a variety of broad leaved species in preference to grasses. Hay making with a single cut each year, rather than multiple cuts for silage, helps to conserve species diversity. The nearer the mowing mimics the grazing of sheep ie. a low cut, the more effective it is in conserving the meadow. The richer the diversity of plants, the greater the variety of insects and other invertebrates that occur, which in turn encourages a greater number of vertebrate species especially birds.

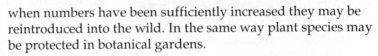

when numbers have been sufficiently increased they may be reintroduced into the wild. In the same way plant species may be protected in botanical gardens.

6. Removal of animals from threatened areas – Organisms in habitats threatened by humans, or by natural disasters such as floods, may be removed and resettled in more secure habitats.

7. Control of introduced species – Organisms introduced into a country by humans often require strict control if they are not to out-compete the indigenous species. Feral animals (domesticated individuals which escape into the wild) must be similarly controlled.

8. Ecological study of threatened habitats – Careful analysis of all natural habitats is essential if they are to be managed in a way that permits conservation of a maximum number of species.

9. Pollution control – Measures to control pollution such as smoke emissions, oil spillage, over use of pesticides, fertilizer run-off, etc, all help to prevent habitat and species destruction. This is especially important in sensitive and vulnerable areas such as river estuaries and salt marshes.

Cane toad eating pygmy possum. Introduced as a means of biological control the cane toad is now a predator of native species

FOCUS

Conservation of fenlands

Wicken Fen

Surrounding the Wash in eastern England there was once a huge area of waterlogged marsh and peatland supporting a rich and unique flora. This fenland has been systematically drained to be used for farming, resulting in a shrinkage of the soil so that the level has fallen about 4.5 metres. For some years now attempts have been made to conserve the remaining patches of undrained land but it is difficult to maintain, or reintroduce if necessary, the original varieties of plants. The fen is now higher than the surrounding farmland and is becoming acidic as the topsoil is leached. This leads to invasion by untypical acid-loving species like *Sphagnum* and the bog myrtle. As water drains off the fen more has to be pumped on to it along special channels to maintain the correct conditions for the vegetation. Typical fenland plants are the sedge, *Cladium mariscus*, and the reed, *Phragmites australis* and these must be cut back every four years in the spring or summer to prevent invasion by scrub such as buckthorn and willows.

Bins for waste recycling

Did you know?

It takes 15 000 recycled sheets of A4 paper to save a tree.

10. Recycling – The more material which is recycled, the less need there is to obtain that material from natural sources e.g. through mining. These activities often destroy sensitive habitats either directly, or indirectly through the dumping of waste which is toxic or the development of roads to transport the products. This can be especially true of metal ores which are often found in mountainous regions, many of which are home to rare species. Recycling paper reduces the demand for 'virgin' paper and hence the need for afforestation with its attendant reduction in species diversity (see Section 14.1.1).

11. Education – It is of paramount importance to educate people in ways of preventing habitat destruction and encouraging the conservation of organisms.

Reclamation of derelict land

As Britain's economic base has shifted from heavy industrial and manufacturing processes to high technology and service industries, more and more land, once occupied by large factories, industries and mines, has been left derelict, some of it heavily polluted. Large volumes of waste associated with these industries have been dumped in spoil and slag heaps. These heaps may be toxic with high levels of heavy metal ions, making it difficult for vegetation to grow on them. Without vegetation they can become unstable and liable to slip. One such slip in the Welsh village of Aberfan in 1966 engulfed a primary school and nearby houses, killing 116 children and 28 adults.

The reclamation of this land is designed to make it safer, aesthetically more pleasing and, if possible, to bring it back into productive use. The establishment of vegetation is vital to this process but is often hampered by the toxicity of the material, its unfavourable pH, a lack of suitable plant nutrients or the absence of organic matter. In addition the particle size of the material is often unsuitable, being too coarse, too fine or simply so compacted that growth is impossible.

The reclamation of any one site firstly involves finding out which factors are preventing plant growth and then remedying them. This may require draining the site, incorporating organic material, levelling the ground, ploughing, adding fertlizers and/or lime and sowing the seeds of appropriate species which can tolerate the conditions. Let us look at two specific examples of reclamation, namely land contaminated by heavy metal ions and by china clay wastes.

Pollution of land by **heavy metal ions** is often the result of the mining of ores to extract metals such as tin, silver, nickel, lead, iron, zinc, chromium and copper. Most of these metals occur naturally as ions in soils, indeed some such as copper, iron and zinc are necessary for plant growth. It is the high concentration of these ions that renders the land unsuitable for plant growth. Reclamation can take a number of forms. Where the degree of pollution is relatively small natural leaching may, over time, reduce the concentration of heavy metal ions to a tolerable level. Alternatively, the area may be covered by unpolluted top soil which will support vegetation. The process is costly and the metal ions may migrate upwards, a process accelerated by the activities of earthworms. Another remedial measure is to treat the affected land chemically in order to precipitate out the toxic ions into a form which cannot be taken up by plants, e.g. iron(II) sulphate may be used to precipitate out chromium ions as chromium(III) sulphate. Lime is used to increase the pH of very acidic land. A further strategy is to establish plants which can tolerate the particular metal ions. A few species of plants have varieties which can tolerate high concentrations of one particular metal ion. For example *Agrostis capillaris* – cultivar *Parys* can tolerate soils heavily polluted with copper

FOCUS continued

China clay spoil heap

Reclaimed landscaped china clay spoil heap

ions. In combination with suitable fertilizers and other after-care methods these species can be successfully established. Further work is then needed to increase the variety of species and so establish a balanced ecosystem.

China clay has been mined in Cornwall since the eighteenth century and this mining has produced large pits, often now flooded, and associated spoil heaps. The fine clay particles in the flooded pits prevent organisms establishing themselves while the spoil heaps are equally inhospitable owing to their low pH, large particle size and deficiency of nitrogen. Reclamation of the spoil heaps has entailed landscaping the contours by redistributing the waste with machinery and adding peat or other organic material to improve water retention and provide a longer-term supply of nutrients. A mixture of different plant seeds is then sown including perennial grasses such as *Lolium perenne* (to establish vegetation quickly and stabilize the land), *Festuca rubra* (a species tolerant of acid conditions and which can survive on soils with poor nutrient levels) and *Trifolium pretense* (a clover which fixes nitrogen and so helps to fertilize the impoverished land naturally). Chemical fertilizers, rich in phosphates and potassium, are applied. If too much is added initially it can inhibit nitrogen fixation by the clover, although once the grasses are firmly established the amount of nitrate can be safely increased.

By these methods, the land can be reclaimed much more rapidly than by natural regeneration and can then be used for low intensity agriculture such as the grazing of Soay sheep - a variety which survives well on low grade pasture.

14.9   Questions

1. The graphs A, B and C show some predictions for the size of the Arctic cod stock at low, medium and high fishing intensities with three different net mesh sizes.

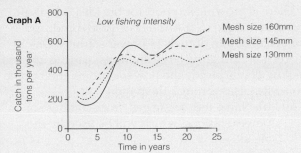

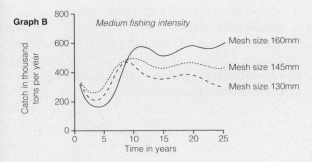

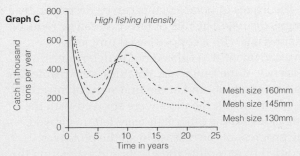

(a) Describe and explain how the following may influence the catch of cod from this fishery
  (i) the intensity of fishing;   *(2 marks)*
  (ii) the mesh size of the net.   *(2 marks)*
(b) Use the information in the graphs to explain the relationship between the productivity of a fishery and the maximum sustainable yield.
                                        (4 marks)
(c) Explain **two** methods by which the intensity of fishing may be regulated.   *(4 marks)*
                                        (Total 12 marks)

NEAB June 1995, Paper BY07, No. 8

2. Spider mites are important pests of cucumbers. The two graphs following show the effects of a trial comparing two different methods of controlling spider mites. Graph 1 shows the results of spraying with an insecticide while Graph 2 shows what happened after the introduction of a predatory mite.

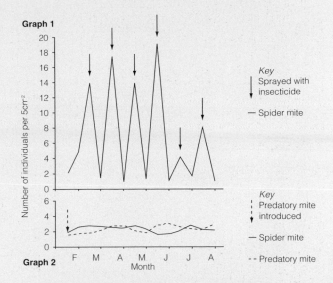

(a) Explain why the spider mite numbers
  (i) remained almost constant after the predatory mite was introduced: *(2 marks)*
  (ii) fluctuated considerably when they were controlled with the insecticide.   *(1 mark)*
(b) Explain why, if the predatory mite is to be successful in controlling the spider mite, it must never completely exterminate the pest.   *(1 mark)*
(c) Explain how integrated pest control could be used to regulate the numbers of spider mites on a cucumber crop.   *(2 marks)*
                                        (Total 6 marks)

NEAB June 1995, Paper BY07, No. 4

3. The diagram shows the Norfolk four-year crop rotation which was widely used in agriculture in the last century.

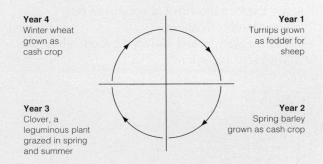

Explain how use of this rotation helped to:
  (a) maintain soil fertility;   *(3 marks)*
  (b) control pests.   *(2 marks)*
                                        (Total 5 marks)

NEAB June 1995, Paper BY07, No. 3

4. The map shows a small area in the Midlands. The sites indicated with letters **A** to **C** are sources of pollution.

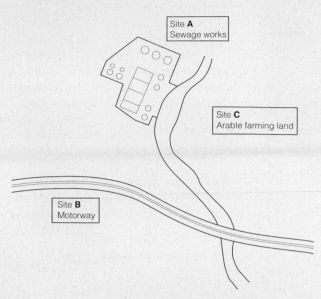

Choose any **two** of sites **A** to **C** and give the letters of your choice in the spaces below. For these sites, suggest the main pollutants associated with **each** and explain how these pollutants affect living organisms and ecosystems. *(12 marks)*

NEAB June 1995, Paper BY05, No. 8

5. Write an essay on **one** of the following topics:
Either A The causes and effects of water pollution.
or B The control of human population size. *(24 marks)*

AEB June 1992, Paper 2, No. 5

6. Coppicing is a technique that is often used when woodlands are managed for conservation purposes.
(a) (i) Describe the technique of coppicing. *(2 marks)*
(ii) Explain the effect of coppicing on a woodland ecosystem. *(2 marks)*
(b) The diagram below shows the foodweb in part of a coppiced woodland.

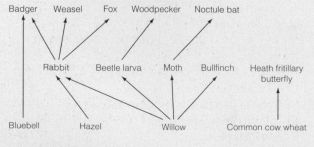

(i) Name the producers in this food web. *(1 mark)*

(ii) Name **one** animal in this food web which feeds at two trophic levels. *(1 mark)*
(iii) State how many trophic levels are shown. *(1 mark)*
(Total 7 marks)

ULEAC June 1995, Paper 1, No. 6

7. There is growing support for the idea of using unicellular algae to absorb waste gases produced from combustion of fuels in power stations. One suggestion is to grow large amounts of algae in shallow ponds beside the power stations and bubble the waste gases through the ponds.
(a) (i) Name **one** waste gas, from combustion in power stations, which will be used by the algae. *(1 mark)*
(ii) Name the process carried out by the algae which needs this gas as a raw material to produce biomass. *(1 mark)*
(b) Suggest **two** uses for the biomass produced by the algae. *(2 marks)*
(c) Describe **one** possible environmental benefit from the process named in (a) (ii). *(2 marks)*
(Total 6 marks)

ULEAC June 1995, Paper 1, No. 2

8. The leaves of potato plants can be destroyed by a fungus disease. The rate of infection can be reduced by spraying with a copper-based fungicide. An experiment was carried out to determine the efficiency of the fungicide. Potatoes were planted in ten separate plots and at the first signs of infection, the plants in half the plots were sprayed with the fungicide and the other half were left unsprayed. The progress of the disease in all the plots was recorded by sampling the plants and estimating the amount of diseased leaves using an arbitrary scale. Measurements were taken every 5 days. The results are given in the table below.

Day	Amount of infection/arbitrary units	
	Unsprayed plants	Sprayed plants
0	0	4.0
5	8.5	7.0
10	15.5	7.5
15	22.0	7.0
20	35.0	8.5
25	43.0	12.0
30	51.0	14.0

(a) (i) Plot the data in a suitable graphical form on graph paper. *(5 marks)*

(ii) Using your graph, find the rate of infection of the unsprayed plants during the period from day 3 to day 12 of the experiment. Show your working. (3 marks)

(b) (i) Comment on the spread of infection in the unsprayed and sprayed plants. (2 marks)

(ii) Suggest a reason for the results obtained for the sprayed plants. (1 mark)

(c) Describe **two** disadvantages of the use of chemicals as fungicides. (4 marks)

(Total 15 marks)

ULEAC June 1994, Paper 1, No. 11

9. Read the information below and answer the questions which follow.

Ideally insecticides should kill harmful insects without causing harm to beneficial insects or other animals, including humans. Chemicals used as insecticides frequently act on the nervous system. The nervous system of insects functions in essentially the same way as that of mammals, so many chemical targeted against insects are also likely to affect humans.

The relative toxicity of various insecticides to mammals and to insects is usually expressed as the *average lethal dose* or LD50. These figures indicate the dose required, either by the mouth (oral) or through the body surface (dermal), to kill half of the animals in the test group.

The table below shows the LD50 values for various insecticides tested on adult houseflies and on rats.

Insecticide	LD50/mg insecticide kg^{-1} body mass		
	Rat (oral)	Rat (dermal)	Houseflies (dermal)
DDT	120–180	18	18
Malathion	2800	50	50
Gamma HCH	90	1.5	1.5
Parathion	8	3	3

DDT and gamma HCH are described as persistent insecticides and can persist for decades in an active form. Malathion and parathion will remain active for only a few months after use.

Parathion and malathion are applied in aerosol form but gamma HCH is applied in a powder form. DDT may be applied in aerosol or powder form but is now banned from use.

Answer the following questions referring to the information given above where relevant.

(a) (i) Which insecticide would be the safest to use in the home to control houseflies? Explain your answer. (3 marks)

(ii) Which insecticide would be the most dangerous if used in the kitchen? Explain your answer. (2 marks)

(b) Many insecticides, such as malathion, are applied as aerosols but gamma HCH is only applied as a powder. Suggest why this is so. (2 marks)

(c) (i) Suggest **one** advantage and **one** disadvantage of using a persistent insecticide such as gamma HCH. Explain your answers. (4 marks)

(ii) DDT is no longer used as an insecticide. Suggest **three** reasons why this is so. (3 marks)

(d) Biological control of pests is frequently preferable to chemical control. Briefly describe **one** example of the biological control of a pest. (2 marks)

(Total 16 marks)

ULEAC June 1993, Paper 1, No. 14

10. The pie charts show changes over the last 5000 years in the vegetation which covers Britain.

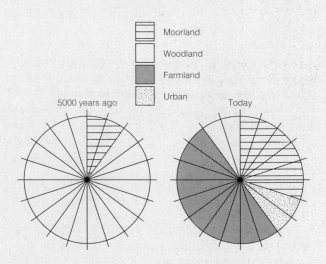

(a) Calculate the difference in the percentage of land covered by woodland 5000 years ago and today. Show your working. (2 marks)

(b) Farmers are now being persuaded to set aside land from food production. Some of this land may revert to woodland naturally.
Briefly explain how and why farmland may revert to woodland naturally. (4 marks)

(c) Give and explain **two** ways in which farming practices prevent farmland from reverting to woodland. (2 marks)

(Total 8 marks)

NEAB June 1995, Paper BY02, No. 6

11. Sugar cane is not native to Australia. Soon after it was introduced it became severely affected by beetles which damaged the plants by eating through the base of the stems.

In South America, the native cane toad keeps down the number of beetles in sugar cane fields. In an attempt to control the beetle in Australia, a small number of cane toads was introduced into one location. The toads soon underwent an explosion in population growth which is still continuing. Cane toads are now a problem in their own right.

(a) Suggest **two** reasons why the cane toad underwent a population explosion when introduced into Australia. *(2 marks)*

(b) Suggest **two** reasons why cane toads might prove a threat to native Australian species. *(2 marks)*

(c) Describe how **one** parasite or predator is used successfully in the biological control of a pest. *(3 marks)*

(Total 7 marks)

NEAB June 1995, Paper BY02, No. 5

12. Discuss the effects of humans on air quality. *(24 marks)*

AEB June 1995, Paper 2, No. 5A

13. Under the separate headings of (a) fertilizers, (b) herbicides and (c) insecticides, write an account of the impact of farm chemicals on the environment.

(a) fertilizers *(9 marks)*

(b) herbicides *(6 marks)*

(c) insecticides *(8 marks)*

(Total 23 marks)

UCLES June 1992, Paper 2, No. 6

14. A student noticed that the density of some plant species appeared to differ depending on how far the plants were from a main road.

The mean density (plants per m²) of three plant species A, B and C was measured at different distances from the main road. The mean density of the same three plant species was also determined at the side of a narrower secondary road in the same locality.

The results of the investigations are shown in the diagrams at the top of the next column.

(a) Describe a procedure the student could have used to determine the mean density of the three plant species. *(4 marks)*

(b) (i) Comment on the relationships between plant density and the distance from the main and secondary road for species A and B. *(4 marks)*

(ii) Comment on the ways in which the distribution of plant species C differs from that of plant species A. *(2 marks)*

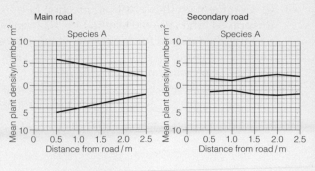

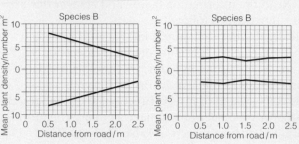

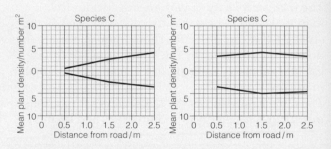

(c) In addition to determining the plant densities, the student measured the pH of soil samples taken in the same distances from each of the roads. The results are shown in the graph below.

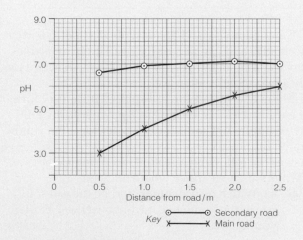

354

(i) Suggest an explanation for the differences between the pH of the soil at the side of the main road and the pH at the side of the secondary road. (2 *marks*)

(ii) Using the data given for pH, suggest an explanation for the distribution of the three species A, B and C. (2 *marks*)

(iii) Suggest one factor, other than pH, which could account for the differences in density distribution of the plant species at the side of the main road. (1 *mark*)

(*Total 15 marks*)

ULEAC June 1996, Paper HB6, No. 5

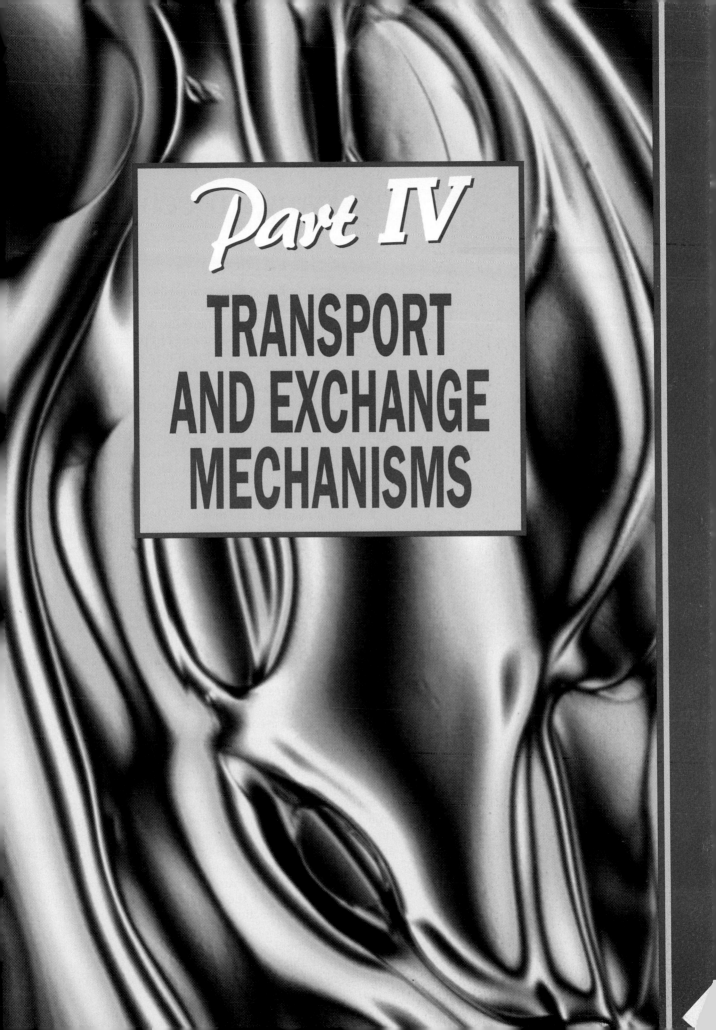

Part IV

TRANSPORT AND EXCHANGE MECHANISMS

Why humans need transport and exchange mechanisms

All organisms need to exchange materials between themselves and their environment. Respiratory gases and the raw materials for growth must pass into an organism and waste products must be removed. This exchange is carried out passively by diffusion and osmosis and actively by active transport, pinocytosis and phagocytosis (Section 4.3). To be efficient, exchange mechanisms require the surface-area over which transfer occurs to be large when compared to the volume of the organism. Where diffusion is involved the exchange surface needs to be moist and the distance across which diffusion occurs must be as small as possible. In small organisms such as protozoans and unicellular algae their surface-area is sufficiently large compared with their volume to allow efficient exchange of most materials over the whole surface of their bodies.

When organisms became multicellular and so grew in size, they could only meet their exchange demands by simple diffusion if their requirements were very modest, for example if they had a very low metabolic rate. An increase in size inevitably meant an increased distance from the surface to the centre of the organism. Even if sufficient exchange occurred at the surface, the centre could still be starved of raw materials, because the rate of delivery was inadequate to supply the demand, if it was dependent on diffusion alone.

These increases in size and/or metabolic rate necessitated the development of specialized exchange surfaces to compensate for a smaller surface area to volume ratio and/or an increased oxygen demand.

Where large size is combined with a high metabolic rate, both specialized exchange surfaces and an efficient means of transport become essential. The solution for large, highly metabolizing, terrestrial organisms such as humans was to develop lungs. These comprise tiny elastic sacs, the alveoli, which are supported by connective tissue. The tubes, called bronchi, leading to these sacs are supported by cartilagenous rings to prevent collapse and the lungs as a whole are supported and protected by a bony cage of ribs. Being located deep within the body and communicating to the outside only by means of a narrow tube, the trachea, evaporative losses are kept to a minimum. The linings of the alveoli are thin and well supplied with blood. Muscular action ensures constant ventilation of the lungs.

With increasing size and specialization of organisms, tissues and organs became increasingly dependent upon one another. Materials needed to be exchanged not only between organs and the environment, but also between different organs. To this end, animals developed circulatory systems. In humans this comprises a series of closed vessels in which blood is circulated by a specialized muscular pump – the heart.

The blood itself must be adapted to transport a wide variety of substances. Many are simply dissolved in a watery solution (the plasma), but others like oxygen are carried by special chemicals (respiratory pigments); these may be contained in specialized cells (red blood cells). Being distributed to all parts of the body, the blood is ideally situated to convey the body's defence and immune system (the white blood cells). The liquid nature of blood, so necessary for rapid transport around the body, suffers the disadvantage that it leaks away when damage is caused to the cavities or vessels containing it. Consequently a mechanism has evolved to ensure rapid clotting in these circumstances.

15 Gaseous exchange

15.1 Respiratory surfaces

All aerobic organisms must obtain regular supplies of oxygen from their environment and return to it the waste gas carbon dioxide. The movement of these gases between the organism and its environment is called **gaseous exchange**. Gaseous exchange always occurs by **diffusion** over part or all of the body surface. This is called a **respiratory surface** and in order to maintain the maximum possible rate of diffusion respiratory surfaces have a number of characteristics.

1. Large surface-area to volume ratio – This may be the body surface in small organisms or infoldings of the surface such as lungs and gills in larger organisms.

2. Permeable

3. Thin – Diffusion is only efficient over distances up to 1 mm since the rate of diffusion is inversely proportional to the square of the distance between the concentrations on the two sides of the respiratory surface.

4. Moist – since oxygen and carbon dioxide diffuse in solution.

5. Efficient transport system – This is necessary to maintain a diffusion gradient and may involve a vascular system.

The relationship between some of these factors is expressed as **Fick's law** which states:

Diffusion is proportional to

$$\frac{\text{surface area} \times \text{difference in concentration}}{\text{thickness of membrane}}$$

Organisms can obtain their gases from the air or from water. The oxygen content of a given volume of water is lower than that of air, therefore an aquatic organism must pass a greater volume of the medium over its respiratory surface in order to obtain enough oxygen.

TABLE 15.1 **Water and air as respiratory media**

Property	Water	Air
Oxygen content	Less than 1%	21%
Oxygen diffusion rate	Low	High
Density	Relative density of water about 1000 times greater than that of air at the same temperature	
Viscosity	Water much greater, about 1000 times that of air	

15.2 Mechanisms of gaseous exchange

As animals increase in size most of their cells are some distance from the surface and cannot receive adequate oxygen. Many larger animals also have an increased metabolic rate which increases their oxygen demand. These organisms need to develop specialized respiratory surfaces such as gills or lungs. These surfaces allow the gases to enter and leave the body more rapidly. There remains the problem of transporting the gases between the respiring cells and the respiratory surface. Generally the gases are carried by the blood vascular system. The presence of respiratory pigments like haemoglobin increase the oxygen-carrying capacity of the blood (Section 16.2.1). The diffusion gradients may be further maintained by ventilation movements, e.g. breathing.

15.2.1 Gaseous exchange in humans

Lungs are the site of gaseous exchange in humans. They are found deep inside the thorax of the body and so their efficient ventilation is essential. The lungs are delicate structures and, together with the heart, are enclosed in a protective bony case, the **rib cage**. There are twelve pairs of ribs in humans, all attached dorsally to the thoracic vertebrae. The anterior ten pairs are attached ventrally to the sternum. The remaining ribs are said to be 'floating'. The ribs may be moved by a series of intercostal muscles. The thorax is separated from the abdomen by a muscular sheet, the **diaphragm**.

Air flow in humans is **tidal**, air entering and leaving along the same route. It enters the nostrils and mouth and passes down the **trachea**. It enters the lungs via two **bronchi** which divide into smaller **bronchioles** and end in air-sacs called **alveoli**. These regions are illustrated in Fig. 15.1.

Regions of the respiratory system
Within the nasal channels mucus is secreted by goblet cells in the ciliated epithelium (Fig. 15.3). This mucus traps particles and the cilia move them to the back of the buccal cavity where they are swallowed. The mucus also serves to moisten the incoming air and it is warmed by superficial blood vessels. Within this region there are also olfactory cells which detect odours.

Air then passes through the pharynx and past the **epiglottis**, a flap of cartilage which prevents food entering the trachea. The **larynx**, or voice box, at the anterior end of the trachea is a box-like, cartilagenous structure with a number of ligaments, the **vocal cords**, stretched across it. Vibration of these cords when air is expired produces sound waves. The trachea is lined with ciliated epithelium and goblet cells. The mucus traps particles and the cilia move them to the back of the pharynx to be swallowed. The trachea is supported by incomplete rings of cartilage which prevent the tube collapsing when the pressure inside it falls during inspiration or if external pressure is applied to it. Between the cartilage rings is soft tissue which allows flexibility e.g. when bending the neck.

The trachea divides into two **bronchi**, one entering each lung. The bronchi are also supported by cartilage. The **bronchioles** branch throughout the lung; as the tubes get finer cartilagenous support gradually ceases. These eventually end in alveoli. Each lung is surrounded by an air-tight cavity called the **pleural cavity**. This is bounded by two membranes, or **pleura**, which secrete **pleural fluid** into the cavity. The fluid is a lubricant, preventing friction when the lungs expand at inspiration.

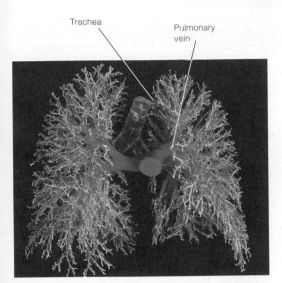

Trachea   Pulmonary vein

Resin cast of pulmonary arteries, trachea and bronchi

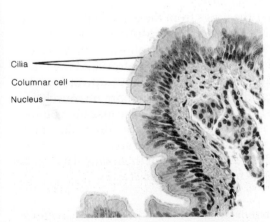

Cilia
Columnar cell
Nucleus

Section of human trachea showing ciliated epithelium (× 150 approx.)

361

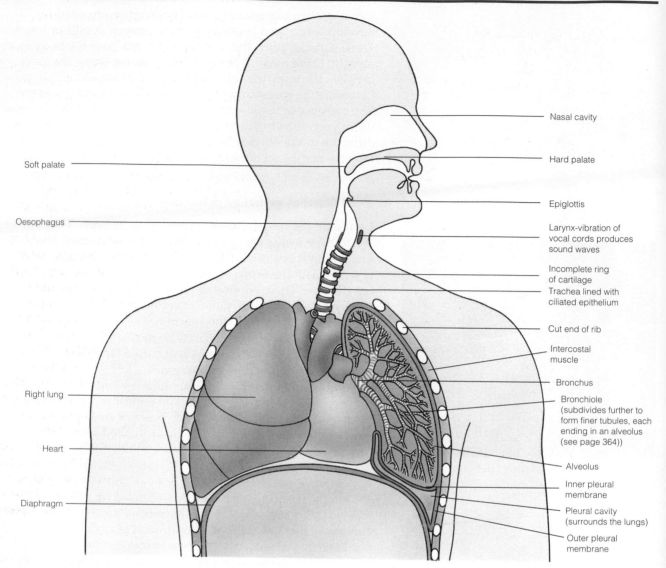

Fig. 15.1 *Ventral view of human thorax*

Labels (from top right):
- Nasal cavity
- Hard palate
- Epiglottis
- Larynx-vibration of vocal cords produces sound waves
- Incomplete ring of cartilage
- Trachea lined with ciliated epithelium
- Cut end of rib
- Intercostal muscle
- Bronchus
- Bronchiole (subdivides further to form finer tubules, each ending in an alveolus (see page 364))
- Alveolus
- Inner pleural membrane
- Pleural cavity (surrounds the lungs)
- Outer pleural membrane

Labels (left side):
- Soft palate
- Oesophagus
- Right lung
- Heart
- Diaphragm

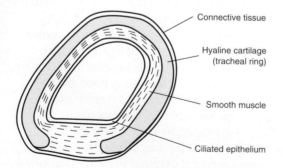

Labels:
- Connective tissue
- Hyaline cartilage (tracheal ring)
- Smooth muscle
- Ciliated epithelium

Fig. 15.2 *Transverse section through the human trachea*

Did you know?

The 700 million alveoli in both human lungs cover an area of 90 m² – almost the size of a tennis court.

Pressure in the pleural cavity is always about 500 Pa lower than in the lungs and this allows them to expand and fill the thorax.

Breathing in (inspiration) in humans

In order for air to enter the lungs from the exterior the pressure inside the lungs must be lower than atmospheric pressure. This lowering of pressure is brought about as follows.

When the external intercostal muscles contract and the internal intercostal muscles relax, the ribs move upwards and outwards (anteriorly and ventrally). The diaphragm muscle contracts and flattens. These two movements cause the volume of the thorax to increase and therefore the pressure inside it falls. The elastic lungs expand to fill the available space and so their volume increases and the pressure within them falls. This causes air to rush into the lungs from the exterior.

Breathing out (expiration) in humans

Breathing in is an active process but breathing out is largely passive. The volume of the thorax is decreased as the diaphragm

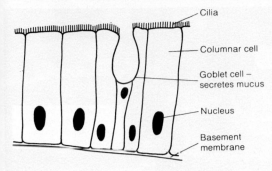

Fig. 15.3 Ciliated epithelium (LS)

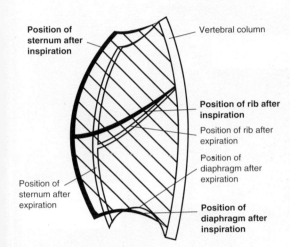

Fig. 15.4 Relative positions of ribs, diaphragm and sternum after breathing in and out

muscle relaxes and it resumes its dome-shape. The external intercostal muscles also relax, allowing the ribs to move downwards (posteriorly) and inwards (dorsally). They may be assisted by contraction of the internal intercostal muscles. As the volume of the thorax decreases, the pressure inside it increases and air is forced out of the lungs as their elastic walls recoil.

Exchange at the alveoli

Each minute alveolus (diameter 100 μm) comprises **squamous epithelium** and some elastic and collagen fibres. Squamous epithelial cells form a single layer attached to a basement membrane. In surface view the cell outlines are irregular and closely packed. The cells are shallow, the central nucleus often forming a bump in the surface. Adjacent cells may be joined by strands of cytoplasm. Such epithelia form ideal surfaces over which diffusion can occur and so are important not only in the alveoli of the lungs, but also in the Bowman's capsule and in capillary walls (Fig. 15.5). Each alveolus is surrounded by a network of blood capillaries which come from the pulmonary artery and unite to form the pulmonary vein. These capillaries are extremely narrow and the red corpuscles (erythrocytes) are squeezed as they pass through. This not only slows down the passage of the blood, allowing more time for diffusion, but also results in a larger surface-area of the red blood cell touching the endothelium and thus facilitates the diffusion of oxygen. The oxygen in the inspired air dissolves in the moisture of the alveolar epithelium and diffuses across this and the endothelium of the capillary into the erythrocyte. Inside the red blood cell, the oxygen combines with the respiratory pigment **haemoglobin** to form **oxyhaemoglobin** (Section 16.2.1). Carbon dioxide diffuses from the blood into the alveolus to leave the lungs in the expired air.

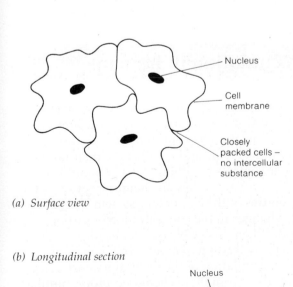

(a) Surface view

(b) Longitudinal section

Fig. 15.5 Squamous epithelium

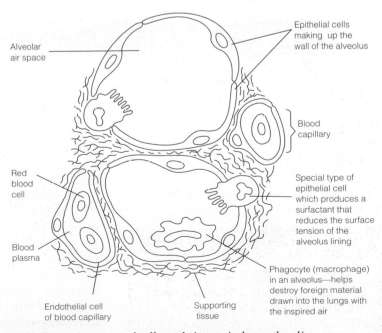

Fig. 15.6 Arrangement of cells and tissues in lung alveoli

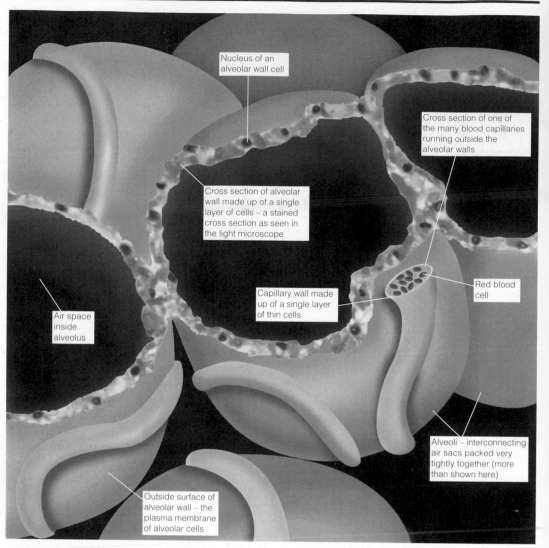

Fig. 15.7 External appearance of a group of alveoli

Magnification ×300 (approx.)

15.3   Control of ventilation in humans

Ventilation of the respiratory system in humans is primarily controlled by the **breathing centre** in a region of the hindbrain called the medulla oblongata. The ventral portion of this centre controls inspiratory movements and is called the **inspiratory centre**; the remainder controls breathing out and is called the **expiratory centre**. Control also relies on **chemoreceptors** in the **carotid and aortic bodies** of the circulatory system. These are sensitive to minute changes in the concentration of carbon dioxide in the blood. When this level rises, for example as a result of physical activity leading to greater cellular respiration in muscles, increased ventilation of the respiratory surfaces is required. Nerve impulses from these chemoreceptors stimulate the inspiratory centre in the medulla. Nerve impulses pass along the phrenic and thoracic nerves to the diaphragm and intercostal muscles. Their increased rate of contraction causes faster inspiration. As the lungs expand, **stretch receptors** in their walls are stimulated and impulses pass along the vagus

Emphysema

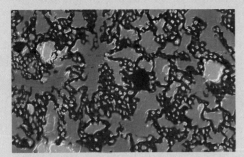

Normal healthy lung tissue

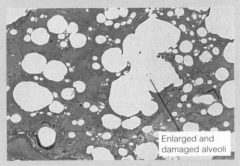

Enlarged and damaged alveoli

Lung tissue damaged by emphysema

One in every five smokers will develop the crippling lung disease called emphysema which, together with other related obstructive lung disorders, kills 20 000 people a year in Britain alone. The disease develops over a period of 20 or so years and it is impossible to diagnose until the lungs have been irreversibly damaged. In its early stages the only symptom is a slight breathlessness but as this gets progressively worse many people are so disabled that they cannot even get out of bed. People with emphysema usually die of respiratory failure, often accompanied by infection. A small number die of heart failure as the heart becomes enlarged and overworked trying to pump blood through arteries which have become constricted as a result of lack of oxygen.

Healthy lungs contain large quantities of elastic connective tissue comprising predominantly the protein elastin. This tissue expands when we breathe in and returns to its former size when we breathe out. In emphysematous lungs the elastin has become permanently stretched and the lungs are no longer able to force out all the air from the alveoli. Little if any exchange of gases can take place across the stretched and damaged air sacs.

The damage is brought about by abnormally high levels of elastase, an enzyme formed in some of the white blood cells, which breaks down elastin. Elastase also degrades other proteins so that, in the latter stages of the disease, breakdown of lung tissue results in large, non-functional holes in the lung.

In healthy lungs elastin is not broken down because a protein inhibitor (PI) inhibits the action of the enzyme elastase. However, in smokers it has been suggested that the oxidants in cigarette smoke inactivate PI, resulting in greater elastase activity and hence a breakdown of elastin.

Elastase is produced by phagocytes which need it so they can migrate through tissue to reach sites of infection. This is part of the body's normal inflammatory response. In smokers, where a large number of phagocytic cells are attracted to the lungs by the particulate materials in smoke, a combination of the release of elastase and a low level of its natural inhibitor leads to a lot of tissue degradation.

Smoking obviously causes much of the damage associated with emphysema but why is it that not all smokers suffer to the same extent? It is possible that the one in five who develop emphysema do so because they have defective repair mechanisms and are unable to counteract the considerable cell damage which occurs during the development of the disease. This may be the result of a genetic defect which limits cell division or production of abnormal connective tissue proteins during smoke-induced stress.

Emphysema cannot be cured and the disease cannot be reversed. The only way to minimize the chance of getting it is not to smoke at all, or to give up – the function cannot be restored to smoke-damaged lungs but giving up can significantly reduce the rate of further deterioration.

nerve to the expiratory centre in the medulla. This automatically 'switches off' the inspiratory centre, the muscles relax and expiration takes place. The stretch receptors are no longer stimulated, the expiratory centre is 'switched off' and the inspiratory centre 'switched on'. Inspiration takes place again. This complex example of a feedback mechanism is illustrated in Fig. 15.8 and further examples of homeostatic control are considered in Chapter 18.

The breathing centre may also be stimulated by impulses from the forebrain resulting in a conscious increase or decrease in breathing rate.

The main stimulus for ventilation is therefore the change in carbon dioxide concentration and stimulation of stretch receptors in the lungs; changes in oxygen concentration have relatively little effect. At high altitudes the reduced atmospheric pressure makes it more difficult to load the haemoglobin with oxygen. In an attempt to obtain sufficient oxygen a mountaineer takes very deep breaths. This forces more carbon dioxide out of the body and the level of carbon dioxide in the blood therefore falls. The inspiratory centre is no longer stimulated and breathing becomes increasingly laboured, causing great fatigue. Given time, humans can adapt to these conditions by excreting more alkaline urine. This causes the pH of the blood to fall, the chemoreceptors are stimulated and so is the inspiratory centre.

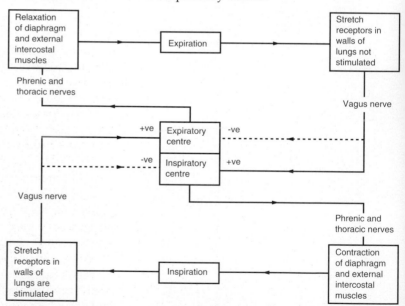

Fig. 15.8 Control of ventilation

15.4 Measurements of lung capacity

Human lungs have a volume of about 5 dm^3 but in a normal breath only about 0.45 dm^3 of this will be exchanged (**tidal volume**). During forced breathing the total exchanged may rise to 3.5 dm^3 (**vital capacity**) which leaves a **residual volume** of about 1.5 dm^3. These terms, and others associated with lung capacity, are illustrated in Fig. 15.9.

Air that reaches the lungs on inspiration mixes with the

Asthma

Asthma is the name given to a group of long-lasting (chronic) disorders which are characterized by some restriction of the airways of the lungs due to muscular spasms, inflammation, excess mucus production or a combination of all three. As a result breathing becomes difficult. Across the world asthma affects around 10% of people and it has increased dramatically in Britain over the past decade where it now accounts for around 2000 deaths each year and is the most frequent cause of children being away sick from school. Many factors may trigger an asthma attack, including anxiety, stress, infection, cold-air, exercise and specific substances to which an individual is allergic.

Why some individuals are allergic to certain substances while others are not is not clearly understood but there may be a genetic predisposition to an allergic response, or the condition may be acquired during early childhood or even when still in the womb. Dietary or environmental factors commonly trigger an attack in a vulnerable individual with certain foods (e.g. milk or eggs), pollen grains, fungal spores and animal hair commonly provoking an attack. One of the most common **allergens** (particles which trigger an attack) are proteases found in the faeces of the house dust mite. Air pollution can make the situation worse; sulphur dioxide and soot particles with a diameter of 10 μm or less have all been shown to provoke an attack. Passive cigarette smoking is also closely linked to the development of asthma and the children of mothers who smoke during pregnancy display a higher than average incidence of the disorder.

Whatever the cause, the reaction to an allergen has two parts: **Sensitization** arises first, as a result of the substance being engulfed by phagocytic blood cells which then produce antibodies to the allergen. These antibodies circulate in the blood before becoming attached to a type of white blood cell called **mast cells**. The patient suffers no symptoms at this stage. **Activation** occurs when the individual is re-exposed to the same allergen, which now binds to the antibodies on the mast cells which as a consequence release a range of chemicals some of which cause spasms of the smooth muscle in the bronchial passages causing them to constrict, while others e.g. histamines lead to inflammation of the lungs. Together these restrict the air-flow to the alveoli and cause the asthma attack.

As would be expected with a complex disorder such as asthma, the treatment is varied, and can include using any combination of the following drugs:

1. Agents which block the synthesis or release of the chemicals which cause inflammation.
2. Antihistamines to counteract histamines – chemicals which cause inflammation.
3. Agents which block inflammatory molecules other than histamines.
4. Agents which prevent cells accumulating at inflammatory sites by blocking the formation of the chemicals which attract the cells.
5. Medicines which block the actions of Platelet Activating Factor (PAF), a chemical which leads to congestion in the small blood vessels of the lung.
6. Agents which act as broncho-dilators and so open up the constricted airways of the lung.

Spirometer attached to a kymograph

TABLE 15.2 **Comparison of inspired, alveolar and expired air**

Gas	% Composition by volume		
	Inspired air	Alveolar air	Expired air
Oxygen	20.95	13.8	16.4
Carbon dioxide	0.04	5.5	4.0
Nitrogen	79.01	80.7	79.6

PROJECT

Use the spirometer to find the effect of exercise on the rate and depth of breathing.

residual air so that it does not 'stagnate' but is gradually changed. This mixing of relatively small volumes of fresh air with a much larger volume of residual air keeps the level of gases in the alveoli more or less constant.

Measurements of respiratory activity may be made using a spirometer attached to a kymograph which records all its movements.

The ventilation rate is calculated as the number of breaths per minute × tidal volume.

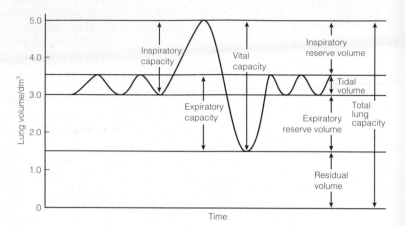

Fig. 15.9 Graph to illustrate lung capacities

15.4.1 Effects of exercise on breathing and gaseous exchange

Exercise entails muscular movement and hence the need for an adequate supply of oxygen to release the energy required for the contraction of muscle fibres. To increase the oxygen supply the rate of gas exchange at the lungs must be increased. This is achieved firstly by increasing the number of breaths per minute from the average of 15 at rest up to 45 at the peak of strenuous exercise. Secondly the amount of air exchanged at each breath is increased from $0.45\,dm^3$ at rest to a maximum of $3.5\,dm^3$ during exercise. These changes help to increase the oxygen consumption of the body to around $4\,dm^3\,min^{-1}$ from the normal resting value of $0.3\,dm^3\,min^{-1}$. This is a thirteen-fold increase although values of up to 20 times are possible in well-trained athletes. This is partly because, with fitness training, the normally passive (and therefore relatively slow) process of expiration is accelerated because both the internal intercostal and abdominal muscles contract forcefully to pull the ribs inwards and the diaphragm upwards. This results in a much more rapid expulsion of air than occurs in an unfit individual, thus allowing more breaths to be taken in a given period of time. Dilation of the bronchioles helps to increase the flow of air down to the alveoli.

Getting more air into the lungs more rapidly would be pointless unless the rate at which oxygen is absorbed from the lungs into the blood is also increased. This is largely achieved by the hormone adrenaline acting on the smooth muscle of the arterioles which supply blood to the capillary network around the alveoli. Dilation of these arterioles improves the blood flow to the lungs and increases the uptake of oxygen into the blood three-fold. The way in which the circulatory system increases the rate of delivery of oxygenated blood to the muscles during exercise is dealt with in Section 16.5.4.

Smoking

Tobacco is responsible for 15–20% of all deaths in Britain, amounting to about 100 000 people every year. The three main diseases closely linked with smoking are:

Coronary heart disease
Smoking increases the likelihood of fatty deposits arising on the inner lining of the arteries (atherosclerosis) which cause the lumen to narrow and so restrict the movement of blood through them. Where this narrowing occurs in the coronary artery it can lead to a heart attack and if in the carotid artery a stroke may be the consequence.

Lung cancer
Cancer is described on pages 116 and 117. There is more than one type of lung cancer but bronchial carcinoma is by far the most common. The tars in tobacco smoke may induce the epithelial cells lining the bronchial tubes to become cancerous. If not treated, the tumor may completely disrupt the functioning of the lung, leaving surgical removal as the only effective treatment. A highly persistent cough, blood in the sputum and chest pains are all symptoms of lung cancer.

Chronic bronchitis
The tars in tobacco irritate the epithelial lining of the bronchial tubes causing it to produce excess mucus. The cilia lining the tubes become damaged and unable to remove this mucus in the usual manner. Only by coughing can the mucus be expelled and in time this leads to scarring and narrowing of the bronchial tubes, causing breathlessness.
Other smoking-related conditions include:
- emphysema (see page 365)
- cancer of mouth, throat, bladder and pancreas
- other cardiovascular diseases
- peptic ulcers
- narrowing of blood vessels in limbs
- damage to the unborn child

Tobacco smoke is a mixture of chemicals, a number of which interact with each other, multiplying their effects. The three constituents which do most harm are nicotine, carbon monoxide and tars.

Nicotine:
- is quickly absorbed into blood, reaching the brain in 30 seconds
- causes platelets to become sticky leading to clotting
- stimulates production of adrenalin leading to increased heart rate and raised blood pressure which puts an extra strain on the heart

Carbon monoxide:
- combines with haemoglobin to form carboxyhaemoglobin, therefore lowering oxygen-carrying capacity of the blood

- may aggravate angina
- seems to slow growth of the fetus

Tars:
- form an aerosol of minute droplets which enter the respiratory system causing thickening of the epithelium leading to chronic bronchitis
- paralyse cilia so dust, germs and mucus accumulate in lungs leading to infection and damage
- contain carcinogens – heavy smokers have a 25% greater risk of cancer than non-smokers.

15.5   Questions

1. An investigation was carried out into the effects of athletic training on respiration in human muscle. In the investigation, a group of trained athletes and a control group of non-athletes exercised at different levels. The levels of exercise were expressed as rates of energy expenditure in $J\,min^{-1}\,kg^{-1}$ of body mass. At each level, oxygen consumption and lactic acid production were measured, and converted into rates per kg of body mass.
The results are shown in the table below. Figures in the table are the means of the measurements made for each group.

Rate of energy expenditure /$J\,min^{-1}\,kg^{-1}$	Rate of oxygen consumption /$cm^3\,min^{-1}\,kg^{-1}$		Rate of lactic acid production /$mg\,min^{-1}\,kg^{-1}$	
	Athletes	Non-athletes	Athletes	Non-athletes
600	30	29	0	0
800	40	39	0	0
1000	50	44	0	185
1200	57	45	85	350
1400	58	45	305	590

Adapted from Margaria, *Scientific American* (226:3)

(a) (i) Compare and comment on the effects of increasing the levels of exercise on rates of oxygen consumption in athletes and non-athletes *(3 marks)*
(ii) Compare and comment on the effects of increasing the levels of exercise on rates of lactic acid production in athletes and non-athletes. *(3 marks)*
(b) Suggest how training may alter the muscles of athletes to bring about these differences in muscle respiration. *(5 marks)*
(Total 11 marks)

ULEAC 1996, Specimen Paper HB3, No. 7

2. Fig. 1 shows a drawing from a photomicrograph of lung tissue.

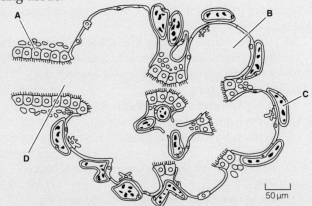

Fig. 1

(a) Name parts **A** to **D** *(4 marks)*
Fig. 2 summarizes a metabolic pathway which occurs in animal and plant cells.

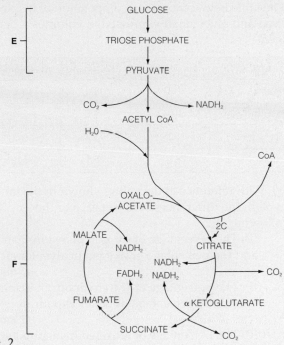

Fig. 2

(b) Complete the table below by
(i) naming the stages labelled **E** and **F**;
(ii) stating the **precise** location in the cell where each of these stages occurs.

	(i) Name of stage	**(ii) Precise location in the cell**
E		
F		

(4 marks)

(c) Describe the fate of the carbon dioxide shown in Fig. 2 when it reaches part **C** in Fig. 1 *(3 marks)*
Fig. 3 shows the way in which breathing is controlled.

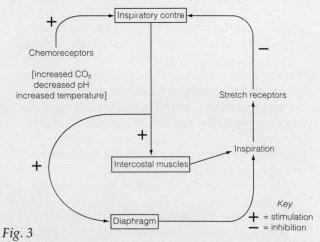

Fig. 3

(d) With reference to Fig. 3, explain how exercise causes a change in the breathing rate. (6 marks)

(Total 17 marks)

UCLES June 1994, Paper 2, No. 1

3. The table below shows the composition of inspired, expired and alveolar air expressed in volumes per cent.

Gas	Inspired air	Expired air	Alveolar air
Oxygen	20.71	14.6	13.2
Carbon dioxide	0.04	3.8	5.0
Water vapour	1.25	6.2	6.2
Nitrogen	78.00	75.4	75.6

(a) With reference to the values shown in the table, explain the differences between each of the following.

(i) The percentage of oxygen in inspired air and the percentage of oxygen in alveolar air (1 mark)

(ii) The percentage of water vapour in inspired air and the percentage of water vapour in expired air (1 mark)

(iii) The percentage of nitrogen in inspired air and the percentage of nitrogen in expired air (1 mark)

(b) Describe **two** effects of smoking on gas exchange. (4 marks)

(c) (i) What is meant by the term *vital capacity*? (3 marks)

(ii) Explain how training can affect the vital capacity of athletes. (2 marks)

(Total 12 marks)

ULEAC June 1993, Paper 1, No. 9

4. (a) (i) Describe how the lungs of a patient with emphysema differ from those of a healthy person. (1 mark)

(ii) Explain why the lungs of an emphysema patient cannot supply the body with sufficient oxygen. (2 marks)

(b) The table at the top of the next column shows the results of a study of 83 patients relating the occurrence of black particles in the lungs and emphysema to the number of cigarettes smoked per day.

Calculate the percentage of people who smoked 16 or more cigarettes per day who had:

(i) severe emphysema (a value of 3 on the scale); (1 mark)

(ii) a large amount of black particles in the lungs (a value of 3 on the scale). (1 mark)

		Number of cigarettes smoked per day	Severity of emphysema/arbitrary scale			
			0	1	2	3
Amount of black particles in lungs/ arbitrary scale	1	0	11	3	0	1
		1–15	1	5	0	0
		16 or more	5	7	3	2
	2	0	1	2	1	1
		1–15	1	1	1	0
		16 or more	0	7	11	9
	3	0	0	0	0	0
		1–15	0	0	0	0
		16 or more	0	1	3	6

(c) Some people are genetically unable to produce a protein called α_1-antitrypsin. Unless they are provided with this protein they will develop emphysema.

(i) Which one of the following techniques would you consider to be of use in detecting inability to produce α_1-antitrypsin?

A Biochemical test

B Endoscopy

C Ultrasound

D X-rays

Give the letter of your choice. (1 mark)

(ii) Suggest why α_1-antitrypsin is not given as a medicine to be swallowed. (1 mark)

(Total 7 marks)

NEAB June 1995, Paper BY08, No. 5

5. Lung cancer is the commonest cancer in the United Kingdom. In 1987, over 40 000 people died from lung cancer; it was the commonest cause of cancer deaths in men, and the second commonest cause in women. The importance of lung cancer as a cause of death has increased during the twentieth century. In 1900 it was a rare disease (at a rate of 10 deaths per 100 000 in men), but by 1980 it was over 100 per 100 000. The figure shows the mortality trends by age and sex for lung cancer from the 1940s to 1985 in England and Wales.

(a) Use the information in the figure to describe the trends in mortality in males and females. (4 marks)

(b) State **one** reason for the use of logarithmic scales in the figure. (1 mark)

(c) Describe briefly the epidemiological evidence that links lung cancer with smoking (4 marks)

(d) Explain how tobacco smoke causes lung cancer. (3 marks)

(e) State **two** withdrawal symptoms of tobacco smoking. (2 marks)

(f) Name **two** other diseases associated with smoking. (2 marks)

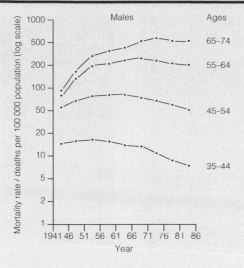

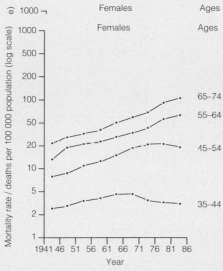

(Source: Factsheet 11, Cancer Research Campaign, 1989)

(*Total 16 marks*)

UCLES June 1993, Paper 3 (Option 2), No. 2

6. (*a*) Describe briefly the structure of the human gaseous exchange system. (*6 marks*)
(*b*) Give an account of the ventilation mechanism and explain how the process of *breathing* is controlled. (*12 marks*)
(*Total 18 marks*)

UCLES June 1993, Paper 2, No. 6

7. In 1970, the Norwegian government announced that it was going to introduce a smoking control programme which would include a ban on all tobacco advertising. The Act came into force in 1975. Fig. 1 shows annual sales of tobacco and cigarettes per person in Norway over the period 1951 to 1981.
(*a*) Suggest **four** further measures, in addition to a ban on advertising, which have been, or could be, implemented to control smoking. (*4 marks*)
(*b*) What evidence is there from Fig. 1 that a ban on tobacco advertising may be effective in reducing cigarette sales? (*1 mark*)

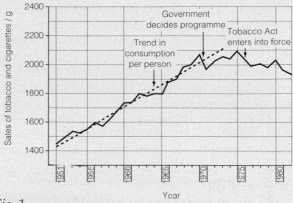

Fig. 1

(*c*) What criticism could be offered against the evidence used in (*b*)? (*1 mark*)
(*d*) Fig. 1 also shows the **trend** in consumption per person for the years 1951 to 1970.
(i) If this trend had continued, what would be the consumption of tobacco and cigarettes have been by the end of 1981?
(ii) Using your answer to (*d*) (i), calculate the percentage reduction in **actual** tobacco and cigarette consumption by the end of 1981. Show the stages in your calculation. (*4 marks*)
Fig. 2 shows the percentage of daily smokers among Norwegian school pupils aged 13–15 years, 1957 to 1980.

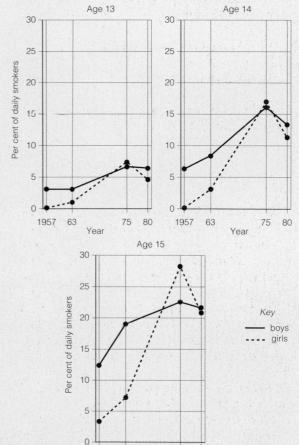

Fig. 2

(e) What further evidence, **for and against** the argument that cigarette advertising affects the volume of cigarette sales, is provided by the data of Fig. 2? *(2 marks)*

(f) The Soviet Union has no cigarette advertising but smoking is widespread. Suggest **four** factors that could be responsible for this. *(4 marks)*

Fig. 3 shows two micrographs of lung tissue. Tissue from a healthy lung is shown on the left, and tissue from the lung of a long-term smoker is shown on the right.

(g) (i) State **two** visible ways in which the tissues differ.

(ii) Briefly account for the differences you have described in *(g)* (i). *(5 marks)*

(h) Tar is regarded as the single most dangerous component of cigarette smoke. Outline the reasons for this. *(4 marks)*

(Total 25 marks)

UCLES June 1992, Paper 3 (Option 2), No. 2

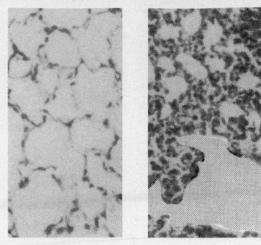

Fig. 3

16 Blood and circulation

As all cells are bathed in an aqueous medium, the delivery of materials to and from these cells is carried out largely in solution. The fluid in which the materials are dissolved or suspended is blood. The cellular components of human blood are described in Section 16.1. While a number of ideas on blood were put forward by Greek and Roman scientists, it was the English physician William Harvey (1578–1657) who first showed that it was pumped into arteries by the heart, circulated around the body and returned via veins.

16.1 Structure of blood

Did you know?

About 3 million red cells are produced, and the same number die, every second in an adult human.

Blood comprises a watery **plasma** in which are a variety of different cells. The majority of cells present are **erythrocytes** or red blood cells which are biconcave discs about 7 μm in diameter. They have no nucleus and are formed in the bone marrow. The remaining cells are the larger, nucleated white cells or **leucocytes**. Most of these are also made in the bone marrow. There are two basic types of leucocyte. **Granulocytes** have granular cytoplasm and a lobed nucleus; they can engulf bacteria by phagocytosis. Some of them are also thought to have antihistamine properties. **Agranulocytes** have a non-granular cytoplasm and a compact nucleus. Some of these also ingest bacteria but the **lymphocytes**, made mainly in the thymus gland and lymphoid tissues, produce **antibodies**. More sparsely distributed in the plasma are tiny cell fragments called **platelets**. These are important in the process of blood clotting.

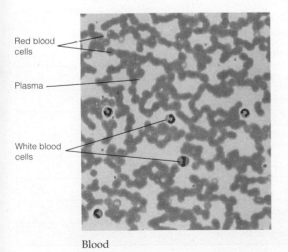

Red blood cells

Plasma

White blood cells

Blood

ERYTHROCYTE

Surface view (disc shaped)

Lateral view (biconcave)

PLATELETS

AGRANULOCYTE

Nucleus

GRANULOCYTES

Nucleus

Neutrophil

Basophil

Fig. 16.1 Composition of blood

375

Formation of blood

In the fetus red blood cells are formed in the liver, but in adults production moves to bones, such as the cranium, sternum, vertebrae and ribs, which have red bone marrow. White cells like lymphocytes are formed in the thymus gland and lymph nodes whereas other types are formed in bones, e.g. the long bones of the limbs, which have white bone marrow.

16.2 Functions of blood

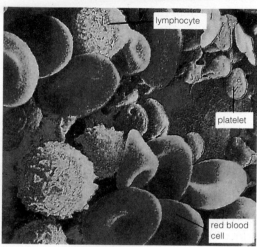

SEM of human blood cells

Blood performs two distinct functions: the transport of materials (summarized in Table 16.1) and defence against disease.

16.2.1 Respiratory pigment – haemoglobin

The solubility of oxygen is low, with only $0.58\,cm^3$ dissolving in $100\,cm^3$ of water at $25\,°C$. At human body temperature ($37\,°C$) the quantity is even less, just $0.46\,cm^3$, because the solubility decreases as the temperature increases. Many animals including humans have evolved a group of coloured proteins capable of loosely combining with oxygen, in order to increase the oxygen-carrying capacity of the blood. These are known as **respiratory pigments**. With a few exceptions, the pigments with large relative molecular mass (RMM) are found in the plasma while those of smaller RMM occur within cells to prevent them being lost by ultrafiltration in the kidneys.

The important property of respiratory pigments is their ability to combine readily with oxygen where its concentration is high, i.e. at the respiratory surface, and to release it as readily where its concentration is low, i.e. in the tissues.

TABLE 16.1   **Summary of the transport functions of blood**

Materials transported	Examples	Transported from	Transported to	Transported in
Respiratory gases	Oxygen	Lungs	Respiring tissues	Haemoglobin in red blood cells
	Carbon dioxide	Respiring tissues	Lungs	Haemoglobin in red blood cells. Hydrogen carbonate ions in plasma
Organic digestive products	Glucose	Intestines	Respiring tissues/liver	Plasma
	Amino acids	Intestines	Liver/body tissues	Plasma
	Vitamins	Intestines	Liver/body tissues	Plasma
Mineral salts	Calcium	Intestines	Bones/teeth	Plasma
	Iodine	Intestines	Thyroid gland	Plasma
	Iron	Intestines/liver	Bone marrow	Plasma
Excretory products	Urea	Liver	Kidney	Plasma
Hormones	Insulin	Pancreas	Liver	Plasma
	Anti-diuretic hormone	Pituitary gland	Kidney	Plasma
Heat	Metabolic heat	Liver and muscle	All parts of the body	All parts of the blood

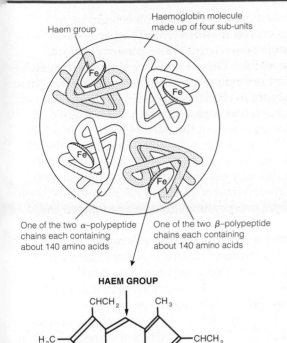

One of the two α–polypeptide chains each containing about 140 amino acids

One of the two β–polypeptide chains each containing about 140 amino acids

Haem group

Haemoglobin molecule made up of four sub-units

HAEM GROUP

Fig. 16.2 The structure of haemoglobin

The best known and most efficient respiratory pigment is **haemoglobin**. The haemoglobin molecule is made up of an iron porphyrin compound – the **haem** group – and a protein – **globin**. The haem group contains a ferrous iron atom, which is capable of carrying a single oxygen molecule. A single molecule of human haemoglobin, has a RMM of 68 000 and possesses four haem groups. It therefore is capable of carrying four molecules of oxygen. The arrangement of the human haemoglobin molecule is given in Fig. 16.2.

16.2.2 Transport of oxygen

An efficient respiratory pigment readily picks up oxygen at the respiratory surface and releases it on arrival at tissues. This may appear contradictory as a substance with a high affinity for oxygen is unlikely to release it easily. Respiratory pigments overcome the problem by having a high affinity for oxygen when its concentration is high, but this is reduced when the oxygen concentration is low. Oxygen concentration is measured by partial pressure, otherwise called the **oxygen tension**. Normal atmospheric pressure is approximately 100 kiloPascals. As oxygen makes up around 21% of the atmosphere, the oxygen tension (partial pressure) of the atmosphere is around 21 kPa.

When a respiratory pigment such as haemoglobin is exposed to a gradual increase in oxygen tension it absorbs oxygen rapidly at first, but more slowly as the tension continues to rise. This relationship between the oxygen tension and the saturation of haemoglobin is called the **oxygen dissociation curve** and is illustrated below.

The release of oxygen from haemoglobin is facilitated by the presence of carbon dioxide – a phenomenon known as the **Bohr**

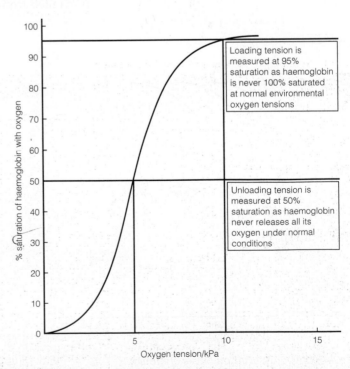

Loading tension is measured at 95% saturation as haemoglobin is never 100% saturated at normal environmental oxygen tensions

Unloading tension is measured at 50% saturation as haemoglobin never releases all its oxygen under normal conditions

% saturation of haemoglobin with oxygen

Oxygen tension/kPa

Fig. 16.3 Oxygen dissociation curve for adult human haemoglobin

effect. Where carbon dioxide concentration is high, i.e. in respiring tissues, oxygen is released readily; where carbon dioxide concentration is low, i.e. at the respiratory surface, oxygen is taken up readily. These effects are shown in Fig. 16.4.

Not only do respiratory pigments vary between species, there are often different types in the same species. In humans, for example, the fetus has a haemoglobin which differs in two of the four polypeptide chains from the haemoglobin of an adult. This gives the fetal haemoglobin a dissociation curve to the left of that of the adult and therefore a greater affinity for oxygen (Fig. 16.5). Only in this way can the fetal haemoglobin absorb oxygen from the maternal haemoglobin in the placenta. At birth the production of fetal haemoglobin gives way to that of the adult type.

Another respiratory pigment in humans is **myoglobin**. It consists of a single polypeptide chain and a single haem group, rather than the four found in haemoglobin. Like fetal haemoglobin, myoglobin has a dissociation curve displaced to the left of that of the adult and therefore has a greater affinity for oxygen (Fig. 16.6). Myoglobin occurs in the muscles of humans, where it acts as a store of oxygen. In periods of extreme exertion, when the supply of oxygen by the blood is insufficient to keep pace with demand, the oxygen tension of muscle falls to a very low level. At these very low oxygen tensions, myoglobin releases its oxygen to keep the muscles working efficiently. Once exercise has ceased the myoglobin store is replenished from the haemoglobin in the blood.

Haemoglobin has a greater affinity for carbon monoxide than it does for oxygen. When carbon monoxide is inhaled, even in small quantities, it combines with haemoglobin in preference to oxygen to form a stable compound, **carboxyhaemoglobin**. The carbon monoxide is not released at normal atmospheric oxygen tensions and the haemoglobin is therefore permanently prevented from transporting oxygen. Below levels of 2%

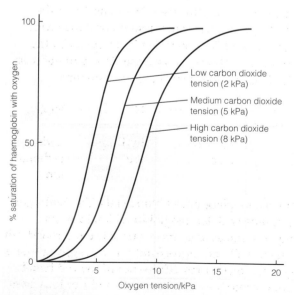

Fig. 16.4 Oxygen dissociation curve of human haemoglobin, illustrating the Bohr effect

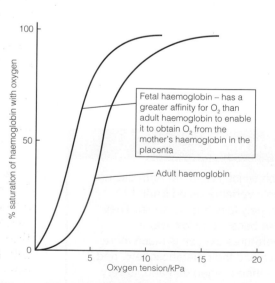

Fig. 16.5 Comparison of the oxygen dissociation curves of adult and fetal haemoglobin

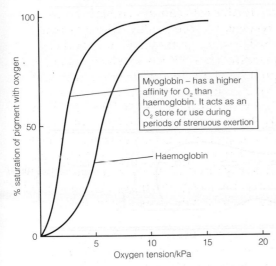

Fig. 16.6 Comparison of the oxygen dissociation curves of human haemoglobin and myoglobin

carboxyhaemoglobin in the blood, there are few if any symptoms. At levels of 2–10% tiredness and loss of concentration can be experienced which increase until the individual is incapacitated at levels of 30–40%. Coma and death from **asphyxia** occur at levels above 70%. As carbon monoxide has no colour or odour it can poison without the victim being aware.

Carbon monoxide arises from two main sources. Firstly it is a constituent of tobacco smoke (see Focus on smoking on page 369). Secondly it results from the incomplete oxidation of fuels such as the petrol burnt in car engines, more especially those that are badly tuned. People whose occupations bring them into regular contact with car exhausts, e.g. taxi drivers, traffic policemen and car park attendants are especially at risk of exceeding the 3% safe limit recommended by the World Health Organization.

16.2.3 Transport of carbon dioxide

Carbon dioxide is more soluble than oxygen in water, but its transport in solution is still inadequate to meet the needs of most organisms. There are three methods of carrying carbon dioxide from the tissues to the respiratory surface.

1. **In aqueous solution** – A small amount, around 5% of carbon dioxide is transported in physical solution in blood plasma.

2. **In combination with haemoglobin** – A little carbon dioxide, around 10%, will combine with the amino groups ($-NH_2$) in the four polypeptide chains which make up each haemoglobin molecule (Hb).

$$Hb-N\begin{matrix} H \\ \\ H \end{matrix} + CO_2 \rightleftharpoons Hb-N\begin{matrix} H \\ \\ COO^- \end{matrix} + H^+$$

| haemoglobin | + | carbon dioxide | carbamino haemoglobin | + | hydrogen ions |

3. **In the form of hydrogen carbonate** – The majority of the carbon dioxide (85%) produced by the tissues combines with water to form carbonic acid. This reaction is catalysed by the zinc-containing enzyme **carbonic anhydrase**. The carbonic acid dissociates into hydrogen and hydrogen carbonate ions.

$$H_2O + CO_2 \underset{\text{anhydrase}}{\overset{\text{carbonic}}{\rightleftharpoons}} H_2CO_3 \rightleftharpoons H^+ + HCO^-_3$$

| water | carbon dioxide | carbonic acid | hydrogen ion | hydrogen carbonate ion |

The above reactions take place in red blood cells. The hydrogen ions produced combine with haemoglobin which loses its oxygen. The oxygen so released diffuses out of the red blood cell, through the capillary wall and tissue fluid into a respiring tissue cell. The hydrogen carbonate ions diffuse out of the red blood cell into the plasma where they combine with sodium ions from the dissociation of sodium chloride to form sodium hydrogen carbonate. It is largely in this form that the carbon dioxide is

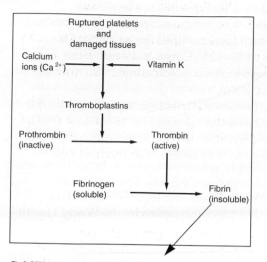

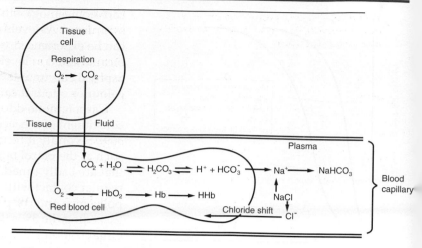

Fig. 16.7 The chloride shift

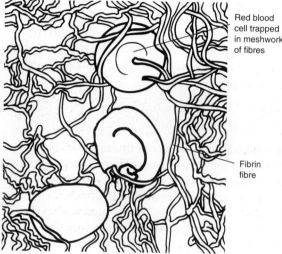

Red blood cell trapped in meshwork of fibres

Fibrin fibre

Fig. 16.8 The clotting process – a summary of the main stages

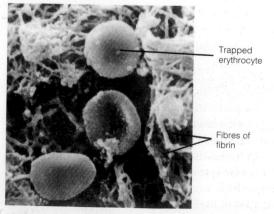

Trapped erythrocyte

Fibres of fibrin

The clotting process (scanning EM) (× 2500 approx.)

carried to the respiratory surface where the processes are reversed, releasing carbon dioxide which diffuses out of the body. The loss of negatively charged hydrogen carbonate ions from the red blood cells is balanced by the inward diffusion of negative chloride ions from the dissociation of the sodium chloride. In this way the electrochemical neutrality of the red blood cell is restored. This is known as the **chloride shift** and is illustrated in Fig. 16.7.

16.2.4 Clotting of the blood

If a blood vessel is ruptured it is important that the resultant loss of blood is quickly arrested. If not, the pressure of the blood in the circulatory system could fall dangerously low. At the same time it is important that clotting does not occur during the normal circulation of blood. If it does, the clot might lodge in some blood vessel, cutting off the blood supply to a vital organ and possibly resulting in death from **thrombosis**. For this reason the clotting process is very complex, involving a large number of stages. Only under the very specific conditions of injury are all stages completed and clotting occurs. In this way the chances of clotting taking place in other circumstances is reduced. The following account includes only the major stages, of what is a more complex process.

Cellular fragments in the blood called **platelets (thrombocytes)** are involved in the clotting or **coagulation** of the blood. At the site of a wound the damaged cells and ruptured platelets release **thromboplastins**. The platelets attract **clotting factors** which create a cascade effect whereby each activates the next in the chain. Amongst these is factor VIII, the absence of which, due to a sex-linked genetic defect, is the cause of haemophilia (Section 7.4.2). At the end of these chain reactions factor X is produced which in the presence of calcium ions and vitamin K causes the inactive plasma protein, **prothrombin**, to become converted to its active form, **thrombin**. This in turn converts another plasma protein, the soluble **fibrinogen**, to

1. *The neutrophil is attracted to the bacterium by chemoattractants. It moves towards the bacterium along a concentration gradient.*

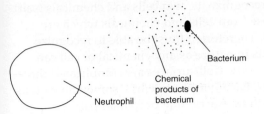

2. *The neutrophil binds to the bacterium.*

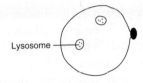

3. *Lysosomes within the neutrophil migrate towards the phagosome formed by pseudopodia engulfing the bacterium.*

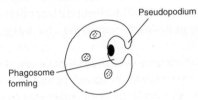

4. *The lysosomes release their lytic enzymes into the phagosome where they break down the bacterium.*

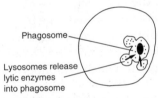

5. *The breakdown products of the bacterium are absorbed by the neutrophil.*

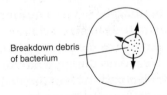

Fig. 16.9 *Summary of phagocytosis of a bacterium by a neutrophil*

fibrin, its insoluble form. The fibrin forms a meshwork of threads in which red blood cells become trapped. These dry to form a clot beneath which repair of the wound takes place. The clot not only prevents further blood loss, it also prevents entry of bacteria which might otherwise cause infection. The clotting process is summarized in Fig. 16.8.

Clotting of blood is prevented by substances such as oxalic acid, which precipitates out the calcium ions as calcium oxalate, and heparin, which inhibits the conversion of prothrombin to thrombin. These substances are known as **anticoagulants**.

16.2.5 Defence against infection – phagocytosis

Two types of white cell, the neutrophils and monocytes, are capable of amoeboid movement. Both types carry out **phagocytosis**. This is the process by which large particles are taken up by cells via plasma membrane-derived vesicles. White cells carry out phagocytosis for two reasons: to protect the organism against pathogens and to dispose of dead, dying or damaged cells and cellular debris.

In protecting against infection the phagocyte is attracted to chemicals produced naturally by bacteria. The recognition is aided by the presence of **opsonins** – plasma proteins which attach themselves to the surface of the bacteria. The phagocytes have specific proteins on their surface that bind to these chemo-attractants. This causes the phagocyte to move towards the bacteria, possibly along a concentration gradient. The phagocyte strongly adheres to a bacterium on reaching it. This stimulates the formation of pseudopodia which envelop the bacterium, forming a vacuole called a **phagosome**. **Lysosomes** within the phagocyte migrate towards the phagosome into which they release lytic enzymes that break down the bacterium. The breakdown products are finally absorbed by the phagocyte. Fig. 16.9 summarizes the process.

Some phagocytic cells called **macrophages** are found throughout body tissues. They are part of the **reticulo-endothelial system** and are mostly concentrated in lymph nodes and in the liver.

Phagocytosis causes **inflammation** at the site of infection. The hot and swollen area contains many dead bacteria and phagocytes which are known as **pus**. Inflammation results when **histamine** is released as a result of injury or infection. This causes dilation of blood capillaries from which plasma, containing antibodies, escapes into the tissues. Neutrophils also pass through the capillary walls in a process called **diapedesis**.

16.3   The immune system

Immunity is the ability of an organism to resist disease. It involves the recognition of foreign material and the production of chemicals which help to destroy it. These chemicals, called antibodies, are produced by lymphocytes of which there are two types: **T-lymphocytes**, which are formed in bone marrow but mature in the thymus gland, and **B-lymphocytes**, which are formed and mature in the bone marrow.

16.3.1 Self and non-self antigens

Effective defence of the body against infection lies in the ability of the lymphocyte to recognize its own cells and chemicals (self) and to distinguish these from cells and chemicals which are foreign to it (non-self). Therefore it must be able to recognize everything which exists in nature as any chemical or cell can potentially invade the body. Cell surfaces are complicated three-dimensional structures. Each lymphocyte has, somewhere on its surface, receptors which fit exactly into one small part (perhaps only a few amino acids) of every cell. Clearly there are many different types of lymphocyte.

The different types of lymphocyte are derived from **stem cells** in the bone marrow, special cells in the embryo which also make red blood cells and platelets. The stem cells, on dividing, actually lose most of their DNA to the lymphocytes, i.e. they donate their genes to the lymphocytes. This they do randomly – dealing out genes in a way similar to dealing a hand of cards. Consider the vast number of combinations of cards in a typical hand. Clearly with hundreds of genes, rather than 52 cards, being randomly distributed there are at least 100 million different types of receptors that can be generated – each one able to fit a different chemical shape.

How then do lymphocytes distinguish between their own cells and those that are foreign? In the embryo the lymphocytes are constantly colliding with their own cells' shapes. Since infection in the uterus is rare, any lymphocytes whose receptors exactly fit cells must be the ones that recognize their own cells. These lymphocytes then either die or are suppressed ensuring that the body's own cells will not be attacked. The body has thus become **self-tolerant**. The remaining lymphocytes have receptors which fit chemical shapes of non-self material. Any material with one of these shapes to which lymphocyte receptors adhere is called an **antigen**.

Immune responses

Once a lymphocyte has become attached to its complementary antigen it multiplies rapidly by mitosis to give a clone of identical lymphocytes. This is known as the **primary immune response** and typically takes a few days during which time the invading pathogen often multiplies and so gives rise to the symptoms of the disease it causes. Some of the lymphocytes in this clone change into cells known as **memory cells**. Unlike the other lymphocytes from the clone which die within a few days these memory cells survive much longer – often for years. Further infections by the same pathogen cause these memory cells to divide immediately. Their numbers therefore build up as fast, if not faster, than those of the invader and so the pathogen is repelled before it can induce the symptoms of the disease. This is called the **secondary immune response** and explains why we only suffer some diseases once in a lifetime, despite frequent exposure to them. Each time a pathogen enters the body more and more memory cells are built up, making future infection even less likely. This progressive increase in the level of immunity to a disease is known as **adaptive** or **acquired immunity**.

The variable region differs with each antibody. It has a shape which exactly fits an antigen. Each antibody therefore can bind to two antigens.

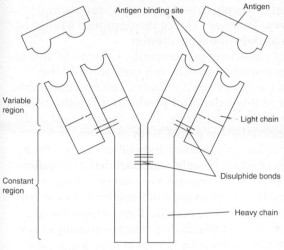

Fig. 16.10 Structure of an antibody

B-lymphocytes and humoral immunity

B-lymphocytes are so called because they both originate and mature in the bone marrow. When a B-lymphocyte recognizes an antigen it divides to form a clone. As most microorganisms possess more than one antigen then many lymphocytes are activated to produce clones in a process known as **polyclonal activation**. Most of the cells in these clones are plasma cells which begin to secrete **antibodies** at the rate of thousands each second.

Antibodies are large protein molecules which comprise four polypeptide chains. One pair of chains is long – **heavy chains**; the other pair is shorter – **light chains**. They are arranged in a Y-shape and have two sites called **binding sites** which fit exactly into the antigen.

There are a number of different antibodies each performing a different function:

1. Agglutination – Because each antibody has two different binding sites it can join to two antigens on two different pathogens. In this way the pathogens can be joined together in clumps making them more vulnerable to attack from other types of antibody.

2. Precipitation – Some antibodies bind together soluble antigens into large units which are thus precipitated out of solution. As such they are more easily ingested by phagocytes.

3. Neutralization – Certain antibodies bind to toxic molecules produced by a pathogen and in doing so neutralize their harmful effects.

4. Lysis – Antibodies which are attached to a pathogen act as binding sites for a number of blood proteins which are collectively known as the **complement system**. Some of these proteins are enzymes which cause the breakdown of the pathogen.

T-lymphocytes and cell-mediated immunity

T-lymphocytes are so called because while produced in bone marrow they mature in the thymus gland. Once attached to their antigen T-lymphocytes divide to form a clone, the cells of which then differentiate into different cell types:

1. T-helper cells – These produce chemicals which activate other white cells such as phagocytes to engulf harmful material. The chemicals attach themselves to the foreign material and so label them as requiring phagocytosis. These labelled chemicals are called **opsonins** (from the Greek meaning 'ready for the table'). The T-helper cells also activate B-lymphocytes to divide to produce plasma cells as well as assisting the T-killer cells to destroy pathogens. Clearly they are essential to a successful immune response – a fact borne out by the consequences of their being rendered inoperable by the Human Immunodeficiency Virus (HIV) leading to AIDS.

2. T-cytotoxic cells (killer cells) – These kill body cells which have become invaded by viruses. They force cylindrical proteins through the cell membrane causing the cell to burst. Since viruses require host cells to reproduce, this sacrifice effectively prevents multiplication of the virus.

3. T-suppressor cells – Once an infection has been eliminated these cells suppress the activities of the lymphocytes and so maintain control of the immune system.

16.3.2 Monoclonal antibodies and their applications

We have seen in Section 16.3.1 that foreign material entering the body will possess more than one antigen and so induces a number of different B-lymphocytes to multiply, producing clones of themselves. The many clones then produce a range of antibodies known as **polyclonal antibodies**.

It is obviously of considerable therapeutic value to be able to produce antibodies outside the body, but until recently the inability to sustain the growth of B-lymphocytes prevented this. However, a cancer of B-lymphocytes produces myeloma cells which continue to divide indefinitely. These can be fused in the laboratory, using polyethylene glycol, with each specific B-lymphocyte to produce cells, called **hybridoma cells**, which produce antibodies of one type only – **monoclonal antibodies**.

The large scale production of antibodies using hybridoma cells is used medically to treat a range of infections. This is not their only application, however. Because they are specific to a single chemical (antigen), to which they become attached, they can be used to separate a particular chemical from a complex mixture. To do this, the monoclonal antibody for the required chemical is immobilized on resin beads which are then packed in a column. The mixture is passed over the beads and only the required chemical becomes attached to the antibodies. The chemical may then be obtained in a pure state by washing the beads with a solution which causes the antibodies to release it.

Monoclonal antibodies are also used in **immunoassays**. Here, the antibody is labelled in some way, e.g. radioactively or by a fluorescent dye, so that it can easily be detected. When added to a test sample they will attach to their specific antigen. Washing in solutions which remove only unattached antibodies leaves only those attached to the antigen. The amount of these in the sample is then apparent from the degree of radioactivity or fluorescence. For example, the presence of a particular pathogen in a blood sample can be detected by use of the appropriate monoclonal antibody tagged with a fluorescent dye.

Another technique is to immobilize the antibodies and pass the solution under test over them. Suppose we are testing for chemical X. If it is present in the solution it will attach to the antibody. A second type of antibody which has an enzyme attached is then added. It combines only with those original antibodies which are linked to chemical X. By adding a substrate which the enzyme causes to change colour, the amount of chemical X will be apparent by the extent of any colour change. This technique, called **Enzyme Linked Immunosorbant Assay (ELISA)**, has many uses including detecting drugs in athletes' urine, pregnancy testing kits and detecting the Human Immuno-deficiency Virus (the AIDS test). It is also possible to link anti-cancer drugs to monoclonal antibodies which are attracted to cancer cells – the so-called '**magic bullets**'. An even more sophisticated technique is to tag monoclonal antibodies with an enzyme which converts an inactive form of the cytotoxic drug (**the prodrug**) into an active form. Once injected these antibodies link to the cancer cells. The prodrug is then administered in a relatively high dose as it is harmless in its inactive state. In the vicinity of normal cells the drug remains ineffective but in the presence of the cancer cells the enzyme on the attached antibody activates the drug which acts upon the cells, killing them. The technique is called **ADEPT (Antibody Direct Enzyme Prodrug Therapy)**.

FOCUS

Pregnancy testing

Home pregnancy testing kits make use of immobilized antibodies on a urine dipstick to detect traces of human chorionic gonadotrophin (hCG), a hormone released from the placenta. Antibodies 'tagged' with blue latex combine with the hormone to produce a readily visible result.

5. Further row of antibodies which combine with latex-tagged antibodies *without* hCG attached

Negative result (blue line in this position)

4. Complex held by immobilized antibodies to form a blue line

Positive result (blue line in this position)

3. hCG bound to antibody to form a complex

2. Antibody tagged with blue latex particle

1. Urine sample containing hCG

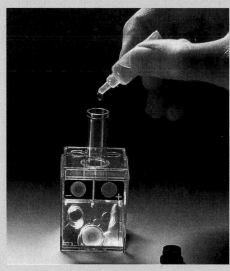

Home pregnancy testing kit

16.3.3 Types of immunity and immunization

There are two basic types of immunity, passive and active.

Passive immunity is the result of antibodies being passed into an individual in some way, rather than being produced by the individual itself. This passive immunity may occur naturally in mammals when, for example, antibodies pass across the placenta from a mother to her fetus or are passed to the newborn baby in the mother's milk. In both cases the young developing mammal is afforded some protection from disease until its own immune system is fully functional.

Alternatively, passive immunity may be acquired artificially by the injection of antibodies from another individual. This occurs in the treatment of tetanus and diphtheria in humans, although the antibodies are acquired from other mammals, e.g. horses. In all cases, passive immunity is only temporary.

Active immunity occurs when an organism manufactures its own antibodies. Active immunity may be the natural result of an infection. Once the body has started to manufacture antibodies in response to a disease-causing agent, it may continue to do so for a long time after, sometimes permanently. It is for this reason that most people suffer diseases such as mumps and measles only once. It is possible to induce an individual to produce antibodies even without them suffering disease. To achieve this, the appropriate antigen must be injected in some way. This is the basis of **immunization (vaccination)** of which there are a number of different types depending on the form the antigen takes.

FOCUS

Allergies

An excessive reaction of the body's immune system to certain substances is known as an allergy. When a foreign substance is detected for the first time lymphocytes produce antibodies, some of which bind to the surface of other white cells called mast cells. If the same substance is encountered again it binds to the antibodies on the mast cells causing the release of chemicals called mediators. The most important mediator is **histamine**. This chemical can produce rash, swelling, narrowing of the airways and a drop in blood pressure. These effects are important in protecting against infection but they may also be triggered inappropriately in allergy. One of the most common allergic disorders, hayfever, is caused by an allergic reaction to inhaled grass pollen leading to allergic rhinitis – swelling and irritation of the nasal passages and watering of the nose and eyes.

Antihistamines are the most widely used drugs in the treatment of allergic reactions of all kinds. Their main action is to counter the effects of histamine by blocking its action on H_1 receptors. These receptors are found in various body tissues, particularly the small blood vessels in the skin, nose and eyes. This helps prevent the dilation of the vessels, thus reducing redness and swelling. Antihistamines pass from the blood into the brain where their blocking action on histamine activity produces general sedation, and repression of various brain functions, including the vomiting and coughing mechanisms.

1. **Living attenuated microorganisms** – Living pathogens which have been treated, e.g. by heating, so that they multiply but are unable to cause the symptoms of the disease. They are therefore harmless but nonetheless induce the body to produce appropriate antibodies. Living attenuated microorganisms are used to immunize against measles, tuberculosis, poliomyelitis and rubella (German measles).

2. **Dead microorganisms** – Pathogens are killed by some means and then injected. Although harmless they again induce the body to produce antibodies in the same way it would had they been living. Typhoid, cholera and whooping cough are controlled by this means.

3. **Toxoids** – The toxins produced by some diseases, e.g. diphtheria and tetanus, are sufficient to induce antibody production by an individual. To avoid these toxins causing the symptoms of the disease they are first detoxified in some way, e.g. by treatment with formaldehyde, and then injected.

4. **Extracted antigens** – The chemicals with antigenic properties may be extracted from the pathogenic organisms and injected. Influenza vaccine is produced in this way.

5. **Artificial antigens** – Through genetic engineering it is now possible to transfer the genes producing antigens from a pathogenic organism to a harmless one which can easily be grown in a laboratory. Mass production of the antigen is then

possible in a fermenter ready for separation and purification before use. Vaccines used in the treatment of hepatitis B can be produced in this way. Vaccination has successfully eradicated smallpox from the world. See Focus on page 541.

16.3.4 Blood groups

Blood groups are an example of an antigen–antibody system. The membrane of red blood cells contains polysaccharides which act as antigens. They may induce the production of antibodies when introduced into another individual. While there are over twenty different blood grouping methods, the ABO system, first discovered by Landsteiner in 1900, is the best known. In this system there are just two antigens, A and B, which determine the blood group (see left). For each of these antigens there is an antibody, which is given the corresponding lower case letter. The presence of an antigen and its corresponding antibody together causes an immune response resulting in the clumping together of red cells (**agglutination**) and their ultimate breakdown (**haemolysis**). For this reason, an individual does not produce antibodies corresponding to the antigens present but produces all others as a matter of course. These antibodies are present in the plasma. The composition of each blood group is therefore as given opposite.

In transfusing blood from one person, the **donor**, to another, the **recipient**, it is necessary to avoid bringing together corresponding antigens and antibodies. However, if only a small quantity of blood is to be transfused, then it is possible to add the antibody to the antigen, because the donor's antibodies become so diluted in the recipient's plasma that they are ineffective. It is not, however, feasible to add small quantities of antigen to the corresponding antibody as even a tiny amount of antigen will cause an immune response. This, after all, is why small numbers of invading bacteria are immediately destroyed as part of the body's defence mechanism. It is therefore possible to safely add antibody a to antigen A and antibody b to antigen B, in small quantities, but not the reverse. For this reason, blood group O, with no antigens present, may be given in small amounts to individuals of all other blood groups. Group O is therefore referred to as the **universal donor**. Individuals of this group are, however, restricted to receiving blood from their own group. In the same way group AB, with no antibodies, may receive blood with either antigen. In other words, group AB can receive blood from all groups, and is therefore termed the **universal recipient**. They can, however, only donate to their own group. When agglutination occurs between two groups, they are said to be **incompatible**. Table 16.2 shows the compatibility of blood groups in the ABO system.

Despite this knowledge and careful matching of blood groups there continued to be inexplicable failures of transfusions up to 1940. It was then that Landsteiner discovered a new antigen (actually a system of antigens) in rhesus monkeys, which was also present in humans. This became known as the **rhesus system** and the antigen as **antigen D**. Where an individual possesses the antigen he or she is said to be **rhesus positive**; where it is absent he or she is **rhesus negative**. There is no naturally occurring antibody to antigen D, but if blood with the

Blood group	Antigens present
A	A
B	B
AB	A and B
O	None

Blood group	Antigen	Antibodies
A	A	b
B	B	a
AB	A and B	None
O	None	a and b

TABLE 16.2 **Compatibility of blood groups in the ABO system**

			Recipient's blood group			
	Group		A	B	AB	O
Group	Antigens		A	B	A and B	None
	Antigens	Antibodies	b	a	None	a and b
Donor's blood group	A	A	b	✓	✗	✓	✗
	B	B	a	✗	✓	✓	✗
	AB	A and B	None	✗	✗	✓	✗
	O	None	a and b	✓	✓	✓	✓

✓ Compatible – bloods do not agglutinate
✗ Incompatible – bloods agglutinate

antigen is transfused into a person without it (rhesus negative), antibody d production is induced in line with the usual immune response. For this reason, before transfusion, blood is matched with respect to the rhesus factor as well as the ABO system.

One problem associated with the rhesus system arises in pregnancy. As blood groups are genetically determined (Section 7.5.1), it is possible for the fetus to inherit from the father a blood group different from that of the mother. The fetus may, for example, be rhesus positive while the mother is rhesus negative. Towards the end of pregnancy, and especially around birth, fragments of blood cells may cross from the fetus to the mother. The mother responds by producing the rhesus antibody (d) in response to the rhesus antigen (D) on the fetal red blood cells. These antibodies are able to cross the placenta. As the build-up and transfer of rhesus antibodies takes some time, and as the problem only arises during the latter stages of pregnancy, their concentration is rarely sufficient to have any effect on the first child. The production of rhesus antibodies by the mother continues for only a few months, but subsequent fetuses may again induce production and are therefore subject to a greater influx of rhesus antibodies. These break down the fetal red blood cells – a condition known as **haemolytic disease of the newborn**. It requires a number of fetal blood transfusions throughout the pregnancy if it is not to prove fatal. Knowledge that the mother is rhesus negative can, however, avert the danger. If this is the case, and the father is known to be rhesus positive, a potential problem exists. In this event rhesus antibodies (d) from blood donors, are injected into the mother immediately after the first birth. These destroy any fetal cell fragments with antigen D, which may have entered her blood, before they induce the mother to manufacture her own antibodies. The injected antibodies are soon broken down by the mother, and in the absence of new ones being produced subsequent fetuses are not at risk.

The proportion of different blood groups varies throughout the world. In the British population the proportions are O–46%, A–42%, B–9%, AB–3%, although there are variations between different areas. In England, for example, numbers with group A slightly exceed group O. Some South American tribes are exclusively group O whereas some North American Indian tribes are three quarters group A. Over a third of European gypsies have group B. The proportion of rhesus positive individuals in most groups is between 75% and 85%.

Tissue compatibility and rejection

We have seen that blood, if adequately matched, can be transfused from one person to another. It should therefore be equally feasible to transplant organs in the same way. The problem lies in the complexity of organs; they possess a far greater number of antigens and so perfect cross-matching can rarely be achieved. In the absence of perfect cross-matching the recipient treats the donated organ as foreign material and so an immune response is initiated. The organ is therefore rejected. Despite these difficulties there have been major advances in the grafting and transplanting of tissues. Clearly if a tissue is grafted from one part of an organism to another, there are no problems of rejection as all material is genetically identical and so compatible. Skin is frequently grafted by this means. Equally transplants between genetically identical individuals like identical twins do not present problems of rejection. Unfortunately, most humans do not have genetically identical brothers or sisters and so depend upon organs from others when the need for a transplant arises. To minimize the chances of rejection, careful matching takes place, to find tissues which are as nearly compatible as possible. This minimizes the extent of the immune response, reducing the risk of rejection. Such compatible tissues are often, but not always, found in close relatives. In addition the recipient is treated with **immunosuppressant drugs** which lower the activity of their natural immune response, so delaying rejection long enough for the transplanted tissue to be accepted. The problem with these drugs is that the recipient is vulnerable to other infections and even minor ones can prove fatal.

More recently two techniques have been developed which suppress the T-lymphocytes responsible for the rejection response while having little effect on the B-cells which produce antibodies. This helps the patient to maintain a resistance to infection. The first technique employs Orthoclone OKT-3, a monoclonal antibody (see Section 16.3.2). Although this has some side effects they are reversible and the antibody has been used successfully to combat kidney rejection. In the second technique human T-lymphocytes are injected into a horse which then produces antibodies to them, known as anti-lymphocyte immunoglobulin (ALG). This is purified and, when injected into a transplant patient, is effective at combating rejection.

16.3.5 Chemotherapy and immunity

The use of chemicals to prevent and cure diseases and disorders is known as **chemotherapy**. The earliest examples used natural chemicals extracted from plants, but nowadays the chemicals are largely synthetically manufactured. Among the most widely used synthetic drugs are the **sulphonamides**. These were found to be effective against certain bacterial infections during the mid-1930s and were used extensively against urinary and bowel infections as well as pneumonia. The development of strains of bacteria resistant to sulphonamides and the wider use of antibiotics have reduced the importance of these drugs.

Antibiotics are chemicals produced by various fungi and bacteria, which suppress the growth of other microorganisms. Since the discovery by Sir Alexander Fleming, in 1928, of **penicillin**, many other types of antibiotics have been marketed, e.g. ampicillin, streptomycin and chloramphenicol. All interfere with some stage of bacterial metabolism and so suppress their growth. Penicillin for example prevents the synthesis of certain components of the bacterial cell wall, while streptomycin, chloramphenicol and tetracycline inhibit mRNA at the ribosomes thus preventing protein synthesis. Polymixin and amphotericin interfere with the proper functioning of the bacterial membrane. Because bacterial cells are prokaryotic, these effects are not experienced by the eukaryotic cells of the host and so antibiotics may be safely used throughout the body. Once again, the development of resistant species has reduced the effectiveness of some antibiotics (see Section 9.2.3).

16.4   The circulatory system

Only very small animals, where cells are never far from the outside, exist without a specialized transport system. The larger and more active an animal, the more extensive and efficient is its transport system. These systems frequently incorporate a pump, valves and an elaborate means of controlling distribution of the blood.

Humans have **closed blood system**. Here blood is confined to vessels. The pumping action of the heart sustains high pressure within these vessels and a combination of vasodilation, vasoconstriction and valves ensures a much more controlled distribution of blood.

Humans have a **double circulation**. Here the blood is returned to the heart after passing over the respiratory surface and before it is pumped over the body tissues. This helps to sustain a high blood pressure and so allows more rapid circulation. The complete separation of the heart into two halves allows oxygenated and deoxygenated blood to be kept separate. This improves the efficiency of oxygen distribution, something which is essential to sustain the higher metabolic rate of an endothermic animal such as a human.

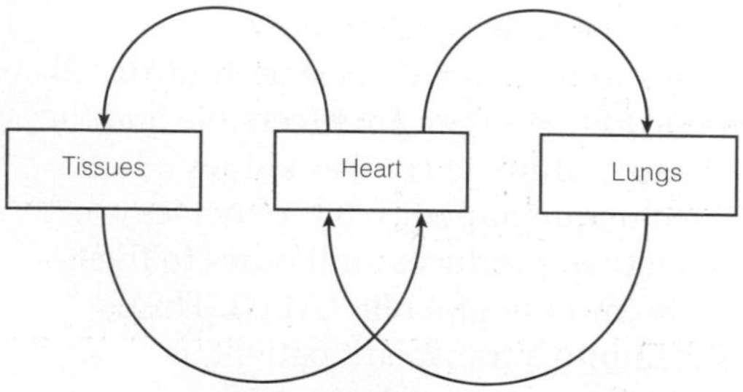

Fig. 16.11 Double circulation

16.4.1 Blood vessels

In the human circulatory system there are three types of vessel. **Arteries** carry blood away from the heart ('a' for 'artery' = 'a' for 'away' from the heart), **veins** carry blood to the heart whereas the much smaller **capillaries** link arteries to veins. A comparison of the structure of these three vessels is given in Table 16.3.

The diameter of arteries and veins gradually diminishes as they get further from the heart. The smaller arteries are called **arterioles** and the smaller veins are called **venules**.

Did you know?

The entire length of arteries, veins and capillaries in the human body is estimated to be 80 000 miles.

TABLE 16.3 **A comparison of arteries, veins and capillaries**

Artery	Vein	Capillary
Thick muscular wall	Thin muscular wall	No muscle
Much elastic tissue	Little elastic tissue	No elastic tissue
Small lumen relative to diameter	Large lumen relative to diameter	Large lumen relative to diameter
Capable of constriction	Not capable of constriction	Not capable of constriction
Not permeable	Not permeable	Permeable
Valves in aorta and pulmonary artery only	Valves throughout all veins	No valves
Transports blood from the heart	Transports blood to heart	Links arteries to veins
Oxygenated blood except in pulmonary artery	Deoxygenated blood except in pulmonary vein	Blood changes from oxygenated to deoxygenated
Blood under high pressure (10–16 kPa)	Blood under low pressure (1 kPa)	Blood pressure reducing (4–1 kPa)
Blood moves in pulses	No pulses	No pulses
Blood flows rapidly	Blood flows slowly	Blood flow slowing

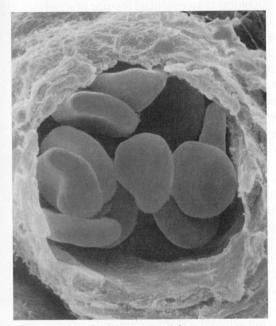

SEM of red blood cells in an arteriole

16.4.2 Human circulatory system

The purpose of the human circulatory system is to carry blood between various parts of the body. To this end, each organ has a major artery supplying it with blood from the heart and a major vein which returns it. These arteries and veins are usually

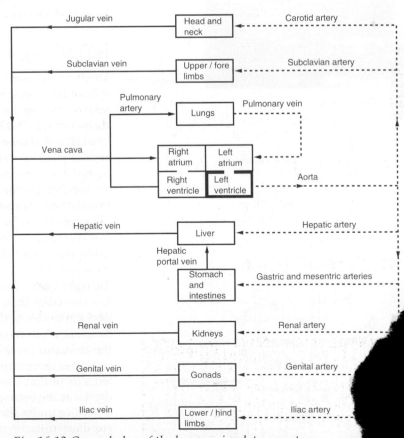

Fig. 16.12 General plan of the human circulatory system

named by preceding them with the adjective appropriate to that organ, e.g. each kidney has a renal artery and renal vein. A general plan of the human circulation is given in Fig. 16.12.

The flow of blood is maintained in three ways:

1. The pumping action of the heart – This forces blood through the arteries into the capillaries.

2. Contraction of skeletal muscle – The contraction of muscles during the normal movements of a person squeeze the thin-walled veins, increasing the pressure of blood within them. Pocket valves in the veins ensure that this pressure directs the blood back to the heart.

3. Inspiratory movements – When breathing in, the pressure in the thorax is reduced. This helps to draw blood towards the heart, which is within the thorax.

16.5   Heart structure and action

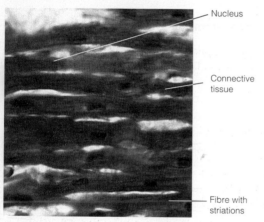

Cardiac muscle

A pump to circulate the blood is an essential feature of most circulatory systems. These pumps or hearts generally consist of a thin-walled collection chamber – the **atrium** or **auricle** – and a thick-walled pumping chamber – the **ventricle**. Between the two are valves to ensure the blood flows in one direction, namely, from the atrium to the ventricle. In a double circulation system there are two atria and two ventricles to allow complete separation of oxygenated and deoxygenated blood. This four-chambered heart is really two two-chambered hearts side by side.

16.5.1 Structure of the human heart

The human heart consists largely of **cardiac muscle**, a specialized tissue which is capable of rhythmical contraction and relaxation over a long period without fatigue. Its structure is shown in Fig. 16.13. The muscle is richly supplied with blood vessels and also contains connective tissue which gives strength and helps to prevent the muscle tearing. The human heart is made up of two thin-walled atria which are elastic and distend as blood enters them. The left atrium receives oxygenated blood from the pulmonary vein while the right atrium receives deoxygenated blood from the vena cava. When full, the atria contract together, forcing the remaining blood into their respective ventricles. The right ventricle then pumps blood to the lungs. Owing to the close proximity of the lungs to the heart, the right ventricle does not need to force blood far and is much less muscular than the left ventricle which has to pump blood to the extremities of the body. To prevent backflow of blood into the atria when the ventricles contract, there are valves between the atria and ventricles. On the right side of the heart these comprise three cup-shaped flaps, the **tricuspid valves**. On the left side of the heart only two cup-shaped flaps are present; these are the **bicuspid** or **mitral valves**. To prevent these valves inverting under the pressure of blood, they are attached to papillary muscles of the ventricular wall by fibres known as the **chordae tendinae**. Fig. 16.14 illustrates the structure of the heart.

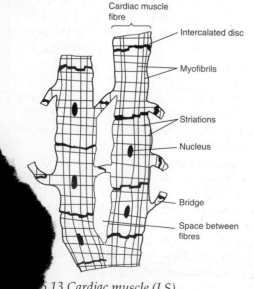

5.13 Cardiac muscle (LS)

1.
Blood enters atria and ventricles from pulmonary veins and venae cavae

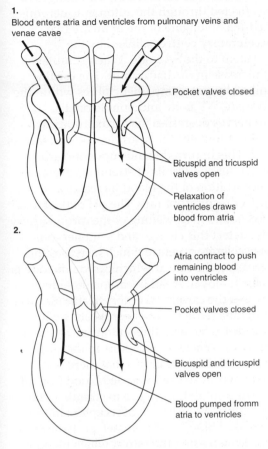

Pocket valves closed

Bicuspid and tricuspid valves open

Relaxation of ventricles draws blood from atria

2.

Atria contract to push remaining blood into ventricles

Pocket valves closed

Bicuspid and tricuspid valves open

Blood pumped fromm atria to ventricles

3.
Blood pumped into pulmonary arteries and the aorta

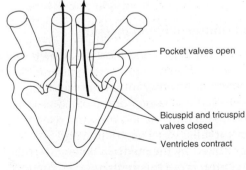

Pocket valves open

Bicuspid and tricuspid valves closed

Ventricles contract

1. *Diastole*
   Atria are relaxed and fill with blood. Ventricles are also relaxed.

2. *Atrial systole*
   Atria contract pushing blood into the ventricles. Ventricles remain relaxed.

3. *Ventricular systole*
   Atria relax. Ventricles contract pushing blood away from heart through pulmonary arteries and the aorta.

Fig. 16.15 The cardiac cycle

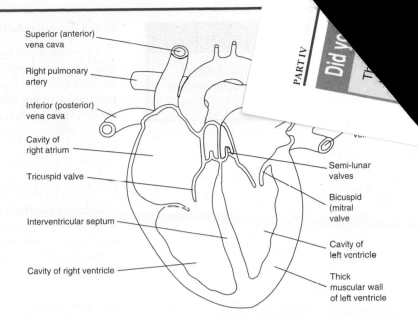

Superior (anterior) vena cava

Right pulmonary artery

Inferior (posterior) vena cava

Cavity of right atrium

Tricuspid valve

Interventricular septum

Cavity of right ventricle

Semi-lunar valves

Bicuspid (mitral valve

Cavity of left ventricle

Thick muscular wall of left ventricle

Fig. 16.14 The structure of a human heart as seen in vertical section from the ventral side

Blood leaving the ventricle is prevented from returning by pocket valves in the aorta and pulmonary artery. These close when the ventricles relax.

16.5.2 Control of heart beat (cardiac cycle)

The human heart is **myogenic**, that is, the heart beat is initiated from within the heart muscle itself rather than by a nervous impulse from outside it. Where a heart beat is initiated by nerves, as in insects, the heart is said to be **neurogenic**.

The initial stimulus for a heart beat originates in a group of histologically different cardiac muscle cells known as the **sino-atrial node (SA node)**. This is located in the wall of the right atrium near where the vena cavae enter it. The SA node determines the basic rate of heart beat and is therefore known as the **pacemaker**. In humans, this basic rate is 70 beats/minute but can be adjusted according to demand by stimulation from the autonomic nervous system. A wave of excitation spreads out from the SA node across both atria, causing them to contract more or less at the same time.

The wave of excitation reaches a similar group of cells known as the **atrio-ventricular node (AV node)** which lies between the two atria. To allow blood to be forced upwards into the arteries, the ventricles need to contract from the apex upwards. To achieve this the new wave of excitation from the AV node is conducted along **Purkinje fibres** which collectively make up the **bundle of His**. These fibres lead along the interventricular septum to the apex of the ventricles from where they radiate upwards. The wave of excitation travels along these fibres, only being released to effect muscle contraction at the apex. The ventricles contract simultaneously from the apex upwards. These events are known as the **cardiac cycle** and are summarized in Fig. 16.15.

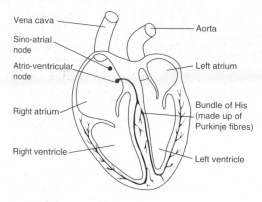

Vena cava

Sino-atrial
node

Atrio-ventricular
node

Right atrium

Right ventricle

Aorta

Left atrium

Bundle of His
(made up of
Purkinje fibres)

Left ventricle

*Fig. 16.16 VS through human heart to show
position of sino-atrial node, atrio-ventricular
node and bundle of His*

16.5.3 Factors modifying heart beat

The human heart normally contracts 70 times a minute, but this
can be varied from 50 to 200 times a minute. In the same way the
volume of blood pumped at each beat can be varied. The volume
pumped (**stroke volume**) multiplied by the number of beats in a
given time (**heart rate**) is called the **cardiac output**. Changes to
the cardiac output are effected through the autonomic nervous
system. Within the medulla oblongata of the brain are two
centres. The **cardio-acceleratory centre** is linked by the
sympathetic nervous system to the SA node. When stimulated
these nerves cause an increase in cardiac output. The **cardio-
inhibitory centre** is linked by parasympathetic fibres within the
vagus nerve, to the SA node, AV node and bundle of His.
Stimulation from these nerves decreases the cardiac output.

Which of these centres stimulates the heart depends on factors
like the pH of the blood. This in turn depends upon its carbon
dioxide concentration. Under conditions of strenuous exercise,
the carbon dioxide concentration of the blood increases as a
consequence of the greater respiratory rate. The pH of the blood
is therefore lowered. Receptors in a swelling of the carotid artery
called the **carotid body**, detect this change and send nervous
impulses to the cardio-acceleratory centre which increases the
heart beat, thereby increasing the rate at which carbon dioxide is
delivered to the lungs for removal. A fall in carbon dioxide level
(rise in pH) of blood causes the carotid receptors to stimulate the
cardio-inhibitory centre, thus reducing the heart beat.

Another means of control is by stretch receptors in the aorta,
carotid artery and vena cava. When the receptors in the aorta
and carotid artery are stimulated, it indicates that there is
distention of these vessels as a result of increased blood flow in
them. This causes the cardio-inhibitory centre to stimulate the
heart to reduce cardiac output. Stimulation of receptors in the
vena cava indicates increased blood in this vessel, probably as a
result of muscular activity increasing the rate at which blood is
returned from the tissues. Under these conditions the cardiac
centres in the brain increase the cardiac output.

16.5.4 Maintenance and control of blood pressure

Changes in cardiac output will alter blood pressure, which must
always be maintained at a sufficiently high level to permit blood
to reach all tissues requiring it. Another important factor in
controlling blood pressure is the diameter of the blood vessels.
When narrowed – **vasoconstriction** – blood pressure rises; when
widened – **vasodilation** – it falls. Vasoconstriction and
vasodilation are also controlled by the medulla oblongata, this
time by the **vasomotor centre**. From this centre nerves run to the
smooth muscles of arterioles throughout the body. Pressure
receptors, known as **baroreceptors**, in the carotid artery detect
blood pressure changes and relay impulses to the vasomotor
centre. If blood pressure falls, the vasomotor centre sends
impulses along sympathetic nerves to the arterioles. The muscles
in the arterioles contract, causing vasoconstriction and a
consequent rise in blood pressure. A rise in blood pressure
causes the vasomotor centre to send messages via the
parasympathetic system to the arterioles, causing them to dilate
and so reduce blood pressure.

Heart transplantation – a medical and moral dilemma

Despite its vital importance to the body, the heart is nevertheless a relatively simple organ whose transplantation is straightforward. Close matching of donor and recipient tissue is necessary to avoid rejection (see Focus on page 389). It was in 1967 that Dr. Christian Barnard carried out the first human heart transplant in South Africa and although many more transplants have taken place since, the recipients have rarely lived more than a further five years, and future developments are likely to centre on the use of the hearts of animals such as the pig. Artificial hearts such as the Jarkik-7 were first implanted in 1982, but the need for external pumps limits the recipient's mobility and so, at present, they are only seen as a temporary measure until a suitable donor heart can be found.

Transplant surgery raises certain moral and ethical issues. To what extent should an individual continue to be given new organs? Does there come a point when they possess so much 'foreign' tissue that they cease to be themselves? Can the cost be justified when other less glamorous areas of medicine may be starved of funds? How much pressure should be put on close relatives to donate their organs as these are most likely to have the best match? With more would-be recipients than donors, how do we select the most worthy case? Is it fair to exclude those who refuse to change their life style, e.g. refuse to cease smoking? At what point does one declare a potential donor dead? Could there be pressure to do so prematurely if suitable recipients of organs are waiting? Who decides whether organs can be donated if there are no instructions left by the deceased? If the next of kin, how appropriate is it to make such a request within minutes of them being informed of their bereavement? Despite these issues, transplant surgery relieves much suffering and looks set to expand.

A rise in blood carbon dioxide concentration also causes a rise in blood pressure. This increases the speed with which blood is delivered to the lungs and so helps remove the carbon dioxide more quickly. Hormones like adrenaline similarly raise blood pressure.

Living at high altitude

The amount of oxygen in the atmosphere is the same at high altitudes as it is at sea level, namely 21%. The respiratory problems associated with living at high altitude are a result of the reduced atmospheric pressure. The reduced pressure means that it is more difficult to load the haemoglobin with oxygen. Above about 6000 m the pressure is inadequate to load haemoglobin effectively. Some human settlements exist at these altitudes and the inhabitants have become **acclimatized**. Acclimatization involves:

1. **Adjustment of blood pH** – The reduced loading of haemoglobin leads to deeper breathing – **hyperventilation** – in an attempt to compensate for lack of oxygen in the blood. This leads to excessive removal of carbon dioxide and a raised

FOCUS

Artificial pacemakers

In Britain about 10 000 people a year receive an artificial pacemaker. The operation takes less than an hour and is performed under local anaesthetic.

Pacemakers are made up of a pulse generator and two electrodes. The pulse generator is about the size of a thin matchbox and weighs 20–60 g. It is powered by a lithium battery and is implanted under the patient's skin. The electrodes are placed intravenously into the right atrium and the right ventricle. Disease or ageing can damage the heart's natural pacemaker and the conduction of impulses through the heart, causing an abnormally slow heart beat. The artificial pacemaker overcomes this by generating electrical impulses artificially and conducting them to the muscles of the heart on demand or when the heart misses a beat.

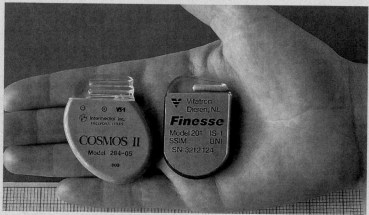

Pacemakers

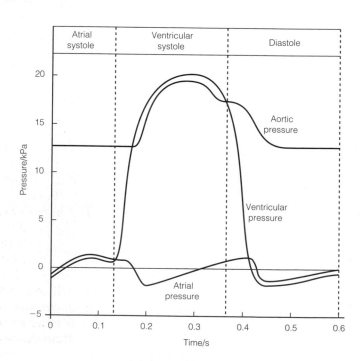

Fig. 16.17 Pressure changes in the atria, ventricles and aorta during one cardiac cycle

Electrocardiogram

An ECG (electrocardiogram) trace follows the electrical activity of nerves and muscles in the heart. There are various characteristic patterns or waves. For diagnostic purposes doctors use three of the waves.

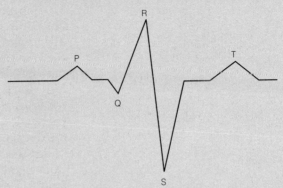

The P wave charts current flow through the atria from the SA node to the AV node. The QRS complex follows the spread of depolarization through the ventricles. Finally the T wave results from currents generated during ventricular repolarization.

Various waves can be picked up as electrical echoes from the heart by connecting the ECG machine's leads to the skin at different sites on the body. By fixing two or three electrodes to the wrists and ankles, doctors get a frontal view of the heart's activity by charting the direction of current flow in two dimensions. Together with horizontal-plane electrodes (six ECG leads strapped across the chest), the ECG can give a three-dimensional picture of the heart's electrical activity, and hence its health.

blood pH. Nervous responses are triggered causing reduced depth of breathing - undesirable in the circumstances. In acclimatized individuals the hydrogen carbonate ions are removed by the kidney, restoring blood pH to normal.

2. **Increased oxygen uptake** – More oxygen is absorbed by the lungs as a result of an improved capillary network in the lungs, and deeper breathing.

3. **Improved transport of oxygen to the tissues** – This is the result of:
   - **increased red blood cell concentration** – this may rise from 45% to 60% of the total blood volume;
   - **increased haemoglobin concentration in red blood cells** – this may rise by 20%.

4. **Changes in haemoglobin affinity for oxygen** – The oxygen dissociation curve is shifted to the right to facilitate release of oxygen to the tissues. Above 3500 m this advantage is offset by the reduced affinity of haemoglobin for oxygen in the lungs and so is not shown by those living at these altitudes, where a shift to the left favours survival.

5. **Increased myoglobin levels in muscles** – With its higher affinity for oxygen this facilitates the exchange of oxygen from the blood to the tissues.

Hypertension

Hypertension or high blood pressure is not always easy to define because there is much individual variation in 'normal' blood pressure and variation as a result of age, general health and degree of activity. Systolic pressure is usually in the range 110–140 mm mercury and diastolic pressure in the range of 70–90 mm mercury. Pressures in excess of 160 mm (systolic) and 95 mm (diastolic) for any length of time are considered by the World Health Organization to indicate hypertension. As one ages, the walls of the arteries become less elastic and this leads to the risk of hypertension increasing as one gets older. It has been estimated that between 10 and 20% of all UK residents suffer from the disease. **Essential hypertension** is the direct consequence of factors which are not fully understood, but which, if left untreated can lead to death from events such as heart failure, heart attack, stroke, kidney failure or diabetes. **Secondary hypertension** is the consequence of some other condition such as kidney problems, hormonal inbalance or the taking of certain medicines. Many other factors can cause high blood pressure, including smoking, excessive alcohol intake, too much salt in the diet, stress, lack of exercise and obesity.

Treatment of hypertension has involved an increasingly sophisticated array of medicines which have reduced the number of deaths from this disease (by 75% between 1958 and 1984). Some of these medications act as diuretics which cause the kidneys to excrete more water thus reducing the volume of the blood and hence lowering its pressure. Others, called **β-blockers**, reduce the cardiac output of the heart or relax the smooth muscle in the arteries, thus reducing their resistance to blood flow. One type acts by blocking the formation of angiotensin II, a chemical released by artery walls which has a vasoconstrictor action.

Effects of exercise on the heart and circulatory system
We saw in Section 15.3 that exercise increases the demand of muscles for oxygen and that to supply this demand, the ventilation rate increases. It follows that if the supply of oxygen to the blood is increased, then to be effective, so must the supply of blood to the muscles. Accordingly, the cardiac output must rise from around 5 dm^3 min^{-1} at rest to a maximum of 30 dm^3 min^{-1} during strenuous exertion, although a four-fold increase to 20 dm^3 min^{-1} is more normal. This rise is achieved by increasing the heart rate from around 70 beats min^{-1} to 190 beats min^{-1} and the stroke volume from 80 cm^3 at each beat to 110 cm^3. A well-trained athlete has a greater cardiac output although the heart rate is normally less than that of an untrained person. This is achieved by repeated exercise increasing the amount of heart muscle and the size of the heart chambers. As a result the stroke volume of a well-trained athlete is as much as 50% greater than that of an untrained person.

FOCUS

Mountain sickness

Although the proportion of oxygen remains the same anywhere in the atmosphere, the pressure of the atmosphere falls as we ascend from the surface of the earth. Atmospheric pressure at Everest Base Camp (5500 m; 18 000 feet), for example, is about half that at sea level. Reduced pressure means there is less oxygen available to the tissues, a condition called **hypoxia**. Both cold and exercise have effects on the body which, added to the effects of hypoxia, may contribute to the illness known as mountain sickness. Speed of ascent is a greater risk factor for mountain sickness than the absolute altitude reached. Those who drive, ride or fly to a high altitude are more at risk than those who walk, and those who climb more rapidly are more at risk than those who take their time. Commonly the symptoms of Acute Mountain Sickness (AMS) appear within 2–4 days of exposure to altitude.

Benign AMS is a fairly harmless form of mountain sickness in which sufferers may experience loss of appetite, headache, nausea, vomiting, sleeplessness and chest discomfort. Some people also develop swelling of the body as fluid accumulates under the skin. These symptoms may be considered an important warning of the more serious form of mountain sickness. **Malignant AMS** may be fatal, affecting the lungs and/or the brain. Pulmonary AMS leads to a build up of fluid in the lungs causing breathlessness and blueness of the lips (cyanosis). Cerebral AMS causes the sufferers to develop headaches, drowsiness, unsteadiness on the feet, abnormal behaviour, impaired consciousness and often coma. Both conditions may occur simultaneously.

There is no general agreement on how AMS is caused but an important factor appears to be the increased blood pressure that results from hypoxia. This may damage capillaries in the brain, eyes and lungs. The small blood vessels in the lungs also show an increased permeability to water which leads to oedema. An increased level of ADH secretion would explain why those suffering from mountain sickness generally pass less urine and retain more water in their body than those people at altitude who do not suffer.

In the event of benign AMS, sufferers should remain at the same altitude for a few days and then, if they recover, proceed cautiously. Malignant AMS sufferers are often in no condition to make decisions for themselves, both their judgement and their physical state being impaired. They should be brought down to lower altitudes at once. Patients with pulmonary AMS will usually improve rapidly after a descent of 2000–3000 feet. Those with cerebral AMS may not regain consciousness for days or even weeks but recovery, when it occurs, is usually complete.

16.5.5 Heart disease

As the organ pumping blood around the body, any interruption to the heart's ceaseless beating can have serious, often fatal, consequences. There are many defects and disorders, some acquired, like atherosclerosis, others congenital, such as a hole-in-the-heart. Some affect the pacemaker leading to an irregular heart rhythm, in others the valves allowing blood to 'leak' back into the atria when the ventricles contract. By far the most common is **coronary heart disease** which affects the pair of blood vessels – the coronary arteries – which serve the heart muscle itself. There are three ways in which blood flow in these arteries may be impeded:

Coronary thrombosis – a blood clot which becomes lodged in a coronary vessel.

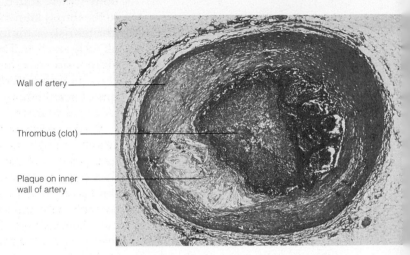

Wall of artery

Thrombus (clot)

Plaque on inner wall of artery

Human coronary artery containing a thrombus

Atherosclerosis – narrowing of the arteries due to thickening of the arterial wall caused by fat, fibrous tissue and salts being deposited on it. The condition is sometimes referred to as hardening of the arteries, and can lead to a thrombosis which further reduces the lumen of the artery.

Spasm – repeated contractions of the muscle in the coronary artery wall.

It is often a combination of these factors, rather than one in isolation, which results in a **heart attack (myocardial infarction)**. If the main coronary artery is blocked, the whole of the heart muscle or **myocardium** may be deprived of blood, resulting in death. If only a branch vessel is affected the loss of blood supply affects only a portion of the myocardium and, after a period of severe chest pain and temporary incapacitation followed by a number of days of complete rest, recovery normally follows. **Angina** is the result of reduced blood flow in the coronary arteries due to atherosclerosis, but sometimes the result of thrombosis or spasm. Chest pain, and breathlessness often occur when an angina sufferer is undertaking strenuous physical effort.

Many factors are known to increase the risk of coronary heart disease. Smoking is a major contributor increasing the likelihood of both thrombosis and atherosclerosis. A raised level of fat, especially cholesterol, in the blood is a major cause of atherosclerosis (see Focus on page 401). The level of cholesterol in the blood is not entirely a matter of diet as there are genetic

Atherosclerosis

Arteriosclerosis is the general term for any condition in which the walls of arteries thicken and lose their elasticity. The most common form of it is **atherosclerosis** in which the thickening is caused by a build-up of cholesterol and other fatty substances. At first these form streaks on the inner wall of the artery but they increase to form patches known as plaques which eventually thicken the wall and narrow the lumen of the artery. These thickenings or **atheromas** most commonly occur in large arteries; arterioles and capillaries are rarely affected. The uneven thickenings cause the flow of blood to be disturbed and this can stimulate the gradual formation of a clot, known as a **thrombus**. The thrombus may grow so large that it blocks the vessel where it forms or small pieces called **emboli** may break off and possibly block small vessels elsewhere.

Both thrombi and emboli may cause the blood supply to a particular tissue to be reduced (**ischaemia**). If this occurs in a coronary vessel, supplying the heart, the person will suffer the symptoms of **angina pectoris**. Commonly these include chest pain when exercising and difficulty in breathing so that a person with angina may have a severely restricted lifestyle. Vasodilator drugs, such as nitroglycerine, may be prescribed which trigger the smooth muscle of the arterial wall to relax so that the vessel dilates. Beta blockers may also be used which can reduce the heart's oxygen requirement by up to 20%. Drug treatments are effective for about 70% of angina sufferers; the rest may require angioplasty or by-pass surgery. **Angioplasty** is a procedure which involves mechanically widening the lumen of an artery affected by atherosclerosis. There are a number of ways of doing this but commonly a deflated balloon attached to a fine catheter is inserted into a partially blocked artery and inflated. The balloon pushes outwards to stretch the lumen of the artery. Other methods include the use of mesh tubes called stents or spinning loops of wire. In a **coronary by-pass** operation veins from other areas of the body, usually the legs, are used to by-pass partial blockages in coronary arteries.

Blockages in arteries may become so severe that areas of tissue deprived of oxygen die (**infarction**). If the dead tissue is cardiac muscle it is known as **myocardial infarction** or a **heart attack**. This is most commonly caused by an embolus or thrombus in the coronary artery. In Britain about half a million people a year suffer a heart attack and almost a third die as a result. The symptoms include severe chest pain, sweating, dizziness and shortness of breath which are not necessarily associated with exercise. It is important that victims are treated quickly to increase their chances of survival and to reduce the likelihood of physiological shock. Anticoagulant drugs and beta blockers are given as well as diuretics to reduce the swelling often associated with infarction.

The atheroma which causes blood clots and blockages may also weaken the wall of an artery. When this happens the weakened point may swell to form an **aneurysm**. This is especially prevalent in the aorta, the arteries at the base of the brain and in those behind the knee. Aneurysms may put pressure on adjacent structures, for example one on an artery at the base of the brain may press on nerves leading to the external muscles of the eye, causing double vision. Another reason aneurysms are dangerous is their tendency to burst, leading to severe haemorrhaging and possibly to death. A brain aneurysm may lead to **cerebrovascular accident (CVA)** otherwise known as a **stroke**. The resulting haemorrhage leads to some areas of the brain tissue becoming ischaemic. A similar effect may also result from an embolism. Strokes vary in severity depending on the amount of tissue affected. Many elderly people have minor strokes, called **transient ischaemic attacks** whose effects are barely noticeable. Other cases have crippling effects and may even be fatal, there being more than 40 000 deaths from CVA in Great Britain each year. Most commonly the aneurysm or embolism affects the middle cerebral artery causing paralysis in one leg and one arm and in the facial muscles of the same side. If the right side is affected there may also be some loss of speech. Damage to other vessels in the brain may lead to disturbances of balance, vision, memory or other brain functions. Although about 20% of CVA victims die within a few days, substantial recovery is often seen in others aided by physiotherapy and speech therapy.

There are a number of risk factors associated with atheroma. Some of these are unavoidable but there is often some way in which we can change our lifestyle in order to reduce our risk. Little can be done about the possible genetic predisposition to develop atheroma. For example, males are more at risk than females and the risk increases with age. However, we can help ourselves by not becoming obese, with its associated risks of diabetes and high blood pressure, by not smoking and by reducing our intake of saturated fats and cholesterol. We need to exercise more and endeavour to reduce the incidence of stress in our lives. It has been estimated that if men between 30 and 59 years of age smoke, have high blood pressure and high blood cholesterol levels their risk of heart disease is eight times as high as that for men of the same age without any of these additional risk factors.

differences which are regulated by several genes (polygenes). As a result some individuals are more sensitive than others to excess cholesterol in the diet. In addition a genetically determined disease called **hypercholesterolaemia** results in a high blood cholesterol level. The defective gene is carried by as many as 1 in 500 people in Britain although it is rare (1 in a million) in its homozygous form, which results in cholesterol levels 3–4 times that of a normal individual. See Focus on cholesterol on page 421 for further details.

Saturated fat of the type found in most meat and animal products, such as milk, is particularly dangerous. High blood pressure or hypertensive disease, a high level of salt in the diet and diabetes are other factors which contribute to atherosclerosis and hence coronary heart disease. Stress is suspected of increasing the risk of heart disease, but scientific evidence is hard to come by as it is difficult to measure stress levels accurately. There appears to be an inherited factor with individuals with a family history of heart disease being more susceptible to heart attacks. Older people are more at risk than younger ones, males more at risk than females. One thing generally accepted is that exercise can reduce the risk of coronary heart disease.

16.6 Lymphatic system

The lymphatic system consists of widely distributed **lymph capillaries** which are found in all tissues of the body. These capillaries merge to form **lymph vessels** which possess valves and whose structure is similar to that of veins. The fluid within these vessels, the **lymph**, is therefore carried in one direction only, namely, away from the tissues. The lymph vessels from the right side of the head and thorax and the right arm combine to form the **right lymphatic duct** which drains into the right subclavian vein near the heart. The lymph vessels from the rest of the body form the **thoracic duct** which drains into the left subclavian vein.

Along the lymph vessels are series of **lymph nodes**. These contain a population of phagocytic cells, e.g. lymphocytes which remove bacteria and other foreign material from lymph. During infection these nodes frequently swell. Lymph nodes are the major sites of lymphocyte production.

The movement of lymph through the lymphatic system is achieved in three ways:

1. Hydrostatic pressure – The pressure of tissue fluid leaving the arterioles helps push lymph along the lymph system.

2. Muscle contraction – The contraction of skeletal muscle compresses lymph vessels, exerting a pressure on the lymph within them. The valves in the vessels ensure that this pressure pushes the lymph in the direction of the heart.

3. Inspiratory movements – On breathing in, pressure in the thorax is decreased. This helps to draw lymph towards the vessels in the thorax.

Lymph is a milky liquid derived from tissue fluid. It contains lymphocytes and is rich in fats obtained from the lacteals of the small intestines. These fats might damage red blood cells and so are carried separately, until they are later added to the general circulation in safe quantities.

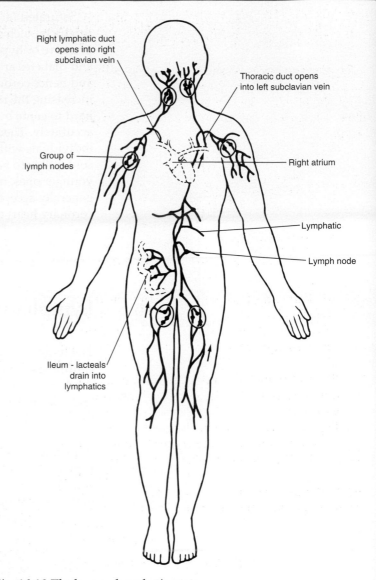

Fig. 16.18 The human lymphatic system

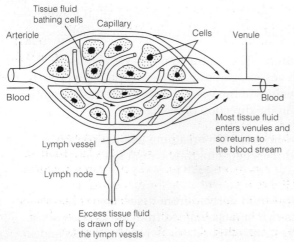

Fig. 16.19 Formation and destination of tissue fluid

16.6.1 Tissue fluid and its formation

As blood passes from arterioles into the narrow capillaries, a hydrostatic pressure is created which helps fluid escape through the capillary walls. This fluid is called **tissue (intercellular) fluid** and it bathes all cells of the body. It contains glucose, amino acids, fatty acids, salts and oxygen which it supplies to the tissues, from which it obtains carbon dioxide and other excretory material. Tissue fluid is thus the means by which materials are exchanged between blood and tissues.

The majority of this tissue fluid passes back into the venules by osmosis. The plasma proteins, which did not leave the blood, exert an osmotic pressure which draws much of the tissue fluid back into the blood. The fluid which does not return by this means passes into the open-ended lymph capillaries, from which point it becomes known as lymph.

16.7   Questions

1. The diagram below shows the processes which take place as blood flows through a capillary bed in mammalian tissues. The hydrostatic pressure and colloid solute (osmotic) potential at X are negligible (0 kPa).

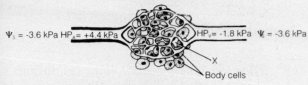

Ψ$_S$ = -3.6 kPa   HP$_A$= +4.4 kPa   HP$_v$= -1.8 kPa   Ψ$_S$ = -3.6 kPa

X
Body cells

HP$_A$ = Hydrostatic pressure in the arteriole
HP$_V$ = Hydrostatic pressure in the venule
Ψ$_S$ = Colloid solute potential (osmotic potential) of the blood

(a)   (i) Name the fluid which occupies the region labelled X.   *(1 mark)*
(ii) With reference to the diagram, describe the formation of the fluid in the region labelled X.   *(2 marks)*
(iii) Calculate the net pressure bringing about this process at the arteriole end. Show your working.   *(2 marks)*
(b) Explain why the osmotic effect of plasma proteins has been taken into account but not that of salts and other dissolved substances in the blood.   *(2 marks)*

(c) In the condition known as *oedema*, excess fluid accumulates at X. Suggest **one** cause of oedema.
                                                      (1 mark)
                                              (Total 8 marks)

ULEAC June 1995, Paper 3, No. 3

2. *(a)* The ABO blood grouping system is based on the presence or absence of antigens (*agglutinogens*) on the cell-surface membrane of red blood cells.
(i) Explain how the ABO blood group of a person can be determined in a hospital laboratory.   *(3 marks)*
(ii) If a person is blood group AB what can be deduced about the respective antibodies (*agglutinins*) present in the plasma?   *(1 mark)*
(iii) Explain why a person with:
1. blood group B can be given a transfusion of blood of group O safely;   *(3 marks)*
2. blood group O is called a *universal donor*
                                                      (1 mark)
(iv) Suggest **one** reason why the antibodies (agglutinins) in a donor's plasma can be ignored during a single transfusion to replace a small amount of lost blood.   *(1 mark)*
(v) Distinguish between the process of agglutination and blood clotting.   *(1 mark)*

(b) The diagram shows a capillary with the pressures involved in causing fluid movement across the capillary wall.

Arterial end

Blood pressure
35 mm Hg   15 mm Hg

Venous end

Plasma osmotic pressure
28 mm Hg   28 mm Hg

Interstitial fluid osmotic pressure
3 mm Hg   3 mm Hg

Units: mm Hg = millimetre of mercury
1 mm Hg = 133.3 kPa

(i) Use the figures in the diagram to suggest how fluid is filtered out of, and reabsorbed back into the capillary.   *(2 marks)*
(ii) Explain why blood pressure falls as blood travels along the capillary.   *(1 mark)*
(iii) More fluid is filtered out of the capillaries than is reabsorbed. The excess is returned to the blood via the lymphatic system. Explain how this movement through the lymphatic system is achieved.   *(3 marks)*
(c) The table shows the change in composition of the blood following a haemorrhage (bleeding).

	Normal	Immediately after haemorrhage	18 hours later
Total blood volume/dm^3	5	4	4.9
Erythrocyte volume/dm^3	2.3	1.9	1.9
Plasma volume/dm^3	2.7	2.1	3.0

(i) Suggest an explanation for the observed changes in total blood volume after the haemorrhage.   *(4 marks)*
(ii) Describe the process by which the body brings about a return to normal levels of erythrocytes.   *(4 marks)*
                                              (Total 24 marks)

AEB June 1995, Paper 2, No. 1

3. Read the following extract:
In Britain about 10,000 people a year receive an artificial pacemaker. The operation takes less than an hour under local anaesthetic and yet it can transform the quality of a patient's life for many years.
One of the most common heart problems is known as heart block. Damage to the atrio-ventricular node of the heart means that electrical impulses are not conducted from the atria to the ventricles. The artificial pacemaker overcomes this by sensing the

level of electrical activity in the atrium and delivering electrical impulses at a corresponding rate to the ventricle. Thus the pacemaker can mimic the natural action of the heart, making it speed up or slow down according to what the body is doing.

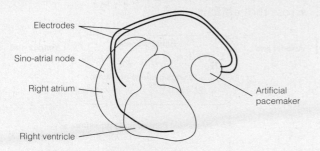

(a) Describe how the contraction of the atria and ventricles is co-ordinated in a single heart beat in a healthy heart. (5 *marks*)

(b) Explain the role of the nervous system in 'making the heart speed up or slow down according to what the body is doing'. (5 *marks*)

(c) In using the artificial pacemaker, suggest why one electrode is attached to the atrium and the other to the base of the ventricle as shown in the diagram. (2 *marks*)

(*Total 12 marks*)

NEAB June 1995, Paper BY03, No. 8

4. A diseased kidney may be replaced with a healthy one transplanted from another person.

(a) Explain how the action of T lymphocytes would normally result in rejection of the transplanted kidney. (2 *marks*)

(b) Describe **two** ways in which the chance of rejection may be reduced. (2 *marks*)

(c) Explain why a kidney may be transplanted from one identical twin to another without risk of rejection. (2 *marks*)

(d) Suggest why some illnesses, normally rare, occur more frequently in both AIDS patients and in those who have received transplants. (2 *marks*)

(*Total 8 marks*)

NEAB June 1995, Paper BY08, No. 4

5. During an expedition to the Himalayas, measurements were made of changes in the climbers' blood. These included blood volume, plasma volume, red blood cell volume and concentration of haemoglobin in the blood.

The climbers spent a period of 18 weeks at altitudes between 4000 m and 5791 m. They spent the next 6 weeks at 5791 m, and then up to 14 weeks at altitudes above 5791 m. The results of the measurements on the blood at the end of each of these periods are shown on the graphs below, expressed as a percentage change compared to sea level values.

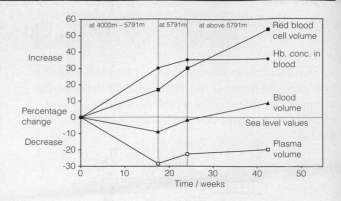

(a) (i) Explain why plasma volume fell during the first 18 weeks of the expedition. (2 *marks*)

(ii) Compare the changes in plasma volume and blood volume over the entire period of the expedition. (2 *marks*)

(iii) Suggest an explanation for the differences between the patterns of change of plasma volume and blood volume during the expedition. (1 *mark*)

(b) (i) Explain the adaptive value to the climbers of the changes in red blood cell volume and haemoglobin concentration during the expedition. (2 *marks*)

(ii) Describe how these changes were brought about, in terms of physiological responses to environmental stimuli. (3 *marks*)

(iii) Suggest an explanation for the differences between the patterns of change of red blood cell volume and haemoglobin concentration. (3 *marks*)

(*Total 13 marks*)

ULEAC June 1995, Paper 4C, No. 2

6. The table below refers to **three** components of human blood. If the statement is correct for the component, place a tick (✓) in the appropriate box and if the statement is incorrect, place a cross (✗) in the appropriate box.

Function	Erythrocyte	Thrombocyte (platelet)	Plasma
Transports carbon dioxide			
Contains enzymes involved in clotting			
Forms antibodies			
Transports hormones			
Carries out phagocytosis			

(*Total 5 marks*)

ULEAC June 1994, Paper 3, No. 2

7. The figure shows the structure of an antibody molecule. The region of the molecule that binds with an antigen is called the *variable region*.

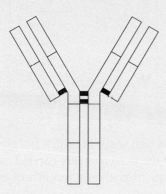

(a) (i) Indicate one of these variable regions on the diagram with a letter **V**.
(ii) What feature of the variable region enables it to bind specifically to an antigen?
(iii) Indicate the position of a heavy polypeptide chain on the diagram with a letter **H**. (3 marks)

One of the most significant advances in immunological technology has been the development of procedures for making large amounts of individual antibodies. The technique involves hybridization of cancer cells with lymphocytes. The lymphocytes make specific antibodies and are obtained from an animal. The different hybrid lymphocytes can be separated from each other and used to produce monoclonal antibodies. The variable region of the antibody is coded for by several hundred genes, only a small number of which are expressed in any one lymphocyte. After the lymphocyte matures, mutations occur in these genes.

(b) (i) What is a *monoclonal antibody*?
(ii) Explain what is meant by *hybridization* of cells.
(iii) What is the advantage of using cancer cells during production of monoclonal antibodies?
(iv) Which type of lymphocyte would be used during production of monoclonal antibodies? (4 marks)

(c) Explain briefly how an animal could be stimulated to produce antibodies. (2 marks)

(d) Describe **one** use of monoclonal antibodies. (2 marks)

(e) Explain the significance of the following statements.
(i) Only a small number of variable genes are expressed in any one lymphocyte.
(ii) Mutations occur in lymphocytes. (4 marks)
(Total 15 marks)

UCLES June 1993, Paper 3 (Option 1), No. 2

8. Fig. 1 shows the patterns of mortality due to diphtheria and measles in children under the age of 15 years in England and Wales from the year 1885 to 1972.

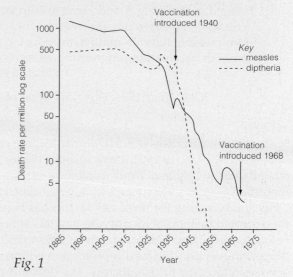

Fig. 1

(a) Explain how the crude death rates for measles and diphtheria have been calculated for Fig. 1. (2 marks)

(b) Fig. 1 shows that vaccination against diphtheria was introduced in England and Wales in 1940. Explain what is meant by *vaccination*. (1 mark)

Before vaccination was introduced, patients suffering from diphtheria could be treated using a serum derived from patients who had recovered from the infection.

(c) What would have been the effective component of the serum? (1 mark)

Some vaccines contain dead organisms, but the measles vaccine contains a living attenuated virus.

(d) Explain the advantage of using
(i) a living virus;
(ii) an attenuated virus. (3 marks)

Fig. 2 shows data on measles **notifications** in England and Wales between the years 1950 and 1991. A measles vaccine was introduced in 1968 and a combined vaccine for mumps, measles and Rubella (MMR) in 1988.

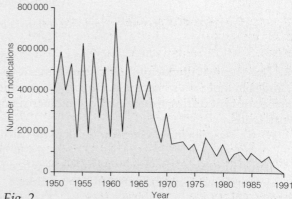

Fig. 2

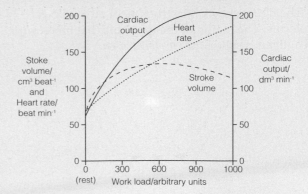

(e) (i) Describe **two** effects of introducing vaccination on measles notifications.
(ii) State **two** reasons why notification of certain diseases is important. *(4 marks)*

(f) Using data from Fig. 1 and Fig. 2 to help you if you wish, give **two** possible reasons **for**, and **two** possible reasons **against**, introducing a measles vaccination programme. *(4 marks)*

(Total 15 marks)

UCLES June 1994, Paper 3 (Option 1), No. 1

9. Coronary heart disease (CHD) is the leading cause of death in the UK. In 1991 it was responsible for 26% of all deaths in England. Epidemiological studies have identified a series of factors which are associated with CHD and screening for these risk factors has become the accepted method of identifying patients at high risk. A political decision was made in 1989 to include disease prevention and health promotion within the services offered by British doctors. The doctor can earn a fee for organizing coronary prevention or health promotion clinics. The Government White Paper 'The Health of the Nation', published in July 1992, included the objective of reducing CHD by 40% by the year 2000 for people aged under 65 years.

(Source, *Lancet*, December 1993)

(a) Explain how coronary heart disease may cause death. *(4 marks)*

(b) Outline the causative link between cigarette smoking and coronary heart disease. *(3 marks)*

(c) (i) Identify **two** factors, other than cigarette smoking, that an epidemiological study would be likely to find associated with coronary heart disease. *(1 mark)*
(ii) Describe briefly how a doctor could screen for the two factors identified in (i). *(1 mark)*

(d) Suggest **two** reasons why the British Government has become active in trying to reduce coronary heart disease. *(2 marks)*

(e) Suggest **three non-medical** measures which the Government could take to try to reduce the incidence of coronary heart disease. *(3 marks)*

(Total 14 marks)

UCLES June 1995, Paper 3 (Option 1) No. 1

10. The graph at the top of the next column shows the changes in a person's heart rate, stroke volume and cardiac output during exercise involving increasing work loads.

(a) (i) Describe how you would calculate cardiac output. *(1 mark)*
(ii) Suggest why stroke volume falls when the work load rises above 600 arbitrary units. *(1 mark)*

(b) Suggest **two** ways in which the graph would be different if the exercise were carried out by the same person after several months of endurance training. *(2 marks)*

(Total 4 marks)

AEB June 1992, Paper 1, No. 7

11. The graph shows a primary and secondary immune response to the same antigen.

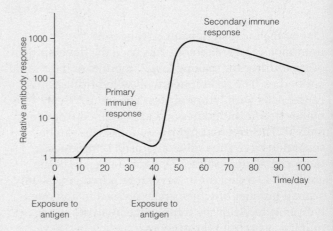

(a) Give **three** ways in which the secondary response is different from the primary response. *(3 marks)*

(b) Give **one** reason for these differences. *(1 mark)*

(c) Why was a log scale used for the vertical axis? *(1 mark)*

(Total 5 marks)

AEB June 1993, Paper 1, No. 12

12. (a) Describe the part played by the sino-atrial node in the initiation of the heart beat. *(2 marks)*

(b) Describe the part played by the automatic nervous system in regulating the heart rate. *(2 marks)*

(c) What is the function of the Purkinje tissue (also called Purkinje fibres)? *(2 marks)*

(Total 6 marks)

AEB June 1993, Paper 1, No. 16

13. The diagram below shows a section of a coronary artery from a person who died of a heart attack, made during a post-mortem examination.

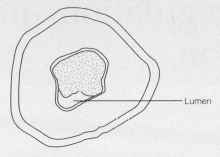

(*a*) (i) Comment on the appearance of this section in relation to the cause of death. (*3 marks*)
(ii) Suggest **two** dietary factors which might have contributed to this appearance. (*2 marks*)
(*b*) What symptoms might this person have experienced prior to the fatal heart attack? (*2 marks*)

(*Total 7 marks*)

ULEAC June 1993, Paper 4B, No. 5

14. Immunization may confer active or passive immunity. Discuss the advantages and disadvantages of each type of immunity in the control of human pathogens. (*Total 10 marks*)

ULEAC 1996, Specimen Paper B/HB4A, No. 8

15. (*a*) Describe the process of phagocytosis and its role in the body's defence system. (*9 marks*)
(*b*) Discuss the social and moral implications of transplant surgery. (*9 marks*)

(*Total 18 marks*)

UCLES June 1993, Paper 3 (Option 1), No. 3b

16. The graph below shows the oxygen dissociation curve for the pigment haemoglobin in a human. The loading tension is the partial pressure of oxygen at which 95% of the pigment is saturated with oxygen. The unloading tension is the partial pressure at which 50% of the pigment is saturated with oxygen.

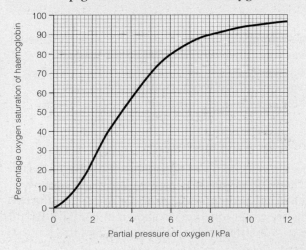

(*a*) Explain why haemoglobin is an efficient respiratory pigment. (*2 marks*)
(*b*) (i) From the graph determine the difference between the loading and unloading tensions of the haemoglobin. Show your working. (*2 marks*)
(ii) Give **one** location in the human body where partial pressures lower than the unloading tension may be reached. Give a reason for your answer. (*2 marks*)
(*c*) Suggest what effects increasing concentrations of carbon dioxide in the blood would have on the loading and unloading tensions of human haemoglobin. Give reasons for your answers. (*4 marks*)
(*d*) The oxygen dissociation curve for fetal haemoglobin lies to the left of the curve for adult haemoglobin. Suggest an explanation for this difference. (*2 marks*)
(*e*) State **three** ways in which carbon dioxide is transported in the blood.

(*3 marks*)
(*Total 15 marks*)

ULEAC June 1996, Paper HB6, No. 4

17. The bar chart shows the relative thickness of parts of the walls of two blood vessels, **A** and **B**. One of these blood vessels is an artery, the other a vein.

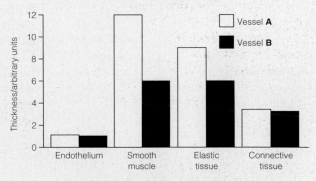

(*a*) Which blood vessel is the artery? Explain the reasons for your answer. (*2 marks*)
(*b*) Explain how the structure of veins ensures the flow of blood in one direction only. (*2 marks*)

(*Total 4 marks*)

NEAB June 1996, Biology Paper I, No. 7

17 Osmoregulation and excretion

Animals such as humans which live on land tend to lose water by evaporation. It is also essential to the proper functioning of their cells that the concentration and proportion of various ions in their body fluids are kept constant. The homeostatic process which maintains a desirable balance of water and ions in the body is termed **osmoregulation**. Homeostasis is the subject of Chapter 18.

The complex chemical reactions which occur in all living cells produce a range of waste products which must be eliminated from the body in a process known as **excretion**. Most nitrogenous waste comes from the breakdown of excess proteins which cannot be stored in the body. The form of these excretory products is influenced partly by the availability of water for their excretion. Animals living under conditions of water shortage cannot afford to lose large volumes of water in order to remove their nitrogenous waste. If water is plentiful it may be used to facilitate excretion.

It is important not to confuse the terms excretion, secretion and elimination. **Excretion** is the expulsion from the body of the waste products of metabolism. **Secretion** is the production by the cells of substances useful to the body, such as digestive juices or hormones. **Elimination**, or **egestion** (see Section 11.5.7), is the removal of undigested food and other substances which have never been involved in the metabolic activities of cells.

17.1 The water molecule

Water is the most abundant liquid on earth and is essential to all living organisms. It is, however, no ordinary molecule. It possesses some unusual properties as a result of the hydrogen bonds which readily form between its molecules. These properties make water an ideal constituent of living things.

17.1.1 Structure of the water molecule

The water molecule is made up of two atoms of hydrogen and one of oxygen. Its basic atomic structure is given in Chapter 1, Fig. 1.4. This is a simplified representation for in practice the two hydrogen atoms are closer together, as shown in Fig. 17.1. By weight, 99.76% of water molecules consist of $^1H_2^{16}O$; the

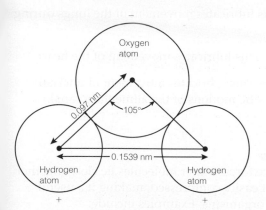

Fig. 17.1 Structure of water molecule

remainder is made up of various isotopes such as ^2H and ^{18}O. The commonest isotope is deuterium (^2H) and when this is incorporated into a water molecule it is known as **heavy water**, as a result of its greater molecular mass. Heavy water may be harmful to living organisms.

17.1.2 Polarity and hydrogen bonding

The distribution of the charges on a water molecule is unequal. The charge on the hydrogen atoms is slightly positive while that on the oxygen atom is negative (Fig. 17.1). Molecules with unevenly distributed charges are said to be **polar**. Attraction of oppositely charged poles of water molecules causes them to group together. The attractive forces form **hydrogen bonds**. Although individual bonds are weak, they collectively form important forces which hold water molecules together. This makes water a much more stable substance than would otherwise be the case.

17.1.3 The importance of water to living organisms

Life arose in water and many organisms still live surrounded by it. Those that left water to colonize land nonetheless keep their cells bathed in it. Water is therefore the main constituent of all organisms – in jellyfish up to 98% and in most herbaceous plants 90%. Even humans consist of around 65% water. The importance of water to organisms is manifold and there is only room here to list a few examples.

Metabolic role of water

1. **Hydrolysis** – Water is used to hydrolyse many substances, e.g. proteins to amino acids, fats to fatty acids and glycerol and polysaccharides to monosaccharides.

2. **Medium for chemical reactions** – All chemical reactions take place in an aqueous medium.

3. **Diffusion and osmosis** – Water is essential to the diffusion of materials across surfaces such as the lungs or alimentary canal.

4. **Photosynthetic substrate** – Water is a major raw material in photosynthesis.

Water as a solvent
Water readily dissolves other substances and therefore is used for:

1. **Transport** – Blood plasma, tissue fluid and lymph are all predominantly water and are used to dissolve a wide range of substances which can then be easily transported.

2. **Removal of wastes** – Metabolic wastes like ammonia and urea are removed from the body in solution in water.

3. **Secretions** – Most secretions comprise substances in aqueous solution. Most digestive juices have salts and enzymes in solution; tears consist largely of water.

Water as a lubricant

Water's properties, especially its viscosity, make it a useful lubricant. Lubricating fluids which are mostly water include:

1. **Mucus** – This is used externally to aid movement in animals, e.g. snail and earthworm; or internally in the vagina and gut wall.

2. **Synovial fluid** – This lubricates movement in many joints.

3. **Pleural fluid** – This lubricates movement of the lungs during breathing.

4. **Pericardial fluid** – This lubricates movement of the heart.

5. **Perivisceral fluid** – This lubricates movement of internal organs, e.g. the peristaltic motions of the alimentary canal.

Supporting role of water

With its large cohesive forces water molecules lie close together. Water is therefore not easily compressed, making it a useful means of supporting organisms. Examples include:

1. **Hydrostatic skeleton** – Animals like the earthworm are supported by the pressure of the aqueous medium within them.

2. **Turgor pressure** – Herbaceous plants and the herbaceous parts of woody ones are supported by the osmotic influx of water into their cells.

3. **Humours of the eye** – The shape of the eye in vertebrates is maintained by the aqueous and vitreous humours within them. Both are largely water.

4. **Amniotic fluid** – This supports and protects the mammalian fetus during development.

5. **Erection of the penis** – The pressure of blood, a largely aqueous fluid, makes the penis erect so that it can be introduced into the vagina during copulation.

6. **Medium in which to live** – Water provides support to the organisms which live within it. Very large organisms, e.g. whales, returned to water as their sheer size made movement on land difficult.

Miscellaneous functions of water

1. **Temperature control** – Evaporation of water during sweating and panting is used to cool the body.

2. **Medium for dispersal** – Water may be used to disperse the larval stages of some terrestrial organisms. In mosses and ferns it is the medium in which sperm are transferred. The build-up of osmotic pressure helps to disperse the seeds of the squirting cucumber.

3. **Hearing and balance** – In the mammalian ear the watery endolymph and perilymph play a role in hearing and balance.

17.2 Excretory products

All animals produce carbon dioxide as a waste product of aerobic respiration and the elimination of this is dealt with in Chapters 15 and 16. Other excretory products include bile pigments, water, mineral salts and nitrogenous substances. There are three main waste products of nitrogenous metabolism: ammonia, urea and uric acid. No animal excretes one of these to the exclusion of the others but the predominance of one over the others is determined by three factors:

1. The production of enzymes necessary to convert ammonia into either urea or uric acid.

2. The availability of water in the habitat for the removal of the nitrogenous excretory material.

3. The animal's ability to control water loss or uptake by the body.

Many aquatic animals excrete mainly ammonia and are called **ammoniotelic**. Other aquatic animals and some terrestrial forms excrete predominantly urea and are said to be **ureotelic**. The remaining terrestrial animals are **uricotelic**, excreting mainly uric acid.

17.2.1 Ammonia

Ammonia is derived from the breakdown of proteins and nucleic acids in the body. Ammonia is very toxic and is never allowed to accumulate within the body tissues or fluids. It is extremely soluble and diffuses readily across cell membranes. In spite of its toxicity it is the main excretory product of marine invertebrates and all freshwater animals.

17.2.2 Urea

Urea, $CO(NH_2)_2$, is formed by the combination of two molecules of ammonia with one of carbon dioxide.

However, its synthesis in living tissues is much more complex than this simple equation suggests. Urea is produced by a cyclic process known as the **urea** or **ornithine cycle**, details of which are given in Section 18.3.2. Urea is much less toxic than ammonia and, although it is less soluble, less water is needed for its elimination because the tissues can tolerate higher concentrations of it.

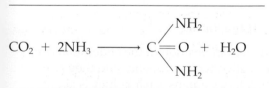

17.2.3 Uric acid

Uric acid is a more complex molecule than urea; it is a purine in the same group as adenine and guanine. Like urea, it involves the expenditure of quite considerable energy in its formation, but this is outweighed by the advantages it confers. Uric acid is virtually insoluble in water and is non-toxic. It requires very little water for its removal from the body and it is therefore a suitable product for animals living in arid conditions, e.g. terrestrial reptiles and insects. Containing little, if any, water, its storage within organisms does not greatly increase their mass. This is an advantage to flying organisms, e.g. birds and insects. It is removed as a solid pellet or thick paste.

Gout

Gout is a disorder which arises when the blood contains increased levels of uric acid. An excess of uric acid can be caused either by increased production or by an impairment of kidney function. The disorder tends to run in families and is far more common in men. The risk of attack is increased by high alcohol intake, the consumption of red meat and some other foods, and by obesity.

When its concentration in the blood is excessive uric acid crystals may form in various parts of the body, especially in the joints of the foot, knee and hand, causing intense pain and inflammation known as gouty arthritis. Crystals may also form in the kidneys as kidney stones.

Drugs may be prescribed to treat an attack of gout or to prevent recurrent attacks that could lead to deformity of the affected joints and kidney damage, but changes in diet and a reduction in alcohol consumption may be an important part of treatment.

17.3 Osmoregulation and excretion in humans – the kidney

In humans the main organ of nitrogenous excretion is the kidney. Kidneys are composed of a number of basic units called **nephrons**. In humans, these nephrons are particularly numerous, with long tubules for water reabsorption.

17.3.1 Gross structure of the kidney

The paired kidneys are held in position in the abdominal cavity by a thin layer of tissue called the peritoneum and they are usually surrounded by fat. In humans, each kidney is about 7–10 cm long and 2.5–4.0 cm wide, packed with blood vessels and an estimated one million nephrons. Each kidney is supplied with blood from the renal artery and drained by a renal vein. The urine which is produced by the kidney is removed by a ureter for temporary storage in the urinary bladder. A ring of muscle called a sphincter closes the exit from the bladder. Sense cells in the bladder wall are stimulated as the bladder fills, triggering a reflex action which results in relaxation of the bladder sphincter and simultaneous contraction of the smooth muscle in the bladder wall. The expulsion of urine from the body via the urethra is known as **micturition**. Although micturition is controlled by the autonomic nervous system, humans learn to control it by voluntary nervous activity.

Within each kidney there are a number of clearly defined regions. The outer region, or **cortex**, mainly comprises Bowman's capsules and convoluted tubules with their associated blood supply. This gives the cortex a different appearance from the

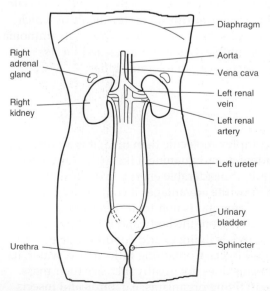

Fig. 17.2 Position of the kidneys in humans

Labels on figure:
Right adrenal gland
Right kidney
Urethra
Diaphragm
Aorta
Vena cava
Left renal vein
Left renal artery
Left ureter
Urinary bladder
Sphincter

inner **medulla** with its loops of Henle, collecting ducts and blood vessels. These structures in the medulla are in groups known as **renal pyramids** and they project into the **pelvis** which is the expanded portion of the ureter.

17.3.2 Structure of the nephron

The main regions of the mammalian nephron are shown in Fig. 17.4, with details in Figs. 17.5 and 17.6. Basically it comprises a glomerulus and a long tubule with several clearly defined regions. The **glomerulus** is a mass of blood capillaries which are partially enclosed by the blind-ending region of the tubule called the **Bowman's capsule**. The blood supply to the glomerulus is from the afferent arteriole of the renal artery; blood leaves the glomerulus via the narrower efferent arteriole. The inner, or visceral, layer of the Bowman's capsule is made up of unusual

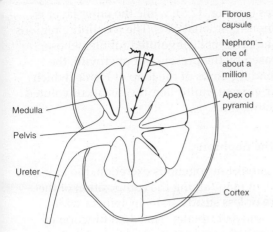

Fig. 17.3 Human kidney to show position of a nephron (LS)

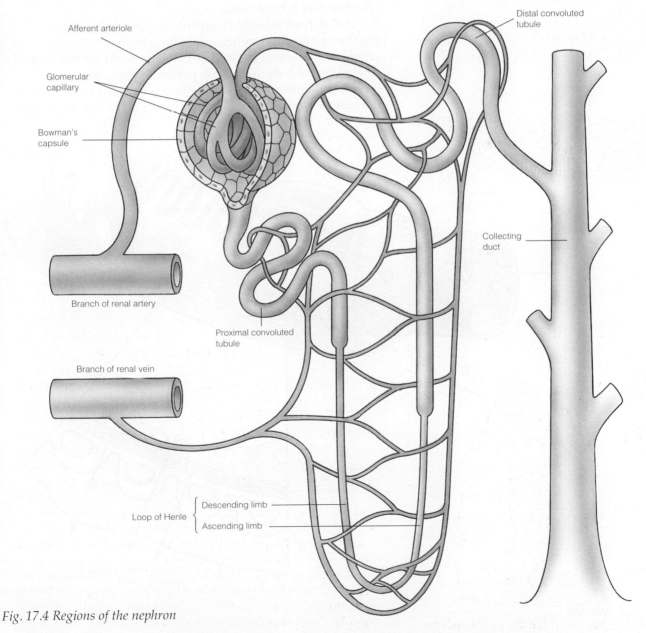

Fig. 17.4 Regions of the nephron

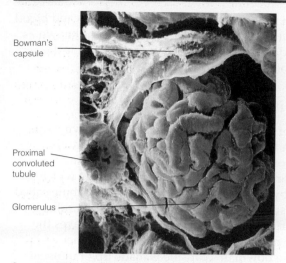

Bowman's capsule

Proximal convoluted tubule

Glomerulus

Scanning EM of nephron showing glomerulus

cells called **podocytes** (see Fig. 17.5), while the outer layer is unspecialized squamous epithelial cells. The remaining regions of the nephron are the proximal convoluted tubule, whose surface-area is increased by the presence of microvilli, the descending and ascending limbs of the loop of Henle, which function as a counter-current multiplier, the distal convoluted tubule and the collecting duct.

17.3.3 Functions of the nephron

Apart from being organs of nitrogenous excretion, the kidneys also play a major rôle in maintaining the composition of the body fluids in a more or less steady state, in spite of wide fluctuations in water and salt uptake. This dual function of excretion and osmoregulation is best studied by a detailed consideration of the functioning of one nephron, the main regions of which are shown in Fig. 17.4.

Ultrafiltration in the Bowman's capsule
The cup-shaped Bowman's capsule encloses a mass of capillaries, the **glomerulus**, originating from the afferent arteriole of the renal artery. The capillary walls are made up of a single layer of endothelial cells perforated by pores about 0.1 μm in diameter. The endothelium is closely pressed against the basement membrane which in places is the only membrane

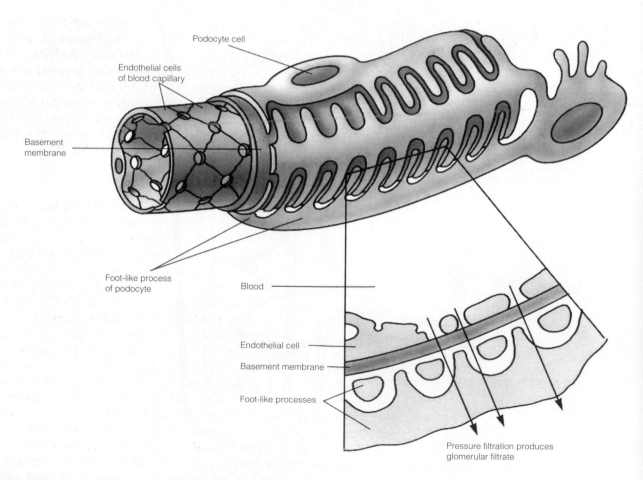

Podocyte cell

Endothelial cells of blood capillary

Basement membrane

Foot-like process of podocyte

Blood

Endothelial cell

Basement membrane

Foot-like processes

Pressure filtration produces glomerular filtrate

Fig. 17.5 Podocyte

Did you know?

Almost a quarter of the heart's output passes through the kidney at each beat.

Did you know?

All the blood in the circulatory system passes through the kidneys every 4–5 minutes.

between the blood and the cavity of the Bowman's capsule (see Fig. 17.4). The blood pressure in the kidneys is higher than in other organs. This high pressure is maintained because in each Bowman's capsule the afferent arteriole has a larger diameter than the efferent arteriole. As a result of this pressure, substances are forced through the endothelial pores of the capillary, across the basement membrane and into the Bowman's capsule by ultrafiltration. The glomerular filtrate contains substances with a relative molecular mass (RMM) less than 68 000, e.g. glucose, amino acids, vitamins, some hormones, urea, uric acid, creatinine, ions and water. Remaining in the blood, along with some water, are red blood cells, white cells, platelets and plasma proteins which are too large to pass the filter provided by the basement membrane. Further constriction of the efferent arteriole in response to hormonal and nervous signals results in an increased hydrostatic pressure in the glomerulus and substances with an RMM greater than 68 000 may pass into the glomerular filtrate. This filtering process is extremely efficient. The glomerular filtrate passes from the Bowman's capsule along the kidney tubule (nephron). As it does so, the fluid undergoes a number of changes, since the urine excreted has a very different composition from the glomerular filtrate. These differences are brought about primarily by selective reabsorption of substances useful to the body. The urine when compared with the glomerular filtrate will contain, for example, less glucose, amino acids and water and a relatively higher percentage of urea and other nitrogenous waste products.

Ultrafiltration is a passive process and selection of substances passing from the blood into the glomerular filtrate is made entirely according to relative molecular mass. Both passive and active processes are involved in the selective reabsorption of substances from the nephron. The composition is further altered by the active secretion of substances, such as creatinine, from the blood into the tubule. Without selective reabsorption humans would produce about 180 dm^3 of urine per day whereas the actual volume produced is approximately 1.5 dm^3.

Proximal convoluted tubule

This is the longest region of the nephron. It comprises a single layer of epithelial cells, with numerous microvilli forming a brush border (see Fig. 17.6). The base of each cell is convoluted where it is adjacent to a blood capillary and there are numerous intercellular spaces. Another notable feature of these cells is the presence of large numbers of mitochondria providing the ATP necessary for active transport. These cells are ideally adapted for reabsorption and over 80% of the glomerular filtrate is reabsorbed here, including all the food substances and most of the sodium chloride and water. Amino acids, glucose and ions diffuse into the cells of the proximal convoluted tubule and these are actively transported into the intercellular spaces from where they diffuse into the surrounding capillaries. The constant removal of these substances from the cells of the convoluted tubule causes others to enter from the lumen of the tubule by diffusion. The active uptake of sodium accompanied by appropriate anions, e.g. chloride, raises the osmotic pressure in the cells and water enters them by osmosis. About half the urea present in the tubular filtrate also returns to the blood by

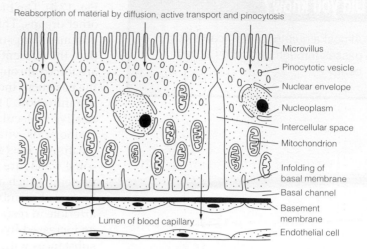

Lumen of proximal convoluted tubule

Reabsorption of material by diffusion, active transport and pinocytosis

- Microvillus
- Pinocytotic vesicle
- Nuclear envelope
- Nucleoplasm
- Intercellular space
- Mitochondrion
- Infolding of basal membrane
- Basal channel
- Basement membrane
- Endothelial cell

Lumen of blood capillary

Fig. 17.6 Detail of cells from the wall of the proximal convoluted tubule

diffusion. Proteins of small molecular mass which may have been forced out of the blood in the Bowman's capsule are taken up at the base of the microvilli by pinocytosis. As a result of all this activity, the tubular filtrate is isotonic with blood in the surrounding capillaries.

Loop of Henle

It is the presence of the loop of Henle which enables humans to produce urine which is hypertonic to the blood. The loop of Henle is made up of two regions, the descending limb which has narrow walls readily permeable to water and the wider ascending limb with thick walls which are far less permeable to water.

The loop of Henle operates as a **counter-current multiplier** system. So how exactly does this work? Consider Fig. 17.7. Sodium and chloride ions are actively pumped out of the ascending limb creating a high solute concentration in the interstitial region. Normally water would follow, being drawn out osmotically. However the walls of the ascending limb are relatively impermeable to water and so little if any escapes. On the other hand the descending loop is highly permeable to water and so water is drawn from it osmotically. This water is carried away by the blood in the vasa recta. As glomerular filtrate enters the descending loop it progressively loses water and so becomes more concentrated. It reaches its maximum concentration at the tip of the loop because as it moves up the ascending limb, ions are removed making it less concentrated.

It might be thought that as the filtrate in the descending limb becomes more concentrated due to the reabsorption of water, osmosis might cease. However the surrounding fluid also becomes more concentrated, ensuring that an osmotic gradient is maintained right down to the tip of the loop of Henle.

In the same way as water is drawn from the descending limb, so it is too from the collecting duct, which runs alongside the loop in the medulla of the kidney. In this way the urine becomes progressively more concentrated (hypertonic) as it moves out of the nephron. The water which is drawn out passes into the blood of the vasa recta which is both slow-flowing and freely permeable, two factors which aid the uptake of water.

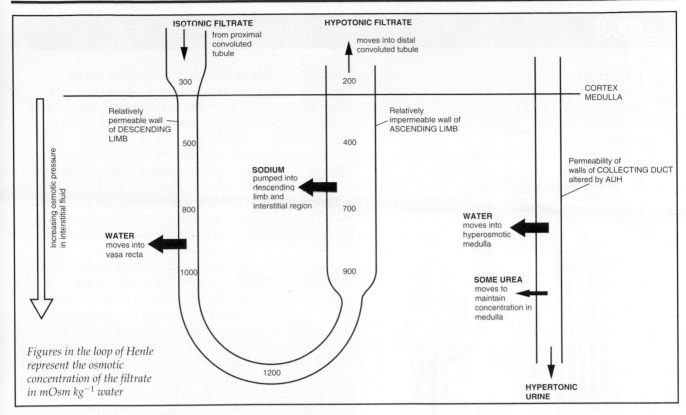

300

200

CORTEX
MEDULLA

Relatively permeable wall of DESCENDING LIMB

500

400

Relatively impermeable wall of ASCENDING LIMB

Permeability of walls of COLLECTING DUCT altered by ADH

Increasing osmotic pressure in interstitial fluid

SODIUM
pumped into descending limb and interstitial region

800

700

WATER
moves into hyperosmotic medulla

WATER
moves into vasa recta

1000

900

SOME UREA
moves to maintain concentration in medulla

1200

Figures in the loop of Henle represent the osmotic concentration of the filtrate in mOsm kg^{-1} water

HYPERTONIC URINE

Fig. 17.7 Counter-current multiplier of the loop of Henle

Distal convoluted tubule

The cells in this region are very similar to those of the proximal convoluted tubule, having a brush border and numerous mitochondria. The permeability of their membranes is affected by hormones (see Section 17.4) and so precise control of the salt and water balance of the blood is possible. The distal convoluted tubule also controls the pH of the blood, maintaining it at 7.4. The cells of the tubule combine water and carbon dioxide to form carbonic acid. This then dissociates into hydrogen ions and hydrogen carbonate ions. The absorption of these hydrogen carbonate ions into the blood raises its pH to compensate for the lowering which results from the production of hydrogen ions during metabolic processes. The hydrogen ions from the dissociation of carbonic acid are pumped into the lumen of the distal tubule. In the lumen hydrogenphosphate ions (HPO_4^{2-}) combine with these hydrogen ions to form dihydrogenphosphate ions ($H_2PO_4^-$) which are then excreted in the urine. The acidic effects of the hydrogen ions is therefore buffered by these hydrogenphosphate ions. The events are summarized in Fig. 17.8.

Not only are hydrogen ions (protons) pumped into the tubule, potassium ions (K^+), ammonium ions (NH_4^-) and certain drugs are also pumped in as a means of controlling blood pH or removing unwanted material. This active removal of substances also takes place in the proximal convoluted tubule and is called **tubular secretion**.

Collecting duct

The permeability of the walls of the collecting duct, like the permeability of those of the distal convoluted tubule, is affected by hormones. This hormonal effect, together with the hypertonic

FOCUS

Dialysis

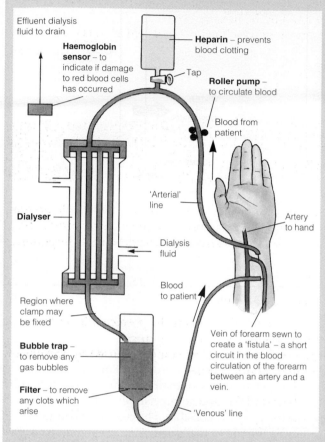

The mechanism of kidney dialysis

Labels on diagram:

Effluent dialysis fluid to drain

Haemoglobin sensor – to indicate if damage to red blood cells has occurred

Heparin – prevents blood clotting

Tap

Roller pump – to circulate blood

Blood from patient

'Arterial' line

Dialyser

Dialysis fluid

Artery to hand

Blood to patient

Region where clamp may be fixed

Bubble trap – to remove any gas bubbles

Vein of forearm sewn to create a 'fistula' – a short circuit in the blood circulation of the forearm between an artery and a vein.

Filter – to remove any clots which arise

'Venous' line

Kidneys may fail as a result of damage or infection. Upon the loss of one kidney the remaining one will adapt to undertake the work of its partner, but the loss of both is inevitably fatal. Survival depends upon either regular treatment on a kidney machine or a transplant. A kidney machine carries out **dialysis**, a process in which the patient's blood flows on one side of a thin membrane while a solution, called the dialysate, flows in the opposite direction on the other side. This counter-current flow ensures the most efficient exchange of material across the membrane. (Section 17.3.3). As the membrane is permeable to small molecules such as urea, this waste product will diffuse from the blood where it is relatively highly concentrated to the dialysate where its concentration is lower. To prevent useful substances like glucose and salts, which are also highly concentrated in blood, diffusing out, the dialysate's composition is the same as that of normal blood. This means that any substance which is in excess, e.g. salts, will also diffuse out until they are in equilibrium with the dialysate. Large molecules such as blood proteins are too large to cross the membrane and there is therefore no risk of them being lost to the dialysate.

A patient's blood needs to pass through the kidney machine many times to ensure the removal of all wastes. Thus, it is necessary for dialysis to take place for up to ten hours every few days. While wastes accumulate in the blood when the patient is away from the machine, adherence to a strict diet ensures they do not build up to a dangerous level before the next treatment.

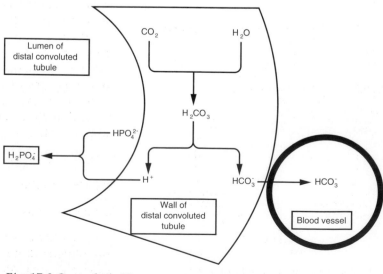

Labels on diagram:

Lumen of distal convoluted tubule

CO_2 H_2O

H_2CO_3

HPO_4^{2-}

$H_2PO_4^-$

H^+ HCO_3^-

Wall of distal convoluted tubule

HCO_3^-

Blood vessel

Fig. 17.8 Control of pH

interstitial fluids built up by the loop of Henle in the medulla, determine whether hypotonic or hypertonic urine is released from the kidney.

If the walls of the collecting duct are water-permeable, water leaves the ducts to pass into the hyperosmotic surroundings and concentrated urine is produced. If the ducts are impermeable to water the final urine will be less concentrated. Hormonal control of the permeability of the walls of the collecting duct to water will be considered in the next section.

The mechanism by which urine is concentrated is illustrated in Fig. 17.7.

17.4 Hormonal control of osmoregulation and excretion

If the kidney is to regulate the amount of water and salts present in the body, very precise monitoring systems are required. The two hormones ADH and aldosterone are particularly important in this respect.

17.4.1 Antidiuretic hormone (ADH)

Antidiuretic hormone (ADH) affects the permeability of the distal convoluted tubule and collecting duct.

A rise in blood osmotic pressure may be caused by any one of, or combination of, three factors:

1. Little water is ingested.

2. Much sweating occurs.

3. Large amounts of salt are ingested.

The rise in blood osmotic pressure is detected by **osmoreceptors** in the hypothalamus and results in nerve impulses passing to the posterior pituitary gland which releases ADH. ADH increases the permeability of the distal convoluted tubule and collecting duct to water. This water passes into the hyperosmotic medulla and a more concentrated (hypertonic) urine is released from the kidney.

ADH also increases the permeability of the collecting duct to urea which passes into the medulla, increasing the osmotic concentration and causing more water to be lost from the descending loop of Henle. If the osmotic pressure of the blood falls owing to

1. large volumes of water being ingested

2. little sweating

3. low salt intake

then ADH production is inhibited and the walls of the distal convoluted tubule and collecting duct remain impermeable to water and urea. As a result, less water is reabsorbed and

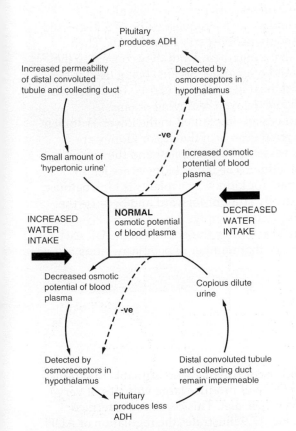

Fig. 17.9 Regulation of ADH production

FOCUS

Kidney transplant

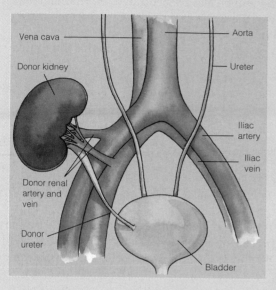

Vena cava

Donor kidney

Donor renal artery and vein

Donor ureter

Aorta

Ureter

Iliac artery

Iliac vein

Bladder

While the kidney machine is an invaluable life-saver, it has many drawbacks. Not only does a considerable time have to be spent connected to the machine, a rigid diet has to be maintained and there is always the risk of anaemia, infection or bone disease. The cost of each treatment is such that there are insufficient machines for all who need them. The preferred solution for many is therefore a **kidney transplant**: a failed kidney must be replaced by a healthy one from a human donor. The donated kidney must be matched so that it is as similar as possible to the failed one since this reduces the chance of it being rejected by the recipient's immune system. A close relative is more likely to have a compatible kidney and therefore live donors are often used. Here a person donates a kidney, safe in the knowledge that he/she can live a normal life with the remaining one. The donor is, however, vulnerable since a disease in the remaining kidney could make dialysis necessary, and there is always a risk in any operation. Against this is the satisfaction of allowing someone to lead a near normal life, free from all the constraints dialysis imposes. However, less than 15% of transplants come from live donors.

The remaining transplants involve the use of healthy kidneys from people who die as a result of other causes. A road accident victim may, for example, provide two functional kidneys. The kidney must be removed within an hour of death, cooled to delay deterioration, and be transplanted within 24 hours. As permission is needed to remove any organ, and as such a request made of a distressed relative is difficult, many people carry donor cards. Their owners sign to say that upon their death they consent to the use of the kidneys (and often other organs) being used for transplants. The card must of course be carried by the owner at all times to avoid any delay in removing organs.

Transplanted kidneys are implanted in the lower abdomen near the groin. The renal vessels of the donor kidney are attached to the iliac vessels of the recipient and the ureter is implanted into the bladder. The failed kidneys are left in place. The survival rate for kidney transplants is high because the operation is relatively straight-forward and because the kidney has a simple vascular supply.

There are around 2000 kidney transplants in the UK each year, with around twice that number of people awaiting a suitable donor.

hypotonic urine is released. Anyone who is unable to produce sufficient levels of ADH will produce large volumes of very dilute urine, whatever their diet. This condition is termed **diabetes insipidus**. Fig. 17.9 illustrates the regulation of ADH production.

17.5 Questions

1. Write an essay on: The structure and functions of the kidney tubule. *(Total 24 marks)*

AEB June 1992, Paper 2, No. 4B

2. The figure shows a cell from the lining of the proximal tubule of the kidney.

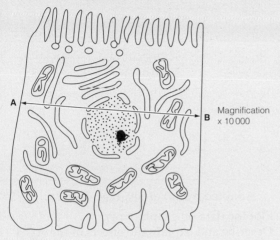

Magnification
x 10 000

(a) Calculate the actual width of the cell measured along the line **A–B**. Show your working. *(2 marks)*
(b) (i) Draw an arrow to indicate the net direction of water movement through the cell.
(ii) What is the process by which water moves across the cell surface membrane? *(2 marks)*
(c) (i) Name **one other** substance which is transported through the membrane of this cell.
(ii) State **two** features of the proximal tubule cell which enable it to transport substances, explaining how each feature is involved in the transport. *(5 marks)*
(Total 9 marks)

UCLES June 1994, Paper 2, No. 4

3. *(a)* If the glomerular filtration rate of the kidneys is $120\,cm^3\,min^{-1}$ and the tubular reabsorption rate is $114\,cm^3\,min^{-1}$, calculate the rate of urine formation per minute. *(1 mark)*
(b) State **two** differences between tubular reabsorption of water in the first (proximal) convoluted tubule and the second (distal) convoluted tubule. *(2 ×1 mark)*
(c) What might reduce the rate of tubular reabsorption of water? *(1 mark)*
(d) The minimum rate of urine production is $300\,cm^3$ per day.
Explain why it is necessary for some urine to be produced each day. *(1 mark)*
(Total 5 marks)

AEB June 1995, Paper 1, No. 6

4. The graph shows the volume of urine collected from a subject before and after drinking $1000\,cm^3$ of distilled water. The subject's urine was collected immediately before the water was drunk and then at intervals of 30 minutes for several hours.

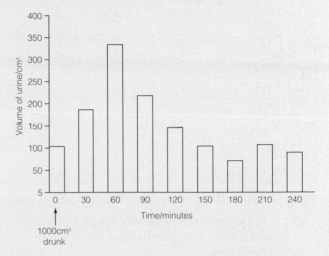

(a) (i) Describe the changes in urine output during the period of the experiment. *(2 marks)*
(ii) Name the process responsible for these events. *(1 mark)*
(b) Explain the difference in the volume of urine collected at 60 minutes and at 90 minutes *(3 marks)*
(c) The experiment was repeated, but this time the subject exercised vigorously for 10 minutes before drinking the water. How would you expect the results of the second experiment to differ from those in the graph? Explain your answer. *(2 marks)*
(d) If, in the original experiment, the subject had drunk 0.9% NaCl solution instead of $1000\,cm^3$ of distilled water, would the same volumes of urine have been collected? Explain your answer.
(Note: 0.9% NaCl solution is isotonic with blood plasma; i.e. it has the same osmotic potential as blood plasma). *(3 marks)*
(Total 11 marks)

AEB June 1994, Paper 1, No. 8

5. An experiment was carried out to investigate the effect of posterior pituitary secretions on urine production in humans.
A person drank $1\,dm^3$ of distilled water, and was at the same time given an injection of posterior pituitary extract. The rate of urine production (in $cm^3\,min^{-1}$) was then measured every 15 minutes for two hours. As a control, the following day the same person again drank $1\,dm^3$ of distilled water, but no injection was

423

given. The rate of urine production was again measured every 15 minutes for two hours. The results of the experiment are given in the table below.

Time/min	Rate of urine production/cm³ min⁻¹	
	After injection of pituitary extract	Control no pituitary injection
0	0.5	0.5
15	0.7	2.0
30	0.8	10.0
45	0.6	16.0
60	0.5	10.0
75	0.4	7.0
90	0.4	5.0
105	0.4	2.0
120	0.4	0.5

Adapted from Green, *Introduction to Human Physiology*

(a) (i) Describe the effect of posterior pituitary extract on urine production, as shown by these data. *(2 marks)*

(ii) Name the component of posterior pituitary extract responsible for this effect. *(1 mark)*

(iii) Describe the mechanism by which this component of posterior pituitary extract gives rise to the effect seen in this experiment. *(3 marks)*

(b) From other experiments it was found that this person's glomerular filtration rate remained constant at 120 cm³ min⁻¹.

(i) Calculate the rate at which water was being reabsorbed in the person's nephrons and collecting ducts at time 0 in both experiments. *(1 mark)*

(ii) Calculate the percentage decrease in the rate of water reabsorption during the first 15 minutes of the control experiment. Show your working. *(2 marks)*

(iii) During the same period the rate of urine production increased by 300%. Comment on the difference between this figure and your answer to part (ii). *(2 marks)*

(c) (i) In the control experiment, during which 15-minute period did the greatest decrease in the rate of water reabsorption take place? *(1 mark)*

(ii) Suggest **two** reasons why the greatest decrease in the rate of water reabsorption occurred during this period, rather than immediately after drinking 1 dm³ of distilled water. *(2 marks)*

(Total 14 marks)

ULEAC June 1994, Paper 3, No. 8

6. Investigations were carried out into the separate effects of sodium chloride and of antidiuretic hormone (ADH) on urine production.

The rate of urine production was measured over a period of 30 minutes. Five minutes after measurements began an intravenous injection was given. On one occasion 10 cm³ of 2.5% sodium chloride solution was injected; on a separate occasion 1 milliunit of ADH was injected. The results are shown in the table below.

Time/min	Rate of urine production/cm³ min⁻¹	
	Sodium chloride injected	ADH injected
0	6.3	5.2
5 injection given	7.0	4.8
10	0.7	2.8
15	0.8	0.5
20	1.2	1.7
25	1.5	3.1
30	1.9	4.0

Adapted from Verney, *Proc. Roy. Soc. B (1947)*

(a) Plot the data on graph paper. *(5 marks)*

(b) Describe and explain the effects of the ADH injection on urine production:
(i) during the period 5–15 minutes; *(2 marks)*
(ii) during the period 15–25 minutes. *(2 marks)*

(c) Discuss the relationship between the two curves on your graph, suggesting reasons for any similarities and differences noted. *(5 marks)*

(Total 14 marks)

ULEAC June 1993, Paper 3, No. 8

7. Nephrosis is a kidney condition in which damage to the glomeruli results in large quantities of protein passing into the glomerular filtrate. This protein finally appears in the urine.

(a) Suggest why this protein is not reabsorbed into the blood in the proximal convoluted tubule of the nephron. *(1 mark)*

(b) As a result of nephrosis large amounts of tissue fluid accumulate in the body, especially in the ankles and feet.

(i) Explain why the loss of protein from the blood results in the accumulation of tissue fluid. *(2 marks)*

(ii) Suggest why this fluid accumulates especially in the ankles and the feet. *(2 marks)*

(c) (i) Explain how the action in the kidney of the hormone aldosterone controls the sodium content of the blood. *(2 marks)*

(ii) Suggest why little aldosterone is produced by a person suffering from nephrosis. *(2 marks)*

(Total 9 marks)

NEAB June 1995, Paper BY03, No. 6

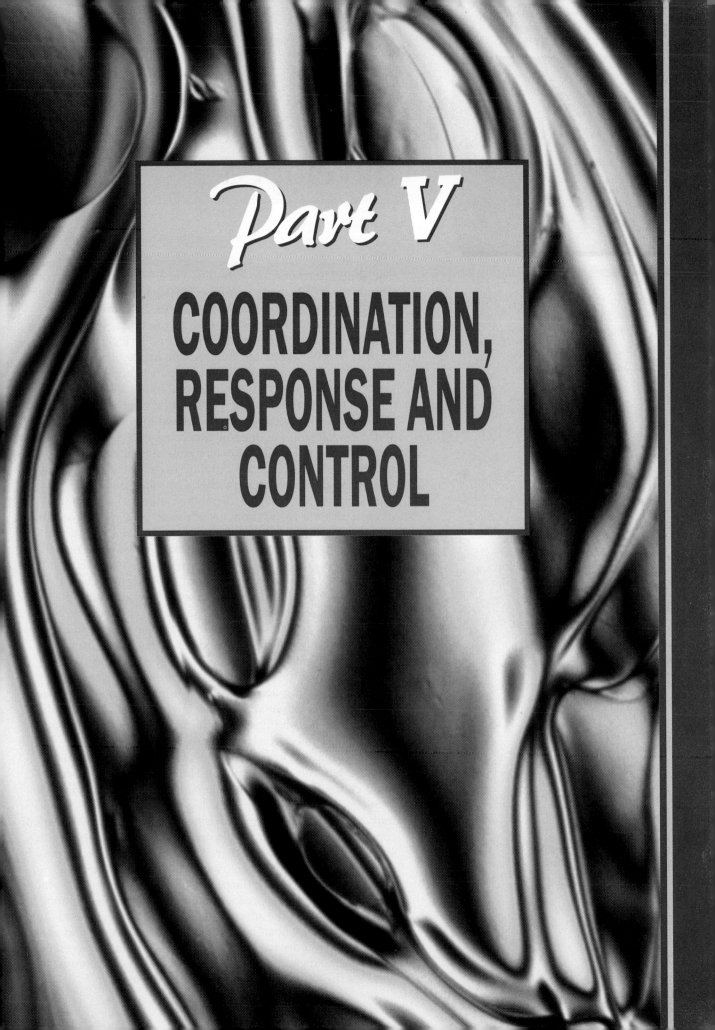

Part V

COORDINATION, RESPONSE AND CONTROL

How control systems developed

The ability to respond to stimuli is a characteristic of all living organisms. While many stimuli originate from outside, it is also necessary to respond to internal changes. In a single-celled organism, such responses are relatively simple. No part of it is far from the medium in which it lives and so it can respond directly to environmental changes. The inside of a single cell does not vary considerably from one part to another and so there are few internal differences to respond to.

With the development of multicellular organisms came the differentiation of cells which specialized in particular functions. With specialization in one function came the loss of the ability to perform others. This division of labour, whereby different groups of cells each carried out their own function, made the cells dependent upon one another. Cells specializing in reproduction, for example, depend on other cells to obtain oxygen for their respiration, yet others to provide glucose and others to remove waste products. These different functional systems must be coordinated if they are to perform efficiently. If, for example, an animal needs to exert itself in order to capture its food, the muscular activity involved must itself be coordinated. The locomotory organs need to operate smoothly and efficiently, with each muscle contracting at exactly the correct time. In addition, more oxygen and glucose will be required and an increased amount of carbon dioxide will need to be removed from the tissues. If breathing is increased so that the oxygen concentration of the blood rises, it is essential that the heart increases its output accordingly. Without coordination between the two systems an increased effort by one could be neutralized by the other. No bodily system can work in isolation, but all must be integrated in a coordinated fashion.

There are two forms of integration in most multicellular animals: nervous and hormonal. The nervous system permits rapid communication between one part of an organism and another, in much the same way as a telephone system does in human society. The hormonal system provides a slower form of communication and can be likened to the postal system. Both systems need to work together. A predator, for example, may be detected by the sense organs, which belong to the nervous system, but in turn cause the production of adrenaline, a hormone. While the nervous system coordinates the animal's locomotion as it makes its escape, the adrenaline ensures that an increased breathing rate and heart beat supply adequate oxygen and glucose to allow the muscles to operate efficiently. The link between these two coordinating systems is achieved by the **hypothalamus**. It is here that the nervous and hormonal systems interact.

All organisms, plant and animal, must respond to environmental changes if they are to survive. To detect these changes requires sense organs. Those detecting external changes are located on the surface of the body and act as a vital link between the internal and external environments. Many other sense cells are located internally to provide information on a constantly changing internal environment. In responding to stimuli, an organism usually modifies some aspect of its functioning. It may need to produce enzymes in response to the presence of food, become sexually aroused in response to certain behaviour by a member of the opposite sex or move away from an unpleasant stimulus. In most cases the organ affecting the change is some distance away from the sense cell detecting the stimulus. A rapid means of communication between the sense cell and the effector organ is essential. In animals the nerves perform this function.

The stimuli received by many sense organs, e.g. the eyes, are very complex and require widely differing responses. The sight of a female of the same species may elicit a totally different response from the sight of a male of the same species. Each response involves different effector organs. The sense organs must therefore be connected by nerves to all effector organs, in much the same way as a telephone subscriber is connected to all other subscribers. One method is to have an individual nerve running from the sense organ to all effectors. Clearly this is only possible in very simple organisms where the sense organs respond to a limited number of stimuli and the number of effectors is small. The nerve nets of cnidarians work in this way.

Large, complex organisms require a different system, because the number of sense organs and effectors is so great that individual links between all of them is not feasible. Imagine having a separate telephone cable leading from a house to every other subscriber's house in Britain, let alone the world. Animals developed a **central nervous system** to which every effector and sense organ has at least one nerve connection. The central nervous system (brain and spinal cord) acts like a switchboard in connecting each incoming stimulus to the appropriate effector. It works in much the same way as a telephone exchange, where a single cable from a home allows a subscriber to be connected to any other simply by making the correct connections at various exchanges.

Where then should the brain be located? The development of locomotion in animals usually resulted in a particular part of the animal leading the way. This anterior region was much more likely to encounter environmental changes first, e.g. changes in light intensity, temperature, pH, etc. It was obvious that most sense organs should be located on this anterior portion. There would be little point locating them in the posterior region, as a harmful substance would not be detected until it had already caused damage to the anterior of the animal. Most sensory information therefore originated at the front. To allow a rapid response, the 'brain' was located in this region. This led, in many animals, to the formation of a distinct head, **cephalization**, concerned primarily with detection and interpretation of stimuli. It was still essential for the brain to receive stimuli from the rest of the animal and to communicate with effector organs throughout the body. An elongated portion of the CNS therefore extends the length of most animals. In vertebrates this is the spinal cord.

With increasingly complex stimuli being received, the brain developed greater powers of interpretation. In particular it developed the ability to store information about previous experiences in order to assist it in deciding on the appropriate response to a future situation. With this ability to learn came the capacity to use previous experience and even to make responses to situations never previously encountered. Thus intelligence developed.

The hormone or endocrine system is concerned with longer-term changes, especially in response to the internal environment. It is an advantage to maintain a relatively constant internal environment. Not only can chemical reactions take place at a predictable rate, but the organism also acquires a degree of independence from the environment. It is no longer restricted to certain regions of the earth but can increase its geographical range. It does not have to restrict its activities to particular periods of the day, or seasons, when conditions are suitable. The maintenance of a constant internal environment is called **homeostasis** and is largely controlled by hormones. In the same way that the brain coordinates the nervous system, the activities of the endocrine system are controlled by the **pituitary gland**.

Responding to changes in the internal and external environments is no less important to survival in plants. Because they lack contractile tissue and do not move from place to place independently, they have no need for very rapid responses. There is therefore no nervous system or anything equivalent to it. Plant responses are hormonal. Their movements are as a result of growth, rather than contractions, and as a consequence are much slower than those of animals.

18 Homeostasis and the endocrine system

We have seen that matter tends to assume its lowest energy state. It tends to change from an ordered state to a disordered one, i.e. tends towards high entropy. The survival of biological organisms depends on their ability to overcome this tendency to disorderliness. They must remain stable. This need for constancy was recognized in the nineteenth century by Claude Bernard. He contrasted the constancy of the fluid which surrounds all cells (*milieu interieur*) with the ever changing external environment (*milieu exterieur*). Bernard concluded: *'La fixité du milieu interieur est la condition de la vie libre.'* (The constancy of the internal environment is the condition of the free life.)

By bathing cells in a fluid, the tissue fluid, whose composition remains constant, the chemical reactions within these cells can take place at a predictable rate. Not only are the cells able to survive but they can also function efficiently. The whole organism thus becomes more independent of its environment.

The term **homeostasis** (*homoio* = 'same'; *stasis* = 'standing') was not coined until 1932. It is used to describe all the mechanisms by which a constant environment is maintained. Some examples of homeostatic control have already been discussed, for example osmoregulation in Chapter 17. Further examples are examined in this chapter.

18.1 Principles of homeostasis

Before examining the detailed operation of homeostatic systems, it is necessary to look at the fundamental principles common to them. Organisms are examples of open systems, since there is exchange of materials between themselves and the environment. Not least, they require a constant input of energy to maintain themselves in a stable condition against the natural tendency to disorder. The maintenance of this stability requires control systems capable of detecting any deviation from the usual and making the necessary adjustments to return it to its normal condition.

18.1.1 Control mechanisms and feedback

Cybernetics (*cybernos* = 'steersman') is the science of control systems, i.e. self-regulating systems which operate by means of feedback mechanisms.

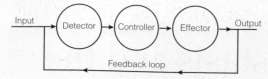

Fig. 18.1 Principal components of a typical control system

The essential components of a control system are:

1. **Reference point** – the set level at which the system operates.

2. **Detector** – signals the extent of any deviation from the reference point.

3. **Controller** – coordinates the information from various detectors and sends out instructions which will correct the deviation.

4. **Effector** – brings about the necessary change needed to return the system to the reference point.

5. **Feedback loop** – informs the detector of any change in the system as a result of action by the effector.

The relationship between these components is given in Fig. 18.1.

An everyday example of such a control system occurs in the regulation of a central heating system in a home, where the various components are:

1. **Reference point** – temperature determined by the occupant, e.g. 20 °C, and set on the thermostat.

2. **Detector** – the thermostat which constantly monitors the temperature of the room in which it is situated.

3. **Controller** – the programmer which can be set to turn the heating on and off at set times. It is connected to the boiler, hot water cylinder, circulation pump and thermostat.

4. **Effector** – the boiler, circulation pump, radiators and associated pipework.

5. **Feedback loop** – the movement of air within the room.

If the temperature of the room falls below 20 °C, the thermostat sends an electrical message to the programmer. The programmer coordinates this information with that in its own programme, i.e. whether the heating is set to operate at this particular time of day. If it is set to operate, it sends appropriate electrical messages which turn on the boiler and the circulation pump. Hot water flows around the central heating system to the radiator in the room. The heat from this radiator warms the air in the room which circulates until it reaches the thermostat. Once the temperature of this air reaches 20 °C, the thermostat ceases to send information to the programmer which then turns off the circulation pump. As the feedback causes the system to be turned off, it is called **negative feedback**. It is possible to have positive feedback systems. Although these are rare in living organisms one example is described in Section 19.1.3.

A similar system operates to control body temperature in humans. Temperature detectors in the skin provide information on changes in the external temperature which is conveyed to the hypothalamus of the brain, which acts as the controller. This initiates appropriate corrective responses in effectors, such as the skin and blood vessels, in order to maintain the body temperature constant. Details of these processes are given in the following section.

18.2 Temperature control

To survive, humans need to exert some control over their body temperature. This regulation of body temperature is called **thermoregulation**. In humans heat may be gained in two main ways:

1. **Metabolism of food.**

2. **Absorption of solar energy** – This may be absorbed directly or indirectly from

  (a) heat reflected from objects;
  (b) heat convected from the warming of the ground;
  (c) heat conducted from the ground.

Heat may be lost in four main ways:

1. **Evaporation of water**, e.g. during sweating.

2. **Conduction from the body** to the ground or other objects.

3. **Convection from the body** to the air or water.

4. **Radiation from the body** to the air, water or ground.

18.2.1 Ectothermy and endothermy

The majority of animals obtain most of their heat from sources outside the body. These are termed **ectotherms**. The body temperature of these animals frequently fluctuates in line with environmental temperature. Animals whose temperature varies in this way are called **poikilotherms** (*Poikilos* = 'various'; *thermo* = 'heat').

Humans maintain a constant body temperature irrespective of the environmental temperature. As our heat is derived internally, by metabolic activities, we are called **endotherms**. As the temperature of the body remains the same, we are sometimes called **homoiotherms** (*homoio* = 'same'; *thermo* = 'heat'). The normal body temperature of humans is 36.7 °C.

The evolutionary advantage of being endothermic is that it gives much more environmental independence. It is no coincidence that the most successful animals in the extremes of temperatures found in deserts and at the poles are the endothermic ones, i.e. mammals and birds. The independence that a constant high body temperature brings allows these groups to extend their geographical range considerably.

18.2.2 Structure of the skin

Most heat exchange occurs through the skin, as it is the barrier between the internal and external environments. It is in mammals that the skin plays the most important role in thermoregulation. Human skin has two main layers, an outer epidermis and an inner dermis.

The epidermis
This comprises three regions:

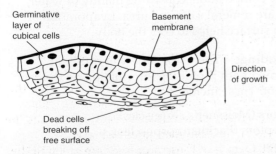

Germinative layer of cubical cells

Basement membrane

Direction of growth

Dead cells breaking off free surface

Fig. 18.2 Stratified epithelium

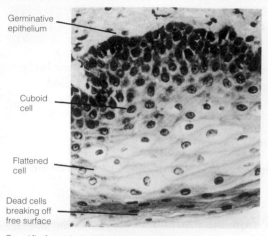

Germinative epithelium

Cuboid cell

Flattened cell

Dead cells breaking off free surface

Stratified epithelial tissue (×200 approx.)

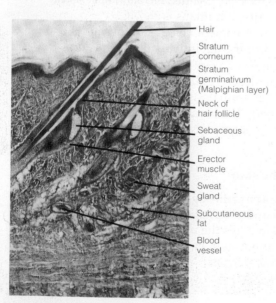

Hair

Stratum corneum

Stratum germinativum (Malpighian layer)

Neck of hair follicle

Sebaceous gland

Erector muscle

Sweat gland

Subcutaneous fat

Blood vessel

VS human skin showing hair (×25 approx.)

1. The Malpighian layer (germinative layer) – The deepest layer made up of actively dividing cells. The pigment **melanin**, which determines the skin colour, is produced here. It absorbs ultra-violet light and so helps to protect the tissues beneath from its damaging effects. The Malpighian layer has numerous infoldings which extend deep into the dermis, producing sweat glands, sebaceous glands and hair follicles. There are no blood vessels in the epidermis and so the cells of this layer obtain food and oxygen by diffusion and active transport from capillaries in the dermis.

2. Stratum granulosum (granular layer) – This is made up of living cells which have been produced by the Malpighian layer. As they are pushed towards the skin surface by new cells produced beneath, they accumulate the fibrous protein, **keratin**, lose their nuclei and die.

3. Stratum corneum (cornified layer) – This is the surface layer of the skin and comprises flattened, dead cells impregnated with keratin. It forms a tough, resistant, waterproof layer which is constantly replaced as it is worn away. It is thickest where there is greatest wear, i.e. on the palms of the hand and the soles of the feet. Through this layer extend sweat ducts and hair.

The dermis
The dermis is largely made up of connective tissue consisting of collagen and elastic fibres. It possesses:

1. Blood capillaries – These supply both the epidermis and dermis with food and oxygen. Special networks supply the sweat glands and hair follicles. They play an important rôle in thermoregulation.

2. Hair follicles – These are formed by inpushings of the Malpighian layer. Cells at the base multiply to produce a long cylindrical hair, the cells of which become impregnated with keratin and die. The more melanin in the hair, the darker its colour. Attached to it is a small bundle of smooth muscle, contraction of which causes the hair to become erect.

3. Sebaceous glands – Situated at the side of the hair follicle these produce an oily secretion called **sebum** which waterproofs the hair and epidermis. It also keeps the epidermis supple and protects against bacteria.

4. Sweat glands – These are coiled tubes made up of cells which absorb fluid from surrounding capillaries and secrete it into the tube, from where it passes to the skin surface via the sweat duct. Sweat has a variable composition, consisting mainly of water, dissolved in which are mineral salts and urea. Evaporation of sweat from the skin surface helps to cool the body.

5. Sensory nerve endings – There is a variety of different sensory cells concerned with providing information on the external environment. These include:

    (a) touch receptors (Meissner's corpuscles);
    (b) pressure receptors (Pacinian corpuscles);
    (c) pain receptors;
    (d) temperature receptors.

6. Subcutaneous fat – Beneath the dermis is a layer of fat (adipose) tissue. This acts both as a long-term food reserve and as an insulating layer.

The structure of human skin is shown in Fig. 18.3.

18.2.3 Maintenance of a constant body temperature in warm environments

When in a warm environment, humans use a range of adaptations to help them maintain a constant body temperature. These adaptations may be anatomical, physiological or behavioural, and include the following.

1. Vasodilation – Blood in the network of capillaries in the skin may take three alternative routes. It can pass through capillaries close to the skin surface, through others deeper in the dermis or it may pass beneath the layer of subcutaneous fat. In warm climates, superficial arterioles dilate in order to allow blood close to the skin surface. Heat from this blood is rapidly conducted through the epidermis to the skin surface from where it is radiated away from the body (Fig. 18.4).

2. Sweating – The evaporation of each gram of water requires 2.5 kJ of energy. Being furless, humans have sweat glands over the whole body, making them efficient at cooling by this means. Humans, may produce up to $1000 \, cm^3 \, hr^{-1}$ of sweat.

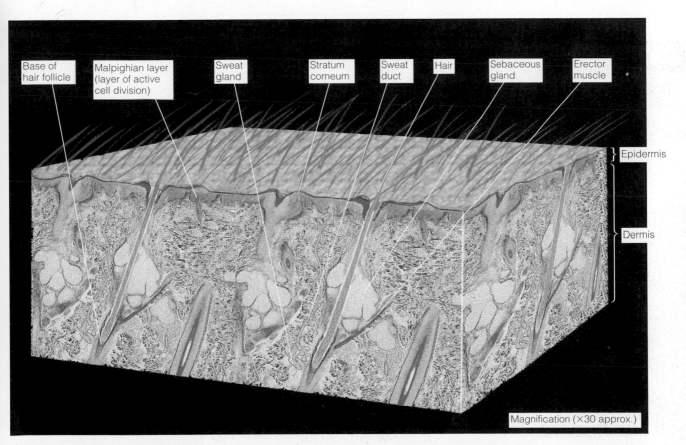

Fig. 18.3 VS through human skin

FOCUS

Heat stress

The mean body temperature of a human is 36.7 °C and the upper 'normal' temperature is 37.5 °C. The body can compensate for any increase in body temperature up to 41.2 °C by such mechanisms as increased sweating and vasodilation of the arterioles in the skin but if the homeostatic mechanism fails **hyperthermia** results, leading to death above 43 °C.

Humans are normally able to adapt to hot climates over the course of several weeks so that the sweat glands produce sweat earlier and for longer, salt is retained in the body and more water is absorbed from the stomach and intestines.

Heat stroke

This serious condition results from the impairment of the heat-regulating mechanisms so that sweating diminishes and the body temperature rises. The skin becomes flushed, severe headaches develop followed by mental confusion and difficulty walking. The higher the temperature, the worse the symptoms. The only treatment is immediate cooling, without which death can result within two to four hours.

Heat exhaustion

Heat exhaustion may result from a restricted water or salt intake and, if untreated, can lead to heat stroke. Patients require cooling and the supply of fluids and salt to relieve the symptoms of thirst, giddiness and severe muscle cramps.

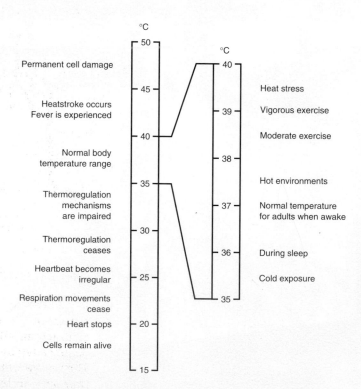

Fig. 18.4 *The range of human body temperature in a variety of circumstances*

PROJECT

A large organism has a relatively large surface-area to volume ratio and this reduces the rate at which heat is lost

1. Translate this statement into a hypothesis which could be tested.

2. Test your hypothesis by comparing heat loss from round-bottomed flasks of different sizes, using temperature sensors and data-logging equipment if possible.

3. Behavioural mechanisms – These are diverse and complex in humans, but include being less physically active (to reduce the amount of heat produced metabolically), seeking shade (to reduce heat absorbed from the sun), finding or creating 'breezy' situations, e.g. use of fans, opening car/house windows (to increase sweat evaporation and hence cooling), wearing lighter coloured clothes (to reflect solar energy), wearing fewer, more loose fitting clothes (to allow sweat to evaporate) and drinking more fluid (to replenish water used in sweating).

4. Large surface area to volume ratio – Over many generations humans have evolved into various races each adapted to suit the prevailing conditions, including environmental temperature. The negroid race is one which has evolved in warm climates. Compared with races which have evolved in colder regions of the world, e.g. Inuit, negroes are taller and thinner, and weigh less. As such they have a larger surface area to volume ratio and so lose heat more rapidly. This is, of course, a long-term adaptation and not one which varies from day to day, although the habit of 'spreading out' rather than 'curling up' on hot days is an example of the same principle.

18.2.4 Maintenance of a constant body temperature in cold environments

The mechanisms used by humans to maintain body temperature in cold environments, include:

1. Vasoconstriction – In cold conditions, the superficial arterioles contract, so reducing the quantity of blood reaching the skin surface. Blood largely passes beneath the insulating layer of subcutaneous fat and so loses little heat to the outside. Both vasodilation and vasoconstriction are illustrated in Fig. 18.5.

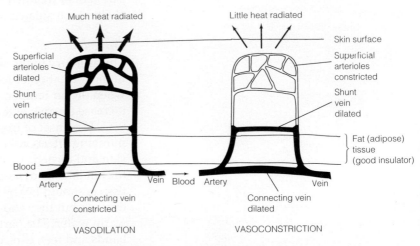

Fig. 18.5 Vasodilation and vasoconstriction

2. Shivering – At low environmental temperatures, the skeletal muscle of the body may undergo rhythmic, involuntary contractions which produce metabolic heat. This shivering may be preceded by asynchronous twitching of groups of muscle. The release of heat energy in this way is called **shivering thermogenesis**. Where heat is released as a result of voluntary, conscious movement, e.g. clapping of hands or stamping of feet, this is known as **non-shivering thermogenesis**.

FOCUS

Cold stress

The lower 'normal' body temperature is 35.8 °C but the body can compensate for falls in body temperature down to 32 °C by increasing the metabolic rate, shivering and vasoconstriction of the arterioles in the skin. Below 32 °C the homeostatic mechanism fails and death from **hypothermia** results below 26 °C.

The human body has no mechanism for acclimatizing to cold corresponding to the way it adapts to hot climates. Instead it must rely on insulation provided by body fat, clothing and shelter. Prevention of the effects of the cold thus depends on the maintenance of body heat by adequate supplies of energy (food and drink), on blocking heat loss and on preservation of an insulating layer of still, dry air. Wind speed has an important effect on human heat balance – the so called wind chill factor.

Hypothermia

This is defined as a core temperature of 35 °C or less. Most at risk are babies with their high surface area to volume ratio, the elderly whose thermoregulatory mechanisms may have deteriorated, and those pursuing outdoor activities such as hiking and potholing. Warning signs include feeling cold, tired and listless, walking slowly and stumbling, unreasonable behaviour and inability to respond to instructions. Bouts of shivering will ultimately cease at about 32 °C and disturbed vision precedes collapse into unconsciousness. Death may occur suddenly below 28 °C as the normal heartbeat is replaced by uncoordinated tremors. The sooner treatment starts the better. The victim must be sheltered, insulated and re-warmed.

Frostbite

This is injury to the skin and sometimes to deeper tissues due to the formation of ice crystals in the cells. It usually occurs when the air temperature is below –12 °C but high winds increase the risk of it developing at air temperatures closer to 0 °C. The onset of frostbite may not be noticed because of the numbing effect of the cold but there may be reddening of the skin and blisters. Clots often form in the blood vessels leading to chilblains and, more seriously, to gangrene. Affected tissues should not be rubbed since this will increase the damage but they should be gently warmed, if possible in warm water. The parts of the body most affected are the hands and feet, ears, cheeks, chin and nose.

Immersion (trench) foot

This may be caused by prolonged exposure to near-freezing temperatures in damp conditions. Lack of mobility, tight boots and wet socks all increase the risk. In the early stages the feet are white and numb; later they become hot, red and very painful and blisters may form. As with frostbite the feet should be gently warmed and the patient may be treated with painkillers and antibiotics.

3. Insulation – Insulation is an effective means of reducing heat loss. While many animals use fur and hair to insulate themselves, the density of hair on the human body is so low for the most part that it is ineffective. Instead we rely on a layer of fat beneath the skin (**subcutaneous fat**). This is effective when used in conjunction with vasoconstriction, but is not a flexible method as the thickness of the layer cannot be altered from day to day. Long periods of exposure to cold do however result in thickening of the layer of subcutaneous fat.

4. Increased metabolic rate – In addition to an increase in heat produced by muscles during shivering, the liver may also increase its metabolic rate during cold conditions. Low temperatures induce increased activity of the adrenal, thyroid and pituitary glands. All these produce hormones which help to increase the body's metabolic rate and so produce additional heat. This requires increased consumption of food.

5. Behavioural mechanisms – These include greater physical activity (to increase metabolic heat production), seeking shelter, e.g. out of the wind (to reduce heat loss by evaporation), wearing more clothes (to increase insulation) and taking in hot food (to warm the body directly and provide for increased metabolic and physical activity).

6. Small surface area to volume ratio – Races of humans who have evolved in colder climates, e.g. Inuit, when compared with those who have evolved in warmer ones, are shorter, bulkier and weigh more. This gives them a smaller surface area to volume ratio and so helps them to conserve heat. While this is a long-term adaptation rather than one which can be modified daily, the practice of 'curling up' when cold uses the same principle of reducing the surface area exposed to the cold outside.

18.2.5 Role of the hypothalamus in the control of body temperature

Control of body temperature is effected by the **hypothalamus**, a small body at the base of the brain. Within the hypothalamus is the thermoregulatory centre which has two parts: a heat gain and a heat loss centre. The hypothalamus monitors the temperature of blood passing through it and in addition receives nervous information from receptors in the skin about external temperature changes. Any reduction in blood temperature will bring about changes which conserve heat. A rise in blood temperature has the opposite effect. These effects are summarized in Fig. 18.6. Although the raising and lowering of hair is ineffective in humans it still occurs and is evident from the 'goose pimples' which sometimes arise in cold weather.

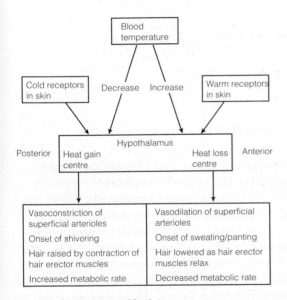

Fig. 18.6 Summary of body temperature control by the hypothalamus

18.3   The liver

The liver, weighing as it does up to 1.5 kg, makes up 3–5% of the body weight. It probably originated as a digestive organ but its functions are now much more diverse, many being concerned with homeostasis.

18.3.1 Structure of the liver

In an adult human, the liver is typically 28 cm × 16 cm × 9 cm although its exact size varies considerably according to the quantity of blood stored within it. It is found immediately below the diaphragm, to which it is attached. Blood is supplied to the liver by two vessels: the hepatic artery which carries 30% of the liver's total blood supply brings oxygenated blood from the aorta, whereas the hepatic portal vein supplies 70% of the liver's blood and is rich in soluble digested food from the intestines. A single vessel, the hepatic vein, drains blood from the liver. In addition, the bile duct carries bile produced in the liver to the duodenum. The relationship of these structures is given in Fig. 18.7.

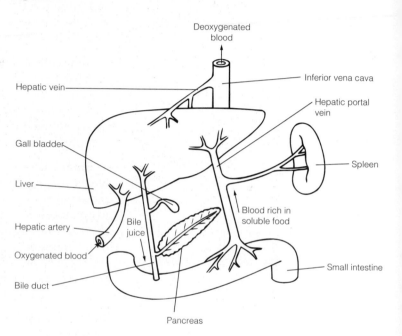

Fig. 18.7 Blood system associated with the mammalian liver

The branches of the hepatic artery and those of the hepatic portal vein combine within the liver to form common venules which lead into a series of channels called **sinusoids**. These are lined with liver cells or **hepatocytes**. The sinusoids eventually drain into a branch of the hepatic vein called the **central vein**. Between the hepatocytes are fine tubes called **canaliculi** in which bile is secreted. The canaliculi combine to form bile ducts which drain into the gall bladder where the bile is stored before being periodically released into the duodenum. The structure of the liver is shown in Fig. 18.8.

The functional unit of the liver is the **acinus**. As blood from the hepatic portal vein and hepatic artery mixes it passes along the sinusoids which are lined with hepatocytes. Materials are exchanged between these cells and the blood. To facilitate this exchange, the hepatocytes have microvilli to increase their surface-area. They also possess a large nucleus, many mitochondria, lysosomes and glycogen granules – all indicate a highly metabolic role for these cells. The canaliculi are also lined with microvilli and these appear to remove bile from the hepatocytes by active transport.

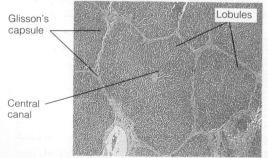

Liver lobule

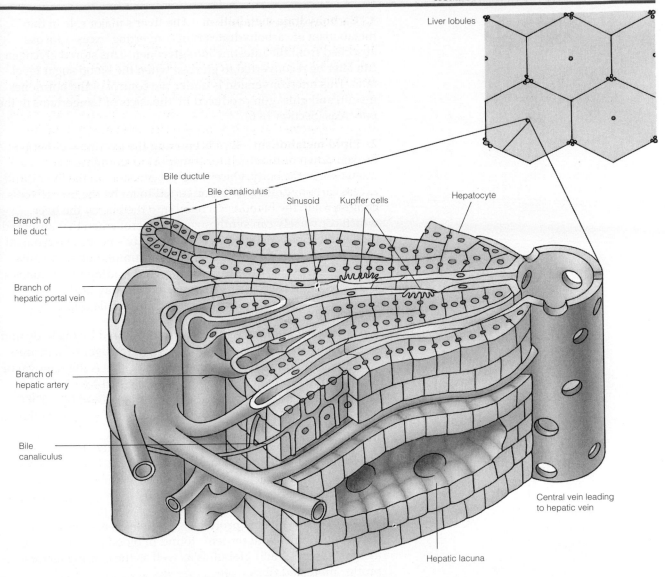

Fig. 18.8 Structure of the mammalian liver

The sinusoids are lined with flattened **endothelial cells**. Their structure is similar to that in many other organs except for the presence of pores up to 10 nm in diameter. In addition, there are specialized cells lining the sinusoid. These are **Kupffer** cells. They are highly phagocytic and form part of the **reticulo-endothelial system**. They are ideally situated for ingesting any foreign organisms or particulate matter which enter the body from the intestines. They also engulf damaged and worn out blood cells, producing the bile pigment bilirubin as a by-product of this process. The bilirubin is passed into the canaliculi for excretion in the bile.

18.3.2 Functions of the liver

The liver is the body's chemical workshop and has an estimated 500 individual functions. Some of these have been grouped under the following twelve headings:

1. **Carbohydrate metabolism** – The liver's major role in the metabolism of carbohydrates is in converting excess glucose absorbed from the intestine into glycogen. This stored glycogen can later be reconverted to glucose when the blood sugar level falls. This interconversion is under the control of the hormones insulin and glucagon produced by the islets of Langerhans in the pancreas (Section 18.6).

2. **Lipid metabolism** – Lipids entering the liver may either be broken down or modified for transport to storage areas elsewhere in the body. Once the glycogen store in the liver is full, excess carbohydrate will be converted to fat by the liver. Excess cholesterol in the blood is excreted into the bile by the liver, which conversely can synthesize cholesterol when that absorbed by the intestines is inadequate for the body's need. The removal of excess cholesterol is essential as its accumulation may cause atherosclerosis (narrowing of the arteries) leading to thrombosis. If in considerable excess its presence in bile may lead to the formation of **gall stones** which can block the bile duct.

3. **Protein metabolism** – Proteins are not stored by the body and so excess amino acids are broken down in the liver by a process called **deamination**. As the name suggests, this is the removal of the amino group ($-NH_2$) to form ammonia (NH_3) which in mammals is converted to the less toxic urea ($CO(NH_2)_2$). This occurs in the ornithine cycle, the main stages of which are shown in Fig. 18.9.

   Transamination reactions whereby one amino acid is converted to another are also performed by the liver. All non-essential amino acids may be synthesized in this way, should they be temporarily deficient in the diet.

4. **Synthesis of plasma proteins** – The liver is responsible for the production of vital proteins found in blood plasma. These include albumins and globulins as well as the clotting factors prothrombin and fibrinogen.

5. **Production of bile** – The liver produces bile salts and adds to them the bile pigment bilirubin from the breakdown of red blood cells. With sodium chloride and sodium hydrogen carbonate, cholesterol and water this forms the green-yellow fluid known as bile. Up to $1\,dm^3$ of bile may be produced daily. It is temporarily stored in the gall bladder before being discharged into the duodenum. The bile pigments are purely excretory. The remaining contents have digestive functions and are described in Section 11.5.4.

6. **Storage of vitamins** – The liver will store a number of vitamins which can later be released if deficient in the diet. It stores mainly the fat-soluble vitamins A, D, E and K, although the water-soluble vitamins B and C are also stored. The functions of these vitamins are given in Chapter 23, Table 23.3.

7. **Storage of minerals** – The liver stores minerals, e.g. iron, potassium, copper and zinc, the functions of which are dealt with in Chapter 2, Table 2.1 and Chapter 23, Table 23.4. It is the liver's stores of these minerals, along with vitamins, which makes it such a nutritious food.

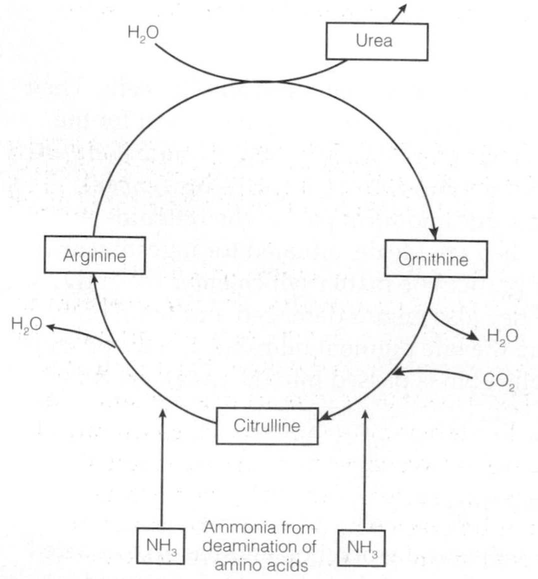

Fig. 18.9 Ornithine (urea) cycle

8. Formation and breakdown of red blood cells – The fetus relies solely on the liver for the production of red blood cells. In an adult this role is transferred to the bone marrow. The adult liver, however, continues to break down red blood cells at the end of their 120-day life span. The Kupffer cells lining the sinusoids carry out this breakdown, producing the bile pigment bilirubin which is excreted in the bile. The iron is either stored in the liver or used in the formation of new red blood cells by the bone marrow. The liver produces **haematinic principle**, a substance needed in the formation of red blood cells. Vitamin B_{12} is necessary for the production of this principle, and its deficiency results in pernicious anaemia.

9. Storage of blood – The liver, with its vast complex of blood vessels, forms a large store of blood with a capacity of up to $1500 \, cm^3$. In the event of haemorrhage, constriction of these vessels forces blood into the general circulation to replace that lost and so helps to maintain blood pressure. In stressful situations adrenaline also causes constriction of these vessels, creating a rise in blood pressure.

10. Hormone breakdown – To varying degrees, the liver breaks down all hormones. Some, such as testosterone, are rapidly broken down whereas others, like insulin, are destroyed more slowly.

11. Detoxification – The liver is ideally situated to remove or render harmless, toxic material absorbed by the intestines. Foreign organisms or material are ingested by the Kupffer cells while toxic chemicals are made safe by chemical conversions within hepatocytes. Alcohol and nicotine are two substances dealt with in this way.

12. Production of heat – The liver, with its considerable metabolic activity, can be used to produce heat in order to combat a fall in body temperature. This reaction, triggered by the hypothalamus, is in response to adrenaline, thyroxine and nervous stimulation. Whether the liver's activities produce excess heat under ordinary circumstances is a matter of some debate.

18.4   The endocrine system

Humans possess two principal coordinating systems, the **nervous system** and the **endocrine system**. The nervous system gives rapid control and details of its functioning are provided in Chapter 19. The endocrine system on the other hand regulates long-term changes. The two systems interact in a dynamic way in order to maintain the constancy of our internal environment, while permitting changes in response to a varying external environment. Both systems secrete chemicals, the nervous system as a transmitter between neurones and the endocrine system as its sole means of communication between various organs and tissues in the body. It is worth noting that adrenaline may act both as a hormone and as a nervous transmitter.

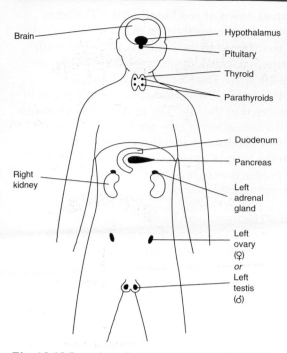

Fig. 18.10 Location of major endocrine glands in humans

TABLE 18.1 **The chemical nature of commonly occurring hormones**

Chemical group	Hormones
Polypeptides (less than 100 amino acids)	Oxytocin Vasopressin Insulin Glucagon
Protein	Prolactin Follicle stimulating hormone Luteinizing hormone Thyroid stimulating hormone Adrenocorticotrophic hormone Growth hormone
Amines (derivatives of amino acids)	Adrenaline Noradrenaline Thyroxine
Steroids (derivatives of lipids)	Oestrogen Progesterone Testosterone Cortisone Aldosterone

This section discusses the principles of the endocrine system, the nature of hormones and the activities of specific endocrine glands. Because of their close association with particular organ systems, the activities of certain endocrine glands are dealt with elsewhere in this book. Reproductive hormones are described in Sections 10.4 and 10.5 and digestive hormones in Section 11.6.

18.4.1 Principles of endocrine control

In humans, two types of gland are recognized: **exocrine glands**, which convey their secretions to the site of action by special ducts, and **endocrine glands**, which lack ducts and transport their secretions instead by the blood. For this reason, the term **ductless glands** is often applied to endocrine glands. The glands may be discrete organs or cells within other organs.

The secretions of these glands are called **hormones**. Derived from the Greek word *hormon*, which means 'to excite', hormones often inhibit actions as well as excite them. All hormones are effective in small quantities. Most act on specific organs, called **target organs**, although some have diffuse effects on all body cells.

Most, but not all, endocrine glands work under the influence of a single master gland, the **pituitary**. In this way the actions of individual glands can be coordinated. Such coordination is essential as hormones work not in isolation, but interacting with each other. Most organs are influenced by a number of different hormones. If the pituitary is considered to be the master of the endocrine system then the **hypothalmus** can be thought of as the manager. It not only assists in directing the activities of endocrine glands, it also acts as the all-important link between the endocrine and nervous systems.

The positions of the major endocrine organs in humans are shown in Fig. 18.10.

18.4.2 Nature of hormone action

Hormones exert their influence by acting on molecular reactions in cells. They achieve this by one or more of the following cell processes:

1. Transcription of genetic information (e.g. oestrogen).

2. Protein synthesis (e.g. growth hormone).

3. Enzyme activity (e.g. adrenaline).

4. Exchange of materials across the cell membrane (e.g. insulin).

While a hormone is transported to all cells by the blood, it only affects specific ones. The explanation is that only target cells possess special chemicals called **receptor molecules** on their surface. These receptors are specific to certain hormones. Both the receptor and the hormone have complementary molecular shapes which fit one another in a 'lock and key' manner, much in the way that enzymes and substrates combine (Section 3.1.2).

There appears to be an alternative means by which this receptor–hormone complex influences the cell. The complex may induce the production of a second messenger (cyclic AMP) which activates enzymes within the cell. The polypeptide and protein hormones act in this way (see Section 18.5.2). Steroid hormones, being lipid derivatives, can pass through the cell

(a) Use of second messenger, e.g. protein and polypeptide hormones such as adrenaline

1. *Hormone approaches receptor site.*

2. *Hormone fuses to receptor site, and in doing so activates adenylate cyclase inside the membrane.*

3. *The activated adenylate cyclase converts ADP to cyclic AMP which acts as a second messenger that activates other enzymes.*

(b) Steroid hormone mechanism of action

1. *Hormone approaches receptor site.*

2. *Hormone combines with the receptor to form a complex.*

3. *Hormone–receptor complex passes across the membrane into the cell where it switches on genes on the DNA which produce specific enzymes.*

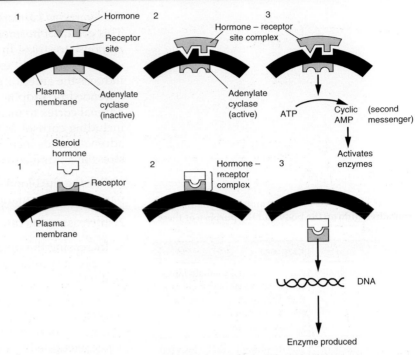

Fig. 18.11 Mechanism of hormone action

membrane. The whole complex enters the cell where it exerts its influence. These mechanisms are illustrated in Fig. 18.11. In some cases the complex simply alters the permeability of the cell membrane. Insulin operates in this manner by increasing the permeability of cell membranes to glucose.

18.5 The adrenal glands

Situated above each kidney in humans is a collection of cells weighing about 5 g. These are the adrenal glands. They have two separate and independent parts:

1. The adrenal cortex – This consists of the outer region of the glands.

2. The adrenal medulla – This consists of the inner region of the glands.

18.5.1 The adrenal cortex

Making up around 80% of the adrenal gland, the cortex produces a number of hormones which have relatively slow, long-lasting effects on body metabolism, kidney function, salt balance and blood pressure. All the hormones produced are **steroids** formed from **cholesterol**. Being lipid-soluble they are able to pass across cell membranes along with their receptor molecule (Section 18.4.2). Hormones from the adrenal cortex are collectively called **corticoids** and fall into two groups:

1. Glucocorticoids which are concerned with glucose metabolism.

2. Mineralocorticoids which are concerned with mineral metabolism.

445

Glucocorticoid hormones

This group of hormones includes **cortisol** which is produced in response to stress. In stressful situations like shock, pain, emotional distress, extreme cold or infection, the hypothalamus induces the anterior pituitary gland to produce adrenocorticotrophic hormone (ACTH). This in turn causes the adrenal cortex to increase its production of glucocorticoids, including cortisol. Where stress is prolonged, the size of the adrenal glands increases. The glucocorticoid hormones combat stress in a number of ways:

1. Raising the blood sugar level, partly by inhibiting insulin and partly by the formation of glucose from fats and proteins.

2. Increasing the rate of glycogen formation in the liver.

3. Increasing the uptake of amino acids by the liver. These may either be deaminated to form more glucose or used in enzyme synthesis.

Mineralocorticoid hormones

This group of hormones includes **aldosterone** which regulates water retention by controlling the distribution of sodium and other minerals in the tissues. Aldosterone cannot increase the total sodium in the body, but it can conserve that already present. This it achieves by increasing the reabsorption of sodium (Na^+) and chloride (Cl^-) ions by the kidney, at the expense of potassium ions which are lost in urine. Control of aldosterone production is complex. In response to a low level of sodium ions in the blood, or a reduction in the total volume of blood, special cells in the kidney produce **renin** which in turn activates a plasma protein called **angiotensin**. It is angiotensin which stimulates production of aldosterone from the adrenal cortex. This causes the kidney to conserve both water and sodium ions. Angiotensin also affects centres in the brain creating a sensation of thirst, in response to which the organism seeks and drinks water, thus helping to restore the blood volume to normal.

18.5.2 The adrenal medulla

The central portion of the adrenal gland is called the **adrenal medulla**. It produces two hormones, **adrenaline** (epinephrine) and **noradrenaline** (norepinephrine). Both are important in preparing the body for action. The cells producing them are modified neurones, and noradrenaline is produced by the neurones of the sympathetic nervous system. These hormones therefore link the nervous and endocrine systems. They are sometimes called the 'flight or fight hormones' as they prepare an organism to either flee from or face an enemy or stressful situation. The effects of both hormones are to prepare the body for exertion and to heighten its responses to stimuli. These effects and their purposes are summarized in Table 18.2.

At a cellular level, adrenaline acts as the first messenger and combines with receptors on the membrane of liver and muscle cells. The hormone–receptor complex on the outer face of the membrane activates the enzyme **adenylate cyclase** which is on the inner face of the membrane. The adenylate cyclase causes the

TABLE 18.2 Effects of the hormones adrenaline and noradrenaline on the body and the purpose of these responses

Effect	Purpose
Bronchioles dilated	Air is more easily inhaled into the lungs. More oxygen is therefore made available for the production of energy by glucose oxidation
Smooth muscle of the gut relaxed	The diaphragm can be lowered further, increasing the amount of air inhaled at each breath, making more oxygen available for the oxidation of glucose
Glycogen in the liver converted to glucose	Increases blood sugar level, making more glucose available for oxidation
Heart rate increased	
Volume of blood pumped at each beat increased	Increase the rate at which oxygen and glucose are distributed to the tissues
Blood pressure increased	
Blood diverted from digestive and reproductive systems to muscles, lungs and liver	Blood rich in glucose and oxygen is diverted from tissues which have less urgent need of it to those more immediately involved in producing energy
Peristalsis and digestion inhibited	Reduction of these processes allows blood to be diverted to muscle and other tissues directly involved in exertion
Sensory perception increased	Heightened sensitivity produces a more rapid reaction to external stimuli
Mental awareness increased	Allows more rapid response to stimuli received
Pupils of the eyes dilated	Increases range of vision and allows increased perception of visual stimuli
Hair erector muscles contract	Hair stands upright. In many mammals this gives the impression of increased size and may be sufficient to frighten away an enemy

Imbalance of adrenal hormones

Where the production of glucocorticoids is deficient, a condition known as **Addison's disease** occurs. Symptoms include a low blood sugar level, reduced blood pressure and fatigue. The condition of the body deteriorates when stresses such as extreme temperatures and infection are experienced. Over-production of glucocorticoids causes **Cushing's syndrome** where there is high blood sugar level mainly due to excessive breakdown of protein. This breakdown causes wasting of tissues, especially muscle. There is high blood pressure and symptoms of diabetes.

Over-production of aldosterone, often as a result of a tumour, leads to excessive sodium retention by tissues; high blood pressure and headaches then arise. The retention of sodium leads to a consequent fall in potassium levels leading to muscular weakness. Under-production of aldosterone leads to a fall in the level of sodium in the tissues. In extreme cases this is fatal.

conversion of ATP to cyclic AMP. The cyclic AMP acts as a **second messenger** (intracellular mediator) in that it moves within the cell to activate enzymes such as those involved in glycogen breakdown. The process is a complex series of enzyme reactions in a chain reaction known as a **cascade effect**. The cascade effect amplifies the response. Fig. 18.11 illustrates the mechanism of adrenaline action.

In one respect adrenaline and noradrenaline differ. Whereas adrenaline dilates blood vessels, noradrenaline constricts them. This difference explains the constriction of blood vessels around the gut while those supplying muscles, lungs and liver are dilated. It appears that receptors on some blood vessels are sensitive to noradrenaline and so constrict while others are sensitive to adrenaline and so dilate.

18.6 The pancreas and control of blood sugar

All metabolizing cells require a supply of glucose in order to continue functioning. The nervous system is especially sensitive to any reduction in the normal glucose level of 90 mg glucose in $100 \, cm^3$ blood. A rise in blood sugar level can be equally dangerous. The supply of carbohydrate in mammals fluctuates because they do not eat continuously throughout the day and the quantity of carbohydrate varies from meal to meal. There may be long periods when no carbohydrate is absorbed from the intestines. Cells, however, metabolize continuously and need a constant supply of glucose to sustain them. A system which maintains a constant glucose level in the blood, despite intermittent supplies from the intestine, is essential. The liver plays a key role in glucose homeostasis. It can add glucose to the blood in two ways:

FOCUS

Diabetes

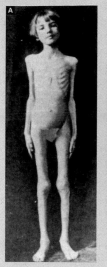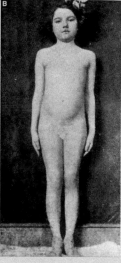

Improvement of health of a diabetic child in response to insulin treatment

Diabetes is a chronic disease where the patient is unable to metabolize carbohydrate, especially glucose, properly. There are over 100 million sufferers worldwide. In Great Britain, 6% of people will suffer diabetes at some time in their lives. There are two distinct forms of diabetes.

Diabetes insipidus is rare and results from a deficiency of ADH, the hormone which controls urine production.
Diabetes mellitus, or 'sugar diabetes' is much more common and occurs in two forms: insulin-dependent, or type 1 diabetes, which usually develops before the age of 20 and non-insulin-dependent, or type 2 diabetes, which often comes on in later life and may be associated with obesity. Insulin-dependent diabetes usually results from a massive loss of insulin-secreting β-cells from the pancreas. The lack of insulin means that the uptake of glucose from the blood after a meal is not promoted. Glucagon continues to convert glycogen to glucose and proteins and lipids are broken down to release even more glucose. This leads untreated sufferers to have a thin, wasted appearance.

Excess blood glucose is excreted via the kidneys and is associated with a considerable loss of water resulting in thirst. The fatty acids from lipid breakdown form ketone bodies which may build up in the blood, lowering its pH and leading to coma. Diabetes was a fatal disease until in 1921 Banting and Best succeeded in isolating insulin from the pancreas of pigs and cows. Insulin is a small protein comprising a total of 51 amino acids in two chains. The sequence of amino acids in insulin was determined by Sanger in the 1950s and more recently the gene for human insulin has been isolated and inserted into the DNA of *Escherichia coli* so that the bacteria can make 'human' insulin on a large scale.

Diabetics must regulate their carbohydrate intake, test their blood glucose level and have regular injections of insulin if they are to lead a normal life and avoid some of the longer-term complications of the disease. These complications include:

- **Coronary heart disease** – three times greater chance than normal – around 70% of diabetics die from this cause;
- **Thrombosis** – diabetics are 50 times more likely than normal to require an amputation due to thrombosis;
- **Strokes** – 15% of diabetics die from this cause;
- **Blindness** – 13 times greater risk than normal;
- **Kidney failure** – greater risk after 10 years of the disease.

Insulin cannot be taken orally because, as a protein, it would be broken down by digestive enzymes.

About 90% of diabetics are non-insulin-dependent diabetics. There seems to be some evidence for a genetic predisposition to this form of diabetes and it may be associated with obesity. Some of these patients seem to have receptors which are less sensitive to insulin than normal but the condition can be controlled by limiting the intake of

FOCUS continued

carbohydrates. Other mature-onset diabetics who secrete low amounts of insulin may be helped by drugs such as sulphonylureas which can be used to stimulate insulin production.

A more recent treatment for some diabetics is a group of drugs called alpha-glucosidase inhibitors. These are taken orally with a meal and slow down carbohydrate digestion, so preventing glucose surges in the blood. The longer-term solution to diabetes may rest with gene therapy (see Section 5.8).

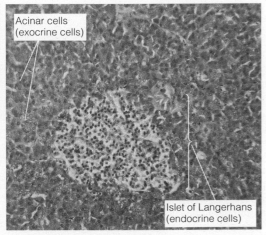

Acinar cells (exocrine cells)

Islet of Langerhans (endocrine cells)

TS of pancreas, showing Islets of Langerhans (×200 approx.)

(i) by the breakdown of glycogen (**glycogenolysis**);

(ii) by converting protein into glucose (**gluconeogenesis**).

It can remove glucose from the blood by converting it into glycogen (**glycogenesis**) which it then stores. A normal liver stores around 75 g of glycogen, sufficient to maintain the body's supply of glucose for about twelve hours. The interconversion of glucose and glycogen is largely under the control of two hormones, produced by the pancreas. The structure of the pancreas and its role as an exocrine gland are described in Section 11.5.4. In addition to being an exocrine gland producing pancreatic juice, the pancreas is also an endocrine gland. Throughout the pancreas are groups of histologically different cells known as the **islets of Langerhans**. The cells within them are of two types: α-cells, which produce the hormone **glucagon**, and β-cells, which produce the hormone **insulin**. Both hormones are discharged directly into the blood. Some hours after a meal, the glucose formed as a result of carbohydrate breakdown is absorbed by the intestines. The blood capillaries from the intestine unite to form the hepatic portal vein which carries this glucose-rich blood to the liver. Insulin from the pancreas causes excess glucose to become converted to glucose-6-phosphate and ultimately glycogen which the liver stores. The same process can occur in many body cells, especially muscle. Some time later, when the level of glucose in the hepatic portal vein has fallen below normal, the liver reconverts some of its stored glycogen to glucose, to help maintain the glucose level of the blood. This change involves a phosphorylase enzyme in the liver which is activated by the pancreatic hormone glucagon.

Should the glycogen supply in the liver become exhausted, glucose may be formed by other means. Once a low level of blood glucose is detected by the hypothalamus it stimulates the pituitary gland to produce adrenocorticotrophic hormones (ACTH) which cause the adrenal glands to release the glucocorticoid hormones, e.g. cortisol. These cause the liver to convert amino acids and glycerol into glucose. In times of stress, another hormone from the adrenal glands, adrenaline, causes the breakdown of glycogen in the liver and so helps to raise the blood sugar level. Further details of these effects are given in Section 18.5.2.

The control of blood sugar level is summarized in Fig. 18.12.

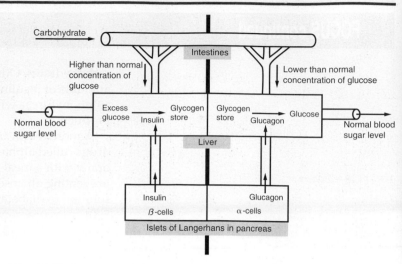

Fig. 18.12 Summary of the control of blood sugar level

TABLE 18.3 **The major endocrine glands and the effects of the hormones they produce**

Endocrine gland	Hormone produced	Effect
Thyroid	Triiodothyronine (T_3) Thyroxine (T_4)	Regulate growth and development of cells by affecting metabolism
	Calcitonin	Lowers calcium level of blood
Parathyroid	Parathormone	Raises blood calcium level while lowering that of phosphate
Adrenal cortex	Glucocorticoid hormones, e.g. cortisol	Helps body resist stress by raising blood sugar level and blood pressure
	Mineralocorticoid hormones, e.g. aldosterone	Increases reabsorption of sodium by kidney tubules
Adrenal medulla	Adrenaline Noradrenaline	Prepare body for activity in emergency or stressful situations
Pancreas (islets of Langerhans)	Insulin (from β-cells)	Lowers blood sugar level by stimulating conversion of glucose to glycogen
	Glucagon (from α-cells)	Raises blood sugar level by stimulating conversion of glycogen to glucose
Stomach wall	Gastrin	Initiates secretion of gastric juice
Duodenum	Secretin	Stimulates production of bile by the liver and mineral salts by the pancreas
	Cholecystokinin-pancreozymin	Causes contraction of the gall bladder and stimulates the pancreas to produce enzymes
Kidney	Renin	Activates the plasma protein angiotensin
Testis	Testosterone	Produces male secondary sex characteristics
Ovary	Oestrogen (from follicle cells)	Produces female secondary sex characteristics
	Progesterone (from corpus luteum)	Inhibits ovulation and generally maintains pregnancy
Placenta	Chorionic gonadotrophin	Maintains the presence of the corpus luteum in the ovary

18.7   Questions

1. The table shows how the concentrations of insulin and glucose in the plasma vary at different times.

When measurement taken	Plasma insulin concentration units per cm³	Plasma glucose concentration mg per 100 cm³
During overnight fast	10	60–100
During a meal	70	110–180
After a meal	10	60–100
During prolonged fasting	5	50–70

(a) Describe the relationship between glucose concentration and insulin concentration in the plasma. *(1 mark)*

(b) Explain the rise in plasma glucose and insulin levels that occurs during the meal. *(3 marks)*

(c) Use information from the table to explain how the control of insulin production is an example of negative feedback. *(2 marks)*

(d) The plasma glucose level is maintained at a minimum of 50 mg per 100 cm³ during prolonged fasting. Suggest how this might be achieved.

(2 marks)

(Total 8 marks)

NEAB February 1995, Paper BY3, No. 4

2. The table below shows the mean voluntary energy intake per day of soldiers stationed in climates with different local mean temperatures.

Local mean temperature /°C	Voluntary energy intake per day /kJ
+35	13 000
+15	15 000
+5	16 800
−5	18 000
−20	20 000
−30	21 000

(a) Discuss the physiological significance of the energy intake in relation to local mean temperature. *(4 marks)*

(b) State **three** ways in which the body acclimatises to **high** temperatures. *(3 marks)*

(c) (i) Compare the body's tolerance to increases and decreases in core temperature. *(2 marks)*

(ii) Describe the effects of cold stress. *(2 marks)*

(Total 11 marks)

ULEAC 1996, Specimen Paper HB2, No. 7

3. Describe the structures and processes involved in the regulation of body temperatures. *(Total 10 marks)*

ULEAC 1996, Specimen Paper HB3, No. 8

4. The diagram shows a section through human skin.

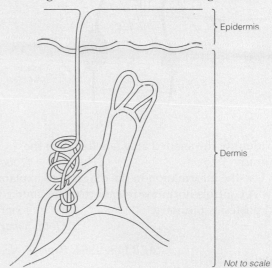

Describe changes which might take place in the structures shown in the diagram as a result of:

(a) exposure to ultraviolet rays in sunlight;

(3 marks)

(b) an increase in body temperature. *(3 marks)*

(Total 6 marks)

AEB June 1992, Paper 1, No. 8

5. *(a)* The table shows some of the hormones produced by the pituitary gland, the organ or gland which they affect, and the effect they produce on this organ or gland. Complete the table.

Pituitary hormone	Target organ/gland	Effect on organ/gland
	Adrenal cortex	Secretes cortisol
		Increased secretion of thyroxin
Luteinising hormone (LH)	Ovary	

(4 marks)

(b) Somatotropic hormone is also a pituitary hormone. It plays an important part in normal growth. Suggest:

(i) how somatotropic hormone may increase growth; *(1 mark)*

(ii) how it acts to oppose the action of insulin.

(1 mark)

(Total 6 marks)

AEB June 1995, Paper 1, No. 13

6. The diagram shows the relationship between the pituitary gland and the floor of the brain.

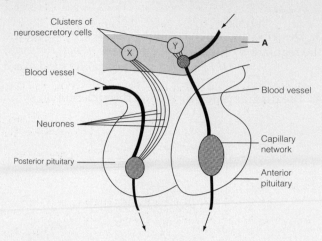

(a) Identify the shaded area labelled **A** in the diagram (*1 mark*)

(b) Use the information in the diagram to explain how **A** controls hormone release from the anterior and posterior pituitary. (*4 marks*)

(*Total 5 marks*)

AEB June 1994, Paper 1, No. 14

7. The diagram shows part of a liver lobule.

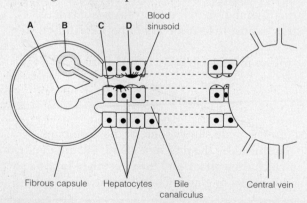

(a) (i) Name vessels **A** and **B**. (*2 marks*)

(ii) Describe the part played by vessels **A** and **B** in liver function. (*2 marks*)

(b) (i) Drawn an arrow in the sinusoid to show the direction of blood flow in the lobule (*1 mark*)

(ii) Explain the function of cells **C** and **D**. (*2 marks*)

(*Total 7 marks*)

AEB June 1994, Paper 1, No. 4

8. An experiment was carried out to investigate the control of body temperature.

A volunteer was kept in a room at 45 °C for one hour. Skin temperature and cranial temperature (measured at the ear drum) were recorded at five minute intervals. After 25 minutes, the volunteer swallowed a small amount of ice.

Both skin and cranial temperatures remained constant during the first 25 minutes. The initial temperatures and results from 25 minutes are shown in the table below.

Time/min	Skin temperature/°C	Cranial temperature/°C
0	36.9	37.5
25*	36.9	37.5
30	37.0	37.4
35	37.5	36.9
40	37.6	37.1
45	37.1	37.3
50	37.0	37.5
55	37.0	37.5

*ice swallowed at 25 minutes

(a) Plot the data on graph paper. You are advised to use a scale for the temperature axis which adequately displays the variation observed.

(*5 marks*)

(b) (i) Explain how, despite the high environmental temperature, both skin and cranial temperatures remained constant during the first 25 minutes. (*3 marks*)

(ii) Describe the change in the cranial temperature during the period 25 to 30 minutes and give **one** reason for this change. (*2 marks*)

(iii) Explain the changes in skin temperature during the period 25 to 50 minutes. In your explanation you should relate the changes in skin temperature to changes in cranial temperature. (*4 marks*)

(*Total 14 marks*)

ULEAC June 1995, Paper 3, No. 7

9. Read through the following passage on the control of blood glucose level, then write on the lines the most appropriate work or words to complete the passage.

An increase in blood glucose concentration to a level above normal is detected by the _____ cells in the pancreas, which respond by releasing the hormone _____. This hormone promotes the uptake of glucose by _____ cells, and its conversion to _____. If the blood glucose level falls below normal, the hormone _____ is released from the pancreas, resulting in the blood glucose level rising again.

The hormone _____, from the _____ cortex, promotes the conversion of _____ to glucose, thus increasing its level in the blood.

(*Total 8 marks*)

ULEAC June 1994, Paper 3, No. 4

10. The graph below shows changes in the levels of glucose and of certain hormones in the blood of a person with diabetes during a 40-minute period of moderate exercise on an exercise bicycle. The person received an injection of insulin at 20 minutes.

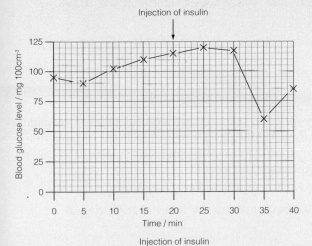

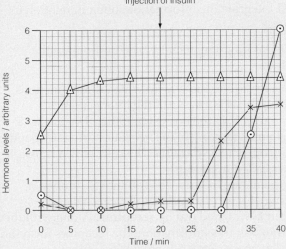

Key
×——× Insulin
⊙——⊙ Glucagon
△——△ Adrenaline

(a) (i) Explain the changes observed in the levels of glucose and of adrenaline during the period 0 to 20 minutes. *(3 marks)*
(ii) Explain the changes observed in the levels of glucose and of the hormones glucagon and insulin during the period 20 to 40 minutes.
(3 marks)

(b) Suggest how the graphs for the period 0 to 20 minutes would have differed in a non-diabetic.
(2 marks)
(Total 8 marks)

ULEAC June 1993, Paper 3, No. 3

11. *(a)* Explain:
(i) what is meant by homeostasis;
(ii) why homeostasis is important in living systems. *(3 marks)*
(b) Hill walkers can encounter extreme changes in environmental conditions. Describe the processes involved in thermoregulation when a walker responds to a rapid fall in external temperature.
(Total 9 marks)

NEAB June 1995, Paper BY01, No. 9

12. Discuss the homeostatic control of plasma glucose, body temperature and blood pressure. *(24 marks)*

AEB June 1995, Paper 2, No. 4a

13. *(a)* What do you understand by the concept of homeostasis? *(6 marks)*
(b) Write an account of the homeostatic functions of the liver. *(17 marks)*
(Total 23 marks)

UCLES June 1992, Paper 2, No. 5

14. Write an essay on: The regulation of the internal environment in human beings. *(20 marks)*

ULEAC 1996, Specimen Synoptic Paper, No. 10

19 The nervous system

The ability to respond to stimuli is a fundamental characteristic of living organisms. While all cells of multicellular organisms are able to perceive stimuli, those of the nervous system are specifically adapted to this purpose.

The nervous system performs three functions:

1. To collect information about the internal and external environment.

2. To process and integrate the information, often in relation to previous experience.

3. To act upon the information, usually by coordinating the organism's activities.

One remarkable feature of the way in which these functions are performed is the speed with which the information is transmitted from one part of the body to another. In contrast to the endocrine system (Chapter 18), the nervous system responds virtually instantaneously to a stimulus. The cells which transmit nerve impulses are called **neurones**.

The nervous system may be sub-divided into a number of parts. The collecting of information from the internal and external environment is carried out by **receptors**. Along with the neurones which transmit this information, the receptors form the **sensory system**. The processing and integration of this information is performed by the **central nervous system (CNS)**. The final function whereby information is transmitted to **effectors**, which act upon it, is carried out by the **effector (motor) system**, which has two parts. The portion which activates involuntary responses is known as the **autonomic nervous system** whereas that activating voluntary responses is termed the **somatic system**. The sensory and effector (motor) neurones are sometimes collectively called the **peripheral nervous system (PNS)**.

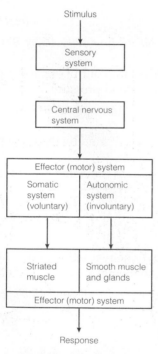

Fig. 19.1 Interrelationships of the various components of the nervous system

---

19.1 Nervous tissue and the nerve impulse

Nervous tissue comprises closely packed nerve cells or **neurones** with little intercellular space. The neurones are bound together by connective tissue.

All neurones have a cell body containing a nucleus. This cell body has a number of processes called **dendrites** which transmit impulses to the cell body. Impulses leave via the **axon** which

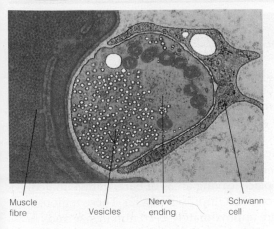

Muscle fibre   Vesicles   Nerve ending   Schwann cell

Transmission EM of neuromuscular junction (×18 500 approx.)

may be several metres in length. Some axons are covered by a fatty **myelin sheath** formed by **Schwann cells**.

Nerve fibres may be bundled together and wrapped in connective tissue to form **nerves**. Nerves may be **sensory**, comprising sensory neurones, **effector (motor)**, comprising effector (motor) neurones, or **mixed**, with both types present.

19.1.1 Resting potential

In its normal state, the membrane of a neurone is negatively charged internally with respect to the outside. The potential difference varies somewhat depending on the neurone but lies in the range 50–90 mV, most usually around 70 mV. This is known as the **resting potential** and in this condition the membrane is said to be **polarized**. The resting potential is the result of the distribution of four ions: potassium (K^+), sodium (Na^+), chloride (Cl^-) and organic anions (COO^-). Initially the concentration of

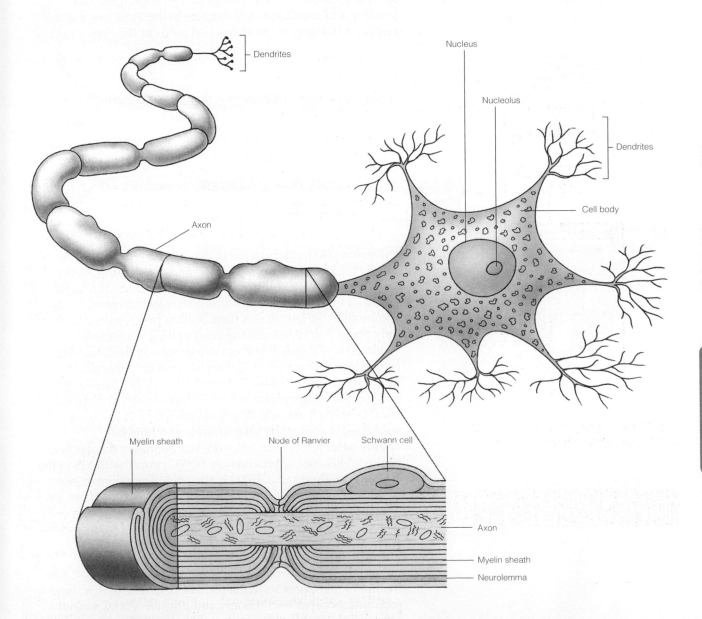

Fig. 19.2 Effector (motor) neurone

FOCUS

Multiple sclerosis and the myelin sheath

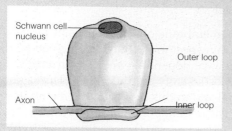

Schwann cell nucleus

Outer loop

Axon

Inner loop

The myelin sheath is produced by the Schwann cell and is rolled around the nerve axon for insulation.

Fig. 1   Schwann cell and axon

On neurones a specialized cell, the **Schwann cell**, wraps itself around the nerve axon to form the numerous concentric layers which comprise the myelin sheath (Fig. 1). This sheath consists of 70% lipid and 30% proteins in the usual bilipid structure; it provides insulation and allows the rapid conduction of electrical signals.

In multiple sclerosis (MS) gradual degradation of the myelin sheath takes place leaving areas of bare, demyelinated axons which cannot conduct impulses (Fig. 2). These regions, known as **plaques**, are approximately 2–10 mm in size and most commonly affect the optic nerve, cerebellum, cervical spinal cord and the area around the ventricles of the brain. Peripheral nerves are unaffected. The most well known symptoms of MS are a weakness of the limbs, 'pins and needles' and numbness, but damage to the optic nerve also results in blurring of the vision and pains in the eyes.

Fig. 2(a) Healthy nerve cell

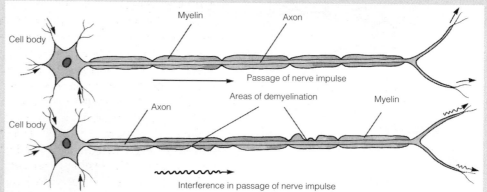

Myelin   Axon

Cell body

Passage of nerve impulse

Areas of demyelination   Myelin

Cell body

Axon

Interference in passage of nerve impulse

Fig. 2(b) Damaged nerve cell in multiple sclerosis

MS has two main patterns of disease development. In some people the condition is progressive and unrelenting, leading to severe crippling, but in most there are periods of relapse followed by spells of remission which may last several years. Although in the later stages there is often progressive disability, only about 1 in 10 MS sufferers end up in a wheelchair.

Multiple sclerosis is one of the commonest diseases of the central nervous system in Europe and yet its cause is still unknown. It affects more women than men, in a ratio of 3 : 2 and there is a high prevalence in countries with a temperate climate; it is uncommon in tropical countries. It has been suggested that possibly diet, lifestyle and physical environment have some influence but no theory has yet been proved. There are approximately 80 000 people with MS in the United Kingdom and 250 000 in the USA. The range of onset of the disease varies from 12 years old to 50 years old but the average age of diagnosis is late 20s to mid 30s.

As yet multiple sclerosis cannot be cured and treatment is very limited. Steroids and ACTH (adrenocorticotrophic hormone) are prescribed during relapse to reduce inflammation and promote a remission but otherwise treatment is supportive in the form of pain relievers, muscle relaxants, occupational therapy and physiotherapy, as well as counselling for the individuals and their families.

(a) Bipolar neurone

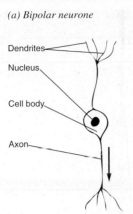

Dendrites
Nucleus
Cell body
Axon

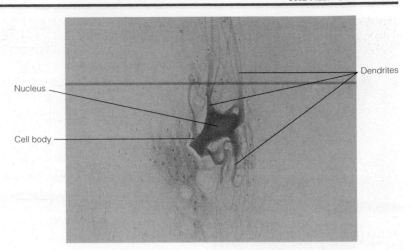

Nucleus
Cell body
Dendrites

Multipolar neurone (×200 approx.)

(b) Branched unipolar neurone

(c) Multipolar neurone

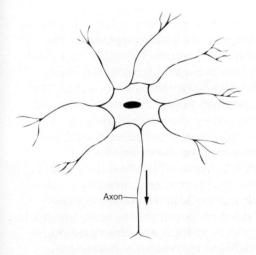

Axon

Fig. 19.3 Types of neurone

potassium (K^+) and organic anions (COO^-) are higher inside the neurone, while the concentration of sodium (Na^+) and chloride (Cl^-) are higher outside. The membrane, however, is considerably more permeable to potassium ions (K^+) than any of the others. As the potassium ion (K^+) concentration inside the neurone is twenty times greater than that outside, potassium ions (K^+) rapidly diffuse out. This outward movement of positive ions means that the inside becomes slightly negative relative to the outside. As more potassium ions move out, the less able they are to do so. In time an equilibrium is reached whereby the rate at which they leave is exactly balanced by the rate of entry. It is therefore the electrochemical gradient of potassium ions which largely creates the resting potential.

The differences in concentration of ions across the membrane are maintained by the active transport of the ions against the concentration gradients. The mechanisms by which these ions are transported are called pumps. As sodium ions (Na^+) are moved in this way they are often referred to as **sodium pumps**. However, as potassium ions are also actively transported they are more accurately **cation pumps**. These cation pumps exchange sodium and potassium ions by actively transporting in potassium ions and removing sodium ions. Being active, this transport requires ATP.

19.1.2 Action potential

By appropriate stimulation, the charge on a neurone can be reversed. As a result, the negative charge inside the membrane of $-70\,mV$ changes to a positive charge of around $+40\,mV$. This is known as the **action potential** and in this condition the membrane is said to be **depolarized**. Within about 2 milliseconds (two thousandths of a second) the same portion of the membrane returns to resting potential ($-70\,mV$ inside). This is known as **repolarization**. These changes are illustrated graphically in Fig. 19.4.

Provided the stimulus exceeds a certain value, called the **threshold value**, an action potential results. Above the threshold value the size of the action potential remains constant, regardless of the size of the stimulus. In other words, the action potential is

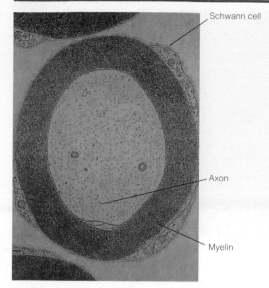

Transmission EM of myelinated nerve fibre

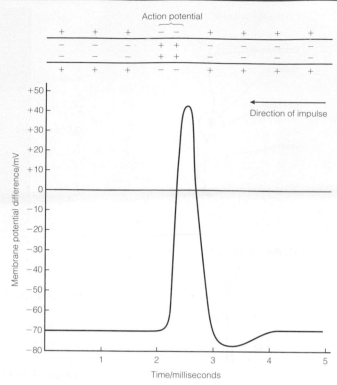

Fig. 19.4 The action potential

either generated, in which case it is always the same, or it is not. This is called an **all or nothing** response. The size of the action potential does not decrease as it is transmitted along the neurone but always remains the same.

19.1.3 Ion movement

The action potential is the result of a sudden increase in the permeability of the membrane to sodium. This allows a sudden influx of sodium ions because there is a high concentration outside which has been maintained by the sodium pump. The influx of sodium ions begins to depolarize the membrane and this depolarization in turn increases the membrane's permeability to sodium, leading to greater influx and further depolarization. This runaway influx of sodium ions is an example of **positive feedback**. When sufficient sodium ions have entered to create a positive charge inside the membrane, the permeability of the membrane to sodium starts to decrease.

At the same time as the sodium ions begin to move inward, so potassium ions start to move in the opposite direction along a diffusion gradient. This outward movement of potassium is, however, much less rapid than the inward movement of sodium. It nevertheless continues until the membrane is repolarized. The changes are summarized in Fig. 19.5.

So why is the movement of ions so rapid? We saw in Section 4.2.2 that some protein molecules span membranes and these have a fine pore or channel through the middle of them. In a neurone membrane some of these channels allow sodium ions (Na^+) to pass through while others permit the movement of potassium (K^+). In the resting state these channels are closed, but when the membrane is depolarized by a stimulus they open.

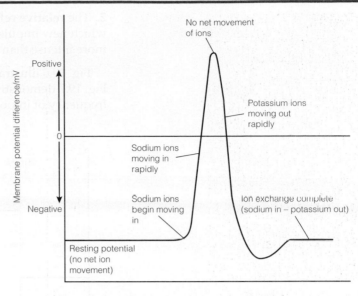

Fig. 19.5 Ion movements during an action potential

They act rather like an entry with a closed gate which can be unlatched. For this reason they are sometimes called **voltage-gated channels**. The gates to the sodium channel open more quickly than those to the potassium channel. This explains why sodium ions entering the neurone cause depolarization followed by the potassium ions leaving which cause repolarization.

19.1.4 Refractory period

Following an action potential, the outward movement of potassium ions quickly restores the resting potential. However, for about one millisecond after an action potential the inward movement of sodium is prevented in that region of the neurone. This means that a further action potential cannot be generated for at least one millisecond. This is called the **refractory period**.

The refractory period is important for two reasons:

1. It means the action potential can only be propagated in the region which is not refractory, i.e. in a forward direction. The action potential is thus prevented from spreading out in both directions until it occupies the whole neurone.

2. By the end of the refractory period the action potential has passed further down the nerve. A second action potential will thus be separated from the first one by the refractory period which therefore sets an upper limit to the frequency of impulses along a neurone.

The refractory period can be divided into two portions:

1. The **absolute refractory period** which lasts around 1 ms during which no new impulses can be propagated however intense the stimulus.

2. The **relative refractory period** which lasts around 5 ms during which new impulses can only be propagated if the stimulus is more intense than the normal threshold level.

Fig. 19.6 illustrates the refractory period in graph form, while Fig. 19.7 demonstrates how the refractory period determines the frequency of impulses along a neurone.

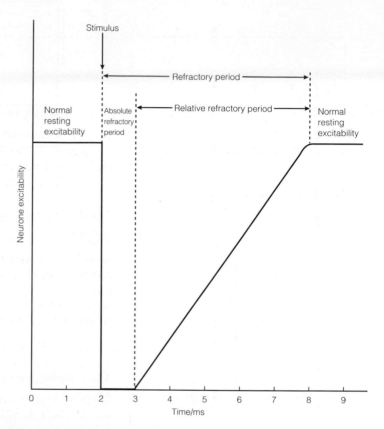

Fig. 19.6 Graph illustrating neurone excitability before and after a nerve impulse

Where the stimulus is at the threshold value the excitability of the neurone must return to normal before a new action potential can be formed. In the time interval shown, this allows just two action potentials to pass i.e. a low frequency of impulses. Where the stimulus exceeds the threshold value a new action potential can be created before neurone excitability returns to normal. In the time interval shown this allows six action potentials to pass, i.e. a high frequency of impulses.

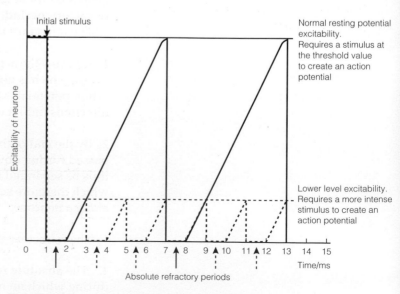

Fig. 19.7 Determination of impulse frequency

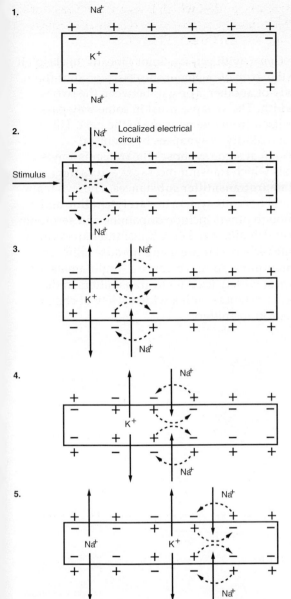

1. *At resting potential there is a high concentration of sodium ions outside and a high concentration of potassium ions inside it.*
2. *When the neurone is stimulated sodium ions rush into the axon along a concentration gradient. This causes depolarization of the membrane.*
3. *Localized electrical circuits are established which cause further influx of sodium ions and so progression of the impulse. Behind the impulse, potassium ions begin to leave the axon along a concentration gradient.*
4. *As the impulse progresses, the outflux of potassium ions causes the neurone to become repolarized behind the impulse.*
5. *After the impulse has passed and the neurone is repolarized sodium is once again actively expelled in order to increase the external concentration and so allow the passage of another impulse.*

19.1.5 Transmission of the nerve impulse

Once an action potential has been set up, it moves rapidly from one end of the neurone to the other. This is the nerve impulse and is described in Fig. 19.8.

According to the precise nature of a neurone, transmission speeds vary from 0.5 metres $msec^{-1}$ to over 100 metres $msec^{-1}$. Two factors are important in determining the speed of conduction:

(a) The diameter of the axon: the greater the diameter the faster the speed of transmission.

(b) The myelin sheath: myelinated neurones conduct impulses faster than non-myelinated ones.

The myelin sheath, which is produced by the **Schwann cells**, is not continuous along the axon, but is absent at points called **nodes of Ranvier** which arise every millimetre or so along the neurone's length. As the fatty myelin acts as an electrical insulator, an action potential cannot form in the part of the axon covered with myelin. They can, however, form at the nodes. The action potentials therefore jump from node to node (**saltatory conduction**), increasing the speed with which they are transmitted (Fig. 19.9).

Fig. 19.8 Transmission of an impulse along an unmyelinated neurone

The insulating myelin causes ion exchange to occur at the nodes of Ranvier. The impulse therefore jumps from node to node.

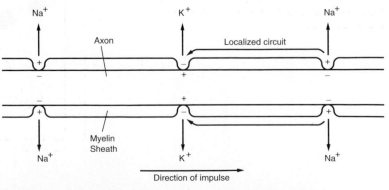

Fig. 19.9 Transmission of an impulse along a myelinated neurone

19.2   The synapse

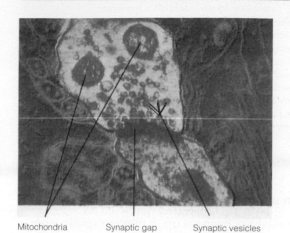

Mitochondria   Synaptic gap   Synaptic vesicles

Transmission EM of synapse (×34 000 approx.)

The word synapse (*syn* = 'with'; *apsis* = 'knot') means 'to clasp'. It is the point where the axon of one neurone clasps or joins the dendrite or cell body of another. The gap between the two is around 20 nm in width. The synapse must in some way pass information across itself from one neurone to the next. This is achieved in the vast majority of synapses by **chemical** transmission, although at some synapses the transmission is **electrical**. Chemicals which transmit messages across the synapse are called **neurotransmitter substances**. The two main ones in the peripheral nervous system are **acetylcholine** and **noradrenaline** although others include dopamine and serotonin. Neurones using acetylcholine as a neurotransmitter are termed **cholinergic neurones** whereas those using noradrenaline are called **adrenergic neurones**. Amino acids, e.g. L-glutamate are thought to be the most widely used neurotransmitters in the brain. In all, over 40 substances with a wide variety of chemical structures act as neurotransmitters.

Did you know?

An average motor neurone may have as many as 15 000 synapses.

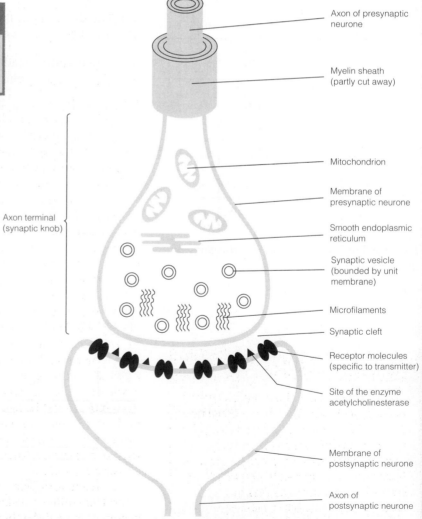

Fig. 19.10 Structure of a chemical synapse

19.2.1 Structure of the synapse

As it is the most frequently occurring type, we shall deal here with the structure of the chemical synapse.

At the synapse the nerve axon is expanded to form a bulbous ending called the **axon terminal (bouton terminale)** or **synaptic knob**. This contains many mitochondria, microfilaments and structures called **synaptic vesicles**. The vesicles contain a neurotransmitter substance such as acetylcholine or noradrenaline. The neurone immediately before the synapse is known as the **presynaptic neurone** and is bounded by the presynaptic membrane. The neurone after the synapse is the **postsynaptic neurone** and is bounded by the postsynaptic membrane. Between the two is a narrow gap, 20 nm wide, called the **synaptic cleft**. The postsynaptic membrane possesses a number of large protein molecules known as **receptor molecules**. The structure of the synapse is illustrated in Fig. 19.10.

19.2.2 Synaptic transmission

When a nerve impulse arrives at the synaptic knob it alters the permeability of the presynaptic membrane to calcium, which therefore enters. This causes the synaptic vesicles to fuse with the membrane and discharge their neurotransmitter substance which, for the purposes of this account, will be taken to be acetylcholine. The empty vesicles move back into the cytoplasm where they are later refilled with acetylcholine.

The acetylcholine diffuses across the synaptic cleft, a process which takes 0.5 ms. Upon reaching the postsynaptic membrane it fuses with the receptor molecules. In **excitatory synapses** this opens ion channels on the postsynaptic membrane allowing sodium ions to enter and thus creating a new potential known as the **excitatory postsynaptic potential** in the postsynaptic neurone. These events are detailed in Fig. 19.11.

Once acetylcholine has depolarized the postsynaptic neurone, it is hydrolysed by the enzyme **acetylcholinesterase** which is found on the postsynaptic membrane. This breakdown of acetylcholine is essential to prevent successive impulses merging at the synapse. The resulting choline and ethanoic acid (acetyl) diffuse across the synaptic cleft and are actively transported into the synaptic knob of the presynaptic neurone into which they diffuse. Here they are coupled together again and stored inside synaptic vesicles ready for further use. This recoupling requires energy which is provided by the numerous mitochondria found in the synaptic knob. Other **neurotransmitters** include **noradrenaline**, **dopamine** and **serotonin**, all of which belong to a group of compounds called catecholamines and probably play a role in motor responses, mood, sleep and pleasure recognition. Two morphine-like neurotransmitters include **enkephalins** and **endorphins** which act as natural pain-killers. Endorphins have a number of effects similar to hormones including reducing thyroxine activity, lowering ventilation and cardiac rate and in conserving water.

The excitatory postsynaptic potentials build up as more neurotransmitter substance arrives until sufficient depolarization occurs to exceed the threshold value and so generate an action potential in the post-synaptic neurone. This additive effect is

Did you know?

The fugu fish is considered a culinary delicacy in Japan. However it contains a highly toxic chemical which kills by blocking the sodium ion channels in nerve membranes. As a result only a few chefs are licensed to prepare this dish – even so some deaths have resulted from eating this fish.

1 The arrival of the impulses at the synaptic knob alters its permeability allowing calcium ions to enter.

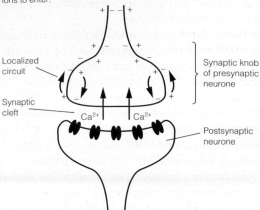

4 The influx of sodium ions generates a new impulse in the postsynaptic neurone.

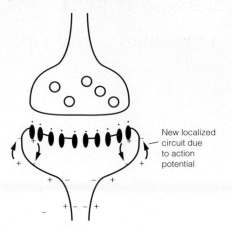

2 The influx of calcium ions causes the synaptic vesicle to fuse with the presynaptic membrane so releasing acetylcholine into the synaptic cleft.

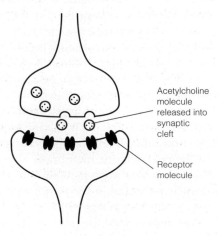

5 Acetylcholinesterase on the postsynaptic membrane hydrolyses acetylcholine into choline and ethanoic acid (acetyl). These two components then diffuse back across the synaptic cleft into the presynaptic neurone.

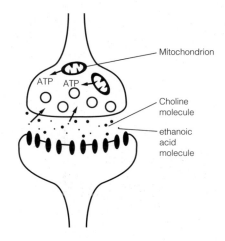

3 Acetylcholine fuses with receptor molecules on the postsynaptic membrane. This causes ion channels to open allowing sodium ions to rush in.

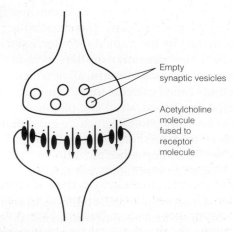

6 ATP released by the mitochondria is used to recombine choline and ethanoic acid (acetyl) molecules to form acetylcholine. This is stored in synaptic vesicles for future use.

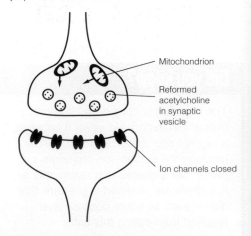

Fig. 19.11 Sequence of diagrams to illustrate synaptic transmission (only relevant detail is included in each drawing)

Drugs and the synapse

There are many different neurotransmitters responsible for information exchange across synapses. Most of the psychoactive drugs available in society today, such as **ecstasy**, **cannabis** and **cocaine**, cause their effects by interfering with the synaptic transmission of one of these messengers. Those drugs which amplify the process of synaptic transmission are called **excitatory** or **agonistic** drugs, while those which inhibit synaptic transmission are known as **inhibitory** or **antagonistic** drugs.

Narcotics such as **heroin** and **morphine** mimic the actions of the neurotransmitters known as endorphins, binding to their specific receptors and blocking sensations of pain. **Nicotine** similarly mimics natural transmitters.

The presence of **caffeine** in the body raises cell metabolism, leading to the release of more neurotransmitters. **Amphetamines** cause increased release of noradrenaline by interfering with storage mechanisms. This leads to excessive activation of neurones and extra information is transmitted around the brain. A user will feel highly aroused but may also suffer damage to organs including the heart.

Some drugs affect the body by interacting with natural neurotransmitters. The **benzodiazepine tranquillizers**, such as Valium, increase the effect of the inhibitory transmitter GABA in the brain resulting in less transfer of information between neurones. In contrast phencyclidine, the active ingredient in **magic mushrooms**, interacts with excitatory transmitters in the brain and inappropriate information is passed between neurones leading to hallucinations.

It is important to remember that neurotransmitters are rapidly absorbed or broken down. **Cocaine** causes noradrenaline to 'linger' in the synapse producing effects similar to those from amphetamines.

£2m Cocaine Seizure

CRACK BARONS TARGET UK

Drugs 'cocktail' caused teenager's death hears court

known as **temporal summation**. All events so far described relate to an **excitatory synapse**, but not all synapses operate in this way. Some, known as **inhibitory synapses**, respond to the neurotransmitter by opening potassium ion channels and leaving the sodium ion channels closed. Potassium therefore moves out causing the postsynaptic membrane to become more polarized. It is thus more difficult for the threshold value to be exceeded and therefore less likely that a new action potential will be created.

465

19.2.3 Functions of synapses

Synapses have a number of functions:

1. **Transmit information between neurones** – The main function of synapses is to convey information between neurones. It is from this basic function that the others arise.

2. **Pass impulses in one direction only** – As the neurotransmitter substance can only be released from one side of a synapse, it ensures that nerve impulses only pass in one direction along a given pathway.

3. **Act as junctions** – Neurones may converge at a synapse. In this way a number of impulses passing along different neurones may between them release sufficient neurotransmitter to generate a new action potential in a single postsynaptic neurone whereas individually they would not. This is known as **spatial summation**. In this way responses to a single stimulus may be coordinated.

4. **Filter out low level stimuli** – Background stimuli at a constantly low level, e.g. the drone of machinery, produce a low frequency of impulses and so cause the release of only small amounts of neurotransmitter at the synapse. This is insufficient to create a new impulse in the postsynaptic neurone and so these impulses are carried no further than the synapse. Such low level stimuli are of little importance and the absence of a response to them is rarely, if ever, harmful. Any change in the level of the stimulus will be responded to in the usual way.

5. **Allow adaptation to intense stimulation** – In response to a powerful stimulus, the high frequency of impulses in the presynaptic neurone causes considerable release of neurotransmitter into the synaptic cleft. Continued high-level stimulation may result in the rate of release of neurotransmitter exceeding the rate at which it can be reformed. In these circumstances the release of neurotransmitter ceases and hence also any response to the stimulus. The synapse is said to be **fatigued**. The purpose of such a response is to prevent overstimulation which might otherwise damage an effector.

19.3   The reflex arc

A **reflex** is an automatic response which follows a sensory stimulus. It is not under conscious control and is therefore involuntary. The pathway of neurones involved in a reflex action is known as a **reflex arc**. The simplest forms of reflex in vertebrates include those concerned with muscle tone. An example of this is the **knee jerk reflex** which may be separated into six parts:

1. **Stimulus** – A blow to the tendon situated below the patella (knee cap). This tendon is connected to the muscles that extend the leg, and hitting it causes these muscles to become stretched.

2. **Receptor** – Specialized sensory structures, called **muscle spindles**, situated in the muscle detect the stretching and produce a nervous signal.

3. **Sensory neurone** – The signal from the muscle spindles is conveyed as a nervous impulse along a sensory neurone to the spinal cord.

4. Effector (motor) neurone – The sensory neurone forms a synapse inside the spinal cord with a second neurone called an effector neurone. This effector neurone conveys a nervous impulse back to the muscle responsible for extending the leg.

5. Effector – This is the muscle responsible for extending the leg. When the impulse from the effector neurone is received, the muscle contracts.

6. Response – The lower leg jerks upwards as a consequence of the muscle contraction.

This reflex arc has only one synapse, that between the sensory and effector neurone in the spinal cord. Such reflex arcs are therefore termed **monosynaptic**. These reflexes do not involve any neurones connected to the brain which therefore plays no part in the response. As the reaction is routine and predictable, not requiring any analysis, it would be wasteful of the brain's capacity to burden it with the millions of such responses that are required each day. Any reflex arc which is localized within the spinal cord and does not involve the brain is called a **spinal reflex**.

Reflexes involving two or more synapses are termed **polysynaptic**. Typical polysynaptic spinal reflexes include the withdrawal of parts of the body from painful stimuli, e.g. removal of the hand or foot from a hot or sharp object. Due to the response involved, such an action is called a **withdrawal reflex**. Fig. 19.12 illustrates a withdrawal reflex where the hand

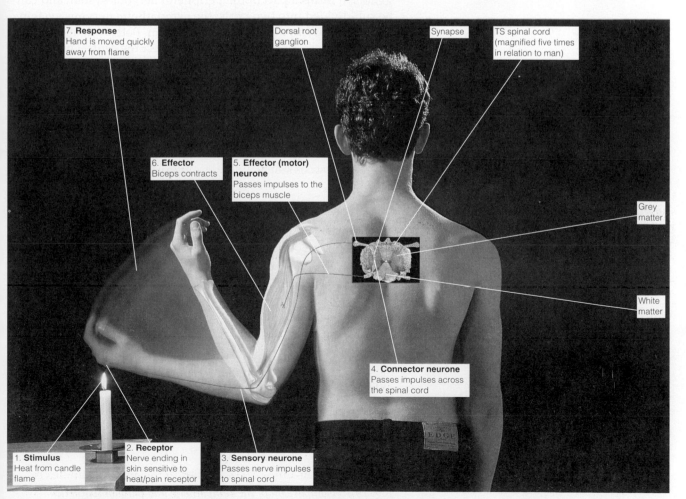

Fig. 19.12 Reflex arc involved in withdrawal from an unpleasant stimulus

is placed near a flame. This reflex involves an additional stage, namely the **connector (intermediate, internuncial** or **relay) neurone**, within the spinal cord.

These simple reflexes are important in making involuntary responses to various changes in both the internal and external environment. In this way homeostatic control of things like body posture may be maintained. Control of breathing, blood pressure and other systems are likewise effected through a series of reflex responses. Another example is the reflex constriction or dilation of the iris diaphragm of the eye in response to changes in light intensity. Details of this are given in Section 19.6.1.

Brain reflexes have neurone connections with the brain and are usually far more complex, involving multiple responses to a stimulus. While reflexes are themselves involuntary, they may be modified in the light of previous experience. These are called **conditioned reflexes** and are discussed in Section 19.7.3.

19.4 The autonomic nervous system

The autonomic (*auto* = 'self'; *nomo* = 'govern') nervous system controls the involuntary activities of smooth muscle and certain glands. It forms a part of the peripheral nervous system and can be sub-divided into two parts: the **sympathetic nervous system** and the **parasympathetic nervous system**. Both systems comprise effector neurones, which connect the central nervous system to their effector organs. Each pathway consists of a **preganglionic neurone** and a **postganglionic neurone**. In the sympathetic system the synapses between the two are located near the spinal cord whereas in the parasympathetic system they are found near to, or within, the effector organ. This, and other differences, are illustrated in Fig. 19.13.

TABLE 19.1 **Comparison of some effects of sympathetic and parasympathetic nervous systems**

Sympathetic nervous system	Parasympathetic nervous system
Increases cardiac output	Decreases cardiac output
Increases blood pressure	Decreases blood pressure
Dilates bronchioles	Constricts bronchioles
Increases ventilation rate	Decreases ventilation rate
Dilates pupils of the eyes	Constricts pupils of the eyes
Contracts anal and bladder sphincters	Relaxes anal and bladder sphincters
Contracts erector pili muscles, so raising hair	No comparable effect
Increases sweat production	No comparable effect
No comparable effect	Increases secretion of tears

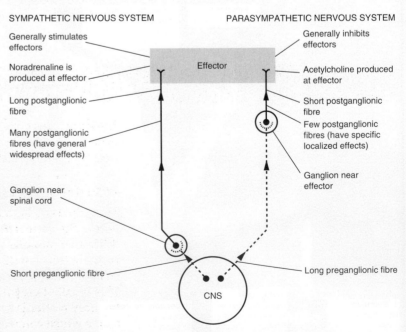

Fig. 19.13 Comparison of the sympathetic and parasympathetic nervous systems

The effects of the sympathetic and parasympathetic nervous systems normally oppose one another, i.e. they are **antagonistic**. If one system contracts a muscle, the other usually relaxes it. The balance between the two systems accurately regulates the involuntary activities of glands and organs. It is possible to control consciously certain activities of the autonomic nervous system through training. Control of the anal and bladder sphincters are examples of this.

Table 19.1 lists some of the effects of the sympathetic and parasympathetic nervous systems.

19.4.1 Control of micturition

Micturition is the removal of urine from the bladder and illustrates how an involuntary reflex and voluntary action can combine to control a process. Up to the age of about two years, micturition is an involuntary reflex, but control gradually becomes voluntary so that most individuals over the age of three years can avoid passing urine at inconvenient times.

When the bladder fills with urine, the urge to micturate may start to be experienced when as little as $150\,cm^3$ has accumulated although in adults at least $350cm^3$ is normally collected before the urge becomes compelling. As the bladder stretches, receptors in its wall send messages to the spinal cord initiating an **emptying reflex**. Impulses pass via the parasympathetic nervous system to the bladder causing contraction of the muscles in its wall and the relaxation of the **internal urethral sphincter**. Urine therefore enters the urethra as far as the **external urethral sphincter**. This one is under voluntary control and prevents micturition until the individual chooses to relax it. Once the bladder is empty the external sphincter is voluntarily closed and the internal sphincter contracts under the influence of the sympathetic nervous system. The brain is also involved in micturition as it integrates the sphincter control, bladder muscle contraction and the contraction of the abdominal and pelvic muscles which aid removal of urine.

19.5   The central nervous system

The central nervous system (CNS) acts as the coordinator of the nervous system. It comprises a long, approximately cylindrical structure – the **spinal cord** – and its anterior expansion – the **brain**.

19.5.1 The spinal cord

The spinal cord is a dorsal cylinder of nervous tissue running within the vertebrae which therefore protect it. It possesses a thick membranous wall and has a small canal, the **spinal canal**, running through the centre. The central area is made up of nerve cell bodies, synapses and unmyelinated connector neurones. This is called **grey matter** on account of its appearance. Around the grey matter is a region largely composed of longitudinal axons which connect different parts of the body. The myelin sheath around these axons give this region a lighter appearance, hence it is called **white matter**.

At intervals along the length of the spinal cord there extend spinal nerves. There are thirty-one pairs of these nerves in humans. They separate into two close to the spinal cord. The uppermost (dorsal) of these is called the **dorsal root**, while the lower (ventral) one is called the **ventral root**. The dorsal root carries only sensory neurones while the ventral root possesses only effector ones; a sort of spinal nerve one-way system. The cell bodies of the sensory neurones occur within the dorsal root, forming a swelling called the **dorsal root ganglion**. The structure of the spinal cord is illustrated in Fig 19.14.

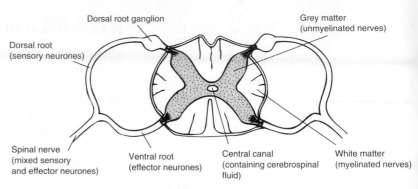

Fig. 19.14 TS through the spinal cord

19.5.2 Structure of the brain

As an elaboration of the anterior region of the spinal cord, the brain has a basically similar structure. Both grey and white matter are present, as is the spinal canal although it is expanded to form larger cavities called **ventricles**. Broadly speaking, the brain has three regions: the **forebrain**, **midbrain** and **hindbrain**.

In common with the entire central nervous system, the brain is surrounded by protective membranes called **meninges**. There are three in all and the space between the inner two is filled with **cerebro-spinal fluid**, which also fills the ventricles referred to above. The cerebro-spinal fluid supplies the neurones in the brain with respiratory gases and nutrients and removes wastes. To achieve this, it must first exchange these materials with the blood. This it does within the ventricles which are richly supplied with capillaries. Having exchanged materials, the fluid must be circulated throughout the CNS in order that it may be distributed to the neurones. This function is performed by cilia found on the epithelial lining of the ventricles and central canal of the spinal cord. The structure of the brain is illustrated in Fig. 19.15.

19.5.3 Functions of the brain

The hindbrain

Medulla oblongata

This region of the brain contains many important centres of the autonomic nervous system. These centres control reflex activities, like ventilation rate (Section 15.3), heart rate (Section 16.5.3) and blood pressure (Section 16.5.4). Other activities controlled by the medulla are swallowing, coughing and the production of saliva.

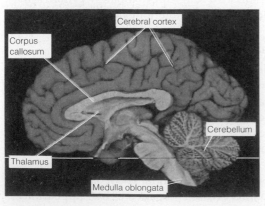

Longitudinal section through a human brain

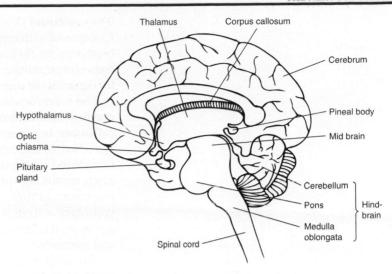

Fig. 19.15 VS through the centre of the human brain

Cerebellum

This is a large and complex association area concerned with the control of muscular movement and body posture. It receives sensory information relating to the tone of muscles and tendons as well as from the organs of balance in the ears. Its role is not to initiate movement but to coordinate it. Any damage to the cerebellum not surprisingly results in jerky and uncoordinated movement.

The midbrain

The midbrain acts as an important link between the hindbrain and the forebrain. In addition it houses both visual and auditory reflex centres. The reflexes they control include the movement of the head to fix on an object or locate a sound.

The forebrain

The thalamus

Lying as it does at the middle of the brain, the thalamus forms an important relay centre, connecting other regions of the brain. It assists in the integration of sensory information. Much of the sensory input received by the brain must be compared to previously stored information before it can be made sense of. It is the thalamus which conveys the information received to the appropriate areas of the cerebrum. Pain and pleasure appear to be perceived by the thalamus.

The hypothalamus

This is the main controlling region for the autonomic nervous system. It has two centres, one for the sympathetic nervous system and the other for the parasympathetic nervous system. At the same time it controls such complex patterns of behaviour as feeding, sleeping and aggression. Another of its roles is to monitor the composition of the blood, in particular the plasma solute concentration, and not surprisingly therefore, it has a very rich supply of blood vessels. It is also an endocrine gland.

Did you know?

Although the brain comprises little more than 2% of the body's weight it uses 20% of the body's energy.

The cerebrum

Compared with other animals, humans have by far the largest cerebrum for their overall body size. In addition, it is highly convoluted, considerably increasing its surface area and hence its capacity for complex activity.

The cerebrum is divided into left and right halves known as **cerebral hemispheres**. The two halves are joined by the **corpus callosum**. In general terms, the cerebrum performs the functions of receiving sensory information, interpreting it with respect to that stored from previous experiences and transmitting impulses along motor neurones to allow effectors to make appropriate responses. In this way, the cerebrum coordinates all the body's voluntary activities as well as some involuntary ones. In addition, it carries out complex activities like learning, reasoning and memory.

The outer 3 mm of the cerebral hemispheres are known as the **cerebral cortex** and in humans this covers an especially large area. Within this area the functions are localized, a fact verified in two ways. Firstly, if an electrode is used to stimulate a particular region of the cortex, the patient's response indicates the part of the body controlled by that region. For example, if a sensation in the hand is felt, then it is assumed that the area receives sensory information from the hand. Equally, if the hand moves, this must be the effector centre for the hand. The second method involves patients who have suffered brain damage by accidental means. If the injured person is unable to move his arm, then the damaged portion is assumed to be the effector centre for that arm.

The association areas of the cerebral cortex help an individual to interpret the information received in the light of previous experience. The **visual association area**, for example, allows objects to be recognized, and the **auditory association area** performs the same function for sounds. In humans, there are similar areas which permit understanding of speech and the written word. Yet another centre, the **speech effector centre**, coordinates the movement of the lips and tongue as well as breathing, in order to allow a person to speak coherently.

Despite the methods outlined above that are used to investigate the functions of the brain, certain areas at the front of the cerebral cortex produce neither sensation nor response when stimulated. These are aptly termed **silent areas**. It is possible that they determine certain aspects of personality as their surgical removal has been known to relieve anxiety. The patients, while tranquil, become rather irresponsible and careless, however. The major localized regions of the cerebral cortex are outlined in Fig. 19.16.

Diffusely situated throughout the brain stem is a system called the **reticular activating system**. It is used to stimulate the cerebral cortex and so rouse the body from sleep. The system is therefore responsible for maintaining wakefulness. The reticular activating system also appears to monitor impulses reaching and leaving the brain. It stimulates some and inhibits others. By doing so it is likely that the system concentrates the brain's activity upon the issues of most importance at any one time. For example, if searching avidly for a lost contact lens, the visual sense may be enhanced. On the other hand, if straining to hear a distant voice, the system may shift the emphasis to increase auditory awareness.

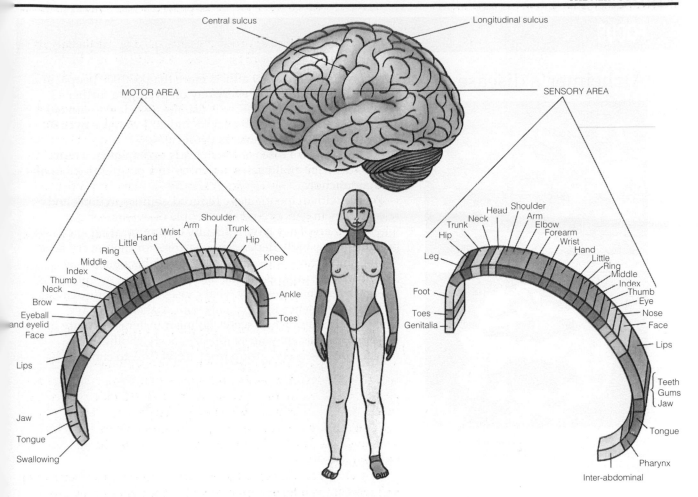

Fig. 19.16 Map of the major regions of the cerebral cortex and their functions

19.5.4 Maintenance of balance

The maintenance of balance provides a good example of how the brain coordinates information from a variety of sources. A series of stretch receptors (**proprioreceptors**) in muscles and joints constantly send impulses to the brain to allow it to be always aware of the precise position of all parts of the body including the legs. The position of the whole body relative to its surroundings is provided by information from the ear which, apart from being an organ of hearing, also functions in maintaining balance.

The parts of the ear concerned with balance are the **semicircular canals**. These are three curved canals containing endolymph which communicate with the middle chamber of the cochlea via the **utriculus** and **sacculus**. Each of the three canals is arranged in a plane at right angles to the other two. A movement in any one plane will result in movement of the canals in the same direction as the head. However, the inertia of the endolymph within the canals means that the endolymph remains more or less stationary. There is relative movement between the canals and the endolymph within them in the same way that there is between a bottle and the liquid within it when the bottle is shaken. The movement of the endolymph is much greater in the canal which is in the same plane as the plane of movement.

Alzheimer's disease

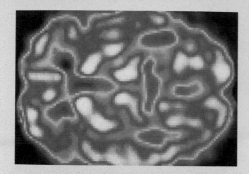

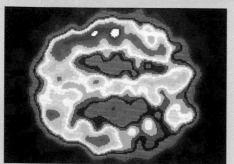

Scans of (top) a normal brain and (above) the brain of an Alzheimer's patient, where the pattern of activity is less symmetrical

Alzheimer's disease now afflicts more than 600 000 people in the United Kingdom and every day on average a further 42 people develop it. The disease is usually associated with old age, affecting 5% of people over 65 and 20% of those over 80. Sadly it can also affect those as young as 40.

Alzheimer's is a disease which leads to dementia, a term used to describe all illnesses which cause a progressive loss of mental function.

People with dementia have reduced abilities to think and reason; they may not remember people or events, who or where they are. They have difficulty communicating and become increasingly dependent on carers for their every need. Although there are some treatments available which may slow down the progress of the disease, there are no cures. No-one even knows exactly what causes Alzheimer's disease.

There is evidence that patients with Alzheimer's have significantly diminished acetylcholine transferase activity in their brains. This enzyme synthesizes acetylcholine by transferring the acetyl group from acetyl CoA to choline:

$$CH_3C(=O)-S-CoA + HO-CH_2CH_2-N^+(CH_3)_2-CH_3 \longrightarrow$$

$$CH_3C(=O)-O-CH_2CH_2-N^+(CH_3)_2-CH_3 + CoA-SH$$

The cause of the disease may also lie in a defect in the neurotransmitter receptors.

Analyses of diseased human brains demonstrate abnormalities in the neurones of various regions, such as the cerebral cortex (the location of many complex mental processes) and an area which plays a vital rôle in memory. In particular the diseased neurones contain accumulations of filaments known as neurofibrillar tangles and areas of the brain are replaced by extracellular deposits called plaques.

These plaques contain aggregates of protein called amyloid which derives from a normal membrane protein (APP – amyloid precursor protein) found in neurones and other cells. Abnormal catabolism of APP results in the production of insoluble fragments which accumulate outside the neurones and form the plaques. Mutations of the APP gene have been shown to be associated with the early onset of Alzheimer's.

Lysosomes may also play some rôle in the degeneration of neurones. APP and similar hydrophobic proteins are difficult to degrade and their accumulation within cells may cause lysosomes to burst and release their hydrolytic enzymes into the cytoplasm of the neurone. This leads to neuronal death and an aggregation of the proteins in the extracellular space.

By the year 2020 about 40% of the population of Britain, North America and Japan will be over 65 years old. This makes research into the dementing illnesses associated with ageing vital to ensure quality of life for sufferers and their carers.

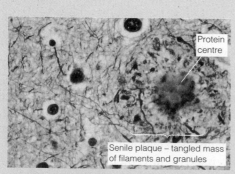

Protein centre

Senile plaque – tangled mass of filaments and granules

LM of brain tissue of an Alzheimer's patient showing a plaque (×250 approx.)

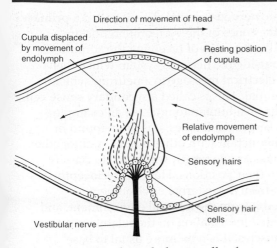

Fig. 19.17 Section through the ampulla of a semi-circular canal

Each of the three canals possesses a swollen portion, the **ampulla**, within which there is a flat gelatinous plate, the **cupula**. The movement of endolymph displaces the cupula in the opposite direction to that of the head movement (Fig 19.17). Sensory hairs at the base of the cupula detect the displacement and send impulses to the brain via the **vestibular nerve**. The brain can then initiate motor impulses to various muscles to correct the imbalance.

The utriculus and sacculus also aid balance by providing information on the position of the body relative to gravity as well as changes in position due to acceleration and deceleration. The information is provided by chalk granules known as **otoliths** which are embedded in a jelly-like material. Various movements of the head cause these otoliths to displace sensory hair cells on regions of the walls of the utriculus and sacculus which respond to vertical and lateral movements respectively. The sensory hair cells thus send appropriate sensory impulses to the brain.

19.5.5 Comparison of endocrine and nervous systems

Both endocrine and nervous systems are concerned with coordination and in performing this function they inevitably operate together. At the same time the systems operate independently and therefore display differences. A comparison of the two systems is given in Table 19.2.

TABLE 19.2 **Comparison of endocrine and nervous systems**

Endocrine system	Nervous system
Communication is by chemical messengers – hormones	Communication is by nervous impulses
Transmission is by the blood system	Transmission is by nerve fibres
Target organ receives message	Effector (muscle or gland) receives message
Transmission is relatively slow	Transmission is very rapid
Effects are widespread	Effects are localized
Response is slow	Response is rapid
Response is often long-lasting	Response is short-lived
Effect may be permanent and irreversible	Effect is temporary and reversible

19.6   Sensory perception

All organisms experience changes in both their internal and external environments. Their survival depends upon responding in an appropriate way to these changes, and they have therefore developed elaborate means of detecting stimuli. To some degree, all cells are sensitive to stimuli, but some have become highly specialized to detect a particular form of energy. These are **receptor** cells. In general terms, these receptors convert whichever form of energy it is that they respond to into a nervous impulse, i.e. they act as **biological transducers**.

In its simplest form, a sensory receptor comprises a single neurone in which a single dendrite receives the stimulus and creates an action potential, which it then conveys along its axon to the remainder of the nervous system. This is called a **primary sense cell**, of which the cones of the vertebrate retina are an example. Sometimes the function of receiving the stimulus is performed by a cell outside the nervous system which then passes a chemical or electrical message to a neurone which creates an action potential. This is called a **secondary sense cell**, of which the taste cells on a human tongue are an example.

Whichever form a sensory cell takes, it is often found in groups, usually in conjunction with other tissues, and together they form **sense organs**. At one time it was usual to classify receptors according to their positions. Hence **exterioceptors** collected information from the external environment, **interoceptors** collected it from the internal environment, and **proprioceptors** provided information on the relative position and movements of muscles. It is now more usual to base classification upon the form of stimulus energy. This gives five categories:

1. **Mechanoreceptors** – detect movements, pressures and tensions, e.g. sound.

2. **Chemoreceptors** – detect chemical stimuli, e.g. taste and smell.

3. **Thermoreceptors** – detect temperature changes.

4. **Electroreceptors** – detect electrical fields (mainly in fish).

5. **Photoreceptors** – detect light and some other forms of electromagnetic radiation.

19.6.1 The human eye

That part of the electromagnetic spectrum which can be detected by the human eye lies in the range 400–700 nm. The eye acts like a television camera in producing an ever-changing image of the visual field at which it is directed.

Each eye is a spherical structure located in a bony socket of the skull called the **orbit**. It may be rotated within its orbit by **rectus muscles** which attach it to the skull. The external covering of the eye is the **sclera**. It contains many collagen fibres and helps to maintain the shape of the eyeball. The sclera is transparent over the anterior portion of the eyeball where it is called the **cornea**. It is the cornea that carries out most refraction of light entering the eye. A thin transparent layer of living cells, the **conjunctiva** overlies and protects much of the cornea. The conjunctiva is an extension of the epithelium of the eyelid. Tears from **lachrymal glands** both lubricate and nourish the conjunctiva and cornea.

Inside the sclera lies a layer of pigmented cells, the **choroid**, which prevents internal reflection of light. It is rich in blood capillaries which supply the innermost layer, the **retina**. This contains the light-sensitive **rods and cones** which convert the light waves they receive into nerve impulses which pass along neurones to the **optic nerve** and hence to the brain. There is an especially light-sensitive spot on the retina which contains only cones. This is the **fovea centralis**. The amount of light entering the eye is controlled by the **iris**. This is a heavily pigmented diaphragm of circular and radial muscle whose contractions alter the diameter of the aperture at its centre, called the **pupil**, through which light enters. Just behind the pupil lies the transparent, biconvex **lens**. It controls the final focusing of light onto the retina. It is flexible and elastic, capable of having its shape altered by the **ciliary muscles** which surround it. These are arranged circularly and radially and work antagonistically to focus incoming light on the retina by altering the lens' shape and hence its focal length. The region in front of the lens is called the **anterior chamber** and contains a transparent liquid called **aqueous humour**. Behind the lens is the much larger **posterior chamber** which contains the transparent jelly-like **vitreous humour** which helps to maintain the eyeball's shape. The structure of the eye is illustrated in Fig. 19.18.

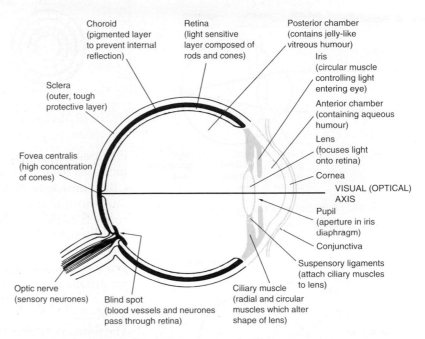

Fig. 19.18 VS through the human eye

Control of the amount of light entering the eye

Controlling the amount of light entering the eye is of importance because if too little light reaches the retina the cones may not be stimulated at all. Alternatively, if the quantity of light is too great the retinal cells may be overstimulated, causing dazzling. Control is exercised by the iris diaphragm as outlined in Fig. 19.18.

Focusing of light rays onto the retina

Light rays entering the eye must be **refracted** (bent) in order to focus them onto the retina and so give a clear image. Most refraction is achieved by the cornea. However, the degree of refraction needed to focus light rays onto the retina varies according to the distance from the eye of the object being viewed. Light rays from objects close to the eye need more refraction to focus them on the retina than do more distant ones. The cornea is unable to make these adjustments and so the lens has become adapted to this purpose. Being elastic, it can be made to change shape by the ciliary muscle which encircles it. The muscle fibres are arranged circularly and the lens is supported by **suspensory ligaments** (Fig. 19.20). When the circular ciliary muscle contracts, the tension on the suspensory ligaments is reduced and the natural elasticity of the lens causes

BRIGHT LIGHT	DIM LIGHT
More photoreceptor cells in the retina are stimulated by an increase in light intensity	Fewer photoreceptor cells are stimulated due to decrease in light intensity
Greater number of impulses pass along sensory neurones to the brain	Fewer impulses pass along sensory neurones to the brain
Brain sends impulses along parasympathetic nervous system to the iris diaphragm	Brain sends impulses along the sympathetic nervous system to the iris diaphragm
In the iris diaphragm, circular muscle contracts and radial muscle relaxes	In the iris diaphragm, circular muscle relaxes and radial muscle contracts
Pupil constricts	Pupil dilates
Less light enters the eye	More light enters the eye
Anterior view of iris and pupil	Anterior view of iris and pupil

Fig. 19.19 Mechanism of control of light entering the eye

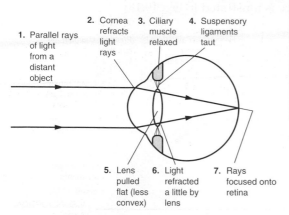

Fig. 19.20(a) Condition of the eye when focused on a distant object

1. Parallel rays of light from a distant object
2. Cornea refracts light rays
3. Ciliary muscle relaxed
4. Suspensory ligaments taut
5. Lens pulled flat (less convex)
6. Light refracted a little by lens
7. Rays focused onto retina

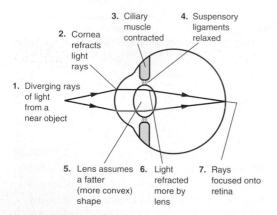

Fig. 19.20(b) Condition of the eye when focused on a near object

1. Diverging rays of light from a near object
2. Cornea refracts light rays
3. Ciliary muscle contracted
4. Suspensory ligaments relaxed
5. Lens assumes a fatter (more convex) shape
6. Light refracted more by lens
7. Rays focused onto retina

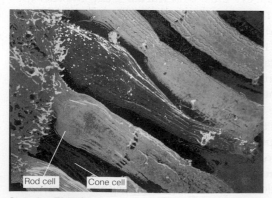

Scanning EM of rod and cone cells

it to assume a fatter (more convex) shape. In this position it increases the degree of refraction of light. When the circular ciliary muscle is relaxed, the suspensory ligaments are stretched taut, thus pulling the lens outwards and making it thinner (less convex). In this position it decreases the degree of light refraction. By changing its shape in this manner the lens can focus light rays from near and distant objects on the retina. The process is called **accommodation**. How the eye accommodates for distant and near objects is shown in Figs. 19.20(a) and (b).

The retina

The retina possesses the **photoreceptor** cells. These are of two types, **rods** and **cones**. Both act as transducers in that they convert light energy into the electrical energy of a nerve impulse. Both cell types are partly embedded in the pigmented epithelial cells of the choroid. The microscopic structure of the retina displayed in Figs. 19.21 and 19.22. shows that the basic structure of rods and cones is similar. However, there are both structural and functional differences and these are detailed in Table 19.3.

Each rod possesses up to a thousand vesicles in its outer segment. These contain the photosensitive pigment **rhodopsin** or **visual purple**. Rhodopsin is made up of the protein **opsin** and a derivative of vitamin A, **retinal**. Retinal normally exists in its *cis* isomer form, but light causes it to become converted to its *trans* isomer form. This change initiates reactions which lead to the splitting of rhodopsin into opsin and retinal – a process known as **bleaching**. This splitting in turn leads to the creation of a generator potential in the rod cell which, if sufficiently large, generates an action potential along the neurones leading from the cell to the brain.

Before the rod cell can be activated again in the same way, the opsin and retinal must first be resynthesized into rhodopsin. This resynthesis is carried out by the mitochondria found in the inner segment of the rod cell, which provide ATP for the process. Resynthesis takes longer than the splitting of rhodopsin but is more rapid the lower the light intensity. A similar process

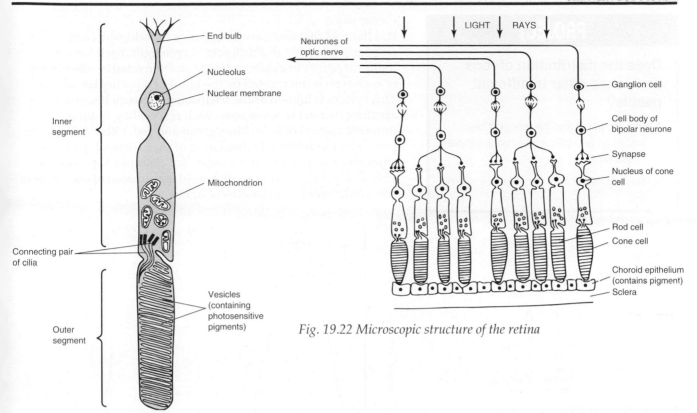

Fig. 19.21 Structure of a single rod cell

Fig. 19.22 Microscopic structure of the retina

TABLE 19.3   **Differences between rods and cones**

Rods	Cones
Outer segment is rod-shaped	Outer segment is cone-shaped
Occur in greater numbers in the retina – being 20 times more common than cones	Fewer are found in the retina – being one twentieth as common as rods
Distributed more or less evenly over the retina	Much more concentrated in and around the fovea centralis
None found at the fovea centralis	Greatest concentration occurs at the fovea centralis
Give poor visual acuity because many rods share a single neurone connection to the brain	Give good visual acuity because each cone has its own neurone connection to the brain
Sensitive to low-intensity light, therefore mostly used for night vision	Sensitive to high-intensity light, therefore mostly used for day vision
Do not discriminate between light of different wavelengths, i.e. not sensitive to colour	Discriminate between light of different wavelengths, i.e. sensitive to colour
Contain the visual pigment rhodopsin which has a single form	Contain the visual pigment iodopsin which occurs in three forms

occurs in cone cells except that the pigment here is **iodopsin**. This is less sensitive to light and so a greater intensity is required to cause its breakdown and so initiate a nerve impulse.

The eye is thus typical of most sense organs in that it functions to collect sensory information (light), to amplify this information (by focusing light and the use of highly sensitive receptors such as the rod cells) and then by acting as a transducer (by converting the light energy into nervous impulses which can be interpreted by the brain).

Colour vision

It is thought that there are three forms of iodopsin, each responding to light of a different wavelength. Each form of iodopsin occurs in a different cone and the relative stimulation of each type is interpreted by the brain as a particular colour. This system is known as the **trichromatic theory** because there are three distinct types of cone, each responding to three different colours of light: blue, green and red. Other colours are perceived by combined stimulation of these three. Equal stimulation of red and green cones, for example, is perceived as yellow. Fig. 19.23 shows the extent of stimulation of each type of cone at different wavelengths of light.

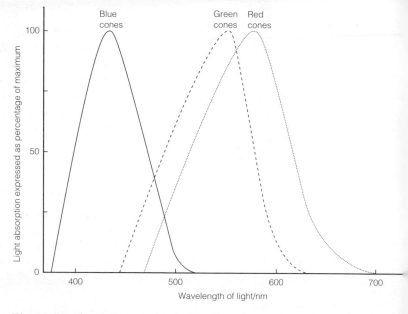

Fig. 19.23 Absorption spectra for the three types of cone occurring in the retina as proposed in the trichromatic theory of colour vision

Colour blindness can be explained in terms of some deficiency in one or more cone type. Deficiencies in the red and green cones, for example, give rise to the relatively common **red–green colour blindness**. The condition is due to a defect on a gene which is linked to the X chromosome (Section 7.4.2). Alternative theories to the trichromatic theory have been put forward in recent years but these have yet to achieve general acclaim.

19.6.2 Role of the brain in vision

All light, of whatever colour, intensity or pattern, which enters the eye is transformed into nerve impulses, all of which are the same. It is up to the brain to visualize these impulses into meaningful shapes. This it does by analyzing and interpreting the frequency of impulses and the origins of the neurones which carry them e.g. from a red cone, or green cone. The visual association areas in the cerebral cortex of the brain are especially important here as they match the incoming information with images already stored in these areas. Hence a corgi would be recognized as a dog even if an individual's previous experience of the species was restricted to labradors.

19.7   Behaviour

In order to survive, organisms including humans must respond appropriately to changes in their environment. Broadly speaking, behaviour is the response of an organism to these changes and it involves both endocrine and nervous systems. Behaviour has a genetic basis and is unique to each species. It is often adapted, however, in the light of previous experience. The study of behaviour is called **ethology**.

19.7.1 Reflexes

Reflexes are the simplest form of behavioural response. Section 19.3 describes a simple reflex response to a stimulus. These reflexes are involuntary responses which follow an inherited pattern of behaviour. How then do these responses improve an animal's chance of survival? The **withdrawal reflex** illustrates their importance. If the hand is placed on a hot object, the reflex response causes it to be immediately withdrawn. In this way damage is avoided.

19.7.2 Innate behaviour

Innate or **instinctive** behaviour is inherited and is highly specific. It is normally an inborn pattern of behaviour which cannot be altered. In practice almost all instincts can be modified to some degree in response to experiences. However, innate behaviour is relatively inflexible when compared to learning. Much instinctive behaviour is highly complex and consists of a chain of actions, the completion of each stage in the chain acting as the stimulus for the commencement of the next stage.

An example of innate behaviour is apparent in young babies who if supported, will instinctively begin to walk when their feet touch the ground. This walking reflex is somewhat uncoordinated but in time becomes modified through learning to allow the highly coordinated walking movement of adults.

19.7.3 Learned behaviour

Learned behaviour is behaviour which is acquired and modified in response to experience. As such it takes time to refine and so is of greatest benefit to animals such as humans with relatively long life spans. The chief advantage of learning over innate behaviour is its adaptability; learned behaviour can be modified to meet changing circumstances.

Associative learning involves the association of two or more stimuli. One form of associative learning is the **conditioned reflex** exemplified by the classic experiments performed on dogs by the Russian physiologist I. P. Pavlov:

1. He allowed dogs to hear the ticking of a metronome and observed no change in the quantity of saliva produced.

2. He presented the dogs with the taste of powdered meat and measured the quantity of saliva produced.

3. He presented the powdered meat and the noise of the metronome simultaneously on 5 to 6 occasions.

4. He presented the noise of a ticking metronome *only* and observed that the dogs salivated in response to it whereas previously they had not done so (Stage **1**).

5. Repetition of Stage **4** leads to a reduction in the quantity of saliva produced until the stimulus fails to produce any response.

The features of a conditioned reflex are:

1. It is the association of two stimuli presented together.

2. It is a temporary condition.

3. The response is involuntary.

4. It is reinforced by repetition.

5. Removal of the cerebral cortex causes loss of the response.

A second form of associative learning is **operant conditioning (trial and error learning)**. This form of learning, studied by Skinner, differs from the conditioned reflex in the way it becomes established. Animals learn by trial and error. If mistakes are followed by an unpleasant stimulus while correct responses are followed by a pleasant one, the animal learns a particular pattern of behaviour.

The features of operant learning are:

1. The associative stimulus *follows* the action, i.e. it does not need to be simultaneous with it.

2. Repetition improves the response.

3. The action is involuntary.

4. While temporary, the association is less easily removed than in a conditioned reflex.

5. Removal of the cerebral cortex does *not* cause loss of the response.

The highest form of learning is **insight** or **intelligent behaviour**. It involves the recall of previous experiences and their adaptation to help solve a new problem. The rapidity with which a solution is achieved excludes any possibility of trial and error. Chimpanzees will acquire bananas fixed to the roof of their cage by piling up boxes upon which they climb to reach them. In the same way sticks may be joined together to form a long pole which is used to obtain bananas which are out of reach outside the cage. Chimpanzees may even chew the ends of the sticks so they can be made to fit one another.

Imprinting is a simple but specialized form of learning. Unlike other forms of learning, imprinted behaviour is fixed and not easily adapted. Newly hatched geese will follow the first thing they see. Ordinarily this would be their mother and the significance of this behaviour is therefore obvious. However, as shown by the Austrian behaviourist, Konrad Lorenz, they will follow humans or other objects should these be seen first. This principle is often used in training circus animals. If a trainer becomes imprinted in an animal's mind, it becomes much easier to train.

PROJECT

Students often express the view that they can study better if there is background music going on at the same time

Find out if they are right or not.

FOCUS

Circadian rhythms

Many of the physiological processes in our bodies appear to vary according to a definite cycle which lasts approximately twenty-four hours. These cycles have therefore been referred to as **circadian rhythms** from the Latin *circa diem*, meaning 'about a day'. It is easy to explain this pattern as a simple response to the 24 hour solar cycle but the pattern continues without external cues. We seem to have an internal **biological clock** which, in the absence of environmental time stimuli, runs in a cycle of approximately 25 hours. However, it is synchronized with the external 24 hour clock by factors known as **zeitgebers**, or 'time-givers'. Without zeitgebers internal and external time become disconnected. Some blind people or people living indoors without social contact get up and go to bed later each day, gradually losing their synchronization with the rest of society. It is a phenomenon also observed in teenagers at weekends and during holidays.

In many ways circadian rhythms operate with homeostasis to improve the interaction between an organism and its environment. Our physiological processes are all controlled homeostatically but the 'setting' is determined by our biological clock. This will maintain our functions at a low level at night to conserve energy, and at a higher level during the day. The environment also plays a part in this by providing an external, or **exogenous**, component to the rhythm as well as acting as a zeitgeber. Humans are less dependent on the natural environment than most organisms but daylight still acts as a zeitgeber, as well as more complex clues such as social conventions.

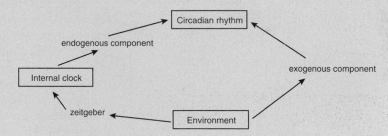

Seasonal Affective Disorder (SAD) is thought to be a human response to long, dark winter nights. During darkness the pineal gland in the roof of the forebrain produces the hormone **melatonin** which effectively 'closes the body down'. Bright light inhibits the production of melatonin and so SAD sufferers buy special lights to give them doses of artificial sunshine.

Our biological clocks control such things as body temperature, sleeping and waking, excretion rate, hormone levels and mental abilities. Our body temperature begins to rise as we approach the time when we normally get up, reaching a peak during the late afternoon and early evening. Fever is most marked in the evening when our body temperature is already highest and more people die in the early morning when body temperature is lowest. Many

FOCUS continued

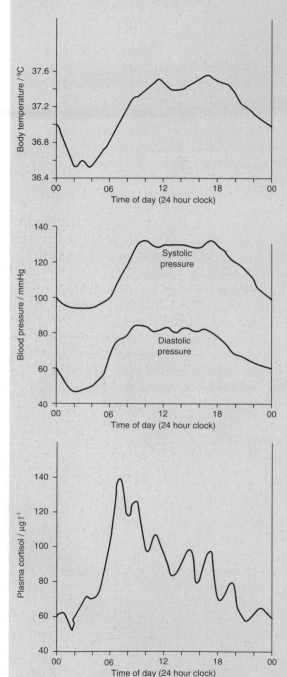

Some daily variables

mental tasks are best approached around dawn when the plasma cortisol level is highest. This hormone, produced by the adrenal gland, helps the body cope with stress. Cortisol is also a natural anti-inflammatory agent and its low level during the night partly explains why asthma attacks and arthritis are worse then.

Both heart rate and blood pressure vary during the course of 24 hours. The heart beats faster during the day than at night, closely following the ups and downs of body temperature. For most people blood pressure begins to rise early in the morning, an hour or so before we wake, peaking in the late afternoon and early evening before falling to a low point around midnight. An awareness of such variation is important when testing patients for particular medical conditions and when administering drugs.

When people move across time zones during jet travel they disrupt their normal circadian rhythms and develop **jet lag**. The body clock cannot reset enough in one jump to match the time zone it is now in, often needing about 5 days to get back to normal. Heart rate and urinary output are affected as well as the ability to concentrate, reason logically and coordinate eye and hand movements. Jet lag is worse when travelling east because sunset is experienced earlier and you are trying to persuade your body clock that it is time to go to sleep earlier than usual. Flying west involves trying to sleep later than normal and this usually causes fewer problems.

Shiftwork causes similar problems this time caused by the conflict between 'home' zeitgebers and 'work' zeitgebers. Adjustment is difficult and shiftworkers may suffer more accidents, more stress and more general ailments than other people. Research has shown the importance of bright light as a zeitgeber for humans and so an attempt is being made to ease some of the problems faced by shift workers by adjusting the light in their workplace and suggesting the use of sunglasses on the way home and thick curtains in bedrooms. Different patterns of shift work bring different problems. Permanent shift, or night, work is good for repetitious work needing physical dexterity and brings few problems of adjustment although socially it may be difficult. People on rapidly rotating shifts with 2 days on each of 3 shifts plus two days off tend to keep themselves orientated to daytime and seem to manage well in problem solving jobs. The most stressful pattern is the slowly rotating shift with one week working days, the next evenings and then nights – all with normal weekends off. This is extremely confusing and is the equivalent of flying across 7 or 8 time zones every 5 days.

19.8   Questions

1. The table below contains statements relating to the functions performed by different regions of the brain. In each box, write the name of the region of the brain which performs the function described.

Function	Region of the brain
Maintenance of posture and muscular coordination	
Regulation of breathing rate	
Transfer of information between right and left cerebral hemispheres	
Osmoregulation	
Accommodation and pupil reflexes	

(*Total 5 marks*)
ULEAC 1996, Specimen Paper HB3, No. 2

2. The diagram shows nerve pathways in the autonomic and somatic nervous systems.

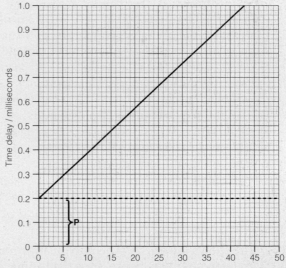

○—< represents a nerve fibre

(a) Identify each nerve pathway by putting a tick in the appropriate box.   (*4 marks*)

Nerve pathway	Autonomic sympathetic	Autonomic parasympathetic	Somatic
P			
Q			
R			
S			

(b) What is the effect of:
(i) parasympathetic stimulation of the bronchi;
(ii) sympathetic stimulation of the skin?   (*2 marks*)
(*Total 6 marks*)

AEB June 1993, Paper 1, No. 17

3. Figure 1 represents a simple spinal-reflex pathway.

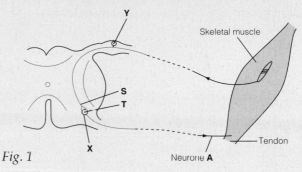

Fig. 1

(a)   (i) Identify feature **X** and feature **Y** in the diagram.   (*2 marks*)
(ii) Name the type of sensory receptor in this reflex pathway.   (*1 mark*)
(iii) Explain how an impulse is transmitted from point **S** to point **T** in this pathway.   (*4 marks*)
(b) Distinguish between a simple reflex and a conditioned reflex.   (*1 mark*)
(c) An experiment was performed to measure the speed of conduction of impulses in a myelinated neurone supplying a skeletal muscle. The nerve was stimulated at varying distances from the muscle. At each distance, the time delay between the application of a stimulus and the contraction of the muscle was recorded. The results are shown in Fig. 2.

Fig. 2   Distance between nerve stimulating point and muscle / mm

(i) Calculate the speed of conduction of the neurone. Show your working.   (*2 marks*)
(ii) Give **three** factors that contribute to the time delay between the application of the stimulus and contraction of the muscle.   (*3 marks*)
(iii) Why is the time delay **P** constant regardless of the distance between stimulating point and muscle?   (*1 mark*)

(d) How would the value obtained for speed of conduction be affected, if at all, if the neurone were:
  (i) unmyelinated but the same diameter;
  (ii) myelinated but half the diameter? (*2 marks*)

(e) Figure 3 shows a recording of a muscle fibre action potential when the skeletal muscle was stimulated via its nerve.

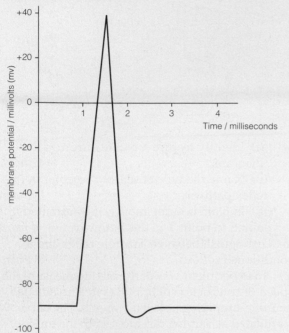

Fig. 3

  (i) The recording shows a negative membrane potential of −90 mV when the muscle cell is at rest (unstimulated). Explain the cause of the resting membrane potential. (*3 marks*)
  (ii) Explain the change in membrane potential from −90 mV to +40 mV following stimulation. (*3 marks*)

(f) (i) What is meant by the *absolute refractory period* of a muscle? (*1 mark*)
  (ii) Unlike skeletal muscle, which has an absolute refractory period of 1.5 milliseconds, cardiac muscle has an absolute refractory period of 200 milliseconds. Explain the advantage of this to the heart. (*1 mark*)
  (*Total 24 marks*)

AEB June 1992, Paper 2, No. 2

4. The figure shows the electrical activity of a neurone.
(a) With reference to the figure, state the resting potential of the neurone. (*1 mark*)
(b) Account for the resting potential of the neurone in terms of the ionic balance across the axon membrane. (*3 marks*)
(c) Describe the sequence of events resulting in the generation of the action potential. (*3 marks*)
An investigation showed that the axon of this neurone transmitted impulses at a maximum frequency of 170 impulses per second.

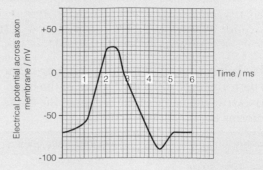

(d) With reference to the figure, explain this result. (*3 marks*)
  (*Total 10 marks*)

UCLES June 1995, Paper 2, No. 5

5. (a) (i) Draw a labelled diagram to show the structure of a **sensory** neurone. (*3 marks*)
  (ii) Indicate on your diagram the direction of movement of nerve impulses in this neurone. (*1 mark*)
(b) Describe **one** feature of the sensory neurone which influences the rate of transmission of nerve impulses (*1 mark*)
(c) Explain the term *threshold* as applied to the generation of nerve impulses. (*1 mark*)
(d) For most neurones the number of nerve impulses which can pass along an axon is rarely more than 200 per second. Suggest an explanation for this observation. (*1 mark*)
  (*Total 7 marks*)

AEB June 1995, Paper 1, No. 16

6. The diagram shows a synaptic knob of a neurone, next to a post-synaptic membrane.

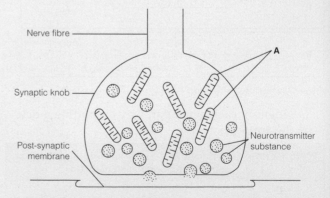

(a) Name the process by which substances, such as the neurotransmitter molecules shown in the diagram, are released from cells. (*1 mark*)
(b) Explain why a synaptic knob contains a large number of the structures labelled **A**. (*2 marks*)
(c) With reference to the information in the diagram, explain why prolonged and frequent stimulation of the nerve fibre would make it temporarily unable to generate any more nerve impulses in the post-synaptic cell. (*2 marks*)

(d) If the neurotransmitter were acetylcholine, what effect would the presence of acetylcholinesterase have on synaptic transmission? Explain why this effect would occur. *(2 marks)*

(Total 7 marks)

AEB June 1994, Paper 1, No. 1

7. The passage below refers to paralysis caused by the disease myasthenia gravis. Use the information in the passage and your own knowledge to answer the questions which follow.

Sometimes a person has very poor transmission of impulses at the neuromuscular junction, an effect that produces paralysis. One cause of this is the condition known as myasthenia gravis, an
5   autoimmune response in which the immune system of the body has developed antibodies against the muscle cell membrane. Reaction of antibodies with the membrane in the synaptic gutter widens the space in the synaptic cleft and
10   also destroys many of the membrane folds. These effects seriously depress the responsiveness of the muscle fibre to acetylcholine.

Adapted from A C Guyton, *Physiology of the Human Body* (1984)

(a) Explain the meaning of each of the following terms.
   (i) Impulses (line 2)   *(2 marks)*
   (ii) Neuromuscular junction (line 2)   *(2 marks)*

(b) Suggest why the response of the muscle fibre to acetylcholine is depressed by each of the following.
   (i) Widening of the space in the synaptic cleft (line 9)   *(3 marks)*
   (ii) Destruction of the membrane folds (line 10)   *(2 marks)*

(c) The passage continues as follows.

Neostigmine is a drug that prevents the destruction of acetylcholine by cholinesterase. Treatment with
15   neostigmine is often highly effective in overcoming the paralysis. This drug allows acetylcholine to accumulate in the neuromuscular junction from one nerve impulse to the next and, therefore, to exert a tremendous effect on the muscle fibre
20   membrane. As a result, persons almost totally paralysed by myasthenia gravis can sometimes be returned almost to normality within a minute of a single intravenous injection of neostigmine.

Explain how treatment with neostigmine overcomes paralysis.   *(4 marks)*

(d) Some chemical weapons inhibit cholinesterase activity. Suggest how this might affect victims of these weapons.   *(2 marks)*

(Total 15 marks)

ULEAC June 1993, Paper 3, No. 7

8. Give **one** example of each of the following types of behaviour:
   (a) habituation: *(1 mark)*
   (b) imprinting: *(1 mark)*
   (c) kinesis.   *(1 mark)*

(Total 3 marks)

NEAB June 1995, Paper BY04, No. 2

9. The diagram shows a vertical section through a human brain.

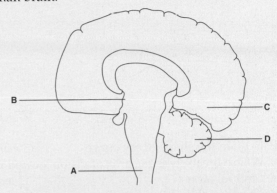

(a) Give the letter of the region of the brain which:
   (i) regulates coordination of the solute concentration of the plasma: *(1 mark)*
   (ii) coordinates the control of the heart rate.   *(1 mark)*
   (iii) receives sensory input from the eyes.   *(1 mark)*

(b) What is the function of the visual association area?   *(1 mark)*

(c) A stroke results from the bursting of a blood vessel on the surface of the brain. As a result of the damage that this causes to the brain, stroke victims may be paralysed in part of the body. Describe how observations made on stroke victims could confirm the function of particular areas of the cerebral hemispheres.   *(1 mark)*

(Total 5 marks)

NEAB June 1995, Paper BY04, No. 6

10. (a) Describe how differences in permeability of the cell surface membrane to particular ions gives rise to a resting potential in an axon.   *(3 marks)*

(b) In the first stage of an action potential, the potential difference across the axon membrane changes from around $-60\,mV$ to approximately $+40\,mV$. Explain how this happens.   *(3 marks)*

(c) Suggest:
   (i) why, although nerve impulses can travel in both directions in an isolated nerve cell, in a whole animal they travel only in one direction;   *(1 mark)*
   (ii) how a single nerve cell can convey information about the strength of a stimulus.   *(1 mark)*

(Total 8 marks)

NEAB June 1995, Paper BY04, No. 7

11. Different parts of the visual cortex receive impulses from specific parts of the retina. The graph shows the area of the visual cortex per unit area of the retina from which it receives impulses.

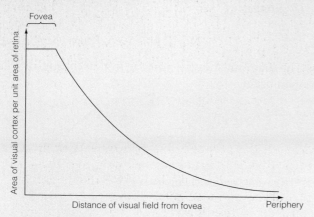

(a) Explain the shape of the curve. *(3 marks)*

(b) Where precisely is the area of vision located in the cerebral cortex? *(1 mark)*

(c) There is a 'blind spot' on the retina of each eye, yet in normal binocular vision there is no blind area in the visual field.

    (i) How does the blind spot differ from the rest of the retina? *(1 mark)*

    (ii) Explain why there is apparently no blind area in the visual field. *(1 mark)*

(d) When a person moves from a lighted area into a darkened room it takes a considerable time before full visual sensitivity is regained.

    (i) What is this process called? *(1 mark)*

    (ii) What happens in the retina during the time that this process is taking place? *(2 marks)*

(Total 9 marks)

AEB June 1993, Paper 1, No. 15

12. The diagram below shows a single rod from a mammalian retina.

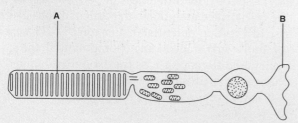

(a) Name the parts labelled **A** and **B** and give **one** function of each. Write your answers in the table below. *(4 marks)*

Part	Name	Function
A		
B		

(b) Draw an arrow next to the diagram to indicate the direction in which light passes through this cell. *(1 mark)*

(c) State **two** ways in which vision using cones differs from vision using rods. *(2 marks)*

(Total 7 marks)

ULEAC 1996, Specimen Paper HB3, No. 4

13. Explain the meaning of each of the following terms.

(a) Operant conditioning *(2 marks)*

(b) Classical conditioning *(2 marks)*

(c) Reinforcement *(2 marks)*

(Total 6 marks)

ULEAC June 1995, Paper 4C, No. 5

14. Fig. 1 shows diagrams of neurones from a part of the forebrain, known as the hippocampus, of people aged 50, 60 and 70 years, and in a 70 year old with Alzheimer's disease.

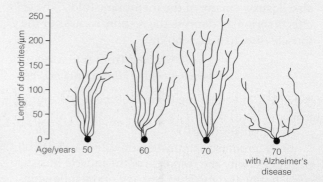

Fig. 1

(a)   (i) With reference to Fig. 1, describe the change in appearance of dendrites in healthy people with increasing age. *(2 marks)*

    (ii) Comment on the appearance of the dendrites of the person with Alzheimer's disease. *(2 marks)*

Studies have shown that about 5% of neurones in the hippocampus disappear with each decade after the age of 50.

(b) For every 100 neurones present in the human hippocampus at age 50, calculate how many will be present by age 70. Show your working. *(2 marks)*

(c) Suggest how the change you identified in *(a)* (i) is related to the loss of neurones with age. *(2 marks)*

(d) Outline the possible mechanisms involved in human long-term memory. *(3 marks)*

(e) Outline **two** consequences of Alzheimer's disease for society. *(4 marks)*

(f) Deterioration of neurones may also occur in the cerebellum. Suggest the likely effects of this on the patient. *(2 marks)*

(Total 17 marks)

UCLES June 1996, Paper 1 (Option 4), No. 2

Muscular movement and support

20

In humans there are three types of muscle: cardiac, smooth and skeletal. **Cardiac muscle** occurs exclusively in the heart where it functions to circulate blood around the body. **Smooth muscle** makes up the walls of most tubular structures, such as the alimentary canal, blood vessels and ducts of the urino-genital system. While both types of muscle have an effector nerve supply from the central nervous system, they are not under voluntary control and will continue to contract and relax rhythmically in the absence of the effector nerve supply. By contrast the third type of muscle, **skeletal muscle**, is under voluntary control and will only contract when innervated by a motor nerve.

20.1 Structure of skeletal muscle

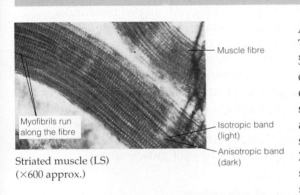

Striated muscle (LS)
(×600 approx.)

Myofibrils run along the fibre

Muscle fibre

Isotropic band (light)

Anisotropic band (dark)

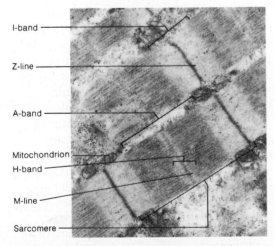

Striated muscle (EM)

I-band

Z-line

A-band

Mitochondrion

H-band

M-line

Sarcomere

An individual muscle is made up of hundreds of **muscle fibres**. These fibres are cylindrical in shape with a diameter of around 50 μm. They vary in length from a few millimetres to several centimetres. Each fibre has many nuclei and a distinctive pattern of bands or cross striations. It is bounded by a membrane – the **sarcolemma**. The fibres are composed of numerous **myofibrils** arranged parallel to one another. Each repeating unit of cross striations is called a **sarcomere** and in mammals has a length of 2.5–3.0 μm. The cytoplasm of the myofibril is known as **sarcoplasm** and possesses a system of membranes called the **sarcoplasmic reticulum**.

The myofibril has alternating dark and light bands known as the **anisotropic** and **isotropic** bands respectively. Confusion between their names can be avoided by reference to the following:

D	L
Anisotropic band	**Isotropic band**
R	G
K	H
	T

Each isotropic (light) band possesses a central line called the **Z line** and the distance between adjacent Z lines is a **sarcomere**. Each anisotropic (dark) band has at its centre a lighter region called the **H zone**, which may itself have a central dark line – the **M line**. This pattern of bands is the result of the arrangement of the two types of protein found in a myofibril. **Myosin** is made

489

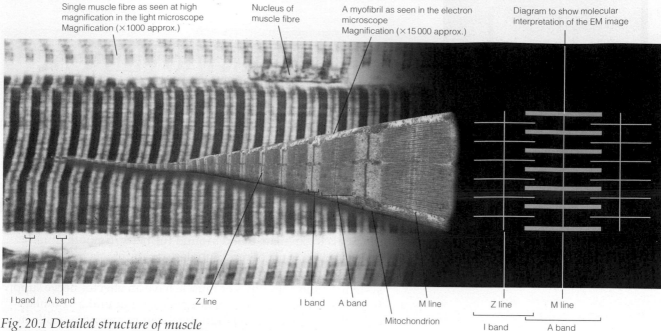

Single muscle fibre as seen at high magnification in the light microscope Magnification (×1000 approx.)

Nucleus of muscle fibre

A myofibril as seen in the electron microscope Magnification (×15 000 approx.)

Diagram to show molecular interpretation of the EM image

I band | A band | Z line | I band | A band | M line | Z line | M line

Mitochondrion

I band | A band

Fig. 20.1 Detailed structure of muscle

Did you know?

Skeletal muscle is the body's most abundant tissue accounting for 23% of the body weight in women and 40% in men.

PROJECT

If you are right-handed presumably you use your right hand more (left-handed people are of course the other way around).

1. Compare muscle strength in left and right hands.

2. Is there any relationship between muscle strength in the hand and handedness?

up of thick filaments and **actin** of thin ones. Where the two types overlap, the appearance of the muscle fibre is much darker. Anisotropic bands are therefore made up of both actin and myosin filaments whereas the isotropic band is made up solely of actin filaments. These arrangements and the overall structure of skeletal muscle are shown in Fig. 20.1.

Myosin filaments are approximately 10 nm in diameter and 2.5 μm long. They consist of a long rod-shaped fibre and a bulbous head which projects to the side of the fibre. These heads are of major significance in the contraction of muscle (Section 20.2.1). Actin filaments are thinner and slightly shorter than those of myosin being approximately 5 nm in diameter and 2.0 μm long. The filaments comprise two different strands of actin molecules twisted around one another. Associated with these filaments are two other proteins: **tropomyosin**, which forms a fibrous strand around the actin filament, and **troponin**, a globular protein vital to contraction of muscle fibre.

20.1.1 The neuromuscular junction

Skeletal muscle will not contract of its own accord but must be stimulated to do so by an impulse from an effector nerve. The point where the effector nerve meets a skeletal muscle is called the **neuromuscular junction** or **end plate**. If there were only one junction of this type it would take time for a wave of contraction to travel across the muscle and so not all the fibres would contract simultaneously and the movement would be slow. As rapid contraction is frequently essential for survival, animals have evolved a system whereby there are many end plates spread throughout a muscle. These simultaneously stimulate a group of fibres known as an **effector (motor) unit**; contraction of the muscle is thus rapid and powerful. This arrangement also gives control over the force generated by a muscle as not all the units need be stimulated at one time. If only slight force is needed only a few units will be stimulated. The structure of an end plate is shown in Fig. 20.2.

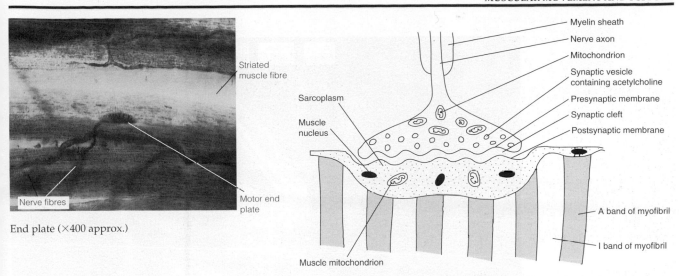

Fig. 20.2 Neuromuscular junction – the end plate

When a nerve impulse is received at the end plate, synaptic vesicles fuse with the end plate membrane and release their acetylcholine. The transmitter diffuses across to the sarcolemma where it alters its permeability to sodium ions which now rapidly enter, depolarizing the membrane. Provided the threshold value is exceeded, an action potential is fired in the muscle fibre and the effector (motor) unit served by the end plate contracts. Breakdown of the acetylcholine by acetylcholinesterase ensures that the muscle is not over-stimulated and the sarcolemma becomes repolarized. This sequence of events is much the same as the mechanism of synaptic transmission (Section 19.2.2).

20.2 Muscular contraction

Muscle cells have the ability to contract when stimulated and are therefore able to exert a force in one direction. Before a muscle can be contracted a second time, it must relax and be extended by the action of another muscle. This means that muscles operate in pairs with each member of the pair acting in the opposite direction to the other. These muscle pairs are termed **antagonistic**. Muscles may be classified according to the type of movement they bring about. For example, a **flexor** muscle bends a limb, whereas an **extensor** straightens it. Flexors and extensors therefore form an antagonistic pair. These and other types of skeletal muscle are listed in Table 20.1.

Skeletal muscle, as the name suggests, is attached to bone. This attachment is by means of **tendons** which are connective tissue made up largely of **collagen fibres**. Collagen is relatively inelastic and extremely tough. When a muscle is contracted, the tendons do not stretch and so the force is entirely transmitted to the bone. Each muscle is attached to a bone at both ends. One attachment, called the **origin**, is fixed to a rigid part of the skeleton, while the other, the **insertion**, is attached to a moveable part. There may be a number of points of insertion and/or origin. For example, two antagonistic muscles which bend the arm about the elbow are the

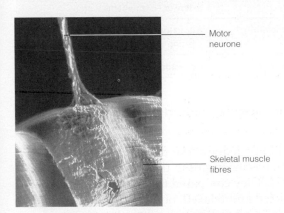

End plate (×400 approx.)

Scanning EM of a neuromuscular junction (×3600 approx.)

Did you know?

There are more than 600 voluntary muscles in the human body.

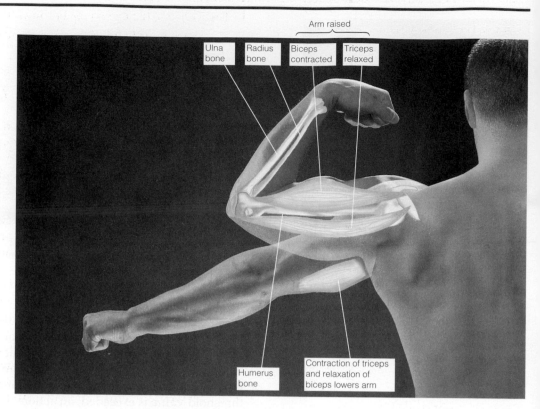

Fig. 20.3 Antagonistic muscles of the forearm

biceps (flexor) and **triceps** (extensor). The biceps has two origins both on the scapula (shoulder blade) and a single insertion on the radius. The triceps has three origins, two on the humerus and one on the scapula and a single insertion on the ulna. These arrangements are illustrated in Fig. 20.3.

TABLE 20.1 **Antagonistic pairs of muscles and the movements they perform**

Muscle action	Opposing muscle action
Flexor – bends a limb	**Extensor** – straightens a limb
Abductor – moves a limb laterally away from the body	**Adductor** – moves a limb from a lateral position in towards the body
Protractor – moves a limb forwards	**Retractor** – moves a limb backwards

20.2.1 Mechanism of muscular contraction – the sliding filament theory

Much of our present knowledge about the mechanism of muscular contraction has its origins in the work of H. E. Huxley and J. Hanson in 1954. They compared the appearance of striated muscle when contracted and relaxed, observing that the length of the anisotropic band (A band) remained unaltered. They concluded that the filaments of actin and myosin must in some way slide past one another – the **sliding filament theory**. It appears that the actin filaments, and hence the Z lines to which they are attached, are pulled towards each other, sliding as they do over the myosin filaments. No shortening of either type of filament occurs. These changes are illustrated in Fig. 20.4. From this diagram it should be clear that upon contraction the following can be observed in the appearance of a muscle fibre:

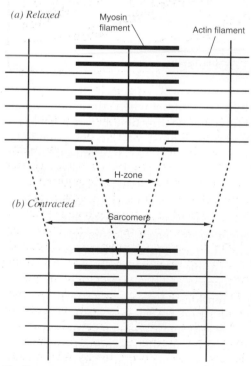

The H-zone, sarcomere and I-band all shorten. The A-band is unaltered

Fig. 20.4 Changes in appearance of a sarcomere during muscle contraction

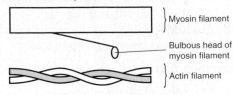

(a) *The head of the myosin molecule is 'cocked' ready to attach to the actin filament*

Myosin filament

Bulbous head of myosin filament

Actin filament

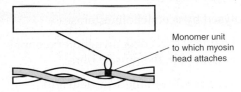

(b) *Myosin head attaches to a monomer unit on the actin molecule*

Monomer unit to which myosin head attaches

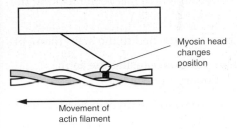

(c) *The myosin changes position in order to attain a lower energy state. In doing so it slides the actin filament past the stationary myosin filament*

Myosin head changes position

Movement of actin filament

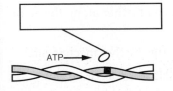

(d) *The myosin head detaches from the actin filament as a result of an ATP molecule fixing to the myosin head*

ATP

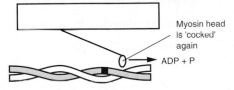

(e) *The ATP provides the energy to cause the myosin head to be 'cocked' again. The hydrolysis of the ATP gives rise to ADP + P*

Myosin head is 'cocked' again

ADP + P

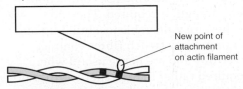

(f) *The 'cocked' head of the myosin filament reattaches further along the actin filament and the cycle of events is repeated*

New point of attachment on actin filament

Fig. 20.5 Sliding filament mechanism of muscle contraction

1. The isotropic band (I band) becomes shorter.
2. The anisotropic band (A band) does not change in length.
3. The Z lines become closer together, i.e. the sarcomere shortens.
4. The H zone shortens.

How exactly do the actin and myosin filaments slide past one another? The explanation seems to be related to cross bridges between the two types of filament, which can be observed in photoelectronmicrographs of muscle fibres. The bulbous heads along the myosin filaments form these bridges, and they appear to carry out a type of 'rowing' action along the actin filaments. The sequence of events involved in these movements is shown in Fig. 20.5.

Each myosin filament has a number of these bulbous heads and each progressively moves the actin filament along, as it becomes attached and reattached. This process is similar to the way in which a ratchet operates and for this reason it is often termed a **ratchet mechanism**. The result of this process is the contraction of a muscle or **twitch**. Having contracted, the muscle then relaxes. In this condition the myosin heads are drawn back towards the myosin filament and the fibrous tropomyosin blocks the attachment sites of the actin filament (Fig. 20.6). This prevents linking of myosin to actin and so stops further muscle contraction. As the separation of the myosin and actin requires the binding of ATP to the myosin head, and as this can only be produced in a living organism, the muscles at death remain contracted. This results in a stiffening of the body known as **rigor mortis**.

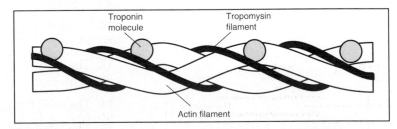

Troponin molecule

Tropomysin filament

Actin filament

Fig. 20.6 Relationship of tropomyosin and troponin to the actin filament

Before a relaxed muscle may be contracted again, the actin filament must be unblocked by somehow moving the tropomyosin so that the myosin heads may once again bind with it. When a muscle is stimulated the wave of depolarization created spreads, not only along the sarcolemma but also throughout a series of small tubes known as the **T-system**. The T-system is in contact with the sarcoplasmic reticulum, both of which are rich in calcium ions (Ca^{2+}). On depolarization they both release these ions. The calcium so released binds to part of a protein molecule called **troponin**. This causes the troponin to change shape and in so doing move the tropomyosin molecule away from the actin filament. This unblocks the actin and so allows the myosin head to become attached to it, causing the muscle to contract. The calcium ions are then actively pumped back into the sarcoplasmic reticulum and T-system ready for use in initiating further muscle contractions.

The energy for muscle contraction is provided by ATP which is formed by oxidative phosphorylation during the respiratory breakdown of glucose. The supply of glucose is provided from the store of glycogen found in muscles. The resynthesis of ATP after its hydrolysis requires a substance called **phosphocreatine**.

The contraction of muscle is apparently brought about by utilizing the energy stored in ATP

1. Suggest a hypothesis that you could test.

2. Design and carry out an experiment which investigates the contraction of muscle fibres from meat using different concentrations of ATP.

20.2.2 Summary of muscle contraction

The events described fit the observed facts of muscle contraction. Further research may reveal additional detail, but the basic mechanism is unlikely to be modified. In view of the complexity of the process, a summary of the main stages is given below:

1. Impulse reaches the neuromuscular junction (end plate).

2. Synaptic vesicles fuse with the end-plate membrane and release a transmitter (e.g. acetylcholine).

3. Acetylcholine depolarizes the sarcolemma.

4. Acetylcholine is hydrolysed by acetylcholinesterase.

5. Provided the threshold value is exceeded, an action potential (wave of depolarization) is created in the muscle fibre.

6. Calcium ions (Ca^{2+}) are released from the T-system and sarcoplasmic reticulum.

7. Calcium ions bind to troponin, changing its shape.

8. Troponin displaces tropomyosin which has been blocking the actin filament.

9. The myosin heads now become attached to the actin filament.

10. The myosin head changes position, causing the actin filaments to slide past the stationary myosin ones.

11. An ATP molecule becomes fixed to the myosin head, causing it to become detached from the actin.

12. Hydrolysis of ATP provides energy for the myosin head to be 'cocked'.

13. The myosin head becomes reattached further along the actin filament.

14. The muscle contracts by means of this ratchet mechanism.

15. The following changes in the muscle fibre occur:
  (a) I band shortens;
  (b) Z lines move closer together (i.e. sarcomere shortens);
  (c) H zone shortens.

16. Calcium ions are actively absorbed back into the T-system.

17. Troponin reverts to its original shape, allowing tropomyosin to again block the actin filament.

18. Phosphocreatine is used to regenerate ATP.

20.2.3 Slow and fast skeletal muscle fibres

There are two kinds of fibre in skeletal muscle. **Fast twitch fibres** contract quickly providing powerful and intense contractions and are hence useful where strength is required. They do however fatigue easily as they are vulnerable to a build up of lactic acid which causes cramp. **Slow twitch fibres** contract more slowly and less powerfully and are hence useful where sustained endurance is required rather than strength as they do not tire easily. Each muscle of the body contains both types of fibre, although the proportion of each varies according to the function that the muscle is usually called on to perform.

20.3   Skeleton and support

Organisms originally evolved in water which gave support. When organisms colonized land, where air provides little support, a skeleton was also necessary to support them against the pull of gravity. Skeletons fulfil three main functions: support, locomotion and protection.

20.3.1 Structure of bone

As bones are usually observed in their dried state, they often give the impression of dead, immutable structures. In fact they are living tissue which is very plastic; capable of moulding itself to meet the mechanical requirements demanded of it. The matrix of compact bone is made up of collagen together with inorganic substances such as calcium, magnesium and phosphorus. These components are arranged in concentric circles, called **lamellae**, around an **Haversian canal** containing an artery, a vein, lymph vessels and nerve fibres. Bone cells, or **osteocytes**, are found in spaces in the lamellae known as **lacunae** and fine channels called **canaliculi** link lacunae. The system of lamellae around one Haversian canal is called an **Haversian system**. Bone is an extremely important and strong skeletal material. It is not static. Its various inorganic components may be deposited or absorbed at different times to meet new stresses put upon the tissue.

When a bone, e.g. the femur, is examined in detail, it is found to have a complex internal structure. There is a hollow shaft, the **diaphysis**, which contains **marrow**, a tissue producing various kinds of blood cell. At each end is an expanded head, the **epiphysis**, which articulates with other bones or to which tendons are attached. While the diaphysis and epiphysis are composed of **hard (compact) bone**, the remainder of the structure is made up of **spongy (cancellous) bone**. This has a honeycomb appearance and provides strength with a minimum of additional mass. A tough, fibrous membrane, the **periosteum**, surrounds the bone. The structure of the femur is shown in Fig. 20.8.

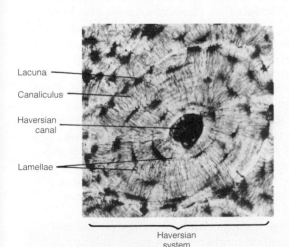

Lacuna
Canaliculus
Haversian canal
Lamellae
Haversian system

Compact bone (TS) (×400 approx.)

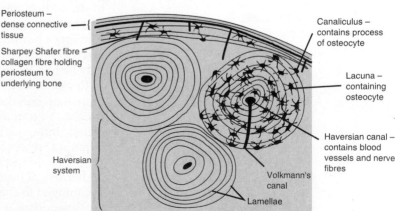

Periosteum – dense connective tissue

Sharpey Shafer fibre = collagen fibre holding periosteum to underlying bone

Haversian system

Canaliculus – contains process of osteocyte

Lacuna – containing osteocyte

Haversian canal – contains blood vessels and nerve fibres

Volkmann's canal

Lamellae

Fig. 20.7 Compact bone (TS)

FOCUS

Osteoporosis and HRT

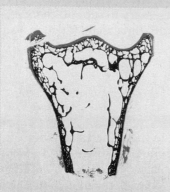

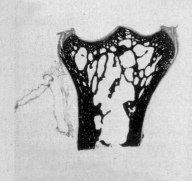

Normal bone (top) and (above) bone showing effects of osteoporosis

Factors which can increase the rise of osteoporosis

- Early menopause
- History of osteoporosis in the family
- Low calcium diet
- High protein diet
- Low fluoride diet
- Smoking
- Lack of exercise
- Excess alcohol intake

Bone is made up of an organic matrix and minerals. The matrix is mainly collagen fibres and the minerals calcium and phosphorus in the form of hydroxyaptite crystals. The surface of bone is covered in cells which continuously remodel it by removing old bone and forming new bone. If the cells remove more bone than is replaced there will be a loss of bone volume which leads to a weakening of the skeleton. This condition is known as osteoporosis.

In the United Kingdom 50% of post-menopausal women will have hip, vertebral or forearm fractures that can be attributed to osteoporosis. Worldwide about 1.7 million people, mostly women, suffer hip fractures as a result of thinning bones – a figure expected to rise to 6 million by 2050.

Long bones consist of an outer layer of cortical bone around the medulla. The latter comprises fat and haemopoietic cells (blood-forming cells) criss-crossed by struts of trabecular bone.

In post-menopausal women the volume of cortical and trabecular bone declines leading to osteoporosis. This has been linked to a fall in their oestrogen production which alters the balance between bone resorption and bone formation.

HRT (hormone replacement therapy) was introduced as a short-term treatment to mitigate the immediate symptoms of the menopause, like hot flushes and night sweats, but the medical indications for HRT have expanded. Some American studies indicate that oestrogen therapy can reduce the chance of fractures resulting from brittle bones, or osteoporosis, as well as halving a woman's risk of suffering a heart attack or stroke. Oestrogen supplements undoubtedly benefit bone density in older women but the hormones may have to be taken for 5 years before they offer any protection against fractures and their effect may decline rapidly when the supplement is stopped. However, oestrogen cannot be the only factor influencing osteoporosis since fracture rates in the western world for both men and women have trebled in the last 30 years.

Some researchers believe that diet plays an important rôle in the prevention of osteoporosis, advocating a diet containing legumes (rich in natural oestrogens) and foods high in vitamin D, like oily fish. Physical exercise also looks promising as an aid in the prevention of osteoporosis, helping to strengthen bones in the elderly. There is even a suggestion that middle-age spread can be good for you! Fat tissue converts a hormone from the adrenal gland into an oestrogenic one so severe dieting in post-menopausal women may be bad for the bones.

Recent research suggests that genes are responsible for more than half the variation in bone density in different people. A group of Australian scientists believes 75% of this genetic influence is the result of a single gene – that for a vitamin D receptor. If the Australians prove to be right, a simple blood test should be enough to identify people at higher risk of brittle bones. Teenagers at risk could be encouraged to change their diet and get more exercise and post-menopausal women might be encouraged to take oestrogen replacement therapy.

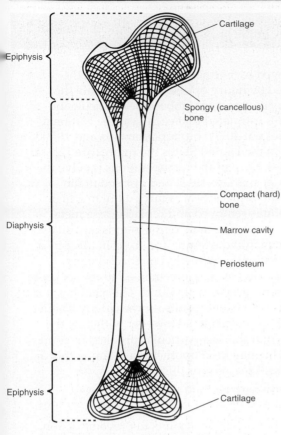

Fig. 20.8 Vertical section through the human femur

Bone has a number of functions:

1. Providing a framework for supporting the body.

2. Providing a means of attachment for muscles which then operate the bones as a system of levers for locomotion.

3. Protecting delicate parts of the body, e.g. the rib cage protects the heart and lungs; the cranium protects the brain.

4. Acting as a reservoir for calcium and phosphorus salts, helping to maintain a constant level in the bloodstream.

5. Producing red blood cells and certain white cells, e.g. granulocytes.

20.3.2 Growth of bone

The skeleton of a human fetus is made up of cartilage which has the same basic shape as the bones it will form. Calcium salts are gradually laid down in the gel-like matrix of this cartilage template in a process called **ossification**. The bones are constantly remodelled as they grow until they assume the characteristic shape and proportions of the adult skeleton. Even then the bones are not static, being constantly changed in shape, size and density to meet the stresses and strains placed upon them. Exercise for example will increase the rate of bone deposition on those parts of the skeleton put under stress. Athletes therefore usually have stronger, denser bones than less active individuals. This constant reshaping of bones is achieved by the activities of **osteoblasts** – cells which lay down bone – and **osteoclasts** – cells which reabsorb bone.

20.3.3 Joints

The skeleton has to fulfil two conflicting functions. On the one hand, it needs to be rigid in order to provide support and attachment for muscles; on the other hand, it needs to be flexible in order to permit movement. In the case of bony endoskeletons this paradox is overcome by having a series of flexible joints between the individual bones of the skeleton. The various types of joint found in a human skeleton can be classified into three groups according to the degree of movement possible:

1. Immoveable (suture) joints – No movement is possible between the bones.

2. Partly moveable (gliding) joints – Only a little movement is possible between individual bones.

3. Moveable (synovial) joints – There is considerable freedom of movement between bones; the actual amount depends upon the precise nature of the joint.

The different joints found in mammals are described in Table 20.2.

In moveable joints, the ends of the bones are covered with a layer of **cartilage**. This prevents damage to the articulating surfaces of bones as a result of friction between them. The joint is surrounded by a fibrous covering called the **synovial capsule**.

FOCUS

Artificial joints

Joints may be damaged by normal wear and tear but the process is accelerated by injury or disease. Commonly the cartilage wears away and movement becomes difficult and painful. In Britain it is estimated that each year the National Health Service carries out 40 000 hip replacements and 16 000 knee replacements; in the United States the figures are 123 000 hips and 95 000 knees. Most of the hip operations involve the Charnley hip, made of stainless steel, and devised in the 1960s. Often a total hip replacement is carried out in which the patient's own joint is removed and replaced by a metal **prosthesis** (artificial part). The 'ball' of the joint is on a shaft which is pushed down into the femur and fixed in place by a cold-setting acrylic cement (polymethyl methacrylate or PMMA). A rigid polyethylene cup is cemented to the socket of the pelvis with the same acrylic compound. This joint has, for many years, produced excellent results for the elderly, lasting 10 to 15 years without replacement. However with time the joint can work loose and this is a particular problem in young and active people who may need another operation within 5 years. There are several reasons for this:

1. Bone bends slightly with use and the stainless steel prosthesis does not.

2. Polyethylene is used on artificial joints to prevent friction. As this wears away, particles build up in the joint and cause inflammation which stimulates osteoclasts (bone destroying cells) to start absorbing bone.

3. The body's immune system responds to the new materials stimulating weak fibrous, rather than bone, repair.

There is now much research into the use of new alloys for replacement joints. A cobalt–chromium alloy is widely used in America and Sweden. This is more resistant to corrosion than stainless steel and can be worked into complex shapes.

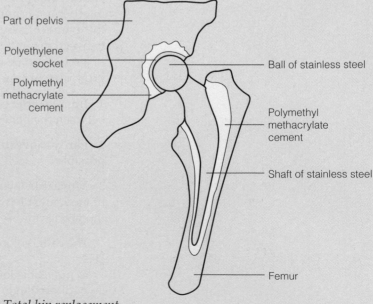

Part of pelvis

Polyethylene socket

Polymethyl methacrylate cement

Ball of stainless steel

Polymethyl methacrylate cement

Shaft of stainless steel

Femur

Total hip replacement

FOCUS continued

Most promising, however, is titanium, often used as an alloy with vanadium and aluminium. Although titanium is soft its 'bendiness' can be an advantage in younger patients. Most important though is its biocompatibility. A stable and unreactive layer of oxide is present on its surface and this reforms within nanoseconds if it is scratched, even when surrounded by body fluids. This oxide layer does not provoke an immune response, so normal bone repair can take place forming a strong bond between the implant and the bone. This is known as **osseointegration** and is thought by many to provide a stronger bond than any cement. There are also trials on the use of growth hormones to stimulate bone repair and the simultaneous transplantation of bone marrow. Breathing in extra oxygen increases the oxygen supply to the bone and appears to promote healing.

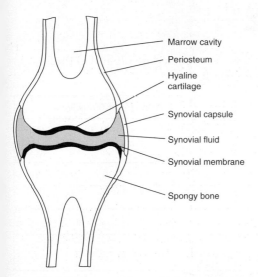

- Marrow cavity
- Periosteum
- Hyaline cartilage
- Synovial capsule
- Synovial fluid
- Synovial membrane
- Spongy bone

Fig. 20.9 Structure of a typical synovial joint

The inner lining of this capsule is known as the **synovial membrane**. It secretes a mucus-containing lubricant fluid called **synovial fluid** which also provides nutrients for the cartilage at the ends of the bones. The structure of a typical synovial joint is illustrated in Fig. 20.9.

The bones of a joint are held together by means of strong, but elastic, **ligaments**.

TABLE 20.2 **Joints of the human skeleton**

Name of joint	Type of joint	Example
Suture	Immoveable	Between the bones of the cranium Between the sacrum and ilia of the pelvic girdle
Gliding	Partly moveable	Between adjacent vertebrae In the wrist and ankle
Pivot	Partly moveable	Between the axis and atlas vertebrae
Hinge	Synovial	In the elbow and knee In the fingers and toes
Ball and socket	Synovial	At the shoulder and hip

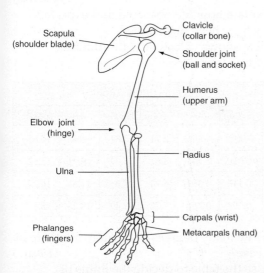

- Scapula (shoulder blade)
- Clavicle (collar bone)
- Shoulder joint (ball and socket)
- Humerus (upper arm)
- Elbow joint (hinge)
- Radius
- Ulna
- Phalanges (fingers)
- Carpals (wrist)
- Metacarpals (hand)

Fig. 20.10 Arrangement of bones in the pectoral girdle (shoulder) and the forelimb of a human

20.4   Questions

1. The photograph is a photomicrograph showing a longitudinal section of striated muscle.

(a) Describe **one** way in which this muscle differs from cardiac muscle.   (*1 mark*)

(b) The photomicrograph is magnified 200 times. What is the diameter in micrometres of the myofibril indicated at the point **A**? Show your working.   (*2 marks*)

(c) Make a drawing of three adjacent sarcomeres from the myofibril labelled **B**. Labels are not required.   (*3 marks*)

(d) Describe how you would expect the appearance of the sarcomeres to differ if:

(i) the muscle were treated with a myosin solvent before the slide was prepared; (*1 mark*)

(ii) the slide had been prepared from contracted muscle instead of relaxed muscle.   (*2 marks*)

A study was carried out to investigate the effect of exercise on the biceps muscle. A sample of 100 young men aged between 18 and 20 years was selected because they did not participate in any active sport.

The arm circumference of each of these subjects was measured at a point midway between elbow and shoulder. It was assumed that the circumference of the biceps muscle bore a constant relationship to arm circumference.

The subjects were then given a two-month work programme designed to exercise their biceps muscles. At the end of this period their arm circumferences were measured again.

The results of the study are shown in the frequency table.

Arm circumference/cm	Number of people in this category	
	Before exercise	After exercise
30–30.9	59	7
31–31.9	36	30
32–32.9	5	63

(e) A χ^2 test was used to test the hypothesis that exercise has no effect on the circumference of the arm.

(i) Copy and complete the table below to calculate the value of χ^2 from the equation

$$\chi^2 = \sum \frac{(O - E)^2}{E}$$

where E is the expected result and O the observed result.

	Arm circumference/cm		
	30–30.9	31–31.9	32–32.9
O	7	30	63
E	59	36	5
$O - E$			
$(O - E)^2$			
$\dfrac{(O - E)^2}{2}$			

$\chi^2 =$ (*2 marks*)

(ii) Explain how the observed and expected figures have been determined.   (*2 marks*)

(f) The table shows values of χ^2 for different degrees of freedom.

Degrees of freedom	Probability value					
	0.99	0.95	0.1	0.05	0.01	0.001
1	0.0001	0.0039	2.71	3.84	6.63	10.83
2	0.020	0.103	4.61	5.99	9.21	13.82
3	0.115	0.352	6.25	7.81	11.34	16.27
4	0.297	0.711	7.78	9.49	13.28	18.47

(i) How many degrees of freedom are there in this case?   (*1 mark*)

(ii) Use the table to decide the limits of probability between which your value of χ^2 falls.   (*1 mark*)

(iii) What information does this give you about the biological significance of the results?
(*2 marks*)

(g) What changes would you expect in the muscle as a result of long-term exercise? (*7 marks*)
(*Total 24 marks*)

AEB June 1993, Paper 2, No. 2

2. Write an essay on:
The structure and functions of bone. (*24 marks*)

AEB June 1992, Paper 2, No. 4(a)

3. Compare and contrast the structure and function of the three types of muscle. (*24 marks*)

AEB June 1994, Paper 2, No. 4(b)

4. (*a*) The photographs show an X-ray of an adult hand (**A**) and that of a very young child (**B**).

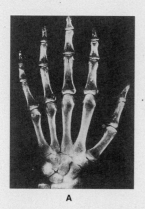
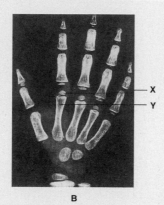

A   **B**

Using the information in the X-rays suggest:
(i) the role of the gap between structures **X** and **Y** on hand **B**: (*1 mark*)
(ii) **one** other piece of evidence which shows that hand **B** is from a younger person than hand **A**. (*1 mark*)
(*b*) The diagram shows the left hand of an adult and two muscles which move the thumb.

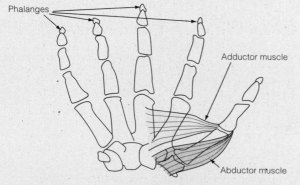

(i) Describe how the thumb can be moved towards the other phalanges. (*1 mark*)

(ii) What advantage do humans have over non-primates in being able to move the thumb in this way? Explain your answer. (*2 marks*)
(*Total 5 marks*)

AEB June 1995, Paper 1, No. 12

5. The diagram below shows the bones of the pelvic region in a person who has had a hip replacement operation.

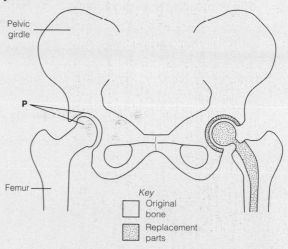

(*a*) Describe the movement which is possible at the joint labelled **P**. (*1 mark*)
(*b*) Explain how friction is reduced in each of the following.
(i) The natural joint (*2 marks*)
(ii) The artificial joint (*2 marks*)
(*c*) Suggest why natural joints usually last for the lifetime of the individual whereas artificial joints do not. (*3 marks*)
(*Total 8 marks*)

ULEAC June 1993, Paper 3, No. 5

6. Fig. 1 shows a sarcomere from a skeletal muscle. Fig. 2 shows a cross-section through this sarcomere as it would appear when seen on an electron micrograph.

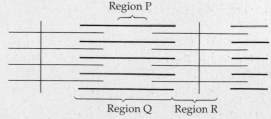

Fig. 1

Fig. 2

(a) Draw a line on Fig. 1 to show from where the cross-section in Fig. 2 was taken.   (1 mark)

(b) Name the main protein found in region **P**.
                                                              (1 mark)

(c) When the muscle contracts, what happens to the length of:
    (i) region **Q**;   (1 mark)
    (ii) region **R**?   (1 mark)

(d) Explain why there is an increase in the rate of respiration of muscle when it contracts.   (3 marks)
                                                              (Total 7 marks)

NEAB June 1995, Paper BY04, No. 4

7. Write an essay on support and movement in animals.

ULEAC June 1996, Paper HB6, No. 11

8. The diagram shows a sarcomere from an myofibril of a striated muscle fibre.

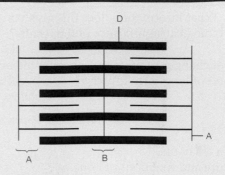

(a) (i) Name the regions labelled A, B and C.
                                                              (3 marks)
    (ii) Name the material which makes up part D.
                                                              (1 mark)

(b) State the change in appearance of B when the muscle fibre contracts.   (1 mark)
                                                              (Total 5 marks)

ULEAC June 1996, Paper HB3, No. 1

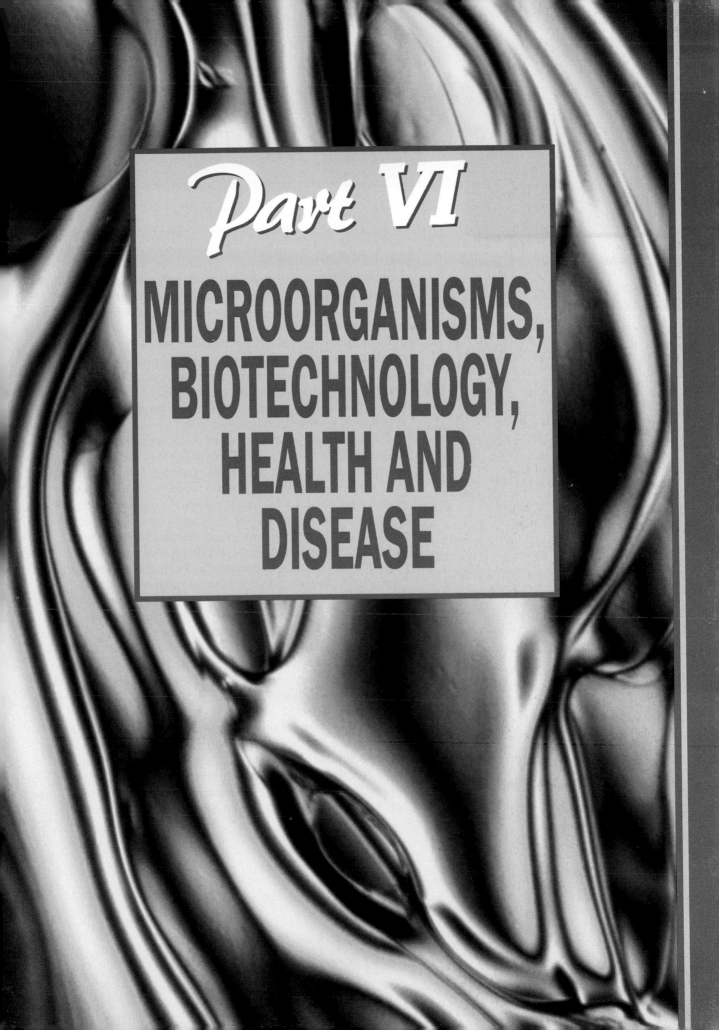

Part VI

MICROORGANISMS, BIOTECHNOLOGY, HEALTH AND DISEASE

Microorganisms

The name 'microorganism' is a general descriptive term rather than a specific scientific one. It refers to those organisms which are not clearly visible to the naked eye. As such it includes representatives from all three of the biological kingdoms, namely all the Prokaryotae, and some members of the Protoctista and the Fungi, as well as all viruses whose place in biological classification is still somewhat uncertain. If microorganisms share the feature of small size, they have little else in common, being very varied in structure and function. Despite the lack of any real biological coherence, the term is nevertheless a convenient, and well-understood, one.

If the structure and functions of microorganisms are diverse, so too are their effects. On the one hand, they are beneficial, indeed essential, to our continued existence; while on the other they are frequently the cause of our demise. Their role in decomposition and recycling is essential to life, while their use in the production of bread, wine, beer and cheese has benefited mankind since ancient times. More recently humans have utilized microorganisms in the production of antibiotics, hormones, fuels and other materials. Their role in genetic engineering may yet prove to be their most significant.

On the other hand, microorganisms are the cause of fatal diseases such as cholera, typhoid, malaria, tuberculosis, influenza and AIDS. They are also a major contributor to famine through being agents of plant disease – the Irish potato famine of 1845–7 (caused by the fungus *Phytophthora infestans*) killed one million people through starvation. Their role in spoiling stored food further exacerbates the problem of feeding the world's population.

Our love–hate relationship with microorganisms may have become more affectionate in recent years as we have developed the biotechnology to exploit the activities of these minute life forms, but the capacity of most microorganisms to evolve rapidly and so thwart our attempts to eradicate the diseases they cause may prevent us becoming completely won over by them.

21 Microorganisms and biotechnology

Biotechnology is the application of scientific and engineering principles to the production of materials by biological agents. Given its recent wide publicity, one could be forgiven for thinking it was a new branch of science. While there is no doubt that recent technological and biochemical advances have led to considerable developments in biotechnology, its origins go back a long way. Food for human consumption has always been vulnerable to spoilage by microorganisms. Ancient civilizations probably found that normally detrimental microbial contamination occasionally conferred some benefit: improved flavour or better preservation for instance. In this way beers would have been developed from 'spoilt' grain and wine from 'spoilt' fruit. Contamination of the alcohol by a different agent led to the production of vinegar which was then used to preserve food. Cheese, butter and yoghurt all resulted from various microbial contaminations of milk.

The modern biotechnology industry had its origins in the First World War. A naval blockade deprived Germany of the supply of vegetable fats necessary for the production of glycerol from which explosives were made. They turned to the fermentation of plant material by yeast as an alternative source. At the same time, the British were using *Clostridium acetobutylicum* to produce acetone and butanol as part of their war effort. In a similar way, the Second World War prompted the mass production of the antibiotic penicillin (discovered by Alexander Fleming in 1929) using *Penicillium notatum*.

Many other chemicals were produced thereafter by use of fermentation techniques, but it was in the 1980s that biotechnology underwent major expansion. This was almost entirely due to the development of **recombinant DNA technology** (Section 5.7.1).

21.1 Classification of organisms

21.1.1 Principles of classification

Before any study can be made of living organisms it is necessary to devise a scheme whereby the enormous diversity of them can be organized into manageable groups. This grouping of organisms is known as **classification** and the study of biological classification is called **taxonomy**

TABLE 21.1 **Classification of humans**

Phylum	Chordata
Class	Mammalia
Order	Primates
Family	Hominidae
Genus	*Homo*
Species	*sapiens*

Taxonomic ranks

It is convenient to distinguish large groups of organisms from smaller subgroups and a series of rank names has been devised to identify the different levels within this hierarchy. The rank names used today are largely derived from those used by Linnaeus over 200 years ago. The largest groups are known as **phyla** and the organisms in each phylum have a body plan radically different from organisms in any other phylum. Diversity within each phylum allows it to be divided into **classes**. Each class is divided into **orders** of organisms which have additional features in common. Each order is divided into **families** and at this level differences are less obvious. Each family is divided into **genera** and each genus into **species**.

With the gradual acceptance that all species arose by adaptation of existing forms, the basis of this hierarchy became evolutionary. Species are groups that have diverged most recently, genera somewhat earlier and so on up the taxonomic ranks.

Every organism is given a scientific name according to an internationally agreed system of nomenclature, first devised by Linnaeus. The name is always in Latin and is in two parts. The first name indicates the genus and is written with an initial capital letter; the second name indicates the species and is written with a small initial letter. These names are always distinguished in text by italics or underlining. This system of naming organisms is known as **binomial nomenclature**.

Living organisms are divided into 5 kingdoms:

Prokaryotae, **Fungi**, **Protoctista**, **Plantae** and **Animalia**. It is difficult to fit viruses into this scheme of classification because they are on the border of living and non-living. For this reason they are dealt with separately.

TABLE 21.2 **Distinguishing features of the 5 kingdoms**

Kingdom	Features
Prokaryotae	Organisms which lack nuclei with membranes, lack envelope-bound organelles and ones with a 9 + 2 microtubule arrangement. Examples include bacteria and blue-green bacteria.
Protoctista	Single celled eukaryotic organisms or organisms which are assemblages of similar cells. A very varied group which includes nucleated algae, protozoa and slime moulds.
Fungi	Non-photosynthetic, eukaryotic organisms which feed heterotrophically using absorptive methods. Their cell walls contain chitin rather than cellulose and they are usually organized into a mycelium of hyphae. They store carbohydrates in the form of glycogen and reproduce by means of spores without flagella.
Plantae	Organisms which are made up of more than one eukaryotic cell which have walls containing cellulose. They photosynthesize using chlorophyll as their main pigment.
Animalia	Non-photosynthetic multicellular organisms with nervous coordination.

21.1.2 Viruses

Viruses are smaller than bacteria, ranging in size from about 20 nm to 300 nm. They cannot be seen through a light microscope and pass through filters which retain bacteria. Many can be crystallized and they can only multiply inside living cells. They do, however, contain nucleic acids such as DNA or RNA and must therefore be considered as being on the border between living and non-living. They are not classified with any other living organisms. They are made up of a nucleic acid core surrounded by a coat of protein called a **capsid** which is made up of subunits called **capsomeres**. Outside cells inert virus particles are known as **virions**. Most viruses found in human cells have the nucleic acid DNA. Other animal viruses and plant viruses contain RNA.

Viruses cause a variety of infectious diseases in humans, other animals and plants. The same virus may have quite different effects in different hosts and these symptoms may be influenced by environmental conditions.

Viral diseases are often difficult to treat because antibiotics cannot be used. Vaccines may be produced but these are not always effective because one virus may exist in a variety of forms. Methods of control therefore depend primarily on prevention, such as breeding resistant species, removal of the source of infection and the protection of susceptible plants and animals.

Life cycle of the influenza virus

The influenza virus is commonly found in the mucus lining of the respiratory tract. Its surface is covered with spikes of two types which are important in infection. The life cycle of the influenza virus is as follows:

1. The rod-shape spikes recognize specific receptor sites on the membrane of the host cell to which they bind.

2. The mushroom-shaped spikes are composed of an enzyme which breaks down the membrane of the host cell.

3. The caspid enters the cell where it breaks down into its constituent capsomeres and molecules of viral enzyme, thus releasing the RNA within it.

4. The RNA and viral enzyme enter the nucleus via a nuclear pore, where they prevent the host cell's DNA from operating in protein synthesis.

5. The viral RNA uses the viral enzyme to start replicating itself and the newly formed RNA acts as a code for the production of all the substances needed to make new influenza viruses.

6. The viral components are produced using the host cell's chemical machinery and assembled by the host cell.

7. Several thousand new influenza viruses are produced which burst out of the host cell to infect other epithelial cells in the respiratory tract. The whole cycle can take less than 24 hours.

It is the damage to the epithelial cells of the respiratory tract which give rise to the symptoms of influenza – sore throat, sneezing, coughing and an excessive discharge of mucus. As the

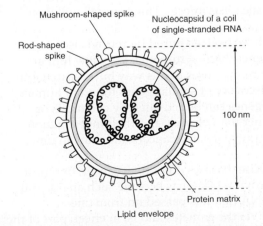

Fig. 21.1 Simplified diagram of an influenza virus

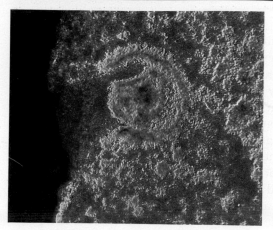

Transmission electron micrograph of a Human Immunodeficiency Virus (HIV) – shown in red – infecting a T-lymphocyte

number of viruses builds up they can be distributed by the bloodstream to other parts of the body giving rise to headache, muscular pain and fever. In the weak and elderly, influenza may cause death, frequently from secondary infections such as pneumonia.

21.1.3 Retroviruses

Probably the best known retrovirus is the Human Immunodeficiency virus (HIV) which causes AIDS (Acquired Immune Deficiency Syndrome), further details of which are given in Section 22.2.5.

The genetic information in a retrovirus is RNA. While many viruses possess RNA, retroviruses are different in that they can use it to synthesize DNA. This is a reversal of the usual genetic process in which RNA is made from DNA and the reason retroviruses are so called (*retro* = behind or backwards).

In 1970 the enzyme capable of synthesizing DNA from RNA was discovered and given the name **reverse transcriptase** (as it catalyses the opposite process to transcriptase which synthesizes RNA from DNA). The discovery of this enzyme, more details of which are given in Section 5.7.2, has considerable importance for genetic engineering.

The DNA form of the retrovirus genes is called the **provirus** and is significant in that it can be incorporated into the host's DNA. Here it may remain latent for long periods before the DNA of the provirus is again expressed and new viral RNA produced. During this time any division of the host cell results in the proviral DNA being duplicated as well. In this way the number of potential retroviruses can proliferate considerably. This explains why individuals infected with the HIV virus often display no symptoms for many years before suddenly developing full-blown AIDS.

When incorporated into the host DNA the provirus is capable of activating the host genes in its immediate vicinity. Where these genes are concerned with cell division or growth, and are 'switched off' at the time, their activation by the provirus can result in a malignant growth known as **cancer**. The RNA produced by these newly activated genes may become packaged inside new retrovirus particles being assembled inside the host cell. This RNA may then be delivered, along with the retroviral RNA, to the next cell the virus infects. This new cell will then become potentially cancerous.

Host genes which have been acquired by retroviruses in this way are called **oncogenes** (*oncos* = tumour). Very few human cancers are caused by retroviruses in this way but research into them has led to the discovery of similar genes found in human chromosomes. These genes can be activated by chemicals or forms of radiation rather than viruses, and their investigation has already helped to prevent some cancers and may, in time, provide a cure.

Retroviruses can cause diseases other than cancer, but most are harmless. Some proviral DNA has become such an integral part of the host-cell DNA that it is passed on from one generation to the next via the gametes and is, in effect, part of the host's genetic make-up. Such a virus is referred to as an **endogenous** virus.

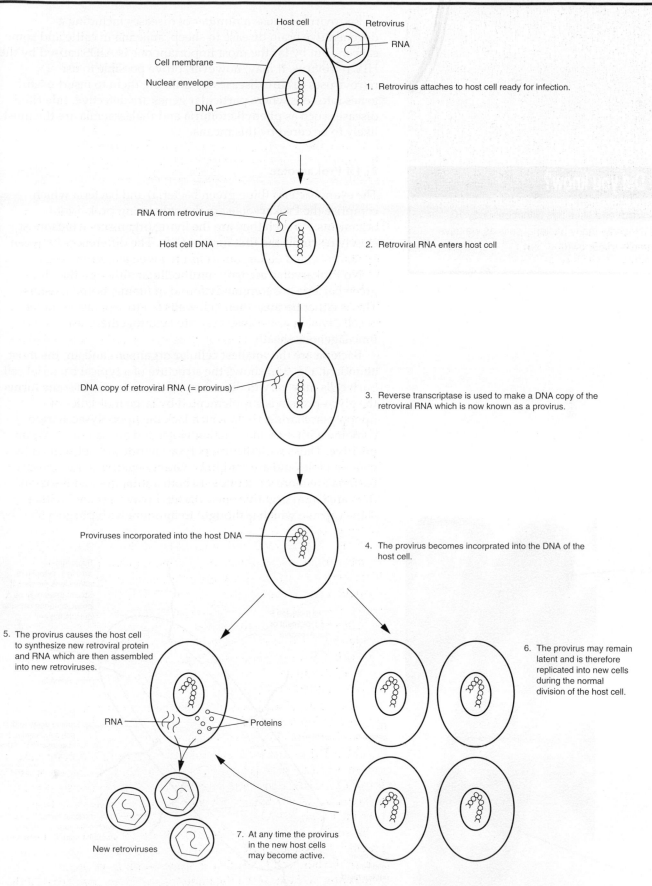

Fig. 21.2 Life cycle of a retrovirus

Retroviruses cause a number of diseases including a degenerative brain disease in sheep, anaemia in cattle and some cancers, but by far the most important one is AIDS caused by the HIV retrovirus. It may, however, prove possible to use retroviruses to cure diseases by utilizing them to insert useful genes into cells where particular genes are defective. Inherited diseases such as phenylketonuria and thalassaemia are the most likely to be cured by this means.

21.1.4 Prokaryotae

The cyanobacteria (blue-green bacteria) and bacteria which comprise the Prokaryotae are the only living prokaryotic organisms. As such they are the living organisms which most closely resemble the first forms of life. The differences between prokaryotic and eukaryotic cells are given in Section 4.1.2.

No Prokaryotae are truly multicellular although the blue-green bacteria are commonly found in filaments and clusters. This is either because their cell walls fail to separate completely at cell division or because they are held together by a mucilagenous sheath.

Bacteria are the smallest cellular organisms and are the most abundant. Fig. 21.3 shows the structure of a typical bacterial cell. Such cells may vary in the nature of the cell wall. In some forms the glyco-protein is supplemented by large molecules of lipopolysaccharide. Cells which lack the lipopolysaccharide combine with dyes like gentian violet and are said to be **Gram positive**. Those with the lipopolysaccharide are not stained by gentian violet and are said to be **Gram negative**. Gram positive bacteria are more susceptible to both antibiotics and lysozyme than are Gram negative ones. Bacteria may be coated with a slime capsule which is thought to interfere with phagocytosis by

> ### Did you know?
>
> Each one of us has within our body 10 times as many bacterial cells as we have cells of our own.

Cell wall

DNA

Cytoplasm

E. coli (EM) (×38 000 approx.)

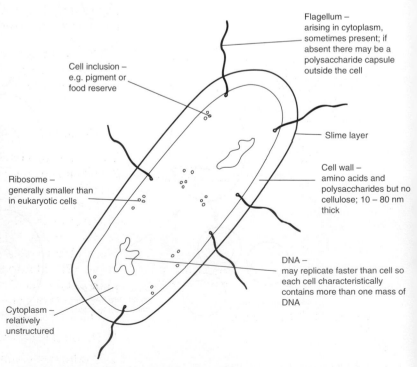

Flagellum – arising in cytoplasm, sometimes present; if absent there may be a polysaccharide capsule outside the cell

Cell inclusion – e.g. pigment or food reserve

Slime layer

Cell wall – amino acids and polysaccharides but no cellulose; 10 – 80 nm thick

Ribosome – generally smaller than in eukaryotic cells

DNA – may replicate faster than cell so each cell characteristically contains more than one mass of DNA

Cytoplasm – relatively unstructured

Fig. 21.3 Generalized bacterial cell

the white blood cells. Bacteria are generally distinguished from each other by their shape. Spherical ones are known as **cocci** (singular – coccus), rod-shaped as **bacilli** (singular – bacillus) and spiral ones as **spirilla** (singular – spirillum).

Cocci may stick together in chains – **streptococcus**, or in clusters – **staphylococcus**. Bacteria show considerable diversity in their metabolism. The majority are heterotrophic and most of these are saprobionts. They are responsible, with the Fungi, for decaying and recycling organic material in the soil. Others are parasitic, some causing disease but many having little effect on their host. Numerous gut bacteria have a symbiotic relationship with their host, for example helping to digest the cellulose ingested by ruminants.

Bacteria reproduce by binary fission, one cell being capable of giving rise to over 4×10^{21} cells in 24 hours. Under certain circumstances conjugation occurs and new combinations of genetic material result. Bacteria may also produce thick-walled spores which are highly resistant, often surviving drought and extremes of temperature.

It is easy to think of all bacteria as pathogens but it is important to remember that many are beneficial to humans. These benefits include:

1. The breakdown of plant and animal remains and the recycling of nitrogen, carbon and phosphorus.

2. Symbiotic relationships with other organisms. For example supplying vitamin K and some of the vitamin B complex in humans, breaking down cellulose in herbivores.

3. Food production, e.g. some cheeses, yoghurts, vinegar.

4. Manufacturing processes, e.g. making soap powders, tanning leather and retting flax to make linen.

5. They are easily cultured and may be used for research, particularly in genetics. They are also used for making antibiotics, amino acids, enzymes and SCP (single cell protein).

Detrimental effects of bacteria include deterioration of stored food and damage to buried metal pipes caused by sulphuric acid production by *Thiobacillus* and *Desulphovibrio*.

21.1.5 Fungi

The Fungi are a large group of organisms composed of about 80 000 named species. For many years they were classified with the plants but are now recognized as a separate kingdom. This separation is based on the presence of the polysaccharide chitin found in their cell walls, rather than the cellulose present in plant cell walls. Their bodies are usually a **mycelium** of thread-like multinucleate **hyphae** without distinct cell boundaries. The Fungi lack chlorophyll and are therefore unable to photosynthesize. They feed heterotrophically, generally as saprobionts or parasites.

Many fungi are beneficial to humans. Examples include:

1. Decomposition of sewage and organic material in the soil.

2. Production of antibiotics, notably from *Penicillium* and *Aspergillus*.

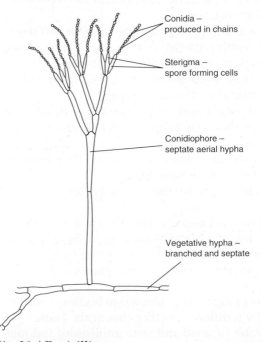

Conidia –
produced in chains

Sterigma –
spore forming cells

Conidiophore –
septate aerial hypha

Vegetative hypha –
branched and septate

Fig. 21.4 Penicillium

3. Production of alcohol for drinking and industry.

4. Production of other foods. Citric acid for lemonade is produced by the fermentation of glucose by *Aspergillus*. Yeasts are used in bread production and the food yeast *Candida utilis* has been investigated as a source of single cell protein (SCP).

5. Experimental use, especially for genetic investigations.

Many fungi are also harmful to humans, causing decomposition of stored foods and deterioration of natural materials such as leather and wood. Fungi more commonly cause disease in plants than in animals but some of the plants infected are of great economic importance to humans. Powdery mildew, caused by *Erysiphe graminae*, causes serious damage to cereal crops.

21.1.6 Protoctista

The kingdom Protoctista is made up of single celled eukaryotic organisms or organisms which are assemblages of similar cells. Apart from this one common feature the kingdom is very varied and includes all nucleated algae, all protozoa and slime moulds. In this section the algae will be used to illustrate the group.

The algae are a varied group of phyla with no one diagnostic feature. They are normally aquatic or live in damp terrestrial habitats. Sub-divisions are mainly associated with biochemical differences related to photosynthesis.

The **Chlorophyta** are green algae which range in form from unicells such as *Chlamydomonas* and *Chlorella* through colonies like *Volvox* and filaments like *Spirogyra* to delicate thalloid genera like *Ulva*. They contain the same photosynthetic pigments as higher plants but the chloroplasts which contain them vary. *Chlamydomonas* has a single bowl-shaped chloroplast and that of *Spirogyra* is spiral. Both have starch deposits called **pyrenoids**. *Chlamydomonas* also has a light-sensitive spot and will swim, by means of flagella, towards the light. Both genera are capable of asexual and sexual reproduction.

Algae are economically important because at least half the carbon fixation of the earth is carried out by algae in the surface layers of oceans. This primary production is at the base of all aquatic food chains. These algae are also responsible for half the oxygen released by plants into the atmosphere.

Algae can be used in some parts of the world as a direct food source for humans and they may be used as fertilizers on coastal farms. Unicellular green algae such as *Chlorella* are easy to cultivate and can be used as a source of a single cell protein (SCP) for human and animal consumption.

Green algae provide oxygen for the aerobic bacteria which break down sewage.

Derivatives of alginic acid found in the cell walls of many brown algae are non-toxic and readily form gels. These alginates are used as thickeners in many products including ice cream, hand cream, polish, medicine, paint, ceramic glazes and confectionery.

Excessive numbers of algae may develop in bodies of water following pollution by fertilizers or other chemicals. These 'blooms' cause the water to smell and taste unpleasant and may lead to oxygen depletion and the death of fish (Section 14.7.2).

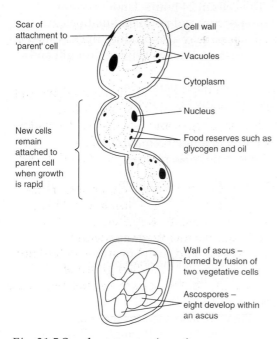

Fig. 21.5 Saccharomyces (*yeast*)

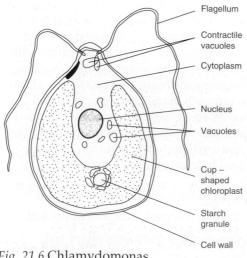

Fig. 21.6 Chlamydomonas

21.2 Growth of microorganisms

Microorganisms (microbes) are found in every ecological niche – from deepest ocean to the limits of the stratosphere, from hot springs to the frozen poles. They are small, easily dispersed and quickly multiply given a suitable environment. They grow on a wide diversity of substrates making them ideal subjects for commercial application. Each species has its own optimum conditions within which it grows best.

21.2.1 Factors affecting growth

The factors which affect the growth of microorganisms are equally applicable to the growth of plant and animal cell cultures.

Nutrients
Growth depends upon both the types of nutrients available and their concentration. Cells are largely made up of the four elements: carbon, hydrogen, oxygen and nitrogen with smaller, but significant, quantities of phosphorus and sulphur. Accounting as they do for 90% of the cell's dry mass, all six are essential for growth.

Needed in smaller quantities, but no less important, are the metallic elements: calcium, potassium, magnesium and iron, sometimes known as **macro-nutrients**. Required in smaller amounts still are the **micro-nutrients (trace elements)**: manganese, cobalt, zinc, copper and molybdenum – indeed not all may be essential to some species. A further group of chemicals, loosely termed **growth factors**, are also needed. These fall into three categories:

1. Vitamins

2. Amino acids

3. Purines and pyrimidines

Up to a point, the more concentrated a nutrient the greater the rate of growth, but as other factors become limiting the addition of further nutrients has no beneficial effect. More details of the nutrients used in culturing cells are given in Section 21.2.4.

Temperature
As all growth is governed by enzymes and these operate only within a relatively narrow range of temperature, cells are similarly affected by it. If the temperature falls too low the rate of enzyme-catalyzed reactions becomes too slow to sustain growth; if too high the denaturation of enzymes causes death. Most cells grow best within the range 20–45 °C although some species can grow at temperatures as low as − 5 °C, while others do so at 90 °C. Three groups are recognized according to their preferred temperature range:

1. **Psychrophiles** (e.g. *Bacillus globisporus*) – These have optimum growth temperatures below 20 °C, many continuing to grow at temperatures down to 0 °C.

515

2. **Mesophiles** (e.g. *Escherichia coli*) – These have optimum growth temperatures in the range 20–40 °C.

3. **Thermophiles** (e.g. the alga *Cyanidium caldarium*) – These have optimum growth temperatures in excess of 45 °C, a few surviving in temperatures as high as 90 °C. These cells have enzymes which are unusual in not being denatured at high temperatures.

pH

Microorganisms are able to tolerate a wider range of pH than plant and animal cells, some species growing in an environment as acid as pH 2.5, others in one as alkaline as pH 9. Microorganisms preferring acid conditions, e.g. *Thiobacillus thiooxidans*, are termed **acidophiles**.

Oxygen

Many microorganisms are aerobic, requiring molecular oxygen for growth at all times: these are termed **obligate aerobes**. Some, while growing better in the presence of oxygen, can nevertheless survive in its absence; these are called **facultative anaerobes**. Others find oxygen toxic and do not grow well in its presence: these are the **obligate anaerobes**. Some of this group, while tolerating oxygen, nevertheless grow better when its concentration is very low. These are termed **microaerophiles**.

Osmotic factors

All microorganisms require water for growth. In most cases this is absorbed osmotically from the environment, although pinocytosis is used in certain protozoa and all groups produce a little water as a product of aerobic respiration. To ensure absorption, the water potential of the external environment must be less negative (higher) than the cell contents. For this reason most microorganisms cannot grow in environments with a high solute concentration – a fact made use of in preserving foods, e.g. salting of meat and fish, bottling of jam and fruit in sugar. A few, called **halophiles**, can survive, however, in conditions of high salt concentration.

Pressure

Although pressure is not a major factor affecting growth in most microorganisms, a few species inhabiting the ocean depths can grow under immense pressure. Some of these **barophiles** cannot grow in surface waters where the pressure is too low for their survival.

Light

Photosynthetic microorganisms require an adequate supply of light to sustain growth.

Water

In common with all organisms, microorganisms require water for a variety of functions. In addition, photosynthetic microorganisms use it as a source of hydrogen to reduce carbon dioxide. Some may use alternative inorganic hydrogen sources, e.g. hydrogen sulphide, for this purpose.

PROJECT

We are advised to keep sugar-reduced jam in the fridge once it has been opened. Investigate the keeping qualities of various preserves.

21.2.2 Measurement of growth

The growth rate of microorganisms in liquid culture (broth) can be estimated in a number of ways. A **haemocytometer** (so-called because it was originally used to count blood cells) is a large microscope slide on to the surface of which is etched one or more grids of known dimensions (usually 25 squares each of side 0.2 mm). The coverslip which is placed over the centre part of the slide is supported in such a way that there is a set depth (usually 0.1 mm) between it and the portion of the slide on which the grid is marked. The volume of liquid above one small square can thus be calculated ($0.2 \times 0.2 \times 0.1$ mm $= 0.004$ mm^3). If a drop of culture containing the cells is placed on the haemocytometer and the coverslip is properly positioned, the number of cells in 0.004 mm^3 of broth can be counted. Many squares should be counted and the average found to obtain more reliable results. The number of cells in 1 mm^3 or 1 cm^3 can be found by multiplying by an appropriate factor (in our example $250 \times$ and $250\,000 \times$ respectively). Where the number of cells is too large to count effectively, the broth should first be diluted by a suitable amount. The final estimate can then be calculated by multiplying the average count by the dilution factor used.

The haemocytometer provides a **total count** of all cells, whether living or dead. Often it is more useful to be able to estimate only the number of living cells in a culture. A technique known as **dilution plating** is adopted for this. Firstly a set of **serial dilutions** are made up. This is done by taking 1 cm^3 of the original culture broth and placing it into 9 cm^3 of distilled water in a second tube and mixing it thoroughly. This solution is now $\frac{1}{10}$th of the concentration of the original. Adding 1 cm^3 of this diluted solution to 9 cm^3 of distilled water and mixing gives a $\frac{1}{100}$th concentration. Continuing this five or six more times provides a range of dilutions. 1 cm^3 of each dilution is then added to a separate agar plate, spread evenly over it, and left to incubate at a suitable temperature for a few days. Each living cell (but only living cells), will give rise to a visible colony growing on the agar plate. Some plates will have so many colonies that separate ones cannot be identified, others will have no colonies at all. At one dilution however, the number of colonies will number 5–50. The actual number is counted and multiplied by the dilution factor to give the number of **living** cells in 1 cm^3 of the original culture. This is called a **viable count**.

The more a broth culture of microorganisms grows, the more turbid (cloudy) it becomes owing to the density of cells in it. Culture growth can hence be measured by a **photometric method** using a colorimeter – an instrument which measures the **optical density** (amount of light absorbed) of a solution. This method provides a measure of the relative growth rate of different solutions. The **actual** growth can be calculated using a calibration graph of a known mass/number of microorganisms in a given volume of water against optical density.

The most accurate method of estimating growth rate is to remove samples from a large broth culture at regular intervals. These samples are filtered, dried and then weighed. The mass of each sample can then be plotted against time to give a graph of growth rate.

A simple, but far less accurate, method is to measure the diameter of a fungal or bacterial colony growing on a solid medium at regular time intervals.

21.2.3 Growth patterns

The growth of a culture of individual cells, e.g. of unicellular yeasts, protozoa or bacteria is, in effect, the growth of a population and follows the same pattern as that described in Section 10.7.2. The typical bacterial growth curve for a batch culture, illustrated in Fig. 21.7, consists of four phases:

1. **The lag phase** – This is the period after **inoculation** (the addition of cells to the nutrient medium) during which the growth rate increases towards its maximum. Growth during this time is slow initially as the bacteria adapt to produce the necessary enzymes needed to utilize the nutrient medium. The rate of cell division gradually increases during this phase.

2. **The exponential (logarithmic) phase** – During this period, with nutrients in good supply and few waste products being produced, the rate of cell division is at its maximum, cells sometimes dividing as frequently as every ten minutes. The culture is in a state of **balanced growth** with the doubling time, cell protein content and cell size all remaining constant.

3. **The stationary phase** – As nutrients are used up and toxic waste products accumulate, the rate of growth slows. The changed composition of the medium results in the production of cells of various sizes with a different chemical make-up. They are in a state of **unbalanced growth**. For the total count, this section of the graph is horizontal because the rate at which new cells are produced is equal to the rate at which dead ones are broken down.

4. **The death phase** – While the total number of cells remains constant, the number of living ones diminishes as an ever-increasing number die from a lack of the nutrients necessary to produce cellular energy, or because of poisoning by their own toxic wastes.

21.2.4 Culture media

The correct balance of nutrients, an appropriate pH and a suitable medium are essential to microbial growth.

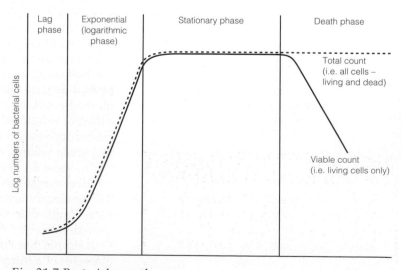

Fig. 21.7 Bacterial growth curve

TABLE 21.3 **A typical broad spectrum medium**

Ingredient	Quantity	Source of
Water	1.0 dm³	Metabolic and osmotic water, hydrogen and oxygen
Glucose	5 g	Carbohydrate energy source
Yeast extract	5 g	Organic nitrogen, organic growth factors
Dipotassium hydrogen phosphate	1 g	Potassium and phosphorus
Magnesium sulphate	250 mg	Magnesium and sulphur
Iron (II) sulphate	10 mg	Iron and sulphur
Calcium chloride	10 mg	Calcium and chloride
Cobalt, copper, manganese, molybdenum and zinc salts	trace	Metallic ion trace elements

The medium itself may be liquid (broth) or solid. Solid media are usually based upon **agar**, a seaweed extract which is metabolically inert and which dissolves in hot water but solidifies upon cooling. The more agar, the more solid is the resulting jelly. Any medium composed to satisfy the demands of a single species is called a **minimal medium**. One which provides the nutrients for a small group of microorganisms with similar requirements, e.g. acidophiles, is known as a **narrow spectrum medium**, whereas a medium for general purposes, designed to grow as wide a range of microorganisms as possible is called a **broad spectrum medium**. It is possible to select for the growth of specific types of organisms by use of **selective media** which permit growth of only a single species. The composition of a typical broad spectrum medium is given in Table 21.3.

21.2.5 Aseptic conditions

Both in the laboratory and on an industrial scale, pure cultures of a single type of microorganism need to be grown free from contamination with others.

A number of techniques are used to sterilize equipment, instruments, media and other materials. Heat, either passing through a flame, dry heating in an oven, or using water in an autoclave (a type of pressure cooker) is effective in sterilizing instruments, small vessels and culture media. Where heating may affect the media, it may be filtered free of microorganisms using especially fine filters. Ultra-violet light can be used on equipment or even whole rooms. Certain other equipment may be sterilized using a suitable disinfectant, e.g. hypochlorite.

21.3 Industrial fermenters and fermentation

Much of modern biotechnology involves the large-scale production of substances by growing specific microorganisms in a large container known as a fermenter. Fermentation should strictly refer to a biological process which occurs in the absence of oxygen. However, the word is taken to include aerobic processes – indeed the supply of adequate oxygen is a major design feature of the modern fermenter.

21.3.1 Batch versus continuous cultivation

In **batch cultivation** the necessary nutrient medium and the appropriate microorganisms are added to the fermenter and the process allowed to proceed. During the fermentation air is added if it is needed and waste gases are removed. Growth is allowed to continue up to a specific point at which the fermenter is emptied and the product extracted. The fermenter is then cleaned and sterilized in readiness for the next batch.

With **continuous cultivation**, once the fermenter is set up, the used medium and products are continuously removed. The raw materials are also added throughout and the process can therefore continue, sometimes for many weeks.

PROJECT

Yeast can respire using different sugars. How would you test the effectiveness of a range of monosaccharides and disaccharides as respiratory substrates?

The continuous process has the advantage of being quicker because it removes the need to empty, clean and refill the fermenter as regularly and hence ensures an almost continuous yield. In addition, by adjusting the nutrients added, the rate of growth can be maintained at the constant level which provides the maximum yield of product. Continuous cultivation is, however, only suited to the production of biomass or metabolites which are associated with growth. **Secondary metabolites**, like antibiotics, which are produced when growth is past its maximum, need to be manufactured by the batch process. The organisms used to produce antibiotics are in any case too unstable for growth by continuous fermentation. In addition, continuous fermentation requires sophisticated monitoring technology and highly trained staff to operate efficiently.

21.3.2 Fermenter design

The basic design of a **stirred-tank fermenter** is shown in Fig. 21.8. It consists of a large stainless steel vessel with a capacity of up to $500\,000\,dm^3$ around which is a jacket of circulating water used to control the temperature within the fermenter. An agitator, comprising a series of flat blades which can be rotated, is incorporated. This ensures that the contents are thoroughly mixed, thus bringing nutrients into contact with the microorganisms and preventing the cells settling out at the bottom.

Where oxygen is required, air is forced in at the bottom of the tank through a ring containing many small holes – a process known as **sparging**. To assist aeration, increased turbulence may be achieved by adding baffles to the walls of the fermentation vessel. A series of openings, or **ports**, through which materials can be introduced or withdrawn, is provided. The **harvest line** is used to extract culture medium. An outlet to remove air and waste gases is needed, as well as one to allow small samples of the culture medium to be removed for analysis. Inlet tubes permit nutrients to be provided and, as the pH changes during fermentation, allow acid or base to be added to maintain the optimum pH. With air being forced into the medium, chemicals often need to be added to reduce foaming. Finally, it is essential to have an **inoculation port** through which the initial inoculum of cells can be introduced once the required conditions in the fermenter are achieved. **Probes**, which constantly register the temperature and pH within the vessel, are used to indicate when adjustments to these factors are necessary.

The stirred-tank fermenter is a well-tried and tested design used extensively in the fermentation industry. It is, however, relatively costly to run, largely as a consequence of the energy needed to drive the agitators and introduce the compressed air. Alternatives have therefore been designed where the air forced into the vessel to provide oxygen is used to circulate the contents, thus making an agitator unnecessary.

One such design, the **pressure-cycle fermenter**, is of two types. In the **air-lift type** the air is introduced centrally at the bottom making the medium less dense. It therefore rises through a central column in the vessel to the top where it escapes. The now more dense medium descends around the sides of the

Fermenter for cloned protein

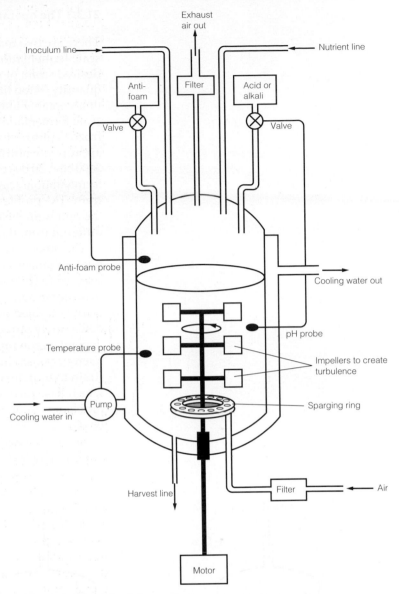

Fig. 21.8 A stirred-tank fermenter

vessel to complete the cycle (Fig. 21.9(a)). Higher pressure at the bottom of the vessel increases solubility of oxygen, while lower pressure at the top decreases solubility of carbon dioxide, which as a consequence comes out of solution. In the **deep-shaft type**, the principle is similar but the air is introduced at the top (Fig. 21.9(b)). This has the advantage of giving a more even delivery of oxygen to the microorganisms.

The **tower-** or **bubble-column** (a variety of the air-lift fermenter) has horizontal rather than vertical divisions (Fig. 21.9(c)). This allows conditions in each section to be maintained at different levels if necessary. A microorganism being carried up from the bottom may therefore pass from a high pH and low temperature to a lower pH and higher temperature to suit each phase of its growth.

While all three types can be used continuously only the air-lift fermenter is used for batch processing. All types must be taller than the conventional stirred-tank vessel to operate effectively.

21.3.3 The operation and control of fermenters

There are two main problems associated with setting up a large-scale fermentation process. Firstly, the inoculum containing the desired strain of microorganism has to be obtained in sufficient quantity; if too little is added to the fermenter, the lag phase is unacceptably long, making the process uneconomic. A small-scale fermentation is set up in a vessel as small as 10 cm³, using frozen culture stock. This is then added to flasks, containing the appropriate nutrient medium, of increasing capacity, e.g. 300 cm³, 3000 cm³, 30 000 cm³, etc., until the final capacity of the end fermentation vessel is reached. This is known as the **fermenter train**. The problem is that the operational conditions that give the optimum yield in a 300 cm³ fermentation flask are often very different from those for a 300 000 cm³ vessel.

The other main problem arises from the fact that the microorganisms used in fermenters have been genetically selected for the properties (e.g. a high product yield) which make them suitable for use in a large-scale fermenter. They are often enfeebled mutant strains which have resulted from deliberately induced mutanogenesis. As efficient production depends upon rapid growth, i.e. many generations of the microorganism in a short period, there is a tendency for the strain to mutate naturally, often reverting to the parent type which has less desirable properties. One way around the problem is to prevent the microorganism producing the desired product until the final fermentation. This reduces the selection pressure which might alter the gene responsible for the product, but is not always feasible. The use of genetically engineered

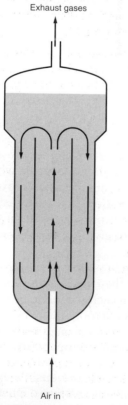

Fig. 21.9(a) Air-lift fermenter

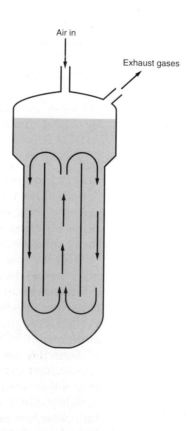

(b) Deep-shaft fermenter

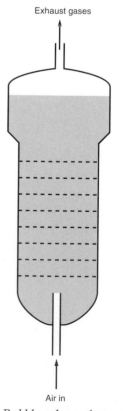

(c) Bubble-column fermenter

stock (Section 5.7) has the advantage that it is much easier to express ('switch on') the desired gene at the appropriate time by use of chemical triggers called **promoters**.

Once a sufficient quantity of the inoculum has been produced, usually between 1% and 10% of the total medium, it is added to the fermenter only after the medium within it is of the correct composition and at the desired temperature and pH. The problem now is to maintain all conditions throughout the fermentation. To achieve this the levels of various nutrients, oxygen, pH and temperature are constantly monitored using probes and the information is fed to a computer for analysis, along with information on the composition of the exhaust gases. The necessary corrective changes can then be made. These may be complex – for example, an increase in oxygen uptake could be countered by reducing the air supply, the pressure within the vessel, the nutrient levels or the agitator speed. Which one is selected has implications for other factors and the choice therefore needs to be made advisedly. While the temperature of the medium may need to be increased initially by piping steam through it, once fermentation is under way the heat generated by the microorganisms necessitates continuous cooling by the water jacket around the vessel.

The processes involved in recovering the product are called **downstream processing**. This often involves separation of the cells from the medium which may be achieved in a number of ways:

1. **Settlement** – The cells may readily settle once agitation and sparging cease. The process can be accelerated by the addition of **flocculating agents**, many of which work by neutralizing the charges on the cells which otherwise keep them in suspension by electrostatic repulsion.

2. **Centrifugation** – The contents of the fermenter are spun at high speed in a centrifuge causing the cells to settle out. Continuous centrifugation is now possible.

3. **Ultrafiltration** – The fermenter contents are forced through filters with a pore size less than $0.5\mu m$ which thereby traps cells allowing only liquid through. Some extracellular protein may also be retained.

Where the desired products are the entire cells themselves, these need only be washed, dried and compacted to complete the process. Where the product is contained within the cells, these must be disrupted by some means, the cell debris removed (e.g. by centrifugation or ultrafiltration), and the desired chemical recovered using precipitation, chromatographic or solvent extraction techniques. Where the product lies in the fermentation liquor rather than the cells, this is separated from unwanted enzymes and metabolites, again by precipitation, chromatography or solvent extraction as appropriate.

21.3.4 Sterilization during and after fermentation

The need for aseptic conditions and the basic mechanisms for achieving them were discussed in Section 21.2.5. In industrial fermentation this presents many practical problems considering that not only a very large vessel needs to be sterilized, but also all associated pipework and probes as well as the nutrients, air-supply, and other agents added during the process.

The equipment is designed so that any nooks and crannies which might harbour microorganisms are minimized. The vessel is highly polished, for example, and all components are designed to allow easy access by sterilizing agents. Having been thoroughly washed all equipment is steam sterilized.

The initial nutrient medium may be sterilized in the fermenter by heating it; any added later may be sterilized by heating *en route* to the vessel, as can all other liquid additions. Concentrated acids and alkalis used to adjust the pH may be so inhospitable to contaminating organisms as not to warrant sterilization.

Filtration is used to remove potential contaminants from the air supply although bacteriophages are small enough to pass through – with disastrous consequences. Heat treatment of incoming air can alleviate this problem. The exhaust air is also sterilized to prevent potentially harmful microorganisms being introduced into the atmosphere.

21.4 Biotechnology and food production

Did you know?

The total bread market in Britain is worth about £3000 million a year.

Until Louis Pasteur showed in 1857 that wine fermentation was the consequence of microbial activity, no one had been aware of the role that microorganisms played in the manufacture of some foods. With Pasteur's discovery came further development of the use of microorganisms in food production, an expansion which continues today.

21.4.1 Baking

The use of yeasts in food production is the oldest, and most extensive contribution made by any group of microorganisms. In bread-making cereal grain is crushed to form flour thus exposing the stored starch. Water is added (making a dough) to activate the natural enzymes, e.g. amylases, in the flour which then hydrolyse the starch via maltose into glucose. The yeast, *Saccharomyces cerevisiae*, is added which uses the glucose as a respiratory substrate, producing carbon dioxide. This carbon dioxide forms small bubbles which become trapped in the dough; upon baking in an oven these expand giving the bread a light texture. Dough is often kneaded – a process which traps air within it. This not only helps to lighten the bread directly but also provides a source of oxygen so that the yeast can respire aerobically producing a greater quantity of carbon dioxide. Some anaerobic respiration nevertheless takes place and the alcohol produced is evaporated during baking.

21.4.2 Beer and wine production

Fermentation by yeasts produces alcohol according to the equation:

$$C_6H_{12}O_6 \longrightarrow 2C_2H_5OH + 2CO_2$$

hexose sugar   ethanol   carbon dioxide

Some alcohol produced in this way is for industrial use, but much goes to make beverages like beers and wines which may

PROJECT

Investigate the effect of Vitamin C on the expansion of bread dough.

Brewing beer

Did you know?

In 1992 purchases of beer in Britain were valued at over £13 million, about 3.5% of consumers' expenditure.

then be distilled to form spirits. The variety of such beverages is immense and depends largely on the source of the sugar and the type of yeast used to ferment it. Various additives further increase the diversity of alcoholic drinks.

To make wine, the sugar fermented is glucose obtained directly from grapes, whereas beers are made by fermenting glucose obtained from cereal grain (usually barley) which results from the breakdown of starch in the grain. The yeast used in wine production is often *Saccharomyces ellipsoideus* as this variety can tolerate the higher alcohol levels encountered in wines. Even more tolerant to high alcohol levels are *S. fermentati* and *S. beticus* and these are primarily used in making sherry. Beers are of two basic types – top fermenting varieties of yeast such as *S. cerevisiae* produce a typical British 'bitter' while *S. carlsbergensis*, a bottom fermenting variety, is used to make lager. In beer production, the barley grain is first malted by soaking it in water for two to three days. The grain is then spread on concrete floors and allowed to germinate (about ten days), during which time the natural amylases and maltases in the grain start to convert starch to glucose. This process is stopped by drying the grain and storing it – a process called **kilning** or **roasting**. The higher the temperature during this process, the darker the resulting beer. The germinated grain is often crushed during this stage. The dried, crushed germinated grain is now added to water and heated to the desired temperature – **mashing**. During mashing the remaining starch is converted to sugar to produce a liquid called **wort**. Yeast is added to the wort to convert it to alcohol, as well as hops and other additives, e.g. caramel, which are used to give each beer its characteristic flavour and colour.

The fermentation itself takes place in large deep tanks of around 500 000 dm³ capacity. No air is introduced as anaerobic respiration is the aim. Although traditionally a batch process, beer production can also be carried out using continuous fermentation. This is more economic and it also allows the carbon dioxide to be collected – a valuable by-product when converted to dry-ice.

The beer is finally separated from the yeast and clarified, and carbon dioxide is added. Sometimes the beer is pasteurized to extend its shelf-life. A good traditional beer, however, retains some yeast in the enclosed barrel which produces the carbon dioxide naturally. Such beers are, for obvious reasons, termed 'live' beers.

21.4.3 Dairy products

Microorganisms have long been exploited in the dairy industry as a means of preserving milk. From this a large number of different products have been manufactured which fall into three main categories: cheese, yoghurt and butter.

Cheese manufacture
An ancient process, cheese-making has altered little over the years. A group of bacteria known as **lactic acid bacteria** are used to ferment the lactose in milk to lactic acid according to the equation:

$$C_{12}H_{22}O_{11} + H_2O \longrightarrow 4CH_3CHOHCOOH$$

lactose   water   lactic acid

Cheese making

Most commercially used lactic acid bacteria are species of two genera – *Lactobacillus* and *Streptococcus*.

Cheese production begins with the pasteurization of raw milk which is then cooled to around 30 °C before a starter culture of the required lactic acid bacteria is added. The resultant fall in pH due to their activity causes the milk to separate into a solid **curd** and a liquid **whey** in a process called **curdling**. The addition of **rennet** at this stage encourages the casein in the milk to coagulate aiding curd formation. Originally extracted from the stomachs of calves slaughtered for food, rennet has now largely been replaced by **chymosin**, a similar enzyme produced by genetically engineered *Escherichia coli*. The whey is drained off and may be used to feed animals. The curd is heated in the range 32–42 °C and some salt added before being pressed into moulds for a period of time which varies according to cheese type.

The ripening of the cheese allows flavour to develop as a result of the action of other milk enzymes or deliberately introduced microorganisms. In blue cheese, for example, *Penicillium* spp. are added. The duration of ripening varies, with Caerphilly taking just a fortnight in contrast to a year required for mature Cheddar. Whereas hard cheeses ripen owing to the activity of lactic acid bacteria throughout the cheese, in soft cheeses it is fungi growing on the surface which are responsible.

Yoghurt manufacture

Yoghurt is made from pasteurized milk with much of the fat removed, and its production also depends on lactic acid bacteria, in particular *Lactobacillus bulgaricus* and *Streptococcus thermophilus*. These are added to the milk in equal quantity and incubated at around 45 °C for five hours during which time the pH falls to around 4.0. Cooling prevents further fermentation and fruit or flavourings can then be added as required.

Butter manufacture

Not essentially a process requiring microorganisms, butter production is nevertheless frequently assisted by the addition to cream of *Streptococcus lactis* and *Leuconostoc cremoris* which help to sour it, give flavour and aid the separation of the butterfat. Churning of this butterfat produces the final product.

21.4.4 Single cell protein (SCP)

Single cell protein comprises the cells, or their products, of microorganisms which are grown for animal, including human, consumption. High in protein, the product also contains fats, carbohydrates, vitamins and minerals making it a useful food. The raw materials for SCP production have included petroleum chemicals, alcohols, sugars and a variety of agricultural and industrial wastes. The microorganisms used to ferment these have been equally diverse – bacteria, algae, yeasts and filamentous fungi. The success of various manufacturing processes has varied. The use of a waste product to produce food seems highly attractive and economical, but the demand it creates for the raw material ceases to make it a waste, its price rises and the process can become uneconomical. Excess food production in some parts of the world has meant the selling off of butter and grain 'mountains' and therefore reduced the need

PROJECT

Investigate the number of viable bacteria in milk or yoghurt samples stored under various conditions.

for alternative sources of food such as SCP. It has not therefore proved the success originally anticipated and many countries have ceased production altogether.

The world's largest continuously operating fermenter (600 tonnes) owned by ICI, produces a single cell protein called **Pruteen**. It comprises 80% protein and has a high vitamin content. The process uses methanol, a waste product of some of ICI's other activities, making the raw material relatively cheap. This is acted upon by the aerobic bacterium *Methylophilus methylotrophus* in a pressure-cycle fermenter with a capacity of 1500 m³ to produce the odourless, tasteless, cream-coloured Pruteen which is used as an animal feed.

Similar projects produce a protein based on the fungus *Fusarium graminearum* which can be grown on flour waste. The product, **mycoprotein**, is intended for human consumption and, being high in protein and fibre, but low in cholesterol, is a healthy addition to the diet.

21.4.5 Enzymes associated with the food industry

Many enzymes used in the food industry are produced by microorganisms. Some examples are given in Table 21.4.

21.4.6 Immobilization of cells and enzymes

One problem with the fermentation processes described so far is that at some point the cell culture is removed and discarded. This is fine when the cells are the desired product, but if it is a metabolite they produce which is required, their removal takes away the manufacturing source which then needs to be replaced. Any mechanism for immobilizing the microorganism and/or the

TABLE 21.4 **Some enzymes produced by microorganisms used in the food industry**

Enzyme	Examples of microorganisms involved	Application
α-amylases	*Aspergillus oryzae*	Breakdown of starch in beer production Improving of flour Preparation of glucose syrup Thickening of canned sauces
β-glucanase	*Bacillus subtilis*	Beer production
Glucose isomerase	*Bacillus coagulans*	Sweetener for soft drinks Cake fillings
Lactase	*Kluyveromyces* sp.	Lactose removal from whey Sweetener for milk drinks
Lipase	*Candida* sp.	Flavour development in cheese
Pectinase	*Aspergillus* sp.	Clearing of wines and fruit juices
Protease	*Bacillus subtilis*	Meat tenderizers
Pullulanase	*Klebsiella aerogenes*	Soft ice cream manufacture
Sucrase	*Saccharomyces* sp.	Confectionery production

Enzymes and fruit juice production

Pectin is a substance which helps to hold plant cell walls together. As a fruit ripens the plant produces proteolytic enzymes which convert the insoluble protopectin of the unripe fruit into more soluble forms, causing the fruit to soften. When fruits are mashed and pressed to form juices these more soluble forms of pectin enter the juice, making it cloudy and causing the colour and flavour to deteriorate. They also increase the viscosity of the juice itself, making it difficult to obtain optimal yields. For fruit juice manufacturers the addition of industrial pectinases between mashing and pressing causes complete depectinization so that a good quality, clear juice is obtained which retains its stability when concentrated. Producers may also use other enzymes such as starch-splitting enzymes to reduce cloudiness, especially with apples, cellulases to improve juice yield and colours, and arabanase to reduce the haze caused by the polysaccharide araban passing from the cell walls into the extracted juice.

PROJECT

The production of fruit juices has been greatly improved by the addition of pectinase

1. Compare the yields of fruit juice from apples with and without the addition of pectinase.

2. Determine the optimum, and thus the most economical, concentration of pectinase.

PROJECT

When enzymes are immobilized by entrapment they appear to be less prone to denaturing at high temperatures

1. From this statement suggest a testable hypothesis.

2. Test your hypothesis by comparing the activity of an enzyme under normal and immobilized conditions.

enzymes they produce, improves the economics of the process. The idea is not a new one – vinegar manufacture and some stages of sewage treatment have used the technique for a century or more.

There are four basic methods of immobilization:

1. Entrapment – Cells or enzyme molecules are trapped in a suitable meshwork of inert material, e.g. collagen, cellulose, carrageenan, agar, gelatin, polystyrene.

2. Encapsulation – Enzymes are held inside partially permeable particles, e.g. alginate beads.

3. Binding – Cells or enzyme molecules become physically attached to the surface of a suitable material, e.g. sand or gravel.

4. Cross-linking – Cells or enzyme molecules are chemically bonded to a suitable chemical matrix, e.g. glutaraldehyde.

However immobilized, the cells or enzymes are made into small beads which are then either packed into columns, or kept in the nutrient medium. The nutrient can be continually added and the product removed without frequent removal of the microorganisms/enzymes. Although the process cannot be continued indefinitely as impurities may accumulate, the semi-continuous nature of the process is a major advantage. Other advantages include:

1. With whole cell immobilization a number of enzymes can act together at the same time in a single process.

2. With enzyme immobilization, the enzyme can be used repeatedly as it is not consumed in the process, making it more economic especially where the enzyme is expensive.

3. Enzymes are vulnerable to changes in temperature and pH. The matrix on/in which they are trapped may buffer them against such fluctuations.

4. The immobilized enzyme and cells, being held in place, cannot contaminate the substance being produced reducing the extent of any purification which might be needed.

Commercial uses of enzymes

Immobilized microbial cell pellets in a packed reactor column used to carry out biotransformations

For many years humans have used enzymes to produce bread, cheese, wine, beer and yoghurts but now they have more diverse commercial applications and the sale of enzymes is a multi-billion pound industry.

The commonest sources of these enzymes are bacteria, yeasts and other fungi. The enzymes may be released from the microbial cell, extracted from it when it is broken or the whole cell may be used. Enzymes or whole cells are usually used in an immobilized form so that the enzyme can be reused many times.

Enzymes are very specific and can be used to produce pure products, often more cheaply than by traditional methods. They may also require less energy and result in less pollution.

The specificity of enzymes enables them to be used for sensitive analytical techniques, such as detecting glucose or cholesterol in blood and the enzyme thermolysin is used to produce aspartame, a sweetener sold as *Canderel* and *Nutrasweet*, much more cheaply than by chemical processes.

There is a great demand by the food industry for high fructose syrups which are as sweet as sucrose and which contain glucose and fructose in approximately equal amounts. These syrups are now produced from starch (itself often a waste product of the food industry) using a combination of four enzymes: α-amylase, glucoamylase, pullulanase and glucose isomerase. The first three catalyze the conversion of starch to glucose and then the glucose isomerase converts the glucose to a 50 : 50 mixture of glucose and fructose.

On a commercial scale enzymes are now providing products for pharmaceutical, agrochemical, food, cosmetic and analytical uses. They are used to manufacture semi-synthetic antibiotics, to degrade wastes and in genetic engineering.

21.5 Biotechnology and pharmaceuticals

Since the antibiotic penicillin was first produced on a large scale in the 1940s, there has been a considerable expansion in the use of biotechnology to produce a range of antibiotics, hormones and other pharmaceuticals.

21.5.1 Antibiotics

Antibiotics are chemical substances produced by microorganisms which are effective in dilute solution in preventing the spread of other microorganisms. Most inhibit growth rather than kill the microorganisms on which they act. Some, like **penicillin**, are only effective on relatively few pathogens – **narrow spectrum antibiotics**, while others, e.g. **chloramphenicol**, will inhibit the growth of a wide variety of pathogens – **broad spectrum antibiotics**. Although around 5000 antibiotics have been discovered only 100 have proved medically and commercially viable.

Antibiotics are made when growth of the producer organism is slowing down rather than when it is at its maximum. They are therefore secondary metabolites and their production takes longer than for primary metabolites. It also means that continuous fermentation techniques are unsuitable and only batch fermentation can be employed.

In penicillin manufacture, a stirred-tank fermenter is inoculated with a culture of *Penicillium notatum* or *Penicillium chrysogenum* and the fungus is grown under optimum conditions: 24 °C, good oxygen supply, slightly alkaline pH. Penicillin production typically commences after about 30 hours, reaching a maximum at around four days. Production ceases after about six days, at which point the contents of the fermenter are drained off. As the antibiotic is an extracellular product, the fungal mycelium is filtered off, washed and discarded. The liquid filtrate containing penicillin is chemically extracted and purified using solvents to leave a crystalline salt. After sterilization the fermenter is available for the next batch.

The development of resistance to antibiotics by pathogens means there is a continuing need to find new types. The emphasis has moved from searching for new natural antibiotics to the development of new strains using genetic engineering. However, this is not easy. Being secondary metabolites, antibiotics are the product of a long metabolic pathway involving numerous genes. Manipulation of these is complex and difficult. Programmes for enhancing the production rate of existing strains and using random mutation and selection methods to develop new ones, are continually developed. Table 21.5 lists some other antibiotics and their producer organisms. Details of the applications of monoclonal antibodies are given in Section 16.3.2.

21.5.2 Hormones

With the advent of recombinant DNA technology it is now possible to use microorganisms to produce a wide range of

TABLE 21.5 **Some antibiotics and their producer organism**

Antibiotic	Producer organism	Type of organism
Penicillin	*Penicillium notatum*	Fungus
Griseofulvin	*Penicillium griseofulvum*	Fungus
Streptomycin	*Streptomyces griseus*	Actinomycete
Chloramphenicol	*Streptomyces venezuelae*	Actinomycete
Tetracycline	*Streptomyces aureofaciens*	Actinomycete
Colistin	*Bacillus colistinus*	Bacterium
Polymyxin B	*Bacillus polymyxa*	Bacterium

Penicillin fermentation

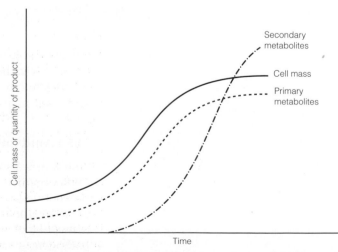

Fig. 21.10 Comparison of primary and secondary metabolite production

FOCUS

Biosensors

Biosensors have been devised which enable a quick and accurate measurement of glucose to be made. This is important industrially but also medically, enabling diabetics to monitor their own blood sugar levels. The method used relies on the specificity of the enzyme glucose oxidase, allowing glucose to be assayed in the presence of other sugars.

Glucose oxidase catalyses the conversion of glucose to hydrogen peroxide (H_2O_2).

$$\beta\text{-D-Glucose} + O_2 \xrightarrow{\text{Glucose oxidase}} \text{Gluconic acid} + H_2O_2$$

This is coupled to a reaction catalysed by peroxidase and utilising the hydrogen peroxide.

$$\underset{\substack{\text{Colourless} \\ \text{hydrogen donor}}}{DH_2} + H_2O_2 \xrightarrow{\text{Peroxidase}} 2H_2O + \underset{\substack{\text{Coloured} \\ \text{compound}}}{D}$$

The glucose oxidase, peroxidase and the colourless hydrogen donor can be immobilized on a cellulose fibre pad. This forms the basis of 'Clinistix', the glucose dipsticks used by diabetics.

More recently the term biosensor has been used to describe the association of a biomolecule, such as an enzyme, with a transducer which produces an electrical signal in response to a charge in the substrate.

Biosensors are not just used for the quantitative detection of glucose. They have also been devised for pregnancy testing kits (see Focus on page 385), to check the freshness of food (there being a correlation between deterioration and the number of microorganisms present) and to detect the presence of pollutants in the environment, as well as for the estimation of many substances, such as urea, ketones and cholesterol, in blood and urine.

hormones which previously had to be extracted from animal tissues. Hormone manufacture using fermentation techniques is relatively straightforward, but the high degree of purity of the final product which is essential, makes downstream processing a complex process. Ion-exchange, chromatography and protein engineering are some of the techniques employed to provide a high level of purity.

Hormones produced in this way include insulin, used in the treatment of diabetes, and human growth factor which prevents pituitary dwarfism. A number of steroids are also manufactured including cortisone and the sex hormones, testosterone and oestradiol. Others with possible commercial and medical value are relaxin which aids childbirth, and erythropoietin for the treatment of anaemia. Bovine somatotrophin (BST), a hormone administered to cows to increase milk yield, is also in current production (see Focus on page 324.

21.6 Biotechnology and fuel production

The rise in oil prices in the early 1970s led to research into alternative means of producing fuel. With only a finite supply of oil available, work continues in this field, accelerated to some extent by the harmful consequences of burning traditional fossil fuels. One method already tried is the fermentation of waste to yield **gasohol** (alcohol) or **biogas** (methane). It may be that in years to come, these fuels will be formed from crops specifically grown for the purpose.

21.6.1 Gasohol production

The 1970s rises in oil price hit oil-importing developing countries, such as Brazil, especially hard, and prompted the initiation of the **Brazilian National Alcohol (or Gasohol) Programme**. The concept was simple – namely to use yeasts to ferment Brazil's plentiful supply of sugar cane into alcohol and so create a relatively cheap, renewable home-produced fuel.

The programme began in 1975 and incorporated research into improving sugar cane production as well as fermenter technology. By 1985 sugar cane production had increased by a third, fermentation conversion by 10% and the fermentation time had been reduced by three quarters. Over 400 distilleries now yield more than $1.2 \times 10^{10}\,\mathrm{dm^3}$ of alcohol annually and all Brazilian cars have been converted to using the fuel, either entirely or mixed with petrol. (Some petrol is added to all alcohol fuels as a disincentive to people drinking them.) It is hoped that by the year 2000 all the country's energy needs will be supplied in this way. What makes the programme so successful in Brazil is that the sugar cane is not only a source of the fermentation substrate, but also a fuel for the distilleries. Once the sugar is extracted from the sugar cane, the fibrous waste, called **bagasse**, can be dried and burnt as a power source for the distillery.

The actual process entails a number of stages:

1. Growing and cropping sugar cane.

2. Extraction of sugars by crushing and washing the cane.

3. The crystallizing out of the sucrose (for sale) leaving a syrup of glucose and fructose called **molasses**.

4. Fermentation of the molasses by *Saccharomyces cerevisiae* to yield dilute alcohol.

5. Distillation of the dilute alcohol to give pure ethanol, using the waste bagasse as a power source.

The special circumstances in Brazil have doubtless contributed to its success but schemes in some other countries, e.g. Kenya, have been abandoned as uneconomic. Nevertheless, the potential for solving both the problem of diminishing oil supplies and disposal of waste at the same time has its attractions. Waste straw, sawdust, vegetable matter, paper and its associated waste, and other carbohydrates are all possible respiratory substrates although many require enzyme treatment to convert them into glucose before yeast can act upon them.

PROJECT

Substances are sold which claim to accelerate the production of compost. Investigate these claims by studying the production of biogas by decomposing vegetable matter.

Biogas generator, Senegal

21.6.2 Biogas production

The capacity of naturally occurring microorganisms to decompose wastes can be exploited to produce another useful fuel, methane (biogas). It has the advantage over alcohol (gasohol) production of not requiring complex distillation equipment – indeed, the process is very simple. A container known as a **digester** is filled with appropriate waste (domestic rubbish, sewage or agricultural waste can be used) to which is added a mixture of many bacterial species. The anaerobic fermentation of these yields methane which is collected ready for use for cooking, lighting or heating. Small domestic biogas fermenters are common in China and India.

21.7   Biotechnology and waste disposal

Did you know?

Removing a year's worth of waste generated by modern Britons would require a nose-to-tail queue of juggernauts stretching six times round the world.

In the previous section we saw how microorganisms could be used not only to dispose of wastes but also to yield a useful by-product at the same time. These are not the only ways in which microorganisms are used to dispose of unwanted material; the disposal of sewage, the decomposition of plastics and the breakdown of oil are further examples. Details of sewage treatment are given in Section 14.7.1.

21.8   Other products of the biotechnology industry

In addition to all the biotechnological applications of microorganisms already discussed, there is an assortment of other products made in this way. Some of these are given in Table 21.6.

In addition to their products, microorganisms may be utilized directly to human benefit. The nitrogen-fixing bacterium *Rhizobium* spp. lives symbiotically in nodules on the roots of certain plants where it forms nitrogenous compounds of use to its host. The addition of this bacterium to the soil, along with the seeds of the plants utilizing them, ensures inoculation of the crop and a resultant better yield in areas where natural inoculation is unlikely.

The bacterium *Bacillus thuringiensis* produces a protein which is highly toxic to insects. By contaminating the natural food of an insect pest with the bacterium, some control can be effected. The ecological consequences of using such 'natural' pesticides need further investigation but it seems likely that they will be less harmful than their artificial counterparts.

A recent, and controversial, development is the use of the bacterium *Pseudomonas syringae* to form artificial snow at winter holiday resorts. The bacterium, which is sprayed with water on to a fan, has surface properties which act as nuclei for the formation of ice crystals. The fact that this process could cause considerable frost-damage if used on food crops illustrates the risks that attend many biotechnological advances if used wrongly, either by accident or with malice.

FOCUS

Biological washing powders

The first biological washing powder was manufactured as long ago as 1913 using an extract from the pancreas which contained trypsin. This had very limited success in the alkaline liquids produced by the washing soda containing it. Since then the detergent industry has become the largest single outlet for industrial enzymes. Proteases remove protein stains such as blood, grass, egg and human sweat; lipases digest oily and fatty stains; amylases remove residues of starch substances. Some washing powders also contain a cellulase complex which modifies the fluffy microfibrils which develop when cotton and cotton-mix garments have been washed several times. This has the effect of brightening the colours and softening the fabric as well as removing some dirt particles.

Most of the enzymes are produced extracellularly by bacteria such as *Bacillus subtilis* grown in large-scale fermenters. The bacteria have been genetically engineered to produce enzymes which are stable at a high pH in the presence of phosphates and other detergent ingredients as well as remaining active at temperatures of 60 °C. Subtilisin, a protease, has also had an amino acid residue replaced with an alternative to make the enzyme more resistant to oxidation. During the 1970s the industry suffered a setback when many of the enzymes were shown to produce allergic reactions. This has been solved by producing encapsulated enzymes which are dust-free.

TABLE 21.6 **A range of other commercial substances produced by microorganisms**

Product	Producer organism	Function of product
Protease	*Aspergillus oryzae*	Detergent additive
	Bacillus spp.	Removal of hair from animal hides
Butanol and acetone	*Clostridium acetobutylicom*	Solvents
Indigo	*Escherichia coli*	Textile dye
Xanthan gum	*Xanthomonas campestris*	Thickener used in food, paints and cosmetics
Cellulases	*Trichoderma* spp.	Brightener in washing powders
Cyanocobalamin (vitamin B$_{12}$)	*Propioni bacterium shermanii*	Food supplement
Gellan	*Pseudomonas* spp.	Food thickener
Glutamate	*Corynebacterium glutamicum*	Flavour enhancer
Streptokinase	*Streptomyces* spp.	Treatment of thrombosis
Interferon	*Escherichia coli*	Treatment of viral infections
Ergot alkaloids	*Claviceps purpurea*	Vasoconstricter used to treat migraine and in childbirth
Cyclosporin	*Cotypocladium inflatum*	Immunosuppressant drug

21.9   Questions

1. The diagram shows part of a haemocytometer grid viewed at a magnification of ×700. The triple-lined square measures 0.2 mm × 0.2 mm. The chamber contains a yeast suspension at a depth of 0.1 mm.

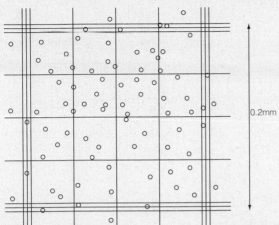

0.2mm

(a) Assuming that this triple-lined square is typical of all the squares on the haemocytometer grid, how many yeast cells are there in 1 mm^3 of the solution? Show your working. *(3 marks)*

(b) The dilution factor of the sample counted was $\times 10^{-3}$. How many yeast cells were there in 1 mm^3 of the original suspension? *(1 mark)*

(Total 4 marks)

NEAB June 1995, Paper BY06, No. 3

2. The graph shows the growth of a bacterial population.

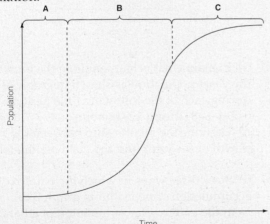

(a) Explain what happens during:
   (i) phase **A**;   *(2 marks)*
   (ii) phase **B**;   *(2 marks)*
   (iii) phase **C**.   *(2 marks)*

(b) Suggest **three** factors which might influence the length of phase **A**. *(3 marks)*

(Total 9 marks)

NEAB June 1995, Paper BY06, No. 4

3. The diagram shows a simplified flow-chart summarizing mycoprotein production.

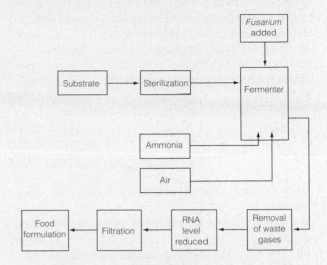

(a) Apart from hydrolysed starch, suggest **two** other ingredients of the substrate. *(2 marks)*

(b) Why is ammonia needed in this process? *(1 mark)*

(c) When the extract is removed from the fermenter, the RNA content is found to be high. Suggest a reason for this. *(1 mark)*

(d) (i) Mycoprotein is produced by a *continuous fermentation* process. Explain what 'continuous fermentation' means. *(2 marks)*

(ii) Suggest **one** advantage and **one** disadvantage of continuous fermentation over batch fermentation. *(2 marks)*

(Total 8 marks)

NEAB June 1995, Paper BY06, No. 6

4. Read the following passage.
Cheese is made from milk by two main processes. Lactic acid is first produced from lactose by bacterial action, which lowers the pH of the milk. Addition of the protease enzyme chymosin then partly breaks down casein proteins, forming a solid mass known as the curd. As the curd matures, further action by chymosin, and bacterial and milk enzymes leads to a variety of flavours and aromas.
Chymosin occurs in rennet, an extract from calf stomach. A genetically engineered chymosin is now available that is produced by cloning the calf chymosin gene in the fungus *Kluyveromyces lactis*. This is used to manufacture a range of so-called vegetarian cheeses.

From *Biochemistry for Advanced Biology* by Susan Aldridge (CUP, 1994).

(a) Explain the procedure by which the calf chymosin gene might have been isolated, inserted into the fungus *Kluyveromyces lactis*, and how chymosin might have subsequently been obtained.
(*4 marks*)

(b) The calf chymosin gene is cloned in the fungus *Kluyveromyces lactis*. Suggest **two** factors which should have been considered when choosing this fungus rather than a different species. (*2 marks*)

(c) Suggest **two** advantages of using chymosin produced by genetically engineered *Kluyveromyces lactis* rather than chymosin extracted from calves' stomachs. (*2 marks*)

(d) Describe **two** other uses of enzymes in industry. (*2 marks*)
(*Total 12 marks*)

NEAB June 1995, Paper BY06, No. 8

5. Immobilized enzymes are often used in industrial processes.

(a) Explain **two** advantages of using immobilized enzymes. (*4 marks*)

(b) The diagram shows a simple biosensor which can be used to measure the concentration of glucose in a solution.

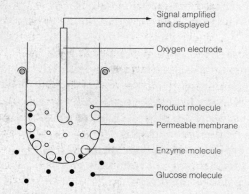

(i) Explain how this biosensor works. (*4 marks*)
(ii) Explain **two** advantages of using a similar biosensor to measure glucose levels in a blood sample, rather than using a chemical test such as Benedict's test. (*4 marks*)
(*Total 12 marks*)

NEAB June 1995, Paper BY06, No. 9

6. The table below refers to some industrially produced enzymes, their action and commercial uses. Complete the table by filling in the spaces.

Enzyme	Action	Commercial use
Amylase		
	Converts lipids to fatty acids and glycerol	Enhance ripening of blue mould cheeses
Pectinase	Degrades pectins	
Protease		Pre-digestion of baby foods

(*Total 5 marks*)

ULEAC 1996, Specimen Paper B/HB4A, No. 1

7. The graphs below show the growth of cultures of two microorganisms in industrial fermenters and the yield of their products.
Graph A shows the growth of the yeast *Saccharomyces* and the yield of its product, ethanol. Graph B shows the growth of the ascomycete mould *Penicillium* and the yield of its product, the antibiotic penicillin.

Graph A

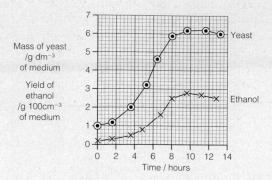

Graph B

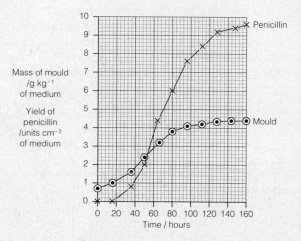

(a) (i) Explain what is happening in the growth of the yeast population as shown in graph A during each of the following time periods: 0–2, 4–6, 8–10 and 12–14 hours. (*4 marks*)
(ii) Describe the relationship between the growth of the yeast and the yield of ethanol. (*2 marks*)

(b) (i) State **three** ways in which the pattern of accumulation of penicillin in graph B differs from the pattern of accumulation of ethanol in graph A. (*3 marks*)
(ii) Ethanol is described as a *primary* metabolite of *Saccharomyces*: it is a direct product of metabolic processes essential for the life of the organism.
Penicillin is described as a *secondary* metabolite of *Penicillium*. It is a product of metabolic processes which are not essential to keep the organism alive.

Suggest how the differences in the patterns of accumulation of these two products may be related to their differing roles in the metabolism of the producer organisms. (*3 marks*)

(*Total 12 marks*)

ULEAC 1996, Specimen Paper B/HB4A, No. 6

8. An experiment was carried out to investigate the efficiency of various antibiotics in destroying a pathogenic bacterium.

Petri dishes of nutrient agar were inoculated with the bacterium using a spreading technique. A paper disc with six different coloured discs attached to it (called a Mastring) was then carefully placed on the surface of the agar in each Petri dish. This is shown in the diagram below.

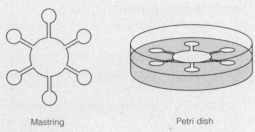

Mastring   Petri dish

Each disc on the Mastring had previously been dipped into a different antibiotic solution and allowed to dry. The Petri dishes were sealed with adhesive tape, turned upside down and incubated.

After 24 hours, the diameter of the clear zone around each disc was measured and used to calculate the area of the clear zone.

The results are given in the table below.

Antibiotic	Area of clear zone/cm²
Chloramphenicol	9.07
Erythromycin	4.90
Novobiocin	3.79
Penicillin G	0.78
Streptomycin	0.00
Tetracycline	2.54

Adapted from Freeland, *Investigations in Applied Biology and Biotechnology*

(*a*) (i) Which antibiotic appeared to be the most effective against the bacterium? Give a reason for your answer. (*2 marks*)

(ii) Compare the relative activities of novobiocin and tetracycline in destroying the bacterium. (*2 marks*)

(*b*) (i) Describe how the spreading technique is carried out. (*3 marks*)

(ii) Why were the Petri dishes sealed with adhesive tape? (*1 mark*)

(iii) What was the reason for turning the Petri dishes upside down before placing them in the incubator? (*1 mark*)

(*c*) Explain why penicillin is produced commercially by batch fermentation, rather than in continuous culture. (*2 marks*)

(*d*) Suggest **two** reasons why commercial yields of penicillin are much greater now than they were when production first started (*2 marks*)

(*Total 13 marks*)

ULEAC June 1995, Paper 4A, No. 1

9. Enzymes are used industrially in a wide range of applications. The majority of these enzymes are extracted from microorganisms such as bacteria and yeasts.

The diagram below represents the stages involved in the production of an isolated enzyme.

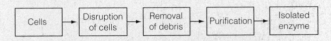

(*a*) (i) Suggest **two** advantages of using micro-organisms as a source of enzymes. (*2 marks*)

(ii) Suggest **two** advantages of using isolated enzymes rather than whole organisms in industrial processes. (*2 marks*)

(iii) Suggest **one** disadvantage of using isolated enzymes in industrial processes. (*1 mark*)

(*b*) Purified enzymes are frequently immobilized. This means that the enzyme molecules are attached to an insoluble support or entrapped within spheres of gel. One simple method of immobilizing an enzyme in the laboratory is to mix it with a solution of sodium alginate and then, using a syringe, allow drops of the mixture to fall into a solution of calcium chloride. The alginate/enzyme mixture forms beads, which are allowed to stand in the calcium chloride solution for 20 minutes to become firm. They are then strained from the calcium chloride solution, rinsed and packed into a column ready for use. The enzyme substrate can be added to the column and the products can be collected at the bottom. These events are summarized in the diagram below.

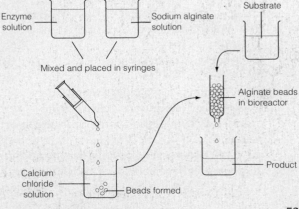

(i) State **two** factors which would affect the rate at which the products would be formed in such a system. *(2 marks)*

(ii) Suggest **two** advantages of using immobilized enzymes rather than enzymes in solution *(2 marks)*

(c) Name **two** enzymes used in the food industry and in each case briefly describe its application. *(6 marks)*
(Total 15 marks)

ULEAC June 1994, Paper 1, No. 12

10. The diagram below shows an industrial fermenter of a type similar to that used in the batch culture of the antibiotic penicillin.

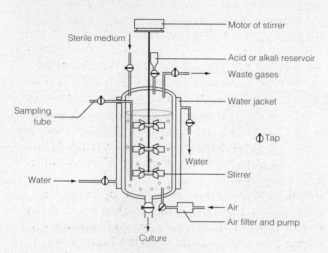

The production of penicillin in such a fermenter is carried out according to the following time scale.

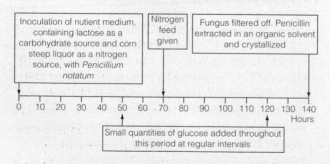

(Adapted from Brock & Madigan, *Biology of Microorganisms*)

(a) What is the function of each of the following?
  (i) Water jacket *(1 mark)*
  (ii) Acid or alkali reservoir *(1 mark)*
  (iii) Air filter *(1 mark)*

(b) (i) Penicillin is a secondary metabolite. Explain why continuous culture is an unsatisfactory method for the production of penicillin. *(2 marks)*

(ii) Give **two** possible reasons for the addition of glucose between 50 hours and 120 hours. *(2 marks)*

(c) In the laboratory *Penicillium* would usually be grown on an agar plate. What advantages are gained from the use of a liquid medium? *(2 marks)*
(Total 9 marks)

ULEAC June 1994, Paper 4A, No. 1

11. The diagram below shows a biogas plant as used by a family in China.

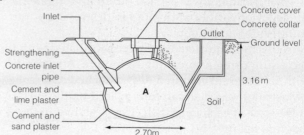

(a) Name **two** constituents of biogas. *(2 marks)*

(b) (i) Describe the processes which occur in **A**. *(2 marks)*

(ii) Explain why the pH within the biogas plant falls during the first stages of gas production. *(1 mark)*

(c) Explain why the biogas plant is normally kept sealed. *(1 mark)*

(d) Suggest why this biogas plant is built underground. *(1 mark)*
(Total 7 marks)

ULEAC June 1993, Paper 1, No. 7

12. The diagram below shows a herpes simplex virus.

(a) Name the parts labelled **A**, **B** and **C**. *(3 marks)*

(b) State **two** structural differences between the herpes simplex virus and the mumps virus. *(2 marks)*

(c) Following infection of a cell, how does the herpes virus replicate? *(2 marks)*
(Total 7 marks)

ULEAC June 1995, Paper 4A, No. 5

13. Describe how the metabolic activities of *Saccharomyces* are exploited in food and drink production.
(Total 10 marks)

ULEAC June 1995, Paper 4A, No. 7

22 Human health and disease

22.1 Principles of human health

Some scientific terms are relatively easy to define, others are more difficult; 'health' and 'disease' fall into the latter category. Some would suggest that 'disease' is merely a disorder of a system's normal functions and that 'health' is the absence of 'disease'. Can a person whose bodily systems are functioning properly but who feels unhappy or depressed be defined as healthy? Can alcoholics or drug-addicts whose habits have not as yet caused any physical harm be likewise described? Clearly health is more than physical well-being, it involves mental and social well-being as well.

If it is difficult to say what we understand by 'health'; to define 'disease' is even more problematic. It is not so much a single entity as a description of certain symptoms which suggest a pattern of future events. Skill and expertise in accurately predicting these future events is what makes an effective doctor.

22.1.1 Classification of diseases

Any classification of diseases into groups invariably leads to problems when one attempts to place a specific disease into a single category. This is because while a number of diseases fit neatly and entirely into one category, some seem to belong to more than one group and yet others combine elements of all types. This being said, six categories are often recognized.

Infections – those communicable diseases which can be passed on from one individual to another. They are almost always caused by other living organisms especially microorganisms, e.g. influenza.

Inherited – genetic diseases which are inherited from one or other parent, e.g. cystic fibrosis.

Degenerative – caused as a result of ageing or the breakdown of the normal structure of a tissue or organ, e.g. senile dementia.

Mental – diseases of the mind, e.g. schizophrenia.

Human inflicted – caused as a result of human activities – often one's own, e.g. alcoholism.

Deficiency – the result of the absence of one or more essential components of the diet, e.g. rickets.

Any disease may be **acute** (appears suddenly and is short-lived) or **chronic** (develops slowly and persists). They may be the result of environmental influences such as radiation or pollutants or they may have no apparent cause. Some diseases, e.g. coronary heart disease, have a series of 'risk factors' each of which increases the chance of developing the illness. Occupation and life style often affect the onset of a particular disease.

22.1.2 Patterns of disease distribution

The incidence of diseases alters both in time and space. In the nineteenth century, infectious illnesses such as smallpox were very common throughout the world. Thanks to vaccination programmes and other medical advances smallpox has now been eradicated entirely.

While many infectious diseases such as malaria and typhoid are still common in the developing world, they are extremely rare in developed countries; here deaths from infectious diseases have given way to those caused by heart disease, cancer and accidents. The relative poverty of the developing nations has restricted the extent of medical care, immunization programmes, health education, clean water supplies and communications, all of which could help reduce the incidence of infectious disease. By contrast, the relative affluence of the developed countries has ensured the control of these diseases, but brought life styles which include tobacco smoking, reduced exercise as a result of car use, excess alcohol consumption, pollution and overeating. These explain in part the alarming frequency of coronary heart disease, cancers and road accidents in these countries.

The effects and global distribution of a disease such as measles illustrates the differences between the developed and developing world. In developed countries where children are well fed and immunization is common, any occurrence of the disease is normally mild and rarely fatal. In developing countries malnutrition and the absence of immunization lead to low resistance and high child mortality especially of those under two years of age. Deaths from measles in the UK dropped from over 4000 in 1930 to around 20 a year in recent times, so while it is not in the 20 major causes of death in the UK it is frequently in the top 5 in developing countries.

22.2 Infectious diseases

The human body is an ideal incubator for most microorganisms. It provides a warm environment of constant temperature, a near neutral pH, a constant supply of food and water in nicely balanced proportions for growth, a transport system which efficiently conveys materials to all parts, a ready supply of oxygen and mechanisms for removing waste materials. Not surprisingly therefore our bodies are naturally colonized by a large number of microorganisms all of which have the capacity to cause disease. The fact that, in most cases, they do not, is the result of our considerable armoury of physical and chemical defences. Many microorganisms live more or less permanently in our bodies benefiting from doing so, but doing us no harm.

Smallpox – the last Jenneration!

There is a certain nicety about the fact that the first disease to be treated by the process of vaccination should be the first major disease to be eradicated by that very process. In the eighteenth century, it had long been known that people did not contract smallpox if they had suffered from the related, but much less dangerous, cattle disease, cowpox. Indeed some brave farmers had deliberately inoculated their relatives with cowpox in order to make them immune. It was however a Gloucestershire doctor, Edward Jenner, who, in 1794, first showed scientifically that cowpox could be used to immunize against smallpox. He took the considerable gamble of inoculating a young boy with cowpox and then, after six weeks, did so with a sample of smallpox. The disease did not take hold and the principle of vaccination (*vacca* is the Latin word for cow) had been discovered.

It was however nearly 200 years later, in 1977, that the scourge of smallpox was eradicated from the world when the last case was reported from Somalia. There has since been a case of smallpox being contracted when a person became infected by a laboratory sample, but no 'natural' recurrence of the disease.

Why then has smallpox succumbed when other diseases such as tuberculosis, measles, malaria and cholera have not, despite, in most cases, worldwide vaccination programmes? Perhaps the most significant factor has been the stability of the smallpox virus which, unlike many other pathogens, did not change its antigens. It did not therefore develop resistant strains against which the vaccine would have been ineffective. Other factors included: the severity of the disease, whose potentially lethal nature made people much more amenable to undergoing vaccination; the ease with which the vaccine could be prepared in bulk; and the simple and painless way the vaccine was administered. The symptoms of the disease were also easy to diagnose allowing rapid isolation of patients before they could spread it further.

These microorganisms are called **commensals**. Other microorganisms, however, cause disease and these are called **pathogens**. The extent to which the pathogen causes damage is known as **virulence**. For a microorganism to be considered a pathogen it must:

1. Gain entry to the host.
2. Colonize the tissues of the host.
3. Resist the defences of the host.
4. Cause damage to the host tissues.

22.2.1 Entry of microorganisms into the body

Entry of pathogens occurs broadly in two ways: via the skin or through natural openings. With its thick, continuous, keratinized layer the skin is an effective barrier to infection. Microorganisms do not readily adhere to it and can easily be removed as the surface cells are shed or during washing. The acidity of secretions from the sweat and sebaceous glands discourage the growth of microorganisms, and the enzyme lysozyme in tears breaks down bacterial cell walls. Invasion therefore normally only occurs when the skin is broken. Cuts and abrasions may occur as a result of injury or certain skin conditions like eczema. Biting insects such as mosquitoes, lice and fleas, or bites and scratches from animals may also allow entry. In many cases the pathogen is deliberately introduced by the bite rather than by a chance opportunity.

The natural openings of the body make suitable access points for microorganisms. Many infectious diseases are respiratory and, despite a mucus layer, lysozymes, cilia and phagocytic cells at various points in the trachea, bronchi and alveoli, diseases such as influenza, tuberculosis and bronchitis infect via the air inhaled along this route. Food and water may carry the agents of typhoid, dysentery and cholera into the stomach and intestines via the mouth. If they do not succumb to the stomach acid and intestinal enzymes they may cause disease. The genital and urinary openings may allow microorganisms to enter. Those requiring direct contact for their transference are easily transmitted during sexual intercourse. Examples include the agents of AIDS, syphilis and gonorrhoea.

22.2.2 Colonizing the tissues of the host

Pathogens need to fix themselves at the site of their infection. This they achieve through a combination of physical modifications (e.g. the protein spikes of the influenza virus) or chemical means (e.g. adhesive substances in some pneumonia pathogens). Once fixed, multiplication occurs rapidly to build up numbers. The need then is to spread the newly formed pathogens throughout the tissue and/or to other regions of the body. Some microorganisms may produce toxins which cause irritation, and this leads to responses such as scratching, coughing and sneezing which help to spread the infection to unaffected areas. Enzymes produced by some pathogens enable them to penetrate cells and so gradually invade a tissue. Via tissue fluid, microorganisms may enter the lymphatic system and so be carried around the body in this way, often entering the blood system and then to all parts of the body. Measles which initially enters via the respiratory system is spread in this way, ultimately affecting areas including the skin and nervous system.

22.2.3 Resisting the host's defences

If the skin and mucus linings of the body represent the first line of defence, then the immune responses of the blood and lymphatic system are the second line. Details of how these operate are given in Section 16.3.

Resisting the second line of defence is achieved in a number of ways including:

1. Interfering with the chemotactic attraction of phagocytes for the pathogen (e.g. the tuberculosis bacterium).

2. Resisting ingestion by phagocytes (e.g. plague bacterium).

3. Avoiding digestion once ingested by phagocytes (e.g. leprosy bacterium).

4. Destruction of phagocytes (e.g. staphylocci).

22.2.4 Damaging the host

The extent of any damage the pathogen causes and hence the onset of its symptoms is related to the rate at which it multiplies. Pathogens like those causing gastro-enteritis divide about every 30 minutes and so produce symptoms within 24 hours of infection. The leprosy bacterium, by contrast, takes up to 3 weeks to divide and so symptoms are not apparent for many months. Some pathogens, e.g. *Salmonella,* will only cause damage if present in very large numbers; others such as the typhoid bacterium cause harm when their numbers are relatively small.

Damage to the host tissues arises as a consequence of one or more of three conditions:

1. **The multiplication of the microorganisms** – Some protozoan infections lead to such a build-up of pathogens that their sheer numbers block the functioning of certain organs. Viruses inhibit the synthesis of DNA, RNA and proteins by the host. The polio virus for example prevents nervous stimulation of muscles by this means.

2. **Toxins from the pathogen** – Most bacterial pathogens produce toxins whose effects are highly diverse. *Clostridium botulinum* which causes botulism produces a neurotoxin which is one of the most potent poisons known. The toxin of *Streptococcus pyogenes* which causes scarlet fever is a vasodilator, while that of *Corynebacterium diphtheriae*, the diphtheria bacterium, inhibits protein synthesis.

3. **As a result of the immune response** – To enable the host to fight pathogens the blood supply to the infected area is increased because of vasodilation. This may lead to inflammation and soreness. The immune response can cause a rise in temperature and consequent fever. Such symptoms are common in most diseases including influenza.

22.2.5 Acquired Immune Deficiency Syndrome (AIDS)

Having first been diagnosed in 1982 AIDS, unlike most other infectious diseases, is a relative newcomer. Such has been the rapidity of its spread that it is now the leading cause of death among 25–45 year old men in the USA and one-third of all adults in Uganda are infected. The World Health Organization estimates that by the year 2000, up to 40 million people will be infected. AIDS is caused by the **human immunodeficiency virus (HIV)**, a spherical retrovirus whose structure is shown in Figure 22.1. More details of retroviruses are given in Section 21.1.3.

Once infected with HIV an individual is said to be **HIV positive**, a condition which persists throughout life. As the virus remains dormant for about eight years, on average, an HIV positive person does not show any symptoms during this period but can act as a carrier, often unwittingly spreading the disease. The virus can be detected in virtually all bodily fluids of an HIV positive individual. However, since it is only in blood, semen or

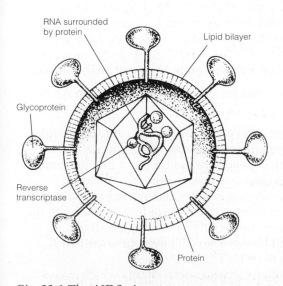

Fig. 22.1 The AIDS virus

RNA surrounded by protein

Lipid bilayer

Glycoprotein

Reverse transcriptase

Protein

vaginal fluid that the concentration is high it is usually spread through sexual intercourse, or transfer of infected blood from one person to another – as when drug users share a hypodermic needle – or from mother to baby during childbirth. There is some evidence that HIV can be transmitted from mother to baby across the placenta as well as in breast milk. The transfusion of HIV infected blood has in the past spread AIDS, although blood is now routinely screened to avoid any risk to patients such as haemophiliacs who depend on transfused blood. Faeces, urine, sweat, saliva and tears have such a low incidence of HIV in an infected person that contact with these substances presents only a very remote possibility of contracting AIDS. In any case, the virus quickly dies outside the human body, and therefore even blood, semen and vaginal secretions must be transferred directly. Thus the risk from contaminated clothing etc. is negligible.

Having entered the blood HIV infects blood cells carrying CD4 receptors (CD4+ lymphocytes) such as T-helper cells (Section 16.3.1) to which the virus readily binds. It becomes enclosed within the cell membrane and so its antigens do not stimulate an immune response from the lymphocytes in the blood. Replication of the virus is controlled and it frequently becomes latent. It is months or years later that replication recommences, so that it is on average eight years before AIDS develops. Most victims then die within two years, usually of opportunist pathogens which take advantage of impaired resistance. Oral thrush is often an early symptom, followed by tuberculosis or pneumonia. All AIDS patients lose weight, some develop a skin cancer called Kaposi's sarcoma. Loss of memory and coordination may occur in the late stages of the disease.

There is, as yet, no cure for AIDS. Much effort is being expended in developing a vaccine but progress is being hampered by the rapid rate at which HIV mutates, the fact that HIV 'hides' itself within the CD4+ lymphocyte cell membrane and the risk that a vaccine from attenuated HIV could induce cancers. Furthermore, as AIDS affects almost exclusively humans, there are no suitable animals on which to test new drugs; humans are the only guinea pigs. Current approaches to trying to find a suitable treatment for AIDS involve the development of:

1. Drugs which inhibit HIV.

2. A vaccine to prevent AIDS.

3. Medicines which boost the immune system of AIDS sufferers.

4. Treatments for the other infections which develop in AIDS sufferers.

Despite these efforts preventative measures are, at present, the best means of containing the disease. Education is paramount and much expenditure has been put into informing the population of the risks and how to minimize them. At highest risk are those sharing needles and syringes and those having unprotected anal intercourse. Avoiding contact with the blood of another person (especially by sharing needles) and using condoms for all forms of sexual intercourse are two obvious precautions to take.

Sadly, AIDS still often carries a social stigma which makes some patients feel ostracized and isolated. The disease also raises moral issues about whether HIV positive individuals should be refused insurance or mortgages or others be required to have an HIV test before being accepted for either.

22.2.6 Influenza

Almost all of us will at some time be infected by the influenza virus. It is therefore sobering to reflect that, what to many of us is just a transient inconvenience, has cost millions of lives this century. The 1918 pandemic alone was estimated to have killed 20 million people worldwide. The structure of the influenza virus and an account of its life cycle are given in Section 21.1.2.

The disease primarily affects the respiratory tract and is spread by inhalation of droplets containing the virus which have been expelled during coughing and sneezing of an infected person. The **neuroaminidase** on the virus's surface allows it to liquefy the protective mucus layer of the throat so that the epithelium beneath is exposed. The **haemagglutinin** spikes on its surface then attach to an epithelial cell. The virus penetrates the cell, injecting its RNA. The virus often spreads throughout the respiratory tract causing sore throat, headache and mild fever. Exposure of the epithelium and reduced resistance as a consequence of fighting the infection can lead to complications from other diseases, most notably pneumonia. It is these secondary infections which more often prove fatal, with the very young and the elderly being most vulnerable. The **incubation period** (the period of time from infection to appearance of symptoms) is normally one to two days.

Treatment for influenza entails taking paracetamol or aspirin to relieve the symptoms and antibiotics may be used to help prevent secondary infections (although they do not treat influenza directly). Vulnerable groups can be immunized, although vaccines are only partially effective, immunity is short and there may be side-effects such as a raised temperature. The constantly mutating nature of the virus means that vaccines quickly become ineffective and new ones have to be developed.

22.2.7 Tuberculosis

Once a common disease in the UK with up to 40 000 cases a year, tuberculosis (TB) is now relatively rare in developed countries, but remains a major killer elsewhere. Significantly there has been a worrying increase in cases both in the UK and the USA.

Mycobacterium tuberculosis, the bacterium causing TB, is rod-shaped and 2–4μm long. It may affect almost any human organ, although pulmonary tuberculosis (infection of the lung) is most common. Infection is most frequently from the inhalation of droplets exhaled during coughing by an infected person, although in a healthy individual whose immune system is operating effectively, the bacteria are normally destroyed rapidly. Transmission occurs most readily in damp, overcrowded conditions. Bovine TB can be passed to humans via infected milk. In the UK, pasteurization of milk and the slaughter of infected cattle has eliminated this source of the disease, but it remains a problem elsewhere in the world.

Initial infection is termed **primary TB** and often displays no symptoms. Some bacteria may, however, remain dormant for up to 30 years and then re-emerge as **post-primary TB** in the lungs

Did you know?

Tuberculosis killed nearly 3 million people worldwide in 1995 – more than in any other year in history.

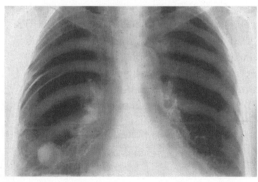

Chest X-ray of a TB infected person

or elsewhere. Without treatment, the bacteria destroy the lung tissue and cause accumulation of fluid in the pleural cavity between the lungs and the chest wall. Treatment involves the administration of anti-TB drugs for a period of six months to ensure its complete eradication. A cocktail of 3 or 4 types is given as there are a number of strains of the bacterium, some resistant to certain drugs.

Prevention of the disease through vaccination has proved the most successful weapon in controlling TB. All children in the UK are routinely tested for their immunity to TB by the injection of a small amount of protein from *Mycobacterium tuberculosis* in what is known as the **Heaf test**. Examination of the injected area some days later may reveal a localized reaction, indicating that the child is already immune. Vaccination of these individuals is unnecessary and dangerous. Those showing no reaction are given the **Bacille Calmette-Guerin (BCG)** vaccine. This is an attenuated (weakened) strain of *Mycobacterium bovis* which causes bovine TB. While this form of mass immunization has been the major reason for the fall in cases of TB in the UK there is no doubt that improved social conditions have also played a part. Better housing, with less overcrowding and less damp conditions, and better nutrition have reduced the ease with which the disease can be transmitted until recently. Now there are signs of a resurgence of the disease in some developed countries. In Britain, for example, there were 10 000 more cases of TB between 1987 and 1993 than would have been expected if the previous downward trend of the last 100 years had been maintained. The reasons for this change are complex but include:

1. A greater number of people living 'rough'.
2. More movement of individuals between countries.
3. Reduced immunity levels in some groups, e.g. AIDS sufferers.
4. A larger proportion of elderly, who are more vulnerable, in the population.
5. Greater antibiotic resistance in strains of the bacterium.

Tuberculosis looks set to remain one of the most significant human diseases in years to come and so presents mankind with one of its greatest challenges.

22.2.8 Cholera

Until 1817 cholera was thought to be a disease of the Indian sub-continent alone, but a series of pandemics in that year affected many other parts of the world. An English scientist, John Snow, suggested in 1854 that it was a disease spread by water or food but it wasn't until 1883 that Robert Koch isolated the causative agent – the curved rod-shaped bacterium *Vibrio cholerae*. Cholera remains endemic to India and parts of Asia where it kills millions of people each year with epidemics arising elsewhere from time to time.

Cholera is transmitted by ingestion of water or food which has been contaminated with faecal material containing the pathogen. Such contamination can arise because water is not purified, sewers leak into water supplies, untreated sewage is allowed into watercourses or organisms, especially shellfish, feed on sewage and are subsequently eaten. Carriers who show no symptoms may unwittingly spread the disease.

The incubation period for cholera can be from 8 hours to 6 days. The most obvious symptom is a watery diarrhoea in which grey liquid stools, called 'rice water', are passed almost unceasingly. This may be accompanied by vomiting. Between them these symptoms can result in immense fluid loss – up to 20 litres a day – causing severe cramps (due to loss of body salts) and eventual collapse. In severe cases death can result within 2 days, but in milder outbreaks or with suitable treatment complete recovery occurs in 1–3 weeks.

The priority in treatment is to replace water and salts which may be given orally (see Focus on oral rehydration on page 259) or in extreme cases, intravenously. This is followed by giving antibiotics such as tetracycline to destroy the pathogen. Prevention methods involve proper sanitation and water purification to sever the normal transmission route. Personal hygiene such as washing hands after defecation and not handling food with uncovered hands also contribute. Flies may act as vectors and so preventing them coming into contact with faeces and food is a further preventative measure. Patients with the disease need to be isolated until they are no longer infected, and their faeces and vomit disposed of safely. Vaccination using killed bacteria is partially effective although the length of immunity is short – a mere six months.

22.2.9 *Salmonella*

Salmonella are a large group of bacteria which can cause a variety of diseases including typhoid, paratyphoid, enteric fever and food poisoning. These infections are collectively called **salmonelloses**. Incidences of food poisoning in the UK have increased in recent years.

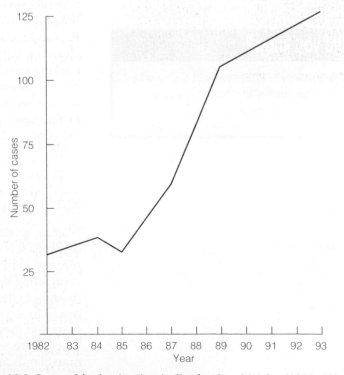

Fig. 22.2 Cases of food poisoning in England and Wales (1982–93)

Food poisoning by *Salmonella* is characterized by diarrhoea, stomach cramps and vomiting. The incubation period can be as short as 12 hours, but the symptoms normally subside after 2–3 days and recovery is complete. In a few cases dehydration or blood poisoning (septicaemia) may arise and can, on rare occasions, lead to death. The very young, the elderly or those with reduced immunity are most at risk. Animals, such as turkeys, chickens, pigs and cattle form a major reservoir of *Salmonella*. If produce from these animals, including eggs and milk, is inadequately cooked before being eaten, food poisoning can result. The faeces of infected humans and domestic pets may also contain *Salmonella*.

Modern factory farming practices such as raising poultry in battery houses, can lead to a build-up of *Salmonella* in the animals as a result of their proximity to each other. Farmers use antibiotics and a range of preventative measures to try to contain such outbreaks but it is notoriously difficult to eradicate the bacterium completely. Humans who harbour the bacteria but show no symptoms (human carriers) may also unwittingly spread *Salmonella* infection.

As with all diseases in which diarrhoea is a symptom, treatment entails administering fluid to prevent dehydration. Otherwise it is largely a matter of resting until the symptoms abate. Personal hygiene is important to avoid contaminating other material, especially food, which could transmit infection to others. Antibiotics can be given but as this encourages the development of strains of *Salmonella* resistant to these drugs, their use is normally reserved for severe cases.

Preventative measures for salmonelloses are centred upon proper hygiene, especially in the preparation and handling of food. In shops and restaurants health regulations control such measures as safe storage and packaging of food, the use of different surfaces for chopping and preparing each type of food, the proper cooking of food, cleaning of utensils and control of flies and rodents. Equally in the home it is important to maintain cleanliness and hygiene when dealing with food. Thorough cooking kills *Salmonella* and is essential for animal meat and animal products. Frozen food must be properly thawed and raw and cooked meats should be stored separately. Personal hygiene and control of vermin, especially flies, reduce the risk of infection as does proper sewage disposal and water purification.

22.2.10 Malaria

Malaria is one of the world's oldest and most devastating diseases. It is estimated that 365 million people are currently infected with a further 2200 million or more being at risk from contracting the disease. Up to one million children each year are thought to die from malaria in Africa alone. It is caused by any one of four parasitic protozoan species of which *Plasmodium vivax* and *Plasmodium falciparum* are the most common. Once much more widespread – there were cases in the Kent marshlands as late as the 1930s – it is now mostly confined to the tropics and subtropics.

Plasmodium has two different hosts during its life cycle – humans and mosquitoes of the genus *Anopheles*. The female mosquitoes suck blood prior to laying their eggs and when they bite a human infected with *Plasmodium* they take in the parasite which then continues its life cycle within the mosquito. When the mosquito later bites another human the parasite passes in with the insect's saliva. Organisms which transmit diseases from human to human or animal to human are termed **vectors**. An anticoagulant is produced by the mosquito to prevent blood clotting during the feeding.

Plasmodium has a complex life cycle of many stages, but basically the parasite in humans initially invades the liver where it multiplies before releasing vast numbers of one of its stages (**merozoites**) into the bloodstream. Here they invade red blood cells where they further multiply at the expense of the cell. When this new wave of merozoites is released it is accompanied by a bout of fever in the host. Re-invasion of other red blood cells, multiplication and release occurs about every 2 or 3 days depending on the species and so leads to a similar pattern of fever bouts in the host. Some cells of this stage develop into male and female stages (**gametocytes**) and remain in the blood until taken up by a feeding female mosquito. In the stomach of the mosquito they mature and fertilize, and the resultant zygote burrows through the stomach wall and encysts. From this cyst large numbers of a further stage (**sporozoites**) are released into the mosquito's blood from where they migrate to the salivary glands ready for injection into the next human host.

The incubation period for malaria is 10–14 days. The symptoms recur in cycles which coincide with the release of merozoites and so the frequency varies with each species, e.g. two days in the case of *Plasmodium vivax*. The cycle of symptoms normally includes the following sequence:

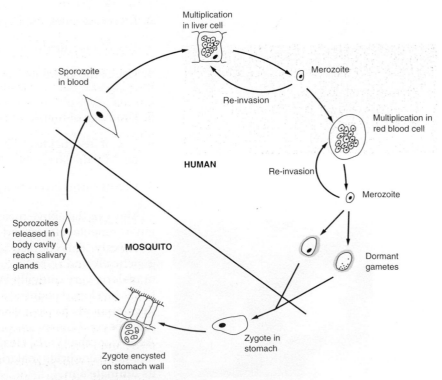

Fig. 22.3 Plasmodium vivax – *simplified life cycle*

1. Headache, tiredness, aching and sometimes vomiting.

2. Shivering, feeling of cold which lasts around 2 hours.

3. Sudden rise in body temperature to 40 °C or above leading to faster heart rate and breathing rate, nausea and fever, lasting about 4 hours.

4. Profuse sweating for between 2 and 4 hours as the body temperature is returned to normal.

If untreated, many bouts of fever may be experienced leaving the patient anaemic and exhausted. This, coupled with possible blockage or rupture of blood vessels, can cause the death of the patient. People who suffer from sickle-cell anaemia have a higher resistance to malaria than those with normal blood cells. This is discussed fully in Section 8.5.3.

Treatment of malaria entails giving anti-malarial drugs such as quinine, chloroquinine and quinacrine, often in combination. These drugs have unpleasant side-effects and *Plasmodium* has developed resistance to them in some cases. Its many stages and strains plus the fact that the parasite is an eukaryotic rather than a prokaryotic cell (see Section 4.1) has made the development of a vaccine very difficult. The latest area of vaccine development has centred on a protein called pfs-25 which attaches itself to the gametocytes prior to them being taken up by the mosquito. The protein seems to prevent the development of sporozoites in the mosquito, breaking the life cycle of *Plasmodium*. While this treatment does not help the patient directly, if successful it could be used to prevent the disease being transmitted to others. Prevention of malaria takes a number of forms:

1. Providing drugs which protect against malaria, e.g. proguanil and pyrimethamine.

2. Use of vaccines – difficult and still being developed (see above).

3. Use of insecticides to kill mosquitoes, especially in homes.

4. Use of mosquito nets to prevent biting by mosquitoes during sleep.

5. Drainage of marshes and swamps where mosquitoes breed.

6. Use of insecticides or oil on water where mosquitoes breed, to destroy the larvae before they develop into adults.

7. Use of carnivorous fish to eat mosquito larvae.

Many of the above measures have highly undesirable environmental effects and are, in any case, difficult to implement effectively. This coupled with the ability of *Plasmodium* to change genetically and so resist drugs and vaccines has made the control of malaria very difficult. With the disease almost eradicated from developed countries the impetus to make further developments has lost some of its momentum, and the costs are often beyond the means of the countries in which it is endemic. As a result the World Health Organization's programme started in 1955 to eradicate malaria has still a long way to go to achieve its ultimate aim.

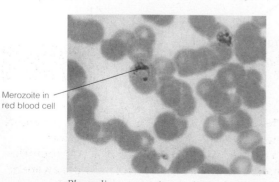

Merozoite in red blood cell

Plasmodium merozoites at signet ring stage

TABLE 22.1   Causes and symptoms of other infectious diseases

Disease	Type of organism	Example	Symptoms	Transmitted by
Dysentery	Bacterium Amoeboid protozoan	*Shigella dysenteriae* *Entamoeba histolytica*	Painful diarrhoea, blood in faeces, frequent abdominal pain. Death may occur as a result of dehydration	Food and water – contaminated with faeces. Flies may be vectors. Human carriers
Botulism	Bacterium	*Clostridium botulinum*	Vomiting, abdominal pain, weakness and paralysis leading to inability to breathe and death	Contaminated food which has not been heated to at least 120°C
Typhoid	Bacterium	*Salmonella typhosa*	Headache, loss of energy, cough and fever followed by swollen abdomen, weakness and delirium and a pink rash	Contaminated food and water. Human carriers
Poliomyelitis	RNA virus	*Poliovirus*	Headache, fever, sore throat and vomiting followed by neck and back pain and ultimately paralysis and death	Contaminated water (mainly). Food and utensils (more rarely). Human carriers
Listeriosis	Bacterium	*Listeria monocytogenes*	Headache, vomiting, aching possibly leading to meningitis and septicaemia	Food contaminated with *Listeria* especially dairy products
Thrush	Fungus	*Candida albicans*	White patches on the tongue and in the mouth and other areas, e.g. vagina. These may simply irritate but infection can spread in immunodeficient patients (e.g. those with AIDS) and ultimately cause death	Normal inhabitant of the body of many humans (commensal)

22.2.11 Athlete's foot

Athlete's foot is caused by the fungus *Tinea pedis*. It is a common infection, especially amongst young adults, which gains its name from the fact that it can be transmitted when the feet are exposed in damp humid conditions as often arise in changing rooms.

The symptoms include irritation of the skin between the toes, which becomes sodden and peels off. The infection may spread to other parts of the feet and sometimes to the hands also. The irritation is often more acute in summer because sweating exacerbates the condition. The skin can become broken and so lead to secondary infections.

The treatment consists of applying a special fungicide to the infected area, normally in the form of a cream. Other than avoiding areas where the fungus is known to occur there is little that can be done to prevent the disease, although thorough drying of the feet after bathing, especially between the toes, and the application of talcum powder with a fungicide will help.

22.3   Inherited disease

The considerable advances made in recent years in our understanding of heredity and genetics has improved our ability to recognize and treat inherited disease in a way that was unthinkable only a decade ago. Perhaps, as developed countries overcame many infectious diseases, they became more aware of alternative causes of death including genetic ones and focused medical attention on curing these. Certainly our mapping of genes in the human genome now allows us to identify the specific gene or genes which lead to many inherited disorders and, through techniques such as gene therapy (Section 5.8), enable us to rectify these. Even where a cure cannot be achieved, amniocentesis and chorionic villus sampling (Focus on page 160) and genetic counselling (Section 8.7.1) can be used to allow individuals to make choices in fuller knowledge of the risks involved.

Information on specific inherited disorders is given elsewhere in this book notably cystic fibrosis (Focus on page 194), haemophilia and colour blindness (Section 7.4.2), Down's syndrome, Klinefelter's and Turner's syndromes (Section 8.5.5) and Huntington's disease (Focus on page 162).

22.4   Degenerative disease

Degenerative diseases are the result of the gradual breakdown in the functioning of tissues or organs as a result of deterioration. This deterioration may be the result of ageing as in the case of some forms of senile dementia or it may occur much earlier in life, e.g. multiple sclerosis (see Focus on page 456). General details of the effects of old age on the various systems of the body are given in Section 10.8.

22.4.1 Dementia

It is not a new phenomenon that mental faculties may deteriorate with age, but as medical care has considerably increased life expectancy, so the frequency of the disease has increased. Dementia adversely effects memory, intellectual capacity, attention span, personality and motor control. **Alzheimer's disease** is not the natural result of ageing but is due to diminished activity of acetylcholine transferase in the brain. Details of the disease are given in the Focus on page 474.

Other forms of dementia are the result of the ageing process. They may, for example, be the result of **atherosclerosis** which causes a narrowing of arteries due to the hardening and thickening of their walls. As a result the blood supply to the brain can be reduced leading to mental deterioration. Thromboses may arise in the vessels leading to a **stroke** or the walls may split resulting in a **cerebral haemorrhage**. Both of these often lead to a sudden, rather than a gradual, onset of dementia.

Treatment for dementia often consists of making the best use of a patient's remaining faculties as we do not, as yet, have any cure for conditions such as Alzheimer's disease. Much care and patience is required by those looking after the patient, especially as failing memory can make individuals a danger to themselves. It is recent rather than long-term memory which often fails first in cases of dementia. Carers often need much support, guidance and periodic relief from their role, if the task is not to prove harmful to their own health; social services, support groups and voluntary organizations such as Age Concern provide welcome assistance in many cases.

Did you know?

Alzheimer's disease, and other forms of senile dementia, affect around 500 000 people in the UK.

22.4.2 Arthritis

Arthritis is the name given to a variety of inflammatory diseases which affect the joints and cause pain and stiffness. They may be the result of a number of factors including old age, injury, infection, genetic influences, gout, cancer, autoimmunity and nervous disease.

Injury may damage the smooth articular surface of a joint, especially in the knees, which are particularly vulnerable to damage when playing many sports. **Infection** of the synovial membrane or other joint tissue can also cause arthritis. One form, called **Lyme disease** is the result of infection by a spirochaete bacterium carried by ticks. **Gout** causes the deposition of uric acid crystals in the joint, which trigger chronic inflammation and tissue damage. See Focus on Gout on page 414. **Cancer** may result in tumours which create damage by deranging the anatomy of the joint. More details on cancer are given in the Focus on page 116. **Nervous disease** may cause the joint to become insensitive or result in abnormal muscular movement. Both may cause injury to joints with consequent arthritis.

Rheumatoid arthritis is a common disease of joints. In Britain it affects 4 in 1000 females and 1 in a 1000 males overall but is much more prevalent in the over 65 age group, affecting 50 in 1000 females and 20 in 1000 males. Although it affects other parts of the body arthritis begins with inflammation of the synovial membrane of a joint. This thickens and becomes filled with white blood cells such as lymphocytes and polymorphs. These begin to attack the cartilage slowly eroding it away. This misdirection of the body's immune system against its own tissues rather than foreign ones is known as **autoimmunity**. The inflamed tissue releases digestive enzymes which further erode the cartilage. The rate of cartilage destruction is very variable taking many years in some patients but as little as a few months in others. Ultimately the ends of the bones are left grinding on one another causing much pain and some bleeding. Tendons may become displaced and shorter adding to the deformity and reduced movement of the joint which is characteristic of this condition.

The causes of rheumatoid arthritis are not clearly understood but it is thought that a combination of genetic and environmental factors may initiate the autoimmunity. Because patients with the condition possess abnormal antibodies, the disease can be diagnosed using a blood test and/or X-ray examination.

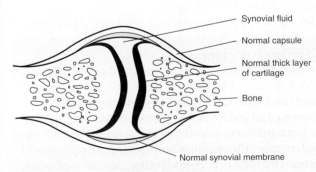

Synovial fluid

Normal capsule

Normal thick layer of cartilage

Bone

Normal synovial membrane

Fig. 22.4(a) Structure of a normal joint

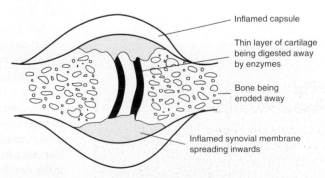

Inflamed capsule

Thin layer of cartilage being digested away by enzymes

Bone being eroded away

Inflamed synovial membrane spreading inwards

Fig. 22.4(b) Structure of a joint displaying rheumatoid arthritis

Treatment of arthritis depends on its cause. Antibiotics are used to treat infection, specific drugs can control gout, while chemotherapy and radiotherapy may alleviate cancers. In the case of rheumatoid arthritis, non-steroid anti-inflammatory drugs (NSAID) such as Voltarol®, Relifex® and Brufen® may be used. Further treatment can involve medicines to block the action of enzymes, immunosuppressive agents and even the use of gold. Despite many years of research and development an effective cure still eludes us.

22.4.3 Osteoarthritis

Osteoarthritis is different from other forms of arthritis in that it does not cause inflammation of the synovial membrane and lacks systemic symptoms. Sometimes known as **degenerative joint disease**, it is characterized by the breakdown of articular cartilage. Old age, stress and damage to the joints all increase the risk of developing the condition.

22.5 Mental illness

The term mental illness covers a broad range of disorders which cause psychological, personality or behavioural symptoms. What constitutes a mental illness may depend upon the 'normal' behaviour of a particular society. What is considered abnormal or deviant in one group, might be perfectly acceptable in another. Nor is there a clear distinction between physical and mental disease, each type often displaying symptoms of the other.

Neuroses cover personality disorders which often result in an exaggerated or irrational response to the ordinary stresses and demands of life. Behaviour, thought processes, emotions and certain body functions may be influenced. Neuroses include phobic, compulsive, obsessive or hysterical behaviour.

Psychoses are mental disorders of a more severe kind which often involve an extensive personality disorder. Disorientation in time and space may occur, hallucinations can be experienced and delusions may arise. One example of a psychosis is **schizophrenia** which is detailed in the Focus on page 555.

22.6 Human inflicted disease

These are a number of disorders and illnesses which are the direct consequence of an individual's premeditated actions. In some cases the harmful consequences of the actions are known at the outset, in other cases the damage only becomes apparent later. Such illnesses include occupational diseases, as well as alcoholism and drug addiction.

FOCUS

Schizophrenia

Schizophrenia is one of the commonest health problems in industrialized societies, affecting half a million people in Britain and two million in the United States at some time in their lives. People with schizophrenia display severe distortion and disorder of thought often leading to delusions, hallucinations, bizarre behaviour and social withdrawal. Without special care schizophrenics can become lonely and isolated and suicide is not uncommon. The causes of schizophrenia are little understood. The illness sometimes runs in families and in many sufferers the brain structure is altered, the ventricles being enlarged. There is also evidence for a link with the brain neurotransmitter dopamine. It seems that schizophrenics may produce abnormally high levels of dopamine or have more receptors to it than would be expected. Consequently drugs which block the dopamine receptors can reduce the symptoms of the disease. Unfortunately they also affect normal dopamine receptors and schizophrenics who are being treated with them may show some symptoms similar to those of Parkinson's disease – though these are reversible.

Increasingly researchers believe schizophrenia to be a syndrome with a number of different underlying causes. If these causes can be isolated drugs may be devised which will make the lives of schizophrenics more tolerable and perhaps, eventually, it will be possible to prevent or cure the condition.

22.6.1 Occupational diseases

Asbestosis is caused by breathing in particles of asbestos, the blue variety being especially dangerous. Asbestos is a virtually indestructible material whose fire-resistant properties make it especially useful in the manufacture of brake and clutch linings, electrical insulation and building construction. It may take 20–40 years after exposure to asbestos for the lung cancer which may result to develop.

Pneumoconiosis literally means 'dusty lungs' and results from the long-term inhalation of a variety of mineral dusts, including silica particles, soot particles and coal dust. These can cause scar tissue to build up in the lung – a condition called **fibrosis**. This results in a lack of elasticity in the lung leading to shortness of breath because the lung cannot be fully extended.

22.6.2 Drug addiction

What is a drug? There are numerous definitions but they usually have in common the concept that a drug in some way modifies the normal mental or physical functions of the body. The term is normally restricted to those substances which are taken into the body rather than ones naturally produced by it. Such a definition not only includes substances commonly accepted as drugs such as paracetamol and heroin, but also substances like caffeine which many may not previously have considered in this light.

This leads us to one mechanism by which drugs can be divided into two categories – according to the way society views them. **Socially acceptable drugs** in Britain include nicotine from tobacco, caffeine in coffee and tea and alcohol in its many forms. Socially unacceptable or **illicit drugs** in Britain include marijuana and LSD. The list differs from society to society with marijuana being acceptable in some countries while alcohol is not. Other drugs such as amphetamines and barbiturates have a perfectly legal and acceptable use as prescribed remedies, but become unacceptable when taken excessively by the patient or by those to whom they are not prescribed. The acceptability of drugs also changes with time. Smoking, once popular and encouraged, is increasingly being perceived as anti-social and alcohol was banned in the USA during the era of Prohibition from 1920 to 1933.

Drug dependence arises when an individual has a particular need to take a drug and removal of it leads to a certain degree of discomfort. **Psychological dependence** occurs when there is an emotional need for the drug and any discomfort experienced is restricted to an altered state of mind such as mild depression. **Physical dependence** occurs when the body has become adapted to the drug in such a way that it, or its products, are necessary for its systems to function normally. Withdrawal of the drug leads to physical symptoms which can cause severe discomfort or pain.

Tolerance arises as a result of the body becoming acclimatized to a drug. As a result over time a larger dose is necessary to produce the same effect. Tolerance may be the consequence of receptors becoming less sensitive to a drug or the tissues becoming more efficient at breaking it down.

Heroin is an example of an opiate drug. Opiates are **narcotic** drugs, i.e. they depress the nervous system and so reduce sensitivity and induce drowsiness or sleep. As a consequence they have therapeutic value as highly effective pain-killers, and natural opiates such as codeine and morphine are widely used in medicine as are synthetic ones like pethidine. Opiates derive their name from the opium poppy from which they can be obtained naturally and they have been used throughout history both medically and recreationally.

Heroin is an addictive drug normally taken for the sense of well-being which it engenders. While small doses, especially if taken orally and intermittently, may not lead to dependence, regular use, especially of injected heroin, can cause physical dependence within a few weeks. Without the drug, addicts develop unpleasant withdrawal symptoms and in time its further use is often to alleviate these effects, rather than for the pleasure it may bring. Tolerance to heroin develops rapidly and so in regular users the dose needs to be progressively increased. While addicts may regularly use doses of 500 mg or more, even 100 mg would usually prove fatal to a non-user. This tolerance rapidly diminishes when a person ceases using heroin and has led to tragic deaths from users taking their previous high doses after a relatively short period of abstinence.

Heroin affects mainly the nervous system where it acts on synapses. There appear to be areas of the brain which have receptors for opiates such as heroin. Heroin influences the neurotransmitters in the brain causing a reduction in the pain threshold and depression of the respiratory centres. Breathing is slowed and there is a general feeling of relaxation, well-being and euphoria.

22.6.3 Alcoholism

Alcohol has been a socially acceptable drug in many parts of the world for centuries and has become part of our social culture. Details of its production are given in Section 21.4.2.

Once consumed, alcohol is absorbed rapidly and almost entirely by the stomach. Small amounts may be oxidized in the stomach and other organs and a little is lost in the breath and urine, but about 80% is metabolized by the liver. The liver converts the ethanol (the alcohol of almost all alcoholic drinks) into ethanal. This is a highly reactive compound which easily combines with $-SH$ and $-NH_2$ groups found in proteins. In so doing it can interfere with the normal functioning of enzymes, and the structural proteins within cells. The ethanal may alter the shape of some proteins so that the body ceases to recognize them and treats them as foreign material by producing antibodies to them. This autoimmune response leads to damage of liver tissue and hepatitis.

The intoxicating effects of alcohol are due to the fact that ethanal reacts with neurotransmitters such as noradrenaline and dopamine which pass messages across nerve synapses. It is thought that these reactions result in the production of morphine-like substances which are the cause of alcohol dependency. A summary of these and other effects of ethanal are given below:

1. Interference with enzyme functioning.

2. Nervous system and brain damage due to the formation of morphine-like substances as a result of reactions with neurotransmitters.

3. Inhibition of protein synthesis, leading to muscle and bone disease.

4. Damage to mitochondria causing slower cellular metabolism.

5. Reactions with phospholipids and some fatty acids causing interference with the functioning of cell membranes.

6. Damage to structural proteins leading to an autoimmune response and hence liver damage.

7. Inhibition of the metabolism of neurotransmitters such as noradrenaline.

These effects can cause damage to most body systems but the nervous system and the liver are especially vulnerable. The damage to cell membranes affects the ability of neurones to generate nervous impulses and hence the ability to respond to stimuli and process information. This is compounded by impaired protein synthesis, mitochondrial functioning and inhibition of neurotransmitter metabolism. The consequences of long-term excessive alcohol consumption can thus result in brain damage leading to memory loss, difficulty in learning new information and poor judgement. In time there may be disorientation, sleep disturbance and dementia. Chronic alcohol users have enlarged brain ventricles due to the shrinkage of brain cells as a result of dehydration.

FOCUS

Cirrhosis of the liver

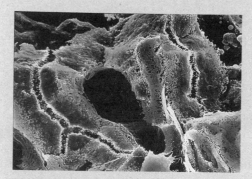

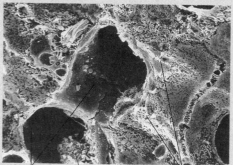

Sinusoids   Phagocytes associated with tissue damage   Connective tissue invading liver

Scanning EMs of cell structure within (top) a healthy liver and (above) one affected by cirrhosis

Worldwide the main cause of the severe liver disease cirrhosis, is infection with the hepatitis B virus but in the western world the commonest cause is alcohol abuse. The chance of developing cirrhosis is related to the amount of alcohol consumed daily. The risks are significantly increased in men with an intake greater than seven units (56 g absolute alcohol) per day and in women exceeding five units (40 g) per day. There is also some evidence that some people are genetically predisposed to develop cirrhosis. Although ethanol itself is toxic the main liver damage is thought to occur as a result of ethanal produced during ethanol metabolism. Ethanal binds to proteins, altering liver structure and function. It inhibits protein secretion from hepatocytes, decreases the activity of many enzymes, encourages cell destruction and stimulates collagen production. The extra collagen produced is responsible for the fibrous scars typical of cirrhosis and has a profound effect on liver function. The collagen deposits in the liver sinusoids depriving the hepatocytes of nutrients. The hepatocytes are therefore unable to produce essential proteins like albumin. The low serum albumin level causes fluid to leak into the tissues and accumulate causing swelling. There is a decreased production of clotting factors leading to a tendency to bleed easily. The liver is unable to carry out its usual functions of dealing with ammonia and other nitrogenous compounds and their accumulation progressively poisons the brain causing confusion and eventually coma.

Many of the severe and irreversible effects of liver damage are preventable if alcohol consumption is reduced and vaccinations against hepatitis viruses are given.

PROJECT

Does alcohol affect the activity of pepsin?

As the organ which metabolizes alcohol, the liver is readily damaged when alcohol consumption is excessive. The alcohol is metabolized in preference to fat which therefore builds up in the liver. Liver cells are damaged leading to inflammation (**hepatitis**) and the development of fibrous tissue. In time **cirrhosis** occurs, a condition in which the liver becomes scarred and fibrous with few normally functioning liver cells remaining (see Focus on this page).

Excessive alcohol use also contributes to high blood pressure, heart disease, gastric and duodenal ulcers, cancer of the mouth, oesophagus and stomach, skin infections, muscle and bone disease and various nutritional problems.

Tolerance arises with excessive alcohol use because the body develops the ability to metabolize it faster and so the user requires greater quantities to achieve the same effect. In addition regular users learn to adapt their behaviour in such a way that the effects of intoxication are less apparent. Abstinence after long-term abuse can produce withdrawal symptoms. In their severest form these include trembling, restlessness, sweating and hallucinating – a condition known as **delirium tremens**.

Abstaining from alcohol does, however, result in rapid recovery from damage, and even when organs like the liver have been seriously affected considerable improvement can be achieved.

The effects of excessive alcohol use are by no means restricted to physical damage. The social consequences can be at least as severe. One major problem is death and injury caused as a result of drinking and driving. The legal limit in the UK is 80 mg of alcohol per 100 cm^3 of blood and even at this level statistics show that a driver is twice as likely to have an accident than someone with no alcohol in the blood. The risk is increased to ten times at blood alcohol levels of 150 mg per 100 cm^3. Apart from the social cost of death and injury as a result of drinking and driving there are also the economic costs of insurance, policing and medical care to be considered.

Aggressive behaviour is a common result of intoxication with alcohol. The loss of inhibition and poor judgement it causes increase the incidence of violent behaviour. This may manifest itself in verbal and physical assaults as well as vandalism. This behaviour may be apparent on the streets or in public houses, from time to time, but is more common, if less obvious, in domestic situations. Intra-family violence often arises between partners and/or immediate relatives. Women and children are especially at risk and increasingly this form of behaviour leads to family breakdown.

Much petty crime such as threatening behaviour, minor theft and vandalism arises when individuals are under the influence of alcohol. More serious crimes such as violent assaults, rape and even murder can also be the direct consequence of excessive alcohol intake.

22.6.4 Effects of tobacco on health

Tobacco smoking is harmful and contributes to the premature death of some 100 000 people each year in the UK. Tobacco smoke is a mixture of chemicals, a number of which interact with each other, multiplying their effects. Carbon monoxide, tar and nicotine have the most influence on health.

Carbon monoxide combines easily with the haemoglobin of the blood to form carboxyhaemoglobin. This lowers the oxygen-carrying capacity of the blood because the carbon monoxide is not released at the tissues and so remains permanently attached to haemoglobin preventing it from carrying oxygen molecules. Regular smokers have around a 5% reduction in the oxygen-carrying capacity of their blood as a result, which leads to breathlessness. Carbon monoxide has also been shown to aggravate angina, a heart condition most often caused by the narrowing of the coronary arteries as a result of atherosclerosis. The growth of the fetus in pregnant women is slowed by the presence of carbon monoxide in the mother's blood.

Tars from the burning of tobacco form an aerosol of minute droplets which enter the respiratory pathways causing thickening of their epithelia which then leads to chronic bronchitis. The tars can paralyse the cilia lining the trachea and bronchi preventing them from removing the mucus secreted by the epithelial lining. As a result dust and germ-laden mucus accumulates in the lungs leading to infection and damage. The cough, typical of many smokers, is the result of trying to remove this build-up of mucus from the lungs. Most significantly, it is the tars in tobacco smoke which have been shown to cause lung cancer. Heavy smokers have a 25% greater risk of this disease than do non-smokers.

Nicotine is quickly absorbed into the blood, taking only around 30 seconds to reach the brain. It stimulates the production of adrenaline by the adrenal glands leading to increased heart rate and raised blood pressure. Because nicotine makes blood platelets more sticky it increases the risk of thrombosis in smokers.

Many diseases are caused by tobacco smoking of which the most common are coronary heart disease, lung cancer and chronic bronchitis. **Coronary heart disease** results because smoking increases the likelihood of fatty deposits arising on the inner lining of the arteries (atherosclerosis) which cause the lumen to narrow and so restrict the movement of blood through them. Where this narrowing occurs in the coronary artery it can lead to a heart attack and if in the carotid artery a stroke may be the consequence. There is more than one type of **lung cancer** but bronchial carcinoma is by far and away the most common. The tars in tobacco smoke may induce the epithelial cells lining the bronchial tubes to become cancerous. If not treated, the tumour may completely disrupt the functioning of the lung, leaving surgical removal as the only effective treatment. A highly persistent cough, blood in the sputum and chest pains are all symptoms of lung cancer. **Chronic bronchitis** is due to the tars in tobacco irritating the epithelial lining of the bronchial tubes causing it to produce excess mucus. The cilia lining the tubes become damaged and unable to remove this mucus in the usual manner. Only by coughing can the mucus be expelled and in time this leads to scarring and narrowing of the bronchial tubes causing breathlessness. Other smoking-related conditions include:

- Emphysema (see Focus on page 365)
- Cancer of the mouth, throat, bladder and pancreas
- Other cardiovascular diseases
- Peptic ulcers
- Narrowing of blood vessels in limbs
- Damage to the unborn child.

> ## PROJECT
>
> Is there a relationship between cigarette smoking and lung capacity?

22.7 Deficiency diseases

Deficiency diseases are caused by the shortage of some essential nutrient in the diet. Perhaps the most dramatic is **kwashiorkor** which results from a deficiency of protein in children. Several diseases result from the deficiency of vitamins and minerals. Reduced levels of vitamin C can lead to scurvy, of vitamin D can lead to rickets, while deficiency of iron causes anaemia. More details of these and other deficiency diseases are given in Section 23.1.5.

22.8 Protection from disease

Protection from any specific disease depends upon the nature of that disease and, in particular, its cause. Clearly a carefully balanced diet will protect against deficiency diseases. This section deals mainly, but not exclusively, with protection from infectious diseases.

22.8.1 Immunity and vaccination

The ability of humans to prevent pathogens establishing themselves on or in their bodies depends largely upon the effectiveness of their immune system. Details of the human immune system are given in Section 16.3.1.

22.8.2 Antibiotics

Alexander Fleming first discovered penicillin in 1929 and this led to the discovery of many other chemicals produced by microorganisms which inhibited the growth of other microorganisms. These are known as antibiotics and more details of them and their method of production are given in Section 21.5.1.

22.8.3 Sterilization and disinfection

Antiseptics and disinfectants are substances used to eliminate or control microorganisms. An **antiseptic** is a substance which is applied to the surface of a tissue or organ (most often the skin) in order to inhibit the growth of potentially pathogenic microorganisms. A **disinfectant** is a substance which destroys all microorganisms, in their vegetative state, which might cause disease. Spore and/or non-pathogenic organisms may not be destroyed. **Sterile** is a term used to denote that the material referred to is completely devoid of any viable form of life.

Sterilization can be achieved by physical or chemical means. A summary of sterilization methods is given in Table 22.2.

22.8.4 Diet and exercise

A properly balanced diet not only diminishes the chances of having a deficiency disease but also ensures that the body is in the best condition to protect itself from infection and to combat any disease that might arise. Such a diet should also ensure that there is no surfeit of a particular food and so prevent disorders such as obesity and alcoholism. Diet and health is dealt with in Chapter 23.

Exercise too can ensure that not only is an individual less likely to suffer certain diseases, but he/she is also in a better state to combat any illness that is contracted. Exercise reduces the risk of cardiovascular disease such as atherosclerosis and thrombosis. It is helpful in rehabilitation from injuries and can

PROJECT

Investigate the effect of exercise and training on pulse rate and recovery time.

TABLE 22.2   Methods of sterilization

PHYSICAL METHODS

Method of sterilization	Mechanism by which it operates
Moist heat	Moist heat at temperatures of 60–80 °C will destroy vegetative microorganisms but not bacterial spores. Boiling in water for up to 6 hours will destroy spores as will heating water to 121 °C in an autoclave for 15 minutes. The heat coagulates macromolecules, especially enzymes.
Dry heat	Dry heat takes longer to inactivate biological molecules and so 1–2 hours at 160–80 °C is required to kill microorganisms. It is effective through dehydration and oxidation of macromolecules.
Cold	Temperatures of 2–6 °C will so reduce the growth of most microorganisms as to prevent growth but not kill them. 0 °C will kill most vegetative forms by the formation of ice crystals which on warming expand and rupture the cell membrane. Spores, being dry, are not destroyed.
Filtration	Membrane filters of cellulose esters and other polymers are manufactured with a range of pore sizes. The smallest can trap even the smallest virus. They are useful for sterilizing liquids and gases.
Radiation	Radiation operates by imparting its energy to molecules in the microorganism and so disrupting them. **Non-ionizing radiation** such as ultraviolet light is absorbed by molecules such as DNA causing mutation and disrupting protein synthesis. **Ionizing radiation** such as X-rays and gamma rays produce oxidizing ions which break up DNA and other macromolecules.

CHEMICAL METHODS

Disinfectant group	Mechanism by which it operates
Phenols	Used by Joseph Lister in 1867. Phenols have high lipid solubility and so disrupt microorganism membranes.
Alcohols	Ethyl and isopropyl alcohol are effective at concentrations between 50 and 80%. They dissolve lipids from cell membranes causing them to rupture and also cause cell dehydration and protein denaturation.
Halogens	Chlorine, bromine, fluorine and iodine are strong oxidizing agents. They inactivate proteins by oxidizing –SH groups, causing them to become denatured. Chlorine is used to disinfect swimming pools and drinking water while iodine is used as an antiseptic for skin wounds.
Soaps and detergents	These primarily work by lowering the surface tension of molecules so that the oily deposits on the skin can mix easily with water and be washed away along with microorganisms. Some act on the cell membrane of microorganisms causing their death.
Alkylating agents	Alkylating agents, such as formaldehyde, glutaraldehyde and ethylene oxide, act by attaching to ionized –COOH, –NH$_2$ and –SH groups in proteins and nucleic acids, disrupting their structure and killing the microorganisms.
Heavy metals	Heavy metals such as mercury and silver bind to enzymes and other proteins, causing them to denature. Silver nitrate solution operates in this way.

remedy ailments such as asthma. It prevents obesity, especially in conjunction with a balanced diet. Many forms of exercise can be relaxing and so reduce stress leading to a reduced likelihood of suffering cardiovascular disease and some mental illnesses. By building strength and flexibility in muscles, bones and joints, the chance of injury, e.g. due to falls, is reduced. Exercise is frequently a social activity. Team games can engender qualities of sharing, responsibility, leadership and comradeship amongst others. Alertness can be improved giving increased awareness to danger and reducing accidents. Being able to perform well and to feel good about oneself can raise confidence and self-esteem and so protect against depression and low self-value which can lead, amongst other things, to drug addiction and crime.

The specific effects of exercise on particular body systems are detailed at various points throughout the book, for example the respiratory system (Section 15.4.1) and the cardiovascular system (Section 16.5.4).

22.9   Detection of disease

There is no question that prevention is better than cure, but experience teaches us that even the best preventative measures sometimes fail and disease occurs. The early detection of any disease considerably increases the chances of it being successfully treated. Modern technology has given the medical profession a formidable array of techniques for providing early warnings of disease and disorders. Screening techniques can be used to examine individuals who are perfectly healthy so that some potentially harmful disease may be detected even before it has produced discernible symptoms. Given that there are not the economic resources, let alone the know-how, to screen everyone for every disease, the process is targeted on the most vulnerable groups for any particular disease, e.g. amniocentesis for pregnant women over 40 years old, who because of their age have a higher risk of bearing children with genetic disorders such as Down's Syndrome. Details of amniocentesis are given in the Focus on page 160. The uses of genetic screening and counselling are discussed in Section 8.7. There are a wide variety of other screening techniques.

22.9.1 X-rays and computerized axial tomography

X-rays are used for body scanning as they penetrate body tissues to a varying degree depending on the density of the tissue. The denser tissues such as bone are resistant to the passage of X-rays and so give a white image on the X-ray plate as the film is unexposed. Less dense tissues are penetrated and the film becomes dark as it is exposed to the X-rays. These softer tissues can be made visible by introducing into them a fluid material which is opaque to X-rays. For example the upper region of the intestine can be seen on an X-ray plate if the patient first swallows a suspension of barium sulphate (barium meal). Once the barium is in the stomach/intestine it resists the penetration of the X-rays and these organs appear white on the X-ray image. The same principle is used in visualizing blood vessels by injecting certain iodine-containing compounds into them.

   Computerized axial tomography (CAT) involves taking many X-rays from a variety of different angles and combining them into one image. This provides an X-ray 'slice' through the body. By stacking together the images taken at slightly different levels in the body, a fully three-dimensional image can be obtained with the help of a computer. There are two drawbacks to the technique. Firstly patients are exposed to relatively high levels of X-rays which increases their risk of developing cancer. Secondly CAT scans do not provide sharp images of soft tissues.

22.9.2 Magnetic resonance imaging (MRI)

The drawbacks encountered with the use of CAT can be overcome using magnetic resonance imaging (MRI). This exploits the fact that 60–70% of the human body is water and water contains hydrogen atoms. When exposed to strong magnetic fields the nuclei of these line up like tiny magnets. If

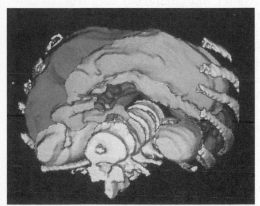

CAT scan of the lower abdomen

Biochemical detection of diabetes

The enzyme glucose oxidase permits an assessment to be made of the amount of glucose in a fluid, even if other sugars are also present – a vital measurement for people suffering from diabetes. Glucose oxidase catalyses the oxidation of glucose to produce gluconic acid and hydrogen peroxide. Biosensors have been developed in which the enzyme is immobilized on a membrane and when it reacts with glucose the product, gluconic acid, causes a change in a transducer which generates electric current. When amplified this can be read on a digital display. The electric current conducted by the acid is proportional to the amount of glucose in the solution.

An alternative approach is to make use of the hydrogen peroxide released by the action of glucose oxidase, coupled with the activity of the enzyme peroxidase. Peroxidase can oxidize a colourless organic compound to a coloured compound using the hydrogen peroxide. The colour given is a measure of the amount of glucose present.

$$\text{Glucose} + \text{Oxygen} \xrightarrow{\text{glucose oxidase}} \text{Gluconic acid} + \text{Hydrogen peroxide}$$

$$\text{Colourless compound} + \text{Hydrogen peroxide} \xrightarrow{\text{peroxidase}} \text{Coloured compound} + \text{Water}$$

Both glucose oxidase, peroxidase and the colourless hydrogen donor can be immobilized on a cellulose fibre pad. This is the basis of the sticks, such as 'clinistix', which enable diabetics to monitor their own blood or urine glucose levels.

exposed to radio waves of the right frequency they will resonate and go out of alignment, absorbing energy. By measuring the signal received from different parts of the body, the number of hydrogen nuclei and hence the number of water molecules can be determined. This tells us the relative density of the tissue and allows a computer to construct an image based on this. The need for special rooms to house the equipment and the very sophisticated computer hardware needed make MRI a very expensive technique, but it is especially useful for scanning the brain.

22.9.3 Endoscopy

Endoscopy is the examination of the interior of the body through an optical instrument called an **endoscope**. The endoscope may be inserted via natural openings or through specially made incisions. With the use of fibre optics, light can be transmitted to allow the instrument to produce accurate images of internal parts of the body such as the heart, intestines, bladder and joints. The **laparoscope** is a form of endoscope used to examine the abdominal cavity via a small incision just below the naval. It can be used to enable minor operations to be carried out without the need for major invasive surgery.

22.9.4 Ultrasound

Rather like light, sound waves can be formed into a beam which is reflected from objects in a way that provides information about their shape. In ultrasound scanning a beam of high frequency sound (usually 1–10 MHz) is directed into the body. The beam is reflected from internal organs and the pattern of echoes produced is detected by the scanner and transduced into pictures on a screen. The technique can be used to view organs such as the heart, but is especially useful for examination of the fetus during pregnancy. Having rapidly dividing cells the fetus is especially vulnerable to the mutating effects of X-rays making this form of examination too dangerous to contemplate. With ultrasound scanning, the size of the fetal head can be determined, giving an accurate estimate of the length of pregnancy so far and hence the likely date of birth. Physical disabilities such as spina bifida or microcephaly are apparent using the technique. Any unusual position of the fetus is also obvious. With this type of information remedial measures can sometimes be taken or adequate preparations for a difficult birth can be made. Ultrasound is used to guide needles during techniques such as amniocentesis and it also has therapeutic uses because it can be used to generate heat in deep-seated tissues. In this way it may reduce stiffness and pain in joints or be used to treat sports injuries such as hamstring pulls.

22.10   Questions

1. Describe how contamination of food with *Salmonella enteritidis* causes food poisoning. How does the spread of *Salmonella enteritidis* differ from that of *Listeria monocytogenes*?

(Total 7 marks)
ULEAC June 1995, Paper 4B, No. 5

2. Either
(a) (i) Describe the effects of amphetamines and cannabis on the nervous system.   *(10 marks)*
(ii) Discuss the measures that society can take to control the use of drugs, such as amphetamines and cannabis.   *(8 marks)*
Or
(b) (i) With reference to nicotine, explain what is meant by the terms *drug* and *drug dependency*.
   (8 marks)
(ii) Discuss the possible consequences of heavy smoking on gaseous exchange.   *(10 marks)*
(Total 18 marks)

UCLES June 1995, Paper 3 (Option 2), Nos. 3(a) and 3(b)

3. Either
(a) (i) With reference to the effects of **named** opiates, explain what is meant by the terms *drug*, *drug dependency* and *drug tolerance*.   *(12 marks)*
(ii) Discuss the effects of illicit drugs on inter-personal relationships.   *(11 marks)*
Or
(b) (i) Give a detailed account of the short- and long-term effects of alcohol on the human body.   *(14 marks)*
(ii) Discuss the social consequences of alcohol abuse.   *(9 marks)*
(Total 23 marks)

UCLES June 1992, Paper 3 (Option 2), Nos. 3(a) and 3(b)

4. Solvents and other volatile substances are mostly abused by children and teenagers. Butane gas in cigarette lighter refills is one of the commonest of these substances to be abused. Butane is also used as a propellant in aerosols such as air fresheners. Manufacturers have used it to replace the chlorofluorocarbons, and by 1989, 90% of domestic aerosols contained butane as a propellant.

The majority of deaths from volatile substance abuse occur in children and teenagers. Between 1971 and 1991, 73.2% of all people who died were under the age of 20. Between 1988 and 1990, 80% of the deaths from volatile substance abuse were related to gas lighter fuel and, in one-third of these cases, it was a first

experiment. The figure shows the number of deaths from volatile substance abuse over the period 1971 to 1991 in the UK.

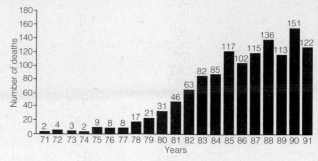

(J.C. Taylor et al. *Trends in deaths associated with abuse of volatile substances 1971–1991*. St. George's Hospital Medical School)

(a) With reference to the figure, comment on:
 (i) the deaths from solvent abuse from 1971 to 1985;   *(2 marks)*
 (ii) the difficulty in drawing conclusions from the number of deaths between 1988 and 1991.
   (2 marks)
(b) Explain why volatile substances are mostly abused by children and teenagers, rather than by older people.   *(2 marks)*
(c) (i) Describe **two** effects of volatile substances on the nervous system.   *(2 marks)*
(ii) Describe **three** ways in which experimenting with volatile substances, such as solvents and butane gas, can lead to the deaths of children and teenagers.   *(3 marks)*

Although deaths from volatile substance abuse now comprise an important proportion of all deaths of teenagers, items in the British press do not reflect this. In the mid 1980s articles about solvent abuse appeared quite frequently. In contrast, in the early 1990s, the press carried far more articles about deaths from 'ecstasy' even though this drug was only involved in 10 deaths in the same period (1988–1990).

(d) Outline **two** advantages and **two** disadvantages of reports appearing in the press of deaths from volatile substance abuse.   *(4 marks)*
(Total 15 marks)

UCLES June 1995, Paper 3 (Option 2), No. 1

5. An investigation was carried out into the effects of alcohol intoxication on memory.
Subjects were tested on their recall of 64 words and all subjects were given the same amount of alcohol. Recall was tested immediately after learning and again after a delay of 20 minutes. Results (to the nearest whole number) are given in the table opposite.

State	Time of recall	Mean number of correct responses
Sober	Immediate	44
Sober	After 20 minutes	19
Intoxicated	Immediate	40
Intoxicated	After 20 minutes	9

(Adapted from H. Weingartner and D.L. Murphy, 1977)

(a) Explain the difference between the figures for immediate recall after 20 minutes when the subjects were sober *(3 marks)*

(b) What is the most significant effect of alcohol intoxication on memory, as shown by these results? Explain your answer. *(2 marks)*

(c) In this investigation there are two different aspects of memory: storage and retrieval.

(i) What do the results suggest about the effect of intoxication on these two aspects of memory? *(2 marks)*

(ii) Explain why the evidence for this is not very reliable. *(2 marks)*

(iii) How might the procedure be modified to demonstrate the effect of intoxication on retrieval alone? *(2 marks)*

(d) Suggest **two** important precautions which would be needed in addition to the above procedure if the results are to be valid. *(2 marks)*
(Total 13 marks)

ULEAC June 1995, Paper 4C, No. 1

6. The blood alcohol levels of three people **P**, **Q** and **R** were measured over a period of time. The results are shown in the figure.

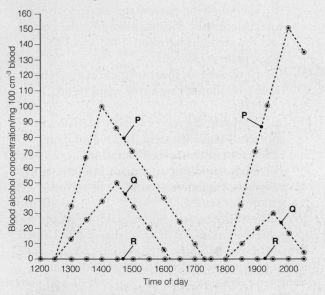

(a) With reference to the figure,

(i) summarize the results shown; *(3 marks)*

(ii) suggest reasons to account for the differences in the blood alcohol levels of **P**, **Q** and **R**. *(4 marks)*

In Britain, the maximum legal limit for driving is 80 mg 100 cm^{-3} of alcohol in the blood. On average, alcohol is removed from the blood at the rate of 30 mg 100 cm^{-3}h^{-1}.

(b) (i) Could **P** legally drive a car at 2230? Explain your answer and show your calculations. *(2 marks)*

(ii) Outline **two physiological** effects of alcohol on the nervous system which would make it dangerous for anyone to drive if they were over the legal limit. *(2 marks)*

(c) Describe the effect of alcohol on (i) urine production, and (ii) body temperature. Explain your answers. *(4 marks)*
(Total 15 marks)

UCLES June 1995, Paper 3 (Option 2), No. 2

7. Influenza is a disease which occasionally becomes pandemic and has proved difficult to eradicate completely.

(a) (i) What is meant by the term *pandemic*? *(1 mark)*

(ii) Suggest **one** reason why influenza has proved difficult to eradicate. *(1 mark)*

(b) Briefly describe the structure of the influenza-causing agent. *(2 marks)*

(c) Outline the events that occur in the host cell after it has been penetrated by the influenza agent. *(3 marks)*
(Total 7 marks)

AEB June 1992, Paper 1, No. 4

8. The figure shows a flow diagram of some of the ways in which pathogens of humans can be transmitted.

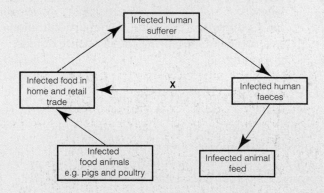

(a) Suggest **two** ways in which the transfer of pathogens from human faeces to food, shown by arrow **X**, is likely to occur. *(2 marks)*

(b) State **one** way in which the transmission of pathogens between infected food animals and humans can be prevented. *(1 mark)*

(c) (i) Explain why socioeconomic factors are often more important in controlling faecal-borne diseases than are antibiotics and vaccination. (4 marks)

(ii) In what circumstances would treatment with antibiotics be preferable to vaccination in controlling a faecal-borne disease? (1 mark)

The cholera vaccine contains heat-killed bacteria and is not very effective, giving partial protection for up to 6 months. However, a recently developed genetically engineered vaccine is expected to give lifelong immunity.

(d) Outline, **in principle only**, a method for preparing a vaccine by genetic engineering. (3 marks)

The figure shows the annual notifications of food poisoning in England and Wales between 1982 and 1992.

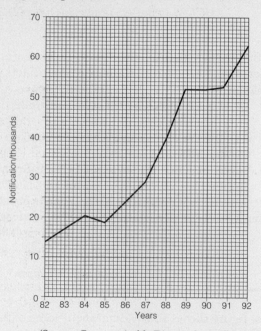

(Source: Communicable Disease Surveillance Centre)

(e) (i) Suggest **two** possible reasons for the trend shown. (2 marks)

(ii) Comment on the value of annual notifications as a means of measuring the incidence of food poisoning. (3 marks)

(Total 16 marks)

UCLES June 1995, Paper 3 (Option 1), No. 2

9. Illicit or controlled drugs are classified in the United Kingdom into three groups, A, B and C. Group A contains the most harmful drugs such as cocaine, LSD and the opiates; group B includes the barbiturates, amphetamines and cannabis; group C includes the minor tranquillizers (e.g. benzodiazepines), the milder stimulants and the less potent analgesics. Drugs seized by the police and by customs are categorized according to this system for the purpose of keeping records. Every year these records are published by the Home Office as part of the *Statistics of the Misuse of Drugs*. Tables 1 and 2 show the number of drug seizures and the quantity of five controlled drugs seized by police and by customs in the UK in 1980, 1985 and 1990.

Table 1

| Drug | Seizures by police | | | | | |
	Number of seizures			Quantity seized/kg		
	1980	1985	1990	1980	1985	1990
Cocaine	365	510	1 410	4.2	6.7	49.6
LSD	244	448	1 772	0.003	0.006	0.020
Heroin	612	3 003	2 321	1.8	32.2	26.9
Cannabis resin	6 218	13 734	43 474	312.2	469.8	57 164
Amphetamines	706	3 401	4 490	5.0	50.2	222.7

Table 2

| Drug | Seizures by customs | | | | | |
	Number of seizures			Quantity seized/kg		
	1980	1985	1990	1980	1985	1990
Cocaine	80	152	395	36.0	78.7	561.3
LSD	24	46	87	0.002	0.004	0.021
Heroin	85	173	272	36.4	334.2	575.8
Cannabis resin	746	1 257	3 295	7 440.3	7 391.4	15 833.1
Amphetamines	23	70	139	0.3	26.5	81.1

(Source: *Statistics of the Misuse of Drugs*: Seizures and Offenders Dealt With, United Kingdom, 1990. Supplementary Tables September 1991)

(a) (i) State **one** reason for classifying a drug as a group A drug. (1 mark)

(ii) Calculate the percentage increase in the total quantity of cocaine seized by the police and the customs between 1980 and 1990. Show your working. (2 marks)

(iii) Comment on the information given in Table 1 by identifying **three** main trends. (3 marks)

(b) (i) Evaluate the use of seizure statistics in determining accurately the level of drug addiction in the United Kingdom. (3 marks)

(ii) Suggest **one** advantage of publishing the number of seizures separately from the quantities seized. (1 mark)

(c) Suggest **three other** statistics which would help to reveal the pattern of drug misuse in the United Kingdom. Explain how each statistic might prove useful in devising policies to try to reduce the number of drug addicts. (3 marks)

(d) Present **one** argument **for** and **one** argument **against** legalizing cannabis in the United Kingdom. (2 marks)

(Total 15 marks)

UCLES June 1994, Paper 3 (Option 2), No. 2

10. Read through the passage and answer the questions that follow.

In 1960 Librium, the first of the benzodiazepines ('minor tranquillizers') to be marketed, was put on sale. Throughout the 60s and 70s the sales of the benzodiazepines increased rapidly. In the UK in 1978, 25.2 million prescriptions were made out at a cost of £28.4 million, with middle-aged women and the elderly receiving above average numbers of prescriptions. The benzodiazepines were welcomed as completely safe replacements for the barbiturates, the main sedative and sleeping pills of the previous 50 years. Ideally, the benzodiazepines used should have a short half-life (less than 8 to 10 hours for half the drug to be removed from circulation). More recently, the numbers of prescriptions have started to fall, but long-term repeat prescriptions accounted for 75% of all UK prescriptions in 1987.

(a) Benzodiazepines are hypnotic drugs. Explain what this means. *(1 mark)*

(b) State **three** advantages of using benzodiazepines compared with barbiturates. *(3 marks)*

(c) Suggest reasons why benzodiazepines are commonly prescribed to the elderly. *(4 marks)*

(d) What would be the consequences of a sedative having a long half-life? *(4 marks)*

(e) (i) State **three** physiological consequences of an overdose of hypnotics.

(ii) Name **one** hormone which might reverse the consequences you have stated. *(4 marks)*

(f) Account for the following changes in the pattern of prescribing benzodiazepines:

(i) the fall in numbers of prescriptions;

(ii) the high proportion of long-term repeat prescriptions. *(4 marks)*

The table shows the range of drugs dealt with by local agencies recently in one county in the UK.

Drug dealt with	Number of local agencies
Alcohol only	2
Tranquillizers only	1
Illicit drugs only	3
Illicit drugs and tranquillizers	6
Alcohol, illicit drugs and tranquillizers	7
Total	**19**

(g) (i) What percentage of local agencies are dealing

with illicit drugs, _____%

with alcohol, _____%

with tranquillizers?_____%

(ii) What criticisms might be offered against this provision by these agencies? *(5 marks)*

(Total 25 marks)

UCLES June 1992, Paper 3 (Option 2), No. 1

11. Measles is a viral disease, mainly of young children. The measles virus is similar to that which causes mumps. Infection with measles usually confers lifetime immunity. The graph below shows the incidence of measles in an American city during the eleven years 1920–1930.

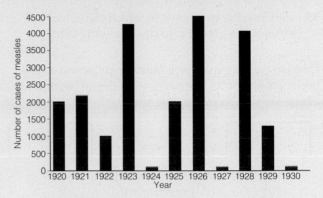

(a) (i) Describe the pattern of incidence of measles during this period. *(2 marks)*

(ii) Suggest **two** possible explanations for the pattern of incidence of measles. *(4 marks)*

(b) (i) Sketch a similar graph to show the pattern of incidence of Human Immunodeficiency Virus (HIV) infection in the United Kingdom for the eleven years 1980–1990. You need not include a vertical scale on your graph.*(2 marks)*

(ii) Suggest reasons for the differences between the two graphs. *(3 marks)*

(Total 11 marks)

ULEAC June 1993, Paper 4A, No. 1

12. *(a)* Suggest why, although chemicals such as phenol may be used as disinfectants, they cannot be used as antiseptics. *(2 marks)*

E. coli bacteria were exposed to a concentration of $4.6\,\text{g}\,\text{dm}^{-3}$ of phenol at various temperatures. The graph shows the percentage of bacteria surviving over a period of 40 hours.

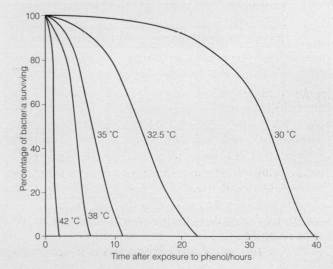

(b) (i) Describe the effect of temperature on the efficiency of phenol as a disinfectant. *(1 mark)*
(ii) Suggest an explanation for the effect you have described. *(1 mark)*
(Total 4 marks)

NEAB June 1995, Paper BY05, No. 3

13. *(a)* Describe **two** ways in which the activity of viruses can give rise to disease symptoms.
(2 marks)

Disease-causing microorganisms gain access to the body via one of its interfaces with the environment. These are shown in the diagram.

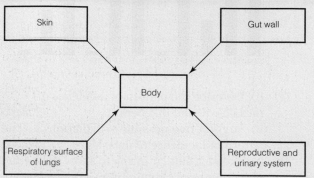

(b) Through which of these interfaces do the following gain access to the body:
(i) an influenza virus? *(1 mark)*
(ii) a *Salmonella* bacterium? *(1 mark)*
(c) How does the human body normally limit the access of microorganisms to the respiratory surface of the lungs? *(2 marks)*
(Total 6 marks)

NEAB June 1995, Paper BY08, No. 1

14. The Misuse of Drugs Act requires doctors in the United Kingdom to notify the Home Office when a person becomes newly addicted to one of several dangerous drugs. These drugs include cocaine, and opiates such as heroin, morphine, methadone and dipipanone. The table shows the numbers of new addicts notified to the Home Office during the years 1981 and 1989 by the type of drug to which addiction was reported.

(a) Suggest **two** features of the notifiable drugs which make them potentially harmful to individuals and society. *(2 marks)*
(b) (i) Calculate the percentage increase in the reported number of new heroin addicts in the United Kingdom between 1981 and 1989. (Show your working.)
(ii) Suggest **two** reasons why the figures published by the Home Office are not likely to be a reliable estimate of the numbers of new heroin addicts. *(4 marks)*
(c) Suggest **two** further statistics which would be useful in assessing the significance of the increase in drug addiction in the period 1981–1989.
(2 marks)
(d) Describe the effects of a **named** opiate on the nervous system. *(2 marks)*
(e) Give **two** reasons why some addicts need to keep increasing the size of the dose of heroin or morphine. *(2 marks)*
(f) Outline **two** methods which can be employed to reduce the number of people becoming addicted to opiates and other notifiable drugs. *(2 marks)*
(Total 14 marks)

UCLES June 1993, Paper 3 (Option 2), No. 1

15. In 1993, a detailed framework for action in the field of public health identified the major health problems which faced developed countries like those in the European Community (EC). One of the problems was an increasingly mobile population due, for example, to greater migration, travel and tourism.
(a) Summarize what is meant by *health*. *(3 marks)*
(b) Suggest **two** criteria that the Government of a developed country could use in judging whether a disease or condition is suitable for action when considering public health. *(2 marks)*

Three diseases or conditions which are causing concern in EC countries are given in the table below.

	Drug						Total*
	Heroin	Methadone	Dipipanone	Cocaine	Morphine	Other	
1981							
England	1 468	409	433	162	314	54	2 015
Wales	18	13	5	6	13	4	34
Northern Ireland	4	1	3	–	1	2	7
Scotland	170	8	32	6	27	12	192
1989							
England	4 550	605	68	500	209	94	5 200
Wales	70	27	6	10	21	14	108
Northern Ireland	5	2	–	3	–	3	10
Scotland	228	48	35	14	29	16	321

*Since an addict can be reported as addicted to more than one notifiable drug, figures for individual drugs cannot be added together to produce the total.

(Regional Trends 26 HMSO, 1991, Central Statistical Office)

Disease or condition	Factors important in prevention or control
Cardiovascular disease	1. _____ 2. _____
AIDS	1. _____ 2. _____
TB	1. _____ 2. _____

(c) Complete the table by stating **two** factors which are important in the prevention or control of each disease. *(3 marks)*

(d) Suggest two reasons why an increasingly mobile population could present a major health problem. *(2 marks)*

A disease that is commonly the subject of action in the field of public health in developing countries is cholera.

(e) (i) Name the causative agent of cholera *(1 mark)*

(ii) Describe **one** way in which cholera is transmitted from one person to another. *(1 mark)*

(iii) State three ways in which the cycle of transmission can be broken, thus preventing the spread of the disease. *(3 marks)*

(Total 15 marks)

UCLES June 1996, Paper 1 (Option 1), No. 1

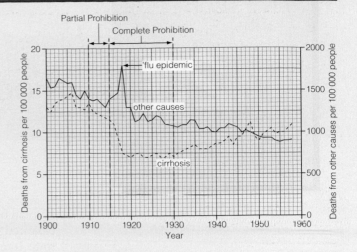

16. Cirrhosis is one of the best indicators of levels of alcohol addiction. The figure shows death rates from alcoholic liver cirrhosis and all other causes in the United States of America from 1900 to 1960. During the period labelled 'Complete Prohibition' in the figure, the manufacture, sale and transport of alcohol was illegal in all States. For a few years before that it was illegal in some States ('Partial Prohibition').

(a) Compare the trend shown for deaths from cirrhosis during the period 1900 to 1960 with that for deaths from other causes. *(3 marks)*

It has been argued that even if the population as a whole reduces consumption of a drug, this will have little impact on the number of addicts.

(b) Do the data in the figure support this hypothesis? Explain your answer. *(2 marks)*

(c) Suggest **two** reasons why cirrhosis is judged to be one of the best indicators of levels of alcohol addiction in a community. *(2 marks)*

(d) Explain how alcohol damages the liver. *(3 marks)*

Heroin addicts commonly report that their reason for starting to use heroin was to try to relieve emotional suffering.

(e) Explain how a knowledge of the biological effects of heroin on the nervous system helps to explain this. *(3 marks)*

(f) Describe the ways in which the behaviour of a heroin addict typically changes as a result of the addiction. *(3 marks)*

(Total 15 marks)

UCLES June 1996, Paper 1 (Option 1), No 2

23 Food, diet and health

Human beings require a constant supply of essential nutrients in balanced proportions in order to maintain themselves in a healthy state. It might therefore be thought that the dietary requirements of all humans are the same – not so. An individual's needs will vary according to size, age, sex, level of activity, state of health and particular personal circumstances, e.g. pregnancy. Even though the requirements of individuals of the same size, age, sex, activity, health and personal circumstances may be the same, the actual diet can differ markedly according to the cultural and economic background of each person as well as their individual beliefs and preferences. Those of us in western Europe with our varied choice of food perhaps too easily forget that in most parts of the world only a few staple foods are available and in many areas even these are lacking in sufficient quantity to sustain the population. Staple foods vary according to the crops grown and these are often determined historically or by climate. Rice is the staple food in South East Asia while maize fulfils this function in Central America. Religious observance may also determine diet to some degree, e.g. Judaism forbids the eating of pork, Hindus are largely vegetarian. Slimmers, vegans and diabetics have their own restricted diets although for very different reasons.

23.1 Balanced diet

In humans **carbohydrates** and **fats** are needed in relatively large quantities as sources of energy and **proteins** are needed in large amounts for growth and repair. **Vitamins** and **minerals** are required in much smaller quantities for a variety of specific functions. **Water** is a vital constituent of the diet for many reasons (see Section 23.1.7) and **dietary fibre** (roughage) is necessary for efficient digestion.

23.1.1 Energy requirements

The amount of energy in foods is expressed in **joules** although for practical purposes the **kilojoule (kJ)** is a much more convenient unit. Some books and magazines still use the former terms calorie and kilocalorie (one calorie = 4.18 joules and one Calorie (= kilocalorie) = 4.18 kilojoules). To measure the amount of energy in different foods, a given mass is burned in oxygen in an apparatus called a **bomb calorimeter**. The total heat generated gives a measure of the food's energy content which is known as its **calorific value**.

PROJECT

Attempt to find a relationship between estimated daily energy intake and estimated energy requirements.

The term which describes the basal metabolic processes needed to keep a human alive is **basal metabolism** and the rate at which energy is used up in maintaining basal metabolism is termed the **basal metabolic rate (BMR)**. It is measured in $kJ\,h^{-1}$ under standard conditions, namely when an individual is completely at rest, lying down in the warmth and at least 12 hours after a meal. Either the amount of heat produced is measured directly or the oxygen uptake (or carbon dioxide output) is measured and from this the energy used can be calculated.

One factor which influences the BMR is body size. As body fat is storage material with a very low metabolic rate, the very variable amounts of fat found in different individuals tends to distort the figures. For this reason the weight of the body excluding fat is normally used as a measure of body size. This is called the **lean body mass**. As women have a higher proportion of body fat than men, as well as being lighter, they have a lower BMR: $251\,kJ\,h^{-1}$ for an average woman (55 kg) compared to $293\,kJ\,h^{-1}$ for an average man (70 Kg). The surface area of the body also affects BMR. The larger the surface area, for any given weight, the greater the heat loss and so the higher the BMR. Age is also a factor. Children have a relatively higher BMR for a given weight than adults (although the actual figure is smaller because of their smaller lean body mass). The maximum BMR occurs at around the age of 20 years diminishing slowly as one ages, e.g. from $293\,kJ\,h^{-1}$ at 20 years old to $259\,kJ\,h^{-1}$ at age 70 years. BMR also increases after taking in food (**diet induced thermogenesis**) as well as with the level of the hormone thyroxine which controls metabolism.

As soon as a person becomes active, the energy requirement increases; the more strenuous the activity the greater the amount of energy needed. Table 23.1 provides examples of the recommended daily energy intake for humans of various ages undertaking various activities.

TABLE 23.1 **Recommended daily intake of energy according to age, activity and sex**

Age/years	Average body weight/kg	Degree of activity/ circumstances	Energy requirement/kJ	
			Male	Female
1	7	Average	3200	3200
5	20	Average	7500	7500
10	30	Average	9500	9500
15	45	Average Sedentary	11 500 11 300	11 500 9000
25	65 (male) 55 (female)	Moderately active Very active Sedentary	12 500 15 000 11 000	9500 10 500 9000
50	65 (male) 55 (female)	Moderately active Very active	12 000 15 000	9500 10 500
75	63 (male) 53 (female)	Sedentary	9000	8000
Any	–	During pregnancy	–	10 000
Any	–	Breast feeding	–	11 500

Did you know?

The energy released from one peanut will keep the brain active for one hour.

PROJECT

Use a simple calorimeter to investigate the suggestion that low fat cheeses contain less energy than full fat cheeses.

23.1.2 Carbohydrates

Details of the chemistry of carbohydrates are given in Chapter 2. Their main function is to provide energy – ideally two-thirds of the total with the remaining third being provided by fats. Sugars and starch are the carbohydrates which provide energy. Sugars are found in most plants in small quantities but are especially concentrated in sugar cane and sugar beet from which the sugar, sucrose, is extracted. Foods made from refined sugar are therefore rich in sucrose and these include jams, biscuits and chocolate as well as many sweetened drinks. Honey is rich in another sugar – fructose. Foods rich in starch include bread, porridge and potatoes.

As carbohydrates are the body's main energy source their inclusion in the diet of athletes is clearly important. It has been shown that endurance athletes who eat a diet rich in carbohydrate for 3–4 days, after several days on a normal mixed diet, can increase their glycogen store from 15 g to 25 g for each kg of muscle. This technique is known as **muscle glycogen loading** and is a means of enhancing athletic performance.

Fruits, vegetables and cereal grains are rich in an insoluble carbohydrate called cellulose. While cellulose therefore provides no direct nutritional value, it is no less important as it is the main constituent of **dietary fibre**. Some components of dietary fibre such as hemicellulose can be fermented in the large intestine to yield fatty acids which can be used to provide energy. Dietary fibre is necessary to give bulk to the food so that it can pass efficiently along the alimentary canal. It has also been shown to lower the cholesterol level in the blood. If the diet is low in fibre the risk of certain diseases is increased. These include constipation, appendicitis, heart disease, haemorrhoids, cancer of the colon and diverticular disease.

23.1.3 Fats and oils (lipids)

Details of the chemistry and functions of lipids are given in Section 2.6. As fat yields more energy for a given weight than carbohydrate it is the main long-term energy store of the body, but its accumulation can lead to obesity and other health problems. For this reason only about a third of the body's energy requirements should come from fat with the remainder being provided by carbohydrate. Foods rich in fat include meat, milk and milk products such as cream, butter and cheese, margarine and baked products like cakes, pastry and biscuits. Any food which is fried is likely to be rich in fat.

Much attention has been focused on the correlation between a high fat intake in the diet and heart disease. It is always difficult to draw direct relationships between one type of food and the incidence of a specific disease because foods contain a wide variety of substances. In addition factors such as exercise, stress and smoking affect an individual's health and the way food is utilised. It does, however, seem that a high intake of fat, especially saturated fat, is a contributory factor in causing heart disease.

23.1.4 Protein

The chemistry of proteins is given in Section 2.7. As a last resort, the body may respire proteins to provide energy, but their main function is as a source of amino acids which are used to

Diseases associated with a low fibre diet

There are a number of diseases of the colon which seem to be linked primarily to eating a diet low in fibre. Fibre adds bulk to food and helps to maintain its normal passage through the alimentary canal by peristalsis. When the diet is low in fibre the segments formed in peristalsis may close completely and build up within them a high pressure. Over the years this tends to push the mucosal lining of the colon into the muscular wall to form balloon-like diverticula often containing faecal material. These diverticula may cause no symptoms and have been found in one third of the population of industrialized countries after middle age. However painful infections may begin in them giving rise to the condition known as **diverticulosis**.

Another disease which develops as a result of a low-fibre diet is **irritable bowel syndrome**. This is characterized by alternating periods of diarrhoea and constipation, by flatulence and a distension of the abdomen. Hard, small stools are passed five or six times a day. It may follow gastroenteritis but often the symptoms appear gradually, usually by the age of 30 and often in teenagers. It is thought to be a stress-related condition since the symptoms worsen in times of anxiety. It seems to result from a lack of coordination in peristalsis so that the waves of contraction become strong and irregular. The symptoms are relieved by increasing the fibre intake although antispasmodic and anti-anxiety drugs may also be used. One-third of all malignant tumours in Western countries are found in the colon and, although there may be a genetic factor involved, the most important factor is thought to be a diet low in fibre. **Cancers of the colon** are rare in Africa and Japan where the intake of dietary fibre is high. If the growth is on the right-hand side it rarely obstructs the colon but it does cause pain, loss of weight, anaemia and fever. Tumours on the left usually cause a blockage leading to pain and distension of the abdomen. Cancers of the colon do not respond well to chemotherapy and so they are removed surgically along with any associated lymph glands. The surgeon then aims to restore the continuity of the colon so that it can function normally. If this is not possible the patient may have a colostomy so that the contents of the large intestine can be voided through the wall of the abdomen into a bag. Four-fifths of people suffering from cancer of the colon make a good recovery.

synthesize new proteins. These proteins are used in metabolism, growth and repair. Of the 20 amino acids needed by humans, 11 can be synthesized by the body and are termed **non-essential amino acids**. The remaining 9 must be provided in the diet and are termed **essential amino acids**. Of these 8 are needed throughout life while one, histidine, is only essential in infancy. The proportions of the 20 amino acids in any protein varies considerably. Clearly proteins with more essential amino acids are of greater value than those with less. More importantly, the proteins with a similar proportion of essential amino acids to the proteins of the human body are of greatest value of all.

Measuring the amount of protein in a food is very difficult and for this reason the amount of nitrogen which is obtained from a protein is used as a more convenient measure. The quality of a protein is measured as its **biological value (BV)**. This is expressed as:

$$\text{Biological value of a protein} = \frac{\text{Nitrogen retained}}{\text{Nitrogen absorbed}} \times 100$$

The amount of nitrogen absorbed by the body is equal to that taken in as food minus that lost in the faeces. The amount retained is equal to that absorbed minus that lost in the urine. We can now express the biological value slightly differently:

$$\text{B.V.} = \frac{\text{Nitrogen intake} - \text{Nitrogen in faeces} - \text{Nitrogen in urine}}{\text{Nitrogen intake} - \text{Nitrogen in faeces}} \times 100$$

The biological value does not take account of how easy it is to digest a protein food. The digestibility of protein is measured as:

$$\frac{\text{Nitrogen intake} - \text{Nitrogen in faeces}}{\text{Nitrogen intake}}$$

The digestibility of a protein depends on the nature of the protein, how it is prepared (i.e. the method of cooking) and individual differences in how easily it is broken down.

Foods rich in protein include meat, fish, eggs, milk, cheese, bread, nuts and some vegetables such as peas. Although plant food contains proportionately less protein, a properly balanced vegetable diet can nevertheless provide all essential amino acids. It is only where there is dependence on just one or two plant foods as sources of proteins that malnutrition results. The amount of protein required in the diet varies with age and with differing circumstances, e.g. pregnancy. Table 23.2 gives the recommended values for various groups.

TABLE 23.2 **Recommended daily amount of protein according to age and sex**

Age (years)	Protein (g)	
	Females	Males
1	27	30
5–6	42	43
9–11	51	56
15–17	53	72
18–34	54	72
65–74	47	60
75+	42	54
Pregnancy	60	—
Lactation	69	—

23.1.5 Vitamins

Vitamins are a group of essential organic compounds which are needed in small amounts for normal growth and metabolism. If the diet lacks a particular vitamin, a disorder called a **deficiency**

disease results. The vitamins required vary from species to species. Table 23.3 lists those needed in a human diet and the roles they play. Vitamins are normally classified as **water soluble** (vitamins C and the B complex) or **fat soluble** (vitamins A, D, E and K). Whereas excess water-soluble vitamins are simply excreted in urine, fat-soluble vitamins tend to accumulate in fatty tissues of the body, and may even build up to lethal concentrations if taken in excess.

Cooking and storage may affect the vitamin content of food. In the case of vitamin C for example, it is highly soluble in water and therefore food boiled in water quickly loses its vitamin C. In addition it is readily oxidized, especially at higher temperatures, high pHs and in the presence of light. Vitamin C can be broken down by an enzyme found in plant cells, but as the two are kept apart in natural conditions, the vitamin is only affected when the food is cut, dropped or bruised. To maintain the highest level of

TABLE 23.3 **Vitamins required in the human diet**

Vitamin/name	Fat/water soluble	Major food sources	Function	Deficiency symptoms
A_1 Retinol	Fat soluble	Liver, vegetables, fruits, dairy foods	Maintains normal epithelial structure. Needed to form visual pigments	Dry skin. Poor night vision
B_1 Thiamin	Water soluble	Liver, legumes, yeast, wheat and rice germ	Coenzyme in cellular respiration	Nervous disorder called beri-beri. Neuritis and mental disturbances. Heart failure
B_2 Riboflavin	Water soluble	Liver, yeast, dairy produce	Coenzymes (flavo-proteins) in cellular respiration	Soreness of the tongue and corners of the mouth
B_3 (pp factor) Niacin	Water soluble	Liver, yeast, wholemeal bread	Coenzyme (NAD) in cellular metabolism	Skin lesions known as pellagra. Diarrhoea
B_5 Pantothenic acid	Water soluble	Liver, yeast, eggs	Forms part of acetyl coenzyme A in cellular respiration	Neuromotor disorders, fatigue and muscle cramps
B_6 Pyridoxine	Water soluble	Liver, kidney, fish	Coenzymes in amino acid metabolism	Dermatitis. Nervous disorders
B_{12} Cyanocobalamine	Water soluble	Meat, eggs, dairy food	Nucleoprotein (RNA) synthesis. Needed in red blood cell formation	Pernicious anaemia. Malformation of red blood cells
Biotin	Water soluble	Liver, yeast. Synthesized by intestinal bacteria	Coenzymes in carboxylation reactions	Dermatitis and muscle pains
Folic acid	Water soluble	Liver, vegetables, fish	Nucleoprotein synthesis. Red blood cell synthesis	Anaemia
C Ascorbic acid	Water soluble	Citrus fruits, tomatoes, potatoes	Formation of connective tissues, especially collagen fibres	Non-formation of connective tissues. Bleeding gums – scurvy
D Calciferol	Fat soluble	Liver, fish oils, dairy produce. Action of sunlight on skin	Absorption and metabolism of calcium and phosphorus, important in formation of teeth and bones	Defective bone formation known as rickets
E Tocopherol	Fat soluble	Liver, green vegetables	Function unclear in humans. In rats it prevents haemolysis of red blood cells	Anaemia
K Phylloquinone	Fat soluble	Green vegetables. Synthesized by intestinal bacteria	Blood clotting	Failure of blood to clot

vitamin C, food should therefore be stored in a cool, dark place, prepared with the minimum of cutting or chopping necessary and cooked in the minimum of water for the least possible time.

23.1.6 Minerals

The principal minerals required in the human diet, and their sources, are given in Table 23.4

Calcium is a particularly important mineral as it is a major component of the skeleton – so much so that, by law, it must be added to all white flour to try to ensure an adequate quantity is available in most people's diet. The absorption of calcium is assisted by vitamin D, without which little would be taken up, and so the consequences of their deficiencies are much the same – namely **rickets** (in children) and **osteomalacia** (in adults). In both cases the bones become soft and weak with the long bones of the legs bending under the body weight as a consequence in the case of rickets. The amount of calcium absorption in women falls around the time of the menopause possibly leading to osteoporosis (see Focus on page 496). Growing children require more calcium than adults as it is needed for growth of bones. The recommended daily intake in children is 600–700 mg, falling to 500 mg in adults. Women need more calcium in the diet

TABLE 23.4 **Some essential minerals required in the human diet**

Mineral	Major food source	Function
Macronutrients Calcium (Ca^{2+})	Dairy foods, eggs, green vegetables	Constituent of bones and teeth, needed in blood clotting and muscle contraction. Enzyme activator
Chlorine (Cl^-)	Table salt	Maintenance of anion/cation balance. Formation of hydrochloric acid
Magnesium (Mg^{2+})	Meat, green vegetables	Component of bones and teeth. Enzyme activator
Phosphate (PO_4^{3-})	Dairy foods, eggs, meat, vegetables	Constituent of nucleic acids, ATP, phospholipids (in cell membranes), bones and teeth
Potassium (K^+)	Meat, fruit and vegetables	Needed for nerve and muscle action and in protein synthesis
Sodium (Na^+)	Table salt, dairy foods, meat, eggs, vegetables	Needed for nerve and muscle action. Maintenance of anion/cation balance
Sulphate (SO_4^{2-})	Meat, eggs, dairy foods	Component of proteins and coenzymes
Micronutrients (trace elements) Cobalt (Co^{2+})	Meat	Component for vitamin B_{12} and needed for the formation of red blood cells
Copper (Cu^{2+})	Liver, meat, fish	Constituent of many enzymes. Needed for bone and haemoglobin formation
Fluorine (F^-)	Many water supplies	Improves resistance to tooth decay
Iodine (I^-)	Fish, shellfish, iodized salt	Component of the growth hormone, thyroxine
Iron (Fe^{2+} or Fe^{3+})	Liver, meat, green vegetables	Constituent of many enzymes, electron carriers, haemoglobin and myoglobin
Manganese (Mn^{2+})	Liver, kidney, tea and coffee	Enzyme activator and growth factor in bone development
Molybdenum (Mo^{4+})	Liver, kidney, green vegetables	Required by some enzymes
Zinc (Zn^{2+})	Liver, fish, shellfish	Enzyme activator, involved in the physiology of insulin

during pregnancy and lactation to satisfy the additional needs of the fetus and new-born. The recommended daily intake for these women therefore rises to 1200 mg.

Iron deficiency leads to **anaemia** because it is a component of haemoglobin in red blood cells. Tiredness, lethargy, dizziness and headaches are all symptoms of anaemia as a consequence of less oxygen being carried by the blood. It is the commonest deficiency disease in Britain, although diet is not the only cause. Anaemia is much more common in women, with around 15% in Britain suffering from the disorder, largely because of the loss of iron in the blood during menstruation.

While it is usually a mineral deficiency which adversely affects health, in the case of **salt (sodium chloride)** an excess is more the problem. High salt intake increases blood pressure (hypertension) leading to, or compounding, other cardiovascular diseases.

23.1.7 Water

Water makes up 60–70% of the total body weight of humans and serves a wide variety of important functions which are discussed more fully in Section 17.1.3. Table 23.5 gives the daily water balance in a human not engaged in active work, i.e. there is no excessive sweating.

23.1.8 Milk

As milk is the only food received by humans in the period after birth, it follows that it must provide all essential materials for growth and development. In this sense it is a balanced diet in itself. It cannot, however, sustain healthy development indefinitely for these reasons:

1. It contains little if any iron – This is no problem to a new-born baby as it accumulates iron from its mother before birth. This store cannot last indefinitely and alternative sources of iron are necessary in later life.

2. It contains no fibre – We saw in Section 23.1.2 the necessity of fibre and the problems associated with its long-term absence from the diet.

3. It contains a high proportion of fat – For a young, actively growing human this is ideal, but as we grow the energy demand is reduced. This could lead to an increase in weight due to storage of the excess fat and a consequent increased risk of heart disease. For the early years, and as a supplement to the human diet in later life, milk nevertheless plays an invaluable role.

23.1.9 Dietary reference values

We have seen throughout this section that the requirement for any particular food depends upon the age, sex and physical condition of an individual. Tables can be constructed which show the **recommended daily amount (RDA)** of each nutrient which any particular group of individuals needs in order to maintain good health. These quantities are also referred to as **dietary reference values (DRV)**.

TABLE 23.5 **Human daily water balance**

Process	Water uptake /cm³	Water output /cm³
Drinking	1450	–
In food	800	–
From respiration	350	–
In urine	–	1500
In sweat	–	600
Evaporation from lungs	–	400
In faeces	–	100
TOTAL	2600	2600

Did you know?

The average human in a lifetime consumes 75 tonnes of water, 17 tonnes of carbohydrates, 2.5 tonnes of proteins and 1 tonne of fats.

The values form a measure which can be used to make comparisons of the nutritional intake of different groups. In themselves they do not show whether or not a person is malnourished as individual requirements differ; they are more a type of 'average' requirement for a particular group. An individual with an intake less than the DRV for a particular nutrient will not necessarily suffer any harm as a result, but could be in danger of doing so.

23.2   Malnutrition

Good health depends upon the consumption of a diet with the relevant balance of nutrients to suit the sex, age and physical condition of an individual. Too much or too little, in part or total, is known as malnutrition and could, in time, lead to ill health. The reasons for malnutrition vary. They can be as a result of disease, e.g. diabetes, a consequence of over-indulgence or due to economic or cultural factors; poor education or a lack of understanding of diet is a common underlying cause. While the members of the more wealthy nations often strive unsuccessfully to reduce their food intake, many of their counterparts in poorer countries struggle equally unsuccessfully to find enough food to survive. While richer nations spend vast sums of money in treating the medical conditions resulting from overeating, people in poorer nations starve for want of a subsistence diet.

23.2.1 Overnutrition

With supermarkets full of food from all over the world and available throughout the year, it is difficult to imagine our ancestors (or indeed those in many countries today) who had to eat what food was available when it was available. Food was often seasonal and long periods might elapse before another meal could be taken. As a result as much food as possible was consumed, some of which was stored to act as an energy source when the external supplies dried up. As this internal store of food added weight to the body, possibly restricting movement, the least heavy type of food – namely fat – was stored. The legacy of this irrefutable logic of evolution is that even when food is readily available we still tend to consume it in quantity, and store it as fat as if we feared that all the supermarkets and local shops were about to go out of business, or close for an extended holiday. As a result a large percentage of people in Britain are overweight increasing their risk of cardiovascular disease, diabetes, certain cancers and gall stones amongst other problems.

The ideal weight for an individual depends upon his/her height. One measure frequently used is the **body mass index (BMI)**. This is the weight (W) in kgs divided by the height (h) squared in metres.

$$\text{BMI} = \frac{W}{h^2}$$

A body mass index of between 20 and 25 represents the least risk

PROJECT

Is there always a relationship between body fat and fitness?

to health. Where the BMI exceeds 27.5 an individual is said to be **obese**, a condition which presents a considerable risk to health.

The causes of obesity are not just an excessive intake of food, but often a lack of physical exercise which is the best means of 'burning off' some of the energy taken in. There may also be a psychological dimension with eating being increased under conditions of stress, boredom or depression. The range, quantity and variety of food available coupled with aggressive marketing increases the temptation to eat more food than is strictly essential. Many convenience foods which can be consumed rapidly and with no preparation, e.g. crisps, biscuits and soft-drinks, are especially attractive in the increasingly busy and hectic world in which we live. These foods are concentrated forms of energy and do not provide much bulk, and so do not give the feeling of fullness which would depress appetite and prevent more from being eaten.

Reduction in weight is best achieved by a combination of reducing the energy intake in the form of food and increasing energy output through physical exercise. Any slimming diet should ensure that there is an adequate supply of essential minerals and vitamins. The intake of carbohydrate and especially fat should be reduced. It is important not to limit energy intake too drastically – typically a daily consumption of 3500–6500 kJ will be effective in losing weight although much depends on the extent of physical activity. There are dangers in reducing energy intake too rapidly because the body needs time to adjust to changes and the diet may prove too unappetizing to be maintained for long. Such diets can only be endured for a short period and so weight is often put on again equally rapidly once it has been abandoned. Equally any diet which is restricted to only one or two foods cannot provide the full range of essential nutrients and there is a high risk of deficiency diseases arising.

23.2.2 Undernutrition

A lack of an adequate quantity of all, or any one, nutrient will adversely affect health. Starvation is the result of a general lack of nutrients of which the absence of adequate protein and energy – **protein energy malnutrition (PEM)** – has the most obvious impact in the form of two conditions, kwashiorkor and marasmus.

Kwashiorkor results when there is severe protein deficiency in the diet. This frequently arises where the diet comprises largely one staple food such as cassava or yams, which is low in protein. It is common in young children particularly after weaning because this results in a change from protein-rich milk to a more carbohydrate-based diet. The symptoms are reduced weight, retarded growth, wasting of muscles and fluid in the tissues (oedema); the latter results in the distended abdomen which is so characteristic of this condition. Providing patients with protein, e.g. dried skimmed milk, will rectify the situation temporarily, but long-term solutions depend on an overall improvement of diet by increasing the protein production of those nations where the disease is common.

Marasmus has similar causes to kwashiorkor, although there is often also a carbohydrate deficiency. The symptoms include a wizened face, wasted muscles but not the oedema common in kwashiorkor.

Eating disorders

The so called 'slimmers disease' **anorexia nervosa**' largely affects adolescent girls. It is estimated that about 1 in 150 are affected, four times the frequency in adolescent boys. Typical symptoms are a severe loss of weight and a refusal to eat, lack of menstrual periods (**amenorrhoea**) and an abnormal fear of being fat and a desire to be thin. It is relatively rare in Afro-Asian populations but is more frequent in Western cultures which tend to admire and idealize slim people. There is also an above average incidence in social classes I, II and III and in certain groups, like ballet schools, where thinness is considered important.

Anorexics grossly overestimate their own body size, even when they are dangerously underweight. They are often people who feel rather inadequate and attempt to control their own lives by refusing to eat. They may be unable to cope with the challenges of puberty and may come from families who, while appearing united on the surface, also find it difficult to cope with changes.

Anorexia often starts with dieting but the weight loss gets out of control; the sufferer may show a great interest in food but will still refuse to eat. Conflicts often begin in the family and the anorexic undergoes severe personality changes. Treatment for anorexia must be prolonged and recovery is often slow. It is often difficult to get an anorexic to admit that there is a problem and then to agree to treatment but it is vital because sufferers can die of starvation. The most severe cases are usually treated in hospital with a caring but strict regime in which weight gain is rewarded with privileges. Psychotherapy is important to prevent relapse but of the most severe cases only 40% recover fully.

Bulimia nervosa is a variant of anorexia, often seen in older girls. Bulimics often have a body weight nearer to normal and may also menstruate. Bulimia is characterized by recurrent episodes of 'binge' eating, frequently on fatty foods or cream cakes. During these spells the sufferer feels a lack of control over eating behaviour. The binges are followed by various methods to prevent weight gain: self-induced vomiting, the use of laxatives or diuretics, strict fasting or vigorous exercise. Such patterns of 'binging' and over-compensating for a high food intake can lead to serious electrolyte imbalances and to recurrent infections. Bulimics are often very strong characters who can become very depressed about their lack of control. They are treated by psychotherapy and by being encouraged to follow strict patterns of eating such as eating at set times and in a particular room and being encouraged to leave something on the plate.

Both anorexia and bulimia are complex conditions with no single cause or cure but perhaps there would be fewer cases if young people were not encouraged to feel that their body shape was so important.

Did you know?

Before 1900, almost three-quarters of children living in poorer industrialized parts of Britain had rickets.

The lack of a single nutrient in the diet leads to specific deficiency diseases. **Vitamin A (retinol)** is essential for the growth and metabolism of cells, for the maintenance of a healthy skin, cornea and mucus membranes and for the formation of rhodopsin (visual purple) a pigment in the retina of the eye. A deficiency of retinol therefore leads to a reduced growth rate in children, **poor night vision** and a condition known as **xerophthalmia**. In extreme cases xerophthalmia causes blocked tear ducts and as a result a dry, inflamed cornea. Prolonged deficiency leads to ulceration of the cornea and blindness.

Vitamin C (ascorbic acid) is needed for the formation of collagen, a major component of connective tissues and it also aids the absorption of iron from the intestines. Deficiency of ascorbic acid causes a condition called **scurvy** whose symptoms include bruising and bleeding under the skin, especially around the gums. Wounds and fractures are also slow to heal.

Iron is an essential component of the haemoglobin found in red blood cells which carries oxygen around the body. It is also part of the myoglobin molecule which carries oxygen in muscle. A deficiency of iron leads to **anaemia**, the symptoms of which are headaches, dizziness and lethargy.

Vegetarian diets are increasingly common for a variety of reasons. Any diet comprising milk, cheese and eggs as well as plant material should provide all the essential nutrients but if the diet is restricted to entirely plant material – **vegan diet** – then greater planning is necessary to ensure that all nutrients are included. Cereals, nuts and pulses are normally necessary to maintain adequate quantities of protein, energy, riboflavin and iron. Even then vitamin B_{12} may be lacking.

23.3 Food preservation

Foods provide us with the essential nutrients we need for our survival but as similar nutrients are required by microorganisms our food is equally attractive to them. In order to obtain the nutrients from the food, microorganisms produce enzymes which digest the macromolecules into smaller units which can then diffuse into the microbial cells and as a result the food deteriorates and becomes unfit for human consumption. This is known as **microbial spoilage**. While many of these microorganisms are saprobiontic and cause no direct harm to humans, others such as *Salmonella*, *Listeria* and *Campylobacter* may cause food poisoning (see Section 22.2.9).

From the moment food is harvested or slaughtered it is not only subjected to microbial spoilage but also decomposition as a result of natural processes within dead cells. The normal active mechanisms which keep various cellular chemicals separate cease upon death and so reactions occur which result in cells digesting themselves. This is called **autolysis** and is largely the result of enzymes acting upon various components of the cell. While this process is useful to some extent in that it tenderizes meat and ripens fruits, for the most part it spoils food, not only making it unpalatable but also more prone to microbial spoilage.

PROJECT

It has been said that fresh fruit juices are 'better for you' than preserved ones.

Use DCPIP to investigate this claim in respect of vitamin C.

Much food is produced only at one season and needs to be stored if it is to be available at other times of the year. Increasingly the points of food production are a long way from the places where they are consumed and so food must be preserved for some time if both quantity and variety are to be available. The preservation of food depends on being able to prevent both microbial spoilage and autolysis. In the short term, blanching or cooking of food destroys the microorganisms and enzymes responsible for spoilage, but long-term preservation requires other mechanisms.

23.3.1 Freezing

The multiplication of microorganisms and the rate of reaction of enzymes are both temperature dependent. Chilling or freezing therefore reduces or halts the activities of both microorganisms and enzymes and so prevents food spoilage. Reducing temperatures to the range 0–10 °C is known as **chilling** and slows, but does not prevent, degradation of the food. Most household refrigerators chill food, typically at around 4 °C.

Freezing entails lowering the temperature to below 0 °C with freezers operating at temperatures down to −20 °C; at this temperature enzyme activity and microbial reproduction ceases. A combination of water being unavailable because it is frozen, the inability to use nutrients/gases and mechanical disruption due to ice crystals results in the death of many microorganisms. Some however survive to resume normal activities once the food has thawed. The ice crystals which destroy microbial cells also disrupt the cells of which food is composed. **Quick-freezing**, in which the food temperature is reduced from 0 °C to −4 °C in less than half an hour, produces smaller ice crystals than slower methods of freezing. These smaller ice crystals cause less disruption of cells, helping to preserve the texture of food once thawed. The main advantages of freezing as a method of food preservation are:

1. Most foods can be frozen.

2. The appearance, flavour and texture of the food is preserved in most cases

3. The nutritive value of the food is preserved.

Briefly immersing certain foods, e.g. fruit and vegetables, in boiling water prior to freezing helps preserve them. This process, called **blanching**, kills most microorganisms and denatures enzymes and so reduces spoilage during the cooling and thawing processes. Blanching however, reduces some of the food's vitamin C content.

23.3.2 Heat treatment

Heat is frequently used to preserve food because raising the temperature of food to a suitable level will both denature enzymes and kill microorganisms. The higher the temperature, the more effective the process, but the greater the damage to the quality of the food.

Pasteurization is a mechanism for extending the shelf-life of food without causing major changes to its flavour or nutrient value. Milk is the food most frequently treated in this way. As

PROJECT

Indicators can be used to assess the level of microbial activity in milk.

Use methylene blue or resazurin to investigate the keeping qualities of milk.

the only food provided for young mammals milk contains an ideal balance of nutrients, making it particularly vulnerable to microbial spoilage. Sterilizing milk by heating it to temperatures of around 105–110 °C for about half an hour will effectively destroy microorganisms and preserve the milk for some time. Unfortunately the process affects the flavour and colour of the milk as well as reducing its protein, vitamin C and thiamin content. In pasteurization, the milk is either heated to between 63 °C and 65.5 °C for half an hour or to 71.5 °C for 15 seconds. In both cases the milk is then rapidly cooled to below 10 °C. The adverse effect on flavour, colour and nutritional value is less than with sterilization although the shelf-life of the resulting milk is shorter.

Canning uses very high temperatures to destroy not only microorganisms but also their spores, and then the sterile food is sealed in a suitable container to prevent infection by microbes. The containers can be plastic or glass as well as the tinned steel traditionally used. Canning usually involves the following processes:

1. Preparation – the food is separated from any inedible material, is washed to reduce the number of microorganisms and chopped into a convenient size as necessary.

2. Blanching – the food is immersed in boiling water or steam to inactivate enzymes.

3. Filling of container – the cans are filled with the appropriate amount of food and any additional liquor eg. syrup, brine.

4. Vacuum emptying – a vacuum is applied to the cans to remove any air.

5. Sealing – the cans are automatically sealed.

6. Sterilisation – the cans are heated under a pressure to 121°C for varying times depending on the size of the can and the food it contains. This process destroys all microorganisms and their spores.

7. Cooling – this occurs slowly to prevent any buckling which could break the seals of the cans.

The high temperature used in the canning process alters the flavour, colour and texture of food. Compare a fresh strawberry for example with those which are canned. The nutritive content is also reduced with proteins, vitamin C and thiamin being especially affected. As heating breaks down the cellular structure, canned foods are more easily digestible and more of the nutrients are released. Macromolecules such as starch and protein are also partly broken down by heating and hence more readily digested.

23.3.3 Chemical inhibitors

Any chemical which kills or prevents the reproduction of microorganisms can potentially be used to preserve food as can those chemicals which inhibit the enzymes which cause autolysis. The chemicals used however must be harmless to health as they will be consumed; they must also penetrate the food to be effective and should not render the food unpalatable.

PROJECT

How is
a) sugar content, and
b) vitamin C content of food affected by
   i) storage time or
   ii) storage conditions?

Did you know?

It has been suggested that the high incidence of stomach cancer in Iceland is due to the large amounts of smoked fish consumed there.

As chemicals which have a direct metabolic effect on microorganisms are likely to be harmful to human metabolism, the inhibitors used to preserve food frequently affect conditions such as osmotic concentration or pH.

Vinegar has long been used as a preservative. As few microorganisms survive in acidic conditions, any substance with a low pH such as vinegar will prevent their growth. The flavour of the food is affected, although it is frequently a matter of taste as to whether this is a detrimental or beneficial change. Lactic, benzoic and sulphurous acids are also used to preserve foods and beverages; these are not always additions to the food, but sometimes a natural product. Yoghurt, for instance, is preserved by the lactic acid produced by the bacteria which convert milk into yoghurt and sauerkraut is cabbage preserved by lactic acid produced by bacteria which ferment it. The addition of salt or sugar to foods creates a solution with a high osmotic potential. As a result water is drawn out of microorganisms in the food and the consequent dehydration kills them. The preservation of jam operates on this principle.

Curing of certain meats, e.g. bacon, is achieved by injecting the meat with a mixture of salts (sodium chloride, sodium nitrate, potassium nitrate and potassium polyphosphate) and then immersing it in a solution of the same. The salts inhibit microbial growth as well as imparting a pink colour to the meat.

Smoking food entails exposing it to the smoke of certain burning woods over a period of time. Substances in the smoke inhibit microbial growth as well as giving the food a distinctive flavour. Bacon, ham, some cheeses and certain fish can be preserved in this way, mostly as an addition to other methods of preservation.

A number of chemicals have direct antibiotic properties; these include sodium nitrite, sodium metabisulphite, nicin and tylosin. The use of these chemicals is closely regulated by law as they can be toxic to humans in high concentrations. More details on preservatives are given in Section 23.4.1.

23.3.4 Dehydration

All microorganisms require water for their growth and reproduction. Equally the enzymes which cause autolysis cannot function without water and so the removal of moisture from food is a highly effective way of preserving it. This is best achieved slowly, otherwise a hard, dry outer layer develops acting as a barrier to the loss of water from the centre. Cereal grains, pulses, fruits, vegetables, meats and milk can all be preserved in this way.

23.3.5 Irradiation

Short-wave ionizing radiation such as X-rays or gamma rays can be used to inactivate microorganisms. Although irradiation produces little if any radioactivity in food, there has been consumer resistance to this method of preservation. The process uses gamma rays from radioactive cobalt–60 or caesium-137 or a beam of high energy electrons produced by a linear accelerator. The process is especially effective against insects and other parasites as these are sensitive to relatively low doses; stored grain can therefore be protected from damage by insects in this way. Irradiation can reduce the levels of vitamins such as ascorbic acid and thiamin in food. It does not prevent autolysis, nor will it render harmless those toxins already present from the activities of microorganisms.

23.3.6 Food packaging

It is clearly advantageous to health to minimize the amount of direct handling of food and this becomes even more important where the food has been sterilized since any handling will contaminate the food. Even exposure to air will lead to loss of sterility and so packaging of food has become a vital part of food preservation. Packages protect food during storage and transport, from a variety of potentially harmful factors such as mechanical damage, climatic conditions and contamination.

The glass, wood, metal, pottery and paper traditionally used for packaging are giving way to synthetic materials such as plastics, celluloses and polythenes. The advantage of these materials is that they can be easily moulded into a suitable shape. In some cases they can be used to **shrink-wrap** food. Here the air, which contains the oxygen needed by microorganisms, can be largely excluded from around the food, helping to preserve it. Where the wrapping material is impervious to oxygen this is particularly effective. **Vacuum packaging** involves actively removing all the air so that oxidation of the contents cannot occur. This is especially useful in packaging margarines and other fats which are readily oxidized. Where sunlight may also cause deterioration of the food, aluminium foil can be used rather than a transparent plastic. It is virtually impossible to remove all the oxygen as small quantities will be trapped within the food and in any case anaerobic microorganisms may continue to degrade it. Some plastic films have very low permeability to water vapour so that there is hardly any weight loss (as little as 2%) when fruit and vegetables are packed in these. Some cellophane films have up to 8–9% weight loss from their contents due to evaporation of water vapour.

A more recent method of preserving foods in their packages has been to modify the atmosphere in the package. Not only can all oxygen be excluded but the replacement gas may have some other beneficial effect, e.g. it may be used to delay ripening. **Modified atmosphere packaging (MAP)**, as it is called, uses gases which may be divided into three broad categories:

1. **Inert blanketing** – using nitrogen.

2. **Semi-reactive blanketing** – using a combination of nitrogen and carbon dioxide.

3. **Fully-reactive blanketing** – using carbon dioxide alone, or in combination with oxygen.

Nitrogen simply replaces the oxygen and so prevents aerobic microorganisms spoiling the food as well as preventing oxidation. Carbon dioxide can exert a powerful inhibitory effect on the growth of many bacteria and moulds, while the addition of oxygen can inhibit growth of some anaerobic microorganisms. To increase the shelf-life of meat from 2–4 days to 5–8 days, it is recommended that it be wrapped in an atmosphere of 60–85%

PROJECT

Investigate weight loss in packaged foods.

oxygen and 15–40% carbon dioxide. The oxygen helps to retain the desirable bright red appearance of the meat while the carbon dioxide inhibits microbial growth; cream on the other hand is packed with 100% nitrogen as any carbon dioxide confers a sharp taste to it.

23.4 Food additives

Substances may be added to food for a number of reasons:

1. So that the food will keep longer by preventing autolysis and/or microbial decay – **preservatives.**

2. To prevent food deteriorating by becoming oxidized – **antioxidants.**

3. To add taste to the food – **flavourings.**

4. To improve the natural taste of the food – **flavour-enhancers.**

5. To make the food appear more attractive – **colourings.**

6. As part of the growing or processing of food – **residues.**

There is legal control of all substances added to food and for these purposes they are classified into six groups:

1. Preservatives

2. Antioxidants

3. Emulsifiers and stabilizers

4. Colours

5. Sweeteners

6. Miscellaneous additives

Each additive is given an **E-number** once its use has been permitted within the European Union. In some cases, the addition of substances to food is compulsory by law in Britain. Potassium iodide, for example, is added to common salt to help prevent goitre – a deficiency disease caused by a lack of iodine in the diet. Margarine for home, rather than catering purposes, has to have vitamins A and D added to help prevent rickets and xerophthalmia. The addition of vitamin B_1 (thiamin) and vitamin B_3 (niacin) to white flour is compulsory, to compensate for the removal of these substances when the germ of the wheat is removed during its production.

23.4.1 Preservatives

Certain food additives are designed to prevent autolysis and microbial decomposition so that food can be stored for longer periods and some of these chemicals were discussed in Section 23.3.3. Preservatives have E-numbers from 200 to 90. One common group of preservatives is the **sulphites and metabisulphites** which are salts of sulphur dioxide. As they leave an unpleasant after-taste they are used largely for foods which will be cooked or boiled, e.g. sausages, as this drives off the sulphur dioxide and leaves the taste unaffected. These preservatives also destroy any vitamin B_1 (thiamin) in the food. **Sorbic acid** and its salts are effective fungicides and so are used for foods liable to be contaminated by yeasts and moulds, e.g. fruit yoghurts and soft drinks. Meats and cheeses are often preserved by the addition of **sodium and potassium nitrites and nitrates** and illustrate the dilemma of using preservatives. They have a clear beneficial effect in that they are especially effective against *Clostridium botulinum* which causes botulism and, but for the use of these salts many more deaths would have resulted from this cause. On the other hand nitrites react with haemoglobin in the blood and reduce its oxygen-carrying capacity leading to dizziness and headaches. In young babies the condition can be life-threatening. For this reason nitrites and nitrates are not yet permitted in baby foods intended for children under six months of age. In addition, nitrites can combine with amines in the stomach to produce nitrosamines, substances with the potential to cause cancer.

Other preservatives include **benzoates** which are used in beer, jams, fruit pie fillings and salad cream and **propionic acid** which helps prevent moulds developing in bread and other baked products.

23.4.2 Antioxidants

Lipids (fats and oils) readily react with oxygen which converts the triglycerides of which they are composed into a variety of aldehydes and ketones. These give the lipids an unpleasant taste and they are said to have become **rancid**. Antioxidants are chemicals which prevent this oxidation process. They have E-numbers between 300 and 322 and include substances such as L-ascorbic acid, tocopherol and lecithins. Apart from their usefulness in preventing rancidity in lipids, antioxidants may be added to certain fruits and vegetables to prevent the browning which can occur due to the effect of a natural enzyme (polyphenol oxidase) which they contain.

23.4.3 Flavourings and flavour enhancers

Flavour is clearly an important factor when it comes to choosing food and manufacturers expend large sums in trying to tempt us to sample their 'tasty' products. Only salt, sweet, sour and bitter tastes can be detected by the tongue; much of what we call taste is really smell. Flavourings are therefore normally highly volatile compounds which readily produce an odour which can be detected by the nose. Many flavours added to food are natural substances derived from other foods. These include oils obtained from natural foods such as oranges, limes, lemons, garlic, ginger, clove and thyme. Other, less volatile, extracts used are obtained from a variety of spices and herbs.

Synthetic flavours may be less popular with consumers but are often cheaper and easier to use by manufacturers. These synthetic flavours are frequently very similar in chemical structure to their natural counterparts although their exact compositions are normally kept secret by the manufacturers. With over so many natural and synthetic flavourings currently in use, their control is more problematic than for preservatives and antioxidants.

PROJECT

Lemon juice can prevent sliced apple going brown

Find out what factors affect the rate of browning in various fruits and vegetables.

Did you know?

Over 3000 different flavourings are added to our food.

FOCUS

Additives, allergies and ailments

The use of food additives is strictly controlled and they have to undergo rigorous testing before their use is licensed. Although tests must show them to be safe, effective and necessary a small number of people still show adverse reactions to some of them. Some additives have been linked to the behavioural disorder known as **hyperactivity** which most commonly affects children and young people. Sufferers become excited and impulsive with a short attention span. They may become aggressive and antisocial and some show a lack of muscular coordination. The Hyperactive Children's Support Group (HASG) recommends avoidance of a number of additives including many colourings, such as tartrazine (E101), quinoline yellow (E104), cochineal (E120) and ponceau 4R (E124). Also listed as possible risk factors are preservatives such as benzoic acid (E210) and antioxidants like butylated hydroxyanisol (BHA or E320).

Other groups who may possibly risk side-effects are asthmatics and those who are sensitive to aspirin. Different people react to different additives but the list of possible ones to avoid includes the preservative potassium benzoate (E212), the antioxidant propyl gallol (E310) and a number of flavour-enhancers. Monosodium glutamate (E621) causes some people to suffer short-lived effects such as palpitations, chest pain and dizziness. Although there is no evidence for any additives causing cancer in humans some, such as nitrates and nitrites (E249–E252) used as preservatives do cause cancers in rodents and may put humans at risk if they are consumed in large amounts (see Section 23.4.1). Their use is not permitted in baby foods. There are a number of antioxidants whose use causes gastric irritation in sensitive individuals. These include the gallates (E310–E312) and the two closely related chemicals butylated hydroxyanisole (BHA) and butylated hydroxytoluese (BHT) (E320 and E321). These antioxidants have also caused cancer in rats when consumed in high doses and they are banned in baby foods.

Flavour enhancers modify the taste of food by seeming to make existing flavours more prominent while themselves being tasteless. Salt and soy sauce have been used as flavour enhancers for many years in China and Japan. It is an ingredient of soy sauce, **monosodium glutamate** which is now the most widely used flavour enhancer; a derivative of the amino acid glutamic acid, it has been commonly used in Chinese cuisine. In large doses monosodium glutamate can cause dizziness, but used sparingly it can enhance the flavour of meats and certain vegetables. It is widely used in canned and dried meats and vegetables as well as in soups.

23.4.4 Colourings

Processing of food often results in loss of colour and yet consumers are particularly careful about colour when choosing food. However appetising and palatable it might be, few would choose to buy blue meat! About 50 colourings are permitted and these have E-numbers from 100 to 180. Many are extracts from natural substances, e.g. beta-carotene from carrots, but others such as the azo dye tartrazine are synthetic. Some examples of permitted colours and the foods they are used in are given in Table 23.6.

TABLE 23.6

Colouring	E-number	Used in
Curcumin	E100	Margarine
Tartrazine	E102	Cake mixes, soft drinks
Cochineal	E120	Alcoholic drinks
Indigo carmine	E132	Blancmange, confectionery
Chlorophyll	E140	Canned vegetables, soups
Beta-carotene	E160	Margarine, soft drinks
Lutein	E161	Egg yolks (added to poultry feed to yellow yolks)
Anthocyanins	E163	Yoghurt, soft drinks
Titanium dioxide	E171	Confectionery

23.4.5 Chemical contamination of food due to agricultural practices

Modern agricultural practices involve the addition of a wide range of chemicals to crops and animal feeds and residues from these chemicals sometimes remain in food consumed by humans. We saw in Section 14.2.8 for example, that pesticides such as DDT can increase in concentration as one moves up the food chain. Where humans form part of a food chain, they are invariably at the top and so at greatest risk from these accumulating residues. Moreover, the residues often build up in one particular tissue where concentrations can become very high. DDT, for example, being fat soluble, accumulates in adipose (fat) tissue and as a consequence many humans possess a higher concentration of DDT in some of their fat than many countries would permit in meat for human consumption.

We also saw in Section 14.7.2 how nitrates from agricultural fertilizers may run off into lakes and rivers. Drinking water taken from these lakes and rivers, despite purification, may contain levels of nitrate which are dangerous to young children because they react with haemoglobin reducing its oxygen-carrying capacity. Even in adults nitrates can react with amines in the stomach to produce the carcinogenic nitrosamines.

Concerns are also being raised about the use of hormones and antibiotics in the raising of animals for human consumption and the possible health risks they may present. Bovine somatotrophin (BST) is one such hormone and the implications of its use are considered in the Focus on page 324.

23.5   Questions

1. Bovine somatotrophin, BST, is a hormone which, when given to cows, will increase milk production. BST used for this purpose is made by genetic engineering. The process is summarized below:

The BST gene is isolated from the DNA of a cow

↓

The BST gene is inserted into a bacterial cell

↓

The bacterium is cloned and the BST isolated

(a) Describe how enzymes may be used to isolate the BST gene from the DNA of a cow and insert this gene into the DNA of a bacterial cell.   *(3 marks)*
(b) BST is a protein. Explain why any BST that gets into the cow's milk will be unlikely to have any effect on a human who drinks milk.   *(1 mark)*
(c) Suggest why cows that are being treated with BST require extra calcium and protein in their diet.
(2 marks)
(Total 6 marks)

NEAB June 1995, Paper BY07, No. 4

2. Complete the table below by writing, in the appropriate boxes, the function of each named nutrient and the name of the disease caused by a deficiency of that nutrient.

Nutrient disease	Function in body	Name of deficiency
Iron		
	Component of rhodopsin (visual purple)	
		Scurvy

(Total 6 marks)

ULEAC 1996, Specimen Paper B/HB4D, No. 1

3. Distinguish between the members of each of the following pairs.
(a) Flavourings and flavour-enhancers   *(2 marks)*
(b) Preservatives and antioxidants   *(2 marks)*
(Total 4 marks)
ULEAC 1996, Specimen Paper B/HB4D, No. 3

4. Discuss the advantages and disadvantages of different methods of food packaging.
(Total 10 marks)
ULEAC 1996, Specimen Paper B/HB4D, No. 8

5. The daily food intake of a 30-year-old woman contains 70 g of protein, 70 g of fat and an unknown amount of carbohydrate.
(a) Assume energy values per gram are 17 kJ for protein, 37 kJ for fat and 16 kJ for carbohydrate.
(i) Calculate the maximum energy yield of the fat in the diet.   *(1 mark)*
(ii) If the energy needs of the woman are 10 800 kJ per day how much carbohydrate must she consume to be in energy balance? Show your working.   *(3 marks)*
(b) (i) Explain the term *essential amino acid*.   *(1 mark)*
(ii) Suggest **one** reason why a person eating an entirely vegetarian diet must usually eat a greater mass and variety of protein per day than a person eating a diet containing animal protein.   *(1 mark)*
(Total 6 marks)

AEB June 1992, Paper 1, No. 16

6. The table below shows the mean daily intake of some substances in the human diet, their potential energy values in kilojoules day^{-1} and the mean daily loss of the substances in the faeces.

Substance	Mean daily intake/g day^{-1}	Potential energy value/kJ day^{-1}	Mean daily loss /g day^{-1}
Proteins	100	1700	6
Starches	300	4800	4
Cellulose	250	4000	240
Unsaturated fat	40	3800	2
Saturated fat	60		3
Calcium	1	0	0.75

(a) The body obtains most of its energy by respiring fat and glucose (derived mainly from starch). Protein is respired only in conditions of starvation.
Doctors recommend that humans should derive less than 30% of their energy intake from fat, and that the fat should be unsaturated rather than saturated.
(i) Does the diet shown in the table follow the doctor's recommendations? Explain your answer.   *(4 marks)*
(ii) Suggest why the doctors recommend that the fat content of the diet should be controlled.   *(2 marks)*
(iii) It is biologically inefficient to use protein as a source of energy. Why is this so?   *(2 marks)*

(b) (i) With reference to the digestive processes involved, explain the difference in starch and cellulose content in the faeces.   (*4 marks*)

(ii) Why is it considered advantageous to humans to have large quantities of cellulose in the diet   (*2 marks*)

(c) How could the efficiency of the calcium absorption of the human be improved?   (*1 mark*)

(*Total 15 marks*)

ULEAC June 1995, Paper 1, No. 14

7. (a) State the meaning of the term *basal metabolic rate*.   (*2 marks*)

(b) The graph below shows the effect of age on basal metabolic rate (BMR).

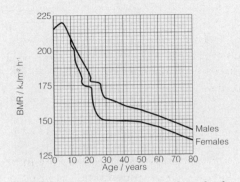

(i) Using the data on the graph, calculate the energy expenditure of a 20-year-old male during an 8-hour period of sleep. Show your working.   (*2 marks*)

(ii) Suggest why basal metabolic rate varies with age and gender.   (*4 marks*)

(*Total 8 marks*)

ULEAC June 1995, Paper 1, No. 10

8. *Staphylococcus aureus* is a bacterium which produces toxins in foods. These toxins are a common cause of food poisoning. *Staphylococcus aureus* grows aerobically and anaerobically, at an optimum temperature of 37 °C. It is killed at temperatures higher than 55 °C. The toxin it produces is heat-stable, and remains active after heating to 100 °C or freezing at −18 °C.

The diagrams at the top of the next column show the sequence of events which led to an outbreak of staphylococcal food poisoning. The outbreak was traced to a manufacturer of processed cold meat.

(a) Comment on the biological principles underlying the following procedures:

(i) storing the meat in brine (concentrated sodium chloride solution) for two days;   (*2 marks*)

(ii) boiling the meat in insulated pans. (*2 marks*)

(b) (i) Suggest the most likely source of contamination of the pressed beef. Explain your reasoning.   (*3 marks*)

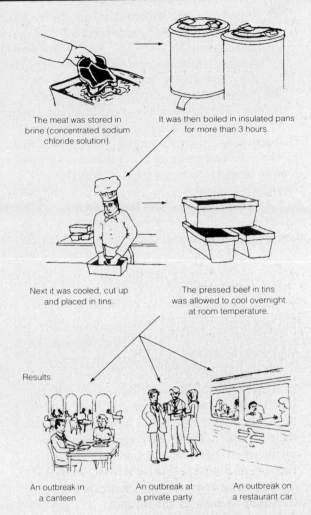

The meat was stored in brine (concentrated sodium chloride solution).

It was then boiled in insulated pans for more than 3 hours.

Next it was cooled, cut up and placed in tins.

The pressed beef in tins was allowed to cool overnight at room temperature.

Results:

An outbreak in a canteen

An outbreak at a private party

An outbreak on a restaurant car

(ii) Suggest **three** ways in which the outbreaks of food poisoning could have been avoided.   (*3 marks*)

(c) State **two** other sources of microbial contamination of food.   (*2 marks*)

(*Total 12 marks*)

ULEAC June 1993, Paper 4B, No. 2

9. Body mass index is given by the equation

$$\text{BMI} = \frac{\text{Mass/kg}}{(\text{Height/m})^2}$$

The maximum BMI value recommended for good health is 25. A person with a BMI value greater than this is probably overweight.

(a) The table below shows the height and mass of six 18-year-old students.

Student	Height/m	Mass/kg
Susan	1.50	54
Nasreen	1.65	71
Rebecca	1.79	77
Chris	1.82	79
Mike	1.60	74
Ashish	1.68	65

(i) Which of these students is/are overweight, according to their body mass indices? Show your reasoning. (4 marks)

(ii) A person is diagnosed as clinically obese if he or she has a body mass 15% or more above the maximum recommended for his or her height. Give the name(s) of any student(s) in the table who would be diagnosed as clinically obese. Show your reasoning. (3 marks)

(b) Describe **one** method, other than measurement of body mass, by which a person might be diagnosed as obese. (2 marks)

(c) Give **three** reasons why the mean life expectancy of clinically obese people is less than that of people of normal body mass. (3 marks)

(Total 12 marks)

ULEAC June 1995, Paper 4B, No. 1

10. (a) In a study of dietary fibre intake in Denmark, people living in rural areas had a mean intake of 18.0 g per day while those living in cities had a mean intake of 13.2 g per day. Suggest an explanation for the difference in dietary fibre intake between these two groups. (2 marks)

(b) Various medical studies have shown that low dietary fibre intake is correlated with a high incidence of constipation and diverticulitis. Explain why it is not possible to say from this evidence that lack of dietary fibre causes constipation and diverticulitis. (2 marks)

(Total 4 marks)

NEAB June 1995, Paper BY08, No. 2

11. A survey was carried out into the relationship between the frequency of unsweetened and sweetened snacks and the occurrence of caries in children's teeth. The results are shown in the table below.

Usual number of snacks /day	Percentage of children with caries	
	Snacks unsweetened	Snacks sweetened
Less than 1	0	26
1	24	29
2	31	27
3	30	42
4	36	45

(a) Describe the relationship between the frequency and nature of snacks and the percentage of children with caries. (3 marks)

(b) Suggest an explanation for the effect of sweetened snacks on the occurrence of dental caries in children. (4 marks)

(Total 7 marks)

ULEAC June 1993, Paper 4B, No. 6

12. The bar charts below show how recommended daily amounts of four essential nutrients (protein, calciferol, calcium and iron) change between babyhood and the age of 21 years.

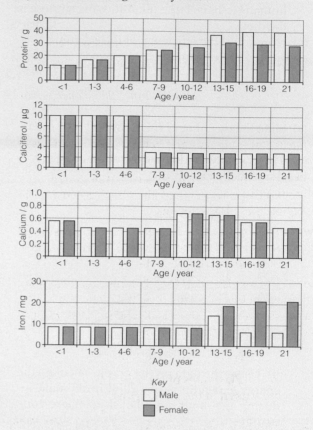

Key
☐ Male
■ Female

(a) (i) For each nutrient in the chart, state one way in which the changes in requirement during growth distinguish it from the other three. (4 marks)

(ii) Suggest an explanation for each of the features stated in (i). (4 marks)

(b) **Sketch** the equivalent bar chart showing how requirements for energy would change in both sexes between babyhood and the age of 21 years. (2 marks)

(Total 10 marks)

ULEAC June 1994, Paper 4B, No. 3

13. Discuss the advantages and disadvantages of adding flavourings and flavour enhancers to processed foods.

(Total 10 marks)

ULEAC June 1993, Paper 4B, No. 7

14. (a) The World Health Organization encourages the development of targets for a national average diet. Discuss the **importance** of developing these targets and summarise the main targets established for Britain. (11 marks)

(b) Outline the **problems** which may be associated with implementing and achieving these targets. *(7 marks)*

(Total 18 marks)

UCLES June 1995, Paper 3 (Option 1), No. 3(b)

15. Describe the processes by which milk may be treated or converted for short-term or long-term storage. *(Total 10 marks)*

ULEAC June 1995, Paper 4B, No. 7

16. In formulating a diet, it is necessary to consider the nutritional value of different component foods.

The *biological value* (BV) of a source of protein is defined as the percentage of absorbed protein that is converted into body protein.

The *digestibility* of a source of protein is a measure of the proportion of that protein which is broken down into amino acids during digestion.

The *net protein utilization* (NPU) is the percentage of protein eaten that is retained by the body. The relationship between the BV, digestibility and NPU is given by the following equation.

$$NPU = BV \times digestibility$$

The BV and NPU values of six different sources of protein are shown in the table below.

Source of protein	BV value	NPU value
Egg	98	96
Meat	80	76
Milk	77	71
Soya flour	70	60
Maize	36	31
Gelatin	9	0

(a) (i) Calculate the digestibility of egg protein. Show your working. *(2 marks)*
(ii) The digestibility of soya flour protein is 0.86. Comment on the difference between this figure for soya flour and that calculated for egg protein in (*a*) (i). *(3 marks)*
(b) The BV of a protein depends on the content of essential amino acids.
(i) Explain what is meant by the term *essential amino acid*. *(2 marks)*
(ii) Suggest why gelatin has a BV of 0. *(1 mark)*
(iii) Suggest why, in the foods given in the table, most animal proteins have a higher BV than the plant proteins. *(2 marks)*

(c) Suggest a reason why protein malnutrition is common in countries where cassava (manioc) is the staple diet. *(2 marks)*

(Total 12 marks)

ULEAC June 1996, Paper B/HB4D, No. 6

17. An investigation was carried out into the effect on blood cholesterol level of eating beans.

For one month before the investigation began, the subjects ate no beans. From Day 0 of the investigation, each subject included in her/his diet 400 g of canned baked beans, each day for two weeks (the 'bean period').

At the end of this time, the subjects went back to their normal diets for two weeks, then had a two-week 'spaghetti period', during which they ate 400 g of canned spaghetti as part of their diet each day. They then returned to their normal diets.

Blood cholesterol levels were measured at intervals during the investigation. The results are shown in the graph below.

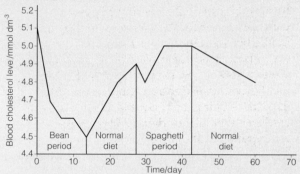

(Walker, *Reading Science*, October 1991)

(a) Describe the effects on blood cholesterol level, as shown in this investigation, of eating the following:
(i) canned baked beans; *(2 marks)*
(ii) canned spaghetti. *(2 marks)*
(b) Explain why it was necessary for the subjects to eat no beans in the period before the investigation. *(2 marks)*
(c) Canned baked beans and canned spaghetti have similar, low, fat levels. Suggest a reason for including the 'spaghetti period' in this investigation *(3 marks)*
(d) It has been suggested that the effect of dietary beans on blood cholesterol is brought about by bacteria in the colon fermenting fibre compounds in the beans into short-chain fatty acids. Suggest how fermentation of this kind might lead to the effects observed. *(3 marks)*

(Total 12 marks)

ULEAC June 1995, Paper 4B, No. 2

Index